U.S. NEWS COVERAGE
OF RACIAL MINORITIES

U.S. NEWS COVERAGE OF RACIAL MINORITIES

A Sourcebook, 1934–1996

EDITED BY
BEVERLY ANN DEEPE KEEVER,
CAROLYN MARTINDALE,
AND MARY ANN WESTON

Foreword by Oscar H. Gandy, Jr.

GREENWOOD PRESS
Westport, Connecticut • London

Library of Congress Cataloging-in-Publication Data

U.S. news coverage of racial minorities : a sourcebook, 1934–1996 /
  edited by Beverly Ann Deepe Keever, Carolyn Martindale, and Mary Ann
  Weston ; foreword by Oscar H. Gandy, Jr.
     p. cm.
    Includes bibliographical references and index.
    ISBN 0–313–29671–5 (alk. paper)
    1. Minorities—Press coverage—United States—History—20th
century. 2. Journalism—United States—History—20th century.
3. United States—Public opinion—History—20th century. 4. United
States—Ethnic relations. I. Keever, Beverly Deepe.
II. Martindale, Carolyn, 1938– . III. Weston, Mary Ann.
IV. Title: News coverage of US racial minorities.
  PN4888.M56N48   1997
  070.4'493058'00973—DC21   96–53850

British Library Cataloguing in Publication Data is available.

Library of Congress Catalog Card Number: 96–53850
ISBN: 0–313–29671–5

First published in 1997

Greenwood Press, 88 Post Road West, Westport, CT 06881
An imprint of Greenwood Publishing Group, Inc.

Printed in the United States of America

The paper used in this book complies with the
Permanent Paper Standard issued by the National
Information Standards Organization (Z39.48–1984).

10 9 8 7 6 5 4 3 2 1

Copyright Acknowledgments

The authors and publisher gratefully acknowledge permission for use of the following materials:

Excerpts from *Operation Crossroads: The Atomic Tests at Bikini Atoll* by Jonathan M. Weisgall,
Annapolis, Md.: Naval Institute Press, 1994. Reprinted by permission of Jonathan M. Weisgall.

Excerpts from *Shaping History: The Role of Newspapers in Hawai'i* by Helen Geracimos Chapin,
Honolulu: The University of Hawaii Press, 1996. Reprinted by permission of the University of
Hawaii Press.

Contents

Foreword

Some fifty years after the recommendations of the Hutchins Commission on the Freedom of the Press were all but ignored, we again hear expressions of concern being raised about the future of news. The threat is no longer the spectre of government regulation, but the mantle of obsolescence. Networked computers and the navigable click stream of the World Wide Web provide a ready alternative to the boring fixity of the printed page and the predictably silly banter of the local broadcast "news team." The target audience, already mistrustful of public relations masquerading as news, reveals little interest in "public journalism" or other efforts to reinvent the press. The press is all but irrelevant to the generation of Americans on which its future depends.

While the challenge of technological alternatives will certainly play a critical role in the demise of the press as we know it, the primary cause is far more complex. As with the other institutions in which we have begun to lose faith, we have come to question whether our reliance on the press is justified or even makes good sense. We now see journalists as automatons, just going through the motions and about as useful as cracked and pitted windshield wipers on a fast car in a driving rain. Even during good times or sunny days, we proceed at our own risk. While the authors who have contributed to this *Sourcebook* have focused primarily on the failures of the press in the coverage and representation of racial and ethnic minorities, these failures are merely symptomatic of a more fundamental myopia. Economic self-interest and a marketplace logic have introduced chips, cracks, and other distortions in a journalistic window already clouded by a thick film of cultural ignorance. We are driving almost blind.

By reviewing how the American news media have from time to time observed, ignored, praised, and condemned the ubiquitous "others" in our midst, the contributors to this book reveal the ways in which the press has performed as a core institution in American society. It may be, as the functionalists suggest, that the media exist to serve the particular needs of society or, at the very least, its readers. It may be the case that settlers actually "needed" to understand the native peoples they encountered as savages, in the same way that the planters needed to believe that their African slaves were less than human and incapable of education, independent assessment, or symbolic communication. Perhaps a similar need governed the creation of an editorial cloaking device that made the Hawaiians and other Pacific Islanders all but disappear into a hazy background mist in order to ease their incorporation into the American empire. Or, as in the case of Japanese Americans, we might see the need for a variable focal length lens that could be adjusted as relations between the United States and Japan grew apart, then closer, only to drift apart once again. As a sourcebook, this volume provides the basis for more finely textured analyses that note similarities and differences in the treatment of Japanese, Chinese, and Pacific Islanders as Asians. This treatment shares much in common with the ways in which Mexicans, Puerto Ricans, and Central and South Americans have been grouped as Hispanics.

We are also reminded that the press serves as a means of communication that meets the needs, or serves the interests of, its owners, investors, and primary clients in addition to the needs of an audience. Strategic framing of particular "others" at appropriate times has served such interests well. However, as several authors in this volume suggest, we ought to question the extent to which the needs of the primary audience, the owners, and the principal clients are ever fully compatible. It seems very unlikely that all interests could be served by the same constructions of reality. Indeed, reflection on this moment in history would suggest that racial and ethnic minorities have not been the only victims of strategic misrepresentation. Racial stereotypes and other media distortions have, over time, introduced a kind of cultural pollution, which, like diesel fuel, dirties the air as it propels the train forward. As a result, we as a people suffer from a disease of the national spirit called racism that has spread among us like cancer.

Most of the resources identified in the *Sourcebook* examine the mainstream press; however, we are also challenged to make sense of the roles that have been performed by the alternative, ethnic, and minority media. We are also invited to speculate about what the future might hold in the context of newer information systems. The broad historical scope of this book helps us to see the ways in which the social function and performance of an alternative and oppositional press has varied as its purpose changed from pacification, to mobilization, incorporation, and eventually the commodification of its audience for sale to the highest bidder. Of course, it may be a long time before the emerging system of networked computers settles into a stable form and becomes recognizable as performing a legitimate news function. Indeed, I would like to suggest that this book is especially useful in the way that it explores the influence of particular individuals acting at particular times in different places and circumstances. Individual action produces what seems like a unique outcome until we move to a higher level of abstraction where we recognize some of the underlying similarities between these different stories. The reward of similar discoveries awaits each reader.

At the same time, we ought not sit idly by and watch the future unfold. As scholars and educators, we have a role to play. Recourses of the sort provided to the Hutchins Commission will not be forthcoming this time because the press no longer fears its government. Indeed, recent debates over the shape of the National Information Infrastructure and the historic revision of the Communications Act virtually ensure smooth sailing for market-oriented corporate communications. With the exception of some expressions of concern about the impact of explicit material on the well-being of impressionable children, concerns about content have been set aside by a belief in the power of the market to correct itself. This is fantasy, and readers of this book will recognize it for what it is. I only hope they will also be moved to write, teach, and organize so that others understand it as well.

Oscar H. Gandy, Jr.
Annenberg School for Communication, Philadelphia

Preface

U.S. News Coverage of Racial Minorities: A Sourcebook, 1934–1996 is a unique reference work. It draws together in one volume the scholarly literature assessing news coverage of Americans of African, Native, Asian, Hispanic, or Pacific Islander origin in the U.S. mainstream media.[1] In terms of time, this book covers the years from 1934 through 1996. Geographically, it covers the fifty states and the territories in the Pacific and the Caribbean that are currently under U.S. governance. No other volume approaches this *Sourcebook* in the breadth and depth of its scrutiny of the intersection of U.S. news and race.[2]

Many empirical studies of news coverage have focused on a single population group, often in one locale or involving one incident, thus providing a fragmented picture of race-related news coverage. The scholarly works themselves are often widely dispersed across decades, regions, and types of news media and are scattered in numerous books, research materials, and academic journals criss-crossing a variety of fields and methodologies.

In contrast, this one-volume *Sourcebook* assembles and analyzes multidisci-plinary materials on news coverage of all five groups. The purposes of its authors were to locate and cite widely scattered, hard-to-find fragments, relate what they have to tell us, and then describe their patterns and significance. The scholarly literature studied primarily concentrated on refereed articles published in academic journals, reports, or other materials produced in an academic setting or on books by experts in the fields. The book's extensive endnotes provide a treasure trove of citations to studies about news coverage of these groups and serve as an unprecedented resource for researchers.

The news media analyzed in the scholarly literature were predominantly English-language print news media, including editorials and cartoons, and to a smaller extent news broadcasting, both of which shape the attitudes of the dominant, general-market English-speaking or -reading population. News outlets serving specific ethnic or racial groups, often disseminated in languages other than English, are important. However, they are outside the scope of the research for this *Sourcebook* except when they provide a critique or appraisal of the mainstream media.

The term *news* as used in this book follows the definition made by communication scholar Mitchell Stephens, who defined news as "new information about a subject of some public interest that is shared with some portion of the public."[3]

The categories of racial and cultural groups selected for this work follow the scheme of the 1990 U.S. Census, which provided the most detailed breakdown of race, ethnicity and Hispanic origin of the American population in the 200 years of the census. Persons of Hispanic origin may be of any race; they are considered to constitute an ethnic or cultural grouping. The Census Bureau indicated that its concept of race in 1990 reflected the self-identification of the respondent and was not intended to signify any biological or anthropological definition.[4]

The authors recognize criticisms of the methodology of the Census Bureau and even its two-century-old practice of classifying people into racial groups. However, discussing these arguments is beyond the scope of this volume. Following the Census Bureau classification has advantages for those who want to compare news coverage of certain population groups to the total numbers of that group.

These five groups are occasionally referred to as *racial minorities* in this book. The authors confronted a daunting problem when challenged to come up with a collective term for these groups. They settled on *minorities* reluctantly, knowing that in many times and places in the United States each of these groups has been—and is—a numerical majority and sometimes a political and economic one as well. The authors also recognize that the term *minority* assumes a white Euro-American point of view. Despite the disadvantages of the term *racial minorities*,[5] we consider it so often used and commonly understood to identify clearly the nonwhite population groups and some cultural groups that share the common experience of having been excluded from the dominant white society and power structures.

Disproportionately high numbers of these racial and cultural groups are at the bottom of the U.S. socioeconomic scale, living in the equivalent of a Third World within the wealthiest nation on the globe. They have fared worse proportionately than other groups historically and even since the 1980s, when the gap between the nation's haves and have-nots began widening, according to one economist, partly because of "an inequality problem based on falling real earnings for low-paid workers that is unparalleled at least since the Great Depression." This economist noted further that the "ultimate cost of increasing inequality lies in the potential for an apartheid economy, one in which the rich live aloof in their exclusive suburbs and expensive apartments with little connection to the working poor in their slums."[6]

The contributing authors also note that many white immigrant groups, especially those whose religion lay outside the mainstream Protestant denominations, have also suffered from exclusion, ridicule, and discrimination. Yet, without distinctive physical characteristics, white immigrants have more easily over time been able to blend in with the dominant elements of white society. Moreover, the physical markers of racial minorities—such as the shape of the eyes or the color of skin—provide easy ways to discriminate in times of crisis or uncertainty. Although usually recognized as being of no biological significance, these physical markers also provide data used in law-enforcement surveillance.[7] In a more positive context, recent academic research has revealed an emerging learning-and-effectiveness paradigm arguing that a business entity that practices true racial and cultural diversity benefits the bottom line in numerous ways beyond legal requirements and political conformity.[8]

For several reasons, 1934 was chosen as the beginning date for this work. First, 1934 ushered in a new phase of broader government-media relations, featuring presidential press conferences, the move to centralize national power, the growth of federal agencies as suppliers of news releases, and, shortly thereafter during World War II, the imposition of voluntary censorship nationwide and of martial law in Hawaii. Second, in Europe, Adolf Hitler was using radio to amplify a brand of racism signifying, as one scholar noted in 1944, that "America had to stand before the whole world in favor of racial tolerance and cooperation and of racial equality."[9] Finally, that year was chosen because the Federal Communications Act of 1934 increased government regulation of broadcasting. This regulation continues today as more and more Americans receive their news— and their views of some reality—electronically and in a rapidly expanding electronic environment.

This book gives parallel treatment to each of these five census groups. Each chapter begins with a history of that group as it came under U.S. jurisdiction. Then, each chapter is divided into six periods suggested by pivotal news events and discusses studies of news coverage of the group during that period. These six time periods and reasons for their selection are as follows:

- 1934 passage of Federal Communications Act to the bombing of Pearl Harbor, December 7, 1941. This prewar period began in 1934, as explained earlier, when official segregation prevailed at home, and it ended with the entry of the United States into World War II, a conventional, ideological war that tested the American creed of racial freedom and equality.[10]

- 1941 bombing of Pearl Harbor to the atomic bombing of Hiroshima, August 6, 1945. This period of global war revealed that the logical limits of an ideology of racial superiority was genocide.[11] The end of the war ushered in an era that brought destructiveness to a new dimension with the dropping of atomic bombs on Hiroshima and Nagasaki.

- 1945 atomic bombing of Hiroshima to the integration of Little Rock, September 1957. The postwar period featured nuclear testing in the Pacific Islands and in the continental United States, the landmark 1954 U.S. Supreme Court decision overturning the separate-but-equal doctrine that had permitted segregated public schools, and finally the use of U.S. troops on September 24, 1957, to enforce court-ordered desegregation of Central High School in Little Rock, Arkansas.

• 1957 integration of Little Rock to resignation of President Richard Nixon, August 9, 1974. The Little Rock school crisis ushered in escalating struggles that made race the most important issue in U.S. domestic life. Then the 1970s Watergate scandal exposed a severe weakening of confidence in U.S. principles, institutions, self-respect, and the integrity of its leaders,[12] and it resulted in the first resignation of a president.

• 1974 resignation of Nixon to the uprising in Los Angeles, April 29, 1992. During this post-Watergate period of mostly Republican presidencies, a new political vocabulary of racial code words was developed, including "inner city," "underclass," "suspect profile," and "affirmative action [that] has been made out to be the exact equivalent of quota systems that discriminated against Jews," according to one source. The Civil Rights Movement for African Americans stalled.[13]

• 1992 uprising in Los Angeles to the presidential election of November 1996. The heavily televised mid-1992 disorders revealed failures of the local police and also the multiracial and -cultural nature of urban problems in Los Angeles. They provided a prelude to the O.J. Simpson trial that again spotlighted the intersection of race and of news about the criminal justice system. The 1996 election campaigns avoided any head-on discussion of racial issues; however, these issues were communicated through code words, such as "immigration," "welfare reform," and "group entitlements."

Despite this book's parallel treatment, some groups were necessarily given more space for a variety of reasons—their numbers, their length of time under U.S. jurisdiction, or the amount of scholarship devoted to them. Also, in many cases, little information was found on broadcast news treatment of the group.

The scholarly literature accessed and analyzed for this *Sourcebook* was made much more comprehensive by the technologies of the Information Age. For example, scanning seventeen on-line database files containing millions of citations produced 1.14 million hits for individual search terms related to the media, to Pacific Islanders and Asian Americans in the United States, or to race. These individual hits were then combined to retrieve relevant citations and abstracts. Such a vast and sweeping search of multidisciplinary literature would have been humanly impossible twenty years ago, and it is virtually impossible to accomplish today without computerized information services and staff.[14]

The scholarly quality of this reference volume is maintained through extensive endnoting on each racial or cultural group, on investigative reporting, and on the federal regulation of broadcasting and telecommunications. But to make the book useful to professional journalists and to attract a readership beyond scholars, the authors have tried to utilize tight, readable writing. Instead of using researchers' names in the text, as is done in academic writing, the authors provided such identification in the extensive endnotes. We have occasionally used in the text the names of researchers whose work is discussed at length or is relied on heavily. For reasons of space, a selected bibliography, rather than a full or enlarged one, appears at the very end of each chapter.

Such an ambitious project as this book could not have been undertaken without an unusually talented and dedicated group of contributors from journalism and mass communication education, most of whom have also worked as professional journalists. Their backgrounds are described in the back of this volume.

Working with the contributors have been the *Sourcebook*'s coeditors, who wrote several chapters, critiqued all the chapters, and contributed ideas for the preface and conclusions chapter; each coeditor also provided a special skill. Bev Keever handled the huge administrative task of keeping the authors, coeditors, and publisher informed of the book's progress at every stage while maintaining a valuable larger view of the book's purpose. Carolyn Martindale, who edited both the initial drafts and final versions of all the chapters, scrutinized every comma and caught a variety of tiny factual errors, while molding a cohesive whole. Mary Ann Weston provided substantive critiques for each initial draft, kept her coeditors on track concerning the book's focus, and wove all the main ideas together into the conclusions chapter.

Many others also assisted in producing this book, and we thank them sincerely. Reading segments of the book and making insightful comments were University of Hawaii professors Robert C. Kiste and Jon Kamakawiwo'ole Osorio, University of Texas at Austin professor Federico A. Subervi-Vélez, Steve Weinberg, former executive director of Investigative Reporters and Editors, and Taylor Alderman, professor emeritus of Youngstown State University. Sharing his expertise on research sampling and statistics was Professor Paul J. Lavrakas, formerly of Northwestern University, now at Ohio State University. Providing immense support for this project from its very inception, and especially for Chapter 8, was Bill Chamberlin, the Joseph L. Brechner Eminent Scholar at the University of Florida.

Offering valuable suggestions for the segment on Chinese Americans were Him Mark Lai of the Chinese Historical Society; Steve Petranik of the *Honolulu Star-Bulletin*, Ann Auman's husband; and developmental psychologist Linda Revilla, Gregory Yee Mark's wife. Others providing guidance at the University of Hawaii were Journalism Department Chair Lowell Frazier; Miles Jackson, ex-dean of the Library School; Rudolf Schmerl, ex-director of research relations, and Professor Terence Wesley-Smith of the Pacific Islands Studies Program. Those giving very special assistance from afar were Julie Marcus of the Center for War, Peace and the News Media in New York; Dr. Hiro Kurashina and Monique Carriveau of the Micronesian Area Research Center in Guam, and Nada Anderson of the National Library of Australia. Peter Parisi of Hunter College of City University of New York graciously provided permission to use information from his 1996 conference paper.

The authors also are grateful to journalism scholars Clint C. Wilson II and Félix Gutiérrez for their theories about phases of news media portrayal of minorities, which are frequently referred to in this book; to Robert M. Entman for his extensive research into local television news portrayals of African Americans; and to Christopher P. Campbell, for his studies that reinforce and extend

Dr. Entman's work on modern white racism in television journalism.

Eileen Finan and Jennifer Hanson, graduate students at the Medill School of Journalism, Northwestern University, scrolled through countless database screens and thumbed through hundreds of pages of paper indexes to locate pertinent studies. Their diligence and resourcefulness were exceptional. Library research or computer database work was performed admirably at the University of Hawaii on several facets of this project by Carolyn Iezza, Ben C. W. Lee, Sooraj Nair, Storm Russell, Jeffrey Stover, and Kumar Vadhri.

Finally, we thank the members of our families for their sacrifices and encouragement, which facilitated the making of this *Sourcebook*.

Beverly Ann Deepe Keever
Mary Ann Weston
Carolyn Martindale

NOTES

1. The term "mainstream media" usually refers to general market English-language print or broadcast products, according to Federico Subervi-Vélez's article "Words We Work and Play With" in *MAC News*, the newsletter of the Minorities and Communication Division of the Association for Education in Journalism and Mass Communication, March 1995, 7.

2. The term "race" as used in this volume means a distinct category of human beings with unchangeable physical characteristics transmitted from one generation to the next. These characteristics in turn are often directly but erroneously linked to psychological or intellectual characteristics and used to distinguish between superior and inferior groups, according to the description of Joe R. Feagin and Clairece Booher Feagin, *Racial and Ethnic Relations*, 5th ed. (Upper Saddle River, N.J.: Prentice-Hall, 1996), 6–7.

3. Mitchell Stephens, *A History of News: From the Drum to the Satellite* (New York: Viking, 1988), 9.

4. U.S. Bureau of the Census, *Statistical Abstract of the United States: 1995*, 115th ed. (Washington, D.C.: U.S. Bureau of the Census, 1995), 4.

5. See, for example, Clint C. Wilson II and Félix Gutiérrez, *Race, Multiculturalism, and the Media*, 2d ed. (Thousand Oaks, Calif.: Sage Publications, 1995), 19–20.

6. Richard Freeman, "Toward an Apartheid Economy?," *Harvard Business Review* 74, no. 5 (September-October 1996), 114–21.

7. See, for example, "Uprising and Repression in L.A.: An Interview with Mike Davis by the *CovertAction* Information Bulletin," in *Reading Rodney King: Reading Urban Uprising*, ed. Robert Gooding-Williams (New York: Routledge, 1993), 142–54. Article originally published in 1992.

8. David Thomas and Robin Ely, "Making Differences Matter: A New Paradigm for Managing Diversity," *Harvard Business Review* 74, no. 5 (September-October 1996), 79–90.

9. Gunnar Myrdal, *An American Dilemma: The Negro Problem and Modern Democracy*, vol. 2 (New York: Harper & Brothers, 1944), 1004.

10. Ibid., 997–1024.

11. This statement extends a concept used to describe Dachau by Ronald Takaki, *A Different Mirror: A History of Multicultural America* (Boston: Little, Brown and Co., 1993), 377.

12. Philip Gleason, "American Identity and Americanization," in *Harvard Encyclopedia of American Ethnic Groups*, ed. Stephan Thernstrom (Cambridge: Belknap Press of Harvard University Press, 1980), 31–58.

13. Patricia Williams, "Conversations about *Brown*: Among Moses' Bridge-Builders," in *Uncivil War: Race, Civil Rights & The Nation 1865–1995*, ed. Eyal Press (New York: The Nation Press, 1995), 170. See also Jimmie L. Reeves and Richard Campbell, *Cracked Coverage: Television News, the Anti-Cocaine Crusade, and the Reagan Legacy* (Durham, N.C.: Duke University Press, 1994).

14. These database searches were conducted through the Dialog Information Services of Palo Alto, California. The searches were made by Rachel Liang of the University of Hawaii Hamilton Library in October 1994 and by Helen Josephine of the UH External Services in June 1996.

1

The Origins and Colors of a News Gap

BEVERLY ANN DEEPE KEEVER

> The Christianized *Indians* in some parts of *Plimouth* have newly appointed a day of Thanksgiving to God for his Mercy. . . . Their Example may be worth Mentioning.
> —*Publick Occurrences Both Forreign and Domestick*, 1690

> While the barbarous *Indians* were lurking about *Chelmsford*, there were missing about the beginning of this month a couple of Children . . . both of them supposed to be fallen into the hands of the *Indians*.
> —*Publick Occurrences Both Forreign and Domestick*, 1690[1]

These two paragraphs in the first newspaper published in England's colonial America serve as a landmark for a printed intersection of news and race in what is now the United States. This landmark preserves for one moment—September 25, 1690—and in one place—Boston—the bifurcated image that an early journalist perceived of the indigenous people. *Publick Occurrences Both Forreign and Domestick* served as a prototype for newspapers that followed.[2]

The first paragraph spoke favorably of the Christianized Indians. Having accepted the Euro-Americans' religion, they instituted a "day of Thanksgiving" that was deemed newsworthy enough to mention. But only two paragraphs later, Indians were described negatively. They were "barbarous" and were "supposed to" have captured several children. The only other dangers highlighted on page 1 were diseases such as smallpox and the Devil, who had struck a pious but melancholy man who had committed suicide, "having newly buried his Wife."

On the other two printed pages, this bifurcated portrayal of the Indians gave way to only negative news. Page 2 of *Publick Occurrences* told of Indians who had captured several French prisoners "whom they used in a manner too barbarous for any English to approve." Another printed page contained news about a Virginia-bound ship that sailed into the wrong port, "where the Indians and French seized her, and Butchered the Master, and several of the men."[3]

Through these articles, *Publick Occurrences* alerted elite settlers who could read English to the threats posed by the Indians to all Euro-Americans. In doing so, the newspaper performed what would become a chief function of its successors: surveillance of the environment, or disclosing threats, problems, or developments to literate individuals and their society.[4] The surveillance function established a pattern of news in the dominant-culture mainstream press about Native Americans, African Americans, Asian Americans, Hispanic Americans, and Pacific Islanders in the over 300 years since *Publick Occurrences* presented them as perceived dangers or problems. This pattern can be seen repeatedly in the chapters that follow.

Conspicuously absent from *Publick Occurrences'* news coverage was any mention of African slaves, who had been brought to the town of Boston shortly after its founding. By 1690, the slaves were not yet considered a danger because they made up only thirteen percent of the population in all twelve colonies.[5] Treated as property rather than humans, they were as numerous in the Northern urban centers as in the Southern tobacco-growing areas, stated one historian;[6] their labor was essential to the prosperity of some colonies. Thus, another news pattern began: labor was imported to benefit the dominant culture economically, but the laborers' economic contributions and plight went unreported on the news pages.[7] This pattern of news invisibility appears often in the chapters that follow.

Later, when the imported labor was no longer needed or allowed, or when sufficient antipathy to the group developed among white U.S. workers and nativist hate groups, the people of color would be attacked verbally, physically, or legally, and thus often were written about negatively by the media. Newspaper successors to *Publick Occurrences* also carried advertisements for slaves, who were transported from Africa by New England shippers, and colonial printers sometimes served as slave sellers for their advertising customers.[8]

Devoid of favorable portrayals, a news gap developed in what Euro-American readers learned about other racial groups in the colonies and later the United States. Fast-forwarding 300 years, the not-guilty verdict in O. J. Simpson's double-murder trial exemplified the results of this news gap. It also dramatized the significant role played by the news media in informing the nation and the world about U.S. race-related public affairs. The jury's finding the celebrated African American not guilty exposed what the media called a racial divide between African Americans and white Americans.[9] Each group held divergent views of mostly white U.S. institutions. To African Americans, local police departments were epitomized by the racist remarks and alleged frame-up of evidence against Simpson by police Detective Mark Fuhrman.[10] African-American women at a battered women's center, for example, cheered when Simpson was acquitted. But many white Americans were stunned by the not-guilty verdict.[11] President Clinton addressed the public reaction to the Simpson verdict by saying that racial divisions are tearing at the heart of America.[12]

More vivid evidence of the news gap had surfaced in 1992, when the acquittal of four officers involved in the beating of Rodney King ignited one of the most destructive urban uprisings in U.S. history, with fifty-three dead, 2,300 wounded and over $1 billion in property damage. Communication scholar Christopher P. Campbell wrote, "Americans who rely on mainstream journalism and prime-time television for their perception of race relations were likely taken aback by the rebellion in Los Angeles." He added, "The popular media in this country have advanced a myth of racial tolerance and assimilation that fails to explain the violent reaction to the Rodney King verdict."[13]

The racial divide exposed by the trial outcome and uprising spotlighted the continuing U.S. dilemma explained in 1944 by economist Gunnar Myrdal: reconciling prejudice, discrimination, and racism with the espoused U.S. ideals of equality and justice.[14] The O. J. Simpson trial outcome also highlighted what might be called the "American Press Dilemma"—the dilemma of critiquing freely, regularly, and systematically a racial, social, economic, and political order of white dominance without subverting or toppling the very order that has granted it a Constitutionally protected position.[15]

This chapter provides a four-layered framework for analyzing the historical underpinnings of the intersection of news and Native Americans, African Americans, Asian Americans, Hispanic Americans, or Pacific Islanders. The four layers, discussed below, describe the early Euro-Americans' sense of racial superiority based on their:

• Bias of religion and pseudo-science
• Bias of the mode of communication
• Bias of the legal construction of race and racism
• Bias in the nature of news.[16]

These four layers contributed to bias in the English-language colonial press, and, as the following chapters demonstrate, vestiges of this bias continue today.[17]

Mainstream *news* coverage of these U.S. racial and ethnic groups has been given little scholarly attention. Although numerous research articles and books have been written about the portrayals of these racial groups in the U.S. mass media of advertising, film, and television entertainment, few have focused on the more limited topic of the *news* media.

Yet, the news media are qualitatively different from other media in several ways. First, the news media are supposed to be or expected to be representing *reality*, the way the world actually is, not a fictional account of it. More simply put, as communication scholars Clint Wilson and Félix Gutiérrez explain, entertainment is "make-believe," but news is "real."[18] Dutch scholar Teun A. van Dijk and others have noted that because large segments of the white public have no contact—or have only superficial contact—with racial minorities either in their neighborhoods or at work, they have few sources except the news media to inform them about racial and ethnic affairs.[19] Also, most news consumers tend to expect these media to portray with some accuracy other groups personally unknown to them. According to van Dijk, "For specific types of social and political events, including those in the field of ethnic relations, the news media are the main source of information and beliefs used to form the interpretation framework for such events."[20] In short, news media help shape their consumers' ideas and beliefs about race sometimes without consumers' conscious awareness.

Second, the press plays a unique and autonomous role in the reproduction of ethnic and racial inequality, according to van Dijk. Furthermore, the news media control the forms of public discourse on ethnic matters. Elites such as business and political interests need the press "to inform both the public at large and each other, to exercise their power, to seek legitimation, and to manufacture consensus and consent."[21] Moreover, what news media say—or ignore—influences the decisions, actions, and priorities of politicians and officials.[22]

Third, the selection of topics to be covered as news indicates how the press is involved in the reproduction of white group and elite dominance, van Dijk has argued. "The press does not primarily focus on issues that are interesting or relevant for the population at large"; instead, the news media focus on topics that concern the elites such as politicians, the judiciary, and the social welfare bureaucracy.[23] In the United States, news coverage about racial and ethnic matters would theoretically be included in the historical mandate of the press to keep citizens informed about government and public affairs, so they can make the intelligent decisions that are the basis of democracy.

News about racial topics is "one of the crucial domestic stories in America's history," a national commission decided thirty years ago in the aftermath of racial disorders in numerous cities.[24] It still is. Future news coverage of these subordinated racial groups is expected to be even more significant because of the U.S. Census Bureau's projected decrease in the number of non-Latino whites as a proportion of the U.S. population. By 2060, the proportion of non-Latino whites in the U.S. population is projected to drop to less than half, down from three-quarters in the 1990 census. Discussions of this demographic shift have had an alarmist tone, especially among Americans of European descent, because many of them fear a loss of white power, privilege, and cultural dominance to subordinated racial and cultural groups.[25]

THE BIAS OF RELIGION AND PSEUDO-SCIENCE

One layer of the culture and ideology that historically has contributed to press bias against people of color rests on the early Euro-Americans' perceived superiority of the dominant Protestant Christian religion over the belief systems of the original inhabitants of North America, of African slaves, and later of Asian Americans, Hispanic Americans, and Pacific Islanders.

The English people who settled the colonies considered the indigenous population heathen and began to expand over their land. According to historian

Winthrop Jordan, "The savagery of the Indians assumed a special significance in the minds of those actively engaged in a program of bringing civilization into the American wilderness."[26]

Taking Western civilization into the American wilderness later went hand in hand with westward-bound frontier printing presses, which often disseminated harrowing accounts of conflict between the two races. Not untypical of Western editors was South Dakota editor L. Frank Baum of the *Aberdeen Saturday Pioneer*. Just ten days before the slaughter at Wounded Knee occurred in 1891, he urged "the wholesale extermination of *all* America's native peoples."[27]

The Whites, by law of conquest, by justice of civilization, are masters of the American continent, and the best safety of the frontier settlements will be secured by the total annihilation of the few remaining Indians. Why not annihilation? Their glory has fled, their spirit broken, their manhood effaced; better that they should die than live the miserable wretches that they are.[28]

Details of the role of the news media in perpetuating later ideologies about and images of Native Americans are presented in Chapter 2.

Europeans also maintained a distinct sense of superiority over Africans, whom they had encountered in voyages of discovery before landing in North America. Unlike the civilizing mission that justified North American expansion, Jordan noted, "The English errand into Africa was not a new or a perfect community but a business trip."[29] Although the Puritans of Boston held ambivalent policies about slaves,[30] by 1698 the shippers and traders from Massachusetts and Rhode Island were the colonies' main slave traders.[31] Originally established as a market for slaves, Wall Street in New York City was selling more slaves than any other commodity by 1711.[32] Thus, by the 1800s, journalism historian David Copeland noted, slavery and slave-trading were "a regular part of American life."[33] The rapid increase in the number of Africans heightened fears of slave revolts, arson, and poisonings; the colonists had created the very conditions they feared.

Jordan traced the roots of racism against Africans in Western culture to Biblical passages: "Negroes" were thought to be descendants of Ham, whose name originally connoted "dark."[34] Ham had been cursed by Noah, which in turn gave rise to the concept that the curse explained their blackness. This argument that the Old Testament stated that slavery was God's punishment upon Africans persisted for two millennia; it appeared in 1770 in an essay published in the *Connecticut Journal*: "The Africans are the children of Ham, which is plain from their being servants of servants to their brethren."[35]

Slavery had existed in "the vast majority of stratified pre-industrial societies,"[36] according to one scholar, and some Africans had been enslaved by Europeans since ancient times.[37] But, he noted, what was peculiar was "the special brand of Western Hemisphere, *racial* slavery." In the United States after the abolition of slavery and the end of the Civil War, he wrote that "a rigid racial dichotomy" was maintained by establishing a segregated system of socializing and mating.[38] How the press helped to perpetuate this segregation and the role it played in desegregation are detailed in Chapter 3.

Later, this religious rationale about the inferiority of nonwhite racial groups was supplemented by what became known as scientific racism, based on pseudo-scientific studies.[39] As one scholar noted, by the 1850s the colonists' religious concern with African Americans and Native Americans "was superseded by theories of evolution and racism."[40] Hierarchies of either races or cultures were established, ranging from the most civilized and advanced to the most barbarous and savage; on any scale, the white man's Indian generally ranked a notch from the bottom, just above the African American.[41] As one scholar explained, such faulty pseudo-scientific arguments "make nature herself an accomplice in the crime of political inequality."[42]

This scientific racism was later exposed and ridiculed by other scientists, but only after centuries of its being used to justify white domination over other races. Today, *race* is generally considered to be socially constructed, meaning that it is important only because people, governments, and institutions say it is important.[43] Ironically, some who have benefited from the race-based classification that undergirded white domination are now calling for a color-blind standard that would ignore the effects of the long-standing inequities endured by subordinated racial and cultural groups in education, health care, employment, and other areas.[44]

The distinction between analyzing the media and race—as opposed to the media and racism—is described by British scholars Paul Hartmann and Charles Husband in *Racism and the Mass Media*:

Race in itself is a matter of no social importance; it is a biological fact as peripheral to essential human nature as differences in height or eye colour. Race as a means of *classifying* people socially, however, is important. This is another way of saying that race is important because people think it is important. It is not race that is the problem but the negative symbolism and meaning which is attached to it, and it is this in turn which makes race a crucial criterion in individual perception and collective action. When people think that differences of race constitute differences in social entitlement you have racism; and *racism*[,] not race[,] is the basis of the British "racial problem."[45]

This "British racial problem" is similar to that in the United States. As U.S. scholar David Sears has noted, "Racism is deeply ingrained throughout Western culture" and over the past five centuries has become "a major complex of national and cultural belief."[46]

THE BIAS OF THE MODE OF COMMUNICATION

The second bias of the culture and ideology that influenced the press in its coverage of race was the attitude of the English colonists and their descendants that their written alphabetized mode of transmitting and storing information was superior to that of the oral-tradition peoples—Native Americans, African Americans, and Pacific Islanders. They also believed it was superior to the pictographic writing system of the Asian Americans. Hispanic Americans did use the same alphabetic writing system as the colonists but it was linked with the Catholic Church, against which the Protestants had struggled in Europe.

As psychologist James M. Jones has pointed out, "The invention of Johann Gutenberg made literacy an important value in Western society." He explained, "African society had an oral tradition, but whites did not see that tradition as simply another way of communicating, teaching, and preserving the past—they saw it as a symptom of basic illiteracy."[47] Westerners slighted the benefits of the oral tradition, including its importance in the discovery of new truth. Furthermore, according to communication scholar Harold Innis, "The oral discussion inherently involves personal contact and a consideration for the feelings of others, and it is in sharp contrast with the cruelty of mechanized communication."[48]

News exchanged in oral cultures through words spoken in face-to-face contact probably dates back tens or even hundreds of thousands of years.[49] However, in England's colonial America—and Western culture—printed news was severed from human interaction; the message was separated from the messenger. News was intrinsically linked with the printing press, which in turn was linked to the alphabet. One scholar noted that the alphabet "is generally considered the greatest invention ever made by man."[50] It created the conditions that contributed to the Western development of codified law, monotheism, abstract science, deductive logic, the printing press, and the Industrial Revolution.[51] As humanities scholar Walter Ong has explained, the alphabet was "democratizing in the sense that it was easy for everyone to learn."[52]

The history of the modern West is a print-based knowledge that is biased in providing monopoly and privilege to those who can read and write its language but works to the disadvantage of those who come from an oral tradition, according to Innis.[53] The print media also favor the establishment of commercialism and empire.[54]

Innis was critical of the press, which, he maintained, came to full flower with special protection in the U.S. Constitution. "We are all familiar with the claims of the printing industry to the effect that it has ushered in a new and superior civilization. No other civilization, we are told, has enjoyed our advantages. Democracy, education, progress, individualism, and other blessed words describe our new heaven."[55]

Likewise, the phonetic alphabet on which the West was built was regarded by Euro-Americans as superior to the pictographic writing system of Chinese characters.[56] Ong indicated that the picture characters of the Chinese language are "stylized and codified in intricate ways which make it certainly the most complex writing system the world has ever known"; the language is also "intrinsically elitist: to master it thoroughly requires protracted leisure."[57] Thus, Chinese and Japanese laborers immigrating to the United States, even if unschooled, came from a civilization utilizing a unique writing system, but it was one perceived by Euro-Americans as unreadable and inscrutable.

The Hispanic Americans' writing system is based on the alphabet. However, this system was linked with Latin learned in school and used by the Catholic Church.[58] The printing press helped to subvert both of these by disseminating information in vernacular languages. This subversion enabled people to turn to the Bible for God's word rather than rely on priests, thus fostering the Protestant Reformation that later took root in the English colonies.

Implications of a shift in the mode of communication from spoken words to alphabet-based writing is discussed in Chapter 6 in a case study of Hawaii. The case study analyzes the transformation of an oral culture to an alphabetic written one and the commercialism and imperialism made possible by the subsequent print media.[59] In this transformation, face-to-face communication, often expressed in dance, song, or gesture, was replaced by written symbols that represented a speaker's sounds even without the speaker. These symbols could be written and stored on materials for long periods in contrast to relying on memory necessitated by the oral tradition. Education once conducted apprenticeship fashion by village experts, often the elders, was replaced by Hawaiian-language newspapers-cum-textbooks. In time, public school instruction in Hawaiian gave way to instruction in English, which led to the near demise of the spoken and written Hawaiian language. The Protestant missionaries' transformation of spoken Hawaiian into a written alphabetic system made possible Western business practices and legal systems too complex to be stored in human memory and transmitted to the next generation. Writing thus paved the way for the Hawaiian monarchy's promulgating a Western-style constitution, instituting private property rights to replace community-held lands, and introducing a capitalistic money economy to replace barter and sharing. Then the Hawaiian monarchy itself was overthrown. The Hawaiian Islands were annexed to the United States in 1898, when Guam, Puerto Rico, and the Philippines also passed from Spanish to American control and Cuba came under the U.S. sphere of influence.

Mode-of-communication differences between orality and literacy gave rise to social and political biases that led to cultural racism, which is more serious than individual or institutional racism.[60] Psychologist James M. Jones described cultural racism as "the most intractable, yet possibly most crucial" because it requires "a new look at cultural assumptions and their manifestations in social organizations."[61] Jones argued, for example, that persons from an oral-tradition culture are at a disadvantage operating under the standards of print-oriented, white Anglo-Saxon Protestants, such as those embodied in high school and college scholastic testing.[62] Thus, he wrote, culture may supersede or overlap with color as a basis for domination.

THE BIAS OF THE LEGAL CONSTRUCTION
OF RACE AND RACISM

The colonists' religious and mode-of-communication biases against Native Americans and African Americans played out in curious political ways. The prerevolutionary press printed a few articles, poems, and letters that equated the enslavement of the Africans with the oppression being suffered by the colonists at the hands of England.[63] But during the Revolutionary War, such items and all antislavery news were absent, giving way to news about the War for Independence.[64]

The Declaration of Independence of 1776 applied only to white men. One scholar noted that critics condemned "the apparent hypocrisy of a people who declared that all men were created equal" and yet deprived "more than an hundred thousand Africans of their rights to liberty and the pursuit of happiness, and in some degree to their lives."[65]

After independence was won, the new government was built on racial distinctions that excluded Native Americans and African Americans from participation. The newly independent press, soon protected by the First Amendment, voiced no new expressions of sympathy for these groups and was unusually silent about "the forces shaping the destiny of our country at this time," media historians noted. "We can learn more by reading reports of foreign observers who visited our shores during the first thirty years of the country."[66] Through silence, the press supported this legal framework that constructed a racial classification and race-based political order designed to preserve and enhance Euro-American predominance. Soon this racial order began to structure major institutions and social relationships.[67]

Under the newly drafted Constitution of 1789, race was a criterion specified in the U.S. Census that was first conducted a year later. Native Americans were not counted at all. African Americans, comprising 19.3 percent of the population, were counted; 92 percent of them were listed as slaves.[68] The Constitution mandated each slave to be counted as three-fifths of a man.

Two hundred years later, the 1990 Census was the most detailed in history. It asked self-identification questions of four racial categories (Native Americans, Caucasians, African Americans, and Asian Americans combined with Pacific Islanders). It also asked for ethnic subcategories for Asian Americans (such as Chinese or Japanese) and for Pacific Islanders (such as Hawaiians, Samoans, or Tongans). It also asked for the specific names of American Indian tribes and a national-origin classification of Hispanic Americans. This 1990 classification scheme differentiated the U.S. population more finely than ever before in ways useful to advertisers, marketers, politicians, economists, and an array of government officials.[69] It also permits the compilation of statistics to show the racial and ethnic composition of the workforce, to construct profiles useful in surveilling or in classifying some population elements, or to enable discriminatory, harmful redlining of certain communities.[70]

Discrimination in American immigration laws started with the Naturalization Act of 1790, which provided for the naturalization of "any alien, being a free white person."[71] After the Civil War, the statute was changed to read that any Chinese person was prohibited from becoming an American citizen, and later this change was interpreted to bar naturalization of any person from Asia. Immigration and naturalization of Chinese were barred from 1882 until 1943, when China became a U.S. ally in World War II.[72] The Japanese could not become naturalized citizens until 1952. As Michael Omi and Howard Winant noted, "It took over 160 years, since the passage of the Law of 1790, to allow all 'races' to be eligible for naturalization."[73]

The antipathy expressed in the colonial press against Native Americans and African slaves did not disappear with the end of the colonists' own perceived enslavement by England. Likewise, as detailed in Chapter 4, the war with Mexico, which began in 1846, expanded U.S. territory into the Southwest and brought more unfavorable press treatment to more indigenous peoples. And, as detailed in Chapter 5, laborers imported from China and Japan in the later 1800s received ambivalent, sometimes outright hostile, press comments.

In 1896 the Supreme Court's *Plessy v. Ferguson* decision approved racial segregation if equal facilities were provided; not until 1954 was segregation in schooling held unconstitutional and ordered dismantled. But in 1996, on the centennial of that landmark separate-but-equal decision, historian Eric Foner noted that "in the legacy of decades of discrimination by federal and state authorities, employers, realtors, educators and others, *Plessy* lives on." Foner noted the "ominous parallels between the time of *Plessy* and our own." The parallels he listed included the key government decisions beginning in the 1980s to weaken affirmative action programs enacted to redress employment imbalances and loosening school district requirements mandating desegregation.[74] Fearing that *Plessy* "may yet enjoy a new lease on life," Foner wrote that the phrase "our Constitution is colorblind," which was hurled at the Supreme Court majority by the lone dissenter in the 1896 decision, "has today been appropriated by those who oppose taking race into account under any circumstances— even to remedy the effects of past injustice and continuing inequity."[75] Other scholars agree that the word *colorblind* has been seized by conservatives as a code word used to imply racial equality but that actually means strategies for rolling back programs set up to overcome disadvantages caused by past segregation.[76]

Despite decades of supposed desegregation since 1954, Sears wrote "that racism continues to pervade white America."[77] Even though "old-fashioned racism" of official segregation has gone underground or out of style, a psychologist stated, it has been replaced by "modern racism." This modern version is an ideology that minimizes contemporary racial discrimination and sees African Americans as pushing too hard and too fast for gains, making unfair demands and using unwarranted tactics.[78] The news media's role in perpetuating modern versions of racism is discussed at the end of this chapter.

Future remedies are unlikely to be simple. Legal scholar Derrick Bell warned that successful remedies are unlikely by the year 2000 without acknowledgement of "the role of racism in the world as it is" and without overturning the legal precedent "under which black rights have been sacrificed throughout American history to further white interests."[79]

The deeply embedded racism in U.S. culture and the news media's general failure to portray and explore that racism constitute a recurring pattern of this book. Again and again, readers will encounter examples of governmental, legal, personal, and news media bias against the racial and cultural groups studied here, and they will wonder why they had never been aware of these episodes. The answer lies partly in the way in which the mainstream U.S. news media have largely ignored the mistreatment of minorities—and in many eras have enthusiastically encouraged it. Exceptions to this pattern are discussed in Chapter 7, which details investigative reporters' exposés about racial injustices and inequities.

THE BIAS IN THE NATURE OF NEWS

The surveillance function of *Publick Occurrences*, as discussed at the beginning of this chapter, entailed furnishing "an Account of such considerable things as have arrived unto our Notice." The surveillance function of news may arise biologically and culturally from the desire of the earliest humans to protect themselves by knowing about their environment; both biology and culture have profoundly affected the form that news content has taken.[80]

By gathering and printing news, the early journalists transformed into writing and print the everyday events and utterances of the oral-based life of the colonies. This information was valuable to the literate but worked to the disadvantage of the illiterate. Copeland noted that this oral-to-print transformation served to make colonial news of an event "official," and it permitted sharing of news, such as about slave revolts, among major towns. Even news of slave insurrections in Jamaica, reprinted from Jamaican papers delivered by ship, was published in Boston and other towns, thus keeping residents on guard against revolts in their vicinity.

Oddly enough, Copeland found, of the thirteen colonies, only in South Carolina was there a noticeable lack of news about slaves and only there did the slave population outnumber whites. In addition, in that one colony, where the threat of insurrection was greatest, slave revolt news almost disappeared, either because of self-censorship or government mandate.[81] Thus, another news pattern emerged: news about the greatest threats to the public may be blacked out or buried if disclosure of them damages the interests of the publisher, the state, or both. This pattern of news blackout also appears in the chapters that follow.

Besides surveillance, *Publick Occurrences* proposed publication so

• "That Memorable Occurrents of Divine Providence may not be neglected or forgotten" and

- "That People everywhere may better understand the Circumstances of Publique Affairs, both abroad and at home, which may not only direct their Thoughts at all times, but at some times also to assist their Business and Negotiations."[82]

Prototypal purposes described by *Publick Occurrences* and persisting over 300 years included this goal of informing people of public affairs and a pledge to correct mistakes. Over time, media analysts have noted, functions of the media have been expanded to cover interpretation of the different parts of society to each other, transmission of social heritage, entertainment, and economic service, especially for the needs of shareholders or fee-paying advertisers.[83]

Publick Occurrences was the colonies' first example of unauthorized news. It had been published without receiving the necessary governor's license—or Countenance of Authority—and four days after publication it was suppressed before a second issue could be distributed.[84]

In 1791 the First Amendment of the Bill of Rights stated, "Congress shall pass no law . . . abridging the freedom of speech, or of the press." That amendment provided the press with special protection supposedly so that it could inform citizens about their government. However, the First Amendment did not immediately change the patterns of covering racial minorities in the established press, which was growing in importance as the "penny press" developed for the common reader. By the late 1820s, a shift came when brand-new publications were established by both Euro-Americans and African Americans to serve as weapons of opposition against slavery.

In 1934 the U.S. government formalized licensing procedures to apply to the emerging electronic media, thus leaving them less protected by the First Amendment. The importance of that 1934 act, its major expansion six decades later with enactment of the Telecommunications Act of 1996, and the impact of both on news coverage of racial and cultural groups are discussed in Chapter 8.

One technological advance of the press related to coverage of racial minorities in an unexpectedly unfavorable way. The invention of half-moon metal stereotype plates needed for high-speed printing revolutionized the newspaper business and prompted a new definition of *stereotype*[85] that in time became attached to news repetitions—often negative—about people of color. That definition is "a person or group considered to typify or conform to a general pattern, lacking individuality."[86] Walter Lippmann, in his 1922 classic *Public Opinion*, warned that the hallmark of the perfect stereotype is that it precedes the use of reason. He also wrote that it "imposes a certain character on the data of our senses before the data reach the intelligence." It is obdurate because it stamps itself upon the facts in the very act of securing the facts.[87] Stereotypes—even unconscious ones—affect the way people process information, form judgements, develop or sustain prejudice, and act.

News media have perpetuated negative stereotypes of racial groups, even now, when they are trying not to do so. What they choose to run as news is often filtered through unconscious stereotypes. This contributes to modern white racism, according to a recent empirical study conducted by communication scholar Robert Entman. He gathered content analysis data from evening news programs on four Chicago television stations in 1989 and 1990. The data suggested that racism still may be indirectly encouraged by traditional crime and political coverage that depict blacks, in crime, as more physically threatening and, in politics, as more demanding than comparable white suspects or leaders. Ironically, he noted, widespread employment of black television journalists suggests to viewers that racial discrimination is no longer a significant social problem. The mix of these two views of blacks encourages modern white racism—hostility toward, rejection of, and denial of black aspirations.[88] In his study, Entman called for systematic, follow-up research to determine whether specific types of news and news practices may be contributing to the metamorphosis and continuation of white racism.[89]

Entman's modern white racism concept was extended in a 1994 study that connected it to national television news coverage of the domestic war on drugs in the 1980s and early 1990s. Scholars described national television news as being "deeply implicated in both publicizing and authorizing the disciplinary operations of the modern drug establishment" that was directed disproportionately against people of color. The scholars noted Ted Koppel's "Nightline" in the aftermath of the Los Angeles upheavals that followed the 1992 not-guilty jury verdicts in favor of four police officers videotaped brutalizing Rodney King. Two rival Los Angeles gang members gave the "Nightline" audience what the scholars described as "an alternative view of the verdict aftermath, arguing that white-collar looters involved in the national savings and local scandal constituted a far more sinister criminal threat to America (and yet most of them never spent time in jail)." Another gang member provided Koppel with a startling view of the Los Angeles Police Department: a rival street gang. The scholars urged thoughtful reporters to consider critically how they deal with "government officials and enterprising experts who have vested interests in cultivating drug hysteria" and how they present certain segments of the population as deviants who are "beyond rehabilitation."[90] Chapter 3 and Chapter 9 present details of newsroom practices that lead to what Entman called modern white racism and to other kinds of racism.

Focusing on race-related issues and practices is more essential than ever before, according to communication scholar Jane Rhodes, in order to begin addressing "the darker side of media history; the tale of a national institution encumbered by a racist past."[91]

In 1923 the American Society of Newspaper Editors adopted its first Canons of Ethics, which indicated that the primary function of newspapers was "to communicate to the human race what its members do, feel, and think."[92] Similarly, in 1947, just as television was emerging as a news medium, the influential Report of the Commission on the Freedom of the Press argued that "the truth about any social group, though it should not exclude its weakness and vices, includes also recognition of its values, its aspirations, and its common humanity.''[93] The commission, also known as the Hutchins Commission, urged news media to project accurately a representative picture of the constituent groups in American society, adding that such coverage would help readers develop an understanding of and respect for each group.[94] The impact of the commission's recommendation for representativeness in news content was significant. Communication scholar Everette Dennis wrote, ''If these recommendations of the commission were at first dismissed as ivory-tower philosophizing, they would later become accepted as dogma for many, if not most, minority critics.''[95]

The consequences of ignoring the commission's recommendations could be serious. Early research found that the scant news coverage of African Americans by two Los Angeles dailies over almost a century created ''black invisibility.'' This led to a sins-of-omission model that confused whites' understanding of racism and that facilitated the exploitation of African Americans by whites. The researchers concluded: ''It may be that inhumanity depends on the invisibility of the victim.''[96]

The racial uprisings that occurred in the 1960s in major urban centers prompted President Lyndon Johnson to appoint the National Advisory Commission on Civil Disorders, often called the Kerner Commission, to investigate the causes of the disturbances. The commission criticized the news media for failing to provide an accurate and representative picture of African Americans. The commission said that the media failed to inform whites about the ''difficulties and frustrations of being a Negro in the United States'' and in so doing had failed in part of their responsibility to the nation and society. Both the Kerner and Hutchins commissions called for a more systematic study of the news media by the profession and other entities.[97]

The urban disorders domestically and the counterculture that arose in opposition to the Vietnam War also raised critical questions about ''objectivity.'' It was the convention journalists had adopted and practiced since the 1920s to duplicate the scientists' rational, disinterested, and detached view of the world. It was developed as a counter to the reality of the journalists' subjectivity.[98]

Of direct relevance to covering racial issues, critics in the 1960s began contending that objectivity in journalism, instead of being an antidote to bias, ''came to be looked upon as the most insidious bias of all,'' sociologist Michael Schudson wrote. He described critics' claims that it ''reproduced a vision of social reality which refused to examine the basic structures of power and privilege,'' it ''represented collusion with institutions whose legitimacy was in dispute,'' and it privileged ''the social structure of news gathering which reinforced official viewpoints of social reality.'' But, from the 1970s on no new ideal had been born to challenge objectivity. Nonetheless, what was required, he wrote, was an individual and institutional ''commitment to caring for truth.''[99]

In 1985 obstacles within newsrooms that blocked better coverage of racial minorities were detailed by Wilson and Gutiérrez. They noted the critical role of the mostly white, mostly male decision-makers who for centuries had defined news, news values and news policies. These decision-makers, commonly called gatekeepers, determine what information is passed on to the public in the form of news and what is held back from dissemination. Wilson and Gutiérrez explained: "Since news reflects what is really important to a society, minority coverage in mainstream news reporting provides insight into the status of minorities. By their professional judgments, the gatekeepers of news reveal how consequential minorities are to American society and determine the ways in which they are interpreted to the majority audience." They said improving mainstream news coverage of racial groups required that "the last vestiges of prejudice and racism must be removed from the gatekeeper ranks." They also called for changes in news policy and the news value system.[100]

They noted that mainstream news coverage about people of color has been characterized historically from the 1830s to the 1990s in these four developmental phases: exclusionary, threatening issue, confrontation, and stereotypical selection. These phases are repeatedly detailed in the chapters that follow.

The news media have a variety of standard values and practices that also contribute to poor coverage of minority groups, and examples of many of these can be found in the following chapters. They include an event-orientation that leads the media to ignore important but long-standing social problems until they erupt into violence. An example is the media's ignoring of the disenfranchisement of black Americans for almost a century—until the protest marches and voter registration drives of the 1960s. Another practice is for the media to then cover the event itself primarily in terms of the conflict, the violence and damage involved, while giving little or no coverage to the conditions leading to the protest. Still another practice is a journalistic proclivity to reduce complex situations to simplistic and misleading terms, such as letting affirmative action programs become framed as "reverse discrimination." An additional problem noted on these pages is the mainstream media's tendency to present debate on issues that deeply affect people of color, such as a proposed civil rights bill or a discussion of atomic testing, primarily as a competition between groups of whites, usually white politicians.

In the 1990s, Wilson and Gutiérrez noted, a fifth—multiracial coverage— phase was embryonic. By then, communication researchers Pamela Shoemaker and Stephen Reese had noted a general proposition about U.S. media coverage: "The more a minority newsmaker has acculturated to white society and the higher his or her socioeconomic level is, the more prominently he or she will be covered."[101] Journalists of racial and ethnic minority background were also underrepresented.[102]

Wilson and Gutiérrez wrote in 1995, "Because people of color are vastly underrepresented in the upper-middle- to upper-class income economic categories, they have been shortchanged in news media coverage." They noted that "a major barrier to more racially comprehensive news coverage has been preoccupation with profit incentive, as media 'marketing' of news has led to, among other questionable practices, an increased emphasis on information targeted to high-economic-profile audiences." They suggested that the news media are fail-

ing in their responsibilities to inform society about the perspectives, contributions, and lives of all its components.[103]

CONCLUSION

In summary, this chapter has reviewed key influences on the news coverage
of Native Americans and African Americans, which began with *Publick Occurrences* in 1690. These influences then continued during the early news coverage
of Asian Americans, Hispanic Americans, and Pacific Islanders. In the chapters
that follow, readers are provided with a longitudinal sweep of patterns of news
coverage of these five groups since 1934 and a short history of each group.
Chapters 7 and 8 explore the significance for these groups of investigative reporting and of federal regulation of broadcasting and telecommunications. Chapter 9 contains conclusions about various patterns of news coverage since 1934.

The *Sourcebook*'s longitudinal sweep comes at a critical juncture. Race relations in the United States are seething to the extent that, as African American
studies specialist Cornel West has explained, "[W]e are on a slippery slope
toward economic strife, social turmoil, and cultural chaos."[104] West stated that
this potential for upheaval stands side by side with "the marvels of the technological breakthroughs in communications and information,"[105] including
news.

Communication scholar Majid Tehranian has noted that these marvels, featuring computers and satellites, have produced a new age of human communication marked by technocratic capitalism as a social system and by national and
global technocracies as dominant communication institutions. These information
technologies are "a double-edged sword," bestowing upon news and other mass
media the hardware, software, and "the underlying cognitive deep structures"
that can lead either to manipulation or to a new dawn. Modern news and other
mass media "have the unique property of creating an illusion of knowledge and
communication without its substance," Tehranian warned. "Systematic distortions in communication are . . . achieved by the power of the modern mass media
through administered silences that impose 'black holes' on public consciousness." But if used interactively for critical public discourse, these technologies
also "have the power to inform and awaken."[106]

These technological marvels are also transforming the U.S. news media
through a new marketing approach to news and a changing environment in
journalistic styles and standards.[107] U.S. newspapers now merging into diversi-
fied information corporations will spearhead an information economy delivered
globally on high-speed fiber optics networks.[108] Supported by this faster, more
powerful media technology, future U.S. news coverage will in unparalleled ways
influence the domestic portrayals of racial and cultural groups, thus potentially
affecting the tranquility of the nation and its image worldwide.

Understanding the impact of future information technologies may be fostered
by recovering the historical perspective and by exposing the contradictions, de-

ficiencies, and promises of the U.S. news media in their coverage of Native Americans, African Americans, Asian Americans, Hispanic Americans, and Pacific Islanders. As a leading African American poet noted: "History, despite its wrenching pain, cannot be unlived, but if faced with courage, need not be lived again" (Maya Angelou, 1993, at William Clinton's Presidential Inauguration).[109]

NOTES

1. *Publick Occurrences Both Forreign and Domestick* (Boston) September 25, 1690, 1. Italics and spellings are in a facsimile copy obtained from the American Antiquarian Society. The original is in the Public Record Office, London.

2. David Alan Copeland, "The Freshest Advices Foreign and Domestic: The Character and Content of Nonpolitical News in Colonial Newspapers, 1690–1775" (Ph.D. diss., University of North Carolina at Chapel Hill, 1994), iii.

3. *Publick Occurrences*, 2, 3; Victor Hugo Paltsits, "New Light on 'Publick Occurrences': America's First Newspaper," *Proceedings of the American Antiquarian Society* 58 (April 1949), 81.

4. Clint C. Wilson II and Félix Gutiérrez, *Race, Multiculturalism, and the Media: From Mass to Class Communication*, 2d ed. (Thousand Oaks, Calif.: Sage, 1995), 34, citing Lasswell; Pamela J. Shoemaker and Stephen D. Reese, *Mediating the Message: Theories of Influences on Mass Media Content*, 2d ed. (White Plains, N.Y.: Longman, 1996), 29.

5. Copeland, "The Freshest Advices," 212.

6. Ibid., citing Gary B. Nash.

7. Ibid., 251.

8. Ibid., 209.

9. This media portrayal of the racial divide also masked a wider range of opinions, with some African Americans disagreeing with the verdict and some white Americans agreeing with it, according to remarks made by Robert McGruder, an African-American journalist with the *Detroit Free Press*, at a videotaped panel discussion of the Associated Press Managing Editors titled "Did We Learn Anything?" (Indianapolis: Freedom Forum, 1995).

10. For an elaboration of how people of color view white institutions, see Joe R. Feagin and Clairece Booher Feagin, *Racial and Ethnic Relations*, 5th ed. (Upper Saddle River, N.J.: Prentice-Hall, 1996), 460–65.

11. Ira Reiner, videotaped remarks made during panel discussion of Associated Press Managing Editors (Indianapolis: Freedom Forum, 1995).

12. "Clinton Calls for Healing," *Chicago Tribune*, 16 October 1995, 1, based on ProQuest's Newspaper Abstracts.

13. Christopher P. Campbell, *Race, Myth and the News* (Thousand Oaks, Calif.: Sage, 1995), 4–5.

14. Phyllis A. Katz and Dalmas A. Taylor, "Introduction," in *Eliminating Racism: Profiles in Controversy*, ed. Phyllis A. Katz and Dalmas A. Taylor (New York: Plenum Press, 1988), 1–16.

15. See Michael Omi and Howard Winant, *Racial Formation in the United States: From the 1960s to the 1990s*, 2d ed. (New York: Routledge, 1994), for their concept of a race-based political order in the United States.

16. This four-layered approach utilizes and extends the social-system level of analysis—where operate some of the most important forces influencing news content—as described by Pamela J. Shoemaker in *Communication Concepts 3: Gatekeeping* (Newbury Park, Calif.: Sage, 1991). She indicated U.S. ideology includes a belief in the capitalistic economic system, the Protestant work ethic, individualism, and liberal democracy. The ideological influences on media content are further articulated by Shoemaker and Reese in *Mediating the Message*, 221–51.

17. This thesis extends to news coverage the important work done in other disciplines, such as that disseminated in Omi and Winant's *Racial Formation* and Feagin and Feagin's *Racial and Ethnic Relations*.

18. Wilson and Gutiérrez, *Race, Multiculturalism, and the Media*, 151.

19. Teun A. van Dijk, *Elite Discourse and Racism* (Newbury Park, Calif.: Sage, 1993); Paula B. Johnson, David O. Sears, and John B. McConahay, "Black Invisibility, the Press and the Los Angeles Riot," *American Journal of Sociology* 76, no. 4 (January 1971), 698–721.

20. van Dijk, *Elite Discourse*, 242.

21. Ibid., 243; Teun A. van Dijk, *Communicating Racism: Ethnic Prejudice in Thought and Talk* (Newbury Park, Calif.: Sage, 1987).

22. David L. Paletz and Robert M. Entman, *Media, Power, Politics* (New York: Free Press, 1981). The authors indicated this finding applied to the mass media, but their book supports this statement largely by analyzing news.

23. van Dijk, *Elite Discourse*, 250.

24. National Advisory Commission on Civil Disorders, *Report of the National Advisory Commission on Civil Disorders* (Washington, D.C.: U.S. Government Printing Office, 1968), 213.

25. Feagin and Feagin, *Racial and Ethnic Relations*, 451.

26. Winthrop D. Jordan, *White over Black: American Attitudes toward the Negro, 1550–1812* (New York: W. W. Norton, 1977), 27.

27. David E. Stannard, *American Holocaust: The Conquest of the New World* (Oxford: Oxford University Press, 1992), 126.

28. Ibid., 108, citing others.

29. Jordan, *White over Black*, 27.

30. Ibid., 66–85.

31. Copeland, "The Freshest Advices," 213.

32. James M. Jones, *Prejudice and Racism*, 2d ed. (New York: McGraw-Hill, 1997), 28.

33. Copeland, "The Freshest Advices," 215.

34. Jordan, *White over Black*, 18; Jane Rhodes, "The Visibility of Race and Media History," in *Gender, Race and Class in Media*, ed. Gail Dines and Jean M. Humez (Thousand Oaks, Calif.: Sage, 1995), 33–39.

35. Copeland, "The Freshest Advices," 248.

36. Pierre L. van den Berghe, "Race and Ethnicity: A Sociobiological Perspective," *Ethnic and Racial Studies* 1, no. 4 (October 1978), 408.

37. Jordan, *White over Black*, 18.

38. van den Berghe, "Race and Ethnicity," 408.

39. Pseudo-scientific studies are critiqued in Stephen Jay Gould, *The Mismeasure of Man*, rev. and exp. ed. (New York: W. W. Norton, 1996). Originally published in 1981.

40. Robert F. Berkhofer, Jr., *The White Man's Indian: Images of the American Indian from Columbus to the Present* (New York: Random House [Vintage Books], 1979), 44.

41. Ibid., 25–69.

42. Gould, *The Mismeasure of Man*, 53, quoting Condorcet.

43. Ibid.; Jonathan Marks, *Human Biodiversity: Genes, Race, and History* (New York: Aldine de Gruyter, 1995), 106–16.

44. Omi and Winant, *Racial Formation*, 117.

45. Paul Hartmann and Charles Husband, *Racism and the Mass Media* (Totowa, N.J.: Rowman and Littlefield, 1974), 205. Emphases are theirs.

46. David O. Sears, "Symbolic Racism" in *Eliminating Racism: Profiles in Controversy*, ed. Phyllis A. Katz and Dalmas A. Taylor (New York: Plenum Press, 1988), 80.

47. James M. Jones, *Prejudice and Racism* (New York: Random House, 1972), 6.

48. Harold A. Innis, *The Bias of Communication* (Toronto: University of Toronto Press, 1991). Reprint with new introduction by Paul Heyer and David Crowley, 191. Originally published in 1951.

49. Mitchell Stephens, *A History of News: From the Drum to the Satellite* (New York: Viking Press, 1988), 22.

50. Robert K. Logan, *The Alphabet Effect: The Impact of the Phonetic Alphabet on the Development of Western Civilization* (New York: William Morrow, 1986), n.p., citing Hitti.

51. Ibid., 58.

52. Walter J. Ong, *Orality and Literacy: The Technologizing of the Word* (London: Methuen, 1982), 90.

53. Innis's work is masterfully synthesized in James W. Carey, "Harold Adams Innis and Marshall McLuhan" in *Communications Control: Readings in the Motives and Structures of Censorship*, ed. John Phelan (New York: Sheed and Ward, 1969), 43–77. Originally published in 1967.

54. James W. Carey, "Innis, Harold (1894–1952)," in *International Encyclopedia of Communications* vol. 2 (New York: Oxford University Press, 1989), 320–21.

55. Innis, *The Bias of Communication*, 139.

56. Logan, *The Alphabet Effect*, 58.

57. Ong, *Orality and Literacy*, 86, 92.

58. Ibid., 112–17.

59. Harold A. Innis, *Empire and Communications* (Toronto: University of Toronto Press, 1972), revised by Mary Q. Innis. Originally published in 1950; also Innis, *The Bias of Communication*.

60. James M. Jones, "Racism: A Cultural Analysis of the Problem" in *Prejudice, Discrimination, and Racism*, ed. John F. Dovidio and Samuel L. Gaertner (Orlando, Fla.: Academic Press, 1986), 279–314.

61. Ibid., 281.

62. James M. Jones, "Racism in Black and White: A Bicultural Model of Reaction and Evolution" in *Eliminating Racism: Profiles in Controversy*, ed. Phyllis A. Katz and Dalmas A. Taylor (New York: Plenum Press, 1988), 117–35.

63. Copeland, "The Freshest Advices," 242–50; Bernard Bailyn, *The Ideological Origins of the American Revolution* (Cambridge, Mass.: Belknap Press of Harvard University Press, 1967), 235–46.

64. Copeland, "The Freshest Advices," 250.

65. Bailyn, *The Ideological Origins*, 246.

66. Michael Emery and Edwin Emery, *The Press and America: An Interpretive History of the Mass Media*, 6th ed. (Englewood Cliffs, N.J.: Prentice Hall, 1988), 105.

67. Omi and Winant, *Racial Formation*, 79. Also, on 162 the authors define "racism" as that fundamental characteristic of policies or activities that creates or reproduces structures of domination based on unchangeable categories of race. Examples of such categories are skin color or other physical markers.

68. Wilson and Gutiérrez, *Race, Multiculturalism, and the Media*, 7.

69. Oscar H. Gandy, Jr., *The Panoptic Sort: A Political Economy of Personal Information* (Boulder, Colo.: Westview Press, 1993).

70. Ibid.

71. Commission on Wartime Relocation and Internment of Civilians, *Personal Justice Denied* (Washington, D.C.: U.S. Government Printing Office, 1983), 28–29, citing others.

72. Ibid., 29.

73. Omi and Winant, *Racial Formation*, 184, footnote 35.

74. Eric Foner, "Plessy Is Not Passé," *Nation* 262, no. 22 (3 June 1996), 6.

75. Ibid.

76. Omi and Winant, *Racial Formation*.

77. Sears, "Symbolic Racism," 78.

78. John B. McConahay, "Modern Racism, Ambivalence, and the Modern Racism Scale" in *Prejudice, Discrimination, and Racism*, ed. John F. Dovidio and Samuel L. Gaertner (Orlando, Fla.: Academic Press, 1986), 91–125, esp. 93.

79. Derrick Bell, "Racism: A Prophecy for the Year 2000," *Rutgers Law Review* 42, no. 1 (1989), 93, 102.

80. Pamela J. Shoemaker, "Hardwired for News: Using Biological and Cultural Evolution to Explain the Surveillance Function," *Journal of Communication* 46, no. 3 (Summer 1996), 32–47.

81. Copeland, "The Freshest Advices," 253–54.

82. *Publick Occurrences*, 1.

83. Wilson and Gutiérrez, *Race, Multiculturalism, and the Media*, 38.

84. "By the Governour and Council" suppression order dated 29 September 1690; facsimile copy obtained from the American Antiquarian Society.

85. Penelope J. Oakes, S. Alexander Haslam, and John C. Turner, *Stereotyping and Social Reality* (Oxford, England: Blackwell, 1994), 15.

86. Richard Weiner, *Webster's New World Dictionary of Media and Communications: The Most Comprehensive Source for Understanding the Language of Writers, Communications, and the Media Industry* (New York: Simon and Schuster, 1990), 464.

87. Walter Lippmann, *Public Opinion* (New York: Macmillan Paperbacks Edition, 1960), 98–99; compare Oakes, Haslam, and Turner, *Stereotyping and Social Reality*. See also Jones, *Prejudice and Racism*, 2d ed., 164–202. This book provides an up-to-date, jargon-free summary of the extensive research conducted by social psychologists on stereotypes, prejudice, and racism.

88. Robert M. Entman, "Blacks in the News: Television, Modern Racism and Cultural Change," *Journalism Quarterly* 69, no. 2 (summer 1992), 341–61.

89. Robert M. Entman, "Modern Racism and the Images of Blacks in Local TV News," *Critical Studies in Mass Communication* 7 (December 1990), 332–45.

90. Jimmie L. Reeves and Richard Campbell, *Cracked Coverage: Television News, the Anti-Cocaine Crusade, and the Reagan Legacy* (Durham, N.C.: Duke University

Press, 1994), 3, 10, 66–67, 260. The authors provided no date for the ''Nightline'' program.

91. Rhodes, ''The Visibility of Race,'' 34.

92. *Problems of Journalism: Proceedings of the First Annual Meeting, American Society of Newspaper Editors* (Washington, D.C.: n.p., 27–28 April 1923), n.p.

93. Commission on the Freedom of the Press, *A Free and Responsible Press: A General Report on Mass Communication: Newspapers, Radio, Motion Pictures, Magazines, and Books* (Chicago: University of Chicago Press, 1947), 26–27.

94. Ibid., 27.

95. Everette E. Dennis, ''Rhetoric and Reality of Representation'' in *Small Voices and Great Trumpets*, ed. Bernard Rubin (New York: Praeger, 1980), 68–69.

96. Johnson, Sears, and McConahay, ''Black Invisibility,'' 718.

97. Commission on the Freedom of the Press, *A Free and Responsible Press*, 96–106; National Advisory Commission on Civil Disorders, *Report of the National Advisory Commission*, 210, 212–13.

98. Michael Schudson, *Discovering the News: A Social History of American Newspapers* (n.p.: HarperCollins, 1978), 159–94.

99. Ibid., 160, 162–63, 193–94.

100. Clint C. Wilson II and Félix Gutiérrez, *Minorities and Media: Diversity and the End of Mass Communication* (Beverly Hills, Calif.: Sage, 1985), 134, 139.

101. Shoemaker and Reese, *Mediating the Message*, 2d ed., 263.

102. Ibid.

103. Wilson and Gutiérrez, *Race, Multiculturalism, and the Media*, 159.

104. Cornel West, ''Learning to Talk of Race,'' in *Reading Rodney King/Reading Urban Uprising*, ed. Robert Gooding-Williams (New York: Routledge, 1993), 257. Originally published in 1992.

105. Cornel West, *Prophetic Reflections: Notes on Race and Power in America* (Monroe, Maine: Common Courage Press, 1993), 43.

106. Majid Tehranian, *Technologies of Power: Information Machines and Democratic Prospects* (Norwood, N.J.: Ablex Publishing, 1990), 67, 20–21.

107. See Everette E. Dennis, *Reshaping the Media: Mass Communication in an Information Age* (Newbury Park, Calif.: Sage, 1989); W. Russell Neuman, *The Future of the Mass Audience* (Cambridge, Eng.: Cambridge University Press, 1991); American Society of Newspaper Editors, *Come the Millennium: Interviews on the Shape of Our Future* (Kansas City, Mo.: Andrews and McMeel, 1994). Christopher J. Feola, ''Newspapers Gain with Technology,'' *Quill* 84, no. 3 (April 1996), 27–29.

108. George Gilder, *Life after Television: The Coming Transformation of Media and American Life*, rev. ed. (New York: W. W. Norton, 1994), 146–216.

109. Maya Angelou, ''On the Pulse of Morning,'' *New York Times*, 21 January 1993, A14.

2

The Native Americans

MARY ANN WESTON AND JOHN M. COWARD

[T]he Indians are children. Their arts, wars, treaties, alliances, habitations, crafts, properties, commerce, comforts, all belong to the very lowest and rudest ages of human existence.

—Horace Greeley, Editor, *New York Tribune*, 1860[1]

Squalid and conceited, proud and worthless, lazy and lousy, [Indian braves] will strut out or drink out their miserable existence, and at length afford the world a sensible relief by dying out of it.

—Horace Greeley, Editor, *New York Tribune*, 1860[2]

It is little wonder that Indian peoples were perceived not as they were but as they "had" to be—from a European point of view. They were whisked out of the realm of the real and into the land of the make-believe. Indians became variably super- or subhuman, never ordinary. They dealt in magic, not judgment. They were imagined to be stuck in the past, not guided by its precedents.

—Michael Dorris, Modoc, 1987[3]

The European discovery and exploration of America was not a neutral event. Early Europeans, in fact, saw the New World largely through medieval eyes, expecting that America was a strange and exotic land complete with monsters, giants, dragons, and barbarous natives.[4] The fantasies of medieval Europe also fueled the search for American cities of gold, a quest that had disastrous consequences for European-native relations in much of Latin America. Christopher Columbus himself was initially ambivalent about the natives, praising their intelligence but also judging their potential to be servants.[5] Indeed, Columbus's first encounter with Native Americans reveals his assumption of superiority. He gave these natives red caps and glass beads "because I recognized that they were people who would be better freed [from error] and converted to our Holy

Faith by love than by force.''[6] But Columbus recognized a superiority beyond religion. He could plainly see that European materialism and technology were advanced well beyond those of the islanders he encountered, and he had no reason to doubt the superiority of European culture and civilization. In short, Columbus and most other European explorers viewed Native Americans as fundamentally different from and inferior to Europeans in significant civilizing ways—everything from religion to material wealth, technology, and culture. Given this perceived inequality, it is little wonder that generations of European immigrants came to America with clear notions about their right to dominate and dispossess the inferior people of the Americas.

The European attitude toward Native Americans was the product of an ideology of civilized progress, a set of beliefs and attitudes that privileged European ways and denigrated all other cultures and societies. In looking at Indians, Europeans saw people in dire need of Christianity, advanced technology, enlightened political arrangements, military organization, and the like. People without such influences, or resistant to them, were inferior and warranted special—and sometimes brutal—treatment. Even Christian charity was not enough to ensure equality or overcome the perceived deficiencies of native people. "Again and again during the centuries of European imperialism," historian Alfred Crosby wrote, "the Christian view that all men are brothers was to lead to persecution of non-Europeans—he who is my brother sins to the extent that he is unlike me—and to the tempering of imperialism with mercy—he who is my brother deserves brotherly love."[7] In the case of American Indians, Europeans recognized inferior people and cultures and then set about converting and coercing Indians to be more like civilized Europeans. It was a path conceived in error and fraught with disaster for both Native and European Americans.

American attitudes toward Native Americans grew directly from such European roots. Two broad stereotypes of the Indian emerged: the noble savage, a simple but natural creature, distinguished by a special innocence and harmony with nature, and the evil Indian, a degraded, barbaric figure most notable for a bloody hatred of civilization. In the eastern colonies, where pressure for native land was building, the evil Indian was naturally dominant. This image was dramatically symbolized in a series of sensational captivity narratives—tales of Indian violence and Christian redemption that were widely read in the colonies. The most famous of these, *Sovereignty & Goodness of God. . . . Being a Narrative of the Captivity and Restauration of Mrs. Mary Rowlandson*, was published in 1682. Mrs. Rowlandson's tale recounted her physical ordeal, her test of faith, and the gift of God's grace. Her story made plain the terrifying inhumanity of the natives. In describing the Massachusetts attack during which she was captured, Mrs. Rowlandson wrote of houses being overrun by warriors and "the father and the mother and a suckling child they knocked in the head." Another villager begged for his life, but the Indians also "knocked him in [the] head, stripped him naked, and split open his bowels."[8] For all who read such stories—and many similar tales followed Mrs. Rowlandson's—Indians were obviously "merciless heathen," subhuman creatures capable of unspeakable evils. In sum, captivity tales reinforced the idea of the savage Indian in the colonial mind.

The first newspaper in the American colonies, Benjamin Harris's *Publick Occurrences, Both Forreign and Domestick*, picked up on these themes. Harris's unauthorized paper, published in Boston in 1690, was suppressed after only one issue. But Harris, like other colonists, identified two types of Indians. The "good" Indians were Christians, praised in *Publick Occurrences* for their decision to worship God with a day of Thanksgiving. But "bad" Indians were also "lurking about Chelmsford," Harris reported, about the same time that two local children disappeared. Although Harris provided no link between the Indians and the missing children, he (and the villagers) assumed that "both of them [are] supposed to be fallen into the hands of the Indians."[9] Thus the first American editor to write about Indians divided them into simple categories that reflected an "us versus them" ideology. Indians who were similar to the colonists—Christians, in this case—were worthy of praise. But "barbarous" natives were obviously different from colonists, so uncivilized that they might very well have kidnapped the Chelmsford children. In this small way, Benjamin Harris began a pattern of positive and negative stereotypes of Native Americans that continued well into the twentieth century.

The "evil" Indian continued to dominate colonial news columns. Given the inevitable cultural misunderstandings and conflicts over land in eighteenth-century America, the image of "the Sculking Indian Enemy" is hardly surprising. A press historian has noted that this phrase was used repeatedly by John Campbell, the editor of the *Boston News-Letter*, a paper founded in 1704.[10] Campbell provided regular reports on Indian conflicts in New England, but he also offered his readers news of Indian violence from up and down the Atlantic coast. The *Boston News-Letter* of May 1, 1704, for example, included extensive news of an attack on a South Carolina farmer, in which Indians had "shot him through the thigh and leggs, then took, Scalpt, kill'd, and stript him Naked."[11] Campbell also provided regular and similarly graphic reports from the Tuscarora War in the Carolinas from 1711 to 1713.

Like Benjamin Harris, colonial editors were quick to blame Indians for kidnapping and violence, even without proof. Boston's *New-England Courant* reported in 1725, for example, that a Stratford, Connecticut, woman lost her child and "concluded it was drown'd." A week later, the child's mutilated body was found two miles away; Indians were suspected and summoned to appear in Stratford.[12] News of Indian hostility and violence increased in the 1760s as western settlement extended to the Appalachians and beyond, fueling the Cherokee War in the South and Pontiac's War in western Pennsylvania, Detroit, and the Ohio Valley. Reports from the battle lines were often confusing and contradictory, however, because news filtered in from the provinces slowly and unreliably from traders, soldiers, and travelers. Despite such inconsistencies, one theme remained constant in news of Indian conflicts: sensationalism. To colonial readers, there was little doubt that the natives were bloodthirsty and cruel, all too willing to slice off limbs and split open heads at the slightest provocation.

A more humane view of native life was provided by Benjamin Franklin, who in 1764 wrote a 10,000-word pamphlet exposing the massacre of twenty Indian men, women, and children in Lancaster County, Pennsylvania, an incident that did not appear in the two Philadelphia papers.[13] Franklin described the murders of Indian families in emotional terms—"the Children clinging to the Parents; they fell on their Knees, protested their Innocence, declared their love for the English, . . . and in this Posture they all received the Hatchet!"[14] Franklin went on to condemn the racism behind the massacre. The killers wanted revenge, Franklin noted, but they attacked the wrong Indians. "The only Crime of these poor Wretches seems to have been, that some had a reddish brown Skin and black Hair," Franklin wrote. And he asked, "Do we come to America to learn and practise the manners of Barbarians?"[15] In contrast to many of his fellow colonists, Franklin recognized that all Indians were not to blame for the actions of a few, and he urged compassion and justice even for evil Indians.

Following the American Revolution, the pressure for new land and opportunity west of the Appalachians ensured that conflicts between whites and Midwestern and Southern tribes would continue. Indeed, one Tennessee historian has suggested that "taking part in the fearless conquest" of new lands motivated some men to move west in the first place. "Tales of blood and cruelty attracted instead of repelled them, and they desired to participate in deeds of valor," Carl Driver wrote about John Sevier, the "Scourge of the Cherokees" who became the first governor of Tennessee.[16] In Driver's view, frontier sensationalism furthered the ideology of civilization, making it plain to expansion-minded Americans that Indians had to be exterminated or removed for the task of nation building to continue.

In fact, this extermination was well under way. As far back as the seventeenth century, when English colonists first encountered Native Americans, they found people and societies decimated by European diseases introduced decades earlier by explorers. Native people had no immunities to such diseases as smallpox and measles, which in some cases wiped out entire communities. Bloody encounters with whites equipped with firearms thinned their ranks further. It has been estimated that the native population of America north of Mexico declined from some ten million to one million in the first centuries following European contact.

When the Constitution was written, Indians were not considered worthy of being counted in the census. Article I Section II of the Constitution excluded "Indians not taxed" from those to be counted to determine the number of representatives each state could send to Congress. However, the phrase was not further defined. It was not until the 1860 Census that Indians were counted as a separate group. Indeed, if whites in the late eighteenth century thought of Indians at all, it was probably as threats or enemies, not as fellow citizens.

However many Indians there were, to whites they were impediments to whites' settlement and expansionist aims. In the early nineteenth century, removal of Indians became the favored option in the South. State officials and private speculators actively promoted the extermination of tribal land claims. Thus the Choctaws, Creeks, Chickasaws, Cherokees, and Seminoles—known collectively as the Five Civilized Tribes for their progressive ways—were, despite this label, routinely pressured to sign away their lands. Southerners supported this policy by arguing that removal was necessary to protect the Indians—people who were, they claimed, a vanishing race, the remnants of a proud but doomed people. Indians might be saved, Southerners argued, if only they were separated from the corrupting influences of civilization.

Voluntary removal in the 1820s was slow and haphazard, which prompted calls for a more vigorous removal policy. The election of Andrew Jackson in 1828 brought such action. With Jackson's approval, the Southern tribes were steadily driven from their homes. The Cherokees, who resisted for a decade, used the first native newspaper, the *Cherokee Phoenix*, to campaign against removal and defend Indian rights. Editor Elias Boudinot was an eloquent spokesman for his people: "Let the Cherokees be firm and united.—Fellow citizens, we have asserted our rights . . . and we will defend them yet by all lawful and peaceful means."[17] The Cherokees appealed to the Supreme Court for relief, winning a decision in *Worcester v. Georgia*. Jackson and the Georgians ignored the decision, despite protests made by Cherokee leaders, Jackson's political opponents, outraged missionaries, and Indian sympathizers. By the mid-1830s, most of the natives had been resettled in Indian Territory (Oklahoma). Many Cherokees remained in the South, however, and in the winter of 1838–1839, all but a few were moved west on the deadly Trail of Tears. Anticipating this final exodus, a Savannah newspaper correspondent expressed the satisfaction of many Southerners: "Georgia is, at length, rid of her red population, and this beautiful country will now be prosperous and happy."[18]

The mainstream press reported the removal controversy, but it was not always a major story. One researcher, in fact, found that partisans on both sides produced much of the news. Indian supporters such as Jeremiah Evarts produced pro-Indian reports, which were answered by letters from federal and state officials. Even *Niles' Register*, one of the most important and even-handed journals of the day, left the debate to activists, never offering its own opinions of the policy.[19] Moreover, many removal stories emphasized not the plight of the Indians but the efficiency of their removal. Routine reports in the Southern press, for example, stressed the transportation aspects of the story: "Migration of Indians.—The Little Rock Times of the 5th inst. states that the steamboat Black Hawk arrived at that place on the Wednesday previous, having on board about 500 Creek Indians, under the charge of Lt. Deas, U. S. Army."[20]

Such reports identified the riverboat and the officer in charge, but no Creeks were named and neither their health nor their traveling conditions were mentioned. Even the Trail of Tears itself—notorious today—was not always a major news story, and many news accounts of the roundup and march originated with U.S. Army and government officials.[21] In any case, such eleventh-hour reports could do nothing to ease the pain of removal or roll back the final tragedy of the policy.

The dispossession of the Western tribes continued as white Americans and immigrants pushed the frontier into the plains and the Southwest, a process aided by the press. In 1836 Texas gained independence from Mexico and promptly began evicting the local Caddo and Hasinai people. A Texas editor anticipated statehood, a time when "the giant arms of the United States will soon sweep the few bands of hostile Indians from our borders."[22]

By 1846 settlers in their heavily laden wagons were crossing the prairies on their way to Oregon, territory recently ceded by England. The Treaty of Guadalupe in 1848 and the Gadsden Purchase of 1853 secured the Southwest as U.S. territory and brought new pressures on the Pueblo tribes. Permanent white settlements and continuing emigration across traditional native lands led to inevitable Indian-white confrontations, a fact not lost on the press. *New York Tribune* editor Horace Greeley, traveling west in 1859 to boost the transcontinental railroad, described Indians as degraded creatures, "slave[s] of appetite and sloth, never emancipated from the tyranny of one animal passion save by the more ravenous demands of another."[23] He recommended an industrial school education, especially for native women, whom he believed to be "the germ of renovation for their race."[24] Without this Indian "renovation," Greeley concluded, "extermination is inexorably certain, and cannot long be postponed."[25]

Some Western editors actively sought extermination. In 1864 William Byers of the *Rocky Mountain News* became increasingly alarmed about Indian threats to Colorado Territory. "Self preservation demands decisive action, and the only way to secure it is to fight them in their own way. A few months of active extermination against the red devils will bring quiet, and nothing else will."[26] These sentiments bore terrible fruit a few months later when the Colorado militia attacked Black Kettle's Cheyenne camp at Sand Creek, indiscriminately killing men, women, and children. Byers cheered: "Bully for the Colorado Boys." But for others, including some humanitarians writing in the Eastern press, the attack on Black Kettle's camp became notorious as the Sand Creek Massacre.[27]

Even as Indian wars were being fought in the Western territories, the federal government was for the first time recognizing Native Americans living in states already admitted to the union. The census law of 1850 extended the census to inhabitants of the territories, but continued to exclude "Indians not taxed" as the framers of the Constitution had done. In the 1860 Census, Indians appeared for the first time in a separate category—"civilized Indians." These were described as "the broken bands and the scattered remnants of tribes still to be found in many States. . . . By the fact of breaking away from their tribal relations, they are regarded as having entered the body of citizens and as subject to taxation." However, it was noted, most were too poor actually to pay taxes.[28] According to the 1860 Census, there were 44,021 "civilized Indians" in a population of 31.4 million. Of course, far more "Indians not taxed" lived within tribal communities.

Press hostility toward Native Americans increased following the Civil War as new waves of farmers, ranchers, and developers began to populate the Western plains. Western editors, never especially sympathetic to Indians, became even more strident when disputes over land and Western migration led to violence. In December 1866, for example, hundreds of Sioux and Cheyenne warriors attacked a party of eighty men under the command of Brevet Lt. Col. William Fetterman on the Bozeman Trail, an ambush that quickly became known as the Fetterman Massacre. The press, East and West, was quick to strike back at the Indians—and at the government's feeble efforts to control them. These were "the same red devils who were furnished with rations, blankets and even ammunition . . . by the United States Commissioners," the *Rocky Mountain News* charged erroneously.[29] "We cannot open a paper from any of our exposed States or Territories, without reading frightful accounts of Indian massacres and Indian maraudings," added the *New Orleans Picayune*.[30]

In the aftermath of the Civil War, some editors actively sought exciting battlefield news as a way of gaining and keeping readers. The Indian Wars of 1866–1867 proved to be a fertile source for such stories. One journalism historian discovered that a Western correspondent's imagination was often more important than his accuracy. Eastern newspapers, the historian wrote, "spread before their readers the kind of highly colored accounts of Indian raids and 'massacres' that the most sensational yellow journalism of a later period would have envied."[31] He also found that some Indian news "was nothing more than propaganda to influence the federal government to send more soldiers . . . thus giving local tradesmen an opportunity to sell more supplies to the troops." One of the most outrageous Indian War stories he documented was the 1867 Fort Buford "massacre," news that appeared in the *New York Semi-Weekly Tribune, Harper's Weekly, Leslie's Illustrated Newspaper*, and elsewhere. The massacre, however, was a hoax. The historian concluded that the story was

compounded of some idle rumor to which were added some of the known details of Fetterman's command (the eighty slain soldiers), plus a liberal amount of imagination on the part of some New York reporter or rewrite man (including the dramatic touch of the commander shooting his wife "to prevent her falling into the hands of the savages").[32]

By 1867, in other words, the Indian War story was sufficiently formulaic that its elements—ruthless natives and helpless wives—could be invented by journalists and recognized by readers as "realistic" frontier news.

Another historian discovered Indian War errors and excesses as well.[33] His comprehensive study of Indian War correspondents, published in 1960, also documented the close physical and ideological relationship between reporters and the army. Soldiers and newsmen rode together, fought together, and generally held similar views of the Indians—views that turned up in their stories. The *New York Herald's* first story on General Custer's 1868 surprise attack on

Black Kettle's Washita River camp, for example, followed Custer's official report "almost paragraph and paragraph."[34] Whatever controversies surrounded
that battle—indeed whether it was a "battle" at all—"Custer reported it a
victory, and so it went into the records and so it went into [the *Herald*'s] dispatches."[35] In short, the evil Indian was very real to Western reporters, even
when they wrote for the supposedly humanitarian Eastern press.[36]

The typical frontier newspaper was not just anti-Indian; it was anti-Washington.
Politicians and bureaucrats were blamed—sometimes fairly, sometimes not—for
all manner of Indian troubles. In Arizona, for example, violence between Arizona
settlers and Apaches simmered for months in the early 1870s, reaching a boiling
point with a series of Apache raids in 1871. Whites blamed the Grant administration for feeding the Apaches, singling out their encampment near Camp Grant,
fifty-five miles north of Tucson. The local papers encouraged revenge. "Would it
not be well for the citizens of Tucson to give the Camp Grant wards a slight entertainment to the music of about a hundred double-barreled shot guns?" the
Weekly Arizonan asked.[37] Eight days later, a handful of white Americans and a
larger number of Mexicans and Papago tribe members slaughtered more than 100
Apaches, most of them women and children. The Arizona papers defended the attack; one editor called it "Righteous Retribution."[38] One researcher concluded
that the Arizona papers reinforced anti-Indian sentiments, although the massacre
probably would have occurred even without this support. He also discovered that
John Wasson, editor of the *Arizona Citizen*, knew about the attack in advance and
could have prevented it by informing the army. He did not, the researcher noted,
because "[t]oo many years of hatred, anguish and villainy" had come between
whites and Apaches in Arizona.[39]

The most famous of all Indian battles, of course, was the 1876 Battle of the
Little Bighorn, where the flamboyant George Armstrong Custer and his men
were overwhelmed by Sioux and Cheyenne warriors. Editorials on the meaning
of Custer's death divided along political lines, but it was always clear that the
Indians had to be punished. James Gordon Bennett's *New York Herald*, a Democratic, anti-Grant paper, used Custer's death as a symbol of the administration's
failed Peace Policy and called for retribution. "Let us treat the Indian either as
an enemy or as a friend—either as a human being or as a savage. Let us ex-
terminate or capture him," the *Herald* editorialized. Of course, this choice offered no peace for Native Americans: "If the Indian will not submit to
civilization, let us cage him as we would a tiger or a wolf."[40]

The press and public clamor over the Little Bighorn also propelled Sitting
Bull to prominence as a national villain, and the once-obscure Sioux leader
became the subject of much speculation and scorn. "Phocion" Howard of the
Chicago Tribune, for instance, erroneously reported that Sitting Bull had been
taught French by a Jesuit priest and had studied Napoleon's military tactics.[41]
Within weeks of the battle, Custer, Sitting Bull, and the controversies of the
Little Bighorn took on mythic characteristics. The gallant Custer came to rep-
resent civilization in all its glorious excesses; Sitting Bull became the proud but

vengeful savage protecting the native past. The Indians won the battle, of course, but they could not win the war. Civilization, progress, and the force of history all required that Sitting Bull and his race recede before the Western expansion that was America's rightful destiny. Most editors stuck to this script. It was, after all, a story they had promoted and, in a vital sense, made "real" in their papers.

But not all native news of the period was anti-Indian. One Western historian profiled two newsmen who saw beyond the clichés and stereotypes. Frederic Lockley, writing for the *New York Times, Chicago Times,* and other papers, and John Hanson Beadle, writing for the *Cincinnati Commercial,* reported from Indian Territory in the 1870s. The historian found that Lockley and Beadle approached Indians "not with hatred but with honesty and fairness" and that they recognized "native peoples as individual and human, rather than as impersonal symbols of uncivilized savagism."[42]

Such reporting foreshadowed an important break in anti-Indian ideology in the late 1870s. Recognizing the hopelessness of the native military situation, reformers and humanitarians renewed their efforts to assist and protect the tribes. In Omaha, a minister turned newspaperman named Thomas Tibbles organized a publicity campaign on behalf of the Poncas, a small tribe forcibly moved to Indian Territory in 1877. When a small group of Poncas under the leadership of Standing Bear attempted to return to the northern plains two years later, Tibbles and other reform-minded Nebraskans used the courts and the press to defend the tribe. As a result, the Poncas soon became idealized Indians, identified as progressive people on the path from savagery to civilization.[43] In contrast to the untamed Sioux and other "wild" tribes, the press praised these natives. "Such Indians have laid aside their savage instincts and customs, and they are now law-abiding, frugal, and industrious," the *Chicago Tribune* declared.[44] The Poncas received favorable coverage again when Tibbles arranged a tour of Eastern cities in late 1879.

In Boston, the Ponca tour had a dramatic effect on journalist and poet Helen Hunt Jackson. She was so moved by the Ponca story that she began researching a history of Indian-white relations. Published in 1881, *A Century of Dishonor* was an emotional exposé of racism and official incompetence toward Indians. The Ponca publicity and Jackson's book brought a wave of sympathy for Indians and a revitalized reform movement in Washington, D.C. The movement succeeded in passing the Dawes Act of 1887, a bill that broke up communal tribal lands and allotted parcels to individual Indians on the assumption that these land-owning individuals would become successful farmers or ranchers and join the American mainstream. Unfortunately, the Dawes Act accelerated the dispossession of many natives, putting Indian lands on the market where speculators and swindlers gobbled up the best parcels and left many Indians worse off than before. In short, neither the idealism of reformers nor the sympathy of the "enlightened" press was sufficient to overcome the social, cultural, and economic constraints that shaped native-white relations in the last decades of the century.

The evil Indian made a powerful and tragic return in 1890 when the Ghost Dance or Messiah movement spread across the plains. Led by a Paiute man named Wovoka, the Ghost Dance religion promised a return to the old ways, when game was plentiful and whites disappeared. Unfortunately, the Ghost Dance also caused great alarm among whites in the West, where signs of Indian renewal were seen as a major threat to Western development. On the Sioux reservations of South Dakota, Indian agency officials and Army officers badly misjudged the situation, resulting in the arrest and murder of Sitting Bull on December 15, 1890, and the massacre of Big Foot's band of some 200 Hunkpapa men, women, and children at Wounded Knee Creek on December 29.

Press coverage of the Ghost Dance religion only made things worse. As the Ghost Dance spread and tensions increased at Pine Ridge, more than twenty reporters from New York, Chicago, and elsewhere traveled to the reservation in search of war. When no war was forthcoming, they filled their columns with speculation and the promise of Indian violence. After reviewing the coverage, one journalism historian concluded that "a large number of the nation's newspapers indulged in a field day of exaggeration, distortion and plain faking."[45] C. H. Cressy of the *Omaha Bee*, for example, reported rumor as fact and became a major source of sensationalism and misinformation about events on the reservation.[46] Another reporter who covered the story was Teresa Dean, unique because of her gender and also because of her willingness to expose the sham reporting of other correspondents. She was especially critical of George Creagor, a *New York World* reporter who claimed to have dressed as an Indian and arranged the surrender of Two Strike, a hostile chief. But Dean knew that Creagor had never left General Miles' headquarters and she said so in her paper, the *Chicago Herald*. Dean also changed her opinion about Indians because of her Pine Ridge experiences. Initially critical of what she perceived as native laziness, Dean developed sympathy and affection for many Indians, although like most other whites, she always judged them by Euro-American standards.[47]

Both economics and traditional news values helped propel the Ghost Dance coverage. As one Western historian has noted, "It was the kind of story, rife with intrigue and the promise of bloodshed, that sold papers."[48] Besides the reporters, several free-lance photographers went to Wounded Knee seeking excitement and action—pictures for what the historian called "a news-hungry nation." When the truth was dull or too confusing, the photographers were as inventive as the reporters. "They learned to fabricate their pictures to meet the demands of the purchaser. In the world of photography of the American Indian, fact became subordinate to stereotype."[49] This analysis of news from Wounded Knee confirms the press's continuing reliance on stereotypes, rumors, and sensationalized "facts" to tell the native story. Despite the growing preference for facts over opinion in nineteenth-century journalism[50] as well as more favorable attitudes toward Indians, the press once again judged natives in conflict with whites less by "truth" than by a predetermined set of ethnocentric ideas that reinforced the inferior status of native people.

By the early twentieth century, white citizens and policy makers generally viewed Native Americans as a "vanishing race" that would die or be assimilated out of existence—a view that was reflected in press coverage. Census counts, however, showed a more ambiguous picture. In 1890 Indians in both states and territories, taxed and not taxed, were counted for the first time. Thus the native population seemed to explode from 66,407 in the 1880 census to 248,253 in the 1890 census (excluding 25,354 Alaska natives). While this number rose and fell somewhat in the next three decades, it stayed just under a quarter of a million—a small fraction of the pre-Columbian population. What did change, however, was the proportion of Native Americans in the general population. Because of the sharp increase in the non-Indian population, the proportion of native people dropped from 0.4 percent in 1890 to 0.2 percent in 1920, according to the census.

Ethnocentric white beliefs that Native Americans must be "civilized" (i.e., become like whites) were reflected in government policies toward Indian lands, education, and citizenship. The Dawes Act and subsequent legislation were intended to hasten the process of assimilation by carving up reservations into individually owned farms and ranches. "Surplus" tribal land not allotted to natives was made available to whites. This policy originally was endorsed both by humanitarians and by whites who coveted Indian lands. The humanitarian argument was that Indians would be "uplifted" to the white man's "civilization" by becoming yeoman farmers on their own plots of land. Others argued that Indian lands ought to be cultivated and if Indians would not do so, whites should. Indians, the argument went, would benefit from seeing white farmers working the land and be inspired to do the same. Historian Frederick Hoxie argued that by 1920 the original goal of total equality and assimilation that drove late nineteenth-century legislation had evolved into something far less idealistic in which Native Americans were placed "on the outskirts of American life" as "junior partners in the national experience."[51]

Certainly by the early twentieth century, the negative consequences of the allotment policy were becoming clear: Native Americans often could not or would not farm successfully. They frequently were forced or tricked into conveying their lands to whites on disadvantageous terms. The laws made inadequate provisions for Indians to pass their allotments on to their heirs. As a result, some allotments were divided up into tiny, unworkable parcels. Through a number of schemes, vast amounts of Indian acreage passed into white hands until native lands were reduced from some 138 million acres in 1887 to about 48 million acres in 1934. Of the remaining Indian lands, nearly half were desert or semidesert.[52] In Oklahoma the transfer of allotted lands of the Five Civilized Tribes (Cherokee, Choctaw, Chickasaw, Creek, and Seminole) from native to white hands became a national scandal. The dimensions of the scandal grew after oil was discovered on some tribal lands. Some Indians who suddenly became enormously wealthy were easy prey for the unscrupulous. State probate courts, rather than the federal government, were given jurisdiction over allottees who were minors or adults who were declared "incompetent" in the legal sense. "Guardians" appointed locally to administer the affairs of these Indians were often grafters who charged exorbitant rates to Native Americans and kept scant records.[53]

Native people also suffered from poor nutrition, health care, and education because of the inadequacies of government programs. The assimilationist philosophy behind government and missionary education programs was the same as that underlying land policies: Indians must rid themselves of their tribal dress, languages, religions, and cultures. Thus the success of Indian schools such as Carlisle in Pennsylvania was measured by the extent to which its pupils rejected their traditional ways. However, when schools ran short of funds, native pupils often lived in squalid, disease-ridden conditions, were forced to work at menial jobs, and were poorly taught.

Native Americans enlisted in significant numbers when the United States entered World War I. They served in all branches of the armed forces and were generally integrated into white units, in keeping with the assimilationist attitudes of the times. Their presence, one researcher found, brought a "barrage of romantic distortions" in the press. Much of the coverage, the researcher found, consisted of rewrites of government press releases such as those from the Committee on Public Information. Stereotypical depictions included myriad variations on the themes of Native American stoicism, bravery, and instinct for battle. Stories also sometimes attributed stereotypical broken English to native servicemen, including those who were college educated. Whatever the distortions, Native American participation in the war was generally praised in the press. For whites, having Indians fighting to defend European civilization seemed to validate the ideology of assimilation. Native Americans' wartime service also led many of them to step up their demands to become U.S. citizens. The demands were met when honorably discharged veterans were granted citizenship in 1919.[54] It was not until 1924 that all Native Americans became citizens. Even then, some states denied them the vote until mid-century.

One of the most colorful and influential figures in Indian-white relations burst on the journalistic scene in the early 1920s. This was John Collier, a white reformer who conducted a splashy public relations campaign in 1922 and 1923 aimed at blocking the Bursum bill, federal legislation that would have deprived New Mexico's Pueblo tribes of some of their valuable lands. Collier's views of the place of native people in national life was radically different from the prevailing ideology of forced assimilation. He recognized the value of native cultures and believed they should be preserved—not only because they were important to tribal people, but also because they contained lessons for white society as well. In short, he advocated cultural pluralism.

Collier, working with reform groups, including the General Federation of Women's Clubs and the Indian Rights Association, put Native Americans in the news columns of papers and magazines throughout the country. He staged media events as a Pueblo delegation went on a cross-country tour to arouse opposition to the bill. Collier personally wrote numerous articles that appeared in national publications. Also, a number of well-known writers who lived at Taos and Santa Fe and who had important connections with Eastern editors took up the Pueblos' cause. A researcher who studied press coverage of the Bursum controversy noted that the *Santa Fe New Mexican*, a paper that covered the matter in detail, mentioned stories from at least forty-nine newspapers, magazines, wire services, and syndicates nationwide. The same researcher found that Pueblo people were overwhelmingly depicted as "good Indians," that is, "noble savages, innocent children of nature, and possessors of secrets of tranquility that had been lost by individualistic, materialistic whites." The research also found that the Pueblos were depicted as "exotic strangers" and "relics of the past." Though many of the articles examined in the study did portray Pueblo people stereotypically— albeit in a positive vein—they also put the idea of cultural pluralism in the public mind.[55]

The defeat of the Bursum bill led to formation of the "dynamic, crusading" American Indian Defense Association headed by Collier, which spearheaded reform efforts in the 1920s.[56] The reform movement was climaxed by Collier's appointment as commissioner of Indian affairs in 1933 in the new Roosevelt administration.

The exposés of Collier and other reformers brought pressure on the government to clean up its administration of Indian affairs. The extent of the problem was detailed in a massive 1928 government study, *The Problem of Indian Administration*, popularly known as the Meriam Report, which documented the failure of government allotment, education, and health care policies and the desperate state of Native Americans.[57] The spate of newspaper and magazine articles depicting Native American conditions and the failure of government policies in the 1920s and early 1930s was described as "an orgy of muckraking" in one study that listed the numerous magazine and *New York Times* articles that exposed betrayals of Indians throughout the West.[58]

Though few scholars have looked at the journalistic treatment of Native Americans during the early years of the twentieth century, numerous historians chronicling the time have used the advocacy journalism of John Collier and others as source material.[59]

1934 FEDERAL COMMUNICATIONS ACT TO PEARL HARBOR ATTACK, DECEMBER 7, 1941

John Collier's tenure as commissioner of Indian affairs brought vast changes to Native Americans. He operated from a philosophy radically different from that of his predecessors who believed the only solution to the "Indian problem" was to force Indians to give up their cultures, religions, and languages and assimilate into white society. Collier, the cultural pluralist, believed native ways were valuable and should be preserved. From this position of cultural strength, he believed, Indians would eventually integrate themselves into twentieth-century Euro-American society.

Collier sought to implement his views through administrative action and far-reaching legislation. Though the Wheeler-Howard bill was a compromise version of the changes he envisioned, it wrought vast changes in Indian life. The measure ended allotment and the loss of Indian lands and accomplished a partial restoration of the tribal land base. Tribes were encouraged to incorporate and write constitutions, even though these institutions also were alien to many tribes' traditional governing practices. The "Indian New Deal" also promoted native arts and crafts and sought to incorporate tribal cultures into native school curricula.[60] Tribes were allowed to decide whether or not to come under the Wheeler-Howard legislation. Some, notably the Navajo nation, refused. Although the changes wrought by the Indian New Deal were duly recorded and disputed in the press, few scholars have studied the news coverage generated by these events.

One researcher who studied portrayals of Native Americans in both national and local press accounts found a variety of images. Ironically, at a time when Indians were struggling with revolutionary changes in their own lives, they were often described in the press according to the same good/bad Indian images that had been a part of literature, popular culture, and journalism virtually since the time of their first contact with Europeans. Indians also were depicted as ancient relics of the past, people who had no contemporary existence. Native people were routinely labeled as "braves," "squaws," or "papooses," and significant events, such as tribal elections, were cast in a humorous vein. The research found such stereotyping was more prevalent in national newspapers and the formulaic writing of newsmagazines than in the local press.

This research also found a new image of Indians in the news at this time: that of the "involved Indian citizen." This was a Native American who, like whites, "was merely a source in a news story, a conduit for information," someone who "spoke for himself without the mediation of a white 'friend' or interpreter." Such images were more likely to be found in local newspapers than in the national press.

Other findings included the following:

• Stories of events involving Native Americans sometimes were selected and organized to emphasize stereotypical aspects over those that had greater intrinsic importance to both white and native readers. An example cited in the study was the coverage of Navajo Tribal Council meetings in 1934 in which the national press emphasized the council's decision to eliminate honorary tribal memberships for celebrities such as movie stars, and ignored or downplayed more important issues such as the government's requirement that Navajos reduce their livestock herds to cut down on overgrazing.

• When Indians performed activities thought to be the province of whites, such as using advertising or engaging in government cost cutting, it was considered newsworthy.

• Straightforward, objective inverted pyramid news stories about Native Americans lacked explanations and cultural context to make them meaningful. Also, "interpretative" stories that provided evenhanded background and explanation and included native voices were scarce.[61]

1941 PEARL HARBOR ATTACK TO ATOMIC BOMBING OF HIROSHIMA, AUGUST 6, 1945

As in World War I, Native Americans performed significant service in World War II, both on the battlefield and on the homefront. An estimated 25,000 Indian men served in the military; additional hundreds of men and women left their reservations to work in defense industries. The war brought many native people and whites into close contact with one another for the first time. Indians did not serve in segregated units as did African Americans or Japanese Americans.

Journalistically, Indians were caught up in the propaganda of the war effort, designed to forge unity at home and a willingness to fight for the nation's war aims. In this, according to one researcher, the stereotypes of warlike Indians were modified in the press to extol the very qualities that had earlier been used to demonize them: enthusiasm for fighting, endurance, scouting and tracking ability, and marksmanship. The study showed that World War II provided an opportunity for news writers to revisit and embellish the old stereotypes of Indians as savages who had an inherent talent for warfare that they were now using to aid their country. Native Americans also were portrayed as patriots who enthusiastically fought for the country that had conquered them and as examples for other colonial peoples who were being called on to fight for their colonizers.[62] (For example, men in British colonies in Africa, India, and elsewhere were enlisted to fight for the Allies.) Native American patriotism, while undoubtedly real and sincere, was used in the press to help justify the war effort. If Indians, who had been slaughtered, demoralized, and pauperized, their lands taken, and their religions outlawed, could fight on behalf of their American conquerers, then the American cause must be valid—or so the reasoning went.

Another researcher, looking at the press portrayals of Native Americans in the war, wrote, "The entire press coverage of American Indians in war was geared to give the impression that Indian people were not only aiding white Americans in the war effort but fervently hoping to share in the victory over fascism and become part of the American democratic way of life."[63] However, this researcher and others also concluded that the enthusiastic press treatment of native servicemen had some unintended negative consequences. For one thing, it helped convince some in government that native people could hold their own in white society and no longer needed federal wardship.

As the war ended, arguments arose in the press to end the "segregation" of Indians on reservations and allow them "freedom" of full participation in American life. The rhetoric was appealing in the postwar atmosphere of victory over totalitarianism. But the reasoning, as some pointed out, was flawed. Such "freedom" in practice amounted to another form of forced assimilation. Indians were not segregated, and reservations were not prisons. Rather, reservations were the last remnant of the once-vast native land base. Also, although they lacked adequate health, education, and economic resources, they were a sanctuary for indigenous people to live and worship according to traditional ways. These explanations, however, were confined to small publications and did not resonate with the public as the "freedom" arguments did.[64]

Such an atmosphere, the researcher argued, set the stage for Congressional moves to "emancipate" Native Americans and led eventually to the infamous "termination" legislation of the 1950s that severed federal relations with some tribes who were ill-prepared and ill-equipped to enter the national economy.

American Indians marched off to war for various reasons; yet, whites took the tribes' participation as an unquestionable act of loyalty to the United States. Whites looked upon it as an American Indian effort to prove themselves worthy of "mainstream society." . . . In this kind of intellectual climate, termination . . . was easily passed as a liberal, democratic method of solving Indian problems.[65]

World War II also gave the press and public some Indian heroes. One was Ira Hayes, the Pima Marine who was photographed with five other Marines raising the American flag on Mount Suribachi during the battle of Iwo Jima. The spectacular success of the photo brought Hayes instant fame and unrelenting publicity. Hayes and the two other surviving flag raisers were brought home to travel the country, reenacting the flag raising to boost war bond sales. After that, Hayes could never escape the media spotlight. Some have argued that the media's star treatment of the shy young man contributed to his alcoholism and death at the age of thirty-two.[66]

A researcher who examined newspaper coverage of Hayes found that he was always referred to as an Indian, making him in effect the symbol of the stereotypical Indian warrior. Such a characterization was likely a torment for Hayes, a shy, inarticulate man who maintained he should not have been treated as a hero ahead of his buddies who were killed in action.[67]

A group of Native Americans whose wartime service made them famous was the Navajo code talkers. This group of Navajo Marines used their native language as code to transmit secret messages during the Pacific campaigns. The Japanese never broke the code. Their contribution was first revealed at war's end in 1945.[68] News depictions of the Navajo code talkers and other native servicemen who used their tribal languages as codes carried dual messages. Clearly they showed the unique contributions Native Americans made to the war effort. But, more subtly perhaps, the portrayals contributed to the image of Indians as exotic people who spoke unknown languages.

1945 ATOMIC BOMBING OF HIROSHIMA TO LITTLE ROCK INTEGRATION, SEPTEMBER 1957

During the postwar era, the pendulum of Indian policy swung again back to assimilation. Collier resigned as commissioner of Indian affairs in 1945, formalizing the end of the policy of cultural pluralism. In the conformist Cold War era of government cost cutting, sentiment grew to withdraw, or terminate, federal services to Native Americans. What was largely lost on the public, and often on officeholders, was that most of these services were the result of treaties in which Indians had ceded valuable lands; they were not charitable handouts.

Nevertheless, Congress sought to terminate federal services to as many tribes as possible and actually succeeded in revoking tribal status of the Menominee of Wisconsin, the Klamath of Oregon, and others. It shortly became clear that the policy was disastrous in human terms because it tossed generally unprepared Indians onto the mainstream economy and society where they often ended up on welfare rolls. It also was a failure financially because paying welfare and other costs associated with breaking up the tribes was a significant economic burden on the states in which tribes were terminated.

A study that examined news coverage of the initial efforts to terminate the Menominee as a tribe—a move that began in 1953, took effect in 1961, and, after much lobbying, was reversed in 1974—found significant differences in local and national news coverage. A local Wisconsin newspaper's coverage in 1953 of the early proposals for termination and the tribe's resistance, the researcher found, was detailed and gave ample airing to Menominees' views as well as the government's. Menominee people were portrayed as involved members of the community. Coverage by regional and national news media, however, seldom explained the negative effects of termination on the Menominee people. Instead, they focused on the Menominee as "people for whom termination would pose no problems."[69] Such portrayals in the national press thus built public sentiment for termination. When the tribe eventually was terminated, the reservation became a county—Wisconsin's newest and poorest. The effects were disastrous for the Menominee people, many of whom were thrown into poverty. Eventually, in 1974, after heavy lobbying by the Menominees and their allies, tribal status was restored.[70]

Another 1950s government initiative for Native Americans was the policy of "relocation," that is, inducing reservation Indians to move to distant cities. The twin goals were to reduce populations on reservations and to assimilate Native Americans into the urban mainstream. Relocation and the informal migration of individuals brought some 80,000 Native Americans to cities between the end of World War II and 1957.[71] The origins of a number of urban Native American communities and social service agencies, such as the Chicago American Indian Center, stem from the relocation era. Some transplanted Native Americans thrived in their new city environment. Others had trouble coping. Some of these returned to their reservations; others became members of the urban poor.

News media accounts of relocation reflected both views. One researcher found that Indians in pro-relocation stories were portrayed as ''good'' Indians, often with special skills or attributes needed by industry, who were ''seeking success through assimilation.'' The portrayal of native people in anti-relocation stories, on the other hand, was of ''desolate, hopeless people who had been uprooted from their traditional ways and dumped into a hostile urban environment.''[72] This negative image in the press was in some ways a variation on the ''bad'' or ''evil'' Indian depiction. Native people, no longer a military threat, were portrayed as a ''degraded'' people who had suffered from their contacts with Euro-Americans, adopting their vices but not their virtues. Similar depictions, in both cultural and journalistic works, dated to at least the nineteenth century. Headline writers sometimes summed up the stereotype with the label ''Lo'' or ''poor Lo.'' This was a reference to the phrase, ''Lo, the poor Indian,'' in Alexander Pope's *An Essay on Man.*[73]

The miserable conditions of Native Americans who migrated from Midwestern reservations to the urban slums of Minneapolis were starkly described in a fifteen-part series in the *Minneapolis Tribune* in 1957. *Time* magazine brought the series to national attention, saying it was ''not only a hard-hitting indictment of the slum conditions in the paper's own back yard but a searching examination of the deep-rooted causes and effects.'' The series' author, Carl Rowan, an African American, brought to his coverage ''a mixture of shrewd news sense and a personal kinship with the Indian,'' according to *Time.*[74] Citation of such local coverage of Native Americans in a national magazine was one of the rare instances of coverage of Native Americans drawing national comment.

An article at least peripherally related to journalistic coverage of Indians appeared in *American Anthropologist* in July 1947. The article reviewed a documentary film in which a group of Hopi described, from their own point of view, some of the problems facing the tribe. Though it did not deal with journalism, the article was significant because it posed a number of questions relevant to journalists about the difficulty of attaining objectivity and of ensuring that the work accurately reflects the whole group, not just the vocal malcontents.[75]

1957 LITTLE ROCK INTEGRATION TO NIXON'S RESIGNATION, AUGUST 9, 1974

Native Americans were often in the news in the 1960s and 1970s as they took direct actions for self-determination. In Chicago in 1961 hundreds of Native American delegates from scores of tribes came together at the landmark American Indian Chicago Conference. The delegates issued a Declaration of Indian Purpose that called on the government to abandon termination and instead to foster Indian participation in programs for tribal betterment in areas of health, education, and economic assistance, among others. At the Chicago conference, a group of young activists formed the National Indian Youth Council which called for self-determination, observance of treaty rights, and an end to assimilationist policies.[76]

While the news media in general were somewhat more sensitive to egregious stereotyping of native people than in previous decades, demeaning images did not vanish. For example, the groundbreaking American Indian Chicago Conference was trivialized in *Newsweek* magazine with phrases such as this: "It was the first time since Hiawatha was knee-high to a tall papoose that braves grown gray had come from every tribe . . . to sit around a mystical council fire."[77]

Native American visibility in the news media increased as activists took direct actions. Thus it was not surprising that news images of young, militant Native Americans asserting their cultural heritage and demanding justice for their people appeared frequently on front pages and in television newscasts. The heightened profile of Native Americans in the late 1960s and early 1970s resulted from the worldwide news coverage of the takeover of Alcatraz Island in 1969; the Trail of Broken Treaties cross-country caravan in late 1972 that led to a brief occupation of the Bureau of Indian Affairs building in Washington, D.C.; the standoff at Wounded Knee, South Dakota, in 1973 when an insurgent faction led by the American Indian Movement (AIM), opposed to the entrenched tribal government of the Pine Ridge Oglala Lakota reservation, took over the historic Wounded Knee site and were surrounded by forces from the federal government; and many other similar, smaller actions.

But media and public attention went beyond crisis coverage. Books by native authors, such as Vine Deloria Jr.'s *Custer Died for Your Sins*, and books explaining the Indian view of historical events, such as Dee Brown's *Bury My Heart at Wounded Knee*, became best-sellers. Indian art and cultural artifacts became fashionable, and Indians became, as one author put it, "positive, though somewhat unreal, symbols for environmentalists, idealistic liberals, and the alienated."[78] The "plight" of Native Americans generated news coverage, too, as journalists, newly attuned to the specter of poverty in America, described Native Americans' privation on reservations and in urban slums. For example, in 1960, the *Denver Post* ran a grim twelve-part series on Native Americans labeled "America's Lost People" that was unrelenting in its descriptions of poverty and hopelessness.[79]

Journalism scholars, too, became interested in Indians, and while a good many studies returned to the nineteenth century for subjects, others examined twentieth-century coverage. Undoubtedly contributing to scholarly interest was the Kerner Commission's 1968 criticism of news coverage of African Americans.[80] When researchers looked at the coverage of Native Americans, they saw ample opportunity for investigation of news coverage along similar lines.

One reporter commented on the superficiality of the coverage of the 1968 Poor People's March in Washington, D.C., where Native Americans, among others, demonstrated to draw national attention to their problems. The media provided only an event-oriented, shallow account of how many persons participated and who spoke, with almost no attempt made to explain the underlying issues involved. This occurred partly, according to the journalist, because the reporters covering the demonstration lacked the background to put the protest in context. But it also was caused by media executives' failure to attempt to have their media understand the grievances and explain them clearly. "Indian hunger is not new; it is not action," the author wrote. "It is old, and it is a first-class news story." But aside from the Indians themselves and some officials, he said, few people knew about it. "If people are ignorant," he added, "somebody isn't informing them."[81]

A 1970 study of the coverage of Native Americans and other minority groups in the *Minneapolis Star* and the *Tribune* foreshadowed the media attention the later South Dakota events would draw. This article concluded that minorities—including Native Americans—actually received more publicity than "established groups," but that the coverage tended to focus on demonstrations rather than on more pacific activities.[82]

The 1973 siege at Wounded Knee, often called Wounded Knee II to distinguish it from the 1890 massacre, brought images of gun-wielding Indians facing off against government forces to the nation's television screens and newspaper front pages. The confrontation also brought a spate of articles and scholarly studies examining the coverage. In addition, numerous books dissecting Wounded Knee II looked also at the role of the news media.

In the weeks and months following the siege, articles in several consumer magazines—those such as *Time* aimed at broad, general audiences—as well as some advocacy journals, such as *The Nation*, took the news media to task for distorting and possibly prolonging the confrontation. Their critique, essentially, was that news workers, especially television reporters, fell for AIM's public relations ploys and went for gaudy pictures of Indians with feathers, guns, and warpaint. This, in turn, encouraged the AIM faction to prolong the event to gain more publicity. At least this was the argument advanced by some federal officials and some news workers. *Time*, for example, seemed to portray journalists as virtually helpless pawns of the AIM insurgents.

Wounded Knee had become a kind of trap, particularly for television. . . . AIM leaders were so successful in getting their side of the story across, and so enthralled by the attention they were receiving, that they seemed willing to prolong the deadlock for the sake of still more publicity. Most newsmen watched helplessly as the thin line between covering and creating news wavered.[83]

Writing in *The Nation*, Desmond Smith called AIM's use of the media a "strategy of political manipulation" and declared that AIM staged "a media coup d'etat." The article claimed that AIM's intent was to use the media to bypass the "orderly processes of government" to bring their grievances to the public. And, it added, "newsmen are helpless victims in the adventurist game of media blackmail."[84]

A third magazine article followed the same line with respect to the AIM insurgents. But the author, Terri Schultz, who covered the Wounded Knee occupation for both the *Chicago Daily News* and *Harper's*, also presented unflattering vignettes of the supporters of tribal chairman Dick Wilson and the local whites. The article criticized reporters on the scene for missing these nuances. "We tightened up the facts, smoothed the edges, covered up the blemishes like portrait artists with fussy clients. We wrote good cowboy-and-Indian stories because we thought it was what the public wanted, and they were harmless, even if they were not all true," the article concluded.[85]

If the press criticized its own coverage at Wounded Knee II, that critique was later endorsed in *The Road to Wounded Knee*, a book coauthored by a journalist sympathetic to the insurgents and by one of the participants in the standoff. They took journalists to task for looking for images to reinforce their stereotypical views rather than seeking the origins of the confrontation, and for reacting with hostility when Indians failed to conform to their preconceived notions.

Newsmen love to think of themselves as hardheaded, cynical, and relentless in their pursuit of truth, even though many prefer to pursue it with maximum comfort and minimum risk. The insult to their objectivity and threats from the government, combined with the long stalemate in negotiations, caused them to take a new tack. By the second month of the Wounded Knee siege . . . [Russell] Means and [Dennis] Banks [two AIM leaders] were no longer portrayed as doomed heroes battling oppression but as a couple of urban toughs trying to seize power. The coverage veered from one unreal extreme to the other, never bothering to assess the facts.[86]

One of the authors of the book cited above called the Wounded Knee insurgents' use of traditional Native American accoutrements, such as war paint and feathers, "Protest as Wild West Show." "Once the Indians found that this formula worked, they flogged it for all it was worth. At Wounded Knee II, the media of the entire world took notice." But the strategy backfired, and some in the media reported Wounded Knee II as "comic opera."[87]

The article criticized the media for making such ploys necessary:

The whole warpath—feathers, paint, and bullets—might never have happened if the media had covered the legislative attacks on Indian land that have taken place in the last 40 years, and the various state and local abuses against Indian lives, with anything like the intensity that these horrible breaches of decency and ethics deserved. But they didn't. The media people fumbled or slumbered, the cheating and exploitation of Indians went on, and it was left to a handful of activists to force the world to pay attention to them.[88]

In sum, the Wounded Knee II insurgents criticized press coverage because of its superficiality and use of outdated stereotypical imagery, but once convinced that use of such stereotypes was the only way to get media attention, the Indians exploited it enthusiastically. The press criticized itself more for allowing itself to be manipulated than for failing to dig out the full story.

Perhaps the most balanced assessment of television's role in the Wounded Knee matter came in a series of articles published in *TV Guide* magazine in December 1973. The author took apart the claims and counterclaims of media manipulation, using interviews not only with government and Native American leaders, but with television news workers who were on the scene. The author took note of the monstrous wrongs Native Americans had suffered outside the news media spotlight, and the powerful provocations to stage "media events"— used successfully by African Americans, students, and others—to claim attention for their causes. He also used accounts by news workers on the scene to show that the AIM insurgents were far less concerned with and adept at media manipulation than their critics claimed. People on all sides of the dispute, the author found, condemned television's coverage. After reading transcripts of all network news broadcasts during the occupation, he concluded that "TV coverage was largely skeletal, one-dimensional, dutiful, chary of treating most of the subtleties inherent in the strife." Nevertheless, it had "a quantity of splendid, old-fashioned derring-do reporting" and "[s]ome of the coverage even ventured into historical background and analysis."[89]

Some nine years after the event, a researcher analyzed the South Dakota press coverage of Wounded Knee II. His article indicated that straight news coverage in the state's major dailies differed little from that of the national press, largely because both used wire service reports. Editorials in South Dakota papers, not surprisingly, criticized the AIM insurgents, arguing that the state was an "innocent victim" of problems created by the federal government and fearing that the tourist industry would suffer because of the confrontation. According to the article, the South Dakota press was similarly critical of the national news media, which exhibited "preconceived and erroneous prejudices against South Dakota and who had trouble keeping the facts straight."[90]

A scholarly treatment of the coverage of Wounded Knee II asked, among other things: "Was the Wounded Knee occupation a 'media event'?" Did the press cause, prolong, or participate in the demonstration? The author argued that the occupation was, indeed, a media event. He cited interviews and articles that indicated that neither side—the Indians' nor the government's—was satisfied with the coverage. Indians complained that the news media did not understand the historical background or causes of the confrontation and that the press relied too much on government sources. Government officials, on the other hand, claimed that the media were too sympathetic to the Indians. Several members of the news media criticized the coverage, too, especially that of television.[91]

The author contended that the "war correspondent's perspective," in which the media used warlike imagery and military terminology, dominated the coverage. He also noted that television coverage veered from a sympathetic, romanticized stance at the beginning of the occupation to one of hostility at the end. Among a wide variety of print articles, he noted, a number on the "plight of the Indian" recited the litany of Native American problems, but did not describe their historical roots. The author concluded that while initial media coverage of Wounded Knee II evoked public sympathy, "[a]s the confrontation continued the American people . . . probably became less sympathetic toward the demonstrators."[92]

Finally, the author concluded, rather gloomily, that the media did not—and perhaps could not—accurately portray the reality of Native American life:

Considering the limitations of the visual media, it seems unlikely that broadcast journalists will ever be able to adequately explain the complex problems facing Native Americans. Moreover, there is an establishment bias in all of the media which holds that Indian problems reflect the failure of the white man's humanitarian efforts rather than his carefully calculated destruction of native cultures. Finally, there is the natural tendency of the press to perpetuate the Hollywood Indian stereotype: Indians on the warpath is newsworthy, Indians living in poverty is not.[93]

Many of the participants and observers at the Wounded Knee II confrontation wrote books about their experiences and often included their assessment of the news media. Most of these analyses were heavily colored by the author's allegiances, whether to the AIM insurgents, the Bureau of Indian Affairs, or others. Generally these accounts treated the news media as monolithic and did not engage in specific examples of good or bad conduct. For example, in *The Road to Wounded Knee*, Robert Burnette and John Koster asserted that "the press people spent most of their time waiting for government press releases, rapping in the Pine Ridge parking lot, drinking coffee at a cafe . . . and hunting for bootleg liquor." The authors acknowledged, however, that "[s]ome AIM leaders, long starved for publicity for their cause and also endowed with healthy egos, went out of their way to cooperate with newsmen," sometimes by repeating events for television cameras.[94] In *Wounded Knee: The Meaning and Significance of the Second Incident*, Rolland Dewing quoted editorials in numerous newspapers around the country to support his contention that a month into the standoff, "much of the media, who had been quite sympathetic on the whole, began to question the authenticity of motives and methods of the besieged Indians. Many newsmen on the scene began to accept the idea that they had been duped."[95]

In examining the images of Native Americans in the news coverage of Alcatraz, Wounded Knee II, and other events of the 1960s and 1970s, one researcher found a variety of depictions. "Images of Indians as militants who spoke for themselves and took direct action to advance their cause were added to popular culture images of Indians as spiritual guides and ecological saviors." While she found more sensitivity to native people than in previous decades, she also noted that reporters seemed too willing to accept without investigation the claims of native activists and of the government.[96]

Broadcast Coverage

The direct actions of Wounded Knee II and other incidents of the early 1970s put Native Americans on television news programs. At the same time, however, a number of native people were exploring use of the broadcast media of radio and television for their own ends in their own communities. One underlying impetus for such efforts lay in the oral nature of native societies. In 1973 Kim Hodgson, director of Ramah Navajo radio in Ramah, New Mexico, described members of that small community walking into the station, sitting down, and recording their views for broadcast. "It fulfills Marshall McLuhan's theory that orally-based cultures adapt naturally to radio."[97]

A second spur to action was the widespread and accurate belief that Native Americans had been ignored and ill-used by the mainstream news media. In the same article, Richard LaCourse (Yakima), news director of the American Indian Press Association News Service and a former Seattle newspaper reporter, observed, "If you look for Indian news in the majority press, you find the Indians practically edited out of existence. The serious concerns, the complex legal entanglements which ensnarl Indian people are almost never accurately or adequately defined through the media."[98]

The widespread stereotyping of Native Americans was analyzed as a form of colonialism by Gerald Wilkinson in an article in the *Indian Historian*. He argued that the "pervasive" nature of the broadcast media distorts Indian images not only for the larger society but for native people themselves. "When these [stereotypical] ideas begin to saturate the hearts and minds of our own people, it becomes a catastrophe superimposed on a disaster." The author urged native people to organize and fight for control of media, particularly cable television, which he saw as having great potential benefits or, conversely, "the greatest cultural threat to Indian people since Columbus," depending on who controlled it.[99]

1974 RESIGNATION OF NIXON TO LOS ANGELES UPRISING, APRIL 29, 1992

As the heightened majority-culture interest in Native Americans faded with the activism of the 1960s and early 1970s, native people themselves sought to consolidate and institutionalize their economic and social gains. While some court decisions and legislation seemed to increase tribal self-determination, cuts in government programs and funds greatly increased unemployment and poverty on reservations. Much of the news coverage of the previous era was spurred by crises and native direct actions; without such eye-catching events to cover, news media interest in Native Americans faded, too.

When commentary was provided on news coverage of native affairs, it usually came in response to crises. For example, the June 1975 incident on the Pine Ridge Oglala Sioux Reservation in which two white FBI agents and a Native American man were killed was examined in Joel D. Weisman's "About That 'Ambush' at Wounded Knee." The article showed how wire services' deadline-driven haste and their reliance on official government sources led to inaccurate and inflammatory accounts of the shootings on the South Dakota reservation.[100]

The article noted that while "many explanations" of the murders were possible, early wire service reports fell back on stereotypes of savagery. "The 'ambush' and 'execution' theories of events reflect an unfortunate commitment to clichés (and perhaps prejudice) on the part of newsmen and officials at the scene." Weisman also noted that one report said the killings "stemmed from" the 1973 Wounded Knee II occupation, when there was no evidence of this at the time the dispatch was filed.[101]

Later it became clear that the incident had its roots in conflicts between supporters of AIM on the one side and the elected tribal government backed by federal authorities on the other, conflicts that had torn the reservation apart since the Wounded Knee II occupation two years earlier. Leonard Peltier was one of four men arrested in the incident. Two of the men were acquitted, the case against one was dismissed, and Peltier was convicted. His supporters, Native American and white, who contended he was wrongfully convicted, were still seeking his exoneration and release from prison in the late 1990s.[102]

Another researcher scrutinized mainstream newspaper coverage of a crisis involving Mohawk groups and whites over Indian seizure of lands in the Adirondack Mountains of New York in the mid-1970s. The article noted that while the takeover happened in May 1974, it was not until some five months later when two non-Indians were shot that the matter became "news." The story then became "not about political conflict but about crime." Drawing on research on social movements and the media conducted by Todd Gitlin, Gaye Tuchman, and Harvey Molotch, the author concluded that

- News coverage was constrained by media frames that emphasize events—particularly violent events—over issues, that "cover political actions that have a certain fit with whatever newsmakers have construed to be 'the story.' " In this case, the matter was framed—misleadingly—as another example of 1970s violent conflict between "militant" groups and the police.

- The national news coverage enabled the Mohawk traditionalists who organized the takeover to air their grievances to a vastly larger audience—both Indian and white—than had been the case before.

- As the "hard news" coverage of violence subsided, the story became framed as a "human interest" story of "the underdog ethnic group struggling to maintain its simple, traditional lifestyle."

- As the press stereotyped the Ganienkeh Mohawks "in the timeless and romantic image of the American Indian," the Mohawks were "quite careful to give the press what it wanted." This, in turn, led to the Mohawks being seen as "hypocrites and skilled public relations men putting up a false front for urban audiences" by local whites, who felt their views were not given as much coverage as those of the Mohawks.[103]

Another study analyzed newspaper coverage in the Skagit Valley of Washington State, the area in which the so-called Boldt decision of 1974 affirmed the rights of local tribes to fish beyond reservation boundaries and awarded half of the state's salmon catch to native fishers. This decision ended decades of state-imposed obstruction of native fishing rights that had been guaranteed by treaty. The article reported on a thematic analysis of coverage of Indians in two local newspapers, the *Concrete Herald* and the *Skagit Valley Herald*, from the early 1900s to the late 1980s. Though the study was confined to two relatively small local papers, its findings echoed those of other studies.[104]

The study found that the volume and nature of reporting on Indians changed dramatically after 1961 when the first native protests and "fish-ins" began. "The predominant media images [in 1961 and 1962] were of Indians who were antisocial or who challenged the status quo by bringing up treaty issues," the author wrote. These images continued from 1971 to 1983, during court proceedings on treaty rights. "The great bulk of reporting . . . in the years 1971–1983 concerned either antisocial Indians or litigious Indians."[105]

Overall, the study found that nearly two-thirds of all reporting over its seventy-five-year span concerned treaty rights or antisocial behavior. "Little attention was given to routine reporting of Indian lives and governance, such as participation in ceremonies, episodes of intergovernmental cooperation, school events, or economic development planning."[106]

The Navajo-Hopi land dispute, a long, complex conflict between these two peoples of the Southwest, was the subject of an article in the *Columbia Journalism Review*, which castigated the "Big Three" newspapers, the *New York Times, Washington Post*, and *Los Angeles Times*, for sporadic coverage that failed to take the issue seriously. The papers, the author said, "have regarded the dispute and its people as little more than material for colorful features."[107]

Two content analyses of native news in English-language Canadian newspapers and one analyzing U.S. newspapers showed quantitatively that crisis or at least conflict drove coverage of native people on both sides of the border. A researcher studying Ontario newspaper coverage of native Canadians from 1971 to 1975 found that the stories about Indians that appeared most frequently in the paper involved their relations with government, and that headline wordings often associated natives with conflict and deviance.[108] An American researcher studying coverage of Native Americans in four U.S. newspapers in 1989 and 1990 found similar results.[109]

A third article described a content analysis of the coverage of Native Indians in the English-language *Montreal Gazette* during the Oka crisis of 1990. The dispute stemmed from the determination of authorities in Oka, Quebec, near Montreal, to build a golf course on land considered sacred to members of the Mohawk tribe. The matter escalated into an armed confrontation. The study found that relatively few stories were published about the dispute while the Indians were protesting peacefully. However, when the Mohawk-led blockade was met by armed police, the coverage increased dramatically. The author also found scant coverage of the "historical roots of Native Indian grievances at Oka."[110]

Some newspapers went beyond crisis coverage, however. A hard-hitting 1987

series published in Phoenix's *Arizona Republic*, for example, revealed in devastating detail how the Bureau of Indian Affairs had betrayed Native Americans.
"Federal Indian programs across the United States are a shambles, plagued by
fraud, incompetence and deceit and strangled by a morass of red tape that has
all but destroyed their effectiveness," the thirty-story series began. Principal
authors of the articles were Mike Masterson, Chuck Cook, and Mark N. Trahant,
the last a member of the Shoshone-Bannock tribes. The series stated that the
federal government had often cooperated with oil and gas companies and had
cheated Native Americans out of profits they should have received. It also stated
that, although the Bureau of Indian Affairs had poured $30 billion into programs
for the Indians in the previous decade, the economies of the reservations had
not been improved and unemployment there averaged 60 percent. In addition,
the series revealed, the bureau had provided seriously substandard housing, education, and health care to Native Americans. Also, confusing federal laws and
jurisdictions had made reservations havens for criminals, and many major
crimes, like murder and rape, were never prosecuted.[111]

Rather than examine only mainstream media coverage, some researchers have
sought to compare the content of native and nonnative news media. Two researchers who compared content of the two types of newspapers in Alaska in
1980 found little difference in the topics of stories covered by the two types of
papers. However, the amount of coverage of Native Alaskans in the nonnative
press was much less—"amazingly low," in the words of the authors. Stories
in both presses were "essentially positive" toward native people.[112] More recently, a researcher compared coverage of the treaty rights dispute between the
Chippewa nation and the state of Wisconsin in a white-owned newspaper and
a native-owned newspaper. The researcher found that in both papers non-Indian
sources were used more often than Indian sources, although use of Indian
sources in the native-owned paper was greater. She also found that the native
paper contained more information favorable to acceptance of Chippewa treaty
rights. The research paper also explained powerful historical and cultural reasons
why this would be the case in a native paper.[113]

Both the local and nonlocal press were faulted for their coverage of a legally
tangled dispute over water rights in Wyoming's Wind River basin. The dispute
involved the Eastern Shoshone and Northern Arapaho tribes who live on the
Wind River reservation and white ranchers who sought to use water from the
Wind River to irrigate their land. The analysis of press coverage was published
in *Extra!*, a publication of Fairness and Accuracy in Reporting (FAIR). It found,
among other things, that the media "often defined the issue in terms of battle
lines, ignoring the spiritual and cultural beliefs that guide the tribes' resource
decisions." In addition, the author wrote, the issue was filtered through "myths"
of the West, such as white pioneers "taming" and settling a "barren" land.
Local media, the author wrote, depicted white irrigators who lacked water in
emotional terms, while tribal members and others sympathetic to their viewpoint
were virtually ignored.[114]

While the number of scholarly treatments of news coverage of Native Americans has been small, the journalism trade press has carried a number of articles, often written by Native American journalists, critiquing mainstream media performance. The critiques have generally emphasized two themes: (1) They have condemned the stereotyping that, they assert, still goes on in the news media, as well as in entertainment, pointing out that less than half of one percent of journalists are Native American; and (2) they have criticized the methods used by news workers in covering Indians and offered advice on how to cover such stories intelligently. Prominent advice has included educating journalists about sovereignty issues and the complex legal status of Indian nations.[115] In 1991 the Minnesota-Dakotas Region of the National Conference of Christians and Jews published *The American Indian and the Media*, a compendium of resources and guidelines for journalists to use in covering Native Americans.[116]

When, early in 1992, the editor of the *Oregonian* newspaper in Portland unilaterally decided to stop using sports team names such as "Redskins" and "Braves" that offended Native Americans, his action drew considerable comment from journalists. On the one hand, some praised the editor, William Hilliard, for his courage; others said the action smacked of censorship.[117] One study of selected coverage of the sports team mascot issue found that the depiction of the issue and of Native Americans protesting mascots changed with time and place. Coverage by Chicago newspapers of a 1989 controversy over the University of Illinois' "Chief Illiniwek" mascot was framed as a political issue and pushed Native American voices to the periphery. But this did not occur in Minneapolis newspapers and the national news media in 1991 when the Atlanta Braves played the Minnesota Twins in the World Series or in 1992 when the Kansas City Chiefs played in the Super Bowl in Minneapolis. In both cases, Native Americans' views were reported prominently, and the protests they led were depicted as a legitimate cause.[118]

Broadcast Coverage

After Wounded Knee II, few if any scholarly studies examined coverage of Native Americans in the mainstream commercial broadcast news media. However, the emerging native broadcast media did receive some attention. Two studies of Native American radio stations emerging in the 1970s found less than positive results. In the case of Ramah Navajo radio, the researcher found that while the station increased the speed of communication among the far-flung Ramah Navajo people and fostered a sense of community, it also contributed to the erosion of Navajo culture and traditions.[119] A second native-run radio station founded in the Southwest at this time, KIPC-FM, radio station of the All Indian Pueblo Council, foundered owing to lack of funds and community support.[120]

A later overview of Native American broadcasting in the United States and Canada found twenty-two native-owned and -operated radio stations in the United States versus some 200 in Canada. This difference the authors largely attributed to the Canadian government's encouragement of the development of native radio. The authors noted that native radio enables indigenous peoples "to speak to one another, and to preserve ancient languages and cultures" and fosters a sense of community. However, they also observed that native journalists face "special problems because traditional journalistic standards are sometimes in conflict with [n]ative cultural norms."[121]

1992 LOS ANGELES UPRISING TO PRESIDENTIAL ELECTION, NOVEMBER 1996

Numerically, Native Americans appeared to be gaining as the century advanced, though they remained near the bottom of indices of income, employment, education, and health. According to the census, the American Indian population increased from 332,397 or about 0.3 percent of the total population in 1930 to 1,959,234 or 0.8 percent of the total in 1990. The Native American population (including Eskimos and Aleuts) nearly quadrupled between 1960 and 1990. The increase may have been partly caused by differing procedures used to determine who was to be counted as an Indian. Before 1960 census takers made classifications based on their own observations. In 1960 and 1970 information was obtained primarily through self-enumeration.[122]

That may help to explain population growth that cannot be accounted for solely by natural increase. Some experts have suggested that increasing racial pride has led more people to identify themselves as Indians. They note that Southern and Eastern states that have not traditionally had large native populations had the biggest increases (118 percent in Alabama and 78 percent in New Jersey) in the 1990 census.[123]

As Native Americans continued to push sovereignty as well as cultural and religious freedom issues, the expansion of Indian gambling raised numerous questions. While it vastly enriched a few tribes and became an economic development vehicle for both natives and whites in a few areas, it also brought complex legal issues involving tribal sovereignty and the relationship between the states and federal government. And, for some groups, it deepened divisions between traditionalists who opposed gambling and others who saw it as a way out of poverty and a spur to general economic development.

Since scholarship naturally lags behind current events, few if any scholarly analyses of the news media coverage of gambling issues had emerged by the mid-1990s. However, several studies in scholarly journals and in the advocacy press decried the mainstream press for ignoring the everyday lives of Native Americans and for distortions in the coverage that did occur—most of it, as in previous decades, in response to crises. Native authors spoke out against institutional neglect of their people in the news media.

An outbreak of a mysterious, sometimes-fatal virus in the Southwest in 1993 brought unwelcome national news media attention to the Navajo nation, where the disease was first reported. Early press accounts incorrectly linked the dis-

ease—which was later discovered to be hantavirus—to Navajos; one paper actually used the term "Navajo flu." Although this error was later corrected, the
outbreak brought a flock of national news workers to the reservation and outraged the Navajo people, who suffered from discrimination because of the
flawed coverage.[124]

An analysis of the cultural and journalistic issues raised by the matter made
these points:

• Cultural clashes between outside news media and Navajo people abounded, including
  intrusion on Navajo religious practices.

• The local press, including the *Albuquerque Journal*, the *Albuquerque Tribune*, and the
  Gallup Independent, covered the crisis in more detail and with more sensitivity than
  did the national media.

• Coverage went beyond "bad reporting based on superficial misunderstanding, misinformation, and speculation," the study's author contended. "Prejudice is involved, and,
  like all prejudice, it is bred in ignorance and manifested in stereotyping."[125]

• News media that did not engage in misinformation or outright stereotyping still were
  guilty of "errors of omission." These media could have been a "rational influence,
  emphasizing the limited nature of the outbreak, taking quick and sure steps to avoid
  conveying even chance misimpressions of Native American lifestyles."[126]

An article describing Alaska's Chukchi News Service argued for the use of
more "cultural journalism" to help explain the daily lives and to dispel stereotypes in the mainstream press of minorities—in this case, Alaska natives. The
author called for "a change in the texture of the content" of news. "The very
institution of journalism, the very concept of news and information, must
change, too."[127] To accomplish that end, the author founded the Chukchi News
and Information Service in 1988 to send writings of his students at Chukchi
College, a branch of the University of Alaska, to the state's mainstream press.
The article noted that the "vast majority" of news and information in Alaska
is generated by nonnatives, although the state's population is from 16 to 18
percent native. The article argued for a cultural journalism that "looks at the
day-to-day activities that are the fabric of life in a particular region" as a way
of countering crisis coverage and dispelling stereotypes. "[M]ainstream news
people must become more reflective of the nation's cultural diversity by opening
their pages to, and indeed seeking out, unorthodox communications such as
cultural journalism as one way to arrive at some level of parity in their coverage
of minorities."[128]

In her examination of news media images of Native Americans, another researcher found more native voices criticizing coverage and a greater range of
images than in the past. "[I]mages of Native Americans in the 1990s press
multiplied. Stereotyping did not end . . . but it was mitigated by a variety of
other portrayals."[129]

An important article in *Newspaper Research Journal* explored the influences that draw Native Americans into journalism and their movement into mainstream or native media. The author, who based her study on a survey of members of the Native American Journalists Association, found that other native journalists were the strongest influence drawing the respondents into journalism. The study also suggested that the Native American cultural value of storytelling was reflected in some Native Americans' decision to enter journalism.[130]

Broadcast Coverage

Though few if any scholarly analyses of treatment of Native Americans in broadcast news media have been done, a trade press article profiled "Heartbeat Alaska," an acclaimed television program that speaks to and about native people. The program's creator, Jeanie Greene, an Inupiat Native Alaskan, indicated the program grew from the failure of Alaskan television to show anything but negative portrayals of Native Alaskans.[131]

The story of emerging native broadcasting, which was often seen as a counterweight to omissions and stereotyping on commercial airwaves, was brought together in a single volume in Michael C. Keith's *Signals in the Air*.[132] In the book Keith profiled all known native broadcast stations, outlined the historical development of native broadcasting, and addressed funding issues and future development, among other things.

CONCLUSION

Inaccurate depictions of Indians were in place even before the first colonial newspaper pulled them into the journalistic realm. The depictions of native people either as noble savages or as evil Indians often were transported intact from literature, popular culture, and other media into the press. Though the status of Native Americans and public policies toward them changed drastically, both attitudes toward Indians and their journalistic depictions were framed by images that had their origins before the time of Columbus. The journalistic and cultural attitudes that led to these portrayals resulted in stereotyping, distortion, and omission of news of significance to the people themselves. And, they have added to and reinforced the misperceptions of non-Indians.

Native cultures in the United States are rich, complex, and diverse. The sovereignty issues that govern Native Americans' unique legal status are intricate and fascinating. The pendulum of public policy toward native people has swung from forced assimilation in the nineteenth and early twentieth century to cultural pluralism during the 1930s and early 1940s, back to assimilation in the 1950s, to rather limited self-determination in the 1960s and beyond.

Most of these issues and policies have been mentioned piecemeal in the mainstream press, but still Native Americans are little known by non-Indians outside their communities. Scholars who have studied news coverage of Native Americans have noted that coverage often reflects the stereotypes found in other media. That is, news stories have often been framed around images of the noble savage or good Indian on the one hand and the evil or degraded Indian on the other. Thus, researchers have found, news about Indians has too often been forced into a mold that does not fit the people or event. Too often, researchers have noticed, coverage came in response to violence, conflict, or crisis. And too often, the resulting stories gave short shrift to the historical causes and underlying issues that led to the explosions.

The scholarly literature on the news coverage of Native Americans is relatively sparse, leaving ample opportunity for further research. Scholars have been more attracted to examinations of news of nineteenth-century Indians than to twentieth-century portrayals. While these nineteenth-century studies are worthy in themselves, they tend to reinforce the notion that Native Americans are people of the past rather than contemporary communities.

In the final decades of the twentieth century, increasing numbers of Native American journalists and scholars have spoken critically about their coverage in the press. In some cases, the news media have responded. It remains for future scholars to determine whether this rising voice of native people and new awareness on the part of the press will result in the kind of balanced, detailed coverage that truly reflects the communities and lives of Native Americans.

NOTES

1. Horace Greeley, *An Overland Journey from New York to San Francisco in the Summer of 1859* (New York: C. M. Saxton, Barker & Co., 1860), 151.

2. Ibid., 153.

3. Quoted in Betty Ballantine and Ian Ballantine, eds., *The Native Americans: An Illustrated History* (Atlanta: Turner Publishing, 1993), 401.

4. Lewis Hanke, *Aristotle and the American Indians* (Bloomington: Indiana University Press, 1959), 3.

5. Christopher Columbus, *The Diario of Christopher Columbus's First Voyage to America, 1492–1493*, trans. Oliver Dunn and James Kelley, Jr. (Norman: University of Oklahoma Press, 1989), 67–68.

6. Ibid., 65.

7. Alfred W. Crosby, Jr., *The Columbian Exchange: Biological and Cultural Consequences of 1492* (Westport, Conn.: Greenwood Press, 1972), 9.

8. Mary Rowlandson, *The Soveraignty and Goodness of God*, quoted in Alden T. Vaughn and Edward Clark, eds., *Puritans among the Indians: Accounts of Captivity and Redemption, 1676–1724* (Cambridge, Mass.: Belknap Press, 1981), 33.

9. Benjamin Harris, *Publick Occurrences, Both Forreign and Domestick*, 25 September 1690, quoted in Calder Pickett, *Voices of the Past: Key Documents in the History of American Journalism* (Columbus, Ohio: Grid, 1977), 20.

10. David Copeland, *Colonial American Newspapers: Character and Content* (Newark, Del.: University of Delaware Press, 1997), 51.

11. Ibid., 59.

12. Ibid., 60.

13. Pete Steffens, "Franklin's Early Attack on Racism: An Essay against a Massacre of Indians," *Journalism History* 5, no. 1 (Spring 1978), 8–12, 31.

14. Quoted in Steffens, 10.

15. Quoted in Steffens, 11.

16. Carl Driver, *John Sevier: Pioneer of the Old Southwest* (Chapel Hill: University of North Carolina Press, 1932; Nashville: Charles and Randy Eller Booksellers, 1973), 2.

17. *Cherokee Phoenix*, 15 May 1830, quoted in Barbara F. Luebke, "Elias Boudinot and 'Indian Removal'," in *Outsiders in 19th-Century Press History: Multicultural Perspectives*, ed. Frankie Hutton and Barbara Straus Reed (Bowling Green, Ohio: Bowling Green State University Popular Press, 1995), 125.

18. *Savannah Georgian*, quoted in *Niles' National Register*, 21 July 1838, 324.

19. John M. Coward, "The Newspaper Indian: Native Americans and the Press" (Ph.D. diss., University of Texas at Austin, 1989), 59–109.

20. *Weekly Western Review* (Franklin, Tenn.), 14 July 1837, 1, quoted in Coward, "The Newspaper Indian," 88. Coward cites two other similar transportation stories, one from 1834 and one from 1836, and suggests that this pattern was common.

21. Coward, "The Newspaper Indian," 91–94.

22. Quoted in Peter Nabokov, "Native America at Mid-Century, 1846–1861," in *The Native Americans: An Illustrated History*, ed. Betty Ballantine and Ian Ballantine (Atlanta: Turner Publishing, 1993), 304.

23. Horace Greeley, *An Overland Journey*, 152.

24. Ibid., 153.

25. Ibid., 156.

26. *Rocky Mountain News*, 10 August 1864, 2.

27. A full treatment of Byers, the *Rocky Mountain News*, and the Sand Creek massacre can be found in David Svaldi, *Sand Creek and the Rhetoric of Extermination* (Lanham, Md.: University Press of America, 1989).

28. Report on Indians Taxed and Indians Not Taxed in the United States (Except Alaska), Department of the Interior, Census Office. New York: Norman Ross Publishing, 1994, 19.

29. *Rocky Mountain News*, 28 December 1866, 4, quoted in Coward, "The Newspaper Indian," 164–65.

30. *New Orleans Evening Picayune*, 31 December 1866, 2, quoted in Coward, "The Newspaper Indian," 170.

31. Elmo Scott Watson, "The Indian Wars and the Press, 1866–67," *Journalism Quarterly* 17 (December 1940), 302.

32. Ibid., 309.

33. Oliver Knight, *Following the Indian Wars: The Story of Newspaper Correspondents among the Indian Campaigners* (Norman: University of Oklahoma Press, 1960). Knight cites the sensationalized reporting of Robert Bogart, who covered the Modoc campaign in California for the *San Francisco Chronicle*, 106–7. Knight also criticizes the "bunkum" of the *Chicago Tribune*'s James William Howard, or "Phocion." About one of his dispatches, Knight commented, "What [Phocion] wrote and the truth don't always appear to have been on speaking terms." See Knight, 223, 230–31. Another view of Indian war news is found in William Dobak, "Yellow-Leg Journalists: Enlisted Men as Newspaper Reporters in the Sioux Campaign, 1876," *Journal of the West* 13, no. 1 (January 1974), 86–112.

34. Knight, *Following the Indian Wars*, 94.

35. Ibid., 101.

36. The Eastern press generally was more sympathetic than the frontier press. But some urban papers were consistently anti-Indian. Richard Slotkin has noted, for instance, that the *New York Herald* was founded by James Gordon Bennett as an expansionist journal and always took a hard line in favor of expropriating Indian lands. See Richard Slotkin, *The Fatal Environment* (New York: HarperPerennial, 1985), 236.

37. *Weekly Arizonan*, 22 April 1871, quoted in William B. Blankenburg, "The Role of the Press in an Indian Massacre, 1871," *Journalism Quarterly* 45, no. 1 (Spring 1968), 65.

38. *Arizona Miner*, 27 May 1871, quoted in Blankenburg, "The Role of the Press," 66.

39. Blankenburg, "The Role of the Press," 70. The hostility of the Arizona press toward Apaches is also documented in John A. Turcheneske, Jr., "The Arizona Press and Geronimo's Surrender," *Journal of Arizona History* 14, no. 2 (1973), 133–48.

40. *New York Herald*, 9 July 1876, n.p. The Little Bighorn was frequently written as three words in the nineteenth-century press, but most modern historians write Bighorn as one word, as it is in the name of the mountain and the river.

41. *Chicago Tribune*, 15 July 1876, 6.

42. Charles Rankin, "Savage Journalists and Civilized Indians: A Different View," *Journalism History* 21, no. 3 (Autumn 1995), 110.

43. John M. Coward, "Creating the Ideal Indian: The Case of the Poncas," *Journalism History* 21, no. 3 (Autumn 1995).

44. *Chicago Tribune*, 19 May 1879, 4.

45. Elmo Scott Watson, "The Last Indian War, 1890–91—A Study of Newspaper Jingoism," *Journalism Quarterly* 20, no. 3 (September 1943), 205.

46. John E. Carter, "Making Pictures for a News-Hungry Nation," in *Eyewitness at Wounded Knee*, ed. Richard Jensen, R. Eli Paul, and John E. Carter (Lincoln: University of Nebraska Press, 1991), 44.

47. Douglas Jones, "Teresa Dean: Lady Correspondent among the Sioux Indians," *Journalism Quarterly* 49, no. 4 (Winter 1972), 656–62.

48. Carter, "Making Pictures," 39.

49. Ibid. The illustrated press also reinforced old stereotypes in coverage of the Wounded Knee massacre. See William E. Huntzicker, "The 'Sioux Outbreak' in the Illustrated Press," *South Dakota History* 20, no. 4 (Winter 1990), 299–322.

50. Michael Schudson, *Discovering the News* (New York: Basic Books, 1978), 71–77.

51. Frederick Hoxie, *A Final Promise: The Campaign to Assimilate the Indians, 1880–1920* (Lincoln: University of Nebraska Press, 1984), 187.

52. Francis Paul Prucha, *The Great Father: The United States Government and the American Indians*, vol. 2 (Lincoln: University of Nebraska Press, 1984), 896.

53. Ibid., 903–9.

54. Russel Lawrence Barsh, "American Indians in the Great War," *Ethnohistory* 38, no. 3 (Summer 1991), 276–303.

55. Mary Ann Weston, *Native Americans in the News: Images of Indians in the Twentieth Century Press* (Westport: Greenwood Press, 1996), 23, 24, 27, 29.

56. Randolph Downes, "A Crusade for Indian Reform, 1922–1934," *Mississippi Valley Historical Review* 32, no. 3 (December 1945), 334.

57. Institute for Government Research, *The Problem of Indian Administration*, Lewis Meriam, technical director (Baltimore: Johns Hopkins Press, 1928).

58. Downes, "A Crusade for Indian Reform," 331–54.

59. See, for example, Lawrence C. Kelly, *The Assault on Assimilation: John Collier and the Origins of Indian Policy Reform* (Albuquerque: University of New Mexico Press, 1983); Kenneth Philp, *John Collier's Crusade for Indian Reform* (Tucson: University of Arizona Press, 1977).

60. Alvin M. Josephy, Jr., "Modern America and the Indian," in *Indians in American History*, ed. Frederick E. Hoxie (Arlington Heights, Ill.: Harlan Davidson, 1988), 253–58.

61. Weston, *Native Americans in the News*, 59–83.

62. Ibid., 85–97.

63. Tom Holm, "Fighting a White Man's War: The Extent and Legacy of American Indian Participation in World War II," in *The Plains Indians of the Twentieth Century*, ed. Peter Iverson (Norman: University of Oklahoma Press, 1985), 157.

64. Ibid., 160–65.

65. Ibid., 165.

66. Albert Hemingway, *Ira Hayes, Pima Marine* (Lanham, Md.: University Press of America, 1988), 129–52; Donald Fixico, *Termination and Relocation: Federal Indian Policy, 1945–1960* (Albuquerque: University of New Mexico Press, 1986), 3–4.

67. Weston, *Native Americans in the News*, 89–90.

68. Ibid., 86.

69. Ibid., 109.

70. For accounts of the Menominee matter, see, among others, Nicholas Peroff, *Menominee Drums* (Norman: University of Oklahoma Press, 1982); and Deborah Shames, ed., *Freedom with Reservation: The Menominee Struggle to Save Their Land and People* (Madison, Wis.: National Committee to Save the Menominee People and Forests, 1972).

71. Fixico, *Termination and Relocation*, 148, 235.

72. Weston, *Native Americans in the News*, 117–18.

73. Pope's quatrain in *An Essay on Man* (1773–1774: Epistle I) said: "Lo, the poor Indian whose untutor'd mind/ Sees God in clouds, or hears him in the wind;/ His soul proud Science never taught to stray/ Far as the solar walk or milky way."

74. "Broken Arrow," *Time*, 4 March 1957, 48–49.

75. Laura Thompson, review of "Hopi Horizons. A Film Study of an Indian Tribe," *American Anthropologist*, July 1947, 464–66.

76. Prucha, *The Great Father*, 1089; Weston, *Native Americans in the News*, 128–29.

77. Quoted in Weston, *Native Americans in the News*, 133.

78. Josephy, "Modern America and the Indian," 267.

79. *The Denver Post*, 3 January 1960, 1; 4 January 1960, 1; 5 January 1960, 1; 6 January 1960, 1; 7 January 1960, 1; 8 January 1960, 1; 10 January 1960, 1; 11 January 1960, 2; 12 January 1960, 2; 13 January 1960, 7; 14 January 1960, 19; 15 January 1960, 17.

80. National Advisory Commission on Civil Disorders (Kerner Commission), *Report of the National Advisory Commission on Civil Disorders* (New York: Bantam Books, 1968), ch. 15.

81. Eric Blanchard, "The Poor People and the 'White Press,' " *Columbia Journalism Review* 7, no. 3 (Fall 1968), 61–65.

82. Fred Fedler, "The Media and Minority Groups: A Study of Adequacy of Access," *Journalism Quarterly* 50 (Spring 1973), 109–17.

83. "Trap at Wounded Knee," *Time*, 26 March 1973, 67.

84. Desmond Smith, "The Media Coup d'Etat," *The Nation*, 25 June 1973, 806–9.

85. Terri Schultz, "Bamboozle Me Not at Wounded Knee," *Harper's Magazine*, June 1973, 46–56.

86. Robert Burnette and John Koster, *The Road to Wounded Knee* (New York: Bantam Books, 1974), 230.

87. John Koster, "American Indians and the Media," *Cross Currents*, Summer 1976, 164–71.

88. Ibid.

89. Neil Hickey, "Was the Truth Buried at Wounded Knee?" *TV Guide*, 1 December 1973, 7–12; 8 December 1973, 33–40; 15 December 1973, 43–49; 22 December 1973, 21–23. Quotes are from 8 December article, p. 38.

90. Rolland Dewing, "South Dakota Newspaper Coverage of the 1973 Occupation of Wounded Knee," *South Dakota History* 12, no. 1 (Spring 1982), 48–64.

91. Edward Justin Streb, "The Rhetoric of Wounded Knee II: A Critical Analysis of Confrontational and 'Media Event' Discourse" (Ph.D. diss., Northwestern University, 1979).

92. Ibid., 140.

93. Ibid., 221.

94. Burnette and Koster, *The Road to Wounded Knee*, 228–29.

95. Rolland Dewing, *Wounded Knee: The Meaning and Significance of the Second Incident* (New York: Irvington Publishers, 1985), 197.

96. Weston, *Native Americans in the News*, 148.

97. "Indians and the Media: A Panel Discussion," *Civil Rights Digest*, Fall 1973, 41–45.

98. Ibid.

99. Gerald Wilkinson, "Colonialism through the Media," *Indian Historian* (Summer 1974), 29–32.

100. Joel Weisman, "About That 'Ambush' at Wounded Knee," *Columbia Journalism Review* 14, no. 3 (September/October 1975), 28–31.

101. Ibid.

102. A detailed and passionate account of the matter is presented in Peter Matthiessen, *In the Spirit of Crazy Horse* (New York: Penguin Books, 1991). The book was first published in 1983, but later withdrawn after the author and publisher were sued for libel—an action the author contended was aimed at curtailing the book's circulation. After eight years of litigation, the book was republished. According to the book's "Afterword" (pp. 593–600), written by Martin Garbus, the attorney who represented the author and publisher in the lawsuits, they were sued by former South Dakota governor William Janklow in 1983; that suit was dismissed in 1988. FBI Special Agent David Price sued Matthiessen and the publisher in 1984; after seven years of litigation, the Supreme Court let stand lower court decisions that the suit be dismissed.

103. Gail Landsman, "Indian Activism and the Press: Coverage of the Conflict at Ganienkeh," *Anthropological Quarterly*, July 1987, 101–13. For research on social movements, see Todd Gitlin, *The Whole World Is Watching* (Berkeley: University of California Press, 1980); Gaye Tuchman, *Making News* (New York: Free Press, 1978);

Harvey Molotch, "Media and Movements" in *The Dynamics of Social Movements*, ed. Mayer Zald and John McCarthy (Cambridge, Mass.: Winthrop Publishers, 1979).

104. Bruce Miller, "The Press, the Boldt Decision, and Indian-White Relations," *American Indian Culture and Research Journal* 17, no. 2 (1993), 75–97.

105. Ibid., 84, 85.

106. Ibid., 90.

107. Jerry Kammer, "The Navajos, the Hopis, and the U.S. Press," *Columbia Journalism Review* 25, no. 2 (July/August 1986), 41–44.

108. Benjamin Singer, "Minorities and the Media: A Content Analysis of Native Canadians in the Daily Press," *Canadian Review of Sociology and Anthropology* 19, no. 3 (August 1982), 348–59.

109. Mary Ann Weston, "Native Americans in the News: Symbol, Substance or Stereotype?" Human Relations Foundation of Chicago Publication, 1992.

110. Marc Grenier, "Native Indians in the English-Canadian Press: The Case of the 'Oka Crisis,' " *Media, Culture & Society* 16 (April 1994), 313–36.

111. Mike Masterson, Chuck Cook, and Mark N. Trahant, "Fraud in Indian Country: A Billion-Dollar Betrayal," *Arizona Republic*, 4–11 October 1987.

112. James Murphy and Donald Avery, "A Comparison of Alaskan Native and Non-Native Newspaper Content," *Journalism Quarterly* 60, no. 2 (Summer 1983), 316–22.

113. Patty Loew, "Voices from the Boatlandings in the Chippewa Treaty Rights Dispute" (Paper presented at Association for Education in Journalism and Mass Communication Convention, Washington, D.C., August 1995).

114. Debra Thunder, "A Hard River to Cross," *Extra!*, July/August 1992, 16–17.

115. Richard Hill, "The Non-Vanishing American Indian," *Quill*, May 1992, 35–37; Tim Giago (Nanwica Kciji), "Indian Country Reporting," *Nieman Reports*, Summer 1991, 48–50; Marshall Cook, "Indian Affairs and the Mainstream Media," *Editor & Publisher*, 23 December 1989, 16–17; Jim Carrier, "Newsrooms Miss Out on a Lot When They Exclude American Indian Journalists," *ASNE Bulletin*, September/October 1988, 20–21; Mercedes Lynn de Uriarte, "Inching Numbers," *Quill*, May 1996, 16.

116. American Indian Media Image Task Force, *The American Indian and the Media* (Minneapolis: National Conference of Christians and Jews, Minnesota-Dakotas Region, 1991).

117. Chris Kent, "Oregonian Shuts Out Redskins, Braves," *Washington Journalism Review* (April 1992), 11–12; William Hilliard, "Stereotypes on the Sports Page," *ASNE Bulletin*, May/June 1992, 20–21.

118. Weston, *Native Americans in the News*, 160–63.

119. Stephen Rada, "Ramah Navajo Radio and Cultural Preservation," *Journal of Broadcasting* 22, no. 3 (Summer 1978), 361–71.

120. Stephen Rada, "KIPC-FM Pueblo Radio: Case Study of a Failure," *Journalism Quarterly* 56, no. 1 (Spring 1979), 97–101, 133.

121. Bruce Smith and Jerry Brigham, "Native Radio Broadcasting in North America," *Journal of Broadcasting and Electronic Media* (Spring 1992), 183–94.

122. *U.S. Census, 1930*. Table 4, Population by Color or Race, for the United States: 1790 to 1930, p. 32; U.S. Census, 1970. Vol. 2, Part 1F, American Indians, p. xi. The authors wish to acknowledge the assistance of Jennifer Hanson of Northwestern University with these data.

123. "Native Americans: Will the Columbus Quincentenary Highlight Their Problems?" *CQ Researcher*, 8 May 1992, 389.

124. Fred Bales, "Hantavirus and the Media: Double Jeopardy for Native Americans," *American Indian Culture and Research Journal* 18, no. 3 (1994), 251–63.

125. Ibid., 254.

126. Ibid., 260.

127. John Creed, "The Value of Cultural Journalism to Diversity in the Mainline Press," *Journalism Educator*, Autumn 1994, 64–71.

128. Ibid., 70.

129. Weston, *Native Americans in the News*, 163.

130. Sheila Reaves, "Native American Journalists: Finding a Pipeline into Journalism," *Newspaper Research Journal* 16, no. 4 (Fall 1995), 57–73.

131. Bert Briller, "For the Forty Ninth State, a New Kind of Television," *Television Quarterly* 27, no. 2 (1994), 57–64.

132. Michael Keith, *Signals in the Air* (Westport, Conn.: Praeger Publishers, 1995).

SELECTED BIBLIOGRAPHY

Athearn, Robert G. *The Mythic West in Twentieth Century America.* Lawrence: University of Kansas Press, 1986.

Axtell, James. *The Invasion Within: The Contest of Cultures in Colonial North America.* New York: Oxford University Press, 1985.

————. "Through a Glass Darkly: Colonial Attitudes toward the Native Americans." *American Indian Culture and Research Journal* 1, no. 1 (1974), 17–28.

Barreiro, Jose, ed. "View from the Shore: American Indian Perspectives on the Quincentenary." *Northeast Indian Quarterly* 7, no. 3 (Fall 1990).

Berkhofer, Robert F., Jr. *The White Man's Indian.* New York: Vintage Books, 1978.

Bernstein, Alison R. *American Indians and World War II.* Norman: University of Oklahoma Press, 1991.

Bieder, Robert E. *Science Encounters the Indian, 1820–1880: The Early Years of American Ethnology.* Norman: University of Oklahoma Press, 1986.

Brown, Dee Alexander. *Bury My Heart at Wounded Knee.* New York: Holt, Rinehart and Winston, 1971.

Burt, Larry W. *Tribalism in Crisis: Federal Indian Policy, 1953–1961.* Albuquerque: University of New Mexico Press, 1982.

Collier, John. *From Every Zenith.* Denver: Sage Books, 1963.

Cornell, Stephen. *Return of the Native: American Indian Political Resurgence.* New York: Oxford University Press, 1988.

Coward, John M. *The Newspaper Indian: Native American Identity in the Nineteenth Century Press.* Forthcoming from University of Illinois Press.

Crosby, Alfred W., Jr. *The Columbian Exchange: Biological and Cultural Consequences of 1492.* Westport, Conn.: Greenwood Press, 1972.

Danky, James, ed. *Native American Periodicals and Newspapers, 1828–1982.* Westport, Conn.: Greenwood Press, 1984.

Debo, Angie. *And Still the Waters Run.* Princeton, N.J.: Princeton University Press, 1940.

Deloria, Vine, Jr. *Behind the Trail of Broken Treaties.* New York: Delacorte Press, 1974.

————. *Custer Died for Your Sins.* New York: Avon Books, 1970.

Deloria, Vine, Jr., ed. *American Indian Policy in the Twentieth Century.* Norman: University of Oklahoma Press, 1985.

Deloria, Vine, Jr., and Clifford M. Lytle. *The Nations Within.* New York: Pantheon Books, 1984.

Dewing, Rolland. *Wounded Knee: The Meaning and Significance of the Second Incident.* New York: Irvington Publishers, 1985.

Dippie, Brian W. *The Vanishing American: White Attitudes and U.S. Indian Policy.* Middletown, Conn.: Wesleyan University Press, 1982.

Horsman, Reginald. *Race and Manifest Destiny.* Cambridge: Harvard University Press, 1981.

Huntzicker, William E. "The 'Sioux Outbreak' in the Illustrated Press." *South Dakota History* 20, no. 4 (Winter 1990), 299–322.

Jackson, Helen Hunt. *A Century of Dishonor.* 1881. Reprint. New York: Harper Torchbooks, 1965.

Johansen, Bruce E. *Life & Death in Mohawk Country.* Golden, Colo.: North American Press, 1993.

Josephy, Alvin M., Jr. *Red Power: The American Indians' Fight for Freedom.* Lincoln: University of Nebraska Press, 1971.

Limerick, Patricia Nelson. *The Legacy of Conquest: The Unbroken Past of the American West.* New York: W. W. Norton, 1987.

Littlefield, Daniel F., Jr., and James W. Parins, eds. *American Indian and Alaska Native Newspapers and Periodicals, 1826–1924.* Westport, Conn.: Greenwood Press, 1984.

———. *American Indian and Alaska Native Newspapers and Periodicals, 1925–70.* Westport, Conn.: Greenwood Press, 1986.

———. *American Indian and Alaska Native Newspapers and Periodicals, 1971–1985.* Westport, Conn.: Greenwood Press, 1986.

Martin, Calvin, ed. *The American Indian and the Problem of History.* New York: Oxford University Press, 1987.

Matijasic, Thomas D. "Reflected Values: Sixteenth-Century Europeans View the Indians of North America." *American Indian Culture and Research Journal* 11, no. 2 (1987), 31–50.

McNickle, D'Arcy. *Native American Tribalism.* New York: Oxford University Press, 1973.

Murphy, James E., and Sharon M. Murphy. *Let My People Know: American Indian Journalism, 1828–1978.* Norman: University of Oklahoma Press, 1981.

Murphy, Sharon. "American Indians and the Media: Neglect and Stereotype." *Journalism History* 6, no. 2 (Summer 1979), 39–43.

Nichols, Roger L. "Printer's Ink and Red Skins: Western Newspapermen and the Indians." *Kansas Quarterly* 3, no. 4 (Fall 1971), 82–88.

Olson, James S., and Raymond Wilson. *Native Americans in the Twentieth Century.* Provo, Utah: Brigham Young University Press, 1984.

Pearce, Roy Harvey. *Savagism and Civilization: A Study of the Indian and the American Mind.* Baltimore: Johns Hopkins University Press, 1953, 1965.

Perdue, Theda, ed. *Cherokee Editor: The Writings of Elias Boudinot.* Knoxville: University of Tennessee Press, 1983.

Price, John A. "The Stereotyping of North American Indians in Motion Pictures." *Ethnohistory* 20, no. 2 (Spring 1973), 153–71.

Riley, Glenda. *Women and Indians on the Frontier, 1825–1915.* Albuquerque: University of New Mexico Press, 1984.

Riley, Sam G. "The Indian's Own Prejudice, as Mirrored in the First Native American Newspaper." *Journalism History* 6, no. 2 (Summer 1979), 44–47.

Rogin, Michael Paul. *Fathers and Sons: Andrew Jackson and the Subjugation of the American Indian.* New York: Alfred A. Knopf, 1975.

Smith, Jane F., and Robert M. Kvasnicka, eds. *Indian-White Relations: A Persistent Paradox.* Washington, D.C.: Howard University Press, 1981.

Steiner, Stan. *The New Indians.* New York: Delta Books, 1968.

Sturtevant, William C., gen. ed. *Handbook of North American Indians.* Vol. 4, *History of Indian-White Relations*, edited by Wilcomb E. Washburn. Washington, D.C.: Smithsonian Institution, 1988.

Taylor, Graham D. *The New Deal and American Indian Tribalism.* Lincoln: University of Nebraska Press, 1980.

Turcheneske, John A., Jr. "The Arizona Press and Geronimo's Surrender." *Journal of Arizona History* 14, no. 2 (1973), 133–48.

Utley, Robert M. *The Indian Frontier of the American West, 1846–1890.* Albuquerque: University of New Mexico Press, 1984.

Voices from Wounded Knee, 1973. Mohawk Nation via Rooseveltown, N.Y.: *Akwesasne Notes*, 1974.

Weston, Mary Ann. *Native Americans in the News: Images of Indians in the Twentieth Century Press.* Westport, Conn.: Greenwood Press, 1996.

White, Robert H. *Tribal Assets.* New York: Henry Holt, 1990.

Woll, Allen L., and Randall M. Miller, eds. *Ethnic and Racial Images in American Film and Television: Historical Essays and Bibliography.* New York: Garland Publishing, 1987.

3

The African Americans

CAROLYN MARTINDALE AND LILLIAN RAE DUNLAP

Maintenance of social, economic, and political privileges over African Americans depended upon the construction of stereotypes. These stereotypes became woven into American life through various cultural forms.
—Bill Gaskins
"The World According to *Life*," 1993[1]

Slavery is an institution that enacted a terrible psychic toll on its perpetrators as well as its victims; it dehumanized whites as well as blacks. In refusing to admit the humanity of Africans and their descendants, white Americans seriously damaged their own spirits as well as the black persons whom they brutalized. The white participants in the slave system—from the sea captains who transported the captured Africans in deplorable conditions, to the slave owners who worked them like beasts and denied them marriages and education and sold family members away from each other, to the Southern slaveholder's wife who had to turn a blind eye to her husband's nocturnal visits to the slave quarters—were aware at some deep spiritual level that they were participating in an obscenity. So like every other human being who takes gross advantage of a weaker person, they found justifications for their actions.

One justification developed by the white American slave traders and holders was that the African was a heathen who in his native land worshipped savage pagan gods, and bringing him to America and exposing him to Christianity was a worthy endeavor surely approved by God. Another rationalization was that the African was a primitive being who lived in such brutish conditions in his homeland that Anglo-Americans were doing him a favor by rescuing him from

Professor Martindale wrote the stereotypes section of this chapter and the entries about press portrayal of African Americans after 1934; Dr. Dunlap wrote the pre-1934 history and the segments on broadcast portrayal of black Americans.

a land of human sacrifice, cannibalism, and other such abominations and bringing him to a civilized land. A third justification was that the African was an ignorant, feckless, childlike being who needed the guidance and care of the paternalistic slaveholder. These rationales were routinely propounded from the pulpit; expressed in literature, newspapers, and magazines; and stated in public and private discourse during the more than 200 years that slavery was practiced in the United States.

Out of this mishmash of white justifications for slavery arose a set of stereotypes about African Americans that persists to this day. The stereotypes portray African Americans, as one expert explains, as a savage or as a Sambo. Contained in the savage stereotype are those qualities that white Americans have attributed to and feared in black Americans: violence, an absence of restraint, sexual prowess and potency, physical strength and ability—the dangerous qualities of the black militant, from Nat Turner to Bobby Seale. The Sambo stereotype includes images of ignorant, lazy, carefree, good-humored blacks like those portrayed in minstrel shows—a childlike, singing, dancing, take-no-thought-for-tomorrow creature who is a permanent child.[2]

These stereotypes were constantly reinforced, in all areas of public and private discourse, for so many years during slavery that when the Civil War ended in 1865 they had achieved a staggeringly tenacious hold on the minds of white Americans. Also, as one source notes, whites by then had a large psychic investment in the belief of white superiority.[3]

In the eleven years of Reconstruction after the Civil War, freed slaves had opportunities that enabled them to begin to break these stereotypes, as will be explained in the next section. But then the political winds shifted in Washington, and by 1876 the federal government had abandoned African Americans. Soon new laws, established by Southern legislatures and upheld by the U.S. Supreme Court, rolled back most of the gains made by African Americans during Reconstruction, and forced blacks into a peonage system only one step up from slavery.

Aiding Anglo-Americans in this renewed repression were the long-standing stereotypes of African Americans that had grown out of whites' guilty consciences over slavery and enabled them to justify denying basic human rights to blacks. By this time, after over 300 years of claims that black Americans were less intelligent, more primitive, and less enterprising than white Americans, many whites believed these claims were true. Reinforcing these convictions was the pseudo-scientific racism that developed. Scientists claimed to have "proved" scientifically that African Americans were not as smart as whites, were less able to learn, had less initiative and less courage. The majority of whites accepted these ideas as proven truths, partly because the ideas agreed with ingrained stereotypes of blacks. Certainly during the next eighty years most whites seemed to suffer few twinges of conscience at permanently denying African Americans an equal opportunity with whites—in employment, education, housing, public transportation, the armed forces, sports, and every other aspect of life. They did not even seem much bothered at the periodic epidemics of lynchings of blacks across the country.

It seems likely that many Anglo-Americans' unacknowledged guilt over white treatment of blacks just drove the stereotypes deeper, because they provided a convenient rationale for denying equal rights to African Americans and then blaming them for it. The stereotypes also enabled whites to feel superior, and were used by business and political leaders who wanted to ensure that poor whites and blacks who were being exploited would not unite against the persons who profited from their exploitation.

Naturally, the stereotypes pervaded popular culture. During the first half of the twentieth century, these images of blacks were perpetuated in radio, film, television, and advertising, as well as in literature, popular fiction, newspapers, and public discourse from both the pulpit and the campaign platform. It was inevitable that these stereotypes would be reflected in mainstream news coverage of African Americans; white reporters and editors were influenced by the same stereotypes and prejudices that affected the rest of white society. The stereotypes seemed to form a sort of mental grid through which news that did not conform to stereotypical images of blacks could not pass.

Not surprisingly, then, until recent decades, the news media in this century have tended to present African Americans almost exclusively as criminals, and also as athletes and entertainers—all portrayals that fit the savage and the Sambo stereotypes. This kind of coverage, combined with the white media's ignoring of discrimination against blacks, ignoring of achievements of individual blacks, and failing to cover the black community, in turn reinforced popular stereotypes of African Americans among readers and viewers. These stereotypical images will appear often in the coverage studies reported on the following pages.

HISTORY BEFORE 1934

"When our history books do not mention the Negro, significant omissions result . . . mentioning him solely in terms of some problem has caused an incomplete, distorted picture to emerge. In either case a more balanced focus is needed," one source has noted.[4]

The largest and most visible American minority has also been the most frequently covered by mainstream media. African Americans were first covered as savages, then as property, later as enemies, and then as strangers.

In 1619, the year before the Pilgrims landed at Plymouth Rock, twenty Negroes on a Dutch frigate arrived at Jamestown, Virginia, as indentured servants. Some scholars say they could not have been slaves because they had already been baptized. By 1640, however, black indentured servants could be sentenced to slavery for life.[5] County records in Virginia for 1646 say a slave owner sold a Negro woman and boy to Stephen Charlton "to the use of him . . . forever." Similarly, six years later, William Whittington sold to John Pott "one Negro girle named Jowan; aged about ten yeares and with her issue and produce . . .

for their life tyme . . . and their successors forever.''[6] More slaves were imported, and by the 1660s slavery was codified in laws, especially in the Southern states. To reduce the chances of the kidnapped Africans cooperating and organizing revolts, blacks were separated from family and village groups when they arrived in this country, and their languages, religions, and culture were ruthlessly suppressed.

At the same time, free Negroes lived in the colonies. In fact, some free Negroes actually owned slaves themselves, but this was not common.[7] By 1790, 757,000 blacks lived in the United States; 60,000 were free. The total number of blacks equaled about 19 percent of the American population, but in some Deep South states they constituted half the population.

Both Northern and Southern states allowed slavery. Southerners defended the institution of slavery primarily because it was absolutely necessary to their economy; the whole plantation system depended upon slave labor. The wealth and power of the slaveholding gentry rose dramatically as a result of slavery, and the white plantation owners were a powerful force in the U.S. economy and federal government from 1800 to the Civil War.[8]

Both Northern and Southern whites sought and found justifications for slavery in religion. Some clerics claimed Negroes were ordained by God to be ''hewers of wood and drawers of water''—to be servants. States passed numerous laws to circumscribe the movement of Negroes regardless of status. Slaves had no rights. But in neither the North nor the South was the free Negro granted political or economic equality. Early news coverage of blacks focused on the transportation and sale of slaves. Posters and newsletters listed auctions and sales and announced slave runaways. So blacks appeared in the press as property or problems.

Many Quaker writers campaigned against slavery. Several eighteenth-century pamphlets reflect their commitment, including works by Benjamin Say, John Woolman, and Anthony Benezet, who published tracts condemning slavery and the slave trade well before the American Revolution. Quakers continued to speak out against slavery and became key participants in the Underground Railroad and instrumental in establishing schools for Negroes.[9]

Slave narratives chronicled the horrors of slavery and the hope that kept blacks committed to survival. Published in newspapers and pamphlets, they revealed the coping strategies of hundreds of slaves, who either remained loyal to their master in servile cooperation, appeared to cooperate while covertly protesting, or refused to adjust to slavery and resorted to suicide, self-mutilation, flight, or open rebellion.[10]

On January 1, 1808, Congress suspended the international trade in African slaves. But the demand for agricultural laborers continued and domestic slave trading thrived. According to one source, ''In Maryland and Virginia, prime male field hands such as were valued at less than $300 in 1790, readily sold for from $1,000 to $1,200 and sometimes more by 1860.''[11]

Despite Congressional action banning the importation of slaves, whites regarded blacks as property that could and should be bought and traded as the economy dictated. One author accurately summarized the position of blacks in America when he said,

People of colour are in every part of the United States considered not merely by the populace but by law as a permanently degraded people; not participating as by right of the civil privileges belonging to every white man, but enjoying what civil privileges they possess . . . as a matter of favor conceded by law, and revocable by law.[12]

After 1815 the abolitionist press grew stronger in the North and in the border states. Among the abolitionist papers were the *Philanthropist* and the *Manumission Intelligencer*, published in Ohio; the *Emancipator*, in Jonesboro, Tennessee; the *Abolition Intelligencer*, in Kentucky; and the *Portrait*, in North Carolina. Another abolitionist, Elijah P. Lovejoy, started the *St. Louis Observer* in 1835. He was killed in 1837 while defending his print shop against a mob.

The first black newspaper, *Freedom's Journal*, appeared in 1827 and also disseminated an antislavery message. The main theme, however, for this and other black papers to come was self-determination and the need for black people to speak for themselves. In the first issue of *Freedom's Journal*, editors Samuel Cornish and John Russwurm wrote: "We wish to plead our own cause. Too long have others spoken for us. Too long has the publick been deceived by misrepresentations, in things which concern us dearly, though in the estimation of some mere trifles." They added that although "there are men in society who exercise towards us benevolent feelings; still (with sorrow we confess it) there are others who make it their business to enlarge upon the least trifle, which tends to the discredit of any person of color."[13]

The *North Star* newspaper, founded by Frederick Douglass, began publishing in 1847 in Rochester, New York. Later called *Frederick Douglass' Paper*, it championed the antislavery cause at a time when most blacks could not read and many states prohibited their learning to do so. At this time it was a crime in Maryland for a free Negro simply to receive a copy of an abolitionist newspaper.

In January 1836, abolitionist William Lloyd Garrison began publication of the *Liberator*. Garrison called for complete and immediate abolition. Southern lawmakers called for his capture and punishment. Northern editors ignored Garrison until they noticed the impact of the *Liberator* on Southerners; then Northern editors defended his right to speak out and be heard.

When the Civil War began, blacks served on both sides of the conflict. In the South many tended the food-producing fields to feed the Confederate troops. Also, 185,000 blacks fought on the Union side despite receiving lower wages, inferior equipment, and daily persecution from white officers and soldiers. They accounted for a tenth of the Union Army soldiers and a third of the Union Navy's casualties.

The Emancipation Proclamation signed by President Abraham Lincoln was announced in January 1863. Because of limited communication channels, thousands of slaves did not get the word about their freedom until months later. Black people still have "Juneteenth" celebrations, acknowledging the confusion around the exact date of freedom for blacks across the South.[14]

Although the Emancipation Proclamation freed the slaves in the rebelling states, it could not guarantee the reception of blacks in society. The Southern response to black liberation was the so-called Black Codes—state laws passed to control former slaves as the slave codes had done before emancipation. For example, the South Carolina code stipulated that in the making of contracts, "persons of color shall be known as *servants* and those with whom they contract shall be known as *masters*." In this same state, the Negro farm worker could not leave the farm without permission.[15]

Laws forbade Negroes from engaging in any vocation other than farming and domestic service, from joining the militia, from riding in first-class passenger cars, from intruding into the assemblies of whites, and from testifying against whites.[16] Negroes did, however, obtain the right to own property, to make contracts, to sue and to be sued, to testify in court in cases involving other Negroes, and to have legal marriages.

At the war's end in 1865, Reconstruction commenced, and Congress created the Freedman's Bureau to help the newly freed slaves, among others. The bureau created a health program, established hospitals, provided legal services, and negotiated contracts for the freedmen.[17] It also established over 4,000 schools. Nearly a quarter of a million former slaves received varying amounts of education through such efforts.

In 1866 Congress passed the Civil Rights Act, which extended citizenship to Negroes. Also passed was the Thirteenth Amendment declaring all people born in the United States citizens. The Fourteenth Amendment of 1868 protects the right to due process and guarantees to all citizens equal protection under the law. The Fifteenth Amendment of 1870 guarantees to former male slaves the right to vote.

One researcher examined the coverage of the Fourteenth Amendment given by thirteen leading newspapers. He found that the views reflected in the papers probably discouraged public support for laws that protected African Americans' civil rights. The views also encouraged among white Americans prejudicial behavior such as segregation and discrimination, which cemented the color line in the late nineteenth century.[18]

The black vote helped Republicans elect state legislators throughout the traditionally Democratic South. Blacks for the first time served as school superintendents, associate justices in state supreme courts, prosecuting attorneys, sheriffs, mayors, and justices of the peace. Also, for the first time, blacks held seats in Congress. Twenty-two Negroes represented eight Southern states. Two of these served in the Senate. Thirteen had been born slaves; some were college trained.

Meanwhile, Southern whites' fear of Northern domination and the enfranchisement of Negroes took the form of open hostility. Secret societies, such as the White League of Louisiana and the Ku Klux Klan, emerged. The Klan's tactics included intimidation, destruction of property, physical punishment, and murder. The lynching of blacks became a favorite tactic of the Klan. State officials in the South began to ignore or circumvent the laws to give power back to Southern whites. The actions of the Klan became hard to prosecute because people were afraid to testify against them and local courts were unlikely to call for punishment of any kind.[19] Systematically and institutionally, blacks were being denied the right to vote. White Southerners changed the polling places without notice and falsely arrested Negroes the day before the election.

The presidential election of 1876 found President Rutherford B. Hayes involved in a deadly compromise. Hayes agreed to remove the remaining federal troops from the South in exchange for political support. The end of Reconstruction opened the way for the "Jim Crow" laws that denied the rights of blacks, including those that should have been protected by the Fourteenth and Fifteenth Amendments to the Constitution. As soon as the conservative Democrats had regained control of state government, they began to reverse the guarantee of equal rights for blacks. Northern interests simply abandoned the cause of African Americans. The *New York Tribune*, with curious logic, said that Negroes, having been given "ample opportunity to develop their own latent capacities," had only succeeded in proving that "as a race they are idle, ignorant, and vicious."[20] One black newspaper editor wrote in 1883, "There is no law in the United States for the Negro. He is an alien in his native land."[21] Over 250 blacks were lynched around the nation in 1892. In 1896 the U.S. Supreme Court sanctioned segregation by letting stand a Louisiana ruling that outlawed integration on railroad accommodations.

One researcher examined nine newspapers—four in the North, two in border states, and three in the South—for their views about African Americans' civil rights in their coverage of the three post–Civil War amendments passed to guarantee black Americans the full privileges of American citizenship. The study found a "diminishing concern for African American rights reflected in the Northern papers, coupled with the increasingly omnipresent view in border and Southern papers that black Americans were not worthy of equal rights." These views, the scholar said, probably helped prevent the development of egalitarian racial attitudes among white Americans.[22] The author reported that newspapers initially showed a mix of strong and pragmatic support for African Americans' civil rights, but after the *Plessy v. Ferguson* decision handed down by the Supreme Court, that support diminished. "In 1883, the eleven Northern and border papers had 95 stories on the Civil Rights Cases decision; in 1896, the same newspapers had only 13 stories on the *Plessy v. Ferguson* ruling."[23] (This decision decreed that separate but equal educational facilities for blacks were Constitutional.)

While many educated blacks embraced the idea of political equality, many others agreed with the sentiment included in Booker T. Washington's "Atlanta

Compromise'' speech given at the Cotton States and International Exposition in 1895. He insisted that "the wisest of my race understand that the agitation of questions of social equality is the extremist folly.''[24]

Washington, who was born a slave of a slave mother and a white father, founded the Tuskeegee Institute in 1881. He reportedly owned interest in several black newspapers around the country that supported his political position. At odds with Washington were blacks who thought that Negroes should have social as well as legal equality. Activist W.E.B. DuBois and William Monroe Trotter, editor of the *Boston Guardian*, became Washington's most outspoken and consistent critics.

By 1909 several black intellectuals and white liberals had participated in the Niagara Movement and formed the National Association for the Advancement of Colored People (NAACP). Among the pioneers were W.E.B. DuBois and journalist Ida Wells Barnett, John Dewey, and muckraker Lincoln Steffens. One year later, the National Urban League opened its doors to help blacks move into mainstream America through employment opportunities.

Up to the late 1890s, most blacks lived and farmed in the South; however, by the end of the 1890s, thousands had begun to migrate to the North. They ran from persecution and toward the prospect of jobs in the rapidly growing industrial North. This Great Migration lasted though the 1920s but peaked between 1915 and 1917.

The year 1914 brought two powerful and opposing events: the opening of D. W. Griffith's film *Birth of a Nation*, and the founding of the Universal Negro Improvement Association by Jamaica-born Marcus Garvey. The film portrayed blacks as less than human and lauded the rise of the Ku Klux Klan. Garvey advocated the liberation of Africa and the connection of American blacks with black people around the globe. These themes resonated with post–World War I American blacks.

Garvey and DuBois sought both to improve the lives of Negroes and to liberate Africa from colonial powers, but they took very different approaches. Garvey, who set up the Black Star Steamship Line and the Negro Factories Corporation, owned the *Negro World* newspaper. DuBois was the editor of the *Crisis* magazine, an organ of the NAACP. The two men exchanged harsh spoken and written words, and newspapers of the day weighed in on the argument. The *Richmond Planet* believed that DuBois was much out of his element for having the audacity to reproach Garvey, the man of action. The *Oakland Sunshine* expressed similar sentiments: "DuBois is talking big things and Garvey is doing big things. We rather admire the man that does rather than talks.''[25]

Blacks returning from service in World War I, in which they had been segregated into largely noncombat units under white officers, were greeted with the same prejudice and discrimination they had left. In many urban areas across the country, blacks rebelled against the injustices of discrimination and racism. Riots erupted in Chicago and other major cities and created what came to be called "The Red Summer of 1919.'' One historian attributed the disturbance to the competition for jobs between blacks and whites and the new experience for whites of having large numbers of black people move into traditionally white neighborhoods. The result of the first great migration had been a dramatic increase in the number of Northern Negroes. The North and the West had over 470,000 more blacks in 1920 than they had had in 1910.[26]

The 1920s witnessed a rebirth of African-American culture in what has come to be called the "Harlem Renaissance." Poets, novelists, musicians, and graphic artists found their voices and shared them with the world.[27] Famous artists of the Renaissance included poets Claude McKay, James Weldon Johnson, Countee Cullen, Jean Toomer, and Langston Hughes.[28]

A principal contributor to the heightened interest in African-American culture was Arthur Schomburg. Born in Puerto Rico, Schomburg became the authority on African-American history and culture. After retiring from a Wall Street firm, he became curator at Fisk University in Nashville. His love of collecting and archiving black books, pamphlets, and artifacts made the Fisk collection unrivaled. He said, "History must restore what slavery took away, for it is the social damage of slavery that the present generation must repair and offset."[29] The black press contributed to this effort.

Although the earliest black newspapers emerged to voice abolitionist protest, and while racial advancement has continued to be a primary concern of the black press, African-American newspapers have traditionally served another important function by providing news about blacks not available in the mainstream white daily press. In particular, black society, sports, and business, as well as crime, have been the major news topics in the black press. The news and editorial columns of the leading twentieth-century black newspapers provide a detailed chronicle of events in the black community and of trends in black protest. They also afford important insights into the views of their readers and of their middle-class black owners. Among the great black newspapers were the *Chicago Defender* (1905), the *Atlanta World* (1928), the *Pittsburgh Courier* (1910), the *Afro American* (Baltimore, 1892; Washington, 1933), the *New York Amsterdam News* (1909), and the *Norfolk Journal and Guide* (1899).[30]

Conversely, scholarly studies of white newspaper coverage of African Americans before 1934 showed that the press provided almost no coverage of blacks, except for black crime news. One study of news about blacks in the Philadelphia press between 1908 and 1932 found that coverage of African Americans constituted only 2 percent of the papers' news space, and between 50 to 75 percent of that coverage was devoted to black crime. Another study of coverage of blacks in seventeen major papers around the nation in 1928 and 1929 found that 47 percent of the news concerned antisocial behavior; the coverage emphasized the bizarre and pathological in black life. In 1922 the Chicago Commission on Race Relations, which condemned the Chicago newspapers' portrayal of blacks, concluded that the 1919 Chicago riots were due partly to hostile attitudes expressed by the local papers. A 1931 study of news about blacks in the Southern press found that the newspapers examined expressed no objections to the lynchings of blacks.[31]

Broadcast Coverage

In 1921 radio station KDKA in Pittsburgh became the first commercially licensed station in the United States. It would be twenty-eight more years before the first black-owned radio station—WERD in Atlanta in 1949—took the air.

The period of 1920 to 1939 saw tremendous growth in the popularity of black music on radio, called "Blackface Radio" by one researcher. The author stated that the advent of radio broadcasting in the United States coincided with the cultural ferment of the Roaring Twenties, the fabled Jazz Age. He laments, however, that the mass distribution of black cultural products diluted these artistic expressions that had awakened Harlem. "Black artists and performers, the inheritors of these art forms, discovered not only that they were exploited financially by the entertainment industry but that they were also forced to compromise their art and often their integrity to get into show business."[32] So black access to the airwaves was very limited, although the black bands of the day broke through any barriers. Even in the 1920s, people could hear the Fletcher Henderson band and the music of Duke Ellington.

People also turned to the radio to hear the minstrel shows. Earlier in the century, white entertainers had blackened their faces and acted like stereotypical African Americans to create blackface minstrelsy, which moved to radio with great success in the 1920s and 1930s. One of the most famous "blackface radio" shows was "Sam and Henry," in which two white male actors played two old black men. The scripts, which featured one stereotype after another, generally showed black people to be ignorant, lazy, and shiftless. Later, the actors went to another station and started a new show, "Amos 'n' Andy." Only the names changed; the theme of making fun of black people remained.[33] By the end of 1920, "Amos 'n' Andy" had become one of the most popular shows on radio among both black and white listeners.

Black newspapers, black ministers, and the NAACP spoke out against the show when it became a national phenomenon. A poem popular at the time was "American Negro, wake up! wake up!/Show radio land you must be treated fair./So get ready to join the mighty force/To push old *Amos 'n' Andy* off the air."[34]

Other popular radio shows in the 1920s and 1930s included "The Jack Benny Show" with Eddie "Rochester" Anderson, his black valet, and "Beulah," a black maid. One black actor noted that, after he received a role in the "Slick and Slim" radio show, "I had to learn to talk as white people believed Negroes talked in order to get the job."[35]

1934 FEDERAL COMMUNICATIONS ACT TO PEARL HARBOR ATTACK, DECEMBER 7, 1941

"When white America catches a cold, black America gets pneumonia."[36] This observation made by a black civil rights activist in 1990 is vividly illustrated by the experience of black Americans during the Great Depression. Because of the job discrimination practiced against African Americans ever since Reconstruction ended nearly sixty years earlier, the black wage earner's income was only about 30 percent of that of the white worker in 1934.[37] Blacks had been the first to lose their jobs when the initial signs of recession occurred in the mid-1920s, so when the Depression hit full force, they were already in dire economic straits. In 1934, 17 percent of whites but 38 percent of blacks were unable to support themselves. Especially in the South, black relief rolls soared. In Atlanta, for example, 65 percent of employable African Americans needed public assistance by 1935.[38]

But, as one historian stated, "[E]ven in starvation there was discrimination." Relief was seldom administered equally to blacks and whites. In many places, African Americans were excluded from soup kitchens, denied relief employment, and given as little as one-sixth the public assistance money given to whites.[39]

In all areas of living, not just in employment, African Americans were second-class citizens—or worse—at this time. Discrimination against them was a way of living and acting that, as one source put it, "was sanctified by custom and tradition and secured by law in many states."[40] African Americans, no matter how distinguished, could not obtain accommodations at most hotels and restaurants, both North and South. In 1939 the Daughters of the American Revolution refused to allow black opera star Marian Anderson to perform at Constitution Hall in Washington, D.C.[41] Only segregated and inferior facilities were available to blacks on trains and buses in the South, to those traveling to the South, to blacks needing admission to a hospital, to black children in schools. In Virginia in 1934, for example, the state's spending on "separate-but-equal" public school education was $47 per capita for white children and $13 for black children.[42] In the Southern states as a whole, for every $7 spent on the education of white children, only $2 was spent on the education of black children.[43]

Also, strict segregation in housing was the rule; outside the rural South, those African Americans seeking a place to live outside of the deteriorated sections of cities were met with bombing and rioting.[44] In addition, in the Deep South states, blacks still were denied the right to vote. The white-only primary, one of several arrangements devised by whites to prevent African Americans from voting, was upheld by the U.S. Supreme Court in 1935.

As late as 1938, the United States' armed forces were strictly segregated, and the black units were largely custodial. Most were not sent into combat—instead they were, as one source noted, "housekeeping troops with military training."[45] African Americans also were largely excluded from professional sports, except for prize fighting and track competitions. Few blacks played professional football, and none were allowed into organized professional baseball or into golf, tennis, or racing.

The lynching of African Americans who had somehow displeased whites was still going on unchecked, primarily in the South. Fifteen blacks were lynched in 1931, and except for the black newspapers and a small organization of Southern white women, few voices were raised in protest.

Not surprisingly, the little coverage of African Americans that white newspapers provided at this time simply reflected the low status and low esteem in which blacks were held. Also, the miniscule coverage of blacks that was provided reinforced both the savage and the Sambo stereotypes—portraying African Americans as violent and dangerous, or as physically strong and talented, as good athletes, singers, and dancers. This kind of coverage of African Americans had been the norm in white newspapers since Reconstruction and was to continue throughout this period and well into the 1950s.

Typical of the coverage was that of four Oregon dailies which, according to one researcher, portrayed none of the advances made by African Americans between 1931 and 1948. Instead, the papers focused their limited coverage of blacks on crime news and items about entertainment and sports personalities.[46] A study of twenty-eight Texas papers' coverage of African Americans in 1935 revealed a heavy emphasis on crime news involving blacks.[47] Another study, which examined the coverage of African Americans in Los Angeles newspapers between 1892 and 1968, found that less than 1 percent of the papers' available news space was devoted to blacks until the 1960s, when the city experienced riots.[48]

One researcher examined the portrayals of black Americans in *Life* between the magazine's inception in 1936 to 1946. *Life* was radically different from most magazines of the day, as it relied primarily upon dramatic photographs. The magazine created the illusion of a nearly all-white American society, the author stated, by ignoring blacks' contributions to the nation and by portraying blacks only infrequently, stereotypically and in dehumanized ways. "The stereotypes conveyed through photographic images made practically indelible impressions on the public consciousness," the author stated. The study found *Life* presented blacks as entertainers and athletes, as violent criminals, in menial roles, as objects of sexual or social voyeurism, or as a social problem. Terms like "mammy," "blackamoor," and "pickaninny" were used frequently.[49]

An exception to this general ignoring of African Americans and denigrating them when they were shown was the coverage provided by the *St. Louis Post-Dispatch* between 1920 and 1950. This paper had a unique standard, was fair and sympathetic toward African Americans, and tried to shape positive opinion toward blacks, one researcher found. "All phases of Negro life and the Negro problem appeared in the *Post* during the sample period. Nevertheless, it would have taken a careful and most detailed reader to ferret them out and piece the picture together" from the infrequent articles that appeared, the author stated.[50]

A more accurate and positive image of African Americans was presented in black newspapers, which during this period increased greatly in circulation and influence. These papers covered everyday life activities of blacks, presented the achievements of individual blacks and African Americans in general, fought for equality, urged readers' support for such organizations as the NAACP, and kept readers informed of issues concerning blacks—all topics that were ignored by white newspapers.

The papers covered with interest the numerous overtures made by Franklin Roosevelt, elected in 1932, and his wife Eleanor, toward African American leaders and organizations. Franklin Roosevelt utilized not only a few black "advisers," as some earlier presidents had done, but also appointed a number of blacks to positions within his administration.[51] Some of the New Deal relief programs set up under Roosevelt's administration did bring some measure of help to African Americans in scattered projects. In the mid-1930s the Committee for Industrial Organization undertook to organize workers in the mass-production industries without regard to race, and many African American workers ultimately benefited from the contracts the union was able to negotiate.[52] Thus, by the time Pearl Harbor was bombed and the country went to war, the situation for black Americans was still bad, but some positive changes had occurred.

Broadcast Coverage

The 1934 Federal Communications Act, like the 1927 Federal Radio Act, challenged broadcasters to operate in the public interest, convenience, and necessity. Commissioners in 1927 and 1934 held that the airwaves belonged to the people and broadcasters could only lease them. But protests from the NAACP over the airing of "Amos 'n' Andy" were ignored by the Federal Radio Commission (FRC) in 1931. *Pittsburgh Courier* editor Robert Vann started the protest that collected 740,000 signatures, which NAACP officers delivered to the FRC. But the show remained on the air and moved to television in the early 1950s using black actors. The NAACP was successful in finally getting the show cancelled in 1952.

1941 PEARL HARBOR ATTACK TO ATOMIC BOMBING OF HIROSHIMA, AUGUST 6, 1945

At the onset of World War II, one historian stated, many black men were not eager to fight to free European nations held captive by fascist forces; instead, "blacks were primarily concerned with the struggle against fascism at home."[53] Even as America was presenting itself to the rest of the world as a defender of democracy, African Americans were still firmly denied any semblance of equality with white Americans. Black people were growing increasingly disillusioned and impatient. They had seen that the black soldier's sacrifices during World

War I had not resulted in any better treatment by whites once he came home. Eleanor Roosevelt herself said, early in the war, "The nation cannot expect colored people to feel that the United States is worth defending if the Negro continues to be treated as he is now."[54]

Leaders of the black press were keenly aware of the increasingly disillusioned and militant mood among African Americans, and they sought to encourage among blacks a more positive attitude about their role in the war. By World War II, the black press had a following second only to the black church, and it was one of the greatest single influences in the black community. Readership of black newspapers was estimated at 4 million African Americans a week, at a time when the black population of the country was 13 million. Black press leaders were convinced that blacks would have to serve in the armed forces in order to achieve equality eventually.[55] To accomplish their aim of transforming black dissatisfaction into a positive attitude toward the war, the press leaders devised the concept of the "Double V" slogan, combining the struggle at home with the fight for victory abroad. "The Army is to fight Hitler and those of us at home will fight hitlerism at home," said one black newspaper.[56]

Ironically, this public-spirited attempt by black press editors to transmute African Americans' deep disillusionment with their country into a willingness to support the war earned the black press a reputation as radical. Black newspapers were widely castigated by whites, even white liberals, for "demanding an overnight revolution in race relations."[57] Meanwhile, J. Edgar Hoover devoted considerable energy and FBI manpower to investigating the black press in an attempt to link it to Communist, Nazi, or Japanese interests. He attempted to obtain sedition indictments against black newspapers throughout the war, but the U.S. attorney general refused to cooperate.[58] In addition, six other federal agencies maintained a surveillance of the black press during the war.

At the same time, the armed services were in no hurry to enlist black men. Under pressure from the White House, the U.S. Army agreed to draft blacks on the basis of their proportion in the population and utilize them in all branches of the service, although in segregated units and under white officers, but this proceeded very slowly. Meanwhile, the Air Corps and the Navy were even slower to train and use African Americans.[59]

Many African Americans who served in the armed forces during World War II were placed in the same kind of noncombat positions to which blacks had been relegated during World War I. They served in ordnance, the quartermaster corps, transportation and construction units, communications groups, and the medical corps. As the war progressed, however, increasing numbers of black volunteers were accepted into the armed forces and trained for combat. In addition, they were gradually accepted into all the services, including the Air Corps and Marines, which previously had been closed to them. Eventually blacks were accepted into officer candidate schools and trained in integrated classes—a first—except in the Air Corps. By the end of the war, about one million African-

American men and 4,000 women had served in the armed forces, half of them overseas.[60]

Many of the African-American combat units performed with extraordinary heroism, stated historian John Hope Franklin. Like the Japanese American combat units in the same war, they won numerous military awards for their gallantry. The heroism and service of the black soldier were praised by the secretary of war, the chief of staff, and top-ranking military officers in many theaters of war. In 1945 the War Department said that volunteer African-American infantrymen had "established themselves as fighting men no less courageous or aggressive than their white comrades." One of the earliest and most famous black military heroes was Dorie Miller, a Navy messman serving aboard the battleship *U.S.S. Arizona.* During the Japanese attack on Pearl Harbor, he took over a machine gun and shot down four enemy planes. Many black servicemen received the Presidential Citation, Distinguished Service Cross, and Distinguished Flying Cross.[61] But not until fifty years later were seven African Americans, six of whom were already dead, awarded the Congressional Medal of Honor for their actions during World War II.

The heroism of black servicemen was not much covered by white newspapers, magazines, and radio, possibly because qualities such as valor and courage under fire did not fit the popular stereotypes of African Americans. However, *Life*, in an unusual 1942 story, documented the movement of African Americans into the military and quoted white instructors of black pilots who praised their students and predicted that they would make crack combat pilots. In the same issue, *Life* admitted,

It is true that U.S. Negroes have never had a square deal from the U.S. white majority, but they know their lot would be far worse under the racial fanatics of the Axis. Now, when their country needs them, they are glad to work and die alongside their fellow white citizens.[62]

Black newspapers and news services sent almost thirty correspondents to cover the efforts of African Americans in the armed forces. Several writers have said that the achievements of black servicemen were largely suppressed or ignored by the white media and received only cursory attention from the war's historians. Black readers in the United States, one researcher explained, "were starved for stories on activities and achievements of their servicemen," and the wartime circulation growth of the black weekly newspapers occurred partly because they were providing such news.[63]

In addition, some noncombat black units were lauded for their unique contributions and valor. In Europe the black ordnance troops fought the Germans on occasion. The 12,500 black Seabees serving in the Pacific were praised by high Navy officials for the work they performed, frequently under severe enemy attack. The 10,000 black troops who constructed the Ledo Road overcame impossible conditions to build a supply route from India through the jungles of

Burma to convey materiel to beleaguered China, and they fought the Japanese at the same time.[64]

As one historian commented, "[M]any more black G.I.'s fought the war with a shovel than with a rifle . . . and did remarkably well on the unglamorous, hard jobs."[65] Black correspondents covered their efforts for the folks back home. Among the unheralded but vital tasks the correspondents reported on was the construction of the Ledo Road, which the British had claimed could never be built. The troops, 60 percent of whom were black, had to push the road through areas with 150 inches of rain a year, new strains of tropical diseases, and 300 kinds of snakes, while the jungle reclaimed some sections faster than they could be cleared, the correspondents reported. Part way through the job, General Joseph Stilwell told the press the road builders were "continuing to do the impossible."[66] African Americans also made up about 10 percent of the American troops who performed one of the nastiest, hottest jobs of all—building a road through Iran, where temperatures could average 140 degrees, to help move Lend-Lease shipments to Russia. This accomplishment did not receive much publicity because secrecy was necessary to prevent the Germans from realizing the size of the operation.[67] Black troops also accounted for about a third of the troops sent to build a highway from the U.S. mainland to Alaska in horrific weather conditions. Their work was covered by a black correspondent, but not by the white press or historians.

Despite their high level of performance, African-American servicemen and women were still subjected to discrimination and racial hostility, especially in the United States, demonstrating the tenacity of stereotypes of blacks deeply embedded in the white American psyche. At many camps, African Americans were discriminated against and were sold inferior merchandise at post exchanges, movie theaters were segregated, and blacks had to wait until all white soldiers had boarded before they could get on a camp bus. Blacks entering the U.S. Army were confronted by hostile white military police and unfriendly white residents in towns near army camps, and the attempts made by black servicemen to resist discrimination led to additional clashes. Numerous violent incidents and sometimes riots erupted at U.S. military camps and towns throughout the war; the worst occurred across the nation in the summer of 1943.[68] At least one black serviceman was lynched while in uniform.

For blacks not in the service, discrimination in the war industries persisted unchecked until late in 1942. When defense industries began to gear up for war in 1940, newly created jobs went first to unemployed whites, and then companies sometimes hired whites from out of town rather than employ local blacks. The situation began to change only because A. Phillip Randolph organized a March on Washington Movement to bring thousands of blacks to the capital to protest the situation. In response, President Roosevelt established the Fair Employment Practices Committee to prevent such discrimination, a move that was heralded as major news by the black press but largely ignored or downplayed by white newspapers.[69] The *Chicago Tribune*'s coverage of a black rally protesting discrimination in defense industry jobs in June 1942 illustrated clearly the mainstream press denial of white racism and foreshadowed the white press practice of turning a fact into an allegation—a practice that would be seen frequently in civil rights–era coverage in the 1950s and 1960s. The *Tribune* reported, "More than 10,000 Negroes packed the Coliseum last night to protest alleged discrimination by the government against members of their race in the armed forces and in war industries."[70]

The decade of the 1940s saw a massive migration of African Americans from the South. Each year during that decade more than 150,000 black Americans moved from the South to the cities of the North and West seeking work. Their attempts to find places to live in cities that had inadequate low-income housing and rigid segregation in housing, plus many whites' perception that they would take jobs from whites, aggravated racial tensions throughout the nation's urban areas. In 1943 mounting tensions touched off a thirty-hour riot in Detroit that saw blacks and whites fighting each other and left twenty-five blacks and nine whites dead. Other riots occurred that summer in Los Angeles and Harlem.

In 1944 Swedish sociologist Gunnar Myrdal published his ground-breaking book *An American Dilemma: The Negro Problem and Modern Democracy.* In it he noted the problems that arise when one segment of the population does not know or understand another segment, despite an abundance of communication resources. He noted that while the black press historically had heralded every victory against discrimination, the white-owned press either limited such coverage or failed entirely to cover racial issues. As a result, "many educated Northerners . . . are well-informed about foreign problems but almost absolutely ignorant about Negro conditions both in their own city and in the nation as a whole. A great many Northerners, perhaps the majority, get shocked and shaken in their conscience when they learn the facts."[71]

Myrdal stated that the Northern newspapers ignored racial problems, except those occurring south of the Mason-Dixon line, and they rarely covered crimes against blacks except for Southern lynchings that made the South look bad. A good example of the Northern papers' ignoring of local racial problems occurred in 1941 when Harlem residents boycotted New York city buses to protest the bus companies' refusal to hire blacks as drivers or mechanics, one researcher noted. Like the Montgomery bus boycott fifteen years later, this protest was led by a young black clergyman, the Reverend Adam Clayton Powell, Jr. Like the later protest, this one organized alternative transportation for black bus users, and it also ended in triumph when the companies agreed to hire blacks. But unlike the later boycott, the *New York Times* and other leading papers did not cover the protest, and most white readers remained uninformed about the issues involved.[72]

Broadcast Coverage

The overriding tendency of the commercially sponsored network radio shows before World War II was to exclude African Americans or allow them to play only stereotypical characters. Often the justification was that Southern sponsors would deny support to black shows or to programs showing blacks nonstereo-typically. The network response sometimes was to air shows about blacks with-out sponsorship. The U.S. Office of Education attempted to fill the void by sponsoring special programs on African-American life—real life. One such pro-gram examined the life of Booker T. Washington. A series called "Freedom's People," which aired on NBC radio in late 1941 and early 1942, was the first series to explore the history and culture of African Americans.[73]

During World War II, black soldiers were often challenged by the enemy to reexamine their decision to defend a country that segregated them in the military and denied them freedom at home. The U.S. government's response was to encourage the networks to produce positive programs about blacks. CBS radio produced a series dealing with ethnic and racial diversity in the military called "They Call Me Joe." Later, in 1945, CBS aired "The Negro at War" to high-light African Americans' service in the wars. Other programs included the CBS broadcast of "An Open Letter on Race Hatred" following the 1943 riots in Detroit. While local police aggressively stopped looters on one side of town, white mobs were allowed to attack black citizens indiscriminately on the other.

1945 ATOMIC BOMBING OF HIROSHIMA TO LITTLE ROCK INTEGRATION, SEPTEMBER 1957

The news media's practice of playing down black victories and ignoring white racism can be observed in the coverage of Jackie Robinson when he became the first African American to join a major league baseball team in October 1945. According to one study, coverage of the event in four metropolitan newspapers failed to emphasize that blacks had previously been barred from major league teams, and most of them did not treat Robinson's signing with the Brooklyn Dodgers as history making. This kind of coverage prevented white readers from realizing how deeply the ugliness of racism was embedded in "the great Amer-ican pastime."[74]

The author quoted one sportswriter's plea that sports reporters should educate readers about baseball's color line. "It's the only way we're going to educate white America, 61% of which clings to the illusion that there is no discrimi-nation," he wrote.[75] But that was not the kind of coverage white-owned news-papers provided.

In contrast to the careful neutrality of the white papers, the four black news-papers examined in the study heralded Robinson's signing as an epochal event and kept the story hot for weeks. Also, it was found that the NAACP's *Crisis*, plus *Collier's*, *Life*, and *Saturday Review*, handled the story in feature fashion, humanizing the event and Robinson and providing the most well-rounded cov-erage of all.[76]

Other researchers examined coverage of Robinson's spring training with the Dodgers' minor league team, the Montreal Royals, in Daytona Beach in early 1946. They studied coverage of the training events and games in black newspapers and a wide variety of mainstream dailies. They found that the black papers reported the events in the context of racial issues neglected by the white press and society at large, while the white press covered the story primarily as a curiosity, without providing social context. Meanwhile, Robinson ignored the taunts and insults hurled at him, and the white press ignored that story.[77]

A reason white Americans were able to cling to the illusion that discrimination did not exist can be glimpsed in another study of three white New York newspapers' coverage of Robinson's first season with the Dodgers in 1947. Robinson was subjected to considerable racial harassment by opposing players throughout the season, but in most of the papers it went virtually unreported.[78] In mid-May two of the papers carried stories about Robinson's receiving threatening letters and about a proposed strike by the St. Louis Cardinals to protest Robinson's presence in the major leagues. Afterward, the papers stopped referring to Robinson as a racial barrier breaker and increasingly covered him like any other rookie. The study's author conjectures that this change may have been motivated by a desire by media managers to cool racial tensions.[79]

Several other studies of press coverage of African Americans during this period reveal highly biased and stereotypical coverage. One researcher studied local news coverage of blacks in five Deep South newspapers from 1950 to 1970. She found that 50 percent of the items found in the 1950s issues examined, and 24 percent of those from the 1970s, were about black crime.[80] Two other studies examined photos of black Americans in three newsmagazines and four major newspapers from 1937 to about 1990. The authors found that between 1937 and 1957, most of the images showed African Americans in highly stereotypical roles, as background servants or as lazy and silly simpletons. Ads in the papers never showed blacks using the items advertised, but instead as servants and porters for white American product users.[81] Another study, of pictorial coverage of African Americans in *Life* magazine from 1937 to 1972, found coverage of blacks amounted to less than 1 percent of the magazine's news space except during school integration controversies or other periods when issues affecting blacks impinged on the broader society. The author also found coverage of the everyday lives of whites averaged 2.7 percent of the total coverage, while portrayal of black everyday life was omitted altogether in half the years, and never reached higher than 0.1 percent.[82] An examination of the images of black Americans in *New Yorker* cartoons from 1946 to 1987 showed that blacks appeared in less than 1 percent of the cartoons, and in the postwar decade all cartoons with U.S. blacks showed them in stereotypical occupations, like maids and bellhops.[83]

One white reporter stated in the 1950s that major Northern newspapers engaged in a conspiracy of silence about oppression and discrimination against African Americans, supposedly to suppress racial tensions. He also noted the papers' unwillingness to cover social news about African Americans, stating that a *New York Times* society editor had said that the paper had run only one black couple's wedding announcement in the newspaper's history. Five other metropolitan dailies reported that they had never carried a photo of an African-American bride.[84]

In most Southern newspapers, an even more active effort to segregate and distort news about African Americans was common. A Southern Regional Council study conducted in the late 1940s concluded that "the Southern newspaper constitutes the greatest single force in perpetuating the popular stereotype of the Negro." One Mississippi editor explained the canons of Southern journalism required the use of the label Negro in all stories about blacks, the omission of the courtesy titles Mr., Mrs., or Miss when referring to blacks, the listing of local services under white and colored categories, and the omission of any photographs of blacks. He added that stories about crimes committed by whites against blacks, and also black-on-black crime, were routinely placed on the paper's back pages if they were carried at all. Stories of black crimes committed against whites, however, were carried on the front page.[85]

Other Southern sources explained that African Americans were always referred to as Negro or colored, usually in lower case.[86] One editor said that, until the early 1950s, it was routine at the *New Orleans Times-Picayune* to airbrush out any black face from crowd photos.[87] One scholar, commenting on the coverage of African Americans in South Carolina newspapers during the mid-1950s, said that blacks were just as thoroughly segregated on the pages of the state's newspapers as they were in public schools or private cemeteries. He said photos of blacks seldom appeared, and few items were run about the black community's schools, civic organizations, businesses, or social or professional activities.[88] Black persons usually appeared in the papers' news columns only as criminals or spokespersons for a racial reform group, which to some readers amounted to the same thing, the scholar noted.[89]

Another study indicated that North Carolina papers covering school desegregation rarely used African-American sources, although blacks would be greatly affected. The researcher also said that only prosegregation sources were given front-page placement.[90] Another source stated that Southern papers were more likely than papers elsewhere to ignore black demonstrations or to place stories about them on inside pages.[91]

However, not all Southern newspaper editors subscribed to the racist attitudes of their time and region, and their convictions were expressed in their editorials and their papers' coverage. Among the exceptions were Mississippi editors Hodding Carter II and Hodding Carter III of the *Delta Democrat-Times* in Greenville, Ira Harkey of the Pascagoula *Chronicle*, and P. D. East of Petal, Mississippi. Other liberal editors were Harry Ashmore of the *Arkansas Gazette*, Harry Golden of the *Carolina Israelite* in Charlotte, and Ralph McGill of the *Atlanta Constitution*.

On the national scene, during the post–World War II period, one of the biggest adjustments white Americans faced, said Franklin, was the new position of African Americans in U.S. society.[92] Black organizations, especially the NAACP, began to press more urgently for equality for blacks. In 1946 the Supreme Court ruled against segregation on interstate buses. President Truman, through executive orders, desegregated the armed forces and established a Committee on Civil Rights. As the 1950s opened, employment opportunities for African Americans improved, black membership and leadership in labor unions increased, and more black people were elected to public office.[93]

In the early 1950s the Supreme Court ruled against segregation in dining cars on interstate railways and ruled for the integration of Washington restaurants. And in 1954, in *Brown v. Topeka Board of Education*, the high court issued its watershed ruling that the "separate-but-equal" education approved in *Plessy v. Ferguson* was inherently unequal and was unconstitutional. The next year it ordered states to proceed with school desegregation "with all deliberate speed."

In 1957 Congress passed the first civil rights act since Reconstruction. The Act called for federal involvement in securing voting rights for African Americans and, as Franklin noted, marked a dramatic reversal of the federal government's historic hands-off policy on civil rights.[94]

Naturally none of these advances occurred without a reaction. Threats, violence, and repressive legislation met most positive changes for African Americans, and during this period White Citizens' Councils—which one Mississippi editor described as a sort of "uptown KKK"—were formed. In several Southern states, the NAACP was branded "subversive" and hounded by legal means. In various parts of the South, persons committed to retaining segregation turned to violence and terrorist tactics.[95]

In 1956 Montgomery blacks organized a boycott of city buses after Rosa Parks, a seamstress, refused to give up her bus seat in defiance of an Alabama law that required blacks to sit in the back of the bus or to stand rather than have whites standing. Parks was arrested and jailed. This one act of courage mobilized the black community, which organized a boycott to protest discrimination and abuses by white drivers against blacks, and to urge the hiring of African-American drivers for routes in black sections. The city immediately arrested about ninety blacks, including their leader, the Reverend Martin Luther King, Jr.

Die-hard segregationists were encouraged by their political leaders' stated determination to resist school desegregation. Many Southern Congressmen, governors, and local leaders vigorously denounced the Supreme Court's decision. Not all Southern leaders behaved this way, and the ones who did were not representative of all white Southerners. However, in the conflict-oriented news media, moderate voices tend to be shouted down and demagogues capture the headlines. The news media's focus on reporting the defiant posturings of the noisiest segregationists, one newsman observed, had the unintended result of giving national credence to the White Citizens' Councils claims that they spoke for the whole South.[96]

Some Southern newspapers contributed to this impression. In a study of the editorial response of five South Carolina newspapers to the school desegregation issue between 1954 and 1964, one researcher concluded that most of the newspapers considered generally failed to offer enlightened editorial leadership in the racial crisis confronting the South. Some editorials welcomed the fact that white mobs had successfully protested voluntary desegregation in West Virginia and Delaware in 1954.[97]

Thus it is not surprising that many Americans, North and South, believed that Southern leaders' vows of "massive resistance" to school integration represented the entire white South. This helped set the stage for rioting in many communities when black students tried to enter previously segregated institutions. In 1956, when Autherine Lucy attempted to attend the University of Alabama, students and townspeople used violence to drive her from the university. The next year, Arkansas governor Orval Faubus personally intervened to try to prevent nine black students from attending Little Rock's Central High School, paving the way for violence and many months of vicious intimidation of the black students.

Violence had long been used by whites to keep African Americans in what whites saw as their place. In fact, 1952 was the first year since 1881 that no blacks were lynched in the United States. White violence against blacks had seldom received much coverage in white-owned newspapers, nor had it aroused much public indignation among white political, religious, or civic groups, until the murder of Emmett Till in 1955.

Till, a fourteen-year-old Chicago resident who was visiting relatives in Mississippi, aroused some whites' indignation when he allegedly whistled at a white storekeeper's wife. He was kidnapped from the home where he was staying, brutally beaten, and shot in the head; his body was thrown into the Tallahatchie River. Black newspapers and magazines, notably *Ebony*, the African-American picture magazine, published the gruesome photos of Till's badly mutilated body. For many African Americans, those photos had the same kind of impact as the video of Rodney King's beating forty years later; they were a brutal and vivid illustration of the viciousness of white racism against blacks.

Several white men were arrested and charged with Till's murder but were tried by all-white, all-male juries. Just as in nearly every other such trial held in the South until that point, they were found not guilty. (Conversely, any black person accused of a crime against a white person also was tried by an all-white jury and was almost always found guilty, no matter what the evidence.)

The case was heavily reported by the white-owned media, both print and broadcast, and was even more intensely covered by the black media. One researcher said that more articles about this case and its aftermath were published in white media than on any other single subject involving a black person in the previous five years.[98]

Southern papers at first denounced Till's murder, the researcher found, but as the Northern white and black papers began covering the story, Southern papers began to express a strong antiblack backlash. Their ire was aroused by statements like one from the *Negro History Bulletin*, which charged, "Lynching may be the work of a small lunatic fringe, but responsible elements have failed to curb this fringe." The NAACP's *Crisis* observed that Mississippi held the nation's seventy-one-year record in lynchings and said that "the white people of Mississippi are directly responsible for this hideous crime." The Southern press retaliated with remarks about "the prejudiced communistic-inspired NAACP."[99]

Another researcher examined coverage of the case in eleven newspapers in various parts of the country and found most of the coverage to be objective. He also noted that Southern papers seldom explained the caste system–like nature of race relations and did not personalize African Americans, while Northern papers did. Papers in both South and North emphasized the violence and injustice of the case.[100]

The *New York Times* and *Life* magazine devoted considerable space to the story and ran editorials critical of the South. The *Times* reporter wrote that the Till murder focused national attention on racial discrimination in the South for the first time.[101]

By the time the trial was over, considerable name-calling and finger-pointing were going on between Northern and Southern newspapers. Some Southern editors felt that the Northern press ignored race problems in its own backyard and covered racial injustices only in the South. One Southern editor wrote that "the race problem cannot be acted upon until the U.S. press at least locates the problem on the map."[102] A Detroit newsman agreed, saying that "Race news is news only if it occurs under a magnolia tree."[103]

Some support for these charges was found in a study comparing coverage of racial tensions in six major Northern and Southern metropolitan papers from 1955 through 1957. The researcher found that the *New York Times* and *Detroit Free Press* tended to present their cities' racial problems as having already been solved; the *Chicago Tribune* ignored local racial conflict completely for the first two years studied. Meanwhile, racial violence in the South was covered regularly by all three papers. Conversely, both the *Montgomery Advertiser* and *Richmond Times-Dispatch* emphasized violent racial conflict when reporting on the North and ignored positive integration efforts from other regions. The *Atlanta Constitution* provided the best local coverage and avoided defensive tactics in coverage, according to the study.[104]

One researcher noted that a Southern editor stated a few years after the Till case that civil rights had not been covered well in the Southern press and that often the minimal coverage provided had been inflammatory and distorted. Another stated that Southern journalists found it hard in the mid-1950s to remain impartial about the race issue, because they were undergoing the same emotional reactions as the larger white population. Hodding Carter III noted, "The failure of the Southern press was in the particularly human desire not to alienate and not be totally alienated from the small community in which one lives."[105]

The year after the Till case, *Time* reported that many editors were dropping the practice of automatically using the race label for African Americans and were developing better methods of covering news in the black community. The *New York Times* management also decided not to use the race label in crime stories unless the description was important and also resolved to provide better coverage of race news.[106]

Broadcast Coverage

By the late 1940s, radio stations around the country had begun programming black-oriented shows. Black music formats attracted millions described by the magazine *Sponsor* as the "new Negro Market."[107] Three principal factors were involved in the sudden emergence of this market: (1) the urban migration of African Americans was relocating them in the major metropolitan radio markets, (2) education and income levels among African Americans were rising, and (3) commercial radio was facing bleak economic prospects due to the arrival of television. For many stations, the choice was embrace the new market or go out of business.

In 1949 "Jockey" Jack Gibson became the first voice heard on the first black radio station in America, WERD Radio in Atlanta. Until this time, black disc jockeys bought time on white-owned stations to present radio shows featuring a variety of black music and news of the day. The DJs became the griots (storytellers) of modern black communities, especially the urban ones. "We were the only leaders," remembers radio disc jockey Martha Jean (The Queen) Steinberg. "You didn't have any political officials elected . . . we were able to bridge the gap of communication between the power structure and the forgotten people. So we were the first activists."[108]

The Committee for the Negro Arts sponsored a conference on Television, Radio and the Negro People in 1949. The committee's report documented the exclusion of African Americans from industry jobs as executives, producers, directors, sound effects technicians, and commentators. It was also critical of the continuing stereotypical portrayal of African Americans on network radio. The report asked if all blacks would be portrayed only as reflections of Amos and Andy and Beulah.[109]

The early 1950s included the hearings of the House Committee on Un-American Activities and its attempts to expose suspected Communists in the United States. Often the investigations included famous Hollywood entertainers, including black entertainers and people sympathetic to black causes. Actor-singer Paul Robeson was targeted by the committee because of his open support of Communism and the Soviet Union. One researcher stated that Robeson was harassed by the government investigations, vilified in the media and the press, blacklisted from employment in show business, and even denied his passport to work abroad.[110]

The old successful radio programs of the 1940s became the new 1950s television programs. When blacks were allowed on screen, they appeared as maids or chauffeurs, but always stereotyped. One author wrote that the only roles open to blacks at the time were the savage African, happy slave, devoted servant, corrupt politician, irresponsible citizen, petty thief, social delinquent, vicious criminal, sexual superman, superior athlete, unhappy nonwhite, natural-born cook, natural-born musician, superstitious churchgoer, chicken and watermelon eater, razor and knife "toter," uninhibited expressionist, and mental inferior. Many of these images persist.[111]

1957 LITTLE ROCK INTEGRATION TO NIXON'S RESIGNATION, AUGUST 9, 1974

Studies of the newspaper treatment of African Americans showed a marked rise in the volume of coverage during the late 1950s and throughout the 1960s. This change occurred because press attention was commanded by the myriad Freedom Rides, sit-ins, school integration attempts, voter registration drives, protest marches, and other projects undertaken by civil rights activists. Media attention also was ensured by the violence directed against the civil rights activists and by the urban riots of the mid-1960s. All these events were clearly good news stories, replete with drama, controversy, and violence. Also, in the case of events occurring in the South, they fit neatly into a good guy–bad guy story line for non-Southern newspapers, with the peaceful civil rights activists as the good guys and the angry Southern racists attacking them as the villains. For the first time, white people across the nation, long sheltered from news about the oppression of blacks and the existence of white racism, were given vivid illustrations of these deeply rooted aspects of American society.

The civil rights demonstrators in the South, trying to change a racist system from outside the system, relied upon the media to convey their message to the wider world. The students trying to integrate segregated schools, the Freedom Riders and lunch counter sit-in students, the marchers and voter registration workers, were in essence offering themselves up to be reviled, beaten, jailed, and even killed for attempting to carry out an activity that any white person could do freely in the South.

President Lyndon Johnson remarked on this phenomenon in 1965 when he noted the heroism of the ordinary African American. "His actions and protests—his courage to risk safety and even life—have awakened the conscience of the nation. His demonstrations have been designed to call attention to injustice, to provoke change and stir reform. He has called upon us to make good the promise of America."[112] In so doing, African Americans relied upon the media to show how they were treated and to convey their message.

This marked a profound change in relations between black Americans and the white-owned media. After several centuries of being largely ignored by the white media, and denigrated when they were portrayed, African Americans were able to use the white media to illustrate some of their problems and help change people's attitudes. For the first time, as one reporter wrote, "black leaders and the news media were *de facto* allies in the fight against Jim Crow." [113]

The reporter stated further that in Louisville, Kentucky, and other cities during the early 1960s, the media contributed to the success of local civil rights activities by bringing demonstrations to the front pages and onto television screens. He suggested that the media coverage helped keep pressure for reform upon white leaders and also helped legitimize the civil rights movement leaders and participants.[114] Although these benefits resulting from coverage by the white media may have been inadvertent, and the alliance between the white news media and black leaders not intentional on the part of white media managers, it remains true that the white-owned media did help advance the cause of civil rights in this period.

One researcher compared five Northern and five Southern newspapers' coverage of the lunch counter sit-in movement that was begun by African-American college students in February 1960 in Greensboro, North Carolina, and within two months had spread to every state in the South. Contrary to her expectations, she found that Southern, not Northern, newspapers did a better job of covering the sit-ins. The stories in the Southern papers included many more black sources, and a greater diversity of sources, than those in the Northern papers. Both types of papers gave the stories roughly the same kind of placement, but the Southern papers published more and longer sit-in stories than the Northern ones, except for the *New York Times*, which devoted many more stories and column inches to the sit-ins than did any of the other papers. The author also noted that the demonstrators ''needed the white press, invited the white press, and welcomed white press attention.''[115]

This idea was echoed by the author of a study of the Nashville sit-ins, also held early in 1960. He stated that the Nashville students saw the media as a friend and ally in winning support for their cause and conveying the message that they were not the persons causing violence or confrontations. As one participant stated, the media helped the public see the contrast between the peaceful students sitting at the lunch counters and the ''hoodlum element that came to beat us up'' or put out lighted cigarettes in the students' hair. The activists emphasized that they relied on the media to get their message out and to convey the nature of their movement to the world.[116]

Several long-range studies measuring the total amount of coverage of African Americans as a percentage of newspapers' available news space found that the coverage rose dramatically during the 1960s, and much of the increase came from civil rights news. For example, a study of the coverage of black Americans in the *Los Angeles Times* over eighty years found that it rose from less than 1 percent in previous periods to 4 to 5 percent now during the 1960s, and 7 percent during the Watts riot. Also, during the late 1950s and the 1960s, civil rights coverage rose from 56 to 68 percent of the *Times'* total coverage of blacks.[117]

Similarly, a study of major newspapers in New York, Chicago, Atlanta, and Boston over thirty years found that coverage of African Americans rose from less than 1 percent in the early 1950s issues sampled to between 2 and 4 percent during the 1960s, and civil rights coverage accounted for from 69 to 79 percent of the 1960s total coverage. Also, even in the 1970s, the coverage continued to rise in two of the papers, and in the other two it remained at from 2 to 4 percent of the total news space.[118] The coverage also changed dramatically in nature. During the early 1950s, when blacks were almost invisible in the newspapers studied, coverage of everyday life activities of blacks, or of blacks as an ordinary part of American society, was rare, and in two of the papers coverage of black crimes accounted for between 22 and 41 percent of the total coverage of African Americans. During the 1960s, as civil rights coverage increased, stereotypical coverage decreased. In the 1970s, everyday life coverage climbed.[119]

A study of newspaper photos of African Americans from 1937 to 1990 found that coverage of news and social conditions affecting blacks rose dramatically during the civil rights era. Crime news stories increased during this period, but so did coverage of everyday life activities, like social matters, politics, business, education, and health. Also, in advertisements, African Americans were more often shown using the products advertised. This change, the author stated, was a clear indication that both advertising agencies and publishers were recognizing the economic resources of blacks and their more equal role in society.[120]

One study of four Chicago newspapers' editorial attitudes toward civil rights between 1954 and 1968 revealed that the papers' commitment was to white people and the rich, not to African Americans and the poor. The researcher pointed out that the papers' editorials proclaimed America's commitment to racial justice and repeatedly criticized racial discrimination. But, in practice, the author stated, all four papers were firmly committed to preserving existing racial inequalities and adamantly opposed any person or policies that sought to alleviate these inequalities. They advocated a laissez-faire policy toward the problems of the poor but urged federal intervention to help business and the upper classes, whose interests they equated with those of the nation. "Ignoring the country's racial inequalities until proposals for change were put forth," the author wrote, "the papers then proceeded to oppose the proposals and discredit those advocating change, regardless of the merit or militancy involved."[121]

Another researcher examined the coverage of black Americans in the *Wichita Eagle* during 1968 and compared the picture presented with empirical data about the black community. He found that the newspaper portrayal was generally accurate but was not adequate in quality or quantity. The empirical data revealed serious economic, social, and political problems in the black community, many of which were not addressed by the *Eagle*.[122]

Although positive and accurate coverage of local demonstrations was provided by some Southern papers, such coverage was not always offered. For example, in 1963, Dr. King led demonstrations in Birmingham for better employment opportunities and an end to segregation. Many schoolchildren joined the demonstrations; police turned high-pressure fire hoses and police dogs on the demonstrators. These much-photographed and televised attacks aroused outrage throughout the country, and sympathy demonstrations were held. But, according to one Northern journalist who covered the events, the two Birmingham dailies tried to insulate readers from "the national impact of the demonstrations" occurring in their city and failed to report in detail on the demonstrators' objectives.[123] One researcher noted that, during the early 1960s, "the most vocal newspaper resistance to civil rights efforts emanated from the Deep South."[124]

Observations about press inattention to the causes of black protest began to appear with increasing frequency in studies of coverage of issues involving African Americans at this time. One reporter covering the Little Rock school integration controversy in 1957 noted that, because of the event orientation of American news media, reporters did a good job of covering what happened at Little Rock but failed to explain *why* it happened.[125] This same criticism would surface again in the 1968 Kerner Commission report on the causes of the urban riots.

An example of press inattention to the causes of civil rights activities was found in one scholar's examination of the *New York Times*' coverage of the 1965 Selma-to-Montgomery march led by Dr. King to encourage African Americans to register to vote and to call attention to their difficulties in trying to do so. The *Times* devoted most of its front page and all of an inside page to this event, running mood pieces, sidebars, and accounts of sympathy marches in other cities. But nowhere in all these hundreds of inches of coverage, the study found, did the *Times* provide information about the number of blacks then registered to vote in Alabama or about the violence, loss of jobs, and other intimidation encountered by those who tried to register. Aside from mentioning white violence against voting rights demonstrators in Selma the week before, the paper provided no background at all that day on the long-standing and flagrant injustices that prompted the march.[126]

In fact, in a study of four major newspapers' coverage of African Americans over thirty years, one researcher found that, during the 1960s, when the papers ran the largest amount of coverage of black protest, they gave explanation of the causes of the protests the least amount of space—between 3 and 11 percent of their total protest coverage. The papers provided more coverage of the causes of black protest in both the 1950s and the 1970s.[127]

A study of these four newspapers' coverage of problems facing black Americans over forty years found almost no attention to black problems in the 1950s issues studied and not much more coverage of problems in the 1960s, although the Civil Rights Movement had been a hot running story for over a decade and some increased attention to the grievances underlying the movement could have been expected. The kinds of problems covered by the papers in the 1960s were poverty and discrimination in the justice system. But news stories from this period conveyed one major problem, according to the researcher: "[T]he white Southerner's implacable determination to maintain a segregated way of life." Stories were found on Southern public schools, restaurants, and amusement parks being closed to avoid integration; a black musician being arrested for trying to check into a Louisiana hotel; a black woman arrested for standing in a "white women only" voting line; civil rights workers in the South being murdered by snipers; and peaceful civil rights demonstrators being beaten while white police stood by watching or did the beating themselves.[128]

The problem of press failure to explore the white oppression of blacks that led to civil rights actions also was pointed out by researcher Sherrie Wilson, who studied eight major newspapers' coverage of the 1960 Civil Rights Act, which was introduced to plug loopholes in the 1957 Civil Rights Act intended to ensure voting rights for blacks in the South. At this time, few black citizens of Deep South states were able to vote because of intimidation and various state laws adopted after Reconstruction. African Americans who attempted to vote were subject to being fired, being evicted, having mortgages called in, and facing violent reprisals. In Alabama in 1960 about 14 percent of the potential number of nonwhite voters were registered, compared with 63.6 percent registration of potential white voters.[129]

The 1960 act was bitterly opposed by Southern senators, who set a twentieth-century record for filibustering. Wilson found that the newspapers' coverage of the efforts to pass the bill "failed to root the legislation in the social conditions that led to its consideration." The impediments blacks faced in trying to vote and the legalized system of segregation in the South received little attention by the newspapers. Instead, the papers tended to emphasize the "political contest" aspects of the effort to pass the bill. Papers referred to the effort to pass the bill as a "marathon battle," "the two-month-old civil rights fracas," and "wrangling over civil rights."[130]

Wilson noted that in 1960 the House and Senate were composed almost exclusively of white males. Thus, in framing or presenting the civil rights debate as a political contest, the papers "portrayed it as a competition between white government officials." This focus on whites could also be found in the sources the newspapers used in covering the story. Except for a few NAACP officials, all the sources used for the story were national and state white politicians. Readers were not told what African Americans thought about the measure, the researcher noted, and the papers' discussion of what impact the bill would have on blacks was "limited and superficial."[131]

Of the papers examined, five expressed some support for the bill, the *St. Louis Post-Dispatch* believed it was too weak, and the *Alabama Journal* vehemently opposed it. Registering a curious objection, one *Journal* editorial stated that the bill's worst feature was that it would "permit Negroes universally to vote merely because they are Negroes."[132]

In 1961 the Congress of Racial Equality (CORE) began sending interracial teams of Freedom Riders on public buses into the South to test segregation in interstate transportation. In Alabama the riders were attacked, beaten, and arrested, which prompted another flood of Freedom Rides. Reacting to pressure from the riders and Attorney General Robert Kennedy, the Interstate Commerce Commission desegregated interstate carriers and terminal facilities. In August 1963 some 200,000 persons, African American and white, participated in a March on Washington to dramatize the need for further action against discrimination in employment, education, and housing. Later, however, four children were killed in the bombing of a black church in Birmingham, and then President John Kennedy, a supporter of civil rights goals, was killed. In June 1964 a civil rights act that was the most far-reaching in support of racial equality was passed by Congress and became law.

One study examined the coverage of the integration crises of 1962 and 1963 in *Life* and *Ebony*. The researchers found far fewer photos showing interracial violence in *Ebony* than in *Life*. They also found about ten times as many photos showing the races together in *Ebony* than in *Life*. They felt *Ebony* placed a strong emphasis on nonviolent resistance and also rejected such groups as the Black Muslims.[133]

Another researcher examined stories in the *New York Times* on the patterns of conflict between New York City's political and business leaders on the one hand, and black and Puerto Rican activists on the other, in the four years preceding the 1964 riots in Harlem and Bedford-Stuyvesant. He concluded that in those years the minority groups had attempted unsuccessfully to expand their involvement in local affairs and to change the behavior of government and other nonminority leaders through peaceful means. They used protests, boycotts, and rent strikes to call attention to racial segregation in jobs, education, and housing, and they also used legal action. Their efforts were resisted by the courts, by businesses, by landlords, by the school board, and by city government, and it eventually became obvious that their actions would not lead to significant reforms.[134]

Among other efforts, the minority groups tried unsuccessfully to persuade officials to set up a police-civilian review board to investigate charges of police brutality. Relations between police and minorities had so deteriorated that any significant incident could have led to a serious outburst, the author stated. The shooting and subsequent death of a black youth by an off-duty police officer was just such an incident, and it provided the spark that set off the 1964 riot.[135]

The author noted that "it was not until nonviolent strategies had been shown to be ineffective that the tendency to use very aggressive tactics and even violence increased." He stated that this pattern conforms to the idea that mass violence by aggrieved groups is more likely to occur when conventional channels for solving problems fail to resolve differences, nonviolent strategies fail to evoke positive responses, and the aggrieved groups have few avenues to bring their case before the public.[136]

A similar idea is expressed by Paula B. Johnson, David O. Sears and John B. McConahay, the authors of a study of blacks, Los Angeles newspapers, and the 1965 Los Angeles riot. They reported that when Dr. King and two other black leaders visited Watts after the riot, they met a group of African-American youngsters who were shouting joyously, "We won! We won!" The men asked the youths why they thought they had won when thirty-four black people had been killed, the black community was destroyed, and white people were using the riot as an excuse for inaction on black grievances. The boys responded, "We won because we made them pay attention to us!"[137]

The authors stated that many African Americans interpreted the riot as an attempt to call attention to police brutality, merchant exploitation, racial discrimination, poor service by public agencies, and deteriorating housing—all long-standing ills that whites had so far ignored. But after the riot, the authors stated, the white public in Los Angeles, local white public officials, and subsequent press coverage were largely unsympathetic to African Americans' grievances. In addition, the Los Angeles newspapers' coverage of black Americans soon returned to its low preriot level, which was less than 1 percent of the papers' available news space.[138]

The two L.A. newspapers' coverage of African Americans during and after the riot, the authors found, tended to reflect white public officials' and the white public's perception of the riot primarily as a threat to public safety, rather than a symptom of serious problems. The authors said the riots gave credence to whites' fears of a rebellious black population, just as black crime stories had done earlier. Instead of becoming more sympathetic to blacks' grievances, threatened and angry whites used the riot to justify continued inaction and repression.[139]

The authors stated that throughout most of the period under study, the white L.A. press's inattention to African Americans enabled whites to feel comfortable ignoring the low status and oppression of blacks. In a society where blacks were not welcomed in white neighborhoods, schools, churches, or businesses, most white people had very little personal interaction with black people, and those interactions were likely to occur with blacks in low-status jobs. The media could have filled an important gap by communicating to whites the attitudes, activities, and problems—even the existence—of African Americans. "Indeed, it is apparent that, without the aid of the media," the authors noted, "most whites are likely to get very little information of any kind about blacks."[140]

The researchers suggested that past black invisibility in the press, plus press attention to acts of bigotry and legalized segregation in the South, had confused whites' understanding of racism. The sins of commission as practiced in the South had blinded whites to the Northern sins of omission. Racial oppression now flowed most often, the authors stated, from the indifference and inattention of well-meaning whites who did not understand how their own attitudes and behavior contributed to racism.[141]

Despite the passage of the 1960 voting rights act, hundreds of thousands of blacks in the South were still barred from voting or were thwarted in their efforts to register. In 1964 civil rights groups sent hundreds of volunteers into the South to help in efforts to register African Americans to vote. Three of the volunteers, two of them white, were tortured and killed near Philadelphia, Mississippi. In Selma, Alabama, a black civil rights worker and then a white minister from Boston were killed by white racists. These acts, and the sheriff's use of tear gas, whips, and clubs against voting rights protesters, attracted worldwide attention.

In 1965 Congress passed another voting rights act, and the attorney general sent federal examiners to register black voters. These moves resulted in the registration of a quarter of a million new African-American voters by the end of 1965.

But discrimination remained a problem in various other areas. African Americans had long been crowded into the already overcrowded and deteriorated housing of inner-city neighborhoods and were confined there by practices of banks, mortgage companies, real estate boards, and white determination not to allow blacks into their suburban or rural neighborhoods. Thus black children were forced to attend substandard schools. In these inner-city neighborhoods, regular city services—from libraries, playgrounds, and youth centers to garbage collection and street lights—were inadequate. One black writer who once lived in the inner city stated that "ghettoes are factories where society manufactures delinquents who eventually evolve into full-fledged criminals and drug addicts."[142]

In the South, by 1965—twelve years after the Supreme Court school desegregation decision—only 6 percent of black children were attending desegregated schools. Economically, the picture was not much better. Even in 1963, a prosperous year, the black unemployment rate was 114 percent higher than that of whites. More than 80 percent of employed African Americans worked at the lowest-paying jobs, compared to 40 percent of employed whites.[143]

An unusual research project examined five leading national white newspapers' coverage of Fannie Lou Hamer, a black civil rights activist from Mississippi. The researcher studied coverage of Hamer from 1964, two years after she embarked upon the dangerous task of registering black voters in Sunflower County, Mississippi, until her death in 1977. One of twenty children of a sharecropping family, Hamer was the founder of the Mississippi Freedom Democratic Party, which attempted, at the 1964 Democratic national convention, to unseat the white Mississippi delegation that refused to register black voters. In an unscheduled appearance before the convention, Hamer "electrified the nation with her harrowing accounts of the brutality and violence against blacks and the killings of black civil rights workers in Mississippi."[144] Her efforts bore fruit at the 1968 convention, when a biracial delegation that she had helped establish was seated. Besides her work in registering black voters, Hamer led a black cotton pickers' strike for decent wages and organized a farm cooperative to help feed poor white and black families in Mississippi. In 1963, in Winona, Mississippi, she was arrested with other protesters and beaten so brutally by Winona police that her foot was left partially paralyzed.[145]

The author noted that white press coverage of the Civil Rights Movement tended to focus on male leadership. Women leaders "were accorded neither the legitimacy nor recognition of their male counterparts." Despite Hamer's outstanding accomplishments and her standing as "one of the most influential and respected crusaders in the freedom struggle of the Deep South,'' Hamer was not covered much by the newspapers studied, and nearly half of their coverage was run when Hamer was on her deathbed. All the papers then said that her struggles, inspiration, and influence placed her at the top of the movement's leadership. If this were the case, the author asked, why had the newspapers given her such scant attention for the previous twelve years?[146]

The researcher hypothesized that the lack of press attention to Hamer occurred partly because she did not fit the newspapers' image of a civil rights leader of the 1960s. She was not male, not a prominent religious figure nor the wife of a civil rights leader, not well educated (she had had six years of schooling), not young, not a student. Gender stereotyping also was found in the stories about Hamer. In 81 percent of the stories examined, Hamer was identified by either clothing or physical description, a kind of detail lacking in accounts about male civil rights leaders.[147]

By the late 1960s signs of change were evident in Southern newspapers' coverage of racial news. Roger Williams, head of *Time-Life*'s Atlanta bureau, observed that, in the late 1950s and early 1960s, many Southern newspapers had played down local racial problems and controversies while focusing on those in the North, and they ''put the blame for the South's racial crisis everywhere but on the South's white leadership.''[148] Stating that historically the Southern newspapers had failed to prepare the people of the South for the changes being thrust upon them, Williams pointed out that one aspect of this failure was their ignoring of local racial problems. He stated that two Birmingham newspapers treated the first of the 1963 disturbances with short stories on inside pages; a policy was observed that news about them could not appear any farther forward in the paper than page two. In Charleston, he added, an African-American boycott in the early 1960s went unreported by two local papers for more than a month.[149]

Another writer observed the same phenomenon. He stated that, during this period, some Southern papers adopted a policy of playing down or suppressing altogether news that reflected the growing restiveness of the local black population. The editors felt, he said, that giving attention to the flare-ups would only make a potentially dangerous situation worse. The result was a deliberate altering of the picture of the world that those newspapers' readers were receiving. The falsity of this picture was exposed only when Northern newspapers, more liberal Southern ones, or national magazines and networks came to town to cover the events.[150]

But by 1967 the performance of Southern newspapers was changing, according to Williams, and they were covering rather than ignoring local racial problems. He stated that no paper did a better job than the Selma paper of covering the 1965 Selma march and the state troopers' beating of the marchers on the Pettus bridge. About that same incident, the *Montgomery Advertiser* editorialized that by ''dumb, cruel and vastly excessive force,'' state leaders had assured the passage of civil rights legislation not considered likely earlier. ''Now is the hour for excuses and elaborate denials," the editor wrote, "for imputing all blame to press and outside agitators, none to inside imbecility."[151]

Also, signs of moderation were noted among many of the Southern papers that had earlier been so opposed to the Civil Rights Movement that they themselves had incited violence. One reason for this new moderation was that the papers had become unpopular in their own communities, because the local power structure had realized that violent opposition to segregation damaged the community. Williams stated that, by 1967, even society pages in Southern papers were becoming integrated and courtesy titles of "Miss" and "Mrs." for black women had become standard.[152]

But changes in attitudes were not uniform among Southern newspapers. A traditionally racist kind of coverage was reported by a Southern newsman analyzing the local newspaper's coverage of lawmen shooting into a women's dormitory at predominantly black Jackson State University in Mississippi in 1970, killing two students and injuring several others. Throughout the coverage of the event, the journalist said, the *Jackson Clarion-Ledger*'s coverage "became a conduit for the police viewpoint to the virtual exclusion of all others." He added that nowhere in the stories was there "a hint that many eyewitnesses dispute the official contention that police fired only in direct reponse to sniper fire." The only eyewitnesses quoted in the stories were the police.[153] The journalist added that people who lived outside Jackson could read more balanced coverage in the Memphis and New Orleans newspapers and from wire service stories than could people who lived closest to the shooting. None of the *Ledger* stories mentioned that the alleged sniper fire drew from lawmen a thirty-second barrage of gunfire that riddled the women's dorm with more than 200 bullet holes, and that no law officers or any of their vehicles showed any evidence of having been hit by sniper fire. The coverage illustrated the newspaper executives' determination to uphold the status quo, to avoid criticizing local and state government, even at the expense of accuracy in reporting, the newsman said.[154]

By 1968 numerous inner-city riots had occurred in cities all across the country. These events, combined with the many other race-related incidents that had been in the forefront of the news for the past decade, prompted considerable soul-searching among media professionals. Numerous seminars and conferences on such topics as "The Media and Race Relations," held across the nation, were attended by news media personnel, college professors, and African-American civil rights and religious leaders. At many of these conferences, the media were castigated for ignoring black communities and for failing to cover them until after violence had erupted.

A Ford Foundation representative said at one seminar, "A race riot is news. But there was news, significant news, in the city before the riot, news of the conditions and forces that led to it. The U.S. press generally . . . has not seen the story, it has not reported the underlying facts." Another seminar participant said that the media had contributed to white lack of understanding of and indifference to the problems and grievances of African Americans.[155]

At many of the conferences, the media's failure to cover any but the most negative aspects of African-American people and communities was noted. This time, journalists seemed to listen. One *Washington Post* editor wrote in 1968, "Is it really true that we *are* just a branch of the power structure . . . and that we carry news about Negroes only when they get in trouble with the law, or the welfare department?"[156]

A by-product of the media's ignoring of black communities was their failure to cover the grievances of African Americans living in inner-city neighborhoods. During the conferences, the media were castigated for having failed to alert their audiences to the severe problems existing in the inner cities, which were the root causes of the urban riots.[157] But one *Los Angeles Times* editor observed that the paper had attempted to explore conditions in the Watts area of Los Angeles before the riots erupted in 1965. In the early 1960s, it had committed staff resources and newspaper space to investigating problems in the city's black neighborhoods and had published numerous stories. But there was no response from white leadership, he said. Nothing changed.[158]

The earlier-mentioned problem of newspapers covering the events of civil rights demonstrations and riots without explaining the long-standing injustices and oppressive conditions that led to the events had a noticeable effect on white readers' understanding of the situations. During the Newark riot of 1967, a Gallup poll found that only one white American in 100 thought that African Americans were being treated badly, and 75 percent thought that blacks were treated the same as whites. The poll also found that the white public blamed the urban violence on "outside agitators" and "Negroes demanding too much."[159] Such incredible ignorance on the part of white Americans as to the true status of black Americans at that time is a powerful illustration of the result of the white media's centuries-old habit of ignoring African Americans and the way they were treated in American society. It also reflected the media's refusal to acknowledge the existence of white racism and its focus on negative images of African Americans.

A National Urban League official noted, during the late 1960s, that the Newark rioters felt that legitimate efforts by responsible black leaders to alleviate their disadvantaged status had failed. They saw that the legislative and judicial gains of the Civil Rights Movement had not altered the character of their lives. [160] An FCC commissioner stated, "A riot is a form of communication. It is a man crying out 'Listen to me, mister. There's something I've been trying to tell you and you're not listening.' "[161]

Researchers who studied press coverage of a 1967 riot in Winston-Salem stated that the press presented the riot almost exclusively from the perspective of law enforcement and the city's white power structure. Reporters made little or no attempt to cover the disorder from the viewpoint of those engaged in the violence; to understand their points of view; to explain the grievances, opinions, and attitudes of African Americans in the riot area; or to explore the conditions there. Because the media covered the riot as a threat to the community and focused on official actions to curb violence and calm racial tensions, the authors stated, white readers were misled about the extent and nature of black discontent.[162]

During the riot-plagued summers of the mid-1960s, a new stereotype of African Americans emerged, according to one researcher. This was the image of the militant black man, making demands and threatening a "long, hot summer" if black demands were not met, or a Black Panther, armed and threatening violence to whites if conditions for African Americans were not improved. To an apprehensive white public largely insulated by its media for centuries from knowledge of white racism (except for that in the South), and ignorant of the oppression under which most African Americans lived, it is not surprising that these demands seemed unreasonable and excessive.[163]

Concerning the causes of the riots, some metropolitan newspapers did attempt to return to the riot areas when the violence had died down, to ask the residents for their opinions. The *Los Angeles Times* ran a series after the 1965 Watts riot; the series included an editorial that called for the kind of preventative action that still has not been undertaken, thirty years later. It called first of all for better police relations with the black community, a stepped-up summer job program for youths, an expanded Head Start program, and an adequate school lunch program, among other projects.[164]

The *Detroit Free Press* twice returned to the area of the 1967 Detroit riots to interview residents about the causes of the riots. Both times, the residents surveyed cited poor relations with police as their primary complaint; they complained that the police treated them without respect, used unnecessary force when making arrests, and were not around when they were needed. They also cited poor housing conditions, poverty, lack of jobs, and other problems.[165]

A very similar list of problems was uncovered by the Kerner Commission when they interviewed black residents of riot areas in cities across the nation about the grievances they felt had caused the riots. As in Watts and Detroit, police practices toward ghetto residents emerged as the primary complaint. Also cited as most serious were inadequate housing, underemployment, and unemployment. In their study of the causes of the riots, the commission uncovered in each innner-city black community a host of serious problems. But they also stated that in each of the scores of riots they studied, the triggering incident was police brutality, or perceived brutality, toward a black ghetto resident.[166]

Another example of black community concern with the problem of police behavior was provided in a seminar set up in the late 1960s between African-American leaders and white journalists and academics. At a University of Washington seminar, one journalism educator noted, although the black participants were willing to discuss the media, they felt such strong animosity toward the police that the presence of journalists was sufficient to unleash a flood of criticism of police. "Black speaker after black speaker," he wrote, "called upon newsmen to direct the media searchlight of truth upon alleged police misbehavior. It was there, that the pain was greatest. It was there, that the sores were rawest."[167]

It should be noted that the subject of police relations with inner-city black communities has been largely ignored by the media and police in the thirty years since these grievances were uncovered. Very few investigations of black citizens' problems with police have been conducted by newspapers and newsmagazines in the past three decades (some exceptions are noted in chapter 7). Not until 1995, when ex-LAPD officer Mark Fuhrman's claims about police attitudes and practices toward blacks were made public, did *Time* run a cover story on the subject. Predictably, most black people were not surprised about Fuhrman's statements, while many whites were shocked, because whites have been insulated from having to face the reality of police behavior toward blacks.

The reasons for this ignoring of police behavior toward inner-city blacks are several. One black leader has noted that middle-class whites have great difficulty believing that the friendly man in blue who helps their children across the street can be indiscriminately hostile and brutal toward African Americans in the inner city.[168] As one black writer and former ghetto dweller noted, "The residents of Black America are consistently subjected to the worst facets and behavior of the policeman. In the ghetto a policeman wields power. He is not the respectful and even humble public servant that he is in middle and upper class communities; he is often a tyrant."[169] Conversely, in the inner cities, police are constantly exposed to the worst behavior of African Americans, too, and, as in Vietnam, the constant danger they face can exacerbate racist attitudes and behavior.

One positive effect of the riots on white news organizations was to illustrate vividly the white media's need for black journalists and their nearly total lack of such reporters. In 1965 the percentage of minority reporters in the nation's newsrooms was less than 1 percent. But news organizations attempting to cover riots quickly discovered the rioters' hostility toward white reporters and also discovered white journalists' extensive lack of knowledge of the black inner city. Many news organizations pressed into service black copy boys, messenger boys, and business office and advertising department personnel. Some of these people remained in reporting, and later white newspapers began hiring reporters away from the black press and encouraging black students to study journalism in college.

This was partly because of the lesson the riots had taught and also because of the 1968 Kerner Commission report. The commission, appointed the year before by President Johnson to investigate the causes of the urban riots, devoted an extensive chapter of its report to the media and their role in race relations. The commission criticized the white media for their failure to hire black reporters, to reflect in their newsrooms the diversity in the nation's population. It also criticized their failure to cover the black community, stating that "far too often, the press acts and talks about Negroes as if Negroes do not read the newspapers or watch television, give birth, marry, die and go to PTA meetings.'' The absence of black faces and black concerns in the media had contributed to the white lack of understanding of African Americans and had helped widen the gap between the races, the commission noted. The commission also castigated the press for failing to provide to white readers any sense of black accomplishment, history, or culture, stating that the media viewed the world from a white man's perspective.[170] Even before the commission's report, various journalists had admitted in media/race relations conferences that, because their papers routinely ignored the ghetto, their staffs were as surprised as the rest of white society when the ghettos erupted.[171]

The Kerner Commission stated that journalists had done a good job of covering the riots, sometimes risking their lives to do so, and had accurately covered the *events* of the Civil Rights Movement. But, in both cases, the commission stated, the media had failed to explain the long-standing grievances that had led to the riots and the whole movement. "The ills of the ghetto, the difficulties of life there, the Negro's burning sense of grievance, are seldom conveyed,'' the commission stated. Tom Wicker of the *New York Times* stated in his introduction to the Kerner Report that "what white Americans have never fully understood— but what the Negro can never forget—is that white society is deeply implicated in the ghetto. White institutions created it, white institutions maintain it, and white society condones it.'' More generally, the commission stated that the press had historically failed to convey to white readers "a feeling for the difficulties and frustrations of being a Negro in the United States.''[172]

The commission's charge that the media had failed to explain the background and causes of the Civil Rights Movement was illuminated in the media's handling of the 1968 Poor People's March, where Native Americans, supported by African Americans, demonstrated in Washington, D.C. Once again, one reporter noted, the media approached the events with a sort of "police blotter'' mentality. They concentrated on the events of the movement, detailing how many people were injured, how many persons participated, and who spoke, and almost completely ignored the issues involved and the underlying causes of this evidence of social unrest. The total effect, the journalist observed, was to reinforce some readers' beliefs that the protesters were criminals and to persuade those who had not yet made up their minds.[173]

A glimpse of the kind of improved coverage that can be achieved through better communications between the media and black communities can be found in a communications professor's report on a media-black council he ran in Seattle for nineteen months in 1968 and 1969. The council was established to inform media decision makers of the concerns of Seattle's black community. It included representatives of the city's two newspapers, four television and several radio stations, and four local black leaders and three young black men from activist or militant black organizations. Frequently, guests from the media and the black community were invited to attend.[174]

During the life of the council, the professor reported, media coverage of black affairs increased considerably. In addition, the two newspapers began running photos and stories of black fashions and foods and carried material on black history, experiences, and attitudes. (Here was an exception to the Kerner Commission's criticism that the media failed to provide white readers with any sense of black accomplishment, history, and culture.) The meetings also opened up channels of communication between journalists and young black activists, which led to better coverage and conflict resolution. In addition, it resulted in alliances between young, activist blacks and older, more moderate ones. The council was disbanded when the funds from the grant for setting it up ran out, but it left behind positive results, including a better understanding by media personnel of black perceptions of white society.[175]

As the demonstrations and urban riots of the 1960s alerted white media executives to the advantages of having minority reporters on their staffs, more journalists of color were hired by mainstream media. By the early 1970s, the number of African-American journalists working in white-owned media had risen from almost none in the late 1950s to 1.5 percent. But these reporters often expressed frustration in their work.

According to a 1972 report on black journalists, very few of them were promoted to decision-making positions where they had any say in the day-to-day handling of news. Also, black reporters stated that they were given little opportunity to deal in depth with issues that affected black people. "There's no commitment [by white editors] to put the black man in honest perspective," one African-American journalist said. He added that, by the time a story written by a black reporter ran the gamut of white editors, it was often "laundered if not eliminated." In addition, he stated, editors continued to filter news about blacks through the old stereotypes of sensationalism, negativity, and criminality. "It's easier to get a piece in on the Panthers or a street gang than on a block club or community news."[176]

Some exceptions were reported. In 1973 the *Sacramento Union*'s "Three Tokens," as they called themselves, were assigned by their publisher to tell the story of the city's black neighborhood, presenting its problems, troubles, and dreams. The reporters—an Asian American, an African American, and a Chicano—produced a twenty-five-part series about the desperate plight of the neighborhood, which one reporter stated "had eluded the attention of the local media for ages except, of course, when somebody got shot or robbed or firebombs were thrown." The series and its frequent follow-up articles about continuing community self-help efforts triggered "an avalanche of goodwill and support," one reporter said. The city council approved $100,000 for a long-stalled multipurpose youth center project, volunteers worked on various community projects, Boy Scout troops were formed, and National Guard units showed up on weekends to do cleanup work. Among the many lessons learned from the project, the reporter stated, was that minority reporters can play a big role if they are allowed to air the unique and pressing problems of minority communities.

They also can help forge an atmosphere for interracial understanding and co-operation.[177]

Meanwhile, by the early 1970s, profound changes had affected the black press. Although more mainstream newspapers had begun to cover news about blacks, they focused mainly on the dramatic and sensational—conflict, militancy, the achievements of "celebrity blacks," and crime—one black reporter noted. The need for the African-American press remained: "When it comes to routine coverage of black communities—social life, church activities, births, marriages, deaths, club and fraternal news, etc.—the black press has an open field."[178]

The thriving black press of the 1940s had declined in subscribers to the point that only one of the old black press giants, the *Baltimore Afro-American*, was among the three largest-circulation black papers in 1970. The other two biggest papers were both propaganda organs of militant groups, the reporter observed. They were the Black Muslims' *Muhammad Speaks* and the *Black Panther*. Among the problems facing the traditional black press, the author noted, was trying not to be too conservative for the revolutionaries, while also trying not to be too revolutionary for the white establishment businesses on whom it was coming to depend for advertising. An additional problem was that black newspapers were becoming training grounds for black journalists who hoped to move on to the white media.[179]

In the late 1960s, white resistance to school integration in the North proved to be just as fierce as it had been in the South during the previous decade. Then, in 1971, President Richard Nixon began blocking the practice of busing to achieve school integration. Two years later, the Supreme Court followed suit by letting stand a lower court decision that banned busing in Virginia, and school desegregation efforts began to falter.[180]

A noted African-American sociologist observed in 1968 that despite the gains of the Civil Rights Movement, the situation of the masses of African Americans had not changed or had even worsened. He observed that the benefits and opportunities achieved by the movement had benefited primarily a small number of middle-class blacks.[181]

One area in which significant change had occurred, however, was in the election of African Americans to political office. In 1966, no American city had a black mayor; by 1973, blacks had served or were serving as mayors of Cleveland, Los Angeles, Atlanta, Detroit, Newark, Gary, and many small towns in the South. Also the number of black state legislators had risen from 97 to 200 in the same period, and the number of African Americans in the U.S. Congress had risen from six to sixteen.[182]

Broadcast Coverage

Research on television and African Americans points to the twin perils of limited roles and a preponderance of negative images.[183] It appears that white media managers accepted and were willing to perpetuate the earlier portrayals of blacks as lazy, ignorant, and shiftless. A 1962 study revealed that of the 398 half-hour units of television that year, no black people appeared in 309 of them. Of the eighty-nine units that did show blacks, twenty-seven featured them only as singers, dancers, and musicians. The next most frequent category was hard news and documentary, primarily because of civil rights activities.[184]

The dramatic events of the Civil Rights Movement required coverage by broadcast outlets. Accustomed to the make-believe world of "I Married Joan" and "Ozzie and Harriet," viewers were shocked by television footage of black men, women, and children civil rights demonstrators being attacked by police dogs in Alabama. Television brought the civil rights struggle into the homes of millions of Americans who had, until then, been able to ignore the existence of racism. Television also showed Southern governors and police defying federal mandates to desegregate. Mal Goode became the first black correspondent for a major television network (ABC) in 1962. It became his job to go into the riot-torn areas where people sometimes refused to talk to white reporters.

All three networks presented documentaries on the Civil Rights Movement in the 1960s. These programs included NBC's three-hour documentary "Crisis behind the Presidential Commitment" and an ABC documentary on the June 1963 integration crisis at the University of Alabama. The massive March on Washington attracted millions to the television to hear Dr. King deliver his now-famous "I Have a Dream" speech in 1963.

WLBT-TV in Jackson, Mississippi, was rebuked by the Federal Communications Commission (FCC) for its slanted coverage of civil rights activities in 1965. In 1969 the United Church of Christ, acting on behalf of Jackson's black community, successfully challenged the license of WLBT.

Each television network produced special coverage of Dr. King's assassination in 1968 and the riots that erupted in major urban areas afterward. The Kerner Commission had sampled six days of television news coverage of 1967 riots in fifteen cities three days before and three days after each riot. The commission reported that the media had failed to give adequate attention to racial problems and had ignored the context of riots, which the media portrayed as black-white conflicts rather than as reactions to slum conditions. They also complained that television news focused on whites although the rioting occurred in black communities.[185]

A 1971 study made of the portrayals of African Americans in network news found that in 52 percent of the newscasts blacks did not appear in speaking roles, were seen in blue-collar jobs, and were often shown in connection with civil rights issues.[186] A similar study of the evening news conducted in 1972 and 1973 found that blacks were again shown mostly in nonspeaking roles relating to school busing, civil rights, and crime.[187]

1974 RESIGNATION OF NIXON TO LOS ANGELES UPRISING, APRIL 29, 1992

By the early 1970s, the protests and demonstrations of the activist 1960s had died down, as had the urban riots, which dwindled sharply after the convulsion of rioting that swept the nation's cities upon Dr. King's assassination in 1968. As the turbulence dwindled, so did the news media's attention to the racial story. A belief that the nation had largely solved its racial problems seemed to pervade the news media and white society alike. Roger Wilkins, a black news executive, observed in 1975 that where racial problems were concerned, America seemed to accept the advice one U.S. senator had proposed earlier about the nation's involvement in Vietnam: "Declare victory and withdraw." He added, "When it became clear that blacks weren't going to destroy the cities," coverage of blacks and the issues affecting them disappeared from newspapers. Lulled by the achievements of a few African Americans who had gained status, white society and journalists simply ignored the fact that 40 percent of the black population was still mired in poverty, black children in urban areas were not being educated, crime rates were rising, and the foundations of urban life were steadily eroding.[188]

During the same period, an African-American journalist noted how coverage of homicides in New York's three dailies reinforced the idea that "some lives are worth caring about and some are not." He stated that the papers gave extensive coverage to a few white middle-class murder victims, largely ignored the murder of twelve people in Harlem at the same time, and ran front-page stories about a Harlem youth sentenced for the murder of a white woman.[189]

He noted, however, that the New York Police Department's records provided a vastly different picture of homicides in the city. According to their records, 50 percent of the city's homicide victims were black and 30 percent were Hispanic; white women accounted for 0.05 percent of the victims. The papers' constant presentation of quite a different picture, he stated, was a way in which the papers restructured reality in accordance with their own racial perceptions.[190]

The journalist noted the discrepancy in coverage was even more notable when the victim was killed by police. When a white youth in a middle-class suburb was shot, the papers gave extensive coverage to bystanders' accounts and the boy's parents' charges against the police. But when a young black man was killed by police with nine shots, five of them in the back, the papers provided scant coverage of bystanders' testimonies and consistently presented the story from the police accounts. The papers also gave very limited coverage to black citizens' protests about the incident.[191]

By 1974 the race story had moved North with a vengeance, over court-ordered busing to desegregate schools. Executives of Boston papers that had sent reporters South in the 1960s to cover the violence there were beginning, one journalist said, to react with the same defensiveness Southerners had shown the decade before. He said the local media attempted to cover the opening weeks of school desegregation as responsibly as possible. Thus when the first day of school was generally quiet, except for the stoning of several school buses in South Boston, the media reported it that way. But the out-of-town reporters could not do so, because of their home offices' preoccupation with violence. One wire-service reporter noted that if a story went out of Boston saying in the lead that the school day was generally peaceful and reported a single episode of violence in paragraph five, the New York office would ask the bureau to move up the paragraph detailing violence. Reporters soon got the message. Bostonians were faced with an eerie discrepancy between the situation their local media reported and the tension and violence trumpeted by the national media.[192]

Several studies of press coverage of black political candidates indicated that African Americans were covered more frequently than whites during elections, although one researcher found stories about them received slightly less favorable display than stories about their white counterparts.[193] Another study, of the coverage of black public officials during political campaigns in nineteen cities between 1970 and 1977, also noted stories about black officials received less favorable display and were less positive, although the stories were longer than stories about white officials.[194] A study of editorial treatment of black and white elected representatives between 1979 and 1983 found that the African-American representatives were more visible than their white counterparts; were more likely to be quoted on local and racial affairs and less likely to be quoted on Congressional, international, and national affairs; were cited as effective leaders less frequently than whites; were more likely to be identified as compassionate and less likely to be identified as moral.[195]

In a study of photos of African Americans in four U.S. newspapers, one researcher found that, during the years from 1972 to 1990, the number of photos increased and the negative racial stereotypes disappeared from news and advertising photographs. African Americans were shown as equal, productive members of society, the researcher said, although in many issues the only African-American images published were of black athletes.[196]

In a study of the coverage of black problems in four major newspapers, one researcher found that the papers' attention to problems facing African Americans tripled in the 1970s over what it had been during the 1960s, despite the newsworthy nature of the civil rights story during the 1960s. The author speculated that this increased attention might have resulted from newspaper executives' increased sensitivity to African Americans because of the Civil Rights Movement. Also, because the racial confrontations of the 1960s had greatly diminished, African Americans and their grievances may have been perceived as less threatening and thus were covered more thoroughly during the 1970s. Among the problems mentioned were that progress toward equality for blacks was slowing as the goal of black equality was being abandoned nationally, and civil rights gains already made were being threatened. Other items noted black Americans' fear and resentment at the lack of public outcry among whites at the resurgence of antiblack hate groups.[197]

During the 1970s, the number of African Americans employed by newspapers rose to around 5 percent of newsroom employees, even though few minority students graduated from traditional college journalism programs. Some students were trained in special programs like the Institute for Journalism Education, begun at Columbia University and revived at Berkeley by Robert and Nancy Maynard in 1977. In 1975 the National Association of Black Journalists was formed. Many African-American reporters contributed greatly to all aspects of their papers' coverage; some of them won Pulitzers. Nevertheless, they believed that their editors had little desire to dig into the problems of inner-city African Americans and other racial issues, partly because of indifference or objections on the part of advertisers and white readers. Also, they agreed that they had to be better journalists than white reporters to even be accepted in newsrooms. Surveys revealed that blacks occupied less than one percent of the policy-making positions on their papers.[198] The black reporters' observations illustrated that simply having more minority journalists in the newsroom does not guarantee more sensitive and accurate coverage of minorities. While journalists of color can bring greater insight and sensitivity to stories about minorities, if they are not promoted to positions in which they can affect decisions about news coverage and display then little will change in a paper's approach to minority coverage.

In 1977 the American Society of Newspaper Editors set a goal that U.S. newsrooms should include by the year 2000 the same percentage of minority journalists as the percentage of minorities in the general population. Partly as a result of that commitment, throughout the 1980s various programs were instituted to attract minority students to university journalism programs and newspapers recruited minority journalists more actively.

In 1979 the Reverend Jesse Jackson told a meeting of the American Newspaper Publishers Association that most blacks distrust the white press because of "the four cardinal sins of the press." He said the press portrays blacks as less intelligent, less hard-working, more violent, and less universal than they really are.[199]

The 1980s opened with a riot in May in the black Liberty City area of Miami, which was caused by a situation that was an eerie foreshadowing of the Los Angeles riot that would occur twelve years in the future. In the Florida case, six white and Hispanic policemen had beaten to death a young black man whom they had arrested after a high-speed chase. The trial was moved to a nearby county, the jury was all white, and the policemen were acquitted. Liberty City exploded in rage; during three days and two nights of violence, eighteen persons, most of them black, were killed.

One analysis of the riot explained that it was caused partly because the verdict was the most recent of a series of inequities that had deepened the local black community's already deep distrust of the justice system. These incidents included a wrong-address drug raid in which a black schoolteacher and his son were beaten by police, and no restitution was ever made, and the sexual molestation of a black girl by a white state trooper who was never brought to trial. In addition, conditions in Liberty City were worse in 1980 than they had been in 1960, when the burgeoning Civil Rights Movement had held out some hope for change. Unemployment in the area was 6 percent in 1960; by 1980, it had tripled. The high school dropout rate had climbed from 30 percent to 50 percent in 1980.[200]

Early in 1983 another riot erupted in Overtown, another poor, black section of Miami. The disturbance was touched off when police killed a young black man. During the three days of violence and destruction that followed, another person was killed by police. The previous autumn, in two separate incidents, local blacks had been killed by white policemen. *Time* reported that African Americans were even angrier because one of the policemen who had killed the black man in January was Hispanic. Some 39 percent of Miami's 1,000-member police force was Hispanic, and only 17 percent was black. The Miami Urban League president said, "Blacks already believe the Cubans have gotten preferential treatment at our expense."[201]

Studies of news coverage of riots occurring in the 1960s, 1970s, and 1980s indicated that every major riot since the 1960s was touched off by police killing or wounding a black man or being acquitted after doing so, and the coverage generally failed to explain the long-standing grievances held by the African-American community toward police and the justice system for past injustices. Also, although in every riot most of those killed were African Americans, the news accounts tended to focus on the white victims and failed to tell the story of the black ones.[202]

A 1980 *Wall Street Journal* series on blacks in America revealed that the black middle class had more than doubled since 1960, and accounted for a third of the black population; in contrast, two-thirds of white Americans had middle-class status. Between 1960 and 1980 the number of African Americans attending college had risen by 400 percent, and black high school graduates were as likely as white graduates to go on to college. Yet the unemployment rate for black college graduates was higher than it was for white high school dropouts.[203]

The *Journal* series also indicated that, despite the Southern states' dismantling of Jim Crow laws, segregated schools, and barriers to black voting, "Blacks still are held firmly at the bottom of the social and economic pyramid."[204] It reported that, although the number of black officeholders had tripled in the past ten years, those elected to higher office usually represented areas where urban decay was so far advanced that it could not be reversed. Representative Shirley Chisholm, one of seventeen African Americans in Congress in 1980, represented a district that included Bedford-Stuyvesant, an area that she said was typical of the "shells white leaders leave behind when they abandon an area politically to blacks."[205]

Another source noted in 1981 that nearly half of all African-American families were poor, two out of every five black children were on Aid to Dependent Children at a time when the economic and political climates were causing cutbacks in such services, a black teenager was five times more likely than a white youth to be killed, and the unemployment rate for black college graduates was almost twice that of whites who never attended college.[206]

A 1981 Gannett News Service series on the situation of African Americans stated that representatives of both the black poor and middle class shared ''the belief that blacks are still unequal and there's no indication that things are getting better. . . . Indeed, there is a growing perception that things are getting worse.'' The report also said that the inner cities were poorer and blacker, and the people there had even less chance of escape.[207]

Conditions did indeed get worse under the Reagan administration, beginning in 1980. The number of African Americans holding government and foreign service posts was sharply reduced. In a stunning reversal, the U.S. Commission on Civil Rights, long a strong voice for justice and equality for African Americans, became an administration mouthpiece, indifferent or hostile to the concerns of blacks, noted historian John Hope Franklin. The president weakened the Legal Enforcement Assistance Administration, thus limiting enforcement of laws against housing discrimination and denying poor people any assistance for redress of grievances against housing abuses. In another sharp reversal, the Justice Department's Civil Rights Division became black Americans' principal *opponent* in their attempts to seek relief through the courts from affirmative action abuses. Reagan's budgets reduced the number of people eligible to participate in federal social programs—food stamps, Medicaid, student loans, unemployment compensation, child nutrition assistance, and Aid to Families with Dependent Children. Meanwhile, Franklin noted, ''the contribution of corporations to federal revenues was reduced from 13 cents to 8 cents for each tax dollar.''[208]

These changes were reflected in an empirical study made of the coverage of the problems facing black Americans in four major newspapers. In the 1980s issues examined, the number of problem stories run declined by about one-third from the number run in the 1970s issues sampled, but the amount of space devoted to black problems increased. Both the problem stories and other stories found presented a clear picture of the federal government's opposing improved equality of opportunity for black Americans. Numerous items described the retreat by the Reagan administration, Congress, the Supreme Court, and the white American public from a commitment to civil rights and affirmative action. Other items chronicled the rise of hate groups and an increased persecution of blacks.[209] The situation bore a strong resemblance to the temper of the government and the white public at the end of Reconstruction, when the cause of blacks was abandoned nationally.

Some of the newly evident racism in American society was expressed in the Howard Beach and Bensonhurst killings of young black men in 1986 and 1989. In the first tragedy, a black youth was run down in New York when he took to the highway to escape a mob of baseball bat–wielding whites. In the second, several young black men who had come to Bensonhurst, New York, to look at a car to purchase were attacked, and one of them was killed by a group of white youths.

By the early 1980s, the proportion of minority reporters in the nation's newsrooms had risen to 5.5 percent, although the rate of hiring of reporters of color had declined consistently during each of the past five years. Some 60 percent of the nation's newsrooms were still all white, and integration had been stalled by economic hard times. Minority reporters stated that they had to prove themselves twice, both as journalists and also as objective reporters of issues concerning minorities. They also pointed out that very few journalists of color had risen into management positions. Other minority journalists noted that many white editors were still using the tired old excuse that they could not find any qualified minority reporters, when the unemployment rate for black journalism graduates was twice the rate of white journalism graduates.[210]

Observers of press portrayals of African Americans noted in the early 1980s numerous stories reflecting whites' hostile reactions to affirmative action and whites' blatant antagonism toward black aspirations. Because the news media gave such extensive coverage to openly racist bigots, one black civil rights leader observed that the media, which used to be allies in the struggle for human rights, were becoming adversaries.[211]

The news media also were charged with failing to explain affirmative action adequately. One black political figure stated that the media had picked up the "reverse discrimination" phrase coined by opponents of affirmative action and used it repeatedly instead of exploring the whole issue of institutional racism and how affirmative action could help redress it. He wondered what the effect would be if the media were to report the extent to which the children of alumni, financial donors, athletes, and similar groups are given priority admission to universities. He said, "It is difficult to overestimate the political power of the media in shaping national policy on large and volatile issues. Attitudes, concepts and code words become deeply imbedded in the public consciousness because of how they are reported, or even how they are headlined."[212]

One educator observed that white racism had become a critical factor in the neglect of the nation's cities and in the news media's failure to explain the urban crisis. He cited another author who described how the plight of black Americans living in the nation's inner cities once again was reported only when disturbances occurred.[213]

Regarding press coverage of black political figures, a study of the *Los Angeles Times'* coverage of the 1982 governor's race between Los Angeles Mayor Tom Bradley and George Deukmejian found that the paper heavily emphasized Bradley's race as an election issue, running numerous major stories, headlines, and polls focusing on his race. By continually highlighting this volatile issue, the researcher stated, the *Times* contributed to Bradley's surprise defeat.[214]

Another researcher studied the coverage in the *Chicago Tribune* and *Sun-Times*, both white-owned papers, and the *Chicago Defender*, a black paper, of the 1983 Chicago mayoral race won by Harold Washington. In all three papers, the researcher found, race received more coverage than seven other traditional campaign issues combined. Although all three papers frequently decried the ugliness of the campaign, they were at least partly responsible for making race an issue by giving it too much coverage and not focusing more on platform issues.[215]

Numerous observers have commented on the newspaper coverage of Jesse Jackson's campaign for the nation's presidency in 1984. Some have noted that he was not covered in the same way as the white candidates and was consistently not presented as a serious candidate. Others have noted how his motivations and agendas were questioned in a way those of white candidates were not. On the other hand, some observers believed that the press coverage of Jackson was "gentle" because of journalists' fear of appearing racist.[216]

The *Washington Post* was the target of a heated protest made by local blacks when it unveiled its redesigned Sunday *Magazine* in September 1986. The issue included a cover story about a black rap musician accused of murdering a drug dealer, a column about a local merchant who had called police when two well-dressed black men entered his store and the columnist's sympathy with his action, a photo "portrait" of Sugar Ray Leonard that featured only his upraised fist, and the appearance of no blacks elsewhere in the magazine, including the ads. Irate blacks held rallies and deposited tens of thousands of copies of the magazine on the newspaper building's steps each week.[217] This kind of insensitive coverage is even more surprising because the *Post* had hired a number of minority reporters. It was a good example of the futility of expecting the presence of minority reporters to make a significant difference in coverage when the major coverage decisions still are made by whites.

In a study of the *Post Magazine*'s coverage before, during, and after the protest, a researcher found that the magazine provided little coverage of African Americans in the four months before the protest, and 65 percent of that was negative. The coverage of blacks rose from 4.5 percent before the protest to 7.7 percent during the four-month protest and to 11.6 percent in the four months afterward. No negative coverage of blacks was found in the four months after the protest, and the only negative portrayals during the protest period itself were found in the debut issue.[218]

In 1986 journalist Kirk Johnson compared one month of news coverage of African Americans by six mainstream and four black-owned print and broadcast outlets in Boston. A striking difference between the two groups' coverage, he discovered, was the news they carried about the city's two predominantly black neighborhoods. In the major media, 85 percent of the stories about these areas dealt with crime, violence, or drug use and reinforced negative stereotypes of blacks. By contrast, 57 percent of the stories about these neighborhoods in the black-owned media portrayed "a black community thirsty for educational advancement and entrepreneurial achievement, and eager to remedy poor living conditions." He also noted that positive events regarded as news in other communities often were not recognized by mainstream media when they occurred in black neighborhoods. For example, black neighborhood activists persuaded Boston's mayor to launch a cleanup campaign in the two neighborhoods by appearing in person to help pick up trash. His appearance was big news in the black-owned media, but it was not even covered by the major newspapers and television stations.[219]

Johnson also found that the black outlets much more often featured stories about education, city government, community and cultural events, the arts, and profiles of educators and entrepreneurs. The black media also showed the true diversity of the black community, occasionally showing blacks as ordinary people, like lifeguards, airline passengers, teachers. Conversely, most of the blacks featured in the white-owned media were entertainers, athletes, criminals, or failing students. He concluded that the major media's news about Boston's black neighborhoods was biased to fit commonly held stereotypes about blacks and the poor, while stories that would reflect the true diversity of the black community were ignored. He also noted that blacks in positions of authority, or with special expertise, frequently were overlooked as reporters sought out the views of white experts, even on issues with a major impact on the black community.[220]

Even more significant was Johnson's finding that even in stories that directly involved racism, the mainstream media either ignored or played down the racism factor. For example, several stories on Supreme Court decisions favoring affirmative action used quotes from white Bostonians stating that they should not have to pay for the sins of their forefathers; no attempt was made to include reactions of minorities. Another story dealt with the discrepancy in test scores between white schoolchildren and minority children in Boston's public schools. No exploration of the past and current roots of the discrepancy was provided. "When a social reality as oppressive as racism is consistently played down," Johnson wrote, the media fail in their responsibility to their readers. He noted that story selection and news coverage "can subtly transform the media from a force for enlightenment to an unwitting perpetrator of racism."[221]

A black journalist and educator noted in 1990 that it seemed to African Americans that "most white people, including journalists, don't see racism as a major problem." She added, "That kind of perceptual dichotomy and denial makes dialogue impossible."[222]

She commented on the Charles Stuart case of the late 1980s, in which a white Boston resident took out a large insurance policy on his pregnant wife, killed her, and wounded himself, then claimed that the shootings had been done by a black man. The journalist said that by concocting "the black guy did it" story, persons like Stuart are tapping into what white people already believe—that black men are violent and criminal.[223] In the early 1990s Susan Smith fabricated a similar story with a similar villain after she drowned her young sons. She also was initially believed because her story fit into many whites' perceptions about the criminality of black men.

A similar use of white racial stereotypes of blacks, this time for political gain, was evidenced by George Bush in his 1988 presidential campaign. In an effort to discredit his opponent, Bush okayed an ad that criticized Governor Michael Dukakis for approving the release from prison of William Horton, a black man later convicted of raping a white woman.[224] The case was not typical; nine out of ten white rape victims have been raped by white men. But the idea of the savage, sexual black man eager to violate white women has been a mainstay of white stereotypes of black men, and a constantly repeated rallying cry of the Ku Klux Klan, for well over 100 years. Thus the Willie Horton ad resonated with many white voters, probably for reasons of which they were not even consciously aware.

Conversely, the 1987 Tawana Brawley case illustrated what African Americans find easy to believe about whites. Brawley, a teenager who had been missing for several days, was found in a garbage bag, smeared with feces, with racial epithets written on her body. She indicated she had been abducted and sexually abused by a group of white men, including policemen. As became evident ten months later, she apparently had concocted the story with her mother to escape her stepfather's anger for some misdemeanor.[225] It is significant that her story initially was perfectly believable to large segments of the black community. Ever since the days of slavery, so many black females have been sexually assaulted by white men, including law officers, that Brawley's story, although bizarre, was not unbelievable. It may have seemed so to white people, partly because their news media have denied them accounts of white male mistreatment of black women, but to many black people it was no more unlikely than Charles Stuart's account, or Susan Smith's, was to whites.

In general studies of minority coverage, one researcher compared Columbus, Ohio's, *Columbus Dispatch*'s coverage of African Americans in 1965 and in 1987 and found that the amount of coverage given to blacks had remained constant. He also discovered that the tone of the coverage was generally much more positive in the later year, although coverage of black crime tripled.[226]

One journalist noted in 1990 that the media's very nature impels them toward the bad news—fires, murder, natural disasters, and controversy. According to one columnist, "We report not the rich diversity of a community but its pathology." Such a focus, however, leaves the media susceptible to being manipulated by demagogues. David Dinkins, New York's first black mayor, frequently noted that radical black activists like the Reverend Al Sharpton received much more media attention than other community leaders who had a more substantive message—a comment frequently voiced by civil rights leaders in the 1960s. One media critic said that the really disturbing aspect of the situation was that television reporters "know they're being manipulated by somebody like Al Sharpton, but they're more interested in getting the good sound bite than they are in not being manipulated."[227]

Increasingly, by 1990, journalists were voicing in trade publications and at conferences the idea that "[t]o cover communities that are increasingly diverse, journalists are going to have to bring to the story a knowledge of and sensitivity to different kinds of people and cultures. It is no longer acceptable to work from a limited personal perspective and yet claim to be objective."[228]

Scholar Carol Liebler did a year-long study of the *Washington Post*'s and the *Atlanta Constitution*'s coverage of efforts to pass the 1990 Civil Rights Act. The bill's objectives were to nullify six recent U.S. Supreme Court decisions that curtailed civil rights and to increase protection against discrimination. Like the researcher who had studied coverage of efforts to pass the 1960 Civil Rights Act, she found that the media focused on the "horse race" aspects of the attempt to pass the bill and were preoccupied with official sources; 70 percent of the news stories about the bill and 86 percent of the editorials focused on the actions and reactions of Congress, the White House, and President George Bush. Liebler also, like the other researcher, found that the coverage largely ignored the "real life" impact of discrimination and how the bill would affect African Americans. For example, 173 civil rights and other organizations went on record in support of the legislation. Yet representatives of these groups were seldom interviewed by the media; the same three black leaders were quoted repeatedly when the civil rights perspective was being sought.[229]

Equally important were her findings about the way in which the bill was framed, the way in which the issues involved were presented. President Bush and his administration were successful in framing the bill as a quota bill, a term the president used 73 percent of the times he was attributed and his administration sources used 41 percent of the time; the president and administration sources accounted for nearly a third of the sources used. Liebler noted that over thirty amendments were made to the bill, largely to avoid it being seen as a quota bill. One amendment specifically stated that nothing in the bill "shall be construed to require or to encourage an employer to adopt hiring or promotion quotas." Yet because the Bush administration continued to define the legislation as a quota bill, and the press picked up this interpretation, proponents of the bill were forced to respond within this framework. After months of debate in Congress and the media, the act was passed by both houses of Congress but vetoed by President Bush. The Senate failed to override the veto.[230]

In 1990 one journalism professor observed that the alliance between the white-owned news media and African Americans that had existed during the 1960s Civil Rights Movement had turned to alienation. He observed that the media are best at telling a story with clear heroes and villains, as the movement had been between the mid-1950s and mid-1960s. But once the urban riots began, the story became more complicated, and the media failed to provide the kind of explanation and analysis "necessary to maintain a sympathetic relationship with the black community." By 1990, he said, distrust of the news media was widespread among African Americans. "Media bashing is a growth industry that seems to be supported by black political leaders, black intellectuals, and even substantial numbers of black newsmen and newswomen themselves."[231]

He stated that one reason for black citizens' distrust of the media is that "blacks are being fit conveniently into a terrible new storyline: black pathology." He and others have noted that blacks are routinely portrayed in the news as drug lords, crack users, violent criminals, unwed mothers, welfare abusers, the homeless, and AIDS victims. At the same time, critics say, coverage of pathologies among whites, such as drug addiction, child abuse, wife beating, white-collar crime, is negligible. The journalism professor noted that the National Institute on Drug Abuse states that blacks are no more likely than whites to use illicit drugs, and that whites sell most of the pure cocaine in the United States and account for 80 percent of its customers.[232]

As one communications professor stated, in the early 1990s, "Nowhere is the racial dichotomy of opinion and perspective more pronounced than on the issue of media treatment of black elected officals." She noted that the arrest of Washington, D.C., mayor Marion Barry on drug charges polarized Washington along racial lines. What whites failed to understand, she suggested, was the black community's frequent experience of seeing "strong blacks being pursued by prosecutorial authorities."[233] The observation is not unfounded. Most people are by now aware that the FBI, under J. Edgar Hoover, devoted considerable manpower and expense to shadowing and investigating Dr. Martin Luther King, Jr., during the 1960s in an effort to find a link to Communism. During the 1980s, members of the U.S. Justice Department and the FBI deliberately leaked to the press information indicating that they were investigating U.S. Representative William Gray for wrongdoing, when they were really investigating the finances of a former member of his office staff. In 1987 the Congressional Black Caucus commissioned a study that concluded that black elected officials at all levels of government were indeed "harassed" by the press, which had served as a "handmaiden" for Justice Department leaks that were for the most part never substantiated.[234] Thus it is not surprising that many African Americans saw the seven years and $3 million the government said it spent on the Marion Barry investigation as another example of a governmental attempt to discredit and bring down a strong black leader.

The 1990 Barry case provides an interesting example of a black backlash that seems to be developing in the United States. The backlash includes an unwillingness of many African Americans to believe the worst, despite the evidence, about a black hero, because they feel the evidence was obtained through racist motives. It also involves an unwillingness to believe a black hero should be convicted, again despite the evidence, because historically so many blacks have been railroaded and treated unequally by the police and in the justice system. Five years after the Barry case, the O.J. Simpson trial was to illustrate similar issues, as well as a similar divergence of perceptions among blacks and whites. As one source noted, "[W]hat one side considers law enforcement, the other may interpret as mere oppression."[235]

In the Barry case, according to a journalism review article, the mayor repeatedly portrayed himself as a victim of politically and racially motivated persecution. Despite the videotaped evidence of him smoking crack, and his lying about it under oath, many African Americans seemed to feel that his wrongdoing was less important than the behavior of the U.S. government in investigating and prosecuting him.[236] Some African Americans pointed out that even law enforcement agencies seldom seek out drug users; drug pushers are considered more important prey. So why did the U.S. Attorney's Office spend seven years and millions of dollars in order to entrap Barry for smoking dope in private?[237]

Several surveys of black elected officials at the local and state levels in the 1980s found that two-thirds of the officials agreed that the coverage of black and white officals was different and unequal, with whites receiving more favorable coverage. Three-fourths of the officials believed that white politicians had more influence with the press.[238]

Several observers have stated that black politicians "suggest that the white press is holding them to a higher standard than white politicians." When several scholars compared the coverage of incumbent black and white congressmen in nine major dailies, they found that the black representatives were given greater visibility and no less favorable display. Black congressmen were used as sources on local and racial issues; the white representatives were quoted on congressional, international, national, state, and county affairs. The scholars also found differences in the presentation of the congressmen's characteristics of leadership, compassion, and morality.[239]

Two studies of minority journalists working for the white press in the late 1980s and early 1990s revealed many of the same problems journalists of color had reported during the 1970s. These included a sense among minority journalists that white reporters resented them as being given preferential treatment in hiring; the feeling that they had been hired because of their race but then not permitted to advance; a sense that they had to perform at a higher standard than their white counterparts to prove their worth; and the perception that a glass ceiling existed that kept minority journalists and women out of top management, decision-making positions.[240]

Complicating the situation was the perceptual gap between black and white Americans. As one set of researchers observed, "There is a sense among white people in America that racism is a thing of the past, an unhappy chapter the nation has put behind it."[241] Because newspaper newsrooms are microcosms of society, the same misperceptions and prejudices exist there as they do in the larger society. This situation has led to very different beliefs among minority and white journalists about what went on in the newsroom.

The study revealed that 85 percent of top newsroom executives were white males. One journalist of color observed, "There's not a lot of generosity in terms of sharing power."[242] The preponderance of white males in newspaper management helps to explain why, two decades earlier, the Kerner Commission had criticized the news media for what two researchers called "a systemic institutional myopia toward the plight of minorities" in the United States.[243] The minority journalists noted that much information about events and situations vitally important to people of color is never printed, because it does not seem important to the gatekeepers—the middle-class white males who determine what the news is.[244]

The 1991 newsroom study suggested that, because racism is not a problem for white people, they seldom realize the nature and effect of biased reporting about minorities. When minority and white journalists were asked how they felt their newspaper covered local minority communities and issues, half the whites felt the paper had done a good job, but 71 percent of the nonwhites said the paper's performance was poor.[245]

A scholar who studied coverage of people of color in press and broadcast outlets in the San Francisco Bay area in 1990 found that people of color still tended to make the news only when they engage in activities like rioting or crime that bring them into conflict with white society, but are otherwise generally ignored by the news media. The study also revealed that virtually all of the few stories found about people of color were written by minority reporters, usually African Americans.[246] The researcher also noted that the news media provide the only routine glimpses the public gets of people who are not like them, and the media can influence racial attitudes by reinforcing racial fears. She added that recent studies suggest that news coverage has contributed to "modern racism"—the belief that racial discrimination no longer exists and that any problems faced by African Americans and other people of color are their own fault.[247]

Since the early 1990s, many black journalists and others have reiterated complaints about news coverage of African Americans that echo the criticisms made by the Kerner Commission in 1968. David Shaw, a *Los Angeles Times* media critic, wrote in 1990,

If all one knew about real-life blacks and Latinos in particular was what one read in the newspaper or saw on television news, one would scarcely be aware that there is a large and growing middle class in both cultures going to work, getting married, having children, paying taxes, going on vacation and buying books and VCRs and microwave ovens.[248]

Shaw also stated that only 15 percent of the poor people in the United States are black, but one gets a very different impression from most press coverage. He added that "most violent criminals, drug users, prostitutes, drunks, illiterates, high school dropouts, juvenile delinquents, jobless and poor people in this country are neither black nor Latino but white." In addition, he stated, the vast majority of African Americans and Latinos, like the majority of whites, are none of the above.[249]

Another researcher, who studied five major newspapers' coverage of the Mike Tyson rape case, stated that the nearly 570 stories he found, written by hundreds of different reporters over nine months, presented just two images of Tyson, both of them demeaning and disempowering: the archetypal African-American male savage, "a crude, violent, sex-obsessed savage who could barely control

his animal instincts," or the victim of horrific social circumstances, venal pro-
moters and the U.S. worship of athletes and heroes. The author noted that both
images were fostered by Tyson's lawyers as well as by journalists, and both
images presented Tyson as helpless before his own sexual appetites or the mach-
inations of others. Also, both "depict a man without self-control or determination, paradoxical for a former world champion." The author stated that both
images served to dehumanize Tyson while confirming demeaning and racist
cultural archetypes about African Americans. [250]

One researcher found 130 accounts of police brutality in major newspapers
between January 1990 and May 1992. White police officers were involved in
over 90 percent of the cases, and blacks or Latinos were the victims in 97 percent
of the incidents. A police officer was punished in only 13 percent of the incidents, and the punishment usually was slight.[251]

One reporter noted that for a full year before the Rodney King beating, black
reporters at the *Los Angeles Times* were deluged with accounts of LAPD mistreatment of African Americans. They suggested that an investigative story be
written on the problem to the *Times* management but were ignored.[252]

In the late 1980s, a grand jury in New York State had refused to indict two
white policemen who had choked to death a twenty-year-old black man outside
a movie theater where he and his friends had caused a commotion. Several years
earlier, a sixty-six-year-old black woman had been killed with two shotgun blasts
fired at point-blank range by one of six white police officers who had gone to
her apartment to evict her for nonpayment of rent; the officer was acquitted of
all charges. The year before, a young black man who had scrawled graffiti on
a Manhattan subway wall died of injuries received when six transit policemen,
in what they said was necessary force to subdue him, hogtied and handcuffed
him and forced a nightstick down on his neck as he lay on a step. These officers
also were acquitted.[253] Stories like this are common in every large city in the
country, and they have been for decades. They help explain the urban riots of
the past and the black rage that exploded at the acquittal of the officers who
beat Rodney King.

In March 1991, King, a twenty-five-year-old African American, was brutally
beaten by LAPD officers after running several stop signs in his car. He suffered
nine skull fractures, a shattered eye socket and cheekbone, a broken leg, a con-
cussion, permanent nerve damage to his face, kidney damage, and permanent
brain damage. The official police report described his injuries as "[s]everal
facial cuts due to contact with asphalt. Of a minor nature. A split upper lip.
Suspect oblivious to pain."[254]

One study said that transcripts of the officers' conversations just after the
beating conveyed a relaxed, jocular tone: "It was right out of *Gorillas in the
Mist*"; "I haven't beaten anyone this bad in a long time."[255] *Time* magazine
reported that "some of the officers involved could be heard swapping racist
jokes and boasting to other cops about the beating. Their lighthearted exchanges,
which they knew were being recorded, sound nothing like the words of men

who fear they have done something reprehensible—or even something out of the ordinary.'' The newsmagazine reported that two of the officers later showed up at the hospital where King had been taken to taunt him. ''We played a little hardball tonight, and you lost,'' one allegedly said.[256]

An area resident videotaped the beating. He was rebuffed when he tried to give the tape to the LAPD; he later sold it to a television station, and it was aired repeatedly on local and national television.[257]

William Solomon studied the *New York Times*' and the *Washington Post*'s news coverage of the beating and the subsequent trial of the police officers. He stated that the news media support the existing social order and act to maintain the systems of liberal democracy and corporate capitalism. As such, he said, the media defer to governmental authority and ''are loath to critique the police or the military, whom they view as protectors of society.''[258] He noted that many people see the police as their protectors from gang violence and urban crime, and he stated that the police's favored status in the press can be observed by comparing the number of police brutality complaints recorded annually with the number of news stories about the complaints.[259] Solomon also claimed that the media are disinclined to focus on the deep and grim cleavages of race and class within U.S. society—the kind of long-standing conditions that underlay the riots that occurred after the verdict was returned.[260]

Solomon found that the views of the underclass were sought immediately after the beating became public, but the coverage soon shifted to the intense power struggle between L.A. Police Chief Daryl Gates and those who sought his resignation. ''The coverage had narrowed to power struggles within the political elite.''[261] (This observation is similar to that of the two researchers who studied attempts to pass the two civil rights acts that also were described by the news media as power struggles among white politicians, while the views of those who would be most affected by the bills were largely ignored.) The papers instead presented a picture of democracy at work, framing the issue as a problem within the 8,300-member LAPD and a situation that could be corrected. (Gates said the problem lay with ''just a few officers, 300 at most.'') The coverage thus ''papered over basic problems of race and class,'' Solomon noted.[262]

The *New York Times* finally published a story that made clear the department's brutality record, which it linked to racism. But, according to Solomon, this racism was presented as an internal problem of the LAPD, unrelated to the city's power structure or the wider social order.[263]

A different researcher argued that what has been described here as the ''savage'' stereotype—the image of black men as violent, uncontrolled, physically powerful, animalistic—helped bring about the acquittal of the four officers tried for beating Rodney King. She noted that this image has been reiterated ceaselessly in popular culture and by the news media for centuries. In her examination of the officers' first trial, she stated that the police officers' defense lawyers tapped into this image when they turned the trial's focus away from the officers' behavior and onto King's physical size, ''inhuman'' strength, and seemingly limitless tolerance for physical pain. In doing so, the lawyers were able to call up an image of the savage black man that already existed in the jurors' minds. The police convinced the jury that because of these traits their extreme behavior was necessary to control King. One police witness to the beating said the situation reminded him of "a movie where the monster gets shot and is still coming at you." According to the author, the monster-like images influenced jurors' perceptions, and despite the videotape the jurors began to believe the beating must have been warranted. One juror even said afterward that King was in full control and could have stopped the beating at any time. Several others said the officers were doing what they had to do to control him.[264]

Several other researchers studied coverage of the subsequent Los Angeles riot, the most serious in this century, partly in an attempt to ascertain whether riot coverage had improved since the disturbances of the 1960s, when newspaper coverage was criticized by the Kerner Commission and others. The researchers noted that the nature of crisis coverage is important because media accounts of crisis situations have a significant influence on the public's perception of the situation, and the public depend upon the media to help them develop informed opinion about important issues.[265]

One pair of researchers who studied the *Los Angeles Times*' coverage of the riot noted that almost 42 percent of the paper's coverage focused on the "dramatic and deadly violence" of the riot. They cited what has become a truism in analysis of journalistic communication—that news reports focus on surface violence but largely ignore the historical context and the underlying social, political, and economic causes. One critic noted that the conditions identified as the causes of the urban riots of the 1960s had worsened by the time the L.A. riots took place. But the *Los Angeles Times* seemed to do slightly better in covering the causes of this riot than it and other papers studied had done in covering the causes of the 1960s riots, the authors stated.[266]

Another researcher came to a different conclusion by using a different method of analysis when she studied the *Los Angeles Times*' coverage of the 1992 riot as compared to its coverage of the 1965 riot in the Watts section of Los Angeles. She found that the newspaper presented the 1992 riot from the view of police, government, and other institutional sources almost as much as it had in 1965. This meant that African Americans were given no more opportunity than in 1965 to express their side of the story, "whether that side was an explanation for why they were looting, what they were upset about, or was a condemnation of the looting and violence" of others. The researcher noted that African Americans and Latinos accounted for 30 and 37 percent, respectively, of those arrested during the riots. She also noted that the police sources used in the 1992 articles were ones that put the police on the defensive.[267]

Her study also found that the explanation of the causes of the riot, such as poverty, segregation, poor educational and employment opportunities, and poor relations with police, was even smaller in the 1992 than in the 1965 coverage.[268]

In addition, the study found in the 1992 coverage much more focus on violence against individuals, notably against Reginald Denny, whose beating was filmed by a helicopter crew, and a white man who was pulled off his motorcycle and killed while on his way to help a black friend start her van. But the stories of other victims were missing, the author said. "An emphasis on white victims is curious," the researcher wrote, because only ten of the fifty-eight persons killed in the riot were white. Of the other victims, twenty-five were black and nineteen were Latino, "but these deaths received almost no attention from the *Times*."[269] Focusing on the stories of white victims and ignoring black victims were also observed in the television news coverage of the 1980 riot in Miami and in general newspaper coverage of crime victims.

The study found that conflict between African Americans and Koreans was mentioned often, with frequent reference to an earlier court decision in which a Korean-American store owner was placed on probation and fined $500 after being convicted of fatally shooting a fifteen-year-old black girl who allegedly attempted to shoplift an item from the store.[270] After the riot, black journalists charged that the white news media exaggerated the conflict between African Americans and Korean Americans while downplaying the involvement of whites and Latinos in the riot.[271]

In addition, the researcher concluded that no more information about the conflict between the African-American community and police was presented by the *Los Angeles Times* in 1992 than in 1965, but the kind of information presented did change. In 1965 the coverage usually gave the police the benefit of the doubt; in 1992, the LAPD "was shown no mercy" by the *Times*. The paper gave prominent coverage to the fact that the police abandoned the riot area when violence first broke out and did not return for hours, despite live television coverage showing motorists being pulled from their cars and beaten. In fact, three of the four people who saved Denny's life said they saw the beating on television and went into the street to rescue him when it became obvious that police were not going to respond.[272]

Broadcast Coverage

Research on the presence of African Americans in television news during the 1970s reveals that blacks were more likely to be portrayed negatively, more likely not to be speaking, more likely to be seen in blue-collar jobs, more likely to appear in stories about traditionally "black issues," and more likely to be seen as criminals and victims.[273] In addition, stories reported by minority newscasters generally dealt with minority problems; minority men in the news were usually criminals or public figures; and nonwhite women in the news usually were experiencing some economic deprivation.[274] Another study, which compared professional football announcers' comments about black and white players, found that blacks received more unfavorable comments than whites. Also, of the players described as unprofessional in their behavior, all were black.[275]

In 1978, Max Robinson became the first black anchor on a national network.

He anchored from the national desk for "ABC World News Tonight" from Chicago. Optimism also grew among blacks when a black ownership group put WGPR-TV (UHF) on the air in Detroit in 1975.[276] The station was subsequently sold to CBS in 1995. One author suggests that WGPR-TV won the distinction of being the first black-owned television station in the continental United States but lost the battle to provide different programming.[277] The owners were unable to produce many shows or to find enough reruns of network shows with positive messages about blacks.

In 1977 ABC presented the miniseries "Roots." Based on Alex Haley's book, *Roots*, the programs reached nearly 38 million people. The series triggered articles in most major newspapers and portrayed blacks as positive protagonists of indomitable spirit. Subsequent network series showcased "A Woman Called Moses" on NBC starring Cicely Tyson as Harriet Tubman in 1978; "Paul Robeson," a one-man show starring James Earl Jones on PBS in 1979; and the four-hour historical drama "Freedom Road," starring Muhammad Ali as Gideon Jackson, a former slave who became a U.S. senator. The year 1979 also brought one of the most talked-about shows on race relations, "Blacks in America: With All Deliberate Speed?" hosted by Ed Bradley on CBS. The show examined twenty-five years of desegregation efforts.

California Newsreels created a documentary in 1985 of four local Miami television stations' coverage of the 1980 riot there after the acquittal of the policemen who had beaten a black man to death. They found that the stations had failed to provide a context for the black community's rage, except for three minutes of background shown several days into the riot. Also, although blacks bore the brunt of the violence, the television newscasts focused on white people killed, white people beaten, and white store owners whose stores were looted or destroyed.[278]

A 1991 California Newsreel documentary, "Color Adjustment," exposed a pattern of racism in television entertainment and news programs from the 1950s through the 1980s. Director Marlon Riggs showed that black actors continued to be cast in minor and demeaning roles throughout this period. The exception in the 1980s was the "Cosby Show," a comedy about a black upper middle-class family of two professional parents and five children that presented them in a positive, realistic context. In January 1985, CBS presented "The Vanishing Family: Crisis in Black America." One author commented that the title of the program suggested that normal everyday life was defined by stable nuclear families. Missing was a recognition that families and communities throughout the country were in the midst of a significant transformation. [279]

The first six parts of "Eyes on the Prize—America's Civil Rights Years" aired on PBS in 1987. The series detailed the events and spirit of the civil rights struggles in America from 1954 to 1965. The final eight parts, "Eyes on the Prize II," aired in 1990 on PBS. The award-winning programs from Blacksides Productions showed the courage and strength of blacks and allowed many viewers to put the civil rights struggle in better perspective for the first time. Each segment highlighted a different development, including the formation of the Black Panthers and the assassinations of Malcolm X and Dr. Martin Luther King.

A 1991 documentary called "Drugs in Black and White," produced by PBS, stated that contrary to the public perception of drug use as an inner-city problem, statistics from national drug institutes indicate that drug use among whites in suburbs and rural areas is twice as high as drug use among African Americans in inner cities. The reason the public believes just the opposite, the documentary said, is that filming drug use among poor blacks on city streets is easy to do; as one television reporter said, "That's where you get the picture." Conversely, filming drug use among whites at private suburban parties is not possible. But the images people see on television get burned into their minds and convince them the drug problem is a black urban problem.[280] One Latino reporter observed, "If you want to get on the air, you go after drug addicts in Central Park, who are minorities. Don't show the ones on Wall Street, who are white."[281]

In the television as in the newspaper industry, people of color were largely unrepresented in positions of authority in the 1980s. Various reports noted that although some minority journalists had been hired for highly visible reporter and anchor positions, they were not in positions to affect news play and content, and the commitment to hire and promote minorities was eroding.[282]

A study of the television news coverage of the 1992 Los Angeles riot found that it focused on the involvement of African Americans as rioters and Koreans and whites as victims, but it significantly downplayed the roles of Latinos, who constituted more than half of the rioters arrested and about one-third of the store owners who lost property in the riot. Also, the study found that the three networks' coverage included substantial commentary on social issues, while local stations "focused almost exclusively on discrete episodes of violence and the restoration of law and order."[283]

1992 LOS ANGELES UPRISING TO PRESIDENTIAL ELECTION, NOVEMBER 1996

Several journalism scholars have noted since the Los Angeles riot that despite the disappearance of overt racism in news coverage and the steady increase in the number of minority reporters in white-owned media, the news media still project inaccurate and demeaning myths about minority groups in this country and reinforce and perpetuate popular "knowledge" about them that is seldom grounded in reality. Two scholars observed that members of these minority groups, as well as society at large, form judgments and act on this "knowledge." "It is a dangerous, divisive and wasteful world that the media create."[284]Another communications scholar suggests that news media portrayal of African Americans contributes to racist police practices and to racism among judges and juries that leads to higher bail, stiffer sentences, and higher rates of incarceration for African Americans than for whites accused of similar crimes.[285]

One black journalist stated, "The news industry is continuing to give to most Americans a negative, distorted concept of people of color and—by extension— racial and ethnic diversity." Like many other journalism scholars, minority journalists, and news executives, she urged a more accurate portrayal of people of color by all journalists, including white ones, and continued commitment to the hiring of minority journalists, despite the "diversity backlash" being reported by media executives.[286] Some progress was evident in the hiring area; by 1996, about 10.5 percent of newspaper newsroom employees were people of color.

Several writers noted during the 1990s that white politicians and members of the public blamed the nation's economic woes on "welfare queens" and "illegal immigrants," scapegoats who appeared frequently in the 1994 congressional elections and the 1996 presidential campaign.[287] The media give wide dissemination to these claims and charges.

Meanwhile, the actions of business, which have a much greater negative impact on the nation's economy, seem to go largely uncriticized in these same media—the rate at which businesses are moving their manufacturing or their purchase of raw materials to foreign countries, or investing heavily in other countries, or laying people off in corporate downsizing to maximize profits for stockholders and CEOs.[288]

Journalist Roger Wilkins pointed out that the industrial manufacturing jobs that once enabled unskilled African Americans and European immigrants to enter the economy are disappearing. An economist stated that the nation lost two million such jobs in the 1980s.[289] These losses were particularly devastating to African Americans. An urban sociologist estimated that seventy thousand manufacturing jobs disappeared from Watts and South Central Los Angeles in the five years between 1978 and 1983. When the 1992 L.A. riots occurred, black male unemployment in the area was around 40 percent.[290] Also, the majority of new jobs in the past two decades in metropolitan areas have been created outside the central city where most poor black Americans live.[291]

Despite the belief of many white Americans that discrimination in employment has disappeared under the influence of affirmative action, the economic situation of African Americans still is not nearly equal to that of whites. For example, the 1990 census indicated that black family income was still between 55 to 60 percent of white family income, where it has been since the 1950s.[292] By the mid-1990s, African Americans were still less likely than whites to hold the better-paid managerial, professional, technical, sales, and crafts positions. In the early 1990s, the Urban Institute sent comparably qualified African American and white applicants to the same employers to apply for jobs. Over one-fifth of the black applicants experienced discrimination at this entry stage.[293]

At the other end of the economic scale, in the mid-1990s, one-third of the nation's 30 million black Americans were living in poverty, and African Americans were three times more likely than whites to live below the poverty line. Low-income blacks were more likely to be laid off in times of recession than were white Americans and were less likely than poor whites to get unemployment when they were laid off.[294]

Yet white people were nearly as ignorant of these economic and racial realities in the early 1990s as they had been in 1967, when 75 percent of whites responded in a Gallup poll that they did not believe that black people were treated any differently than whites. In the early 1990s, polls conducted by both the *Los Angeles Times* and the Associated Press found that 60 percent of whites did not believe that racial discrimination was the main reason blacks had worse jobs, income, and housing than whites but believed that blacks had the same opportunities as whites.[295] The reason for such amazing ignorance among whites lies largely where it did twenty-five years earlier. Because residential segregation has been so firmly entrenched in this country, which has resulted in segregated schools, and because of long-standing discrimination in hiring, most white people do not know much about the lives of African Americans other than what they read in the newspaper or see on television. And the news media continue to deny the existence of white racism in everyday life. They also ignore evidence of white discrimination against people of color and focus on pathology in poor black communities, sending the message that all problems faced by black people are due to black laziness and criminality. Portrayals of blacks in the entertainment media, both television and movies, largely reinforce white stereotypes of blacks.

Meanwhile, many white Americans continue to cling to their stereotypical beliefs about African Americans, and these too are reinforced by news coverage that focuses on black pathology. A nationwide survey in 1992 found that 38 percent of white respondents felt that African Americans were more prone to violence than people of other races; 35 percent felt that blacks preferred welfare over work; 13 percent believed that blacks were less intelligent than people of other races. In addition, a 1994 Times-Mirror national survey found that 51 percent of whites agree that equal rights have been pushed too far in the United States. In similar surveys, a majority of whites said they felt black Americans were too demanding, paranoid, and pushy. One scholar defines "modern racism" as the white view that black Americans are making unreasonable demands for changes.[296]

Ignored in nearly all discussions of such matters is the extent to which whites have benefited from two centuries of slavery and another century of legalized oppression of African Americans in the North as well as the South. Wilkins noted that by the end of the Civil War, the belief in black inferiority "had become a foundation stone of U.S. culture." Whites have amassed generations of advantage in the accumulation of education, wealth, employment, and the practice of reserving the best opportunities for themselves and for European immigrants.[297]

Wilkins stated in 1992 that for only twenty-seven of the previous 373 years, ever since Africans were brought to the American colonies, "have we had something other than slavery or legal and cultural racial subordination." He added,

"The habits of racism that built up over these centuries are tenacious; they haven't died. The most powerful habit is that of defining blacks for the convenience and profit of whites."[298]

The news media, of course, have played and still play a large role in reinforcing those definitions. In 1995 the National Association of Black Journalists charged that newspaper reporters and headline writers have helped created confusion over affirmative action, using words like "bias benefit" and "preferences" that confused readers about the issues. The organization's media-watch project revealed that many newspapers had picked up words used by opponents of affirmative action and employed these terms in reporting on affirmative action.[299]

Early in 1996 the federal court that covers Texas, Louisiana, and Mississippi ruled that the University of Texas law school could not use different admission standards for minority applicants than it does for whites. *Time* noted that the decision was "a frontal assault on the current law of the land" decided in the 1978 Bakke decision, which prohibits quotas but allows schools to consider race as a factor in college applications.[300]

The court decision was an excellent example of institutional racism, which accepts practices giving preferences to whites as business as usual but criticizes as racist any attempt to create opportunities for minorities. After the decision, minority groups argued that screening for special skills or family connections amounts to affirmative action for white students. In an instance of newspapers helping to *clarify* affirmative action issues, the *Los Angeles Times* reported that UCLA routinely gives preference to the children of "major donor prospects," admitting rich students over thousands of applicants with higher grades. Other newspapers reported that several University of California regents—including Governor Pete Wilson—who had voted to end affirmative action had used their influence to get the children of relatives, friends, and business partners into the college of their choice. One University of Texas student leader said, "Affirmative action is not a handout. It's an opportunity. The window of opportunity has only been open for 20 years. Discrimination has existed for 300 years."[301]

The new threat to affirmative action admissions is made worse by the fact that in 1996, forty-two years after the *Brown v. Topeka* Supreme Court decision declared that segregated public schools were inherently unequal, most children of color still do not have equal educational opportunities. Since the 1980s, when the Reagan and Bush administrations opposed mandatory school desegregation and cut back programs to aid schoolchildren of color, resegregation has occurred in many public schools. In 1996 two-thirds of black students attended schools that were predominantly nonwhite. The most intensely segregated schools were those in central cities; schools that had the highest proportion of black students also had the highest rates of poverty.[302]

In addition, programs that will further victimize poor children of color have been political rallying cries frequently voiced in the 1994 Republican Contract with America and also by Democratic leaders. In the past several years, politi-

cians have found instant voter approval by attacking welfare, school lunch programs, Aid to Families with Dependent Children, Head Start programs,
educational enhancement programs for inner-city schools, job training projects,
and any other government program aimed at helping a segment of the population
popularly supposed to be loafing on welfare and bleeding the government dry.
Several commentators have noted, however, that the job market has collapsed
under the urban poor, and none of the politicians, scholars, and journalists "now
obsessed with bad black behavior and welfare reform has lifted a finger to pull
them back into the economy."[303]

Many African Americans see white racism behind the considerations that the
white-dominated government and voters apply to questions of what is worth
funding. They point out that the government seems willing to waste billions of
dollars on the military in multimillion-dollar bombers that will never be used,
in gigantic cost overruns, even on $45 wrenches and $200 toilet seats. And
Congress and recent administrations will fund welfare to the well off in the form
of tax breaks for businesses and the rich and junk bond takeovers. But they will
spend no money on the inner cities, where many of the black poor live, and
they want to save money by cutting programs for school lunches, Head Start,
Aid to Families with Dependent Children, and enhanced educational programs
for inner-city schools—all the programs that can help prevent the development
of another generation of impoverished and alienated juveniles who become criminals. One observer commented on the irony of a public and politicians so concerned with black crime but oblivious to the fact that the cuts they are proposing
and enacting will result in the suffering and death of poor black children.[304]

The politicians and public, of course, do not intend to attack these children,
but their parents, who are seen as lazy, parasitic, and criminal. Oddly enough,
several in-depth accounts of poor black people written by minority journalists
in 1994 may have helped strengthen that perception. Leon Dash, an acclaimed
African-American reporter for the *Washington Post*, won a Pulitzer Prize for his
eight-part series on an impoverished black woman who used heroin, sold drugs
and stole to feed her children, sold her eleven-year-old daughter into prostitution,
and supported her adult children's drug habits with her welfare checks. Dash
said he wrote the series to shed light on a crisis, but many readers objected that
he had put so much effort into depicting a highly dysfunctional black family,
thereby reaffirming the views many whites have of blacks in Washington,
D.C.[305]

A journalism scholar analyzed another in-depth series, this one written by an
African-American journalist for the *New York Times* and focused on a single
block in Harlem. The three-part series, presumably portraying an entire urban
community, was presented completely through personal profiles of such people
as an eighteen-year-old college student, an unemployed and unwed teenage
mother, a thirteen-year-old drug dealer, and a welfare mother. The scholar contended that, although some features of language and presentation gave the series

a compassionate air, in the end it made these people into objects who are symptoms of social problems and reinforced stereotypical conceptions of urban blacks. Also, the scholar stated, by omitting historical context, demographic data, and the subjects' own comments on larger social life, the series failed to report clear signs of social cohesion and self-help attempts made in the neighborhood.[306]

Another journalism scholar analyzed the media representations of boxer George Foreman and concluded that both Foreman and the media have constructed for him a Sambo image that reinforces racist views of African Americans. "Foreman has managed to tap into the American racial memory and pull out a personality that conforms nicely to past stereotypes of the African-American male as a lazy, carefree, subservient buffoon." The media have cooperated in the creation of this image, which is a nonthreatening one for white Americans. He believes that this image, plus Foreman's role as a prize fighter, accounts for Foreman's continued phenomenal popularity and marketability in the more than twenty-five years since he won the heavyweight title.[307]

In the summer of 1994, football hero and actor O.J. Simpson was arrested and charged with the brutal murder of his ex-wife and her friend. The situation tapped into the 100-year-old black experience of thousands of black men falsely accused and lynched, or given an unfair trial and sentenced to imprisonment or death by all-white juries and racist white judges. For many African Americans, it aroused the same memories and emotions as were activated by the Marion Barry trial and to some extent the Mike Tyson trial. White Americans, largely ignorant or forgetful of the almost universally negative nature of black men's experience with police and the criminal justice system, focused primarily on the nature of the evidence and the occasionally sensational revelations of the trial.

The black press routinely focused on Simpson's race because, as one black publisher stated, "Black folks are sympathetic to any black folks caught in the criminal justice system, because it is a racist system." Noticeably absent from the black media debate on Simpson and the case, one account said, was the possibility that Simpson might be guilty. Within hours of the killings, the source wrote, many African Americans were convinced that the police and the white media were working together to bring Simpson down.[308]

Another source noted that African-American and white reactions to the verdict illustrated vividly the bipolar views the races hold about the nation's criminal justice system. According to an ABC-TV poll, 63 percent of whites felt that a black man who was clearly guilty of murdering two whites (based on the televised trial evidence) was found not guilty by a predominantly black jury. In contrast, the poll revealed that 83 percent of black respondents felt that a justice system that whites had never questioned "when it was killing, maiming and framing blacks," one source said, "had finally had its comeuppance."[309]

Early 1995 saw the beginning of a long series of burnings of black churches in the South; by the end of 1996, over seventy had been burned. Perhaps not surprisingly, since the U.S. government is a microcosm of American society just as media newsrooms are, the initial response by federal investigators from the FBI and Alcohol, Tobacco and Firearms agencies was tinged with racism, according to black pastors and church members. Ignoring the recent upsurge in vocal outpourings of antiblack hate groups in the United States and the KKK's long history of burning black churches as an intimidation tactic, the investigators failed to pursue vigorously the possibility that the fires had been set by white hate groups, according to the black victims. Instead, they said, the investigators tended to suspect and harass black pastors and congregations for the burnings.[310]

In mid-1996, after congressional hearings were held on the investigators' behavior and some congressional action was taken to help rebuild the churches, the investigative situation apparently improved. An FBI official still noted the difficulty of conducting an investigation when numerous groups are suspect. What was difficult and unnerving, he said, "is the fact that what we're facing isn't a national conspiracy but a mind-set of a large segment of our society."[311] Less well publicized was the fact that, by the end of 1996, only 20 percent of the persons arrested and convicted for church burnings were motivated by racial hatred; other motives were religious hatred and financial gain. Also seldom reported was the fact that an equal number of white churches had been burned in the South during the same time period.[312]

In October 1995 the controversial Nation of Islam leader Louis Farrakhan organized the Million Man March that brought over 600,000 black men to Washington, D.C., for a day of unity. Although the event attracted at least three times as many people to the capital as had the much-heralded March on Washington in 1963, the significance of the event was not very much analyzed and commented upon afterward in the white media. At the time, authorities seemed unable to determine how many people attended, although by a week after the event the official number was given as 600,000 and perhaps more. Black media used the figure of a million. Whatever the number, it was obviously one of the largest groups ever to assemble in Washington, and the event was clearly significant. But the white media seemed disinclined to seek out that significance; coverage and commentary seemed instead to focus on the controversial nature of Farrakhan's remarks. Commentators in the black media expressed a range of opinions, but the predominant theme seemed to be that the participants had gathered for a day of unity, mutual reinforcement, and a renewal of commitment to themselves, their race, and their families.[313]

Broadcast Coverage

Studies of television news portrayals of African Americans indicate that television seems to prefer the coverage and discussion of crime. In late 1993, ABC News presented a special, "Viewpoint: Crime, Violence and TV News." Ted

Koppel and his guests asked if blacks are overrepresented as violent criminals and what can be done differently to present a more accurate portrayal of blacks. Writer Ishmael Reed complained that news about blacks features black pathology but is conspicuously silent on the pathology of whites. Reed insisted, "Though television networks run footage of black small-time drug dealers all day, seldom do they carry stories about money laundering, presumably because the banks are some of the principal stockholders of the networks." [314]

The 1994 O.J. Simpson case revealed the black-white dichotomy in U.S. society. Blacks tended to think that Simpson was innocent, while the overwhelming majority of whites polled thought he was guilty. The televised trial, which lasted nearly a year, provided daily fare for television stations around the world and attracted uprecedented media attention. It commanded such attention partly because it embodied so many traditionally divisive racial images: Simpson, a *wealthy black sports figure* married to *a white woman*, was accused of *using a knife to violently kill her* and her friend, *a white man*. The televised proceedings illustrated clearly the differences between the experiences of black and white Americans, even if they did not promote greater understanding. One hundred and fifty million people watched the announcement of the not-guilty verdict from a predominantly black jury. Many hours of analysis followed as people found it difficult to accept the jury's decision. Simpson was later found liable for violating the victims' civil rights and ordered to pay millions of dollars to their families.

A thirteen-month study of a large-market television news station demonstrated that local news programs are significantly distorted in two respects: they project the ideas that crime is violent and criminals are black. In effect, viewers are "primed" to consider crime through the lens of their racial stereotypes. And, although the home city of the station includes a larger number of Hispanics than blacks, the news producers prefer to present crime as a black-and-white issue.[315]

The broadcasting industry lacks diversity among its decision-makers. Studies of the employment of African Americans in broadcasting revealed that in 1995 blacks held only 9 percent of the jobs in television, down from 10.1 percent the previous year, and 6 percent of those in radio. In 1995 African Americans accounted for only 1 percent of news directors in television and 5 percent of those in radio.[316] Increased numbers of nonwhites in these positions could improve the coverage of minorities.

Scholar Robert Entman analyzed crime and political stories in the evening news on four Chicago television stations. He found the names of African Americans accused of crime were less likely to be provided than those of white suspects, thus making the black accused seem less a person and more a representative of a category of persons outside the white viewers' own group. Also, African-American suspects were less likely to be shown in motion than white ones, thus making them seem less individual. In addition, black suspects were less likely than whites to be shown well dressed and more likely to be shown in jail clothing. Finally, African Americans were more likely to be shown being physically grasped by police than white suspects. All these findings, Entman said, contributed to a picture of black suspects as being less individualized, less human, and more dangerous than white ones.[317]

In his analysis of the portrayal of African Americans in political stories, Entman said, "News about blacks who acted politically conveyed the notion that they spoke and behaved more than whites to advance 'special interests' against the public interest."[318] Later, in an analysis of television network news, Entman reported that the networks presented more stereotypical impressions and a narrower range of positive roles for blacks than for whites. In political stories, whites were more often shown championing either or both sides, but blacks were more likely to be seen complaining about something. Black political leaders were seen most often in connection with criminal activity.[319]

In another study, Entman noted that Caucasian suspects tended to be filmed with their attorneys, while minority suspects were typically shown being handcuffed and taken into custody. He also found that a prodefense sound bite was included three times more often when the accused was white. Thus the black suspects were depersonalized and shown as being more dangerous and violent than the white ones. Entman concluded that the overall image of crime and violence in local news was one in which minorities, especially blacks, played a large role in causing violence, but contributed disproportionately little toward helping society cope with it.[320]

Some researchers have discussed the prevalence of stereotypes in the news as a reflection of myths that whites hold about nonwhites. The news product, then, may not be the result of racism among journalists, editors, and producers; instead, news about nonwhites may be created out of what white journalists believe is true about "them."

Christopher P. Campbell examined local television newscasts from twenty-nine cities across the country for coverage of events surrounding the Martin Luther King holiday in January 1993, and also studied newspaper coverage of the events in five of the cities. The 900 stories examined showed overwhelmingly white news sources; African Americans were usually seen in crime or sports stories. Campbell noted that the coverage reflected a picture of nonwhite Americans as different from white Americans. The limited coverage of African Americans provided encouraged white viewers to retain the myth that all blacks act and react like the few who appear on television.

Campbell concluded that racist stereotyping had persisted in local television news coverage in the 1990s. The stereotypes were not as blatant as their predecessors; rather than minstrels and Sambos, viewers saw a more subtle mythology about minority life that was the product of majority culture stereotypes inadvertently communicated by journalists.[321]

CONCLUSION

Press Coverage

In summary, over the time period addressed in this study, newspaper coverage of African Americans has clearly improved. From ignoring black citizens or printing only negative news about them through the 1940s, the press provided illuminating and largely sympathetic accounts of the Civil Rights Movement in the 1950s and 1960s. Since then newspapers have provided much more coverage, and more complete and representative coverage, of African Americans and their improved position in society. In addition, they have slowly hired more minority reporters, from about 2 percent in the early 1970s to 11.5 percent in 1996, and these reporters are providing increased coverage of minority issues and situations to their newspapers.

However, partly because of deeply ingrained prejudices, newspaper coverage still seems to focus on black pathology, to ignore severe problems facing African Americans, and to provide biased and misleading coverage of such issues as affirmative action, school resegregation, and welfare. Newspapers also seem to focus on the pathology but to ignore the plight of poor blacks in the inner cities, where the situation is worse now than it was in 1968 when the Kerner Commission criticized the news media for ignoring the frustrations and "justifiable rage" of poor urban blacks. The papers have come a long way, but the staggeringly tenacious hold that stereotypes of African Americans have on white perceptions still controls coverage to a large extent. Until these stereotypes are abandoned, white-owned media cannot begin to provide accurate coverage that will help interpret the various segments of American society to each other and help close the widening black-white schism in this nation.

News executives also need to guard more carefully against letting their media be used by white politicians pandering to racist fears, government officials seeking to cast suspicion on the integrity of African-American politicians and other black leaders, and racist and nativist groups seeking to blame the country's woes on poor people of color and immigrants. They also need to remember that they are, as the Kerner Commission stated, looking at the world out of white men's eyes and thus need to seek out the views and the knowledge of people unlike them. Perhaps most of all, they need to realize that the press plays a vitally important role in the relations between the races, whether it desires such a role or not. Newspapers can help promote stereotypes, reinforce prejudices, and fail to make the reality of minority life understandable to the white majority, as they have done until the past several decades. Or they can help to expose the truth about the stereotypes, can present facts about issues like affirmative action and welfare rather than just parroting the arguments of opponents, and can promote understanding between racial groups. Martin Luther King once said, "We must learn to live together as brothers or we will perish together as fools." One of the few institutions in the nation with the resources and power to help the races learn to live together as brothers is the news media.

Broadcast Coverage

The daily parade of shackled black prisoners on television news paints a picture of blacks as violent and threatening toward whites, self-interested and demanding toward society—continually causing problems for the law-abiding tax-paying majority. [322] And since journalists belong to this tax-paying group, it would be naive to assume they are not affected by the images too. By their professional judgments, the gatekeepers of news project how consequential minorities are to American society and determine the ways in which they are interpreted to the majority audience. When covering stories about black individuals, journalists may not merely be reporting a single newsworthy event in which a black person happens to be involved. Instead, they effectively may be defining blacks for millions of whites.

A group of researchers looked at the effects of heavy exposure to 1985–86 entertainment and news programs. Findings indicated that greater exposure to television entertainment was associated with beliefs that black Americans enjoyed a relatively higher socioeconomic position than they did in reality, while higher exposure to television news was associated with perceptions that black Americans were relatively worse off in income, social class, and educational achievement than they actually were.[323]

Most Americans get their news and derive their image of black people from television. So they tend to believe, in spite of the facts, that blacks are more violent, less patriotic, more emotional, less intelligent, more athletic, less likely to care for their children, less well educated, and less financially responsible—in sum, more of a problem than a solution in America. This image of African Americans deprives the nation of the richness of diversity and the rewards that can come only from the unique perspective of African-American experiences.

NOTES

Many of the works cited in these notes are research papers presented at conventions of the Association for Education in Journalism and Mass Communication (AEJMC). To save space, the organization will be referred to by its acronym in these notes.

1. Bill Gaskins, "The World according to Life: Racial Stereotyping and American Identity," Afterimage 21, no. 3 (Summer 1993), 14.

2. Joseph Boskin, "Denials: The Media View of Dark Skins and the City," in Small Voices and Great Trumpets: Minorities and the Media, ed. Bernard Rubin (New York: Praeger, 1980), 141–43.

3. From Andrew Hacker, Two Nations: Separate, Hostile and Unequal, quoted in Roger Wilkins, "White Out," Mother Jones 17, no. 5 (November/December 1992), 47.

4. Benjamin Quarles, The Negro in the Making of America (New York: Simon and Schuster, 1966), 18.

5. Ibid., 44.

6. Winthrop Jordan, *White over Black: American Attitudes toward the Negro, 1550–1812* (Chapel Hill: University of North Carolina Press, 1968), 53.

7. Ibid.

8. Joe R. Feagin and Clairece Booher Feagin, "African Americans," in *Racial and Ethnic Relations*, 5th ed. (Upper Saddle River, N.J.: Prentice-Hall, 1996), 237.

9. See Herbert Aptheker, "The Quakers and Negro Slavery," *Journal of Negro History* 25, no. 3 (July 1940), 331 ff.

10. Charles Nichols, *Many Thousand Gone* (Bloomington: Indiana University Press, 1963), 73.

11. Frederic Bancroft, *Slave Trading in the Old South* (Baltimore: J. H. Furst, 1931), 198.

12. Quarles, *The Negro*, 79.

13. Martin Dann, *The Black Press 1827–1890* (New York: G. P. Putnam's Sons, 1971), 34.

14. William H. Wiggins, *O Freedom!: Afro-American Emancipation Celebrations* (Knoxville: University of Tennessee Press, 1987).

15. Quarles, *The Negro*, 154.

16. Ibid., 155.

17. Ibid.

18. David Domke, "Whither the Fourteenth Amendment? The Implications of a 'Let the Negroes Take Care of Themselves' Policy in the Press" (Paper presented at AEJMC convention, Washington, D.C., August 20, 1995).

19. Quarles, *The Negro*, 166.

20. Jean Folkerts and Dwight Teeter, Jr., *Voices of a Nation: A History of Mass Media in the United States*, 2d ed. (New York: Macmillan, 1994), 231.

21. Donald Drake, "Militancy in Fortune's New York Age," *Journal of Negro History* 55 (October 1970), 309.

22. David Domke, "African Americans and 'Delusive Theories of Equality and Fraternity': The Role of the Press in the Institutionalization of Racial Inequality" (Paper presented at AEJMC convention, Atlanta, August 1994).

23. David Domke, " 'Unfortunate to Say the Least': The Press, Social Change and the Nadir of African Americans" (Paper presented at AEJMC convention, Washington, D.C., August 1995), 17.

24. Folkerts and Teeter, *Voices of a Nation*, 292.

25. Elliot Rudwick, "DuBois versus Garvey: Race Propagandists at War," in *Promises to Keep*, ed. Bruce Glasrud and Alan Smith (Chicago: Rand McNally, 1972), 277.

26. Quarles, *The Negro*, 227.

27. James McPherson, Laurence Holland, James Banner, Jr., Nancy Weiss, and Michael Bell, eds. *Blacks in America* (Garden City, N.Y.: Anchor Books, 1972).

28. See Nathan Huggins, *Harlem Renaissance* (New York: Oxford University Press, 1971).

29. Alain Locke, *The New Negro: An Interpretation* (New York: Arno Press, 1968).

30. See Warren Brown, *Checklist of Negro Newspapers in the United States 1827–1946* (Jefferson City, Mo.: Lincoln University School of Journalism 1946). McPherson et al. list in *Blacks in America* wonderful sources for further research of black newspapers and their courageous and ingenious editors. Jannette Dates and William Barlow include

a good chapter on the black press in *Split Image: African Americans and the Mass Media* (Washington, D.C.: Howard University Press, 1994). See also Dann, *The Black Press.*

31. See George Simpson, *The Negro in the Philadelphia Press* (Philadelphia: University of Pennsylvania Press, 1936); Noel Gist, "The Negro in the Daily Press," *Social Forces* 10, no. 3 (March 1932); Chicago Commission on Race Relations, *The Negro in Chicago* (Chicago: University of Chicago Press, 1923); Selma Warlick, "Negro News in the Southern Press" (Master's thesis, Columbia University, 1931).

32. Dates and Barlow, *Split Image,* 176.

33. "Black Radio: In the Beginning" (Program no. 1) (Washington, D.C.: Smithsonian Institution, 1996).

34. Arnold Shankman, "Black Pride and Protest: The Amos 'n' Andy Crusade," *Journal of Popular Culture* 12, no. 2 (1979), 240.

35. Dates and Barlow, *Split Image,* 188.

36. C. T. Vivian (Speech delivered at 3rd National Conference on Racial and Ethnic Relations in American Higher Education, Santa Fe, New Mexico, June 1990).

37. P. L. Prattis, "Race Relations and the Negro Press," *Phylon* 14 (December 1953), 378.

38. John Hope Franklin, *From Slavery to Freedom: A History of Negro Americans,* 3d ed. (New York: Vintage Books, 1969), 496.

39. Ibid., 496–97.

40. Prattis, "Race Relations and the Negro Press," 374.

41. William J. Leonhirth, "The Civil Rights Movement in the 1940s: A Communication Context" (Paper presented at AEJMC convention, Atlanta, August 1994), 9.

42. Leonard Ray Teel, "Seeking an 'American Gandhi': Black Press Opinion in the Early 1930s" (Paper presented at AEJMC convention, Minneapolis, August 1990), 11.

43. Franklin, *From Slavery to Freedom,* 547.

44. Prattis, "Race Relations and the Negro Press," 374.

45. Ibid., 377.

46. Florence Rebekah Beatty-Brown, "The Negro as Portrayed by the St. Louis *Post-Dispatch* from 1920 to 1950" (Ph.D. diss., University of Illinois at Urbana-Champaign, 1951), 10.

47. Ibid., 11.

48. Paula B. Johnson, David O. Sears, and John B. McConahay, "Black Invisibility, the Press and the Los Angeles Riot," *American Journal of Sociology* 76, no. 4 (January 1971), 706–7.

49. Gaskins, "The World According to *Life,*" 14–15.

50. Beatty-Brown, "The Negro as Portrayed," 294.

51. Franklin, *From Slavery to Freedom,* 530–34.

52. Ibid., 540–45.

53. Lee Finkle, "The Conservative Aims of Militant Rhetoric: Black Protest during World War II," *Journal of American History* 60 (December 1973), 707.

54. Franklin, *From Slavery to Freedom,* 599.

55. Finkle, "The Conservative Aims," 704.

56. Ibid., 693–94, 710.

57. Ibid., 696.

58. See Patrick Washburn, *A Question of Sedition: The Federal Government's Investigation of the Black Press during World War II* (New York: Oxford University Press, 1986), 8, 167.

59. Finkle, "The Conservative Aims," 698–99.

60. Franklin, *From Slavery to Freedom*, 581–85.

61. Ibid., 586, 590–91.

62. Mary Alice Sentman, "Black and White: Disparity in Coverage by *Life* Magazine from 1937 to 1972," *Journalism Quarterly* 60, no. 3 (Autumn 1983), 507.

63. William Brower, "The Black War Correspondents," *Media History Digest* 1, no. 1 (Fall 1980), 47, 49.

64. Franklin, *From Slavery to Freedom*, 585, 587, 588.

65. John D. Stevens, "Black Correspondents of World War II Cover the Supply Routes," *Journal of Negro History* 57 (October 1972), 395.

66. Ibid., 398–401.

67. Ibid., 395–97.

68. Franklin, *From Slavery to Freedom*, 589–90.

69. Finkle, "The Conservative Aims," 699–700; Leonhirth, "The Civil Rights Movement," 11.

70. Leonhirth, "The Civil Rights Movement," 21.

71. Ibid., 6, 24.

72. Ibid., 7–8, 22.

73. "Black Radio: In the Beginning," (Program no. 2) (Washington, D.C.: Smithsonian Institution, 1996).

74. William G. Kelley, "Jackie Robinson and the Press," *Journalism Quarterly* 53 (Spring 1976), 138.

75. Ibid., 138–39.

76. Ibid.

77. Chris Lamb and Glen Bleske, "A Different Story: How the Press Covered Baseball's First Integrated Spring Training" (Paper presented at AEJMC convention, Anaheim, California, August 1996), 1, 24.

78. Pat Washburn, "New York Newspapers and Robinson's First Season," *Journalism Quarterly* 58 (Winter 1981), 641–43.

79. Ibid., 643.

80. Helen Louise Tatro, "Local News Coverage of Blacks in Five Deep South Newspapers, 1950 to 1970," *Journalism Abstracts* 10 (1972), 336.

81. Paul Martin Lester, "African-American Photo Coverage in Four U.S. Newspapers, 1937–1990" (Paper presented at AEJMC convention, Montreal, Quebec, August 1992), 10. See also Paul Lester and Ron Smith, "African-American Photo Coverage in *Life, Newsweek* and *Time*, 1937–1988," *Journalism Quarterly* 67, no. 1 (Spring 1990), 128–36.

82. Sentman, "Black and White," 505, 506, 508.

83. Ruth Thibodeau, "From Racism to Tokenism: The Changing Face of Blacks in *New Yorker* Cartoons," *Public Opinion Quarterly* 53, no. 13 (Winter 1989), 482–94.

84. Ginny Whitehouse, "Only under the Magnolia: Regionalized Reporting of Racial Tensions in the 1950s" (Paper presented at AEJMC, Kansas City, Missouri, August 1993), 4, 6–7.

85. Jane Rhodes, "Racial Coverage of the 1950s Print Media and the Case of Emmett Till" (Paper presented at AEJMC convention, San Antonio, Texas, August 1987, 3–4.

86. Ibid., 3.

87. Ira Harkey, Jr., *The Smell of Burning Crosses*, 1st ed. (Jacksonville, Ill.: Delphi Press, 1967).

88. Andrew Secrest, "In Black and White: Press Opinion and Race Relations in South Carolina, 1954–1964" (Ph.D. diss., Duke University, 1972), 100.

89. Ibid.

90. Roy Carter, "Segregation and the News: A Regional Content Study," *Journalism Quarterly* 34, no. 1 (Winter 1957), 3–18, cited in Sherrie L. Wilson, "Newspaper Coverage of the 1960 Civil Rights Act" (Paper presented at AEJMC convention, Atlanta, August 1994), 6.

91. Sharon Bramlett-Solomon, "Southern vs. Northern Newspaper Coverage of the Dime Store Demonstration Movement: A Study of News Play and News Source Diversity," *Mass Comm Review* 15 (1988), 24–30.

92. Franklin, *From Slavery to Freedom*, 608.

93. Ibid., 609–14.

94. Ibid., 622.

95. Ibid., 614–19.

96. Harry Ashmore, "The Story behind Little Rock," *Nieman Reports* 12, no. 2 (April 1958), 5–6.

97. Secrest, "In Black and White," 102–3.

98. Rhodes, "Racial Coverage," 8.

99. Ibid., 11–12.

100. Warren Breed, "Comparative Newspaper Handling of the Emmett Till Case," *Journalism Quarterly* 35, no. 3 (Summer 1958), 291–98.

101. Rhodes, "Racial Coverage," 13, 14, 16.

102. Ibid., 16–17.

103. Whitehouse, "Only under the Magnolia," 4.

104. Ibid., 26.

105. Rhodes, "Racial Coverage," 19–20.

106. Ibid., 20–21. See also Edward Beiser and Peter Swift, "Race and Place in *The New York Times*," *Social Science Quarterly* 53 (June 1972), 129–35.

107. *Sponsor*, October 1949, 3.

108. Jacquie Gales Webb, Lex Gillespie, and Sonja Williams, "Black Radio . . . Telling It Like It Was," Program no. 9 (Washington, D.C.: Smithsonian Institution, 1996).

109. Dates and Barlow, *Split Image*, 195.

110. Ibid.

111. P. Noble, *The Negro in Films* (Port Washington, N.Y.: Kennikat Press, 1969).

112. Franklin, *From Slavery to Freedom*, 638–39.

113. Wilson, "Newspaper Coverage," 3.

114. Ibid.

115. Bramlett-Solomon, "Southern vs. Northern Newspaper Coverage," 24, 26.

116. David Sumner, "The Media's Role in a Nonviolent Movement: The Nashville Student Movement" (Paper presented at AEJMC convention, Kansas City, Missouri, August 1993), 7–9, 11.

117. Johnson, Sears, and McConahay, "Black Invisibility," 707, 711, 712.

118. Carolyn Martindale, *The White Press and Black America* (Westport, CT: Greenwood Press, 1986), 79–80, 84.

119. Ibid., 79, 83–85.

120. Lester, "African-American Photo Coverage," 10.

121. Thomas James Kelly, "White Press/Black Man: An Analysis of the Editorial Opinion of the Four Chicago Daily Newspapers toward the Race Problem, 1954–1968" (Ph.D. diss., University of Illinois at Urbana-Champaign, 1971), 429, 431–32.

122. Robert Latta, "A Content Analysis of News of Black Americans As Presented by the Wichita *Eagle* and a Comparison with Empirical Data," *Journalism Abstracts* 9 (1971), 225.

123. Roger Williams, "A Regional Report: Newspapers of the South," *Columbia Journalism Review* 6 (Summer 1967), 27.

124. Wilson, "Newspaper Coverage," 11.

125. Ashmore, "The Story behind Little Rock."

126. Martindale, *The White Press*, 96.

127. Ibid.

128. Carolyn Martindale, "Significant Silences: Newspaper Coverage of Problems Facing Black Americans," *Newspaper Research Journal* 15, no. 2 (Spring 1994), 106–8.

129. Wilson, "Newspaper Coverage," 19.

130. Ibid., 23–24, 27.

131. Ibid., 27.

132. Ibid., 17, 19.

133. Leslie Sargent, Wiley Carr, and Elizabeth McDonald, "Significant Coverage of Integration by Minority Group Magazines," *Journal of Human Relations* 13 (4th quarter 1965), 486–88.

134. Daniel J. Monti, "Patterns of Conflict Preceding the 1964 Riots: Harlem and Bedford-Stuyvesant," *Journal of Conflict Resolution* 23, no. 1 (March 1979), 41, 47.

135. Ibid., 50–51.

136. Ibid., 41, 65.

137. Johnson, Sears, and McConahay, "Black Invisibility," 699.

138. Ibid., 698, 713, 715.

139. Ibid., 717, 719.

140. Ibid., 701–2.

141. Ibid., 717–18.

142. Claude Brown, "The Ghetto View of Crime," *Race Relations Reporter*, November 1974, 18.

143. Franklin, *From Slavery to Freedom*, 642, 644.

144. Sharon Bramlett-Solomon, "Civil Rights Vanguard in the Deep South: Newspaper Portrayal of Fannie Lou Hamer, 1964–1977," *Journalism Quarterly* 68, no. 3 (Fall 1991), 517.

145. Ibid.

146. Ibid., 515–16, 519.

147. Ibid., 516, 519–20.

148. Williams, "A Regional Report," 26.

149. Ibid., 27.

150. John Hulteng, *The Messenger's Motives: Ethical Problems of the News Media* (Englewood Cliffs, NJ.: Prentice-Hall, 1976), 192.

151. Williams, "A Regional Report," 27, 32.

152. Ibid., 28, 30.

153. Edwin Williams, "Dimout in Jackson," *Columbia Journalism Review* 9, no. 2 (Summer 1970), 56–57.

154. Ibid., 57–58.

155. Ben Gilbert, "Race Coverage," *ASNE (American Society of Newspaper Editors) Bulletin* 515 (January 1968), 1.

156. Ibid., 2.

157. Michelle Bender, "The Black Community—Whitewashed in the News? Can Coverage Be Improved?" *American Press* 86, no. 7 (May 1968), 31.

158. Paul Fisher and Ralph Lowenstein, eds., *Race and the News Media* (New York: Praeger, 1967), 37–40.

159. Frank Stanley, Jr., "Race, Poverty and the Press," *ASNE (American Society of Newspaper Editors) Bulletin* 511 (September 1967), 2.

160. Ibid., 13.

161. Gilbert, "Race Coverage," 13.

162. David Paletz and Robert Dunn, "Press Coverage of Civil Disorders: A Case Study of Winston-Salem, 1967," *Public Opinion Quarterly* 33 (1969–1970), 339–40, 345.

163. Martindale, *The White Press*, 86.

164. Jack Jones, "The View from Watts," *Los Angeles Times*, 17 October 1965.

165. Philip Meyer, "Return to 12th Street: A Follow-up Survey of Attitudes of Detroit Negroes, October 1968," *Detroit Free Press*, 1968, 8.

166. National Advisory Commission on Civil Disorders, *Report of the National Advisory Commission on Civil Disorders* (New York: New York Times Co., 1968), 40, 120, 143.

167. Lawrence Schneider, *The Newsman and the Race Story*, report of a symposium for newsmen of Washington and Oregon, 28–29 June 1968 (Seattle: University of Washington School of Communications, 1968), 17.

168. James Farmer, *Lay Bare the Heart: An Autobiography of the Civil Rights Movement* (New York: Arbor House, 1985), 284.

169. Brown, "The Ghetto View of Crime," 18.

170. National Advisory Commission on Civil Disorders, *Report of the National Advisory Commission*, 184, 366, 383.

171. Jack Lyle, ed., *The Black American and the Press* (Los Angeles: Ward Ritchie, 1968), xiii.

172. National Advisory Commission on Civil Disorders, *Report of the National Advisory Commission*, vii, 366, 373, 383.

173. Eric Blanchard, "The Poor People and the 'White Press,' " *Columbia Journalism Review* 7, no. 3 (Fall 1968), 61–65.

174. Lawrence Schneider, "A Media-Black Council: Seattle's 19-Month Experiment," *Journalism Quarterly* 47, no. 3 (August 1970), 440–42.

175. Ibid., 446–49.

176. Dorothy Gilliam, "What Do Black Journalists Want?," *Columbia Journalism Review* 11, no. 1 (May/June 1972), 49–50.

177. K. W. Lee, "Minority Reporters Call Attention to Social Ills," *Editor & Publisher*, 4 August 1973, 14.

178. L. F. Palmer, Jr., "The Black Press in Transition," *Columbia Journalism Review* 9 (Spring 1970), 32–33.

179. Ibid., 31–33.

180. John Hope Franklin and Alfred A. Moss, Jr., *From Slavery to Freedom: A History of Negro Americans*, 6th ed. (New York: McGraw-Hill, 1988), 457–58.

181. Ibid., 461.

182. Ibid., 463.

183. Dates and Barlow, *Split Image*; Marilyn Fife, "Black Images in American TV: The First Two Decades," *Black Scholar*, November 1974, 7–15; Paula Poindexter and Carolyn Stroman, "Blacks and Television: A Review of the Literature," *Journal of Broadcasting* 25 (1981), 103–22; Carolyn Stroman, Bishetta Merritt and Paula Matabane, "Twenty Years after Kerner: The Portrayal of African Americans in Prime-Time Television," *Howard Journal of Communications* 2 (Winter 1989–1990), 44–56; Robert M. Entman, "Blacks in the News: Television, Modern Racism and Cultural Change," *Journalism Quarterly* 69, no. 2 (Summer 1992), 341–61; B. S. Greenberg and J. E. Brand, "Minorities and the Mass Media: 1970 to 1990," in *Perspectives on Media Effects*, ed. Jennings Bryant and Dolf Zillman (Hillsdale, N.J.: Lawrence Erlbaum Associates).

184. Robert Lewis Shayon, "Living Color on Television," *Saturday Review* 45 (24 November 1962), 25.

185. National Advisory Commission on Civil Disorders, *Report of the National Advisory Commission*, 369–78.

186. Churchill Roberts, "The Portrayal of Blacks in Television Network Newscasts," *Journal of Broadcasting* 15, no. 1 (1971), 45–53.

187. Churchill Roberts, "The Presentation of Blacks in Television Network Newscasts," *Journalism Quarterly* 52, no. 1 (1975), 50–55.

188. Roger Wilkins, "Further More: From Silence to Silence," *More*, July 1975, 27.

189. Clinton Cox, "Meanwhile in Bedford-Stuyvesant . . . ," *More*, April 1976, 18. Over twenty years later actor Bill Cosby spotlighted this same phenomenon when he expressed concern for the family of a black youth shot in South Central Los Angeles the same day Cosby's son Ennis was killed in an affluent section of the city.

190. Ibid.

191. Ibid., 19–20.

192. Edwin Diamond, "Boston: The Agony of Responsibility," *Columbia Journalism Review* 13, no. 5 (January/February 1975), 9–11.

193. John Barber and Oscar Gandy, Jr., "Press Portrayal of African American and White United States Representatives," *Howard Journal of Communications* 2, no. 2 (Spring 1990), 214.

194. Thom Lieb, "Protest at *The Post*: Coverage of Blacks in *The Washington Post Magazine*" (Paper presented at AEJMC convention, Portland, Oregon, July 1988).

195. Barber and Gandy, "Press Portrayal," 223.

196. Lester, "African-American Photo Coverage," 10–11.

197. Martindale, "Significant Silences," 108.

198. Bill Kirtz, "Coverage of Minorities and Hiring Improves," *Editor & Publisher*, 1 December 1979, 32.

199. John Consoli, "Why Blacks Distrust the Press," *Editor & Publisher*, 28 April 1979, 87.

200. *Race against Prime Time*, California Newsreel, San Francisco, 1985.

201. Kurt Andersen, "Miami's New Days of Rage," *Time*, 10 January 1983, 20–21.

202. National Advisory Commission on Civil Disorders, *Report of the National Advisory Commission*; *Race against Prime Time*; Paula Reynolds, "From 'Burn Baby Burn' to 'No Justice, No Peace': How the *Los Angeles Times* Covered the Los Angeles Riots of 1965 and 1992" (Paper presented at AEJMC convention, Atlanta, August 1994), 18–19.

203. Ronald Alsop, "Minority Report: Middle-Class Blacks Worry about Slipping, Still Face Racial Bias," *Wall Street Journal*, 3 November 1980, 1.

204. Neil Maxwell, "Minority Report: In Much of the South, Separation of the Races Still Is Key Fact of Life," *Wall Street Journal*, 17 November 1980, 1.

205. David Blum, "Minority Report: Black Politicians Fear They Can't Do Much to Help Their People," *Wall Street Journal*, 29 October 1980, 1.

206. Pamela Douglas, "The War on Black Children," *Black Enterprise*, May 1981, 22–27.

207. Gannett News Service Special Report, *Equality: America's Unfinished Business* (Washington, D.C., June 1981), 3.

208. Franklin and Moss, *From Slavery to Freedom*, 473–75.

209. Martindale, "Significant Silences," 108, 110.

210. Pamela Moreland, "Minorities—1: You Editors Make Me Angry," *ASNE (American Society of Newspaper Editors) Bulletin*, May/June 1982, 6–8; Lee Stinnett, "Minorities in the Newsroom," *ASNE Bulletin*, May 1981, 32–33.

211. The Reverend Joseph Lowery, cited in John DeMott, "White Racism in the Newspaper," *The Masthead* 33, no. 4 (Winter 1981), 6.

212. Carl Stokes, cited in DeMott, "White Racism," 10.

213. DeMott, "White Racism," 8, 9 citing Joel Dreyfuss.

214. J. Gregory Payne, "Shaping the Race Issue: A Special Kind of Journalism," *Political Communication and Persuasion* 5, no. 3 (1988), 146–47, 155.

215. Timothy Grainey, Dennis Pollack, and Lori Kusmierek, "How Three Chicago Newspapers Covered the Washington-Epton Campaign," *Journalism Quarterly* 61, no. 2 (Summer 1984), 354–55.

216. Daniel Riffe, Don Sneed, and Roger Van Ommeren, "Political and Racial Adversaries: Southern Black Elected Officials and the Press" (Paper presented at AEJMC convention, Minneapolis, August 1990).

217. Lieb, "Protest at *The Post*," 1.

218. Ibid., 8.

219. Kirk Johnson, "Black and White in Boston," *Columbia Journalism Review* 26, no. 1 (May/June 1987), 50–51.

220. Ibid.

221. Ibid., 52.

222. Linda Wright Moore, "Can the Press Do the Right Thing? I. How Your News Looks to Us," *Columbia Journalism Review* 29, no. 2 (July/August 1990), 21.

223. Ibid., 24.

224. Feagin and Feagin, "African Americans," 262.

225. Robert McFadden, Ralph Blumenthal, M. A. Farber, E. R. Shipp, Charles Strum, Craig Wolff, *Outrage: The Story behind the Tawana Brawley Hoax* (New York: Bantam, 1990).

226. Edward Pease, "Kerner Plus 20: Minority News Coverage in the *Columbus Dispatch*," *Newspaper Research Journal* (Spring 1989), 17–27.

227. Andy Court, "Can the Press Do the Right Thing? III. What *Is* the Right Thing?" *Columbia Journalism Review* 29, no. 2 (July/August 1990), 28.

228. Moore, "How Your News Looks to Us," 23.

229. Carol Liebler, "Sources, 'Quotas,' and Civil Rights: The Press and the Civil Rights Act of 1990" (Paper presented at AEJMC convention, Boston, August 1991), 7, 10.

230. Ibid., 1, 8, 11.

231. William Drummond, "Blacks and the News Media: From Alliance to Alienation," *Current*, January 1991, 4–6.

232. Ibid., 8–9.

233. Moore, "How Your News Looks to Us," 24.

234. "A 'Rising Star': The Political Career of Rep. William Gray," Joan Shorenstein Barone Center on the Press, Politics and Public Policy, John F. Kennedy School of Government, Harvard University, 1990.

235. Richard Rubenstein, "Resolving Racial Conflict in the United States: A New Perspective Is Needed," *Peace in Action*, Winter 1990–1991, 26.

236. Jeff Kamen, "Marion Barry Tries the Press," *Washington Journalism Review* 12 (November 1990), 40–41.

237. Rubenstein, "Resolving Racial Conflict," 27–29.

238. Daniel Riffe, Don Sneed, and Roger Van Ommeren, "The Press and Black Elected Officials at Three Levels of Public Office" (Paper presented at AEJMC convention, Washington, D.C., August 1989), 8.

239. Riffe, Sneed, and Van Ommeren, "Political and Racial Adversaries," 2, 3.

240. Edward Pease and Guido Stempel III, "Surviving to the Top: A Study of Minority Newspaper Executives" (Paper presented at AEJMC convention, Washington, D.C., August 1989), 4, 7.

241. Ted Pease and J. Frazier Smith, *The Newsroom Barometer: Job Satisfaction and the Impact of Racial Diversity at U.S. Daily Newspapers*, Ohio Journalism Monograph Series no. 1 (Athens, Ohio: Bush Research Center, E. W. Scripps School of Journalism, Ohio University), July 1991, 32.

242. Ibid., 4, 31.

243. Ibid., 5.

244. Ibid., 22–23.

245. Ibid., 25–26.

246. Erna Smith, *What Color Is the News? An Ethnic Content Analysis of Bay Area News Media* (San Francisco: San Francisco State University, 1991), 4, 17, 18.

247. Erna Smith, "Commentary: The Color of News," *Muckraker*, Summer 1992, 3.

248. Dorothy Gilliam, "Editorial Content: Is It Fair? Is It Accurate?" in *Kerner Plus 25: A Call for Action*, Unity 1994, March 1993, 19.

249. Ibid.

250. Jack Lule, "The Rape of Mike Tyson: Race, the Press and Symbolic Types" (Paper presented at AEJMC convention, Kansas City, Missouri, August 1993), 9, 10, 26.

251. Kim Lersch, "Current Trends in Police Brutality: An Analysis of Recent Newspaper Accounts" (Master's thesis, University of Florida, 1993); Feagin and Feagin, "African Americans," 584.

252. Lisa Baird, "That Special Perspective They *Say* They Want" in "L.A. Stories: A City Ablaze Casts a Glaring Light on the Press," *CJR (Columbia Journalism Review)* 31 (July/August 1992), 27.

253. *Outrage*, 33.

254. William Solomon, "Deconstructing Violence: Press Coverage of the L.A.P.D./ Rodney King Beating and First Trial" (Paper presented at AEJMC convention, Kansas City, Missouri, August 1993), 5.

255. Ibid., 22.

256. Lance Morrow, "Rough Justice," *Time*, 1 April 1991, 19.

257. Solomon, "Deconstructing Violence," 6.

258. Ibid., 3, 5, 18.

259. Ibid., 13, 21.

260. Ibid., 3, 4.

261. Ibid., 7–8, 15–16.

262. Ibid., 8, 16, 22.

263. Ibid., 14.

264. Venise Berry, "Mediated Messages: Black Men and the Rodney King Incident" (Paper presented at AEJMC convention, Atlanta, August 1994), 19–20, 5.

265. Tony Atwater and Niranjala Weerakkody, "A Portrait of Urban Conflict: The *L.A. Times* Coverage of the Los Angeles Riots" (Paper presented at AEJMC convention, Atlanta, August 1994), 4.

266. Ibid., 3, 6, 12, 18.

267. Reynolds, "From 'Burn Baby Burn'," 12–13.

268. Ibid., 14, 21.

269. Ibid., 17.

270. Ibid.

271. Gilliam, "Editorial Content," 19.

272. Reynolds, "From 'Burn Baby Burn'," 19–20, 28.

273. Roberts, "The Portrayal of Blacks," 45–51; Roberts, "The Presentation of Blacks," 50–55; United States Commission on Civil Rights, *Window Dressing on the Set: Women and Minorities in Television* (Washington, D.C.: U.S. Government Printing Office, 1977) and *Window Dressing on the Set: An Update* (Washington, D.C.: U.S. Government Printing Office, 1979).

274. U.S. Commission on Civil Rights, *Window Dressing*, 1977.

275. Raymond Rainville and Edward McCormick, "Extent of Covert Racial Prejudice in Pro Football Announcers' Speech," *Journalism Quarterly* 54, no. 1 (1977), 20–26.

276. James Phillip Jeter, "WGPR-TV, 1975–1995: Rest in Peace" (Paper presented at AEJMC convention, Anaheim, California, August 1996).

277. Ibid.

278. *Race against Prime Time.*

279. Herman Gray, "Television, Black Americans and the American Dream" in *Gender, Race, and Class in Media*, ed. Gail Dines and Jean Humez (Thousand Oaks, California: Sage, 1995), 430–37.

280. "Drugs in Black and White," PBS Video, 1991.

281. Michael Massing, "Blackout in Television," *Columbia Journalism Review* 21, no. 4 (November/December 1982), 42.

282. Ibid., 38–44.

283. Erna Smith, "Transmitting Race: The L.A. Riot in TV News," San Francisco State University, draft 10/93 for Center for Urban Affairs and Public Relations Conference on Media, Race and Governance, Northwestern University.

284. Jannette Dates and Edward Pease, "Warping the World: Media's Mangled Images of Race," *Media Studies Journal* 8, no. 8 (Summer 1994), 92–93.

285. Gilliam, "Editorial Content," 19.

286. Ibid., 18, 20.

287. Dave Berkman, "Career vs. Race," *Shepherd Express* (Milwaukee), 4 April 1996.

288. Feagin and Feagin, "African Americans," 246.

289. Wilkins, "White Out," 48.

290. Ibid., 46.

291. Feagin and Feagin, "African Americans," 255.

292. Ibid., 255.

293. Ibid., 251–53.

294. Ibid., 256–57.

295. Ibid., 244.

296. Ibid., 243.

297. Wilkins, "White Out," 47.

298. Ibid., 45–46.

299. Steve Geimann, "NABJ Protests Language in Debate," *SPJ Press Notes*, 7 August 1995, 1.

300. S. C. Gwynne, "Undoing Diversity," *Time*, 1 April 1996, 54.

301. Ibid.

302. Feagin and Feagin, "African Americans," 270–271.

303. Wilkins, "White Out," 48.

304. Berkman, "Career vs. Race."

305. Alicia Shepard, "Free Press: An Intimate Dispatch from the Underclass," *American Journalism Review* 16, no. 2 (November 1994), 14–15. The woman of whom Dash wrote died of AIDS early in 1996, and later that year Dash's book about her, *Rosa Lee*, was published.

306. Peter Parisi, "The New York Times Looks at One Block in Harlem: Narratives of Race in Journalism" (Paper presented at AEJMC convention, Anaheim, California, August 1996), 10–13, 18.

307. David Engen, "The Making of a People's Champion: An Analysis of Media Representations of George Foreman," *Southern Journal of Communication* 60, no. 1 (Winter 1995), 142.

308. E. R. Shipp, "OJ and the Black Media," *CJR* (*Columbia Journalism Review*) 33 (November/December 1994), 40–41.

309. David Berkman, "Media Musings: O.J. Aftermath," *Shepherd Express* (Milwaukee), 12 October 1995.

310. Jack E. White, "First the Flame, Then the Blame," *Time*, 17 June 1996, 35.

311. David Van Biema, "After the Burning," *Time*, 1 July 1996, 52–54.

312. "Civil Rights Commission Says Racial Tensions High in States with Church Burnings," *Jet* 90, no. 24 (28 October 1996), 4.

313. Nikki Giovanni, "A Million Reasons to Hope," *Black Collegian* 26, no. 3 (1 April 1996), 28.

314. Ishmael Reed, *Airing Dirty Laundry*, Reading, Massachusetts: Addison-Wesley, 1993), 5.

315. Franklin Gilliam, Jr., Shanto Iyengar, Adam Simon, and Oliver Wright, "Crime in Black and White," *Harvard International Journal of Press/Politics* 1, no. 3 (1996), 6–23.

316. Robert Papper, Michael Gerhard, and Andrew Sharma, "More Women and Minorities in Broadcast News," *Communicator*, August 1996, 8–15.

317. Entman, "Blacks in the News," 341–61.

318. Ibid., 355.

319. Robert Entman, "Representation and Reality in the Portrayal of Blacks on Network Television News," *Journalism Quarterly* 71, no. 3 (Autumn 1994), 509–601.

320. Robert Entman, "African Americans according to TV News," *Media Studies Journal* 8, no. 3 (Summer 1994), 29–39.

321. Christopher Campbell, *Race, Myth and the News* (Thousand Oaks, Calif.: Sage, 1995), 58, 62, 82.

322. Entman, "African Americans according to TV News," 29.

323. G. Blake Armstrong, Kimberly Neuendorf and James Brentar, "TV Entertainment, News, and Social Perceptions of College Students," *Journal of Communication* 42, no. 3 (Summer 1992), 153–76.

SELECTED BIBLIOGRAPHY

Beatty-Brown, Florence Rebekah. "The Negro as Portrayed by the St. Louis *Post-Dispatch* from 1920 to 1950." Ph.D. diss., University of Illinois at Urbana-Champaign, 1951.

Berry, Venise. "Mediated Messages: Black Men and the Rodney King Incident." Paper presented at Association for Education in Journalism and Mass Communication Convention, Atlanta, August 1994.

Bramlett-Solomon, Sharon. "Southern vs. Northern Newspaper Coverage of the Dime Store Demonstration Movement: A Study of News Play and News Source Diversity." *Mass Comm Review* 15 (1988), 24–30.

Campbell, Christopher P. *Race, Myth and the News.* Thousand Oaks, Calif.: Sage, 1995.

Cox, Clinton. "Meanwhile in Bedford-Stuyvesant . . ." *More*, April 1976, 18–21.

Dates, Jannette, and William Barlow, eds. *Split Image: African Americans and the Mass Media.* Washington, D.C.: Howard University Press, 1994.

DeMott, John. "White Racism in the Newspaper." *The Masthead* 33, no. 4 (Winter 1981), 6–11.

Entman, Robert M. "African Americans according to TV News." *Media Studies Journal* 8, no. 3 (Summer 1994), 29–39.

———. "Blacks in the News: Television, Modern Racism and Cultural Change." *Journalism Quarterly* 69, no. 2 (Summer 1992), 341–61.

———. "Representation and Reality in the Portrayal of Blacks on Network Television News," *Journalism Quarterly* 71, no. 3 (Autumn 1994), 509–601.

Feagin, Joe R., and Clairece Booher Feagin. "African Americans." In *Racial and Ethnic Relations*, Joe R. Feagin and Clairece Booher Feagin, 234–89. 5th ed. Upper Saddle River, N.J.: Prentice-Hall, 1996.

Finkle, Lee. "The Conservative Aims of Militant Rhetoric: Black Protest during World War II." *Journal of American History* 60 (December 1973), 692–713.

Franklin, John Hope, and Alfred A. Moss, Jr. *From Slavery to Freedom: A History of Negro Americans.* 6th ed. New York: McGraw-Hill, 1988.

Gaskins, Bill. "The World according to *Life*: Racial Stereotyping and American Identity." *Afterimage* 21, no. 3 (Summer 1993), 14–16.

Gilliam, Dorothy. "Editorial Content: Is It Fair? Is It Accurate?" In *Kerner Plus 25: A Call for Action.* Unity 1994, March 1993, 18–20.

———. "What Do Black Journalists Want?" *Columbia Journalism Review* 11, no. 1 (May/June 1972), 48–52.

Johnson, Kirk. "Black and White in Boston." *Columbia Journalism Review* 26, no. 1 (May/June 1987), 50–52.

Johnson, Paula B., David O. Sears, and John B. McConahay. "Black Invisibility, the Press and the Los Angeles Riot." *American Journal of Sociology* 76, no. 4 (January 1971), 698–721.

Kamen, Jeff. "Marion Barry Tries the Press." *Washington Journalism Review* 12 (November 1990), 40–45.

Leonhirth, William J. "The Civil Rights Movement in the 1940s: A Communication Context." Paper presented at Association for Education in Journalism and Mass Communication Convention, Atlanta, August 1994.

Liebler, Carol. "Sources, 'Quotas,' and Civil Rights: The Press and the Civil Rights Act of 1990." Paper presented at Association for Education in Journalism and Mass Communication Convention, Boston, August 1991.

Lule, Jack. "The Rape of Mike Tyson: Race, the Press and Symbolic Types." Paper presented at Association for Education in Journalism and Mass Communication Convention, Kansas City, Missouri, August 1993.

Martindale, Carolyn. "Significant Silences: Newspaper Coverage of Problems Facing Black Americans." *Newspaper Research Journal* 15, no. 2 (Spring 1994), 102–15.

———. *The White Press and Black America*. Westport, Conn.: Greenwood Press, 1986.

Monti, Daniel J. "Patterns of Conflict Preceding the 1964 Riots: Harlem and Bedford-Stuyvesant." *Journal of Conflict Resolution* 23, no. 1 (March 1979), 41–69.

National Advisory Commission on Civil Disorders, *Report of the National Advisory Commission on Civil Disorders*. New York: New York Times Co., 1968.

Parisi, Peter. "The New York Times Looks at One Block in Harlem: Narratives of Race in Journalism." Paper presented at Association for Education in Journalism and Mass Communication Convention, Anaheim, California, August 1996.

Prattis, P. L. "Race Relations and the Negro Press." *Phylon* 14 (December 1953), 373–83.

Quarles, Benjamin. *The Negro in the Making of America*. New York: Simon and Schuster, 1966.

Reynolds, Paula. "From 'Burn Baby Burn' to 'No Justice, No Peace': How the *Los Angeles Times* Covered the Los Angeles Riots of 1965 and 1992." Paper presented at Association for Education in Journalism and Mass Communication Convention, Atlanta, August 1994.

Rhodes, Jane. "Racial Coverage of the 1950s Print Media and the Case of Emmett Till." Paper presented at Association for Education in Journalism and Mass Communication Convention, San Antonio, Texas, August 1987.

Schneider, Lawrence. "A Media-Black Council: Seattle's 19-Month Experiment." *Journalism Quarterly* 47, no. 3 (August 1970), 439–49.

Stevens, John D. "Black Correspondents of World War II Cover the Supply Routes." *Journal of Negro History* 57 (October 1972), 395–406.

Wilkins, Roger. "Further More: From Silence to Silence." *More*, July 1975, 23, 27.

———. "White Out." *Mother Jones* 17, no. 5 (November-December 1992), 44–48.

Wilson, Sherrie L. "Newspaper Coverage of the 1960 Civil Rights Act." Paper presented at Association for Education in Journalism and Mass Communication Convention, Atlanta, August 1994.

4

The Hispanic Americans

MICHAEL B. SALWEN AND GONZALO R. SORUCO

I'll build that security fence [between Mexico and the United States], and
we'll close it, and we'll say, "Listen José, you're not coming in this time!"
—Republican presidential contender Patrick J. Buchanan, speaking before
an almost all-white audience at a rally in Waterloo, Iowa, January 1996[1]

We didn't cross the border; the border crossed us.
—A slogan popular among Chicanos[2]

Despite their long history and large numbers, Latinos have been an "invisible minority" in the United States. Until recently, few social scientists and
policy analysts concerned with understanding stratification and social problems in the United States have noticed them.
—Joan Moore and Raquel Pinderhughes[3]

[I]t will take years to understand the multifaceted and far-reaching implications of this cultural transformation, the move of Hispanics from periphery to center stage. I believe that we are currently witnessing a
double-faceted phenomenon: Hispanicization of the United States, and An-
glocization of Hispanics. Adventures in Hyphenland, explorers in El Do-
rado, we Hispanics have deliberately and cautiously infiltrated the enemy,
and now go by the rubric of Latinos in the territories north of the Rio
Grande. Delaying full adaptation, our objective is to assimilate Anglos
slowly into ourselves.
—Ilan Stavans, Mexico-born critic and author[4]

Unlike other immigrant groups who came to the United States or—in the case
of African Americans—were brought here against their will, for many Hispanics
of Mexican ancestry there was no movement across borders. Rather, as a result
of political upheavals, the borders changed under their feet.[5] Hispanics differ
from many of the other groups discussed in this book because they are not a

race but an ethnic group. The more than 22 million Hispanics in the United States today (according to the 1990 Census) include Caucasian Hispanos of European descent, peoples from Latin America who trace their roots to the inhabitants before the Spanish conquistadors, and African Americans who trace their lineage to slaves and mestizos (persons of mixed parentage, usually Spanish or Portuguese and Native American). It is stating the obvious to say that there is no one Hispanic group, but rather national origin groups such as Mexican Americans, Puerto Ricans, Cuban Americans, Dominicans, and so forth. Most Hispanics prefer to identify themselves by these groups. Still, the inclusive term "Hispanic" or "Latino" offers a convenient way to classify people who, despite their differences, share some commonalities in their ancestry.

Mexican Americans, the first Hispanics in the United States in large numbers, came through forced annexation as well as immigration. The expansion of the Santa Fe Trail to the West and the Mexican American War of 1846–1848 triggered the first widespread portrayals of a Hispanic group in the U.S. media.[6] Many U.S. newspapers were advocates of America's expansionist "manifest destiny" policy, although some newspapers and magazines questioned U.S. involvement in the Mexican American War.[7] The war was by no means universally popular, and such notables as Abraham Lincoln, Ulysses S. Grant, and Ralph Waldo Emerson protested U.S. involvement.[8] Nonetheless, the dominant war fever coverage in the popular press did much to spread popular images of "cruel" and "bloodthirsty" Mexicans, a stereotype that traces its roots to General Antonio López de Santa Anna's "massacre" at the Alamo in 1836.[9]

The image of Mexicans in the press reflected widely held attitudes and beliefs on race and ethnicity.[10] Not only the news media, but also the popular romance fiction books of the mid-nineteenth century, known as "dime novels," developed a cottage industry exploiting Mexican stereotypes. One writer in particular, Ned Buntline, had a tremendous following that contributed to what one writer described as "the inflated patriotism of the superior thinking Anglo-Saxons."[11]

One of the nation's first Spanish-language newspapers, *La Patria* of New Orleans, established on October 1, 1847, offered a more sober account of the war hostilities.[12] Its correspondents stationed in Mexican cities offered a Mexican perspective on the hostilities. But *La Patria*, like other segments of the Mexican-American community, was suspect during this time of strong war fever in the United States. The paper was criticized by its English-language competitors for what were perceived as its frequently pro-Mexican editorials.[13]

As a result of the harsh 1848 Treaty of Guadalupe Hidalgo following the war, the United States acquired huge territories from Mexico in what is now the southwestern United States.[14] With the new territory, the United States added 80,000 Mexicans to its population; nevertheless, the U.S. government virtually ignored the needs of the new people under its authority. The territory of New Mexico, which attained statehood in 1912, did not even establish a public school system until 1890.[15] Despite the United States' acquisition of vast new territories, for the next 100 years the Spanish-speaking people on the land were an "invisible minority." America's press noticed them only during times of civil disturbance, disasters, and other bad news events.

The late nineteenth century witnessed increased press xenophobia against the Spanish. Spaniards were portrayed as aggressors in the popular American press because they held territory in North America, an area considered by Americans to be part of the United States' "sphere of influence."[16] Cuba's War of Independence against Spain in 1898 (known in the United States as the Spanish-American War) represented a nadir in U.S. press stereotyping of Spaniards. The "yellow press," led by publishers William Randolph Hearst and Joseph Pulitzer, engaged in exaggerated and racist discourse, portraying the Spaniards as ruthless killers.[17]

As America's leading press lord, Hearst, a xenophobic patriot with political aspirations, wielded his influence over public opinion to bring the United States into the war. Before the war, Hearst's *New York Journal* prepared public opinion for entry into the war with atrocity stories—many of them apocryphal—describing how the Spaniards were "attacking hospitals, outraging women, poisoning wells, imprisoning nuns and roasting twenty-five Catholic priests alive."[18]

Hearst and Pulitzer hired famous war correspondents, including Richard Harding Davis and novelist Stephen Crane (who wrote *The Red Badge of Courage*), to chronicle the Spanish atrocities. Hearst, for example, hired the popular artist Frederick Remington (famous for his paintings of the old West that were reprinted in popular magazines) to create drawings to accompany the atrocity stories. The flamboyant Davis glorified Theodore Roosevelt and his "Rough Riders" in his best-selling account of the war, *The Cuban and Porto Rican Campaigns* (1898).[19] Hearst repeatedly wired his correspondents in Cuba to report about Spanish atrocities. According to the legend, Remington wired back that everything was quiet in Cuba and he anticipated no war. In response, Hearst reportedly wired Remington: "Please remain. You furnish the pictures and I'll furnish the war."[20]

When the American battleship *Maine* exploded in Havana Harbor on February 15, 1898, leaving 260 Americans dead, the Spaniards denied involvement in the explosion and sent their regrets. Hearst's newspaper nonetheless implied the Spanish were responsible and offered a $50,000 reward for "the detection of the perpetrators of the *Maine* outrage."[21] President William McKinley, under intense public and press pressure, took no political position on Spanish involvement in the sinking and—in an action unusual for a president—allowed Congress to decide whether to go to war, which it promptly chose to do. With the headline "Now to Avenge the Maine" reveling in America's entry into war, Hearst and the *Journal* were satisfied.

The U.S. victory over Spain left the United States with Spain's colonial possessions in North America—Puerto Rico and Cuba—plus the Philippines and Guam. As with the war with Mexico fifty years prior, the United States again found itself with Hispanic peoples under its control. Many Puerto Ricans and Cubans, long resentful of Spain's colonial control, were discouraged when the

United States failed to grant independence to their homelands. Cubans were granted independence from the United States in 1902 but under terms that explicitly permitted the United States to intervene militarily in the island's political affairs to "protect" Cuba. U.S. military forces invaded Cuba in 1906, 1912, and 1917.

Puerto Rico was governed by the United States until the 1940s, when President Harry Truman granted it greater autonomy.[22] A mostly elite class of politically motivated Puerto Ricans, who had established New York City as their government-in-exile, had lived in the United States since the nineteenth century.[23] After the Spanish American War, Puerto Rican leaders led a largely peaceful fight for their island's independence from the United States. During the early twentieth century, middle- and lower-class Puerto Ricans came to the United States, mostly to New York City, and created small neighborhoods called *colonias*.[24]

The passage of the Jones Act in March 1917, over the objections of political leaders on the island, made Puerto Ricans U.S. citizens (unless they explicitly refused citizenship, which would involve giving up many basic civil rights). This political act was undertaken so that the United States could draft Puerto Ricans to fight during World War I. The act brought increased numbers of Puerto Ricans to the U.S. mainland, with an estimated 35,000 Puerto Ricans in New York City by 1918.[25] As their numbers increased, America's welcome toward the former proindependence advocates who fought the Spanish aggressors waned, and the press joined in the rising tide of bigotry. As one writer observed, "In New York and other U.S. cities, the transition to American rule over Puerto Rico had unsettling effects on Puerto Ricans in these settings. American newspapers such as the *Boston Globe* and the *New York Times* projected derogatory images of Puerto Ricans as 'aborigines,' people 'incapable of governing themselves.' "[26]

The early twentieth century, like the late nineteenth, saw more instability in Latin America and more Hispanics migrating to the United States. Mexico's 1910 revolution brought a wave of Mexican immigrants to the United States. Media depictions of the violent revolution cultivated images of the new Mexican arrivals as a dangerous and violent people.[27] Aggravating the situation, their arrival occurred during a period of violent border clashes. These new Mexican immigrants settled primarily in the American Southwest.

Some years later, in early 1917, with the United States officially neutral at the start of World War I, the loyalty of Mexico, and by extension Mexican Americans, became suspect after a confidential German telegram was intercepted by London and passed on to the Americans. The dispatch, known as the "Zimmermann telegram," exposed Germany's plans to seek an alliance with Mexico if the United States entered the war on the side of the Allies. The telegram stated, in part,

In case we should not be successful in this [keeping the United States neutral], we propose Mexico an alliance upon the following terms: Joint conduct of the war. Joint conclusion of peace. Ample financial support and an agreement on our part that Mexico shall gain back by conquest the territory lost by her at a prior period in Texas, New Mexico and Arizona.[28]

At first, incredulous American officials suspected the telegram was a British forgery, to get the United States involved in the war on the side of the British. But soon afterward the Germans acknowledged that the telegram was genuine.[29] The telegram was made public and received wide attention in the U.S. press. Although there is no evidence that the Germans actually made the overture to Mexico, the disclosure nevertheless raised alarms in the United States, fueling suspicions that Mexican Americans were disloyal. A number of "nativist" U.S. politicians aggravated attitudes toward Mexico and Mexicans by repeatedly bashing Mexico in the press. In April, after the United States entered the war against Germany, U.S. officials remained concerned about Mexico's joining the war as a German ally.[30] An editorial published in the *Los Angeles Times* illustrated the national xenophobia against Mexico and Mexican Americans:

If the people of Los Angeles knew what was happening on our border, they would not sleep at night. Sedition, conspiracy, and plots are in the very air. Telegraph wires are tapped, spies come and go at will. German nationals hob-nob with Mexican bandits, Japanese agents and renegades from this country. Code messages are relayed from place to place along the border, frequently passing six or eight people from sender to receiver. Los Angeles is the headquarters for this vicious system, and it is there that the deals with German and Mexican representatives are made.[31]

Meanwhile, an image of Mexicans as violent, dirty, and lazy was being perpetuated in popular entertainment media. Silent movies and early sound movies with titles such as *Bronco Billy* and *The Greaser's Revenge* (both in 1914) portrayed Hispanics in "greaser" films as either threatening bandits or buffoons.[32] While the focus of this chapter is on the news media, it is worth noting that Spanish-language newspapers in the Southwest actively sought to correct these negative popular culture portrayals.[33]

In 1918 Francisco Chapa, the publisher of *El Imparcial de Texas* in San Antonio, led an editorial campaign against derogatory film depictions of Hispanics; his efforts resulted in a ban against exhibiting films in Texas that depicted Hispanics in a disparaging manner.[34] In 1919 similar successful campaigns were undertaken by *La Prensa* in Los Angeles and *El Mosquito* in Tucson. The newspapers' campaigns were noticed in Latin America, and several Latin American republics protested Hollywood films with negative Hispanic images.[35] By the early 1920s, Mexico and several South American nations had banned the importation of films that they believed depicted Hispanics as lazy or as criminals.[36] The protests against the films in the United States, and especially the protests from Latin American republics, had the desirable effect of curtailing the negative images. A more favorable stereotype of Hispanics emerged in subsequent years.[37] Chapa's campaign illustrated the important role of the Hispanic media as a cultural change agent.

In addition, radio broadcasting targeted to a Hispanic-American audience made itself felt as early as the mid-1920s.[38]

While most scholarly research concerning the Hispanic media during this period was largely historical and biographical in nature, describing Hispanic newspapers and their founders such as Chapa's *El Imparcial de Texas*,[39] groundbreaking sociological research during the 1920s conducted by Robert Ezra Park, at the University of Chicago's "Chicago School" of sociology, applied a "symbolic interactionist" approach to study the contribution of ethnic news media in the socialization of the immigrant.[40] Park, a former journalist, in his landmark *The Immigrant Press and Its Control* (1922), gave particular attention to the role of the ethnic press in immigrant assimilation.[41] Although many community leaders and editors of foreign-language publications hoped that the ethnic press would forge ethnic cultural ties and impede unwanted assimilation, Park, a political progressive, believed that assimilation was an inevitable and desirable consequence of the ethnic press:

The immigrant press, despised by foreign intellectuals for its vulgarity, has power among its readers rarely equaled by more literary journals. Having created its reading public, it monopolizes it to a great extent. Nationalistic editors seek to use this monopoly to keep their readers' interest and activity focused on the home country. But under the terms of its existence the press is apt to aid rather than prevent the drift toward American community.[42]

Park's research provided the first comprehensive data-based analysis of foreign-language newspapers in the United States. Spanish-language newspapers, according to Park's research, accounted for the third largest number of foreign-language newspapers in the United States in 1920 (100), behind German- (276) and Scandinavian-language newspapers (111).

It will be apparent in this chapter that immigration is a central theme in understanding news media depictions of Mexican Americans. Although immigration often led to periods of intense public hostility toward Mexican immigrants, because Americans viewed them as competitors for jobs (even though most Americans would not perform the jobs that the immigrants did), it is ironic that U.S. business interests actively and successfully lobbied the Congress to relax restrictions on Mexican laborers entering the United States when domestic labor shortages occurred. Even when anti-immigrant and anti-Mexican feelings were high, as for example during the period after the disclosure of the "Zimmermann telegram" and the subsequent U.S. entry into the war, Congress— under pressure from agricultural, railway, mining, and other commercial interests—eased restrictions on Mexican immigration to alleviate the labor shortage created by the war.[43]

When the United States experienced economic downturns, Congress passed legislation to reduce the flow of Mexican immigration as easily as it had passed legislation to increase the flow when cheap labor was needed. With the economy failing in 1929, Mexican immigration to the United States was sharply curtailed with the passage of the Immigration Act. The creation of the Border Patrol a few years earlier, tight enforcement of immigration laws, and bilateral agreements between Mexico and the United States contributed to a sharp reduction in Mexican immigration. With Americans fearing that immigrants were taking jobs from American workers, more than 400,000 Mexicans were deported during the Great Depression of the 1930s.[44] In some cases, racist and overzealous federal agents deported Mexicans who were U.S. citizens. Officials in Los Angeles were particularly aggressive in enforcing deportation laws during the Depression. In an effort to intimidate Mexicans into leaving on their own, local police and Department of Labor agents invited the press to accompany them during raids.[45]

Mexicans were not the only Hispanics to come to the United States during this period. With far less notice, Hispanics from the Basque region of Europe's Iberian peninsula were settling in the Great Basin region of the United States after Francisco Franco's government cracked down on them, outlawing public displays of the Basque culture. They established sheepherding communities in Nevada, southwestern Oregon, and parts of Idaho. An estimated 50,000 to 100,000 Americans of Basque heritage live in the United States today.[46]

1934 FEDERAL COMMUNICATIONS ACT TO PEARL HARBOR ATTACK, DECEMBER 7, 1941

Hispanics in the United States before World War II, overwhelmingly Mexicans, were largely ignored by both the public and the news media. Most Mexicans in the United States lived in the West and Southwest where they were largely segregated from the rest of society in jobs and neighborhoods. Also a burgeoning Hispanic community of Puerto Ricans existed in the Northeast. In addition, a small but growing community of Mexicans was emerging in Chicago, where they were employed in steel production, meat packing, construction, trucking, and other industries.[47] Despite the public's and the media's ignoring of Hispanics, the emergence of prominent Hispanics in Southwestern politics and the growth of Spanish-language newspapers in these regions foretold the future prominence of Hispanics in the United States.[48]

Hispanic political representatives from the Southwest were bringing a Hispanic perspective to national issues. This was particularly evident in New Mexico, where Mexico-born Octaviano Larrazola served as governor in 1919. In 1926 a *New York Times* editorial stated that "Spanish is as much the official language of the New Mexican Legislature as is English."[49]

Most notable among the nation's earliest and most prominent Hispanic leaders was New Mexico's Mexican-American Senator Dennis Chávez, who was active in the state's politics beginning in the 1920s. Ever since Chávez, Hispanics have exerted significant political influence in New Mexico. As historian Thomas Weyr observed, ''[Hispanic] self-governance [in New Mexico] is a tradition, one reason the territory of New Mexico was admitted to the Union as a state only in 1912. Anglos feared the political competition.''[50]

Chávez was appointed the state's senator in 1934 after the sitting senator died in office. He was elected in 1936 and served until his death in 1962, at which time he held the fourth highest position in seniority and two key chairmanships. During the Roosevelt administration, he was a supporter of the New Deal; during the Johnson administration, he supported the Great Society. Chávez was considered the first national-level ''Hispanic role model.''[51]

The migration of large numbers of Mexicans to the United States after Mexico's 1910 revolution led to the establishment of many small newspapers that served the budding Mexican-American communities in the Southwest.[52] Most important among these was *La Opinión* in Los Angeles, launched in 1926 by Ignacio E. Lozano, who later purchased *La Prensa* in San Antonio.[53] *La Opinión*, which is still published today, is considered an ethnic press ''success story.''[54] Lozano remained active as publisher until February 1953.[55]

The early Spanish-language newspapers were not solely neutral transmitters of news. They were seen by their readers as part of the community and expected to champion Hispanic causes. They took up this challenge with zeal. As noted earlier, during the 1910s and 1920s, *El Imparcial de Texas* in San Antonio and other Spanish-language newspapers led campaigns against negative stereotyping of Hispanics in motion pictures. Years later *El Imparcial* and *El Heraldo de México* supported campaigns against the death penalty, which was viewed in the Hispanic community as disproportionately imposed against Mexican Americans. Spanish-language newspapers also crusaded against the light punishment in courts of whites convicted of murdering Mexicans.[56] During one notorious episode in 1935, two whites in Tucson, earlier convicted for killing two Mexicans, were released after the jury could not reach a verdict. The two men had successfully appealed their convictions. After the county attorney refused to seek another trial, claiming it would be too costly to taxpayers, an editorial in *El Tucsonense* railed against the decision: ''If the victims had been Americans killed by Mexicans, then the cost would have been no object; but justice for Mexicans is measured in grams.''[57]

The issue of Hispanic immigration to the United States has been of enduring concern to Hispanic Americans and the general public. As noted later in this chapter, the general market news media were and still are accused of portraying Hispanic immigrants in insensitive and even racist terms. But did Spanish-language newspapers such as *La Opinión* cover the immigration issue any better? Scholar Ricardo Chavira, in a rare comparative longitudinal analysis of news coverage of Hispanic immigration in the general market and Spanish-language press, suggested that *La Opinión*'s coverage could have been better.[58] He studied how *La Opinión* and the *Los Angeles Times* reported Mexican emigration and deportations during the 1930s, 1950s, and 1970s. While *La Opinión* was more compassionate than its English-language counterpart, Chavira still criticized *La Opinión* for not defending the rights of Hispanic immigrants to the extent that he believed it should have as a newspaper written for the Mexican-American community.

Meanwhile, Hispanics of largely Puerto Rican heritage who settled in the Northeast during the late nineteenth and early twentieth centuries saw themselves primarily as political refugees. It is therefore not surprising that many of the early Spanish-language newspapers in New York during this time were aimed at an elite, politically concerned readership.[59] But when the number of Puerto Rican immigrants to New York swelled in later years, a community newspaper that addressed community concerns was needed.[60] José Campubri founded *La Prensa* in New York City in 1913 as a weekly tabloid to meet this need. It was originally directed at residents whose roots were in Spain, but it later oriented its editorial content to the burgeoning Puerto Rican community. *La Prensa* became a daily in 1918. As Virginia Sánchez-Korrol wrote of *La Prensa*'s community news coverage:

It did not confine its services to reporting foreign and domestic news, but fully involved itself in community affairs. Besides advertising for local businesses, special sections reported the arrivals and departures of individuals to and from Spanish-America. Classified ads informed the Spanish-reading public of employment opportunities. Calendars of community events merited regular reporting as did the myriad activities of community groups throughout the city's *colonias*.[61]

1941 PEARL HARBOR ATTACK TO ATOMIC BOMBING OF HIROSHIMA, AUGUST 6, 1945

Hispanics remained a largely neglected minority during the years of World War II, even though Mexican Americans served in the U.S. military disproportionately to their numbers.[62] Mexican Americans were concentrated in the Southwest, far from the nation's political and economic centers in the Northeast. Even in the Southwest, where many were employed as low-paid agricultural workers, they were often segregated from white Americans in both employment and their neighborhoods. Also, Mexican farm workers were highly migratory and followed the crops through Midwestern states as far north as Michigan, Montana, Indiana, and Ohio.[63]

The number of Mexican immigrants coming to the United States, along with some Central Americans, increased during and after World War II when the United States faced an acute labor shortage and desperately needed cheap labor.[64] To ease the problem, Congress passed the *bracero* (low-paid agricultural contract laborer) program, which permitted temporary entrance to foreign workers.

The war years were marked by America's recognition of Mexico's concern about America's treatment of Mexico's citizens and Americans of Mexican extraction in the United States. The Mexican government's criticisms caused discomfort in U.S. government circles because the United States depended upon Mexico as an ally in the war. Hensley Woodbridge's investigation of the Mexican newspaper coverage of Mexicans in the United States offers a unique perspective of the plight of U.S. Mexicans during this period.[65] Below are three representative examples of Woodbridge's findings:

- In the United States, they despise us. They call us greasy and dirty and do not consider us worthy to associate with them. In the United States they send our consuls to eat in the kitchen or they do not serve us at all (in *Lectura*).

- For many citizens of the United States the Mexican is a contemptible person. . . . North Americans are waging a war against Germany and against the ideas for which Germany is fighting, one of which is the superiority of the Aryan. But that group of North Americans who despise the Mexican has become seduced by the racial ideas of Germany (*Lectura*).

- There is no doubt that Mexican workers in the state of Oregon are and continue to be the victims of anti-Mexican phobia. . . . This discriminatory action is eloquent testimony that we can use to measure and understand the degree of esteem in which Mexicans are held in the United States (*Mañana*).

In an article published in *Common Ground* titled "The Forgotten Mexican," Carey McWilliams, a long-time advocate of civil rights for many disenfranchised groups and the editor of *The Nation* for two decades (1955–1975), noted that in the name of President Franklin Roosevelt's "Good Neighbor" policy the United States government—with the cooperation of private, commercial media interests in the United States—launched a large-scale radio propaganda blitz to Mexico, Central America, and South America to counter anti-Americanism in the region.[66] The idea for the radio blitz was due in no small part to the efforts of Senator Dennis Chávez of New Mexico. He called upon the Department of State to construct shortwave radio facilities to "show Latin America that in addition to our pilgrim ancestors a considerable portion of our country has a history of distinct Iberic origin."[67]

McWilliams noted in the *Common Ground* article that many Mexicans living in the United States on territory that once was part of Mexico viewed the United States with the same suspicion as Latin American nations: "When we broadcast Good Neighbor programs in Spanish, it seldom occurs to us that there is a sizeable Mexican population in our midst and that the Good Neighbor policy might very well start at home within our own borders."[68]

The war years witnessed the rise of Hispanic ghettos in Los Angeles and elsewhere that would plant the seeds for a variety of social problems that would affect Hispanic life in later years.[69] Many young Mexicans had formed "gangs" with reputations for violence and flashy dress. The gangs adopted names such as the Mateo Bombers, the Main Street Zooters, the Califa, the Black Legion, and the Sleepy Lagoon. The young Mexicans' distinctive "zoot-suit" apparel included long, baggy pants pegged at the cuffs and wide-collared "zoot suit" suitcoats down to the knees. The outfit also typically included wide-brimmed "pork pie" hats. The "pachucos" or "zoot suiters," as they were known, often greased their hair down so it shone and lay flat.

The growth of the Los Angeles ghetto, with some 220,000 persons of Mexican ancestry, gained national attention during the notorious zoot-suit riot in 1943. Although the common term to refer to this incident is the zoot-suit "riot," it will be evident that most of the Mexican Americans did not foment violence and were in fact the victims of violence. It was the vigilantes who spurred the riot. On June 4, vigilante soldiers and sailors, accompanied by some civilians, entered the Mexican district armed with bats. The mobs attacked Mexicans, reportedly singling out those dressed in zoot suits, often forcing them to undress before beating them.

The incident caused a good deal of national soul-searching when Americans tried to explain how so many young Americans—especially servicemen—could engage in such organized violent activity. An editorial in the *Christian Century* referred to the vigilantes as "native fascists."[70] Thomas J. McCarthy, writing in the *Commonweal*, claimed that Los Angeles newspapers showed little remorse for their contribution for the incident: "[A]t least two metropolitan newspapers treated the whole 'incident' in a carnival spirit. There were streamer heads about navy task forces taking over downtown Los Angeles and one could read in accounts a kind of approval for the whole thing."[71]

Governor Earl Warren created a committee to investigate the violence. Mexican government authorities, meanwhile, launched a series of "informal exchanges" with Secretary of State Cordell Hull, threatening an international incident. Axis government propaganda broadcasts to Latin America gave a good deal of attention to the zoot-suit incident at a time when the U.S. government was trying to maintain good relations with Latin American governments.[72]

A year before the zoot-suit incident, the U.S. government had taken notice of the disparaging depictions of Mexicans in Los Angeles' newspapers. Government agencies informally passed word to the newspapers that their coverage was impairing the nation's war efforts.[73] McWilliams, writing in the *New Republic*, claimed that the English-language Los Angeles press deserved much of the blame for the zoot-suit disturbance because of its portrayals of Hispanics as criminals:

Immediate responsibility for the outbreak of the riots must be placed upon the Los Angeles press and the Los Angeles police. For more than a year now the press (and particularly the Hearst press) has been building up anti-Mexican sentiment in Los Angeles. Using the familiar Harlem "crime-wave" technique, the press headlined every case in which a Mexican had been arrested, featured photographs of Mexicans dressed in "zoot suits," checked back over criminal records to "prove" that there had been an increase in Mexican "crime" and constantly needled the police to make more arrests.[74]

McWilliams was appointed California's commissioner of immigration and housing in 1938. In 1939 he published *Factories in the Field*, which sympathetically described the plight of the largely Hispanic migrant workers.[75] The book earned him the enmity of the state's powerful produce growers. In 1942, with the support of the growers, Governor Warren fired him.[76] After the zoot-suit riot, McWilliams, who also wrote fiercely against anti-Semitism in Germany and elsewhere in Europe, wrote a column in a New York newspaper comparing mob violence against Jews in Germany and elsewhere in German-occupied Europe with the violence against the Mexicans in Los Angeles: "There is a deadly parallel between the pictures of naked Mexican boys lying on the ground in pools of blood—with grinning mobs standing around—and the pictures one began to see a few years ago of Jews being made to clean the streets of Vienna."[77]

The long-suspected role of the general market press in fomenting the zoot-suit disturbance was corroborated in a systematic manner some years later by two sociologists.[78] They confirmed that for years before the episode the *Los Angeles Times* had carried a steady stream of negative press portrayals of the city's Mexican community.[79] Their research focused on how the coverage cultivated a climate for the eventual violent "crowd behavior." The press's repeated use of the phrases "zooters" and "zoot-suiters" drew together "the most reprehensible elements of the old unfavorable themes, namely sex crimes, delinquency gang attacks, draft-dodgers, and the like."[80] The negative press coverage stigmatized young Mexicans and transformed them into negative symbols that were prime targets of violence:

Unlike the symbol "Mexican," the "zoot-suiter" symbol evokes no ambivalent sentiments but appears in exclusively unfavorable contexts. . . . [T]he symbol "zoot-suiter" could become a basis for unambivalent community sentiment supporting hostile crowd behavior more easily than could "Mexican." . . . It [the term zoot-suiter] evoked only the picture of a breed of persons outside the normative order, devoid of morals themselves, and consequently not entitled to fair play and due process. Indeed, the zoot-suiter came to be regarded as such an exclusively fearful threat to the community that at the height of rioting the Los Angeles City Council seriously debated an ordinance making the wearing of zoot-suits a prison offense.[81]

The zoot-suit incident in Los Angeles was followed by similar, albeit smaller and isolated, incidents in San Diego, Detroit, Philadelphia, Baltimore, and even Toronto, Canada.[82] It seemed that Mexicans were an invisible minority ignored by the press when they labored in the fields doing work that most Americans refused to do for low wages. They became visible when news about them was negative, as when riots erupted.

1945 ATOMIC BOMBING OF HIROSHIMA TO LITTLE ROCK INTEGRATION, SEPTEMBER 1957

The economic "good times" after World War II were marked by apathy and blissful national ignorance regarding the plight of America's racial and ethnic minorities. Mexicans and Central Americans were still coming to the United States, working in squalid conditions and picking the food for dinner tables in an increasingly affluent and materialistic postwar America. McWilliams summed up their status: "They are the victims of a well-organized caste system which dooms them to restricted types of employment, visits upon them a complex and comprehensive system of social discrimination, and makes for chronic maladjustment. The system, moreover, tends by its very nature to be self-perpetuating."[83]

Up to now, the history of Hispanics in America was largely that of Mexicans. But the postwar years would bring other Hispanics, most notably Puerto Ricans, to the United States in significant numbers. While the United States experienced a postwar economic boom, Puerto Rico experienced severe economic problems. Many of these problems stemmed from the changing economy on the island caused by U.S. economic domination. This contributed to the "great migration" of Puerto Ricans to the mainland, primarily New York City, after World War II.[84] The increasing presence of Puerto Ricans was accompanied by a spate of news stories about "the first airborne diaspora in history."[85] Today the United States has about 6.3 million Puerto Rican citizens, about 2.3 million of whom reside on the mainland and 900,000 in New York City alone.

A Puerto Rican ghetto known as "Spanish Harlem" was burgeoning in Manhattan's upper East Side to rival that of East Los Angeles.[86] The increasing numbers of Puerto Ricans in the New York metropolitan area, where they were heavily concentrated as low-paid employees in sweatshops, caused alarm. When *Scribner's Commentary* published an article titled "Welcome Paupers and Crime: Puerto Rico's Shocking Gift to the U.S.," the Puerto Rican community led a vigorous protest.[87]

The influx of Puerto Ricans led to public demands to halt the immigration tide. But unlike Mexicans, who had to make their way, often covertly, across a border, Puerto Ricans were American citizens and could legally take a one-way flight to the United States. In fact, a small cottage industry existed to bring Puerto Ricans to the U.S. mainland legally.[88]

In 1948 Columbia University sociologist C. Wright Mills, with Clarence Senior and Rose Kohn Goldsen, published *The Puerto Rican Journey*, which concluded that Puerto Ricans, like the waves of immigrants before them, were coming to the United States for economic reasons to better their lives.[89] Although Puerto Ricans were American citizens, mainland Americans often looked upon them with suspicion. The postwar years were marked by a paranoia about Communism, and many non-Hispanic Americans considered Puerto Ricans to be Communist sympathizers. The fact that a relatively small number of Puerto Rican nationalists invoked Communist rhetoric when they called for their home-land's independence fostered this unfounded image.

The issue of Puerto Rican independence gained prominence when, on October 30, 1950, anti-U.S. nationalists on the island led an uprising, with rebels firing on the Governor's Palace in an attempt to slay Governor Luis Muñoz Marín. The uprising, which sparked violence and arson in towns throughout the island, left twenty-three dead. Two days later, two Puerto Rican nationalists attempted to assassinate President Truman. The failed assassination further fueled suspi-cions about the political loyalties of Puerto Ricans in the United States. In a move to discredit the rebels, Governor Muñoz Marín attempted to link the rebels on the island to the Truman assassination. Rebel leaders, however, claimed no involvement in the assassination attempt. They came out of the hills and sur-rendered their weapons rather than face retaliation.

As the 1950s progressed, Puerto Ricans were making headway into New York City's important institutions. By the late 1950s they, along with recently arrived Italian immigrants, predominated in the city's powerful garment district unions, which only a generation earlier had been associated with the city's Jewish im-migrant population.[90]

The widespread diffusion of television as a mass medium during the 1950s brought some unwanted recognition to the plight of another Hispanic group, Mexican Americans. Non-Hispanic Americans could now see television images of Mexicans wading across the Rio Grande to come to the United States. The press gave extensive and often insensitive news coverage of the government roundup and often brutal deportation of undocumented Mexican workers in the mid-1950s, dubbed "Operation Wetback." However, as scholar Juan García noted, despite its insensitive tone, the intense media coverage focused a spotlight on the Immigration Service and forced the agency to restrain itself, except in California, where the media favored the crackdown.

Not only had the media played an instrumental role in encouraging large numbers of "illegals" to flee the country before the drive began, but it [sic] also served the purpose of giving wide exposure to a reorganized, revitalized Immigration Service. Yet the wide publicity given to the operation was a double-edged sword in that any slipup by the service would come to the surface. The service had to be careful not to injure or harm any of the apprehended "aliens," for such an incident would surely cause serious po-litical and international repercussions. . . . And occur they did, although they were not given much press coverage in California. . . . [T]he California media was [sic] very fa-vorable toward the Immigration Service in its reporting activities. This situation was probably due to the climate of cooperation on the part of many growers in California. As much as the media was [sic] either controlled or strongly influenced by grower in-terests and large numbers of people favored the roundup, the media saw little reason to take a critical view of the operation and some of the incidents surrounding its imple-mentation.[91]

The newsmagazines during the 1940s and 1950s, following the lead of *Time* magazine's founder Henry Luce, invoked picturesque language to "enliven" the news and make it entertaining. This practice fostered insensitive news coverage of Mexicans. The newsmagazines used the "wetback" term prominently in headlines to capture attention. Perhaps partly cognizant of the derogatory nature of the term, the newsmagazines often shunned the "wetback" term in the copy, and when the word did appear in copy, the editors carefully placed it inside quotation marks, leaving readers with the message that the newsmagazines were not responsible for using the slur. In later years, this rationale to justify repeating common slurs would no longer be considered defensible.

Newsweek magazine was especially enamored of the "wetback" term. Headlines such as "The Mexican Wetbacks" (November 25, 1948, p. 80), "War with the Wetbacks" (June 28, 1954, p. 22), "Wetback Flood" (May 25, 1953, p. 56), or simply "Wetbacks" (March 11, 1946, p. 70) were common in its pages. The magazine carried the headline "Wetbacks in the River" (September 12, 1949, p. 22) to describe how many Mexican Americans crossing the Rio Grande were drowning and washing up on the Texas side of the border.

Time carried a story headlined "The Ants" (April 27, 1953, p. 29) based on a quotation by a Border Patrol worker: "Like ants; they're swarming over the desert like ants." In addition to the newsmagazines, other publications employed the "wetback" label: "Wetback Invasion in Texas" (*The Nation*, August 20, 1949, p. 168) and "Wetbacks Swarm In" (*Life*, May 21, 1951, p. 33).

In 1955 the *Science News Letter* (December 10, p. 372) carried a public health story with the ludicrous yet serious headline "Wetbacks Bring Insects" to describe the health hazards posed by Mexicans crossing the border. According to the article, these Mexican laborers were "introducing one of the world's most destructive insect pests, the pink bollworm, into uninfested areas of the nation." In frightening terms, the article quoted authoritative sources to suggest that little could be done to stop the threat:

Wetbacks are a constant threat to keeping the bollworm out of non-infested areas, but not too much can be done about them, Dr. Hoyt said. About the only effective way to keep wetbacks out would be to station a guard along every two or three feet of the border, 24 hours a day, Dr. Hoyt pointed out.

In this xenophobic atmosphere, a thirty-year-old *San Diego Union* reporter named Gene Fuson donned "a pair of old dungarees, a week's beard, [and] a straw sombrero" to pose as a "wetback" who moved across the border with ease.[92] In a series of front-page stories, Fuson described how he had purchased identity papers and an American birth certificate in Tijuana and managed to cross the border twice even though he identified himself to his Tijuana sources as a "Czech Communist agent." The "Communist" angle of the story was perhaps the most alarming element. Writing in the 1950s, during the "Red Scare," Fuson claimed that Communist agents were active among the "wetbacks.'' In reporting about Fuson, *Newsweek* concluded its story by noting that two months earlier the Senate killed a $2 million request to beef up the Border Patrol. As a result, ''[t]he wetbacks—and possibly Communist agents—will keep coming, too.''[93]

Not all news coverage of Mexican immigration was negative during this time. Texas newspapers published by R. C. Hoiles, which included the *McAllen Monitor*, the *Harlingen Star*, and the *Brownsville Herald*, were in the forefront of a campaign conducted against the Border Patrol's crackdown on Mexican workers during the 1950s. The newspapers' criticisms were not solely the result of sympathy for Mexicans, but rather sympathy for growers in a state that depended on low-paid Mexican laborers. As García wrote, ''Editorials [in these newspapers] strongly criticized the militaristic approach of the Border Patrol to round up 'illegals,' depriving respectable citizens of much-needed labor.''[94]

The postwar years and 1950s witnessed the evolution of some Spanish-language newspapers in metropolitan areas into thriving economic industries. Critics were concerned that wealthy non-Hispanic entrepreneurs, as well as Hispanic ones, both driven by profit, would ''devour'' and ''subvert'' emerging Spanish-language publications.[95]

Their fears appeared to be realized when the respected *La Prensa* of New York City fell upon economic hard times in the face of competition and was purchased by a New York entrepreneur. *La Prensa*—which had a reputation as a ''dignified spokesman for the Spanish-speaking community''—had long dominated New York's Hispanic newspaper market.[96] Another New York newspaper, *El Diario de Nueva York*, founded in 1948 by a wealthy Dominican doctor named Porfirio Domenicci, competed against *La Prensa* by ''translating the tabloid formula of sex, crime, features, and pictures into everyday Spanish,'' according to *Newsweek*.[97] *El Diario*'s slogan was ''Champion of the Puerto Ricans and Hispanos.''

Domenicci hired a longtime New York newsman named Stanley Ross to manage the paper.[98] The fact that Domenicci did not hire a Hispanic raised some eyebrows and further fueled concern that Spanish-language newspapers were not serving their Hispanic communities. But Ross proved to be an able manager who understood the role of *El Diario* in the history of New York journalism and as a voice of Puerto Ricans. As Ross said of his editorial management of the paper:

We're successful because, in a sense, we do for Puerto Ricans what Tammany Hall did for the older immigrants 50 years ago. We don't give [Puerto Ricans] buckets of coal, but we try to help them adjust to urban life. . . . Sure I hit teen-age crime hard. But I try to balance this with stories showing the positive side of Puerto Rican life. In this paper, it's news when a Puerto Rican buys a house in the suburbs or gets a civil-service job.[99]

With its formula of sex and crime, the colorful *El Diario* tabloid tripled its circulation to 70,000 between 1948 and 1955. Meanwhile the staid and dignified

La Prensa saw its circulation plummet. In 1960 it was purchased by the brothers Fortune and Anthony Pope, owners of the Italian-language *Il Progreso*. In March 1962, entrepreneur O. Roy Chalk purchased majority stock in *El Diario* and later a majority holding in *La Prensa*, merging the two newspapers in 1963 as *El Diario de Nueva York–La Prensa*. At the time of the merger, *El Diario* had an audited circulation of 70,000, making it the largest audited Spanish-language newspaper, compared to *La Prensa*'s claimed circulation of 33,000 (because it was not audited, this figure was probably highly inflated). *El Diario–La Prensa* published three editions daily, with copies air-shipped to Chicago and the West Coast.[100]

1957 LITTLE ROCK INTEGRATION TO NIXON'S RESIGNATION, AUGUST 9, 1974

The rise of civil rights movements during the 1960s created a national awareness of the Hispanic plight, one that elicited both concern and apprehension. A story published in *U.S. News & World Report*, with the headline "Another Civil Rights Headache," reflected many non-Hispanic Americans' fears that with protests and claims of discrimination by African Americans, the United States did not need complaints from another ethnic or racial minority group.[101]

Prior to the 1960s, the Hispanic label was commonly used by the popular press to describe a homogenous, pan-Hispanic group in the United States. The 1960s, however, brought about an increased recognition that distinctive social-cultural differences existed among various Hispanic groups. This recognition grew during the 1970s because of increased awareness of the concerns and demands of all minorities during the 1960s. It was also due to the arrival of Cuban immigrants to U.S. shores in the wake of that island republic's revolution that brought Fidel Castro to power. The first waves of Cuban immigrants were largely white. Many were affluent and, because they were on the losing end of the revolution, fiercely anti-Communist. Many of them identified with the conservative part of America's political spectrum—challenging the stereotype that all minorities (let alone Hispanics) were associated with liberal politics.

For years Hispanics had been coming to the United States in increasing numbers, but they remained a largely invisible minority except during brief and violent circumstances, such as civil disturbances. During the 1950s and 1960s, Hispanics were aggregating in sizable numbers in metropolitan areas other than the Southwest. During the decades of the 1960s and 1970s, they were starting to organize and gain attention to their plight. In this regard, Hispanics were following political tactics practiced by the black Civil Rights Movement to gain press coverage.[102]

The blatantly negative press portrayals—and even the derogatory term "wetback"—were still to be found in press coverage during the late 1960s. After a truckload of forty-seven Mexican-American laborers smuggled across the border were locked in their truck—"an airless, oven-hot space"—resulting in one death, *Time* ran the story under the headline "Deathtrap for Wetbacks."[103] Worse, the story used the term "wetback" throughout as a noun and adjective without quotation marks.

Also during this period television commercials for Frito-Lay corn chips used a cartoon character stereotype of a gun-toting, mustachioed Mexican bandit in a wide-brimmed sombrero named the "Frito Bandito." The Frito Bandito was "clever" and "sneaky." In the commercials, he was depicted sneaking into houses and stealing corn chips, so mothers were warned to purchase two bags.[104]

Although the press and entertainment media still used offensive Hispanic stereotypes, these portrayals no longer went uncriticized.[105] The Mexican American Anti-Defamation Committee complained of several commercials, pointing to the Frito Bandito commercial as the "most blatant offender."[106] Frito-Lay, Inc., at first balked at withdrawing the Frito Bandito character.[107] After a series of protests and boycotts, several local television stations refused to carry the Frito Bandito advertisement, and, in 1970, Frito-Lay canceled the highly successful advertising campaign.[108]

While advertisers still produced offensive advertisements, they became more sensitive and quickly withdrew the most offensive advertisements with little prodding.[109] As an example of the effectiveness of the organized protests against the Frito Bandito commercial and other offensive television commercials, ten years after the Frito Bandito incident, Tostitos, another corn chip produced by Frito-Lay, drew on a more favorable Mexican stereotype to promote its product. It used a tall, distinguished "Latin Lover" type who reminisced in a Spanish accent how, as a youth, he could not wait to return home after school and find warm corn chips waiting for him. To be sure, this was still a stereotype, but a more favorable one. It did not draw angry letters, protests, or boycott threats. As media scholars Clint Wilson and Felix Gutiérrez wrote of the Tostitos advertisement:

This time Frito-Lay had struck the right chord with Latinos and non-Latinos. The company played on the accepted imagery of Latinos and Latin America, but instead of reinforcing the image of the sneaky Mexican bandit, the company played on the romantic image of the distinguished, cultured Latino, perhaps more a product of Spain than of Mexico.[110]

While organizations such as the Mexican American Anti-Defamation Committee were countering negative images of Mexicans in the media, on another front actions were being taken to foster positive images and public awareness of Hispanic issues. During the 1960s, the Chicano Press Association (CPA) was formed as a semiofficial "confederation" to share news stories with the estimated fifty Chicano newspapers in the United States.[111] The CPA also made its service available to "all other publications committed to improve the news media in the Spanish-speaking community."[112]

Scholars in the burgeoning field of communications study also deserve credit for increasing public recognition of negative Hispanic stereotypes and neglect. "Content analysis" of media coverage was being used by journalism scholars to chronicle media portrayals of Hispanics and other ethnic and racial minorities. An array of empirical studies demonstrated negative portrayals of Hispanics in the general market news media.[113]

A landmark content analysis study by Joshua Fishman and Heriberto Casiano reported on the treatment of Puerto Ricans in four New York City dailies—two printed in English and two in Spanish—during a six-month period in 1967.[114] The authors looked at the frequency with which Puerto Ricans were mentioned in the newspapers' pages, the major focus of the reference, whether needs or problems of the Puerto Rican community were addressed, and whether Puerto Ricans were viewed positively or negatively, or as Americans or foreigners. They found the English-language newspapers were less likely to report about Puerto Ricans than were their Spanish counterparts, and when they did so it was usually to report a crime, looting, or rioting. The authors also found that both English- and Spanish-language newspapers focused on intergroup relations between the Puerto Rican and the dominant "Anglo" society. The English-language newspapers also made few references to solutions for the problems facing the Puerto Rican community while the Spanish-language newspapers gave more coverage to solutions-oriented stories.

A content analysis of a variety of minority groups in the *New York Times* from 1934 to 1994 reported that Hispanics were a largely invisible minority until the 1990s.[115] The researcher noted that over the sixty-year span of the study Hispanics were framed in crime stories far more frequently than any of the other three minority groups examined. Even in the 1990s, Hispanics still did not receive anything near the coverage that African Americans received. Noting that the most recent census indicated that Hispanics accounted for 9 percent of the U.S. population, second only to African Americans among ethnic and racial minority groups, the author stated,

Given these facts, it is surprising that the amount of coverage of Latinos found in this study was so much less than the coverage of African Americans. The number of Latinos in the population is three-fourths the number of African Americans, yet the amount of coverage of Latinos found was less than a tenth the amount found on African Americans. This seems extremely disproportionate.[116]

The earliest news reports to arouse national concern about the plight of Hispanics of largely Mexican descent in the United States involved exploited farm workers, which was by no means a new issue. But the still-young mass medium of television would thrust the issue onto the media and public agendas.[117]

In 1960, the day after Thanksgiving Day, a "CBS Reports" investigative television documentary hosted by the famed CBS journalist Edward R. Murrow and titled "Harvest of Shame" described squalid migrant labor camps along the East Coast. The program documented the workers' de facto servitude. The program was a work of passion and "clear-cut advocacy journalism . . . in the muckraking style of Ida Tarbell and Lincoln Steffens," one scholar noted.[118] While the program did not focus on Hispanic migrant workers, it set the stage for later news reports involving the exploitation of Hispanic farm laborers.

The cause of Mexican-American farm laborers was taken up by César Estrada Chávez, a Mexican American who had worked in California vineyards during his boyhood. Chávez, who understood the importance of getting press attention for his cause, organized farm workers in California's agricultural belt and created the United Farm Workers (UFW) organization during the early and mid-1960s. He was trained in labor organizational skills by Saul Alinsky,[119] a well-known social activist who believed that minority groups needed to organize to achieve their demands. Alinsky impressed Chávez with the belief that the political system can work and violence is not needed.[120]

A competitor for the mantle of Hispanic leadership and media attention was firebrand speaker Reies López Tijerina, known as "Rey Tigre" (King Tiger). Tijerina organized the Alianza Federal de las Mercedes (Federal Land Grant Alliance) and captured media and public attention by demanding the establishment of "free city states" for Mexican descendants of landless peasants in 2,500 square miles of New Mexican territory that he claimed was stolen by the United States from the Spanish more than 100 years earlier. On June 5, 1967, he led a gun-toting group of insurrectionists on a courthouse raid in Tierra Amarilla with the intention of making a citizen's arrest of the district attorney for the earlier arrest of Tijerina's followers.[121] One scholar stated, "The raid was news and made headlines across the country. Tijerina was good copy, and for a while liberals supported him."[122]

Rodolfo "Corky" González, another important Chicano leader during this period, founded the Crusade for Justice in Denver and penned the epic poem *Yo Soy Joaquín*, which became a rallying cry of the Chicano movement. He also espoused Tijerina's separatist goals. González called for the United Nations to hold a plebiscite to establish an independent homeland for Hispanics in the Southwest to be called Aztlán, the name given to the land the ancient Aztecs were supposed to have inhabited before moving southward to Tenochitlán (present-day Mexico City).[123]

In contrast to Tijerina and other Chicano leaders perceived by the general public as radicals, César Chávez gained respect as a spokesperson for Hispanic causes, both in Hispanic and in politically liberal non-Hispanic circles as well. Chávez gained nationwide attention after securing a stunning victory over grape growers who were forced by public pressure and boycott threats to recognize Chávez's UFW union.[124] Part of Chávez's success was his ability to get his causes portrayed favorably and sympathetically in the general market news media. He emphasized nonviolence and was regularly photographed beside posters of Martin Luther King, Jr., and Mahatma Gandhi. A devout Catholic, he prayed in public, led UFW workers in prayers, and made the Virgin of Guadalupe a symbol of his movement. As F. Arturo Rosales observed, Chávez was aware that his opponents characterized him as a "radical," linking him with Castro and the Cuban revolution. He thus carefully and calculatingly cultivated an image that would make him palatable in what were regarded as mainstream circles. Scholar Arturo Rosales wrote:

But Chávez was careful to never endorse any radical ideas that opposed capitalism, primarily because he himself did not espouse revolution. . . . Indeed, Chávez obtained support from a dazzling inter-denominational array of religious groups. This helped sustain the union through its most difficult times, but it would have been impossible if the union had projected a radical image. The rallying cry became simply, "¡Justicia para los campesinos y viva la Virgin de Guadalupe!" [Justice for the field workers and long live the Virgin of Guadalupe!] Such symbol manipulation was deliberate but not cynical.[125]

Thanks to Chávez, it became fashionable at Manhattan parties to boycott grapes and shun Gallo wine. Chávez offered a human face to the exploited migrant workers.[126] He regularly appeared among the 1960s liberal "beautiful people" set, which included Robert Kennedy and the folk-singing group Peter, Paul, and Mary. In February 1968, Chávez began a fast "as an act of penance, recalling workers to the nonviolent roots of their movement."[127] With an underlying tone of cynicism about how Chávez was putting forward a moderate image, *Time* magazine reported on the very public nature of Chávez's fast:

Although he insisted that his decision was essentially a private one, the fast took on a certain circus aura and raised suspicions that its motivation was more theatrical than theological. . . . One woman solemnly asked him if he were indeed a saint. When the fast ended, Senator Robert Kennedy knelt next to him to receive Communion. Some 8,000 others joined them in Delano's Memorial Park for a bread-breaking ceremony.[128]

After the grape boycott victory, Chávez was successful in his "boycott lettuce" campaign. He was so mainstream that his cause was warmly received at the Democratic National Convention in 1972, with Senator Edward Kennedy addressing the convention, "Greetings fellow lettuce boycotters!"

Chávez's contribution was to organize Mexican laborers and help them use the news media to gain attention for their cause. He also started a union newspaper and two radio stations to forward his programs. As a case study using content analysis, scholar Stephan Rada documented how a small group of Chicano strikers in fiercely antiunion Texas during 1968, through the careful staging of demonstrations and other events in the tradition of Chávez, managed to gain positive news coverage. In this way, the strikers cultivated favorable public opinion and support for their quest to be represented by a union.[129] Rada demonstrated that union leaders had cleverly overcome anticipated hostile local news coverage of their strike, including having Chávez arrive in Austin as part of "César Chávez Day" and speak in favor of their cause.

Public attention was riveted on Hispanics in August 1970, when police and Chicanos clashed in Los Angeles after Vietnam War protests turned violent, resulting in 260 arrests, sixty wounded, and three dead. One of those killed was Rubén Salazar, a *Los Angeles Times* columnist. Salazar had gained a reputation for providing sympathetic coverage of the Chicano movement in the general market press since the movement's inception.[130] He had also exposed police brutality in the barrios.[131] During the rioting in Los Angeles in 1970, a Los Angeles deputy sheriff, responding to what he claimed was a gunman holed up in a bar, shot a tear gas canister into the bar. The canister hit Salazar in the head. "To this day, many believe he [Salazar] was silenced because he wrote about the Chicano/Latino civil rights movement."[132]

This chapter has described how Hispanics of Mexican heritage formed ethnic enclaves in the West and Southwest and, later, how Hispanics of mostly Puerto Rican heritage settled in New York and elsewhere in the Northeast. Cubans, a third major group of Hispanics, made their way to the United States in significant numbers during the 1960s. Endemic social and economic inequalities in Cuba that had fermented since the turn of the century created an atmosphere that was ripe for rebellion. Following the Cuban revolution, when Fidel Castro took power on January 1, 1959, many Cubans, unhappy with the increasingly Marxist tint of Castro's government, fled the island. Fewer than 50,000 Cubans had lived in the United States before the Cuban revolution of 1959. In that year, 27,000 Cubans arrived here, with Miami as their port of entry. By the end of 1960, another 60,000 had sought asylum in the United States.[133]

At first many Miamians believed the Cubans' stay would be only temporary. But the Cubans remained, and they changed the character of the community from a tourist-based economy to an international trade center.[134] Many Cuban refugees, who had been business leaders in Cuba, used their experience and connections in Latin America to make Miami a center for Latin American trade. Pre-Castro Cuba also had a thriving journalistic community, and many of the exiles with journalistic experience entered Spanish-language print and broadcast journalism in the United States.[135] The less-well-to-do Cubans took low-paying jobs in the city's thriving tourist industry, displacing many African Americans, a fact that would be partly responsible for the later frictions that developed between the city's Cuban and African-American communities.[136]

The Cuban diaspora to the United States that began in 1959 would, by the middle of the 1980s, bring an estimated one million Cubans to the United States, of which about half would settle in south Florida. By 1980 Miami had the second largest Cuban population in the world after Havana. The first wave of immigrants, known as the "Golden Exiles," consisted disproportionately of the island's upper and middle classes.[137] The Cuban immigrants transformed sections of Miami into replicas of old Havana. Calle Ocho (Eighth Street) became a bustling area with restaurants and nightclubs. Some restaurants, such as the Versailles and Centro Vasco (no longer in business), became meeting spots for the Cuban community's political leaders.

In sharp contrast to the Chicanos in the Southwest, who were portrayed in the news media as political "militants" and "radicals," Miami's Cubans were portrayed as fiercely anti-Communist and even patriotic Americans. Also in contrast to the stereotype of "lazy" Mexicans, Cubans were portrayed as hard-working, industrious and entrepreneurial, and a "model minority." It was typical for the press to refer to the Cubans' "historic propensity for hard work."[138] Studies of Cuban immigration and settlement, however, showed a more complex picture of Cuban immigrant success in America than that portrayed in the popular press.[139]

There was surprisingly little public outcry or negative press portrayal of Cuban immigrants as competitors for jobs, partly because the Cubans' reputations as anti-Communists made them welcome during the national paranoia of the Cold War, partly because of the vibrancy of the U.S. economy, and partly because the Cuban immigrants, unlike the Mexicans and Puerto Ricans coming to the United States, were largely professional, educated, and of white European descent.[140]

Broadcast Coverage

The 1960 "Harvest of Shame" documentary televised on CBS helped sensitize the viewing public to the oppressive situation of migrant workers in the United States. Although the program did not focus on Mexican-American migrant farm workers per se, the documentary's spirited advocacy journalism and the respect commanded by host Edward R. Murrow helped pave the way for later investigations by the news media and direct action by Mexican Americans.

After the 1970 Vietnam War protest clashes between police and Chicanos, other mass market news media started to give sympathetic coverage to the plight of Hispanics. During October 1971, CBS carried an acclaimed documentary titled "Chicano." It was hosted by Hughes Rudd and produced by Gene DePoris. "Chicano" was praised as a "balanced" report that focused on the growing Chicano movement in Los Angeles and the Southwest; nevertheless, "Chicano" was an all-too-common example of critically praised news coverage that failed to translate into significant ratings. The public was still not interested in Hispanics.[141]

This lack of interest was illustrated in John Seggar's study of television depictions of females and minorities between 1971 and 1975. The study reported improvements in television portrayals of African Americans, but Hispanics, coded under "other minorities," showed "only a minimal gain." The fact that a major ethnic minority group such as Hispanics could be dispensed with in the "other" category illustrated the media's neglect of Hispanics.[142]

Spanish-Language Broadcasting. Spanish-language radio broadcasting in the United States as a community medium dates to the mid-1920s, when English-language stations sold flat-rate time segments to Hispanic brokers.[143] By the 1970s, the brokerage system was ending "in favor of the more independent, full-time stations in AM and subsequently FM—many transmitting up to twenty-four hours per day," one writer stated.[144] During the 1970s, national

Spanish-language broadcast media gained prominence. The growth of Spanish-language radio and especially television caught the attention of Hispanic and non-Hispanic entrepreneurs, who saw Spanish-language media as potentially profitable enterprises.[145]

As early as the 1940s, broadcast media tycoons in Latin America had recognized the potential of the Spanish-language market in the United States. During the 1950s, Cuban media magnate Goar Mestre, who along with his brothers controlled Cuba's premier CMQ radio network, briefly expanded into radio in Puerto Rico, but he never expanded his operations to the U.S. mainland.[146]

It was clear that television was becoming a major medium to reach Hispanic audiences in the United States. Mexico's wealthy Emilio Azcárraga set his sights on the growing Hispanic population of the United States, but he was barred by Federal Communications Commission (FCC) rules from holding a majority interest in a U.S. broadcasting outlet because he was not an American citizen. The resourceful Azcárraga circumvented the FCC regulation by creating alliances with several U.S. citizens. With an eye on the Latin American and U.S. market, in the late 1950s, Azcárraga created Televicentro. The company, located in Mexico City, boasted a large television production center with live television production facilities, twenty-four studios, and a transmission tower.[147] To market his films and Televicentro's programs in the United States, Azcárraga created Productora de Teleprogramas de México (ProTele).[148]

In the United States, Azcárraga was instrumental in the creation and development of the Spanish International Network (SIN). This network, which started with a couple of stations in San Antonio and Los Angeles in the late 1950s, began to dominate the Spanish-language market during the 1970s and 1980s. The use of communication satellites simplified and expedited the transport of programming and news between Televicentro's studios in Mexico and SIN's stations in the United States.[149]

1974 RESIGNATION OF NIXON TO LOS ANGELES UPRISING, APRIL 29, 1992

As the 1970s drew to a close, leaders in the Hispanic community had great expectations for the decade of the 1980s. In a fit of enthusiasm, Miami Mayor Maurice Ferre declared the 1980s "the Decade of the Hispanic."[150] As the 1980s drew to an end, *Time* magazine made a similar prediction for the coming decade with its July 11, 1988, special issue on Hispanic influence in the United States. Actor (and role model) Edward James Olmos, of the then-hit television show "Miami Vice," was featured on the cover. The thrust of the *Time* special issue was that Latin culture was quickly becoming part of the general American culture: "America, the great receiver. From every culture to arrive within its borders, it embraces some new ingredient. . . . Nowadays the mainstream is receiving a rich new current. More and more, American film, theater, music, design, dance, and art are taking on a Hispanic color and spirit."[151]

The sheer magnitude of the Hispanic population growth attracted the attention of academics in political science, sociology, ethnology, and mass communications. These researchers began to study Hispanic migration trends, settlement patterns, labor fluctuations, consumer behavior, and depictions in the mass media. The "Latinamericanization of the United States" and the pros and cons of cultural assimilation became the topic of many studies.[152] At the same time, within the Hispanic community, a movement began to gain recognition and acceptance by the larger American community.

This chapter has thus far focused on the three main Hispanic groups in the United States: Mexicans (63 percent), Puerto Ricans (12 percent), and Cubans (5 percent). In the late 1970s and early 1980s, new groups began to arrive. With the triumph of the Sandinistas in Nicaragua, Central American—especially Nicaraguan—immigration on a large scale began in 1979. Guerilla wars elsewhere in Central America brought Guatemalans and Salvadorans to the United States as well, mostly as low-wage domestic employees and restaurant workers.[153] By 1990 Los Angeles County had as many as one million Central Americans, the majority probably undocumented. Of these, an estimated 300,000 to 500,000 were Salvadorans, and 120,000 to 200,000 were Guatemalans.[154]

Other Hispanic immigrants from elsewhere in Latin America settled on the East Coast. By the mid-1980s, from 300,000 to 500,000 Dominicans had come to the United States, establishing enclaves in northern Manhattan and the Queens borough in New York City.[155] They resided in the same areas as middle-class Colombian immigrants escaping political violence at home.[156] Similar upheavals during the 1970s and 1980s also brought middle-class immigrants from Chile and Argentina.[157]

Although the earlier Cuban exiles had been accepted, if not welcomed, into the United States as warriors in the vanguard against the Cold War, the waves of Cuban exiles arriving since 1980 have been of a different strain from the original exiles. While they still were anti-Castro, their reasons for leaving Cuba were economic as well as political.[158] Many were nonwhite. Partly because of racial reasons, their poverty, and the end of the Cold War, the later waves of Cubans were not as easily accepted into the United States as the earlier generation of Cubans had been.[159]

Sociologists count as many as five major Cuban migrations to the United States, including the "Marielito exodus" starting in the mid-1970s.[160] A sixth wave, known as the "Balsero" wave, occurred during the summer of 1994, when about 70,000 Cubans crossed the Florida straits in small boats and makeshift vessels.

The "Marielitos," in particular—so named because they fled from the Cuban port city of Mariel—had the burden of overcoming the image of being Cuba's dregs, foisted on the United States by a clever Castro. Castro boasted that he had expunged Cuba of its "scum" by opening the island's jails and releasing its most hardened criminals to the United States while President Carter welcomed the exiles with "an open heart and open arms." But only a small number of the Marielitos were murderers or rapists, and the news coverage as a whole suggested that "most of those arriving here, if guilty of anything, had simply shown too great a distaste for Castro and his government."[161]

During the first two months of the exodus, the press gave little coverage to the large number of gays among the refugees, although many journalists were aware of them. In an important and controversial piece published in the *Columbia Journalism Review*, Michael Massing, *CJR*'s executive editor, accused the news media of ignoring the gays among the Marielitos. He declared the incident exposed "the timidity and awkwardness of the American press in handling stories about gays."[162] The press might have continued to ignore the gay angle had not a White House leak confirmed the large number of gays among the refugees.

Many journalists, aware that the public would react negatively to so many gays among the Marielitos, were uncomfortable about how to report the gay angle. The incident was something of a watershed in the history of press coverage of Hispanics. Journalists as a group, who in an earlier period thought nothing of describing Hispanics as "wetbacks" and casting doubt on their loyalty to the United States, now recognized that they had some responsibility in shaping a national consciousness about minority groups. But, as Massing's article made clear, there was no clear answer regarding whether the press had made the right decision to minimize the gay angle.[163]

In Miami, many Cubans were disturbed by negative media portrayals of the *recién llegados* (the recently arrived).[164] In a highly publicized reaction to the perceived negative depictions of the Marielitos, the Miami City Commission succeeded in barring most of the film production of Brian de Palma's remake of *Scarface* in Miami. The remake, released in 1983, featured a Marielito drug king in Miami.[165]

The relatively rapid Latinization of Miami caused growing pains in the city's general market news media. While this was happening throughout the country,[166] the relatively rapid transformation in Miami serves as an exemplar case. A wave of "Hispanic panic" overtook the *Miami Herald* newsroom, said one scholar, as the newspaper tried to cope with the challenge of serving the concerns of its growing and increasingly critical Cuban population.[167]

Long considered one of the finest newspapers in the Knight-Ridder chain, the *Herald* saw its circulation remain static as the local population surged. Cuban community leaders castigated the *Herald* for what they perceived as its "insensitivity" toward Cubans for refusing to take a tougher editorial stance against Castro and Cuba.[168] The establishment of the Cuban American National Foundation (CANF), the city's most powerful Cuban exile group, exacerbated the paper's problems with the Cuban community. In October 1987, the CANF purchased a full-page ad in the *Herald* claiming the paper was aggressive in its "ignorance of our people." The situation became further aggravated in early 1992 when Jorge Mas Canosa, the chief executive officer (CEO) of a Miami construction company and head of the CANF, declared a campaign against the

Herald and the Spanish-language *El Nuevo Herald*. Among other complaints, Mas Canosa was angered because the *Herald* failed to endorse emphatically legislation aimed at tightening the embargo against Cuba in its editorial pages. "The *Miami Herald* usually takes and assumes the same positions as the Cuban government," Mas Canosa declared over a leading Spanish-language radio station in the city. "But we must confess that they [*sic*] were once more discreet about it, trying to place a certain distance between themselves and Castro."[169]

Within three months of Mas Canosa's declaration, the CANF had purchased large signs on city buses with messages declaring, "I Don't Believe *The Herald*" (in English and in Spanish). The organization also distributed fliers with examples of "unfair" stories published in the *Herald*, such as travel stories about Cuba in the travel section being an example of the *Herald*'s insensitivity to the Cuban community. So fierce was the anti-*Herald* campaign that the Miami-based Inter-American Press Association, an organization dedicated to freedom of the press in the Western Hemisphere and usually known for condemning press restrictions by authoritarian Latin American governments, criticized the CANF campaign against the *Herald*: "Campaigns of denunciation and criticism based on emotions run the risk of inflaming some members of the community to the point of violence."[170]

Well before the brouhaha with the CANF, the *Herald* sought to address its Hispanic problem. Most notably, the paper published *El Herald* as a largely Spanish-language translation insert starting in 1976. After complaints from the city's Cuban community that *El Herald* was not serving Spanish-speaking readers and with Knight-Ridder (which owns the *Miami Herald*) research indicating a significant market for a trendy Spanish-language newspaper, *El Herald*, which had been in continuous publication as an insert in the *Miami Herald* since March 29, 1976, was revamped as *El Nuevo Herald* in November 1987.[171] In an attempt to give *El Nuevo Herald* its own identity, the slick-looking newspaper, graphically influenced by *USA Today*, was published in separate facilities from its English-language parent with a separate staff. As scholar Gonzalo Soruco wrote of Knight-Ridder's plan for its Spanish-language newspaper:

Fearful of losing additional readers, Knight-Ridder formulated changes designed to reach, attract, and retain Hispanics. Some of *The Herald*'s changes were cosmetic, others substantial; many were unpopular. In the early 1980s, the newspaper began hiring Hispanics for mid-level management positions. It also softened its coverage of issues that were delicate for Cubans and invited members of the Hispanic community, particularly Cubans, to write commentaries for its op-ed pages.[172]

The 1970s and 1980s witnessed the beginning of a programmatic body of research on both news and entertainment media portrayals of Hispanics.[173] A study by Charles Ericksen, founder and editor of Hispanic Link, Inc., a Washington, D.C., news service, bemoaned the absence of Hispanic leaders and experts as sources in the news.[174] The "irresponsible" U.S. media, Ericksen argued, do not give Hispanic spokespersons visibility in the general market press. Describing six "dimensions of irresponsibility," Ericksen described how U.S. newspapers neglected Hispanics. He argued that the press did not allow Hispanics to be authorities on general issues and "even in areas where Hispanics have the obvious expertise."[175] As a result, even in the late 1970s and early 1980s, he was able to chronicle insensitive headlines and stories in the general market press. The following are just two examples cited by Ericksen: "State Threatened by Alien Horde" (banner headline in the *Los Angeles Examiner*, August 8, 1977) and "No Greenbacks for Wetbacks" (*Washington Monthly*, December 1980).

Content analysis studies confirmed negative media portrayals of Hispanics. A study made by media scholar Félix Gutiérrez, which sampled 144 articles about undocumented immigration that appeared in California newspapers between January 1977 and March 1978, found that almost half the articles used the term "alien" or "illegal alien" in the headlines to describe people who were burdens on society and problems for law enforcement.[176] In a similar vein, Francis Matera analyzed stories dealing with Cuban issues in the *Miami Herald* and *El Herald/El Nuevo Herald* from 1976 to 1988.[177] The study reported a pattern of negative images of Cubans that formed a stereotypical image.

Not all the research yielded negative findings. Robert Logan and Bruce Garrison's study of newspaper coverage of the 1980 Mariel boatlift of Cubans to the United States indicated that mass market press coverage of Hispanics depended upon political and ethnic differences in U.S. cities.[178] In their comparative content analysis, the authors found that the Miami newspaper reported significantly more news about the influx of Cubans to the United States than did a newspaper in Saint Petersburg, Florida. They claimed that the influx of Hispanics into the United States was having an impact on local governments and the news media's coverage and interpretation of international news.

Bradley Greenberg and his colleagues, reporting on newspaper coverage of Mexican Americans in six Southwestern dailies in 1980, also found that Mexican Americans were covered proportionate to their communities' populations, although the majority of local stories met this requirement only because they contained Spanish surnames.[179] However, the researchers also found that the more detailed news stories focusing primarily on Mexican Americans accounted for only 10 percent of the local news. Elsewhere, Greenberg and his colleagues claimed that "sports news and photo coverage get high marks for their inclusion of Hispanics. . . . [L]ocal news coverage exclusive of sports gets a passing grade—good, not excellent, but better than it is currently receiving credit for."[180] A cross-media study made of local Hispanic-American news in Southwestern cities also showed that Hispanics are covered often by the local media.[181]

In another study that warned against assuming uniformly negative news coverage, Judy VanSlyke Turk and her colleagues, in a study of the Albuquerque *Journal* and San Antonio *Express*, found that Hispanics received fair treatment in the local press.[182] "Hispanics and Hispanic issues are present in the news-paper newshole in proportion to their presence in the population."[183]

1992 LOS ANGELES UPRISING TO PRESIDENTIAL
ELECTION, NOVEMBER 1996

The 1990s were marked by a number of issues relevant to media images of Hispanics. Some enduring topics such as police brutality continued to be im-portant. In April 1996, a television news crew in Los Angeles videotaped sheriff's deputies clubbing two Mexicans after stopping a truck full of Mexican immigrants after a high-speed chase. The scene, which was repeated on the local news for weeks, bore an eerie similarity to the violent police beating of Rodney King. But the beating of the Mexicans occurred during a heated debate in the state about curbing the flow of immigrants from Mexico and denying them basic benefits. As a result, many Mexican community leaders were stunned by how many Americans and the press sympathized with the police.

One of the most important issues relevant to Hispanics in the 1990s was the "English First" or "Official English" movement undertaken to make English the official language of business and government in the United States. Critics see the calls for English as the official language as a throwback to the fiercely anti-immigrant and anti-Catholic Know-Nothing Party (also known as the Amer-ican Party), which briefly enjoyed political success during the 1850s.[184] The period from 1850 to 1920 had been marked by a series of state acts that effec-tively blocked non-English speakers from access to voting, public education, and other rights.[185] Since the first decade of the twentieth century, with increas-ing fear of immigration, various states passed legislation mandating public (and sometimes private) school instruction be in English. By 1923 thirty-four states had approved such legislation.[186] Only in the late 1950s and early 1960s, with the increasing demands made by African Americans for civil rights, did the Supreme Court overturn literacy tests and, by extension, language requirements for voting and other basic rights.[187]

To be sure, not all supporters of the U.S. English movement can be dismissed as racists or xenophobes. Early in the Official English debate, supporters of English First included such progressives as former CBS broadcaster Walter Cronkite, author Saul Bellow, and Alistair Cooke. It also included many His-panic leaders. These well-meaning supporters, however, withdrew their support when they realized that many supporters of official English had a hidden agenda. The group's reputation became tainted when, in 1987, John Tanton, the group's founder, remarked that Hispanics have "greater reproductive powers."[188]

Fear of growing numbers of Hispanics and of the cultural and economic consequences of their numbers fostered legislation to restrict immigration during the 1990s. In California, Proposition 187 (known as the "Save Our State" initiative) was endorsed by Governor Pete Wilson. Wilson made "Prop 187" one of the cornerstone issues in his failed bid for the 1996 Republican presidential nomination. The proposition was overwhelmingly approved by California voters in November 1994. If upheld by the courts, it would deprive state residents who are not legal residents of numerous social services, including use of public schools and nonemergency health care. On August 1, 1996, the House of Representatives passed the English Language Empowerment Act. The measure was meant to limit strictly the use of languages other than English for government business. One of the act's requirements calls for members of Congress to issue press releases and newsletters in English only.

Evidence suggests that journalists are extremely uninformed about immigration issues. They often report data about the harmful social consequences of immigration to society by relying on sources hostile to immigration while ignoring the beneficial social and economic aspects of immigration. According to John J. Miller, the associate director of the Manhattan Institute's Center for New American Community in Washington, D.C.,

The common accusations about high costs, neighborhood decline, welfare use and job competition serve as covers for closet xenophobes who won't admit in public that they are uncomfortable with the racial and ethnic make-up of today's immigrants. That these complaints don't have much empirical support makes their case a tough sell, but sloppy journalism turns a complex and encouraging reality into a simplistic and ominous fiction.[189]

Frank del Olmo of the *Los Angeles Times* claims that journalists reporting immigration are easily manipulated by sources with vested interests because journalists lack a sense of history about immigration. "Overall," he maintains, "too much of the coverage is done in a quick, dirty, and sexy way." As a result, well-meaning journalists were duped by politicians who exploited the immigration issue during the 1990s. Although by and large del Olmo claims that politicians, not the press, created the paranoia over immigration, the press is to blame for cultivating the climate of fear that allowed politicians to exploit the issue.[190]

The approval of Proposition 187 caused anger in Hispanic communities throughout the nation. Its passage stirred debates in Spanish-language media organizations over the appropriateness of those media openly advocating positions against Proposition 187. Hispanic journalists' self-questioning about the appropriateness of the objectivity model of journalism was triggered by a team of college-educated Hispanic journalists who posed as Mexican laborers looking for work in California, driving a beat-up pickup truck, for a story that was aired on ABC's "Prime Time Live." The story documented the exploitation of Mexican workers in California and, in contrast to charges that these laborers were bleeding the state's economy, showed that they were necessary to the economic growth of the state.[191]

The "Prime Time Live" story and other investigative stories like it, in which Hispanic journalists appeared actively to expose problems in the Hispanic community, have ignited journalistic debates regarding the role of Hispanic jour-nalists.[192] It was the subject of much debate during the meetings of the National Association of Hispanic Journalists (NAHJ). As New York *Daily News* col-umnist Juan González said during a recent NAHJ meeting: "Throughout your career, there are editors and publishers and owners who will tell you differently, [that you] must be 'objective, above the fray.' I am challenging that."[193]

CONCLUSION

Empirical research conducted on media portrayals of Hispanics has failed to document evidence of changes over the years. Most of the research undertaken narrowly focused on certain Hispanic subgroups (or did not distinguish among Hispanic subgroups) in limited—often local or regional—media outlets during limited periods.[194] This is a failing since even a cursory historical analysis in-dicates that the general market news media have responded to social changes regarding Hispanics in America. Before World War II, the news media neglected the "invisible minority." After the war, historical evidence suggests that news coverage was uniformly negative, focusing on the "dangers" of Hispanics as criminals, burdens on the social system, and cultural threats to the dominant English-speaking society. Since the tumultuous 1960s and 1970s, the media seem to have been influenced by heightened social awareness of the plight of minorities. Some news media began shifting from conceiving of Hispanics as a monolithic group and recognized cultural and political differences among His-panic subgroups. Much of the insensitive, even racist, coverage has waned, and some favorable coverage might be expected.

Empirical research is needed to corroborate the anecdotal evidence that news coverage changed with social circumstances. In addition, researchers need to examine whether the coverage went through progressive improvement over the years or whether there were roadblocks and even setbacks. For example, with the current paranoia over immigration, some critics have argued that the country is experiencing a revival of insensitive press coverage of Spanish-speaking Americans.

Perhaps it is unfair to put the full onus of responsibility for any group's depictions on the media. The media are part of the larger society and cannot be disconnected from events and attitudes in the society. Still, as central cultural organs, the news and entertainment media must take some responsibility for the society's images of its minority groups.

After signs of improvement in the news media coverage of Hispanics were noted, some people began to fear that an ugly trend is now reemerging—that the news media will portray Hispanics as foreigners and a threat. This regressive trend is attributed to the fear associated with the increase in the nation's Hispanic population, the rise of Hispanic population in urban centers such as Los Angeles, New York, Miami, and elsewhere, and a growing xenophobia over immigration that has been fostered by some unscrupulous political leaders. The immigration issue was deftly exploited by Republican presidential aspirants Pete Wilson and Pat Buchanan during the 1996 campaign. Buchanan, in particular, often used insensitive language to assail Hispanics. He repeatedly used the name "José" to refer to all Mexicans *en masse* and referred to "a landfill called multiculturalism." With special regard to Hispanics, he promised to erect a wall or lay down a trench along the Mexico border to keep Mexicans from coming to the United States, as was noted in the quotation at the beginning of this chapter.

Did the news media perpetuate the increasing xenophobia? The Unity Project, sponsored by the National Association of Hispanic Journalists as well as other minority journalism associations, noted a series of disturbing news media reports published during the 1990s.[195] For example, in 1993, a *Time* magazine cover story featured "Miami: The Capital of Latin America." The Unity Project report claimed that the cover story left the impression that Miami's Cubans and other Hispanics were not real Americans. The Unity Project also noted with some alarm that terms such as "alien" and "illegal" were creeping into mass market news reports about Hispanics.

The news media are technologies. The tendency to criticize them for every social problem ignores the fact that they are what journalists and society make of them. Journalists of course must report the news—the good and the bad. And sometimes the news media are indeed unfairly criticized for being the bearers of news that people would rather not know. But, as the history of news coverage of Hispanics in the United States also shows, the news media have at times exacerbated some of society's worst fears about immigrant "invasions." But just as the news media can play on people's fears, they can also contribute to social understanding.

NOTES

The authors gratefully acknowledge the insightful comments of Federico Subervi-Vélez, of the University of Texas at Austin, which greatly improved the manuscript. The authors, however, are responsible for any deficiencies in the chapter.

1. James Bennet, "Candidate's Speech Is Called Code for Controversy," *New York Times*, 25 February 1996, A22, late edition.

2. Patricia Gonzáles and Robert Rodríguez, "A Homage to Rubén Salazar: Honoring the First Amendment," in *Sin Fronteras: Window of Opportunity*. National Association of Hispanic Journalists, 13th Annual Convention, El Paso, Texas, and Juárez, Mexico, June 1995, 12.

3. Joan Moore and Raquel Pinderhughes, "Introduction," in *In the Barrios: Latinos and the Underclass Debate*, ed. Joan Moore and Raquel Pinderhughes, (New York: Russell Sage Foundation, 1993), xi–xxxix.

4. Ilan Stavans, *The Hispanic Condition: Reflections on Culture and Identity in America* (New York: HarperCollins, 1995), 9.

5. David Weber, *Foreigners in Their Native Land: Historical Roots of Mexican Americans* (Albuquerque: University of New Mexico Press, 1973).

6. The United States acquired Louisiana (1803) and Florida (1821) before the Mex-

ican conquest. Since Hispanics in these territories were mainly European whites, Americans "did not vilify the Hispanics of the Southeast. But the Anglos did despise the racial mixture of northern Mexicans, deeming it a mongrelization of the lowest order. And by subordinating northern Mexicans as inferior, they built up a case for appropriating their lands, even through violence." F. Arturo Rosales, *Chicano! A History of the Mexican American Civil Rights Movement* (Houston: Arte Público Press, 1996), xxii.

7. Frank Luther Mott, *A History of American Magazines, 1741–1850* (Cambridge: Harvard University Press, 1938). See pp. 454–56 for American magazine coverage of the war, which included a surprising amount of antiwar coverage.

8. Himilce Novas, *Everything You Need to Know about Latino History* (New York: Plume/Penguin, 1994), 82–83.

9. Cecil Robinson, *Mexico and the Hispanic Southwest in American Literature* (Tucson: University of Arizona Press, 1977).

10. Arnoldo De León, *They Called Them Greasers: Anglo Attitudes toward Mexicans in Texas, 1821–1900* (Austin: University of Texas Press, 1983); Stephen Gould, *The Mismeasure of Man* (New York: W. W. Norton, 1981); Sarah Sharbach, *Stereotypes of Latin America, Press Images, and U.S. Foreign Policy* (New York: Garland Publishing, 1993).

11. Norman D. Smith, "Mexican Stereotypes on Fictional Battlefields," *Journal of Popular Culture* 13 (1980), 526–40; quotation on p. 537.

12. Wilson and Gutiérrez date the first Spanish-language newspaper to 1808, with the publication of *El Misisipí* of New Orleans. Clint C. Wilson II and Félix Gutiérrez, *Minorities and the Media* (Beverly Hills: Sage, 1985).

13. Tom Reilly, "The War of New Orleans: 1846–1848," *Journalism History* 13 (Autumn/Winter 1986), 86–95.

14. Richard Griswold del Castillo, *The Treaty of Guadalupe Hidalgo: A Legacy of Conflict* (Norman: University of Oklahoma Press, 1990). With the Gadsden Treaty in 1854, the United States purchased another 30,000 square miles of territory from Mexico.

15. Robert T. Bach, "Mexican Immigration and the American State," *International Migration Review* 12 (Winter 1978), 536–58; Carey McWilliams, "The Forgotten Mexican," *Common Ground* 3 (Spring 1943), 65–78.

16. Charles Brown, *The Correspondents' War: Journalists in the Spanish-American War* (New York: Charles Scribner's Sons, 1967); Joyce Milton, *The Yellow Kids: Foreign Correspondents in the Heyday of Yellow Journalism* (New York: Harper & Row, 1989); David J. Weber, "The Spanish Legacy in North America and the Historical Imagination," *Western Historical Journal* 23 (February 1992), 5–24; Joseph E. Wisan, "The Cuban Crisis As Reflected in the New York Press (1895–1898)," *Columbia University Studies in History, Economics, and Public Law* 403 (1934), 455–60.

17. Ilia Rodríguez, "News Reporting As Colonial Discourse: Press Coverage of the U.S. Invasion of Puerto Rico during the Spanish-American War" (Paper presented at Association for Education in Journalism and Mass Communication Convention, Washington, D.C., August 1995).

18. W. A. Swanberg, *Citizen Hearst* (New York: Charles Scribner's Sons, 1961), 110.

19. Richard Harding Davis, *The Cuban and Porto Rican Campaigns* (New York: Charles Scribner's Sons, 1898).

20. Ibid., 110.

21. Ibid., 138.

22. Virginia Sánchez-Korrol, "In Their Own Right: A History of Puerto Ricans in the U.S.A," in *Handbook of Hispanic Cultures in the United States: History*, ed. Alfredo Jiménez (Houston: Arte Público Press, 1993), 281–301.

23. Juan Casasús, *La Emigración Cubana y la Independencia de la Patria* (Havana, Cuba: Lex, 1953); César Andreu Iglesias, *Memorias de Bernardo Vega: Una Contribución a la Historia de la Comunidad Puertorriqueña en Nueva York* (Rio Piedras, Puerto Rico: Ediciones Huracán, 1980); Clara Rodríguez, *Puerto Ricans: Born in the U.S.A.* (Boston: Unwin Hyman, 1989); Virginia Sánchez-Korrol, *From Colonia to Community: The History of Puerto Ricans in New York City, 1917–1948* (Westport, Conn.: Greenwood Press, 1983).

24. Sánchez-Korrol, "In Their Own Right."

25. Angelo Falcón, "A History of Puerto Rican Politics in New York City: 1860s to 1945," in *Puerto Rican Politics in Urban America*, ed. James Jennings and Monte Rivera (Westport, Conn.: Greenwood Press, 1984), 15–42.

26. Ibid., 23.

27. John Bodnar, *The Transplanted: A History of Immigrants in Urban America* (Bloomington: Indiana University Press, 1985); Lewis Gann and Peter Duignan, *The Hispanics in the United States: A History* (Boulder, Colo.: Westview Press, 1986), 46; George Kiser and Martha Woody, *Mexican Workers in the United States: Historical and Political Perspectives* (Albuquerque: University of New Mexico Press, 1979), 19.

28. Cited in Percy Alvin Martin, *Latin America and the War* (Baltimore: Johns Hopkins Press, 1925), 533.

29. Martin Gilbert, *The First World War: A Complete History* (New York: Henry Holt, 1994); Rosales, *Chicano!*, 60.

30. Martin, *Latin America and the War*, 535–36.

31. Quoted in W. Dirk Raat, *Revoltosos: Mexico's Rebels in the United States* (College Station: Texas A&M University Press, 1981), 276–77.

32. Blaine Lamb, "The Convenient Villain: The Early Cinema Views of the Mexican American," *Journal of the West* 14 (1975), 75–81.

33. For a comprehensive overview on entertainment media depictions of Hispanics, see Federico A. Subervi-Vélez, Charles Ramírez Berg, Patricia Constantakis-Valdés, Chon Noriega, Diana Ríos, and Kenton Wilkinson, "Mass Communication and Hispanics," in *Handbook of Hispanic Cultures in the United States: Sociology*, ed. Félix Padilla, Nicolás Kanellos, and Claudio Esteva-Fabregat (Houston: Arte Público Press, 1994), 304–57.

34. Chapa is considered one of the most important crusading Hispanic publishers of this period. For more on Chapa, see Charles Harris, III, and Louis Sadler, "The 1911 Reyes Conspiracy: The Texas Side," in *Border Revolution*, ed. Charles Harris III and Louis Sadler (Las Cruces: Center for Latin American Studies, New Mexico State University, 1988), 31–33.

35. Rosales, *Chicano!*, 60.

36. Helen Delpar, "Goodbye to the Greaser: Mexico, the MPP DA, the Derogatory Films, 1922–1926," *Journal of Popular Film and Television* 12 (1984), 34–40.

37. Arthur G. Pettit, *Images of the Mexican American in Fiction and Film* (College Station: Texas A&M University Press, 1980); Linda Williams, "Type and Stereotype: Chicano Images in Film," in *Chicano Cinema*, ed. G. Keller (Binghamton, N.Y.: Bilingual Review, 1985), 59–63; Allen Woll, *The Latin Image in American Film* (Los Angeles: Latin American Center for Publication, University of California, 1980).

38. For more on early radio broadcasting targeted to a Hispanic-American audience, see Jorge Reina Schement and Loy A. Singleton, "The Origins of Spanish-Language Radio: The Case of San Antonio," *Journalism History* 4, no. 2 (1977), 56–58, 61; Subervi-Vélez et al., "Mass Communication and Hispanics," 327–29.

39. Harris and Sadler, "The 1911 Reyes Conspiracy."

40. Everett M. Rogers, *A History of Communication Study: A Biographical Approach* (New York: Free Press, 1994).

41. Robert Ezra Park, *The Immigrant Press and Its Control* (New York: Harper & Brothers, 1922).

42. Ibid., 79.

43. Rosales, *Chicano!*, 42–47.

44. Carey McWilliams, "The Forgotten Mexican"; Cary Davis, Carl Haub, and JoAnne L. Willette, "U.S. Hispanics: Changing the Face of America," in *The Hispanic Experience in the United States: Contemporary Issues and Perspectives*, ed. Edna Acosta-Belén and Barbara R. Sjostrom (New York: Praeger, 1988), 3–55; Leonard Broom and Eshref Shevky, "Mexicans in the United States: A Problem of Social Differentiation," *Sociology and Social Research* 36 (1952), 150–58; Tom Watkins, *The Great Depression: America in the 1930s* (Boston: Little, Brown, 1993), 68–70.

45. Rosales, *Chicano!*, 50.

46. Novas, *Everything You Need to Know*, 36.

47. Ibid., 102.

48. Subervi-Vélez et al., "Mass Communication and Hispanics."

49. "The Southwest's Immigration Problem," *New York Times*, 10 November 1926, 26.

50. Thomas Weyr, *Hispanic U.S.A.: Breaking the Melting Pot* (New York: Harper & Row, 1988), 136.

51. Leah Beth Ward, "An American Statesman," *Hispanic Business*, April 1993, 46.

52. Ramón Chacón, "The Chicano Immigrant Press in Los Angeles: The Case of *El Heraldo de México*, 1916–1920," *Journalism History* 4 (Summer 1977), 48–50, 62–63; Juan Gonzáles, "Forgotten Pages: Spanish-Language Newspapers in the Southwest," *Journalism History* 4 (Summer 1977), 50–51; Edward Kemble and Helen Bretnor, *A History of California Newspapers, 1846–1848* (Los Gatos, Calif.: Talisman Press, 1962); Herminio Ríos and Guadalupe Castillo, "Toward a True Chicano Bibliography: Mexican-American Newspapers, 1848–1942," *El Grito: A Journal of Mexican-American Thought* 3 (1970), 17–24; James Shearer, "Periódicos Españoles en los Estados Unidos," *Revista Hispanica Moderna* 20 (1954), 45–57; Porter A. Straton, *The Territorial Press of New Mexico, 1834–1912* (Albuquerque: University of New Mexico Press, 1969); Henry Wagner, "New Mexico Spanish Press," *New Mexico Historical Review* 12 (1937); Subervi-Vélez et al., "Mass Communication and Hispanics"; Kirk Whisler, "The Growth of Hispanic Print Media," *Caminos* 5 (January 1984), 26–30.

53. While Lozano's *La Opinión* of Los Angeles and *La Prensa* of San Antonio stand out among Mexican-American newspapers, *El Espectador*, a weekly published in California's San Gabriel Valley east of Los Angeles from 1933 to 1961 by Ignacio (Nacho) López also deserves attention. López was described as a "Mexican American muckraker" as a result of his articles and editorials that spanned the New Deal era to the rise of the Chicano movement. See Mario García "Mexican American Muckraker: Ignacio

L. López and *El Espectador,*" *Mexican Americans: Leadership, Ideology, & Identity, 1930–1960,* (New Haven, Conn.: Yale University Press, 1989), 84–112.

54. Carlos E. Cortés, "The Mexican-American Press," in *The Ethnic Press in the United States: A Historical Analysis and Handbook,* ed. Sally Miller (New York: Greenwood Press, 1987), 247–90, quotation on 247. Also see Francine Medeiros, *"La Opinión,* a Mexican Exile Newspaper," *Aztlán* 11 (Spring 1980), 65–87; Mary Ann Sterling, "Spanish-Language Print Media in the United States: A Case Study of *La Opinión,* a Los Angeles Daily" (Master's thesis, University of Southern California, 1984).

55. Cortés, "The Mexican-American Press."

56. Rosales, *Chicano!,* 66–70. Rosales also reports the stories of crusading Mexican-American journalists who wrote against the death penalty.

57. Ibid., 69.

58. Richaro Chávira, "A Case Study: Reporting of Mexican Emigration and Deportation," *Journalism History* 4, no. 2 (Summer 1977), 59–61.

59. Joseph Fitzpatrick, "The Puerto Rican Press," in *The Ethnic Press in the United States,* ed. Sally Miller (New York: Greenwood Press, 1987), 303–14; Kal Wagenheim and Olga Jiménez de Wagenheim, *The Puerto Ricans: A Documentary History* (New York: Praeger, 1973).

60. For more about *La Prensa* and other Puerto Rican newspapers and magazines established in New York, see Sánchez-Korrol, *From Colonia to Community,* 69–77.

61. Sánchez-Korrol, *From Colonia to Community,* 70–71.

62. Carl Allsup, "Who Done It? The Theft of Mexican-American History," *Journal of Popular Culture* 17 (Winter 1983), 150–55; Raúl Morín, *Among the Valiant: Mexican Americans in World War II and Korea* (Los Angeles: Tottden Publishing, 1963).

63. McWilliams, "The Forgotten Mexican"; Francisco Rosales, "Mexican Immigration to the Urban Midwest during the 1920s" (Ph.D. diss., Indiana University, 1978).

64. James D. Cockcroft, "The Unrecognized: Mexican Immigrant Workers and America's Future," in *The Hispanic Experience in the United States: Contemporary Issues and Perspectives,* ed. Edna Acosta-Belén and Barbara R. Sjostrom (New York: Praeger, 1988), 209–26.

65. Hensley C. Woodbridge, "Mexico and U.S. Racism," *Commonweal,* 22 June 1945, 234–37.

66. McWilliams, "The Forgotten Mexican"; see also Michael B. Salwen, "Propaganda without the Pain: America's World War II Experiment with Hemispheric Radio" (Paper presented at Association for Education in Journalism and Mass Communication Convention, Atlanta, August 1994). See also Fred Fejes, *Imperialism, Media, and the Good Neighbor: New Deal Foreign Policy and United States Shortwave Broadcasting to Latin America* (Norwood, N.J.: Ablex Publishing, 1986).

67. U.S. Congress, House of Representatives, *A Government Radio Station to Further Pan American Relations,* radio address of the Honorable Dennis Chávez of New Mexico, 3 March 1938, 75th Cong., 3d Sess., 4 March 1938, 873–74; also see Salwen, "Propaganda without the Pain."

68. McWilliams, "The Forgotten Mexican," 65.

69. Ricardo Romo, *East Los Angeles: History of a Barrio* (Austin: University of Texas Press, 1983).

70. "Portent of Storm," *The Nation,* 23 June 1943, 734–36, quotation on p. 736.

71. Thomas J. McCarthy, "Report from Los Angeles," *Commonweal,* 25 June 1943, 243–44, quotation on p. 244.

72. "Zoot Suits and Service Stripes: Race Tensions behind the Riots," *Newsweek*, 21 June 1943, 35–40.

73. "Portent of Storm."

74. Carey McWilliams, "The Zoot-Suit Riots," *New Republic*, 21 June 1943, 818–20, quotation on p. 819.

75. Carey McWilliams, *Factories in the Field*, 3d ed. (Hamden, Conn.: Shoe String Press, 1969; originally published in 1939).

76. Glenn Fowler, "Carey McWilliams Is Dead at 74; Edited *The Nation* for 2 Decades," *New York Times*, 28 June 1980, A18.

77. "Portent of Storm," 735.

78. Ralph Turner and Samuel Surace, "Zoot-Suiters and Mexicans: Symbols in Crowd Behavior," *American Journal of Sociology* 67 (July 1956), 14–20. See also Gary Norman Van Tubergen, "Racial Attitudes of Gatekeepers" (Ph.D. diss., University of Iowa, 1988), 1–5.

79. These findings were particularly damning because this was not the Hearst-owned newspaper, which was thought to be particularly hostile to Hispanics.

80. Turner and Surace, "Zoot-Suiters and Mexicans," 20.

81. Ibid., 19–20.

82. "Zoot Suits and Service Stripes."

83. McWilliams, "The Forgotten Mexican," 66.

84. There are conflicting estimates of the size of the great migration. For more information, see Joseph Fitzpatrick, *Puerto Rican Americans: The Meaning of Migration to the Mainland*, 2d ed. (Englewood Cliffs, N.J.: Prentice-Hall Ethnic Groups in American Life Series, 1987), 14–27.

85. Sánchez-Korrol, *From Colonia to Community*, 4.

86. Patricia Cayo Sexton, *Spanish Harlem* (New York: Harper Colophon Books, 1965).

87. Falcón, "A History of Puerto Rican Politics in New York City."

88. "Puerto Rican Drift to Mainland Gains," *New York Times*, 31 July 1947, A18.

89. C. Wright Mills, Clarence Senior, and Rose Kohn Goldsen, *The Puerto Rican Journey* (New York: Harper and Row, 1948).

90. Howard Morley Sachar, *The Course of Modern Jewish History*, exp. ed. (New York: Delta, 1977), 343.

91. Juan Ramon García, *Operation Wetback: The Mass Deportation of Mexican Undocumented Workers in 1954* (Westport, Conn.: Greenwood Press, 1980), 193–94.

92. "Wetback Reporter," *Newsweek*, 1 September 1952, 41–42.

93. Ibid., 41.

94. García, *Operation Wetback*, 214.

95. Félix Gutiérrez, "Spanish-Language Media in America: Background, Resources, History," *Journalism History* 4, no. 2 (Summer 1977), 34–41, 65; Félix Gutiérrez and Jorge Reina Schement, "Chicanos and the Media: A Bibliography of Selected Materials," *Journalism History* 4, no. 2 (Summer 1977), 52–55.

96. "Our Puerto Rican Press," *Newsweek*, 28 September 1959, 114–15.

97. Ibid., 115.

98. Fitzpatrick, "The Puerto Rican Press."

99. "Our Puerto Rican Press," 115.

100. "The Chalk Line," *Newsweek*, 4 June 1962, 92–93. Chalk sold the paper to the Gannett Company in 1981. For more on the history of these and other Spanish-language

newspapers after the period discussed in this section, see Subervi-Vélez et al., "Mass Communication and Hispanics," 318–23.

101. "Another Civil Rights Headache," *U.S. News & World Report*, 6 June 1966, 46.

102. Frank del Olmo, "Voices for the Chicano Movement," *Quill*, October 1971, 8–11; Frank del Olmo, "Chicano Journalism: New Medium for New Consciousness," in *Readings in Mass Communication*, 2d ed., ed. Michael Emery and Ted Curtis Smythe (Dubuque, Iowa: William G. Brown, 1974), 306–12; Francisco Lewels, *The Uses of the Mass Media by the Chicano Movement: A Study in Minority Access* (New York: Praeger, 1974).

103. "Deathtrap for Wetbacks," *Time*, 11 October 1968, 24–25.

104. William Raspberry, "How about Frito Amigo?" *Washington Post*, 2 June 1971, A19.

105. Félix Gutiérrez, "Advertising and the Growth of Minority Markets and the Media," *Journal of Communication Inquiry* 14, no. 1 (1990), 6–16; Charles Taylor, Ju Yung Lee, and Barbara Stern, "Portrayals of African, Hispanic, and Asian Americans in Magazine Advertising," *American Behavioral Scientist* 38 (February 1995), 608. For an up-to-date review of advertising portrayals of Hispanics see Octavio Emilio Nuiry, "Ban the Bandito!," *Hispanic* (July 1996), 26–32.

106. "Mexican Americans Assail Commercials," *New York Times*, 10 December 1969, A40.

107. "Ban the Bandito?," *Newsweek*, 22 December 1969, 82, 86; Thomas Martínez, "How Advertisers Promote Racism," *Civil Rights Digest*, Fall 1969, 8–9.

108. For more on advertising to minority markets, see Gutiérrez, "Advertising and the Growth of Minority Markets."

109. Although they withdrew the most offensive stereotypes, they still portray Hispanics "filtered through Anglo eyes." Nuiry, "Ban the Bandito!"

110. Wilson and Gutiérrez, *Minorities and the Media*, 110.

111. Lewels, *The Uses of the Mass Media by the Chicano Movement*.

112. del Olmo, "Chicano Journalism: New Medium for New Consciousness," 307.

113. Armando A. Arias, Jr., "Mass Mediated Images of Undocumented Mexicans" (Paper presented at annual conference of the Western Society of Criminology, Reno, Nevada, June 1985); Chávira, "A Case Study: Reporting of Mexican Emigration and Deportation," 59–61; Sylvia Anne Lee, "Images of Mexican Americans in San Antonio Newspapers: A Content Analysis" (Master's thesis, University of Texas at Austin, 1973); Francisco Lewels, "Racism in the Mass Media—Perpetuating the Stereotype," *Agenda* 8 (January/February 1978), 4–6; Félix Gutiérrez, "Making News—Media Coverage of Chicanos," *Agenda* 8 (November/December 1978), 21–22; Félix Gutiérrez, "Latinos and the Media in the United States: An Overview" (Paper presented at the International Communication Association meeting, Acapulco, Mexico, May 1980); Leo Anthony Sánchez, "Treatment of Mexican Americans by Selected U.S. Newspapers, January–June 1970" (Master's thesis, Pennsylvania State University, 1973).

114. Joshua Fishman and Heriberto Casiano, "Puerto Ricans in Our Press," *Modern Language Journal* 53 (1969), 157–62.

115. Carolyn Martindale, "Only in Glimpses: Portrayal of America's Largest Minority Groups by *The New York Times*, 1934–1994" (Paper presented at the Association for Education in Journalism and Mass Communication Convention, Washington, D.C., August 1995).

116. Martindale, "Only in Glimpses," 16.

117. For a discussion of the news media's ability to raise the awareness or salience of issues among the public, the agenda-setting function of the press, see Maxwell McCombs and Tamara Bell, "The Agenda-Setting Role of Mass Communication," in *An Integrated Approach to Communication Theory and Research*, ed. Michael B. Salwen and Don W. Stacks (Mahwah, N.J.: Lawrence Erlbaum Associates, forthcoming).

118. Ann Sperber, *Murrow: His Life and Times* (New York: Freundlich, 1986), 604.

119. Novas, *Everything You Need to Know*, 117.

120. Farnsworth Fowle, "Saul Alinsky, 63, Poverty Fighter and Social Organizer, Is Dead," *New York Times*, 13 June 1972, 46.

121. Patricia Bell Blawis, *Tijerina and the Land Grants: Mexican Americans in Struggle for Their Heritage* (New York: International Publishers, 1971); Peter Nabokov, *Tijerina and the Court House Raid* (Albuquerque: University of New Mexico Press, 1969).

122. Weyr, *Hispanic U.S.A.*, 138.

123. Novas, *Everything You Need to Know*, 121–22.

124. T. Calvo Buezas, "Mito, Rituales, y Símblos en el Movimiento Campesino Chicano, *Revista Española de Antropología Americana* 11, 259–71; Mark Day, *Forty Acres: César Chávez and the Farm Workers* (New York: Praeger, 1971); J. E. Levy, *César Chávez: Autobiography of La Causa* (New York: Norton, 1975).

125. Rosales, *Chicano!*, 139.

126. John Hammerback and Richard Jensen, "The Rhetorical Worlds of César Chávez and Reies Tijerina," *Western Journal of Speech Communication* 44 (Summer 1980), 166–76.

127. "The Little Strike That Grew to *la Causa*," *Time*, 4 July 1969, 16–21, quotation on p. 19.

128. Ibid., 19.

129. Stephen Rada, "Manipulating the Media: A Case Study of a Chicano Strike in Texas," *Journalism Quarterly* 54 (1977), 109–13.

130. Pete Dimas, "Perspectives on the Career and Life of Rubén Salazar" (Master's thesis, Arizona State University, 1980).

131. William Drummond, "The Death of the Man in the Middle: Requiem for Rubén Salazar," *Esquire*, April 1972, 75–81.

132. Gonzáles and Rodríguez, "A Homage to Rubén Salazar," 12.

133. Alejandro Portes and Robert Bach, "Immigrant Earnings: Cuban and Mexican Immigrants in the United States," *International Migration Review* 14 (1980), 315–41.

134. James Russell, "Airlines, AC and Castro Were Key to Miami's Business Transformation," *Miami Herald*, 28 July 1996, 1F, 2F.

135. Michael B. Salwen, *Radio and Television in Cuba: The Pre-Castro Era* (Ames: Iowa State University Press, 1994).

136. Patrick May, "Miami: Where Hype Is Hip," *Miami Herald*, 21 July 1996, 1A, 18A.

137. María Cristina García, "Cuban Exiles and Cuba-Americans: A History of an Exile Community in South Florida, 1959–1989," (Ph.D. diss., University of Texas at Austin, 1990); Richard Fagen, Richard Brody, and Thomas O'Leary, "Cubans in Exile: Disaffection in the Revolution" (Stanford, Calif.: Stanford University Press, 1968).

138. "Havana, Fla.," *Newsweek*, 1 September 1969, 59.

139. Thomas Boswell and James Curtis, *The Cuban-American Experience: Culture, Image and Perspectives* (Montclair, N.J.: Rowman and Allenheld, 1984); *Migration To-*

day 46, special double issue dedicated to Cuba (Fall 1983); Yolanda Prieto, *Cuban Migration in the 60s in Perspective* (New York: New York University, Occasional Papers, April 1984).

140. Edna Acosta-Belén, "From Settlers to Newcomers: The Hispanic Legacy in the United States," in *The Hispanic Experience in the United States* ed. Edna Acosta-Belén and Barbara R. Sjostrom, (New York: Praeger, 1988), 81–106; Tom Alexander, "Those Amazing Cuban Emigres," *Fortune,* October 1966, 144–49; David Reiff, "Cubans in America: From Exiles to Immigrants," *Miami Herald,* 6 August 1995, 1M, 4M.

141. John O'Connor, "Kvetched at Any News Shows Lately?," *New York Times,* 7 November 1971, Section II, 17.

142. John Seggar, "Television's Portrayal of Minorities and Women, 1971–1975," *Journal of Broadcasting* 21 (Fall 1977), 435–46.

143. Schement and Singleton, "The Origins of Spanish-Language Radio"; Subervi-Vélez et al., "Mass Communication and Hispanics."

144. Subervi-Vélez et al., "Mass Communication and Hispanics," 328.

145. Sarah Acosta, "Big Waves in Radioland," *Hispanic Business,* December 1993, 48–49, 50; Steve Beale, "A Hallmark in the Takeover of Spanish TV," *Hispanic Business,* May 1988, 20–32, 48; David Bollier, "Targeting the Nation in Its Own Tongue," *Channels,* December 1987, 83; David Bollier, "Into the Mainstream," *Channels,* December 1988, 104; Ramíro Burr, "Television's New Pot of Gold," *Hispanic Business,* April 1993, 28, 30; Juan Coto, "Spanish TV Upgrading Its Image," *Miami Herald,* 2 April 1989, 1K; Juan Coto, "Spanish News Gives CNN Ratings Lesson," *Miami Herald,* 9 July 1989, 1K; Juan Coto, "New Battle for Hispanic Viewers," *Miami Herald,* 22 June 1989, 1C, 2C; Humberto Lópes, "Musical Chairs at TV Networks," *Hispanic Business,* July 1992, 8–9; Humberto Lópes, "Bad Vibes but Good Business?," *Hispanic Business,* February 1993, 30, 32; Rick Mendosa, "The Television Wars, Part II," *Hispanic Business,* December 1993, 52–54; Rick Mendosa, "Turning Point for Spanish Radio," *Hispanic Business,* April 1993, 24, 26.

146. Salwen, *Radio and Television in Cuba.*

147. Pablo Arredondo-Ramírez and Enrique Sánchez-Ruiz, *Comunicación Social, Poder y Democracia en México* (Guadalajara, Mexico: Universidad de Guadalajara, 1986).

148. "Se Habla Español," *Forbes,* 21 July 1986, 14–15; Gonzalo Soruco, "The Rise and Fall of Spanish-Language Television in the United States" (Paper presented at the Association for Education in Journalism and Mass Communication Convention, Washington, D.C., August 1995).

149. Elisabeth Malkin, "The Rupert Murdoch of Mexico?," *Business Week,* 11 December 1995, 61.

150. Maurice Ferre, "Decade of the Hispanic," *Advertising Age,* 15 February 1982, M14, M16, quotation on p. M14.

151. Richard Lacayo, "A Surging New Spirit," *Time,* 11 July 1988, 46.

152. Reilly, "The War of New Orleans"; Federico Subervi-Vélez, "Hispanics, the Mass Media, and Politics: Assimilation vs. Pluralism," (Ph.D. diss., University of Wisconsin, Madison, 1984); Federico Subervi-Vélez, "The Mass Media and Ethnic Assimilation and Pluralism: A Review and Research Proposal with Special Focus on Hispanics," *Communication Research* 13 (1986), 71–96; Melanie Wallendorf and Michael Reilly, "Ethnic Migration, Assimilation, and Consumption," *Journal of Consumer*

Research 10 (December 1983), 292–302; J. Zubrzycki, "The Role of the Foreign Language Press in Immigrant Assimilation," *Population Studies* 12 (1958), 73–82.

153. A. J. Good, "Guatemala's Hidden Refugees," *Christian Century*, 9 May 1990, 499–501.

154. Norma Chinchilla, Nora Hamilton, and James Loucky, "Central Americans in Los Angeles: An Immigrant Community in Transition," in *In the Barrios*, ed. Joan Moore and Raquel Pinderhughes (New York: Russell Sage Foundation, 1993), 51–78.

155. Gann and Duignan, *The Hispanics in the United States*, 117; Sherri Grasmuck, "Immigration, Ethnic Stratification, and Native Working Class Discipline: Comparisons of Documented and Undocumented Dominicans," *International Migration Review* 18 (Fall 1984), 692–713; Antonio Ugalde, Frank Bean, and G. Cárdenas, "International Migration from the Dominican Republic: Findings from a National Survey," *International Migration Review* 13 (1979), 235–54; Kathryn Wolford, "From American Dream to Dominican Hope," *Christian Century*, 5 December 1990, 1137–39.

156. S. Sassen-Koob, "Formal and Informal Associations: Dominicans and Colombians in New York," *International Migration Review* 13 (1979), 314–32.

157. George Church, " 'Hispanics': A Melding of Cultures," *Time*, 8 July 1985, 36–39.

158. Antonio Jorge, Jaime Suchlicki, and Adolfo de Varona, eds., *Cuban Exiles in Florida: Their Presence and Contribution* (Miami: University of Miami North-South Center, 1991).

159. Heriberto Dixon, "Black Cubans in the United States," *Unveiling*, September/November 1984, 20–23; Heriberto Dixon, "Who Ever Heard of a Black Cuban?," *Afro-Hispanic Review* 1 (September 1982), 10–12; Susan Greenbaum, "Afro-Cubans in Exile: Tampa, Florida, 1886–1984," *Cuban Studies/Estudios Cubanos* 15 (1985), 77–93.

160. Michael Massing, "The Invisible Cubans," *Columbia Journalism Review* 19 (September/October 1980), 49–51.

161. Ibid., 49.

162. Ibid.

163. It is not clear whether the press underplayed the gay angle or did not fully fathom the enormity of the situation. Most likely a combination of these factors accounted for the gay angle's being minimized in the initial news reports. But it is clear that many liberal journalists felt uncomfortable with the possibility of demeaning a minority group. Massing, "The Invisible Cubans."

164. "A Question of Intolerance," *Miami Herald*, 14 July 1996, sect. I.

165. Ibid.

166. Mark Fitzgerald, "Reaching Out to Chicago Hispanics," *Editor & Publisher*, 18 September 1993, 12; Félix Gutiérrez and Clint C. Wilson, II, "The Demographic Dilemma," *Columbia Journalism Review* 17, no. 5 (January/February 1979), 53–55.

167. Gonzalo Soruco, *Cubans and the Mass Media in South Florida* (Gainesville: University of Florida Press, 1996).

168. Reese Cleghorn, "The Battle in Miami: Too Easy to Ignore," *Washington Journalism Review* 14, no. 4 (May 1992), 4; Sally Deneen, "*The Miami Herald* Takes Some Heat," *Washington Journalism Review* 14, no. 3 (April 1992), 11; Alex Jones, "The Tough Question for the *Herald* Is in Spanish," *New York Times*, 11 May 1987, B7; William Labbee, "Cuba Over and Out," *New Times* (Miami), 21–27 November 1990, 20–27; Anne-Marie O'Connor, "Trying to Set the Agenda in Miami," *Columbia Journalism Review* 31, no. 1 (May/June 1992), 42–43; Thomas Rosenstiel, "Latinos and

Paper Clash in Miami," *Los Angeles Times*, 9 January 1987, 1A; John Rothchild, "The Cuban Connection and the Gringo Press," *Columbia Journalism Review* 23, no. 3 (October 1984), 48–51.

169. Sally Deneen, "Case Study—Miami: The *Herald* and Miami's Cuban Community," *Media Studies Journal* 6, no. 4 (Fall 1992), 136–47, quotation on p. 138.

170. Ibid., 143.

171. Ana Veciana-Suarez, *Hispanic Media: Impact and Influence* (Washington, D.C.: Media Institute, 1987).

172. Soruco, *Cubans and the Mass Media in South Florida*, 75.

173. We discuss primarily news media portrayals here. For more on entertainment media, see Subervi-Vélez et al., "Mass Communication and Hispanics."

174. Charles A. Ericksen, "Hispanic Americans and the Press," *Journal of Intergroup Relations* 9, no. 1 (1981), 3–16.

175. Ibid., 5.

176. Gutiérrez, "Making News."

177. Francis R. Matera, "Ellipsis and Eclipse As Indicators of Bias: *The Miami Herald*'s Coverage of Cuban Issues," *American Journalism* 8 (Winter 1991), 35–47.

178. Robert Logan and Bruce Garrison, "Factors Affecting News Coverage: Two Florida Papers and the Mariel Refugee Influx," *Newspaper Research Journal* 5 (Fall 1983), 43–52.

179. Bradley S. Greenberg, Carrie Heeter, Judee Burgoon, Michael Burgoon, and Felipe Korzenny, "Local Newspaper Coverage of Mexican Americans," *Journalism Quarterly* 60 (1983), 671–76.

180. Bradley S. Greenberg, Michael Burgoon, Judee Burgoon, and Felipe Korzenny, *Mexican-Americans and the Mass Media* (Norwood, N.J.: Ablex Publishers, 1983), 223.

181. Carrie Heeter, Bradley Greenberg, Bradley Mendelson, Judee Burgoon, Michael Burgoon, and Felipe Korzenny, "Cross Media Coverage of Local Hispanic American News," *Journal of Broadcasting* 27 (Fall 1983), 395–402.

182. Judy VanSlyke Turk, Jim Richstad, Robert Bryson, Jr., and Sammye Johnson, "Hispanic Americans in the News in Two Southwestern Cities," *Journalism Quarterly* 66 (Spring 1989), 107–13.

183. Ibid., 113.

184. Tarla Peterson, "Reconstituting Ethnocentrism: The American Ethnic Coalition and Official English," *Howard Journal of Communications* 1 (Fall 1988), 99–112; Brant Short, "Mandating a 'Mother Tongue': Historical and Political Foundations of the English First Movement," *Howard Journal of Communications* 1 (Fall 1988), 86–98.

185. David Marshall, "The Question of Official Language: Language Rights and the English Language Amendment," *International Journal of the Sociology of Language* 60 (1986), 7–75.

186. Arnold Leibowitz, "English Literacy: Legal Sanction for Discrimination," *Notre Dame Lawyer* 45 (1969), 7–67; Marshall, "The Question of Official Language."

187. Joshua A. Fishman, "Bilingualism and Separatism," in *The Annals of the American Academy of Political and Social Science*, ed. Rita Simon (Beverly Hills: Sage, 1986), 169–80; Leibowitz, "English Literacy"; Marshall, "The Question of Official Language."

188. Francis R. Matera and Michael B. Salwen, "Support for Radio Martí among Miami's Cubans and Non-Cubans," *International Journal of Intercultural Relations* 16 (1992), 135–44.

189. John Miller, "Immigration, the Press and the New Racism," *Media Studies Journal* 8 (Summer 1994), 19–28, quotation on p. 28.

190. Frank del Olmo, "Covering Civil Rights in the 1990s: The Perspective from California" (Keynote address at annual meeting of Association for Education in Journalism and Mass Communication, Anaheim, California, August 1996).

191. Joseph Tovares, "Mojado Like Me," *Hispanic*, May 1995, 20–26, quotation on p. 22.

192. Valerie Menard, "The Latino Angle," *Hispanic*, September 1995, 14–18.

193. Debra Gersh, "Portrayals of Latinos in and by the Media," *Editor & Publisher*, 31 July 1993, 12–13, quotation on p. 12.

194. A rare exception is the work of Chávira, cited earlier. See Chávira, "A Case Study."

195. Center for Integration and Improvement of Journalism, *News Watch: A Critical Look at Coverage of People of Color* (San Francisco State University: Unity '94 Project, 1994).

SELECTED BIBLIOGRAPHY

Bananas Is My Business. A ninety-minute independent documentary on "Brazilian Bombshell" Carmen Miranda that exposes the stereotypes of "hot-tempered" South Americans in the U.S. cinema. An International Cinema release. 1995.

Chicano! History of the Mexican-American Civil Rights Movement. A four-hour series that appeared on PBS in 1996 and chronicled the movement during the tumultuous years from 1965 to 1975. Available for purchase by contacting the National Latino Communication Center, 1–800–722–9982.

Ericksen, Charles A. "Hispanic Americans and the Press." *Journal of Intergroup Relations* 9, no. 1 (1981), 3–16.

Greenberg, Bradley S., Michael Burgoon, Judee Burgoon, and Felipe Korzenny. *Mexican-Americans and the Mass Media*. Norwood, N.J.: Ablex Publishers, 1983.

Gutiérrez, Félix. "Spanish-Language Media in America: Background, Resources, History." *Journalism History* 4, no. 2 (Summer 1977), 34–41, 65.

Gutiérrez, Félix, and Jorge Reina Schement. "Chicanos and the Media: A Bibliography of Selected Materials." *Journalism History* 4, no. 2 (Summer 1977), 52–55.

Hispanics on Deadline. A fifteen-minute educational video of interviews with nine Hispanic journalists. American Society of Newspaper Reporters, 11690B Sunrise Valley Drive, Reston, Va. 20191.

Lichter, S. Robert, Linda S. Lichter, Stanley Rothman, and Daniel Amundson. "Prime-Time Prejudice: TV's Images of Blacks and Hispanics." *Public Opinion*, July/August 1987, 13–16.

McWilliams, Carey. *North from Mexico: The Spanish-Speaking People of the United States*. Westport, Conn.: Greenwood Press, 1968.

Murphy, Sharon. *Other Voices: Black, Chicano, and American Indian Press*. Dayton, Ohio: Pflaum/Standard, 1974.

Murrow, Edward R. "Harvest of Shame." VCR Video. CBS News. FoxVideo, Inc., P.O. Box 900, Beverly Hills, Calif. 90213. Fifty-five minutes, 1992 (first aired 25 November 1960).

Richard, Alfred Charles, Jr. *Censorship and Hollywood's Hispanic Image: An Interpretive Filmography, 1936–1955*. Westport, Conn.: Greenwood Press, 1993.

Rosales, F. Arturo. *Chicano! A History of the Mexican American Civil Rights Movement.* Houston: Arte Público Press, 1996.

Smith, Norman D. "Mexican Stereotypes on Fictional Battlefields." *Journal of Popular Culture* 13 (1980), 526–40.

Soruco, Gonzalo. *Cubans and the Mass Media in South Florida.* Gainesville: University of Florida Press, 1996.

Subervi-Vélez, Federico A. "The Mass Media and Ethnic Assimilation and Pluralism: A Review and Research Proposal with Special Focus on Hispanics." *Communication Research* 13 (1986), 71–96.

Subervi-Vélez, Federico A., Charles Ramírez Berg, Patricia Constantakis-Váldes, Chon Noriega, Diana Ríos, and Kenton Wilkinson. "Mass Communications and Hispanics." In *Handbook of Hispanic Cultures in the United States: Sociology,* ed. Félix Padilla, Nicolás Kanellos, and Claudio Esteva-Fabregat. Houston: Arte Público Press, 1994, 304–57.

Time (special issue). "Hispanic Culture Breaks Out of the Barrio." 11 July 1988.

Turner, Ralph, and Samuel Surace. "Zoot-Suiters and Mexicans: Symbols in Crowd Behavior." *American Journal of Sociology* 67 (July 1956), 14–20.

Wilson, Clint C. II, and Félix Gutiérrez. *Minorities and the Media.* Beverly Hills: Sage, 1985. A second edition was published under the title *Race, Multiculturalism, and the Media: From Mass to Class Communication.* Thousand Oaks, Calif.: Sage, 1995.

5

The Asian Americans

The Chinese Americans
ANN ELIZABETH AUMAN AND GREGORY YEE MARK

This is emphatically a white man's country, and a white man's government, (and) the Chinaman is not and cannot be a white man.
—*Sacramento Union*, 1881[1]

The study of images of Chinese Americans and their history in the United States is a relatively new and emerging field. Most scholarly publications concerning Chinese Americans cover the immigration and exclusion of the Chinese in the United States, or their general history. Little scholarly research has been done on media images.[2] News coverage is tied to the broad history of Chinese Americans: immigration, exclusion, the Asian American civil rights movement, and the emergence of Chinatown youth gangs. Chinese media images also have been related to the history of U.S. business, labor, politics, and immigration policies, as well as American trade and political interests in China and Asia.

Him Mark Lai of the Chinese Historical Society noted that scholarly works on the Chinese in America first appeared in the 1880s and 1890s, but during the first half of the twentieth century, less academic research was undertaken because "the Chinese question" had become less important.[3] The Chinese in America were not in the limelight, probably because there were fewer Chinese in this country than in previous decades.[4] Scholarly research is needed on the post–World War II period and, in particular, on the success stories that promoted the model minority image and on the coverage of hate crimes against Chinese Americans.

This chapter describes the portrayal of the Chinese in the United States in mainstream American news media, primarily newspapers from 1850 through 1996. The descriptions are drawn from scholarly literature concerning the Chinese in the news media and from representative examples of newspaper stories.

Chinese immigration to the United States began around 1850, shortly after the discovery of gold in California, but images of China and its people preceded the arrival of the first Chinese immigrants to the United States. Images such as the "opium-addicted heathen" were promulgated by traders and missionaries, even though it was the Western nations that flooded China with opium.[5]

In the nineteenth century, deteriorating social, economic, and political conditions in China contributed to the migration of Chinese people to the United States in search of gold, jobs, and a better life. Chinese immigrants built railways and engaged in mining, agriculture, fishing, light manufacturing, and other labor and domestic jobs. From 1865 to 1868, the Chinese constituted the majority of the labor force that built the western portion of the Transcontinental Railroad, and they worked quickly and hard. According to one account, Chinese railway workers laid ten miles of track in the desert in one day.[6] Chinese immigrants not working in the mines or on the railways provided services in work camps, towns, and cities as laundrymen, cooks, and cleaners, but racism restricted job opportunities. Even though the Chinese worked in menial jobs that others often shunned, they were criticized for taking jobs away from white men and women.

In the late 1870s and 1880s, anti-Chinese sentiment became widespread in the United States. After the passage of the Chinese Exclusion Act in 1882, many Chinese were driven out of their jobs and homes; some were even massacred. Negative images of the Chinese in the media played a major role in building anti-Chinese sentiment throughout the nation, and these negative stereotypes continued well into the next century.[7]

One account from the *San Francisco Chronicle* in 1878 said that San Francisco's first immigrant from China arrived in 1847, found gold, then "wrote to a friend in China who spread the news that brought many of his countrymen to California."[8] The *Chronicle*'s news article on the growth of Chinatown depicted the Chinese as a menacing octopus and described "How the Mongolian octopus developed and fastened its tentacles upon the city."[9]

The concept of "hordes" of Chinese was beginning to take root, even though the number of Chinese in the United States was relatively small—63,200 by 1870,[10] up from 34,900 in 1860. Yet some positive images appeared in the media. In December 1851, San Francisco's *Alta California* newspaper reported a meeting of 300 Chinese in San Francisco at which an adviser was appointed for them. Another account published in the *Alta* discussed the Chinese without prejudice, offering a straightforward report of their activities:

About 200 Chinamen have come over who have formed an encampment on a vacant lot at the head of Clay Street. They have put up about 30 tents which look clean and white, and around and in which are scattered the various articles of Chinese wares and tools which they have brought over. They look cheerful and happy and will no doubt make good citizens and voters in a few years.[11]

The *New York Times* was neutral in the 1880s on Chinese immigration because it was "more a matter of concern to Americans out West than to those in the East," according to a study made of print media coverage of immigration.[12] The newspaper did publish some editorials discussing the issue; two editorials criticized the anti-Chinese sentiment and said it was organized by people who did not want to work.[13]

Many West Coast newspaper accounts were negative despite the contributions of the Chinese, who were called "heathen, crafty, moon-eyed celestials" and dirty thieves.[14] A study made of newspaper articles published in Astoria, Oregon, cited mostly negative accounts: "It is just as natural for a Chinaman to steal as it is for a sponge to absorb water." And "They are alien in spirit, thought, language, tradition, education, religion, morality and humanity."[15]

Astoria newspapers attempted to justify repressive acts performed against the Chinese in the 1870s: "If these immigrants were all intelligent and industrious, and so many producers added to the ranks of labor, the objection to their coming would not be so strong or so general." Another article stated, "This class of servants is being encouraged at the expense of white people, so we need not expect a source of first class white laborers for any kind of service." Yet another said, "Every Chinaman is a faucet inserted into the land, draining a stream of gold, small or large, into the land of his birth."[16]

These negative images were widespread in the print media but were not universal. In a study made of the *Sacramento Union*, from 1850 to 1882, Cheryl L. Cole showed that the paper's three editors had mixed views on the question of Chinese immigration, at least until the late 1870s.[17]

On cultural and social matters they were often as anti-Chinese as most Californians; on economic questions, however, their capitalist and business interests forced them to recognize the many benefits that the Chinese labor force afforded for the rapid development of California's economy. In politics on the state and national level, they represented Republican party interests that felt particularly bound to uphold the idea of justice under the law for all persons, regardless of race, and to condemn the anti-Chinese rioters who hoped to force the Chinese from California by physical terror."[18]

By 1870 Sacramento ranked second only to San Francisco in the number of Chinese inhabitants. Most historians have relied on San Francisco newspaper accounts, particularly papers that represented the interests of the Democratic party and primarily the Workingmen's Party, which was anti-Chinese and initiated riots.[19]

Cole, in analyzing *Sacramento Union* editors' viewpoints, noted that they "often expressed alarm" at Chinese immigration. "The *Union* editors' opinion undoubtedly reflected that of most Californians who were alarmed at the increasing presence of so alien a people, and who believed the Chinese to be a racially inferior people who could never settle in California as the social equals of whites."[20]

Throughout the 1850s, Chinese were discouraged from mining after a tax was levied on foreign miners, most of whom were Chinese. Yet the state became heavily dependent on the income from that tax, which amounted to one-half the state's total income. After 1855, 98 percent of the miners' taxes came from Chinese.[21] *Sacramento Union* editors pointed out the state's dependence on Chinese labor as well as the income from their taxes.

Sacramento Union editors also believed that the Chinese were particularly well-suited for certain types of domestic and difficult agricultural labor. "The editors concluded that the presence of Chinese was tolerable as long as they undertook 'labor which Americans would not consent to perform,' such as menial or domestic service, and 'accept(ed) compensation which Americans would not receive.' " The *Union* was also well aware that California's capitalists and merchants, a small yet influential group, supported the use of Chinese labor.[22]

Sacramento Union editors were ambivalent about Chinese labor because of the editors' attachment to Republican Party morality. They felt that the Chinese were a "cultural blight" in California; at the same time, they insisted on the equal treatment of Chinese under California's laws, and they were interested in expanding trade with Asia.[23] Business people noted that the Transcontinental Railroad, completed with much Chinese labor, made trade with Asia possible at last. As a result, the *Union* continued to support good relations with China. The Workingmen's Party, however, supported anti-Chinese agitation and the exclusion of Chinese laborers, regardless of treaties or trade potential.[24] The anticipated Chinese trade never materialized, and the Chinese issue became a political football tossed between the Workingmen's Party and business interests. By that time, the *Sacramento Union*, even though it was dominated by railroad interests, was concerned about the ability of the Chinese to assimilate into American culture, and it criticized Chinese opium dens and houses of prostitution.[25]

It has also been noted that the *San Francisco Chronicle* and the *Morning Call*, engaged in a circulation war, publicized the anti-Chinese labor sentiment and were responsible for anti-Chinese activity.[26] Both newspapers, in particular the *Chronicle*, also questioned the ability of the Chinese to assimilate.[27] The *New York Times* supported restrictive immigration and stated in 1888 that the Chinese could not assimilate with Americans.[28]

Republican interests stalled and then mitigated exclusion legislation but did not stop it from becoming law in 1882. The Chinese Exclusion Act was renewed in 1892, and in 1902 it was made "permanent" until it was repealed in 1943, when a quota of 105 was established. This was only after negative stereotypes were replaced by more positive images, and after the United States and China became allies during World War II.[29] However, Chinese exclusion was not really terminated until 1965. Exclusion reduced the Chinese American population by curtailing immigration and encouraging those disgusted by discriminatory laws to leave the country. The 1890 Census reported 107,500 Chinese residents in the United States. Ten years later there were 89,863, and in 1910 there were 71,500.[30] The Immigration Act of 1924 further stifled immigration by denying immigration to virtually all Asians except Filipinos, who were considered "American nationals."[31]

Anti-Chinese feeling also existed on the East Coast as a result of both West Coast and East Coast anti-Chinese news reports. Jack L. Hammersmith cited evidence from a study made of New York and Massachusetts newspapers and demonstrated that West Virginia editors were equally racist in presenting dehumanizing images of Chinese immigrants.[32] For example, the Point Pleasant, West Virginia, *Weekly Register* attempted to stir up fears of an influx of Chinese being employed in mines and factories, and they were described as "almond-eyed, pig-tailed, rat and rice-eating hordes" and as "heathen Chinee."[33] William Randolph Hearst's *New York Evening Journal* charged that exclusion was jeopardized by big business, and that no thought had been given to the impact upon the American worker.[34] In 1870 a trainload of Chinese was brought to North Adams, Massachusetts, as strikebreakers to work in a shoe factory after a newspaper report had informed the factory's owner of the successful use of Chinese laborers in a San Francisco shoe factory.[35] The Chinese laborers, who did not join with American workers, soon had a reputation for complacency. New Jersey's *Newark Advertiser* linked the burning of a hat factory to the bitterness among workers that Chinese were to be employed in the factory. Nevertheless, other business men were soon contracting Chinese labor.[36]

Animal imagery was used to dehumanize the Chinese, and later the Japanese and Filipinos. Media portrayals of them as animals, or as another species, no doubt helped to build public support for policies that restricted Chinese immigration and denied the Chinese rights enjoyed by white Americans.[37] According to Richard Austin Thompson, in his study of Yellow Peril literature from 1890 to 1924, West Coast media and politicians fanned the growing fear of a "Chinese invasion," which led to use of the phrase "Yellow Peril" to describe the danger to Western-white-Christian civilization from the perceived growing power of Oriental peoples. Thompson explained that it is not clear where the phrase Yellow Peril came from, but in 1895 a German monarch commissioned a picture of a Buddha and a Chinese dragon high in the smoke of the burning cities of Christian Europe, with words exhorting people to defend their faith and their home.[38]

Some "positive" images were found of the Chinese who had become Christians or were noted for their industriousness. According to one account in an Oregon newspaper, "a pagan with a Christian heart in him" tried to save a woman from being enslaved by a "heathenish monster from the flowery kingdom."[39] Another described a leading Chinese merchant who died: "Ah Kow was well liked by the business community of Astoria and was as near a white man as we ever met without the blood of the white race coursing through his veins."[40] Chinese were portrayed in a positive light when they were associated with commonly accepted Western traits such as religious beliefs or industriousness.

After the passage of the Chinese Exclusion Act in 1882, anti-Chinese sentiment continued to grow and culminated in anti-Chinese riots. One of the best known involved the massacre of twenty-eight Chinese in Rock Springs, Wyoming, in 1885.[41] The first newspaper to print anti-Chinese articles in Wyoming was the *Frontier Index* of Green River City, according to scholar A. Dudley Gardner.[42] The editor, Legh Freeman, headed his editorial column with the words, "The Motto of This Column: Only White Men to Be Naturalized in the United States." Gardner also cites racist attitudes in other papers, such as the *Cheyenne Daily Leader*: "We are being ruined by Chinese thieving." The *Montana Radiator* (Helena) reported that "Mongolian hordes" were preventing "Helena women from making a living washing clothes."[43]

In 1885 the bulk of the railway and mine laborers were Chinese. They were employed to work for the Union Pacific Railroad and in the company's coal mines.[44] Also, they filled an important niche as domestic labor. Yet newspapers did not acknowledge their role positively. According to Gardner, in 1882, an attaché to the Chinese embassy in Washington, D.C., visited Wyoming and criticized the press for not portraying the Chinese in a favorable light. He accused the newspapers of creating the nationwide anti-Chinese sentiment that existed at the time, which led to the Chinese Exclusion Act.[45]

In the 1890s, *New York Times* editorials focused on legislation that kept Chinese laborers from coming to the United States and on smuggling. Yet, in 1893, the *New York Times* also criticized a law requiring registration of all Chinese residents in the United States as discriminatory. It noted that Americans on the West Coast feared and hated competition from the Chinese, who were considered to be "industrious, patient and frugal."[46]

During the last two decades of the nineteenth century, a significant number of Chinese on the U.S. mainland lived in Chinatowns—the result of discrimination and anti-Chinese labor activities. Their crowded living conditions contributed to negative images for a while, but during the early part of the century, more favorable ones began to emerge when the Chinese were seen as less of a threat as their numbers decreased. The *New York Times* saw the Chinese as more desirable than some other immigrants. It called policies toward Japanese and Chinese immigrants "brutal and insulting."[47] On the one hand, the *San Francisco Chronicle* attacked the migration of Chinese women, some of whom were forced into prostitution, and complained that the Chinese introduced opium into the country. But in 1905 the paper "castigated the white guides of Chinatown for giving the city a bad name by creating fake opium dens as tourist attractions after the Chinese had actually stamped out the real dens." Also, the traffic in Chinese prostitutes had died out by then.[48] Anti-immigrant feelings were then unleashed onto the increasing numbers of Japanese immigrants.

One scholar noted that, between 1910 and 1922, the Chinese "were depicted as a harmless and defeated people."[49] As a contained and nonthreatening population, resident Chinese came to be perceived as potential contributors to the U.S. economy largely through tourism, working in laundries and restaurants, and as consumers of goods imported from China.[50] She cited a 1916 story from the *San Francisco Chronicle* on the Chinese Consolidated Benevolent Association, also called the Chinese Six Companies, praising the services they provided to the Chinese community: ''The general welfare of the Chinese is the keynote of the association . . . a worthy Chinese need never want either monetary assistance or help in time of trouble.'' At other times, journalists pointed out virtuous Chinese qualities that Americans lacked, such as eating melon seeds rather than drinking alcohol.[51] One author in the *Atlantic Monthly* stated that the Yellow Peril was more imaginary than real, and that even ''the most violent activities of the Chinese race'' would be ''kindly and gentle compared with the White Perils.''[52]

More positive images, yet still mixed, prevailed throughout the second decade and into the 1920s. These images reflected the editorial policy of each publication. On the one hand, Chinese Americans were depicted as having acculturated: Chinatown had been burned down during the San Francisco earthquake, a modern one had been built, and the tong wars had ended. Tourism in the Chinatowns, the Japanese immigration ''threat,'' and a desire to help modernize the newly established Republic of China in 1912 and promote trade may have contributed to this improved image.[53]

On the other hand, some articles presented negative images and focused on the smuggling of illegal immigrants into the United States.[54] Much of the smuggling, no doubt, was the result of repressive immigration policies and the long detention and interrogation of Chinese immigrants at Angel Island after the immigration and detention center was established in San Francisco Bay in 1910. The *New York Times* ran editorials that advocated keeping out illegal immigrants and supported restrictions that it believed were ''fair and humane.''[55] Later, the *Saturday Evening Post* contributed to the passage of the restrictive immigration act of 1924.[56] The magazine was pro-immigration until the second decade of the twentieth century, when the tone of the articles changed. In contrast, the *New York Times* in the 1920s discredited the notion of a superior white race. The paper noted that the Chinese and Japanese ''worked harder and lived more simply than Americans and got ahead of their neighbors through diligence.''[57] Later, in the early 1930s, the *New York Times* protested immigration laws against the Chinese and Japanese, as well as the detention of immigrants.[58]

1934 FEDERAL COMMUNICATIONS ACT TO PEARL HARBOR ATTACK, DECEMBER 7, 1941

In the 1930s, positive images of Chinese Americans began to emerge more frequently owing to the significant decline in population and because the Chinese no longer posed such a perceived threat to American society. The images tended to promote Chinatown as a tourist attraction and focused on the ability of Chinese Americans to weather the Great Depression successfully.[59] It was said that the Chinese took care of their own and that there were no hungry people in Chinatown because of the support of the Chinese benevolent associations and strong family ties.[60]

Throughout the Depression and later, Chinese Americans were praised for their financial contributions to help China's war against the Japanese and against natural disasters. Many stories were run of impoverished Chinese giving up their last dimes for the "mother" country. The *San Francisco Chronicle's* coverage of various fund-raisers and "rice bowl parties" was extensive.[61] The February 1940 rice bowl party held in San Francisco raised more than $50,000 in two days.[62] One scholar noted that

sending American-earned money to China, once an abhorrent act used as evidence of unassimilability and the parasitic nature of Chinese in the United States, came to symbolize a type of American "patriotism," as if the high degree of loyalty the Chinese showed for China was indicative of the equally high degree of love they had for the United States. Not one word of criticism accompanied the descriptions of Chinese fund-raisers. Instead they seemed to be used as yet another example of the organized and industrious nature of the Chinese in the United States.[63]

Many Chinese were absorbed into the war industries, where they were seen as valuable contributors to the war effort.

Chinese Americans wanted to make it clear that they were not Japanese, and some articles in the press tried to show the differences. An article published in *Life* magazine on December 22, 1941, tried to make this point: "How to tell Japs from the Chinese," but it was dehumanizing in its portrayal. Photos of the Chinese economics minister and of Japan's Premier Hideki Tojo were displayed, with an explanation that the Chinese person "never has rosy cheeks" and has a "parchment yellow complexion." Tojo "sometimes (has) rosy cheeks" and an "earthy yellow complexion." On the next page, northern Chinese brothers— "tall and slender"—were pictured alongside Japanese admirals who were called "short and squat." *Life* Publisher Henry R. Luce, the son of missionary parents, was sensitive to the issue because he had grown up in China. Throughout the war, Luce brought the war in China home to Americans through words and pictures in *Time* and *Life* magazines. According to David Halberstam, "It was not just his magazines, but his 'March of Time' newsreels, showing the brave Chinese standing up to the barbarism of the Japanese, which became perhaps the most successful and influential propaganda of its time in making Americans care and think about China and identify with Chiang Kai-shek."[64]

The war improved the image of Chinese Americans; at the same time, Chinese Americans and others were actively promoting an exotic Chinatown image to boost tourism. According to a story printed in *BusinessWeek* magazine in 1938, Chinatown was San Francisco's number 1 tourist attraction.[65]

1941 PEARL HARBOR ATTACK TO ATOMIC BOMBING OF HIROSHIMA, AUGUST 6, 1945

After Pearl Harbor was bombed on December 7, 1941, and China and America became allies against the Japanese, a more positive image of Chinese Americans emerged.[66] Madame Chiang Kai-shek's tour of the United States in the spring of 1943 was covered favorably in the media.[67] During her visit to San Francisco, the *San Francisco Chronicle* ran twenty articles and editorials about her. The *New York Times, Chicago Tribune, San Francisco Examiner*, and *Los Angeles Times* also gave her positive coverage. According to one scholar, "Chinese Americans, now equated with Madame Chiang, were portrayed as modern, intelligent, proud, tolerant and Christian."[68] Chiang and other notable Chinese Americans who appeared to have Western traits helped change the image of Chinese Americans. Several months after her visit, the sixty-one-year-old Exclusion Act was finally repealed on December 17, 1943. The improved image of Chinese Americans had enabled them successfully to lobby for and change immigration policies.

Support for change in immigration laws was reflected in popular newspapers and magazines. The *New York Times*, from the end of the nineteenth century on, attacked the U.S. immigration policy, sometimes championing the cause of the Chinese.[69] An editorial published in the *Saturday Evening Post* in 1943 called for an end to Chinese exclusion, in part because the Japanese used it in their propaganda effort in China. Several scholars note that the Japanese informed the public in Asia about the harassment of Chinese at immigration detention centers and the social and economic pressures that forced them into ghettos and menial jobs in America. Some Americans argued that bringing the Chinese under the normal quota system would right a wrong and "help avert a potential disaster" ("combine canniness with good manners," as the *Saturday Evening Post* phrased it).[70] Pressure to repeal the act also developed because of a labor shortage during the war.[71]

1945 ATOMIC BOMBING OF HIROSHIMA TO LITTLE ROCK INTEGRATION, SEPTEMBER 1957

World War II left many Chinese, particularly students and professionals, stranded in the United States at a time when civil war and the rise of the Communist party were creating chaos in China. After the People's Republic of China was established in 1949, some Chinese Americans were filled with patriotism and went back to China to help rebuild the country, but most chose to stay in America. These newcomers, unlike the laborers who preceded them, commanded the respect of the Americans, who wanted to help them because they were educated and would probably make scientific and technological contributions to the United States.[72] Henry Luce, the publishing magnate, donated his New York home to Chinese students.[73] Henry Shih-shan Tsai has commented that these few thousand professionals constituted only a small percentage of the Chinese population in the United States, but their achievements and their struggle for equality in America not only helped instill in the U.S.-born Chinese a sense of national pride and ethnic consciousness, but also created a more favorable Chinese image among the American people.[74]

John Dower noted, however, that even after the Exclusion Act was repealed, "anti-Oriental" sentiment could not be reversed immediately.[75] Chinese immigration was still limited to 105 Chinese a year.[76] Other significant immigration laws included the following:

• The War Brides Act of 1945 allowed entry to Chinese war brides of American soldiers.
• The Immigration and Naturalization Act of 1952 (the McCarran-Walter Act) made all races eligible for naturalization and eliminated race as a bar to immigration. But China's quota remained at 105. The act created special-preference categories for immigrants with special technical or other skills and increased the number of non-quota immigrants, including immediate relatives of citizens and permanent residents.[77]
• The Refugee Relief Act of 1953 provided asylum for refugees and expelled and displaced persons, including Chinese.

China was isolated after 1949 until the early 1970s, and anti-Communist sentiment was strong in America. Chinese Americans, remembering the internment of the Japanese during World War II, wanted to make it clear that they were not Communists. The growth of the Cold War and anti-Communist sentiment was reflected in various news articles. By 1959 the *Saturday Evening Post* supported the screening of immigrants to keep out potential subversives and criminals. On the other hand, the *New York Times* denounced the McCarran-Walter Act for barring the entry of anyone who was in any way connected with the Communist Party and members of Nazi, Fascist, or other non-Communist totalitarian organizations. The *Times* argued that certain immigrants may have once been involuntarily associated with these groups and should be admitted. It also argued that it was absurd to keep out supporters of democracy.[78]

Leftist activities by Chinese Americans came to public attention when a scuffle broke out in 1949 between pro-Mao and Kuomintang partisans during a Chinese Workers' Mutual Aid Association meeting in San Francisco's Chinatown. The event drew the attention of NBC. As a result, the association's membership dwindled.[79] In 1954 the All-American Overseas Chinese Anti-Communist League held its first meeting in New York City to let the American public know that overseas Chinese were against Communism. This and other organizations were involved in a movement to head off the potential mass deportation of Chinese who had entered the country illegally.[80] Nevertheless, many Chinese organizations, particularly those with leftist tendencies, were under scrutiny. For example, in 1952, the Senate Internal Security Committee subpoenaed Eugene Moy, the editor of the left-wing *China Daily News* of New York City.[81]

1957 LITTLE ROCK INTEGRATION TO NIXON'S RESIGNATION, AUGUST 9, 1974

During this period, media images of Chinese Americans reflected Cold War politics, the Vietnam War, and a growing sympathy for immigrants and refugees.

According to one account, the "red" anti-Communist fear in the 1950s and during the Vietnam War was reflected in the *Saturday Review*. A *Review* columnist in 1966 repeated a rumor that, in preparation for war with China, the U.S. internment campus used to incarcerate Japanese Americans were being prepared for the Chinese to prevent them from committing acts of sabotage. The camps were never used.[82]

Rita Simon and Susan Alexander have demonstrated that, during the 1960s, the news coverage reflected less prejudice and promoted more liberal immigration policies. The *Saturday Evening Post* ran excerpts from a book written by John F. Kennedy encouraging a generous immigration policy, which eventually led to the elimination of the national origin immigration system in 1965.[83] The *New York Times* also came out in support of liberalized immigration and refugee relief policies. In 1962 Kennedy signed a presidential directive that allowed more than 15,000 refugees from China to enter the United States over a period of three years. In 1965 the Hart-Celler Act terminated discrimination against Asian immigrants. The ceiling was raised, and each country was allocated 20,000 immigrants. Chinese immigration rose from 1,000 immigrants per year in the decade before 1965 to 9,000 in 1975.[84]

Despite more liberal immigration policies, the perception that immigrants from Asia would have trouble adjusting to America was still evident. *U.S. News and World Report* published in 1970 and 1971 stories and data on immigrants and where they came from and stated that they might have trouble adjusting, but that their skills would help them cope.[85]

Exclusionary laws had created an unnatural situation in which there were always significantly more men than women in the Chinese American community, which explained the earlier existence of the houses of prostitution in Chinatowns. By 1970, however, there were about 435,000 Chinese in the United States, and the ratio between males and females was equal.[86] About 60 percent were native born, and more than half lived in five cities: Honolulu, San Francisco, Oakland, Los Angeles, and New York.

In the 1960s, the African-American Civil Rights Movement helped create an Asian American civil rights movement that increased ethnic awareness and concern about social justice in the Chinese American community. At the same time, the influx of immigrants from Hong Kong increased, and more Chinese American publications appeared, including some English-language newspapers, such as *East/West*. Chinese American newspapers had existed since the *Golden Hills' News* was established in 1854 in San Francisco. All were intent on changing negative images of Chinese as "opium addicts, hatchet men and slave girls."[87] The *Chinese Digest*, established in 1935, was eager to dispel the image of the "sleepy Celestial enveloped in mists of opium fumes." It was active in calling for the repeal of the Chinese Exclusion Act in 1943.[88] In the mid-1960s, *Truth Weekly* was more sensational. *East/West* was more concerned with local community problems and cultural identity, especially among the younger Chinese.[89] Increasing ethnic consciousness among Chinese Americans helped them form a sense of community and created a transitional period from a foreign-born to an American-born population.

During the ten years after the immigration act of 1965 was passed, more immigrants from Hong Kong arrived, and they tended to gravitate toward the Chinatowns in the big cities. In 1967 the *San Francisco Examiner* criticized the deteriorating economic and social conditions in San Francisco's Chinatown. A series of articles described the ghetto conditions as a feudal enclave for immigrants whose inhabitants were diseased, oppressed, and afraid. The writer blamed the Six Companies (the Chinese Consolidated Benevolent Association) for the sweatshop conditions endured by laborers from Hong Kong.[90] On the other hand, the Six Companies, which had become less political and more social in its activities, preferred to promote the exotic Chinatown image in order to attract tourists. A few months after the articles were printed, the Six Companies called a press conference and dismissed the articles as one-sided and a "blanket indictment of the entire segment of the Chinese people of San Francisco."[91]

In the 1960s and 1970s, Chinese youth gangs began to form, and the popular press noticed. The stories quoted individuals, including politicians, who commented that the new Chinese immigrants were having difficulty adjusting, but that it was safe for Caucasians to go to Chinatown. The implication was that only Chinese were being killed. According to a story appearing on page 1 of the *San Francisco Chronicle* in 1972, the mayor of San Francisco, Joseph Alioto, concerned over a wave of gang murders and beatings in Chinatown, "nevertheless pronounced that area the safest place in town for tourists and Caucasians."[92]

1974 RESIGNATION OF NIXON TO LOS ANGELES UPRISING, APRIL 29, 1992

Throughout the 1970s, plenty of stories appeared on crime and Chinatown youth gang violence, but little scholarly research was done. An article published in the *San Francisco Examiner* in 1974 was titled: "Gang War Erupts Again in Chinatown."[93] An Associated Press story that ran in the *Honolulu Star-Bulletin* in 1977, headlined "The Dark Side of Chinatown," focused on the difficult, dirty conditions there.[94] A caption under a photo noted that "Harry Woo got a bullet wound in the leg for his efforts in working with (New York's) Chinatown's gangs." The *San Francisco Examiner* and the *San Francisco Chronicle* and other publications covered a massacre that occurred in Chinatown's Golden Dragon Restaurant in 1977 in which five people were killed and eleven were wounded.[95] The *Chronicle*'s page 1 headline and deck read: "Chinatown Massacre: Five Slain in Restaurant. 11 Wounded in S.F.'s Worst Mass Slaying."[96] The life of an eighteen-year-old immigrant who was arrested for the crime was described in the *Examiner* this way: "These kids are new . . . they get involved with gangs," according to a large pull-quote from a teacher in the half-page story.

The Media Alliance, a San Francisco–based organization of journalists, photographers, publicists, and filmmakers, complained that a *New Times* magazine article about the Golden Dragon incident had "racist overtones."[97] A National News Council study described the six points made in the complaint, which focused on a story titled: "The Golden Dragon Labor Day Massacre," which appeared in the October 28, 1977, issue of *New Times*. It says that the story had an unrelated photo of an Asian smoking an opium pipe, a retouched photo of Marlon Brando giving him certain stereotyped features associated with Asians, an old photo of a tong war, and a caption "Clazy Joey," among other things. *New Times* editors responded that they had made some stupid mistakes but were not racist except for the "Clazy Joey" caption. The National News Council commended them for apologizing.

A study of the *New York Times* coverage of Chinese Americans over an eighty-year period showed an abundance of crime coverage. Most of the coverage of Chinese Americans came in the 1970s, followed by the 1920s and then the 1910s.[98] An incident of police brutality in New York's Chinatown in 1975 attracted much coverage. The study notes that half of the coverage analyzed was crime related, followed by coverage of political events (24.7 percent), routine other news, and culture. Another study of *Times* coverage of minorities from the 1930s to the 1990s noted that of the total coverage of Asian Americans, Chinese Americans appeared in 27 percent of the coverage, most of it concerning crime, in nine stories.[99] (Other studies of the newspaper coverage of the Chinese in Oregon in the 1870s and 1880s also had noted the disproportionately high numbers of arrests of Chinese.[100])

During the 1980s, youth gangs became more organized, more sophisticated, less publicly violent, and less frequently involved in drug trafficking and "all the old vices," according to an article published in the *San Diego Union*.[101] Consequently, Chinese gangs were not in the news as much as they had been during the previous decade. Instead, the model minority and competitive images of Chinese Americans, evident in *New York Times* articles since the 1880s, were on the rise.[102] The increasing number of Chinese immigrants who have enrolled at well-known universities, such as the University of California at Berkeley, has helped contribute to the image of Chinese Americans as ardent rivals, hard working and obedient.

Such stereotyping has negatively affected all Asian Americans, not just Chinese Americans. A 1991 *Wall Street Journal* and NBC News poll of voters' opinions revealed that the majority of American voters believe that Asian Americans receive "too many special advantages" and were not discriminated against,[103] but a study of Asian Americans conducted by the U.S. Commission on Civil Rights showed that Asian Americans face many barriers to full participation in U.S. society and have been victims of hate crimes.[104] Chinese Americans who have suffered from hate crimes have sometimes been mistaken for members of another Asian racial group. Being of Chinese ancestry had no relevance.

Hate crimes have increased so much that the federal Hate Crimes Statistics Act was created in 1990 so that data are now published about crimes that manifest prejudice against all minorities.[105] The first hate crime against a Chinese American that was covered by the media occurred in 1982. Vincent Chin, a young Chinese American engineering student celebrating at his own bachelor party in Detroit, was chased and brutally beaten to death by two white auto workers who apparently thought he was Japanese and blamed him for the troubles of the U.S. auto industry. His dying words were, "It's not fair."[106] The killers received a sentence of three years' probation and a $3,780 fine; they never served a single day in jail. The sentence sparked protests from Asian Americans who felt it was too lenient. One of the men was acquitted five years later of federal charges of violating Chin's civil rights, a verdict that overturned a twenty-five-year sentence he had received the year before. This event unified many different elements in the Chinese American community during the 1980s, including the younger and older generations.

Seven years after Chin was killed, Ming Hai (Jim) Loo was beaten to death in Raleigh, North Carolina, by white men who blamed him for the death of U.S. service personnel in Vietnam, according to quotes from the killers printed in the *Greensboro News and Record*.[107] Loo and his friends were called "chinks" and "gooks."[108] Both killers received light sentences. Another incident, an attack in 1989 on a Chinese grocer in Castro Valley, California, received much local news media attention. When a local newspaper reported that a lawsuit had been filed against the attackers, the family received a telephone death threat. Neither of the attackers served any prison time. After some female students of Chinese descent were harassed at the University of Connecticut at Storrs in 1987, the *Hartford Courant* reported that "deep-seated prejudice at UConn has bred a climate in which harassment based on race, sex, ethnic background and sexual preference is tolerated by administrators, students, faculty and staff members."[109]

The 1970s and 1980s also witnessed growing interest by U.S. businesses in re-establishing relations with China and expanding trade. On January 1, 1979, diplomatic relations between the United States and China were established. After the Tiananmen massacre took place in Beijing in June 1989, Americans had an increasing awareness of the plight of pro-democracy students in China. *U.S. News & World Report* ran an article a few months later that continued to support open immigration policies: "The President's advisors will argue that room must be left for refugees from other hot spots—China for instance . . . but that some of the flow must be diverted to other nations."[110]

Most non-Asian Americans have difficulty distinguishing among the different Asian groups. This is also true of media representatives, who tend to lump all Asians together. Part of the fault lies with news and entertainment images and with the U.S. government classification systems. The broad Asian American category covers immigrants from certain Pacific Islands to Bangladesh. Virginia Mansfield-Richardson, who chronicled the lack of research on Asian Americans, concluded that "the very basic problem of determining who is an Asian American may be one obstacle that is preventing the media from correctly covering Asian Americans and Pacific Islanders.''[111] This assumption makes even more sense, she said, because radio and television, in particular, tend to oversimplify to fit a tight time spot. She cited *New York Times* stories that presented slanted, negative images of minorities.[112]

Broadcast Coverage

As a minority group, Chinese Americans in recent times generally have been portrayed as model minorities by the news media. One source noted that, during the late 1980s and early 1990s, every major newsmagazine and television network featured glowing reports of the achievements of Asian Americans in occupations and education.[113] Some Chinese Americans who have risen to prominent positions, such as news reporter Connie Chung, formerly of NBC and CBS; Hawaii Senator Hiram Fong; world-renowned architect I. M. Pei; ice-skating champions Tiffany Chin and Michelle Kwan; and tennis star Michael Chang have received considerable media coverage. Despite her fame, Chung was once referred to as ''Connie Chink'' by Cliff Kincaid, a Washington, D.C., radio personality, according to the *Washington Post*.[114] He argued it was a slang term, but the Asian American Journalists Association (AAJA) defines ''chink'' as a racial slur.[115] However, Chung is credited with setting off a boom in female Asian-American network newscasters, who usually sit as anchors beside white males. The networks, it seems, are not comfortable with the reverse.[116]

The AAJA encourages news organizations to avoid stereotyping Asian Americans as model minorities, as competitive, as a threat to Americans' jobs, or as gang members. Its members have created a handbook to help print and broadcast journalists create realistic images and to ''show how heroes and villains can be used to create a balance without distorting a story line.''[117] The handbook provides examples of how Asians can be cast in mainstream roles, as well as examples of positive and negative images, starting with films from the early 1900s. Although the current stereotype that Asians are intelligent, affluent, and well-behaved is better than the Yellow Peril stereotype of decades past, many Asian Americans chafe under the model minority label, according to the handbook.[118] News organizations are urged to cover Asian Americans as they would other groups.

Although no studies of television news portrayals of Chinese Americans were found, it should be noted that the Detroit broadcast media played an active role in carrying stories of the Chinese American protests against the light sentences given to Vincent Chin's killers in the early 1980s and thus helped build pressure for a new federal trial. In addition, the local stations ran stories investigating various aspects of the case. (Additional information on this situation can be found in Chapter 7.)

David Liu, an Emmy award-winning producer, said about network news, ''There's always coverage of a Chinatown gang murder or of a Chinese New

Year's celebration. . . . There should be more coverage of a case like Vincent Chin's [murder] in the Detroit area; there's not nearly the proportion of coverage there should be."[119]

In the early 1990s WNYE, a PBS affiliate in New York, started a weekly thirty-minute prime time program in English called "Asian America," which covered social, political, economic, and cultural topics concerning Asian Americans. The first person interviewed on the show was Nora Chang Wang, New York Mayor Rudolph Giuliani's employment commissioner.[120]

1992 LOS ANGELES UPRISING TO PRESIDENTIAL ELECTION, NOVEMBER 1996

Project Zinger, a media watch publication of the AAJA and the Center for Integration and Improvement of Journalism at San Francisco State University, examines any periodical or broadcast report that perpetuates an ethnic stereotype, and the problem is discussed with the journalists in an effort to sensitize them.[121] For example, the *San Francisco Chronicle* used a drawing of a Chinese child to accompany a story called "Japanese Kids Get '24-hour Love.' " The child's hair is worn in a queue.[122] Project Zinger's advisory board stated that the AAJA's *Asian American Handbook* notes that cartoonists frequently exaggerate an individual's unique physical features, but they need to be aware of the problem of stereotypes and they need to learn more about the diverse backgrounds of Asians and Asian Americans. The AAJA's New York chapter criticized New York's *Newsday* for a story perpetuating a stereotype that Chinese Americans are gamblers: "Gambling is an accepted part of New York's Chinatown culture. Always has been. Probably always will be."[123] One board member commented that the article was "an example of how pop sociology and stereotypic, simplistic images of Asian American communities can discredit an otherwise well-reported piece."[124]

The Center for Integration and Improvement of Journalism at San Francisco State University has published *News Watch: A Critical Look at Coverage of People of Color*, as part of its Unity '94 project. The examples chronicled in that publication note continued stereotypes of Chinese Americans as gang members, as part of an Asian invasion, and as exotic (eating worms, for example, or eating domesticated animals). One cartoon published in the *San Diego Union-Tribune* (September 5, 1993) drew criticism from readers: "Chinese Food Has High Fat Content," a newspaper headline read. A man replied: "What worries me is the cat content."[125]

The U.S. Commission on Civil Rights has also taken action to fight stereotypes. In its February 1992 Civil Rights Report, the commission noted that "the public's perceptions and attitudes towards Asian Americans are heavily influenced by the way Asian Americans are portrayed by the media. Many of the civil rights problems confronting Asian Americans are fashioned by stereotypes, especially the model minority stereotype, that are promoted by the media."[126]

Recommendation 39 suggests, "The media should make every effort to provide balanced, indepth, and sensitive coverage of Asian Americans and to improve the representation of Asian Americans in their decision-making ranks."[127]

When Bill Wong, a columnist for the *Oakland Tribune*, was fired in March 1996 after writing for the paper for sixteen years, some Asian American journalists "found in Wong's dismissal a dark subtext: a lack of respect for Asian journalists generally," according to the *Columbia Journalism Review*.[128] Some residents of Oakland felt betrayed and rallied outside the newspaper's offices to get Wong reinstated. He had been considered a voice for minority readers and "kind of an icon for many Asian Americans in his profession." The editor in chief at the time insisted that the firing had nothing to do with race or politics, but was over salary and the editor's decision to use the money for other purposes. "Tone-deaf to the racist implications" was the way one ex-employee described management's attitude.[129]

CONCLUSION

The history of the portrayal of Chinese Americans in the mainstream American news media reflects U.S. immigration policies, politics, big business, and labor interests as well as U.S.–China relations. Coverage that was largely negative in the 1870s has changed somewhat with the growth of the model minority image, but more research must be done on recent coverage to examine the degree to which the images of Chinese Americans have changed, particularly in light of hate crimes. Little scholarly literature has been published on the post–World War II period, particularly from the 1960s. A content analysis of the portrayal of Chinese Americans in the mainstream news media that includes placement and story play is needed. Such a study could show how stereotypes of Chinese Americans have changed and whether their coverage is being integrated into mainstream coverage.

Part of the problem of stereotyped, biased, and confused coverage may be due to the fact that Chinese Americans account for less than 1 percent of the U.S. population. Many Americans may not even know any Chinese Americans—much less know them well. Given this, representatives of news organizations will frequently justify coverage of Chinese Americans when it is deemed newsworthy by their standards—for instance, when it involves a cultural event, riot, or success story—but the reporters usually do not have enough interest or knowledge to explain the context of the story. These news values, ingrained in years of white male journalistic training, are part of the culture of newsrooms and of the mass media. Is it possible to change this culture and improve coverage of Chinese Americans? Change should come from management; it may be impossible for individual reporters and photographers to go against the tide by covering news in a nonstereotypical way because their stories and photos may not be chosen by editors to run in the paper. Competition for space is great because of the shrinking newshole in newspapers, and stories that are not deemed newsworthy may not be published. Also, high-level editors are influenced by what a publisher might want to see in the paper. Broadcast organizations face the same type of cultural newsroom environment, heightened by competition among reporters seeking to become "stars" and by the extremely limited airtime available for news stories.

If publishers and owners are willing to adopt new standards, then a strategy to change newsroom culture can be implemented. The News 2000 program created by the largest news organization in the United States, Gannett Co. Inc., has the potential to achieve this. The program requires that all Gannett's news organizations make efforts to appeal to readers by getting to know them better, including ethnically diverse groups. In addition, its newspapers, as well as those owned by other companies, strive to create diversity in newsrooms by hiring women and racial minorities. Reporters need training in covering non-Caucasian groups, and this will require resources. It will take time to train reporters to cover Chinese Americans as they would Caucasians, and to use them as sources of information. On the other hand, perhaps reporters and editors will initiate a new attitude from their grassroots position.[130]

It may be an uphill battle to improve the coverage of Chinese Americans in most American news organizations because of the economic environment in which mass media operate. As Clint Wilson and Félix Gutiérrez and others note, the media are forced to act as businesses aiming to make a profit.[131] They tend to support common and popular themes. As a result, the opinions of ethnic and other minority groups often have been ignored.[132] Wilson and Gutiérrez note five stages that have characterized the development of news media portrayals of minorities in the United States after the 1830s "Penny Press."[133] These can be applied to the coverage of Chinese Americans.

1. Exclusionary—Early period of Chinese immigration. Chinese Americans were ignored or treated as if they were sub-human because they were not white. This was evident in the dehumanizing language and cartoons used frequently from the 1870s through the 1920s by the media. Words such as "heathen," "pig-tailed" and "yellow" were common.

2. Threatening issue—Chinese immigrant labor threatened American workers' jobs. Chinese Americans were criticized for coming as laborers, learning a white man's business, then beating him at it.[134] It was feared that they would monopolize businesses and land in California, for example. In more recent times, fear of competition from Chinese Americans and others of Asian ancestry has focused attention on UC Berkeley and other universities.

3. Confrontation—The news media, having exacerbated the perceived threat and brought it to the public's attention, then covered the response, which was sometimes violent. From the 1880s, the media in the Western states, in particular, have been influential in promoting anti- and pro-Chinese sentiment. For example, the *San Francisco Chronicle* had an active role in promoting the anti-Chinese cause in the 1880s and the resulting riots and violence. Henry Luce's *Time* and *Life* magazines were active in the pro-Chinese cause during World War II, which helped sway American sentiment

in favor of abolishing the exclusion laws.

4. Stereotypical selection (of news)—Model minority characterizations. The Chinese have been stereotyped as intelligent and industrious; on the other hand, Chinese Americans have most typically been portrayed as less than human, competitive, conniving, and untrustworthy, or as youth gang members and criminals.

5. Integration—Chinese Americans in the future will be reflected in all types of news, as are Euro-Americans.

We may possibly be at the beginning of the last stage, but much more needs to be done. Some media executives in communities with many Chinese Americans are realizing that, for economic reasons, they must appeal to all readers. Some are increasing the number of minorities on staff in an effort to improve reporting. But do these staff have the resources and time to understand fully the complexity of the various minority groups? Will they be respected or seen as dispensible? The unique qualities of the various types of Chinese American people cannot be ignored. There are American-born Chinese Americans of several generations, and those of Chinese ancestry who were born in China, Taiwan, Hong Kong, and Southeast Asia. Some are bicultural and function comfortably in Chinese and American cultures, and some want to assimilate. Efforts like those of *Project Zinger*, the U.S. Commission on Civil Rights, and others to raise cultural awareness, and indeed to change newsroom culture, may influence news media representatives to integrate people of all ethnic backgrounds into news coverage.

NOTES

1. Cheryl L. Cole, "Chinese Exclusion: The Capitalist Perspective of the *Sacramento Union*, 1850–1882," *California History* 57, no. 1 (1978), 23.

2. Some of the classic works of this period are Mary Roberts Coolidge, *Chinese Immigration* (New York: Harry Holt, 1909); and Henry Shih-shan Tsai, *The Chinese Experience in America* (Bloomington: Indiana University Press, 1986).

3. Him Mark Lai, "Chinese American Studies: A Historical Survey," *Chinese America: History and Perspectives* Serial (San Francisco State University: Chinese Historical Society of America, 1988), 12.

4. Ibid., 13–14. Lai points out that the Chinese in Hawaii were not subject to the Chinese Exclusion Acts until after annexation of the territory in 1898. Hawaii continued to receive immigrants until the turn of the century. "The absence of a large white middle class in the Hawaiian kingdom also gave the Chinese a chance to carve out a niche for themselves as entrepreneurs and skilled workers," according to Lai.

5. H. M. Lai and P. P. Choy, *Chinese-American Studies Planning Group* (San Francisco Chinatown: Self-published, 1973). Also see Colleen Valerie Jin Fong, "Tracing the Origins of a 'Model Minority': A Study of the Depictions of Chinese Americans in Popular Magazines" (Ph.D. diss., University of Oregon, 1989), 77.

6. Susan Gall and Irene Natividad, "Who Are the Chinese Americans?" in *The Asian American Almanac*, ed. Susan Gall and Irene Natividad (Detroit: Gale Research, 1995), 46.

7. Fong, "Tracing the Origins of a 'Model Minority,' " 75–76, 192.

8. Reva Clar and William M. Kramer, "Chinese-Jewish Relations in the Far West: 1850–1950," *Western States Jewish History* 21, no. 1 (1988), 27. According to an account from the *San Francisco Chronicle* in 1878.

9. Ibid.

10. Sucheng Chan, *This Bitter-Sweet Soil: The Chinese in California Agriculture, 1860–1910* (Berkeley: University of California Press, 1986), 43.

11. Gall and Natividad, eds., *The Asian American Almanac*, 41, quoting the *Alta California*, 22 August 1851.

12. Rita J. Simon and Susan H. Alexander, *The Ambivalent Welcome: Print Media, Public Opinion and Immigration* (Westport, Conn.: Praeger, 1993), 197.

13. Ibid.

14. Liisa Penner, *The Chinese in Astoria, Oregon, 1870–1880* (Astoria: Self-published, 1990). A look at local newspaper articles, the census, and other related materials.

15. Ibid., 3, 5.

16. Ibid., 8.

17. Cole, "Chinese Exclusion," 8.

18. Ibid.

19. Ibid., 9. Cole cites Edward Kemble, *A History of California Newspapers, 1846–1858*. Sacramento, Calif: *Daily Union*, 1858. Also see Jules Becker, *The Course of Exclusion, 1882–1924: San Francisco Newspaper Coverage of the Chinese and Japanese in the United States* (San Francisco: Mellen Research University Press, 1991).

20. Cole, "Chinese Exclusion," 11.

21. Ibid., 12.

22. Ibid., 13–14.

23. Ibid., 13.

24. Ibid., 14, 16.

25. Ibid., 21, 23.

26. Richard Austin Thompson, *The Yellow Peril: 1890–1924* (New York: Arno Press, 1978), 9–10.

27. Ibid., 205.

28. Simon and Alexander, *The Ambivalent Welcome*, 201.

29. The Exclusion Act did allow children born of males already in the United States to enter the United States. Chinese men would return to China to father children. Also see Paul Pederson, Juris Draguns, Walter Lonner, and Joseph Trimble, eds., *Counseling across Cultures* (Honolulu: East-West Center, Culture Learning Institute, University Press of Hawaii, 1981).

30. Gall and Natividad, eds., *The Asian American Almanac*, 49.

31. Ibid., 50.

32. Jack Hammersmith, "West Virginia, the 'Heathen Chinee,' and the California Conspiracy," *West Virginia History* 34, no. 3 (Charleston, W.Va.: State Department of Archives and History, 1973), 291–96. He cites a study of New York and Massachusetts newspaper accounts by Stuart Creighton Miller, *The Unwelcome Immigrant: The American Image of the Chinese, 1785–1882* (Berkeley: University of California Press, 1969), 291.

33. Hammersmith, "West Virginia, the 'Heathen Chinee,' " 293.

34. Thompson, *The Yellow Peril*, 103.

35. Gunther Barth, *Bitter Strength: A History of the Chinese in the United States, 1850–1870* (Cambridge: Harvard University Press, 1964), 198.

36. Ibid., 205–6.

37. John W. Dower offers a thorough discussion of animal imagery and stereotyping of the Japanese in *War without Mercy: Race and Power in the Pacific War* (New York: Pantheon Books, 1986), 81–93.

38. Thompson, *The Yellow Peril*, 2–3.

39. Penner, *The Chinese in Astoria*, 33.

40. Ibid., 61.

41. A. Dudley Gardner, "Chinese Emigrants in Southwest Wyoming, 1868–1885," *Annals of Wyoming* 63, no. 4 (Fall 1991), 139–44. Also see Gall and Natividad, eds., *The Asian American Almanac*, 49, which puts the number killed at 40 and says another 500 were driven into the desert.

42. Gardner, "Chinese Emigrants."

43. Ibid., 140.

44. Ibid.

45. Ibid., 142.

46. Simon and Alexander, *The Ambivalent Welcome*, 203, quoting the *New York Times*, 18 June 1893.

47. Ibid., 206.

48. Thompson, *The Yellow Peril*, 201–2.

49. Fong, "Tracing the Origins of a 'Model Minority,' " 218.

50. Ibid., 219.

51. Ibid., 223, 226.

52. Ibid., 227. She cites J.O.P. Bland, "The Real Yellow Peril," *Atlantic Monthly* (June 1913), 734–44.

53. Ibid., 228. Also see p. 235 on the desire of Americans to shape China's future and support the modernization and democratic movement of Sun Yat-sen, who had traveled extensively in the United States.

54. Ibid., 247.

55. Simon and Alexander, *The Ambivalent Welcome*, 211.

56. Ibid., 70–71, 202, 248.

57. Ibid., 212, quoting the *New York Times*, 15 April 1924.

58. Ibid., 215, quoting editorials in the *New York Times*, 1931 and 1933.

59. Fong, "Tracing the Origins of a 'Model Minority,' " 255.

60. Ibid., 256.

61. Ibid., 261. Fong cites several articles from the *San Francisco Chronicle* and other publications.

62. Ibid., 262.

63. Ibid., 262–63.

64. David Halberstam, *The Powers That Be* (New York: Alfred A. Knopf, 1979), 69.

65. Fong, "Tracing the Origins of a 'Model Minority,' " 230. See *BusinessWeek*, 12 March 1938, 28.

66. According to Roger Daniels, William Peterson, a University of California Berkeley professor, first coined the term "model minority" in the mid-1960s to describe the Japanese Americans. Other social scientists soon applied the term to other Asian Amer-

icans. Roger Daniels, *Prisoners without Trial: Japanese Americans in World War II* (New York: Hill and Wang, 1993).

67. Tsai, *The Chinese Experience*, 114.

68. Ibid.

69. Simon and Alexander, *The Ambivalent Welcome*, 242–43.

70. Dower, *War without Mercy*, 185–86.

71. Simon and Alexander, *The Ambivalent Welcome*, 14.

72. These positive images also emerge among the American-born Chinese Americans after World War II.

73. Tsai, *The Chinese Experience*, 121–22.

74. Ibid., 124.

75. Dower, *War without Mercy*, 166.

76. Gall and Natividad, eds. *The Asian American Almanac*, 51. The change granted naturalization rights and allowed family members to immigrate.

77. Dower, *War without Mercy*, 267.

78. Simon and Alexander, *The Ambivalent Welcome*, 218.

79. Tsai, *The Chinese Experience*, 133.

80. Ibid., 135.

81. H. M. Lai, "To Bring Forth a New China, to Build a Better America: The Chinese Marxist Left in America to the 1960s," *Chinese America: History and Perspectives* Serial (San Francisco: Chinese Historical Society of America, 1992), 60.

82. Jacobus tenBroek, Edward Barnhart, and Floyd Matson, *Prejudice, War and the Constitution* 3rd ed. (Berkeley: University of California Press, 1968), vi.

83. Simon and Alexander, *The Ambivalent Welcome*, 80–81.

84. Ibid., 267.

85. Ibid., 187, quoting *U.S. News & World Report*, 5 October 1970.

86. Gall and Natividad, *The Asian American Almanac*, 51.

87. Him Mark Lai, "Chinese American Studies: A Historical Survey," *Chinese America: History and Perspectives* Serial (San Francisco State University: Chinese Historical Society of America, 1990), 15.

88. Julie Shuk-yee Lam, "The Chinese Digest, 1935–1940," *Chinese America: History and Perspectives* Serial (San Francisco State University: Chinese Historical Society of America, 1987), 119–37.

89. Paul Slater, "San Francisco's Chinese Newspapers: A Lingering Institution," *Journalism Quarterly* 46, no. 3 (Autumn 1969), 606.

90. Tsai, *The Chinese Experience*, 137–38. He cites the *San Francisco Examiner*, 14, 15, 18 August 1967.

91. Ibid., 138, quoting a Six Companies press release, 2 October 1967.

92. "Alioto Says Chinatown Is Mostly Safe," *San Francisco Chronicle*, 30 June 1972, 1.

93. "Gang War Erupts Again in Chinatown," *San Francisco Chronicle*, 13 June 1974, 19.

94. Peter Arnett, "The Dark Side of Chinatown," *Honolulu Star-Bulletin*, 27 March 1977, C4.

95. Annie Nakao and Raul Ramirez, "Massacre: The Story of a Teen-age Suspect," *San Francisco Examiner*, 31 March 1978, 6.

96. *San Francisco Chronicle*, 5 September 1977, 1.

97. *In the Public Interest II: A Report by the National News Council, 1975–1978*

(New York: National News Council, 1979), 269–70.

98. Chin-yao Jennifer Mu, "Coverage of Chinese Americans in the *New York Times*, 1900–1980" (Master's thesis, University of Texas at Austin, 1982), 46–52.

99. Carolyn Martindale, "Only in Glimpses: Portrayal of America's Largest Minority Groups by the *New York Times*, 1934–1994" (Paper presented at the Association for Education in Journalism and Mass Communication Convention, Atlanta, August 1995), 14.

100. Herman B. Chiu, "Power of the Press: How Newspapers in Four Communities Erased Thousands of Chinese from Oregon History" (Paper presented at the Association for Education in Journalism and Mass Communication Convention, Anaheim, California, August 1996), 25. Also see Robett Edward Wynne, *Reaction to the Chinese in the Pacific Northwest and British Columbia 1850–1910* (New York: Arno Press, 1978).

101. "Chinese-Organized Crime Burgeons on West Coast," *San Diego Union*, 6 March 1988; chronicles the growth of organized crime.

102. U.S. Commission on Civil Rights, *Civil Rights Issues Facing Asian Americans in the 1990s*, Washington, D.C.: U.S. Government Printing Office, 1992, 19. For a discussion of the model minority image, see Ki-Taek Chun, "The Myth of Asian American Success and Its Educational Ramifications," *IRCD Bulletin* 15, no. 1–2 (Winter/Spring 1980), 1–12. Also see Grace Yun, ed., *A Look beyond the Model Minority Image: Critical Issues in Asian America* (New York: Minority Rights Group, 1989); and Kwang Chung Kim, "The 'Success' Image of Asian Americans: Its Validity, and Its Practical and Theoretical Implications," *Ethnic and Racial Studies* 12 (October 1989), 512–38.

103. Michel McQueen, "Voters' Responses to Poll Disclose Huge Chasm between Social Attitudes of Blacks and Whites," *Wall Street Journal*, 17 May 1991, A16.

104. U.S. Commission on Civil Rights, *Civil Rights Issues*, 1.

105. Specifically, the Hate Crimes Statistics Act of 1990 was created to enable the attorney general to acquire and publish data about crimes that manifest prejudice based on certain group characteristics.

106. See "Chinese-American Rights Case Ends in Acquittal," *Honolulu Star-Bulletin* Associated Press article, 1 May 1987, A7. Also see Leon Daniel, "Asian-Americans Victims of Detroit Hard Times," *Honolulu Sunday Star-Bulletin & Advertiser*, 21 August 1983, A9.

107. Seth Effron, "Racial Slaying Prompts Fear, Anger in Raleigh," *Greensboro News and Record (N.C.)*, 24 September 1989.

108. U.S. Commission on Civil Rights, *Civil Rights Issues*, 26–27.

109. See Katherine Farrish, "UConn Students Reflect on State of Race Relations," *Hartford Courant*, 6 April 1989, B1. See also U.S. Commission on Civil Rights, *Civil Rights Issues*, 43.

110. Simon and Alexander, *The Ambivalent Welcome*, 194, quoting *U.S. News & World Report*, 18 September 1989.

111. Virginia Mansfield-Richardson, "Asian Americans and Mass Communication in the United States: A Wake-up Call" (Paper presented at the Association for Education in Journalism and Mass Communication Convention, Washington, D.C., August 1995), 15.

112. Ibid., 27–28.

113. Joe R. Feagin and Clairece Booher Feagin, "Japanese Americans," in *Racial and Ethnic Relations*, 5th ed. (Upper Saddle River, N.J.: Prentice-Hall, 1996), 404.

114. U.S. Commission on Civil Rights, *Civil Rights Issues*, 44. See Jeffrey Horke,

"On Radio, A Racial 'Joke' '": WNTR Host Takes on Connie Chung," *Washington Post*, 24 March 1990, C1.

115. U.S. Commission on Civil Rights, *Civil Rights Issues*, 44–45.

116. Darrell Y. Hamamoto, *Monitored Peril: Asian Americans and the Politics of TV Representation* (Minneapolis: University of Minnesota Press, 1994), 244–45.

117. Asian American Journalists Association, *Asian American Handbook* (Chicago: Asian American Journalists Association, Chicago Chapter, and the National Conference of Christians and Jews, Chicago and Northern Illinois Region, 1991), 1.1.

118. Ibid., 3.11.

119. Gall and Natividad, eds., *The Asian American Almanac*, 597.

120. Ibid.

121. Ibid.

122. *Project Zinger: A Critical Look at News Media Coverage of Asian Pacific Americans* (Washington, D.C.: Center for Integration and Improvement of Journalism and Asian American Journalists Association, 1992), 14.

123. Ibid., 4.

124. Ibid.

125. *News Watch: A Critical Look at Coverage of People of Color*, A Unity '94 Project (San Francisco: Center for Integration and Improvement of Journalism, San Francisco State University, 1994), 11.

126. U.S. Commission on Civil Rights, *Civil Rights Issues*, 204.

127. Ibid.

128. J. Michael Robertson, "The Wong Affair: A Case of Ethnic Insensitivity, or Just the Bottom Line?," *Columbia Journalism Review* 35, no. 2 (July/August 1996), 15.

129. Ibid.

130. In Paul Lester's book, *Images That Injure: Pictorial Stereotypes in the Media* (Westport, Conn.: Praeger, 1996), he urges news people to change.

131. Clint C. Wilson II and Félix Gutiérrez, *Minorities and Media: Diversity and the End of Mass Communication* (Beverly Hills, Calif.: Sage, 1985), 37. Also see their new edition: Wilson and Gutiérrez, *Race, Multiculturalism and the Media* (Thousand Oaks, Calif.: Sage, 1995).

132. Fred Fedler, "The Media and Minority Groups: A Study of Adequacy of Access," *Journalism Quarterly* 50, no. 1 (Spring 1973), 109.

133. Wilson and Gutiérrez, *Minorities and Media*, 135–42.

134. Thompson covers the "economic peril" of the Chinese in *The Yellow Peril*, 91–140.

SELECTED BIBLIOGRAPHY

Asian American Journalists Association. *Asian American Handbook*. Chicago: Asian American Journalists Association, Chicago Chapter, and the National Conference of Christians and Jews, Chicago and Northern Illinois Region, 1991.

Chan, Sucheng. *Asian Americans, an Interpretive History*. Boston: Twayne, 1991.

———. *This Bitter-Sweet Soil: The Chinese in California Agriculture, 1860–1910*. Berkeley: University of California Press, 1986.

Choy, Philip, Lorraine Dong, and Marlon Hom. *The Coming Man: 19th Century American Perceptions of the Chinese*. Seattle: University of Washington Press, 1994.

Cole, L. Cheryl. "Chinese Exclusion: The Capitalist Perspective of the *Sacramento Union*, 1850–1882." *California History* 57, no. 1 (1978), 8–31.

Coolidge, Mary Roberts. *Chinese Immigration*. New York: Harry Holt, 1909.

Fong, Colleen Valerie Jin. "Tracing the Origins of a 'Model Minority': A Study of the Depictions of Chinese Americans in Popular Magazines." Ph.D. diss., University of Oregon, 1989.

Gall, Susan, and Irene Natividad. "Who Are the Chinese Americans?" In *The Asian American Almanac*, edited by Susan Gall and Irene Natividad. Detroit: Gale Research, 1995.

Lai, Him Mark. See various articles in *Chinese America: History and Perspective* Serial. San Francisco: Chinese Historical Society of America.

Miller, Stuart Creighton. *The Unwelcome Immigrant: The American Image of the Chinese, 1785–1882*. Berkeley: University of California Press, 1969.

Project Zinger: A Critical Look at News Media Coverage of Asian Pacific Americans. Washington, D.C.: Center for Integration and Improvement of Journalism and Asian American Journalists Association, August 1992.

Simon, Rita J., and Susan H. Alexander. *The Ambivalent Welcome: Print Media, Public Opinion and Immigration*. Westport, Conn.: Praeger, 1993.

Takaki, Ronald. *Strangers from a Different Shore: A History of Asian Americans*. Boston: Little, Brown, 1989.

Thompson, Richard Austin. *The Yellow Peril: 1890–1924*. New York: Arno Press, 1978.

Tsai, Henry Shih-shan. *The Chinese Experience in America*. Bloomington: Indiana University Press, 1986.

U.S. Commission on Civil Rights, *Civil Rights Issues Facing Asian Americans in the 1990s*. Washington, D.C.: U.S. Government Printing Office, February 1992.

The Japanese Americans
Thomas H. Heuterman

The only American citizens who were detained in assembly centers and later transported under guard to barbed-wire concentration camps were those of Japanese ancestry.
—Joe R. Feagin and Clairece Booher Feagin[1]

Japanese Americans faced a social environment of almost unrelenting hostility from 1869 until well after World War II.[2] First came a crisis of immigration and adjustment from 1869 to 1906. Next, state and federal legislation brought a crisis of exclusion, extending to 1926 and beyond. An interval of accommodation followed but ended with World War II and evacuation. The return from internment camps and readjustment prompted a final crisis that continued on into the 1950s.[3] During those eighty years, the Issei (the immigrants from Japan) and Nisei (their children) could take scant comfort from the constitutionally protected press as they sought to exercise their rights. In the remainder of the twentieth century, no overt crises occurred but neither did the press generally even acknowledge the Japanese-American community.

Historians debate whether the hostility experienced by Japanese Americans was merely a continuation of that first faced by Chinese Americans, or whether a new set of circumstances led to efforts to exclude the Issei and Nisei. Evidence exists that, at least initially, distinctions were made between these immigrants from Asia. In 1869 the *San Francisco Chronicle* observed "objections raised against the Chinese . . . cannot be alleged against the Japanese [who are] gentlemen of refinement and culture [who] have brought their wives, children, and . . . new industries among us."[4] In fact, historian Roger Daniels claimed he failed to find "a single word" of protest against the early immigrants from Japan.[5]

As early as 1865, sugar plantation owners in Hawaii sought to employ low-wage Japanese laborers as an economical way to develop their land. When the *City of Tokyo* berthed in Honolulu in 1885, the *Pacific Commercial Advertiser* viewed the arrival of nearly 1,000 men, women, and children most favorably: "The arrival of the steamer from Japan with the first lot of immigrants will afford great satisfaction, and the arrangements now contemplated should lead to a large immigration in the next few months."[6] Of course, the Hawaiian king saw the laborers as future subjects who could offset the threat posed by the white elite to his monarchy.[7]

The major period of sustained immigration started in 1886, when the Meiji regime permitted peasant males from southern Japan to seek their fortune in foreign lands. Between 1886 and 1897, roughly 26,000 workers went to Hawaii.[8] During this period, the *Hawaiian Gazette* observed, "The asiaticizing of the Hawaiian Islands is proceeding at such a rapid rate that those citizens who know what such a course must lead to, may well stand appalled before such a prospect."[9]

Early Japanese immigrants to the U.S. mainland may have been so few in number that they were perceived as no threat. Before the passage of the Chinese Exclusion Act in 1882, the numbers of newcomers from Japan were negligible. After the act was passed, they came in response to the efforts of labor recruiters, who were seeking replacements for the Chinese on railroads, on farms, in mines, and in canneries.[10] Only 148 Japanese Americans were living in the United States in 1880 and about 2,000 in 1890, but by the turn of the century over 24,000 lived on the mainland. The majority at any time lived in California.[11]

It has also been observed that the Japanese inherited not so much the anti-Chinese hostility as the same conditions, at least in California, that gave rise to anti-Chinese sentiments. Not the least of these factors was the racism of the Native Sons and Daughters of the Golden West, the California Joint Immigration Committee, and the California Farm Bureau Federation.[12] In May 1905, delegates from sixty-seven organizations met in San Francisco to form what became the Japanese Exclusion League (the Asiatic Exclusion League), led primarily by labor groups whose motives were both racial and economic. By 1908 the league had over 100,000 members—more people than the number of Japanese Americans then living in the United States—and 238 affiliated groups.[13]

Although the racist intensity may have been greatest in California, an image of the Japanese was spreading nationally. In 1907 a classic racial stereotype was published in *Collier's* magazine. Deemed typical of the newcomers was the buck-toothed, bespectacled, arrogant, and wordy figure mouthing phrases such as "Honorable Sir" and "So sorry, please."[14] This image has never died out.

On March 18, 1907, President Theodore Roosevelt signed an order prohibiting aliens, primarily Japanese, from settling on the mainland.[15] The Japanese government agreed to stop issuing passports to laborers wanting to go to the United

States in the reciprocal action that became known as the Gentlemen's Agreement.[16] From 1907 through the end of the decade, newspapers in Washington and Oregon wrote at length to disassociate themselves from the "California position," which sought to prohibit Japanese immigration completely and to bar Japanese children from the San Francisco public schools.[17] By 1910 the U.S. Japanese-American population stood at 72,000.[18]

It made little difference to William Randolph Hearst whether the "Yellow Peril" was composed of the Chinese or Japanese.[19] His father, George Hearst, had used anti-Chinese sentiment as a means of gaining a U.S. Senate seat in 1886. The younger Hearst unleashed his own anti-Japan tirade in the *New York American* in 1915 and 1916.[20] In 1917 Hearst's International Film Service Corporation produced *Patria*, which, like the American Legion's later *Shadows of the West*, portrayed Japanese immigrants as sneaky, treacherous agents of a militaristic Japan. The *Saturday Evening Post* and Hearst's *Cosmopolitan* magazine serialized novels about the dangers of Japanese land ownership.[21]

Sentiment cooled during World War I while Japan was an ally of the United States and Japanese Americans on the West Coast raised food for the war effort. Officials seldom enforced California's new Alien Land Law, which prohibited Japanese Americans from owning land.[22] However, in 1919, V. S. McClatchy, the editor and publisher of the *Sacramento Bee*, returned from an Asian trip incensed over Japanese censorship. He formed, and dedicated the remainder of his life to, the California Joint Immigration Committee supported by the Native Sons of the Golden West, the Grange, the State Federation of Labor, and the American Legion.[23] The committee's goal was to exclude Japanese from the United States.

Reflecting one view of Caucasians in the Pacific, the *Pacific Commercial Advertiser* in Honolulu in 1919 hinted that the Constitution might not apply to the Japanese:

The Constitution, it is true, grants to every man the right to worship according to the dictates of his own conscience, but that does not mean that a religion hostile of our principles shall be taught the children of residents of America, children who are some day to exercise the right of franchise and perhaps help make our laws.[24]

In the Pacific Northwest, the *Spokesman-Review* of Spokane, Washington, observing the increased immigration, said the numbers of "little brown men from Japan" were a "worriment to many."[25] But racism had no influence on those who recognized the desirability of Japan as a Pacific trading partner. The *Business Chronicle* of the Pacific Northwest in Seattle in 1919, possibly recognizing the creeping influence of McClatchy's California Committee, editorialized:

Somewhere within Seattle—or is it from without?—an as yet unidentified influence is raising a hue and cry against the Japanese. It is not good business practice to slap one's best customer in the face, nor is it good form to slam the door when friendly neighbors call. . . . Seattle was chosen as the terminus of the great Japanese steamship lines, and it is the simple truth to state that Seattle has become great as a world port because the Japanese have in large measure made it such.[26]

Obviously not holding such a global view, the *Los Angeles Times* in 1920 stated that "assimilation of the two races is unthinkable. It is morally indefensible and biologically impossible. An American who would not die fighting rather than yield to this infamy does not deserve the name."[27]

In Hawaii, when the Federation of Japanese Labor joined 2,600 Filipino sugar plantation workers on strike in 1920, newspaper reaction made it obvious that this was more than a labor dispute. The *Pacific Commercial Advertiser* asked whether Hawaii was to be an American territory or an Oriental province. The newspaper denounced Buddhist priests, Japanese newspaper editors, and other "subjects of the Mikado" as agitators.[28] By the 1920s, nearly half of Hawaii's population was composed of Issei or Nisei, who were served by the Japanese language press, itself divided over how to combat the racism of Americanism that assaulted Japanese institutions such as the language schools. While the *Nippu Jiji* (Japan Times) urged passive assimilation, Fred Kinzaburo Makino of the *Hawaii Hochi* (Hawaii News) took his campaign for equal rights into the courts. The *Honolulu Star-Bulletin* and the *Advertiser*, in opposing the latter course, called for the muzzling of Makino's *Hochi*.[29]

Joining Hearst and McClatchy on the mainland in intensity, if not in scope, was James Scripps, the son to whom E. W. Scripps had turned over his newspapers in Seattle, Spokane, and Portland in 1911. Scripps's *Seattle Star* matched Hearst's vehemence when the U.S. House Committee on Immigration and Naturalization came to Seattle in 1920 for hearings on immigration quotas. The work of committee chairman Albert Johnson, publisher of the Hoquiam, Washington, *Washingtonian*, led to the National Quota Act of 1921, legislation anticipated by the *Star*'s sensational coverage of the Seattle hearings.

"Will You Help to Keep This a White Man's Country?" asked the *Star* in a front-page five-column headline over an editorial in colored ink. The editorial said it was the solemn duty of the community to aid in presenting to the members of Congress facts and figures about the "growing menace of Oriental aggression" that Japanese colonization and competition illustrated.[30]

By 1920 the U.S. Japanese-American population had reached 111,000. Washington Governor Louis F. Hart had already told Congressman Johnson that the situation in the "Southern state" (California) was grave, and conditions in Washington State were "greatly similar."[31] The irony that the journalistic racism was also greatly similar there apparently was not noted.

Voices of moderation did exist. The *Fresno Republican* favored civil rights and justice for the Issei and Nisei. Editor Chester Harvey Rowell may have been a racist, but as he observed the California legislature's consideration of the 1913 anti-alien land law, he wrote,

Injustice has been the only American way of dealing with a race problem. We dealt unjustly with the Indian, and he died. We deal unjustly with the Negro, and he submits. If Japanese ever come in sufficient numbers to constitute a race problem, we shall deal unjustly with them—and they shall neither die nor submit.[32]

The *Monterey Cypress* and the *San Jose Mercury* regarded the Issei as good employers. "The Japanese give their farm hands white sheets and treat them like white men," a San Jose city official was quoted as saying.[33] The *Morning Olympian* at the Washington State capital asked for a sincere effort to understand the viewpoint of the Japanese, "a people who have raised themselves to undisputed standing among the first class nations of the world."[34] The *Portland Telegram* in Oregon regretted that the Pacific Coast was handling the Japanese question in such a way as to create in the Japanese government a "distinctly unfriendly feeling."[35]

The *Yakima Morning Herald* in Washington State responded that the peaceable Americans could rely on Japan's large antimilitarist party for peace in the Pacific. But illustrating how such press moderation was less than pervasive, the *Herald* itself within a month stated that a race that inherently clings to its own different traditions was "an insoluble lump in the melting pot" and a menace to the future of the country. To keep the United States the great land that it was, "the Mongolian nations must be forbidden to make this a dumping ground for their people."[36] This all echoed the sentiment of the *Christian Science Monitor*, which expressed concern about "the millions . . . of an alien sort" pouring into the country from new sections of Europe and "even Asia."[37]

Such polite opposition to immigration paled in the face of the blatant racism published in the agriculture-rich Yakima Valley of Washington State in 1920. Buried on page 12 of the weekly *Wapato Independent* under a one-column headline stating simply "Anti-Alien Land Law" stood a statement made by a Wapato attorney that ranked with the rhetoric of the *Seattle Star*. Reacting to the efforts being made to pass in Washington State a law against aliens owning land, which was essentially identical to the California law, Joseph C. Cheney said that the Anglo-Saxon and "the Jap" could not mix. "White and yellow skins will not blend into a veril [sic] nation." Intermarriage would produce a low mongrel race, he contended; the Japanese Americans reproduced faster, made more intense use of the land, and could make a living off less area. He said that he would rather see his children dead than married to Japanese, "and so would you." American men and women could not live "or even exist" under conditions "the Jap" tolerated. "Show your colors now," he concluded. "The slogan of the day is THE JAP MUST GO. Make your choice. Are you White or are you yellow?"[38]

Not only did the *Wapato Independent* editor insert this diatribe into the news columns, but he remained silent editorially. Racism by editorial silence was too often a hallmark of the press during the decades prior to World War II. Moreover, racism by such silence and by fear-mongering editorials and columns completely ignored the existence of federal and state laws that prohibited Japanese immigrants from marrying whites, becoming citizens, and directly owning land.

Washington State did adopt an anti-alien land bill in 1921, prohibiting land ownership by noncitizens. Passage came amid *Seattle Star* headlines such as "House Committee Unanimous for Anti-Jap Bill!," "Pro-Japs Fail to Delay Bill," and "Further Delay Is Treason!" Publisher James Scripps had died just as the legislature was convening, but his death obviously had no effect on his paper's continuing frenzy.[39] Thus the press of the state shared major responsibility with Republican politicians and special interest groups in perpetuating the fear of land holdings by Japanese Americans.[40] The press influence came not by journalistic design, but rather through a passive and uncritical role—as a conduit—of "objectively" conveying the news of the American Legion and the Anti-Japanese League rather than by editorial campaigns. The racism by silence was evident again.

The *Seattle Post-Intelligencer* had continued to show moderation. In a thoughtful editorial it said that legislators, who came from all parts of Washington State, should have had too comprehensive a view than to follow the example of California. The demand for the legislation did not come from citizens, labor, capital, or churches, but from California by "wholly artificial means. We do not recall any time in history when California seemed so solicitous about legislation in Washington."[41]

The questions of whether the Washington State anti-alien land law could be enforced on the federally administered Yakama Indian Reservation further exacerbated tension for the Japanese Americans and frustration for the American Legion. The Ku Klux Klan brought its recruiting efforts into this setting in 1923, and although no violence resulted, the presence of the white robes, hoods, and burning crosses provided justification for the *Seattle Star* to emphasize this threat. "Yakima Valley in Jap War!," the eight-column front-page banner *Star* headline reported without any basis in fact.[42]

The *Star* did tell readers of the Caucasian supporters of the Japanese Americans, a group that was never acknowledged by the local *Wapato Independent*. But a citizens' meeting held to petition the secretary of the interior to enforce state antialien land laws on the Yakama Indian Reservation prompted still another Seattle headline, "Yakima Valley Unites to Oust Jap Invaders."[43] Even more menacing was the *Star*'s rhetoric: "The devil's cauldron is boiling. Behind the shadow of the Rising Sun of Japan, which has already cast its blighting shadow upon the valley, a second and even more sinister omen is crouching." The story referred to the Ku Klux Klan, and the reporter told of hearing dark threats and whispers about the Klan.[44] But other than possibly affecting a Wapato school board election, the Klan is credited with no overt action. Yet the Yakima Valley press again exhibited its racism in its editorial silence on such issues, and Japanese Americans were forced to tend to their truck farms and rear their children in this hostile climate.

A study made of the *Wapato Independent* found that two-thirds of the paper's stories that were hostile to Japanese Americans or that favored excluding them from white institutions in the two decades prior to Pearl Harbor were printed during the four-year period of the antialien land law controversy between 1920 and 1923. Of the editorials on the topic printed prior to World War II, 83 percent were published during those four years.[45] Significantly, none supported the Japanese Americans.

When William Randolph Hearst acquired the *Seattle Post-Intelligencer*, the journalistic climate in the Pacific Northwest became even more negative for Japanese Americans. In a letter meant for publication in all of his newspapers during the Congressional debates held on the 1924 National Quota Act, which would exclude Japanese immigration, Hearst said he strongly favored Japanese exclusion "to prevent these Orientals swarming into the country and absolutely overrunning it." Americans wanted to preserve their country not merely for white races, but for Occidental standards of wages, standards of living, and labor conditions. He saw the highest achievements of U.S. civilization in its high morals and standards of living, the morals dependent upon the ability to take care of the family comfortably, to send the children to school, and to maintain the household on an independent and self-respecting basis. Furthermore, "We do not want in this country the demoralizing competition of low Oriental labor conditions, poor standards of living, and contaminating Oriental morals. This is not race prejudice. It is race preservation."[46]

Reaction to the National Quota Act was not restricted to California; editorials appeared across the country. If they were like those printed in the *New York Times*, the *New York Herald Tribune*, the *Chicago Daily Tribune*, the *Louisville Courier-Journal*, the *San Francisco Chronicle*, and the black-owned *Chicago Defender*, nearly all supported the exclusion of immigrants from Japan while denying that racism was a factor.[47] In addition, public opinion polls in the 1920s and 1930s revealed that prejudice against the Japanese was commonly accepted among white Americans, especially on the West Coast. A 1927 survey made of the views of white students in California, for example, found frequently mentioned stereotypes of Japanese as dishonest, treacherous, and unfairly competitive.[48]

Not until 1952 did the federal government allow first-generation Japanese Americans to become naturalized citizens, and only in the mid-1960s were anti-Asian restrictions removed from the U.S. immigration laws.[49]

In Hawaii, in the early 1920s, legislators authorized licensing of Japanese language schools and examination of instructors. In 1927 the U.S. Supreme Court declared the 1922 statute unconstitutional. The *Honolulu Advertiser* supported the Court, but during the 1930s, the newspaper tangled with the *Star-Bulletin* on the issue. The *Advertiser* claimed that alien teachers conveyed a strain of thought not in accordance with American ideals. The *Star-Bulletin* countered that no disloyalty had been cited among Americans of Oriental descent "and so the attack is being made on the language schools."[50]

Considerable amicable interaction between Japanese Americans and Caucasians did take place. The Issei improved their English and built commercial ties in their communities. In Hawaii, Japanese Americans by 1930 operated 49 percent of the retail stores and made up 74 percent of the farmers and 56 percent of the fishermen.[51] On the mainland, the Nisei entered schools, made friends, and played on sports teams. At the institutional level, Japanese churches, language schools, and associations held joint programs with community groups. All of this cooperation received press attention.[52]

Yet Japanese Americans in the states of Arizona and Washington suffered violence during the Great Depression, which obviously exacerbated the racial situation. As early as 1931, "Farmer John," an otherwise-unidentified citizen, wrote a letter to the *Wapato Independent* in the Yakima Valley complaining about the expense of educating Japanese-American children whose families worked untaxed land leased from Indians.[53] By 1933 the hostility moved to the Japanese farms, where use of Filipino labor antagonized the Caucasians. In a four-week period that spring, dynamite damaged seven farms before the perpetrators were arrested. The nearby *Independent* failed to condemn the acts—still another example of racism by editorial silence. The regional *Yakima Daily Republic* recognized that the bombings had outraged the state, but it seemed general disorder rather than the effect on Japanese Americans was the primary concern: "[P]eople cannot go around over this county blowing up homes, garages or haystacks without having to account to the law enforcement officials."[54] In Arizona a year later, Japanese Americans faced not only dynamite attacks but also shootings and flooded crops.[55]

1934 FEDERAL COMMUNICATIONS ACT TO PEARL HARBOR ATTACK, DECEMBER 7, 1941

In Hawaii, the two Honolulu newspapers split on the issue of statehood in the 1930s, each viewing the role of Americans of Japanese ancestry as justification. The *Advertiser* criticized Japanese businesses for paying wages lower than white employers, Japanese language schools for allegedly teaching loyalty to Japan, and Japanese Americans for exhibiting dual loyalties. The *Bulletin* countered, stating that evidence of disloyalty was lacking, thousands were growing up as loyal citizens, and statehood opponents were using devious and roundabout methods to preserve the political status quo.[56]

Although Japanese Americans generally enjoyed a period of accommodation in the 1930s, even where no dynamite was thrown or shots were fired, conflict was never far below the surface. According to one source, "Half a century of agitation and antipathy directed against Japanese Americans, following almost 50 years of anti-Chinese and antiforeign activity, had by 1941 diffused among the West Coast population a rigidly stereotyped set of attitudes toward Orientals which centered on suspicion and distrust."[57]

By 1932 the Department of State and the U.S. Navy, fearing that U.S. immigration policies and the Japanese occupation of Manchuria could lead to war, were joined by the Commerce and Justice departments and Army Intelligence in a clandestine surveillance of the U.S. Japanese-American population.[58] The Japanese invasion of China in 1937 heightened the worry, and the press reflected the country's concern.

Increasingly hostile newspaper coverage toward Japan paralleled governmental scrutiny, at least on the Pacific Coast. The term "Jap" was increasingly used in news accounts of Japan's actions. The Yellow Peril threat idea surfaced again in Sunday newspapers.[59] In Hawaii, however, both the *Advertiser* and *Star-Bulletin* in 1941, prior to the bombing of Pearl Harbor, frequently expressed faith in the loyalty of the Nisei and Issei. In fact, a patriotic rally sponsored by a Nisei group on June 13 prompted the strongest favorable press reaction.[60]

In October 1941, J. Edgar Hoover instructed field agents to "take immediate steps to secure and develop confidential informants of the Japanese race."[61] Over 2,000 suspects had already been identified among the U.S. population of 127,000 Japanese Americans; some were considered dangerous, prompting intense observation.[62]

On December 5, 1941, Hoover instructed his agents to prepare for "the immediate apprehension of Japanese aliens who have been recommended for custodial detention." Less than forty-eight hours after the attack on Pearl Harbor, agents began the mass roundup not only of the "most dangerous" aliens, but also those on secondary lists.[63] Both government and public sentiment for interning the entire Japanese-American population followed shortly.

1941 PEARL HARBOR ATTACK TO ATOMIC BOMBING OF HIROSHIMA, AUGUST 6, 1945

The first weeks of the war encouraged the church, social service, and civil liberties organizations sympathetic to Japanese Americans. Acts of public hostility were infrequent and minor; public officials pleaded for fairness.[64] Such support was disarming for such groups as the Northern California Committee on Fair Play for Citizens and Aliens of Japanese Ancestry and the President's Committee on Fair Employment Practices.[65] Letters to public officials contained no groundswell for evacuation during the first six weeks after the bombing of Pearl Harbor, but thereafter efforts of pressure groups proved effective.[66] It was just a matter of time until the California Joint Immigration Committee, the American Legion, the Native Sons and Daughters of the Golden West, chambers of commerce, and agricultural and business groups weighed in with their views.[67]

Newspapers generated their own hostility. As early as December 8, the *Los Angeles Times* said that California was a "zone of danger." It pointed out that some Japanese Americans were good Americans; however, "What the rest may be we do not know, nor can we take a chance . . . that treachery and double-dealing are major Japanese weapons."[68] It was a philosophy that prompted the government to close the *Nippu Jiji* and the *Hawaii Hochi* in Hawaii from December 11 to January.[69]

On January 5, 1942, Los Angeles Mutual Broadcasting commentator John B. Hughes initiated a campaign for "drastic action" against the Japanese Americans. *San Francisco Chronicle* columnist Henry McLemore on January 29 wrote that the Issei and Nisei should be removed "to a point deep in the interior" and not "a nice part of the interior either." Westbrook Pegler urged that the Japanese Americans in California should be under armed guard "and to hell with habeas corpus until the danger is over."[70]

Pressure groups representing labor and agricultural interests, who saw Japanese Americans as competition, and nativist groups, who resented non-Caucasian peoples, constituted the primary constituency for evacuation. The press not only carried their views, but became itself "the primary means" by which the evacuation was achieved, according to one source.[71] The *Los Angeles Times* illustrated the shift in opinion. In the first days after the bombing of Pearl Harbor, the newspaper urged public restraint; "Let's Not Get Rattled," an editorial said. By the end of January, the newspaper maintained that "the rigors of war demand proper detention of Japanese and their immediate removal from the most acute danger spots."[72] In early 1942 the *Honolulu Advertiser* and the *Star-Bulletin* expressed alarm over a possible fifth column in Hawaii, but the fear quickly subsided and rarely appeared again in 1943 and 1944.[73]

The weekly *Hood River News* in Oregon, in opposing internment, did not have the influence of the *Los Angeles Times*, but it illustrated the existence of the pockets of moderation on the West Coast. Editor Hugh Ball, who had lived in Japan, saw the complexities of the issue. On February 6, in opposing evacuation, he cited the existing labor shortage, the importance of the fruit crop to the Columbia River economy, and the possibility that those removed would be forced onto the public dole. A later editorial observed, "Wars inevitably have ends, and hysteria gives place to sorrow and regrets . . . [and] many of the old hates are forgotten."[74]

Congress had no such foresight. On February 10, a congressional joint committee recommended the complete evacuation of all Japanese Americans from the Pacific Coast. The action was taken despite testimony from the Department of Agriculture regarding the importance of the $32 million farm production of Japanese Americans toward the war effort.

On February 12, columnist Walter Lippmann, writing from San Francisco, said that Washington held the view that a citizen may not be interfered with unless an overt act had been committed. But he went on to say, "The Pacific Coast is officially a combat zone. Some part of it may at any moment be a battlefield. And nobody ought to be on a battlefield who has no good reason for being there. There is plenty of room elsewhere for him to exercise his rights."[75]

Meanwhile, the *Christian Science Monitor* ran no editorials supporting internment but ran two opposing it in December 1941 or January 1942; the *New York Times* ran one supporting and three opposing internment, and the *Arizona Republic*, published in Phoenix, ran ten supporting internment and two opposing it before February 1. After the Executive Order, during March and April, only the *New York Times*, among the three newspapers, ran one editorial questioning internment.[76]

On February 19, President Roosevelt issued Executive Order 9066 authorizing evacuation.[77] But the president was reacting not only to the Congressional recommendation. As Lippmann's column attests, sentiment for the action came from an admixture of public and political sentiment, all carried by the press.[78]

An example came on the floor of the House of Representatives the day before the president's action. Mississippi Congressman John Rankin told his colleagues, "This is a race war. . . . The white man's civilization has come into conflict with Japanese barbarism. . . . I say it is of vital importance that we get rid of every Japanese, whether in Hawaii or on the mainland. . . . Damn them! Let us get rid of them now!"[79]

In the Senate, Tom Stewart of Tennessee said that the Japanese Americans "are cowardly and immoral. . . . A Jap is a Jap anywhere you find him, and his taking the oath of allegiance to this country would not help, even if he should be permitted to do so."[80]

The press indirectly had influence even within the White House. Colonel Frank Knox, the secretary of the navy, had been the publisher of the *Chicago Daily News*, and prior to that he had been the general manager of the Hearst press while it was conducting its crusades against the "Yellow Peril." He became the most blatant voice in the Roosevelt administration calling for the imprisonment of all Japanese Americans.[81]

Pursuant to the president's evacuation directive, a series of orders poured from the office of Lieutenant General John L. DeWitt, the commander of the Fourth Army and the military chief of the Western Defense Command in San Francisco. Early in the war, DeWitt had observed, with a bizarre logic, "The very fact that no sabotage has taken place to date is a disturbing and confirming indication that such action will be taken."[82]

In fact, however, no Japanese American was ever proven to have collaborated with the enemy during World War II. The entire paranoia about Japanese-American spies and sabotage, and the resultant rationale for interning Japanese Americans, grew out of racist notions in the minds of many white Americans and was fanned by white politicians and labor leaders and disseminated in the press.[83]

In March, DeWitt broadened to the whole Western Defense Command the area in which Japanese Americans had to register.[84] Another proclamation established a curfew, prohibited alien travel beyond five miles, and placed firearms, radios, and cameras—already confiscated—on a contraband list.[85] A later series of orders called for the mass evacuation of Japanese Americans in five days in the Puget Sound, Los Angeles, and San Diego areas.[86] Construction of assembly centers was under way by April, and in May General DeWitt announced evacuation plans for each West Coast county. Army troops were dispersed throughout the West to process evacuees and board them on the trains for the assembly centers.

One source notes that Japanese-American homes and businesses had to be sold quickly and at a loss. The evacuation interned about 120,000 Japanese, more than two-thirds of whom were native-born U.S. citizens "whose only crime was to be perceived by whites as racially different."[87] The fact that the evacuation and internment were flagrant violations of their Constitutional rights seems to have been easily overlooked by the press and the government, as well as by ordinary citizens.

In Hawaii, the military pursued a moderate policy regarding relocation. Approximately 1,440 persons, or less than 1 percent of all local Japanese, were taken into custody, including agents of the Japanese consul, Shinto and Buddhist priests, language school personnel, and community leaders. The assistant secretary of war announced, on March 27, 1942, the impracticality of massive relocation for Hawaii's Japanese Americans. The difference in treatment of Japanese Americans in Hawaii as opposed to those on the mainland stemmed from the important role Japanese Americans played in Hawaii's economy and the more ethnically mixed and racially tolerant nature of the territory. Besides, millions of dollars would have had to be spent in housing and feeding one-third of the territory's population.[88] In addition, the government's action concerning Japanese Americans on the mainland was a political decision; in Hawaii, it was a military one.[89]

By May, anti-Japanese films were playing in mainland theaters across the country. An octopus figure with the head of a Japanese with an evil, toothy face illustrated newspaper advertisements for *Menace of the Rising Sun*, promoted by the headline, "The Beast of the East Threatens Civilization."[90] All of this, of course, illustrated the need to vilify the enemy, as had been done in World War I when libraries burned German-language books, symphonies removed German compositions, schools stopped teaching German, universities fired professors of German, and the federal government clamped down on German-language newspapers.[91]

In 1942, however, only the identifiable Japanese Americans, not the German Americans, were uprooted from their homes. In fact, one source noted that the West Coast military commander had established the western parts of California, Washington, and Oregon and the southern part of Arizona as areas where no Japanese, Italian, or German aliens could reside. But only Japanese Americans were evacuated; the 200,000 Italian and German aliens were not pressured to move from their homes.[92]

Another source stated,

For many Japanese-Americans, the verbal stripping of their humanity was accompanied by humiliating treatment that reinforced the impression of being less than human. They were not merely driven from their homes and communities on the West Coast and rounded up like cattle, but actually forced to live in facilities meant for animals for weeks and even months before being moved to their final quarters in the relocation camps.[93]

As U.S. Army troops began to process evacuees and board them on the trains for the assembly centers, the editor of the *Wapato Independent*, Wapato, Washington, a center for the area's 1,000 Japanese Americans, regarded his town's experience as an army town short-lived but pleasant. The soldiers were well-behaved, and residents of the community—"not to mention some of the girls''—were sorry when they left, he wrote.[94] He said nothing about the Japanese Americans. Departure of the uniformed acquaintances of a few hours generated more editorial expression of regret than the evacuation of a population that for forty years had helped sustain the local economy, had performed for community nights, had topped scholastic honor rolls and athletic teams, and had held joint church services with local congregations.

The *Los Angeles Times* maintained its support for mass relocation after the president's action on February 19. While the *Times* had felt that many Japanese Americans were fully loyal, and before Roosevelt's action would have accepted less restrictive measures than evacuation, the *San Diego Union* was consistent in supporting incarceration in both periods. Among large California newspapers, the *San Francisco Chronicle* retreated the most from its concern that both Japanese Americans and Japanese aliens would be persecuted because of race. Once the evacuation order was issued, it, too, supported government policy.[95]

By the middle of January, editorials in and letters to 112 California newspapers that favored evacuation or other restrictive measures exceeded sentiment in favor of fair treatment for Japanese Americans.[96] Likewise, more than 88 percent of the editorials in twenty-seven newspapers in Washington, Oregon, and California supported evacuation and internment before Executive Order 9066 as well as after.[97]

However, no groundswell of public opinion was behind these editorials. Surveys of California citizens taken in January 1942 indicated that a majority felt existing controls to be adequate. A second study conducted during the second week of February in all three Pacific Coast states found only 14 percent of the citizens felt it necessary to detain Japanese Americans. A third survey found that 54 percent judged security measures against Japanese Americans adequate before Executive Order 9066, but only 40 percent did so by the end of February. This swing in public opinion was confirmed by a national survey in March in which 93 percent approved the removal of Japanese aliens and 59 percent the removal of Japanese-American citizens.[98]

In Hawaii, editorials in the *Advertiser* and *Star-Bulletin* reflected distrust of the Japanese after the bombing of Pearl Harbor, but an underlying current of trust was also evident. Until January 1943, any positive trend was less dominant than statements of suspicion, but by mid-1943, editorials favoring the Japanese far outnumbered those reflecting suspicion. Efforts of the Issei and Nisei to prove their loyalty through participation in the war were thus proven effective. Publicity about Japanese defense workers and Nisei soldiers reduced the suspicion of both newspapers. The *Advertiser* went so far as to claim that living next door to the Japanese had given islanders keen insight into Japanese loyalties whereas the mainlanders were blinded by prejudice.[99]

One researcher examined the editorial position on the internment of the *New Republic*, one of the most liberal and influential journals of the period. The author found that, although the weekly's editors issued continued calls for the preservation of civil liberties and warned against the dangers of repeating the xenophobic excesses of World War I, the journal essentially supported the internment while calling for a different treatment of "loyal" and "disloyal" Japanese Americans. The *New Republic* did refrain, throughout the war, from using derogatory images and terms for the Japanese and Japan. It also published letters written by internees and articles supporting them, providing an opportunity for their views to be heard.[100]

The regional press in areas where a major internment center was to be located may have favored internment in the abstract, but not near its communities. In Arkansas, Jerome and Rohwer were selected as sites for internees to arrive at in the fall of 1942. Many citizens were indignant, but the *Arkansas Gazette* of Little Rock appealed for tolerance and pointed out that three-fourths of the Japanese Americans were citizens. The paper sent a reporter to the centers to determine that the rationing program all U.S. citizens faced was being observed.[101]

Reaction in Wyoming was far less moderate, and internee food consumption became the flash-point issue. One letter writer in February 1942 felt that bringing the population to Wyoming would be "too good for them." When L. L. Newton of the Lander *Wyoming State Journal* proposed that the state greet the Japanese Americans in "a democratic and Christian manner," he was held up to public ridicule in a Cheyenne *Wyoming Eagle* editorial entitled, "Has Mr. Newton Gone Berserk?"[102]

The governor and other political leaders, too, wanted no importation of Japanese Americans unless strict federal supervision was provided. "Mere removal of a fifth columnist from California to Wyoming leaves him a fifth columnist, still, pregnant with potentiality for causing damage, bloodshed and death here," according to Cheyenne's *Wyoming State Tribune*.[103]

Once the Issei and Nisei were moved from the assembly centers and set up housekeeping in the tarpaper-covered concentration camps, possessing only what they could carry, journalistic attention turned to concern over the luxurious conditions in which the evacuees might be living.[104] One of the most famous cartoons of the era appeared in the *Denver Post* in March 1943. It showed a toothy, repulsive-looking Japanese family sitting around a dinner table while a tall, smiling Uncle Sam loomed nearby, standing like a waiter at attention with a trayful of items labeled "meat" and "luxuries." A buck-toothed little "Jap" is saying, "Home was never like this," while the family grins happily. An American couple with a child, all looking thin and wan, are pictured outside gazing hungrily in through the window.[105]

In response to this outrageous portrayal, editor Bill Hosokawa, in his "Frying Pan" column published in the *Heart Mountain Sentinel*, the Wyoming concentration camp newspaper, wrote,

We are against government regulation or restriction of newspapers because we believe in journalistic responsibility. But surely the manner of presentation and circumstances surrounding the publication of this cartoon indicate an utter lack of a sense of responsibility. Its publication can be termed only as malicious, and we have no place for that sort of journalism in this country, especially when we are striving for national unity.[106]

Ironically, a little more than three years later, Hosokawa went to work for the *Denver Post*.

Not long after the cartoon appeared, the *Denver Post* assigned sportswriter Jack Carberry to do a series of stories on the conditions at the Heart Mountain camp. He was primed by an assistant who had been fired for mishandling surplus food storage at the camp and who had contacted a state politician. Indeed, the camp had overstocked rationed foods to compensate for the shortages it had experienced the previous fall. Because it was complying with new federal rationing rules, it could not distribute the stock as rapidly as planned.

The situation prompted predictable headlines in the *Post*: "Food Is Hoarded for Japs in U.S. While Americans in Nippon Are Tortured" and "America's Jap 'Guests' Refuse to Work but Nips Enslave Yankees." Carberry described the carloads of luxury fruits and rare vegetables he found "hidden" at Heart Mountain, failing to mention all were consumed in accord with rationing regulations. A complete fabrication was the alleged trading of rationed foods for whiskey by evacuees, who were actually fed at a cost of 35 cents per person per day.[107]

All of this was justification for the *Post* to editorialize that "when the war is over, every Jap in this country should be sent back to what is left of Japan, and no Jap should ever again be allowed to land in the United States." Hosokawa fought back:

[W]e protest, in the name of justice that the *Post* claims to espouse, the cruel, distorted and untrue allegations about pampered treatment and our ingratitude. As a frail, small voice replying to the *Post*'s thunderings, we protest the viciously editorialized headlines coldly calculated to inflame public opinion against loyal American citizens whose only crime was that of being born with Japanese faces.[108]

The federal government tried to minimize such attention to the camps through positive news releases. No attempt was made to censor the news, as it was recognized that a truthful presentation of events was the best control. A press relations representative was assigned at each assembly center. Whenever journalists arrived, they were referred to the representative, who provided information and conducted escorted tours.[109] But the government could not control inflammation of public opinion when American Legion posts throughout Wyoming adopted hostile resolutions against the camps and the Japanese Americans.[110]

In January 1943 the U.S. Army announced the formation of an all-Nisei unit. When the announcement was made in Hawaii that 1,500 Nisei volunteers would be accepted, 9,507 men responded, 2,686 of whom were accepted due to low mainland response. (Only 5 percent of the eligible internees in concentration camps volunteered.) *Time* magazine ran a picture of the enlistees with the cutline, "There Are Good Japs." The *Honolulu Star-Bulletin* ran the most extensive coverage, describing the pride of families that the youths "are entrusted with the patriotic mission of fighting for their country."[111]

The 100th Infantry Battalion of the U.S. Army's 442nd Regiment arrived at Salerno, Italy, later that year, "knee-deep" in journalists who were intrigued by the novelty of Japanese-American soldiers. But none of the journalists' stories saw print until at least a month later; only after the Nisei had proven themselves at the front did the Army clear the stories. Because these were all released at about the same time, a barrage of coverage ensued across the country. Hearst newspapers carried no stories, however, and the *Los Angeles Examiner* stated in 1943 that, for training, "Japs" were "swarming into the state; evacuees supplied with guns." But the *Des Moines Register*, in March 1944, ran an interview with an officer in the 100th who said,

These Hawaiian Japanese call themselves Hawaiians or just plain Americans. They've earned the right to call themselves anything they damn well please. I've never been so mad in my life as I have been since I returned to the United States and have heard cracks made about Japs fighting on our side in Italy.[112]

After three weeks of fighting in the first two waves at Cassino, the 1,300 men of the 100th were reduced to fewer than 500.

In September 1944, the 442nd was attached to the 36th Division and transferred to France. The unit entered the Vosges mountains with 2,943 men. Six weeks later, they had 161 dead, 43 missing, and 2,000 wounded, 882 seriously. Rumors began to spread that the Nisei troops were being used as cannon fodder. Little media coverage appeared about this action, perhaps because the Army, sensitive to the charge of using the troops as cannon fodder, held back all stories. On March 28, 1945, the 442nd left again for Italy, prompting an avalanche of positive coverage.[113]

By the end of the war, the 442nd had a combat record unequalled in U.S. military history. It took three times the casualties of the average unit and won over 18,000 individual decorations for bravery, including a Congressional Medal of Honor.[114]

A study that has analyzed the coverage of the 442nd found that, when the unit was mentioned, coverage was almost universally favorable. A directly inverse relationship existed between the amount of coverage of the unit and the amount of anti–Japanese American coverage carried by a newspaper or magazine, as illustrated by the lack of coverage by the racist Hearst newspapers. *Newsweek* carried only one story on the unit, but published numerous stories reflecting anti–Japanese American sentiment. Conversely, the *New York Times* covered the 442nd extensively while stressing the rights of all citizens regardless of race.[115]

Newspaper comic strips, as well as news columns, addressed the internment issue. Superman on June 28, 1943, was called on by his creators to "stop destruction by subversive and disloyal Japanese in concentration camps."[116] Clark Kent and Lois Lane were sent to "Camp Carok" to report to readers. They met with "Major Munsey," who informed them of the difficulty of mingling loyal Americans "of Jap ancestry" with enemy sympathizers. Kent's X-ray vision revealed sinister-looking internees in the woodworking shop planning an escape with smuggled firearms. Kent ducked out to return as Superman, but not before Lane and the major were captured by the conspirators. He saved them and returned to confront the villains, whom he dispatched. But he spied Caucasian thugs in a nearby forest: "White men co-operating with the enemy!"—a turn of events that took him on to related adventures with a "slant-eyed opponent."[117]

In the last frame of the series, Superman directly faced his readers and, in words perhaps inspired by the Office of War Information and War Relocation Authority, said, "It should be remembered that most Japanese-Americans are loyal citizens. Many are in combat units of our armed forces, and others are working in war factories. According to government statements, not one act of sabotage was perpetrated in Hawaii or [the] territorial U.S. by a Japanese-American."[118]

The irony of why, if they were this loyal, the Issei and Nisei were in the camps at all was apparently missed by both Superman and his readers.

Some photographic records of the camps were more realistic. Dorothea Lange, famous for her pictures of the Great Depression, and Ansel Adams both photographed the Manzanar Relocation Center in California. But their photographs showed contrasting interpretations. Adams's showed smiling people, small camp businesses, and serene landscapes that emphasized the success of the internees in adapting to their environment. Lange's, however, showed oppressive circumstances and attempted to reveal the internment as an injustice. Adams's photos were widely used at the time; Lange's were not shown much until the 1960s and 1970s.[119]

Considering all the institutional and individual racism exhibited toward the Japanese Americans, it is surprising that in September 1944, when the public was polled regarding the immigration of foreign nationalities, 20 percent still favored allowing immigration from Japan. Seventy-five percent would stop Japanese immigration, the lowest among foreign groups.[120]

Starting in 1944, small numbers of internees from the camps were released to excluded areas, the same year 61 percent of the public said that Caucasians should receive first chance at postwar jobs. Among those who felt no economic discrimination should be made against Japanese Americans, more than half qualified their replies by adding, "If the Japanese are loyal."[121] In December of that year, the West Coast was completely reopened for settlement.[122] As late as October 1945, however, some Issei still had to receive permission to leave camps to return to their homes.

Most of those imprisoned returned to the West Coast to find their farms or businesses in the hands of whites or in ruins, their household possessions destroyed, and local whites hostile and sometimes even violent. Their economic losses were estimated as at least $400 million. They were compensated in 1948 for less than 10 percent of these losses.[123]

1945 ATOMIC BOMBING OF HIROSHIMA TO LITTLE ROCK INTEGRATION, SEPTEMBER 1957

Because of the hostility and even violence directed at Japanese Americans when they returned to their homes, self-employment continued to be an important factor in their economic endeavors. Many Japanese Americans were involved in gardening, grocery, and laundry businesses. The next generation of Japanese Americans, however, began moving into white-collar jobs.[124] Before the internment, U.S.–born Japanese-American men over the age of twenty in California had an average educational level of 12.5 years; the figure for Japanese-American women was also high.[125] After the internment, Japanese Americans continued to prize educational achievement, and they sent their children to college. As a result, they began to achieve professional status, paving the way for the "model minority" stereotype that developed in later decades.

The story of Japanese Americans as a constituent group in society was largely ignored by newspapers in the postwar years. Japanese Americans received scant attention in the *New York Times* in the 1940s and in subsequent decades. Coverage of all Asian Americans combined received an average of only 0.39 of an inch per issue in the *Times* in the 1940s; 28 percent of that was devoted to the military actions of World War II or its aftermath. Not until the 1980s did coverage of Asian Americans improve significantly in the *Times*—to an average of 7 column inches per issue—and 20 percent of that was devoted to crime news, much of that among Chinese Americans.[126] Of the minority groups studied in the 1934 to 1994 period, Asian Americans received the least press attention, and Japanese Americans, with a 1980 population of 716,000, received a tiny percentage of that, as the *Times* failed to reflect the complexity of constituent Asian groups.[127]

1957 LITTLE ROCK INTEGRATION TO NIXON'S
RESIGNATION, AUGUST 9, 1974

Because of the racism of the U.S. naturalization laws, first-generation Japanese Americans were not allowed to become citizens until the 1950s. Most Nisei, or second-generation Japanese Americans, were not old enough to vote until the 1940s, but the internment delayed their efforts to participate in political life. Most political gains for Japanese Americans came first in Hawaii, then in California.[128]

Some Japanese Americans had been elected to political office in Hawaii as early as the 1930s. Later, several returning World War II veterans were elected to Hawaii's legislature, and they helped influence Congress to grant Hawaii statehood in the late 1950s. War hero Daniel Inouye was elected the first Japanese American in Congress as a representative from Hawaii. Later Spark Matsunaga and Patsy Takemoto Mink were elected to the House, and Inouye became a senator. Also in the 1960s a few Japanese Americans were elected to city office in California, and in 1972 a Japanese American was elected a county commissioner in Washington State.[129]

1974 RESIGNATION OF NIXON TO LOS ANGELES
UPRISING, APRIL 29, 1992

Just as the *New York Times* failed fully to reflect the nation's Asian groups from 1934 to 1994, it also ignored White House action in 1976 when President Gerald Ford proclaimed, "We know now what we should have known then: not only was evacuation wrong, but Japanese-Americans were and are loyal Americans." Only a letter to the editor brought readers' attention to the proclamation.[130]

The *Times*, however, did give front-page coverage in 1983 to the release of the report of the Commission on the Wartime Relocation and Internment of Civilians, *Personal Justice Denied*. The report concluded that evacuation was prompted not by military necessity but by race prejudice, war hysteria, and a failure of political leadership.[131]

The Ford proclamation and the findings of the commission contributed to the political climate that enabled Congress to pass the 1988 Civil Liberties Act. Among its provisions, Congress allocated $20,000 to each survivor who had been incarcerated. Payments began in 1990, but not without opposition, even from the *New York Times*. The editors admitted that incarceration was a "cruel and pointless surrender to panic," something they had not said at the time, but suggested instead a symbolic "gesture of atonement," such as a scholarship fund.[132]

The opposition of the *Times* was genteel compared to that expressed in a guest column published in the Hearst *Los Angeles Herald Examiner* on October 5, 1987. Written by Dr. Howard D. Garber, director of Citizens for Truth, the column criticized the newspaper for failing to report "the facts" concerning U.S. treatment of evacuees. He alleged a well-organized Japanese fifth column existed on the West Coast amid widespread espionage. In seeking redress for internment, Garber stated that the "powerful and deceitful Japanese-American lobby" had engaged in a national campaign of vilification and lies. As an example, he cited the "voluntary" nature of the relocation centers, with internment only for enemy aliens about to be deported. "Those who chose relocation centers over settlement in the other 44 states were free to leave those centers for colleges and war plants."[133] Garber was joined by the Americans for Historical Accuracy, "a coalition against the falsification of USA history." Also, S. I. Hayakawa, a former U.S. senator from California, claimed that relocation was neither cruel nor unjust, but necessary for military reasons and for the protection of the Japanese people themselves from the hostility of their white American neighbors.[134]

By using terms such as "relocation," Garber and Hayakawa illustrate the use of euphemistic terminology by citizens some forty-five years after the government masked the true nature of the actions taken against the Japanese Americans. The term "relocation" camps avoids the facts that people had been confined, detained, imprisoned, and restrained. "Evacuation centers" were decidedly not concentration camps, according to the government. One source has stated that most newspapers, normally critical of public relations euphemisms, printed army press releases verbatim in those days, and many city rooms became an extension of the army public relations office. Former classmates and their parents became "Japs," "Nips," "Aliens," "enemy aliens," or "dangerous aliens." At least the *Tacoma News-Tribune* saw through all the rhetoric when, as early as 1942, it labeled this practice euphemistic.[135]

During periods of economic recession in the 1980s and 1990s, resentment toward Japan's growing preeminence in the automotive, electronics, and other industries spilled over onto Japanese Americans. During World War II, many white Euro-Americans had seemed unable to distinguish between the government of Japan and the Japanese Americans who had been born in the United States. Similarly, in recent decades, many whites have found Japanese Americans handy targets for their resentment against the actions of Japan's government and business community.

In 1987 U.S. Representative Daniel Inouye, a Japanese American who lost an arm fighting for the United States in World War II, received hate mail telling him he should "go home to Japan where you belong."[136] In recent years, Japanese-American community centers have been vandalized; anti-Japanese-American graffiti, such as "Look out for the Asian invasion" and "Stop the Yellow Hordes," has appeared on college campuses and highway overpasses; and Japanese Americans have been assaulted, threatened, and harassed in their homes, businesses, and places of employment.[137]

Although Japanese Americans have achieved significant economic success, they still face discrimination in business. Several sources have reported that

Japanese Americans are sought after for engineering and technical jobs, but are denied promotion to managerial and executive positions.[138] One source noted that, in 1980, positions in the highest-level administrative, professional, and managerial levels have been closed to Japanese and other Asian Americans, particularly on the West Coast, and that whites with weaker credentials or less ability have been promoted more quickly.[139]

A similar imbalance exists in politics. In 1990 about one of ten Californians was Asian American, but only three members of the state's forty-seven-member Congressional delegation and no members of the state legislature were Asian American. Only 1 percent of the state's city council and school board positions were held by Asian Americans.[140]

The model-minority stereotype that was featured in every major newsmagazine and television network in the late 1980s and early 1990s grew out of the economic and educational attainments of Japanese Americans and other Asian Americans.[141] The 1990 Census revealed that the median income for Japanese-American families was more than one and one-third that of white families; only 3.4 percent of Japanese-American families fell below the federal poverty line; and the unemployment rate of Japanese Americans was half that of whites. In addition, Japanese-American men and women were more likely to hold managerial or professional jobs than their white counterparts.[142]

In educational achievements, the census data show that 88 percent of Japanese Americans over twenty-four years of age are high school graduates and 35 percent are college graduates, compared with 79 percent and 22 percent of whites in these age groups. Among Japanese Americans between the ages of sixteen and nineteen, only 3 percent are high school dropouts, compared to 9 percent of whites. Some 64 percent of Japanese Americans aged from eighteen to twenty-four are enrolled in college, compared with 37 percent of whites.[143]

Broadcast Coverage

Japanese Americans have occasionally been presented on television, but the portrayal frequently has been insensitive. Even the well-known "Farewell to Manzanar," broadcast in 1976 on NBC, dramatizing the complexity of the daily life of an Asian-American community at an internment camp, was criticized by Japanese Americans for focusing on an atypical family while ignoring white racism. The medium thus here, too, reduces issues to melodrama, operating at the emotional and visceral level, and denies or downplays the existence of white racism. "Farewell" was, however, the most complex portrait of the Japanese-American community that had been broadcast by a network.[144]

As in newspaper coverage, television news has at times failed to avoid clichés or provide comprehensive reports. Too often on the fiftieth anniversary of the attack on Pearl Harbor, critics contend, did news divisions use war imagery when discussing contemporary economic relations between the United States and Japan, as in "Nightline" and "Frontline" episodes, or in reports on the "buying up" of America, seen as an invasion. Only PBS's "The Color of Honor" was seen as exploring the complex issues and contradictory demands faced by a Japanese-American community divided over the issue of volunteering for military service from the concentration camps.[145]

1992 LOS ANGELES UPRISING TO PRESIDENTIAL ELECTION, NOVEMBER 1996

The Asian American Journalists Association, among other ethnic press groups, has long contended that the constituent groups of society cannot be comprehensively reflected in the press unless people of color are on the staffs of America's newspapers. Yet, as late as 1994, only 10.5 percent of those employed on U.S. newspapers come from these minority cultures, and only a small number of those were Asian Americans.[146]

Although few academic studies of the newspaper coverage of Asian Americans in the post–World War II period have been published, those that have been found confirm that the press devoted minimal attention to Japanese Americans. Also, a recent study reported a "serious lack" of scholarly research on Asian Americans and mass communication since 1982. Only three theses dealt with the topic generally, and only three others studied Japanese Americans and the press; all covered the internment period. These statistics led to the conclusion that the wealth of the Japanese-American experience, both before and after World War II, has "literally been forgotten and ignored" among the theses and dissertations of the last fifteen years.[147]

Quality of coverage is as important as quantity. Numerous anecdotal examples of stereotypical coverage were found in a 1993 project of the Asian American Journalists Association that collected examples of potentially offensive portrayals and solicited opinions about them from Asian-American newspersons. The project found that stereotypical images of Japanese Americans as having "buck teeth, heavy glasses and slits for eyes" did not end with World War II. Cartoonists today continue to draw Asians and Asian Americans in this manner, sometimes while bashing Japanese auto manufacturers. One such cartoon published in the *New York Post* added this quote from Japan's Prime Minister Kiichi Miyazawa to make his point: "So sorry dat honorable president [Clinton] think I mean 'no' when I say 'yes,' maybe you have me confused with Gennifer?"[148] The *Detroit Free Press* in 1992 depicted two Japanese businessmen buying silicone breast "imprants," with the sign reading "Crearance Sale." A *Dallas Morning News* cartoon showing President Bush vomiting behind the dinner table in Japan had one Japanese official saying, "I think Bushie-san think trade deal not so hot."[149] Nor did the term "Jap" fall from use with the end of the war. As recently as 1992 the *Village Voice* wrote about "Jap bashing."[150]

Sports writer Frank Deford professed surprise that his *Newsweek* cover story on Olympic figure skater Kristi Yamaguchi in 1992 caused offense. At a time when all Asians walk a tightrope between asserting pride in their cultural and ethnic heritage and the desire to be fully accepted as fellow citizens, one source said, he wrote about the "irony" that the United States was represented by a Japanese American "when so many Americans are blaming the Japanese, rounding on them, making devils of them . . . and not pausing to check birth certificates." Critics said the article made too much of the Japanese background of Yamaguchi, a fourth-generation citizen. They could have added that the article came close to the model-minority stereotype, which ignores the psychological and social problems many Asian Americans still experience. The "success" argument also implies that nonwhite people can succeed only if they work hard, and if they do not succeed, it is because of their own shortcomings, the source said. Thus the success thesis can prompt invidious comparisons among ethnic minority groups and become a justification for institutional racism.[151]

Kristi Yamaguchi is one of the many Japanese Americans who have been victimized by the recent scapegoating of Japanese Americans for the competitive business practices of Japan itself. Previous gold medal figure skaters of Euro-American background, like Dorothy Hamill, have been sought by advertisers for profitable endorsements. But it was thought that because many white Americans have strong anti-Japanese prejudices, it would not be wise to use Yamaguchi to endorse products, and indeed, one source noted, she has received fewer major endorsements than have whites with similar achievements. Yamaguchi herself was puzzled about why the current anti-Japan sentiment should apply to her. "I certainly don't think it should affect me," she said. "I'm a fourth generation American. I went to the Olympics for America."[152]

CONCLUSION

Both weak and insulting coverage of Japanese Americans and Constitutional issues involving them have been the major concerns of this chapter. On few occasions here have we seen that the Constitutionally protected press raised significant concerns about the abridgment of the Constitutionally protected freedoms experienced by Japanese Americans, not only in wartime, but in the whole series of crises from immigration to their resettlement after the incarceration experience.

Dissenting U.S. Supreme Court Justice Frank Murphy in 1944 raised such concerns when, in his minority opinion in the Korematsu case, he described the internment roundup of Japanese Americans as "one of the most sweeping and complete deprivations of constitutional rights in the history of this nation in the absence of martial law."[153]

Fred Korematsu was arrested on the streets of San Leandro, California, shortly after World War II broke out, for violating the U.S. Army's evacuation order. He was convicted, placed on probation for five years, and sent off to a concentration camp. He appealed the conviction in a case that led to the Supreme Court's 1944 6-to-3 decision that upheld the Constitutionality of the military orders that led to the evacuation and internment.[154] In 1983 Korematsu filed a petition to erase his wartime criminal conviction and find that the U.S. government had erred. The government agreed to set aside the conviction, but it did not answer the allegations concerning its own misconduct. A judge set aside Korematsu's conviction and said that the government's meek response was tantamount to admitting error.[155] The error the government should have faced was the existence of documents from 1942 that showed that it had altered and destroyed evidence that contradicted the claim that evacuation was necessary because of the disloyal activities of Issei and Nisei.[156]

Coverage of the 1983 Korematsu case proceedings by six major newspapers—the *New York Times*, the *Washington Post*, the *Los Angeles Times*, the *San Francisco Chronicle*, the *Honolulu Star-Bulletin*, and the *Honolulu Advertiser*—showed that, aside from the California newspapers, the newspapers were conspicuous in their pro-government selectivity by virtually ignoring the paper trail of court exhibits documenting the government's suppression of evidence that contradicted the policy decision to evacuate the Japanese Americans. News coverage was thus tilted favorably toward the government side.[157] Newsmagazines, as well, failed to criticize government policy.[158] (When the Reagan administration was considering reparations for the Issei and Nisei in 1981, the magazines indicated that internment was wrong. Although the publications attributed the internment to prejudice, hysteria, and the failure of political leadership, only *Time* attributed any blame to the mass media for its role in contributing to the hysteria.[159])

The wartime findings are similar to those assessing the performance of twenty-seven newspapers in Washington, Oregon, and California during two World War II periods. Many of these newspapers seem not to have evaluated government policy—their Constitutional duty—"but blindly supported it," the author stated. "In so doing, they appear to have relinquished their watchdog role to become government publicists."[160] It was therefore concluded that, although the press has at times been termed the loyal opposition to government, this may not always be the case in periods of crisis. Thus concern about press controls in wartime might not be what information the press is allowed to gather in regard to national security, but the press's interpretation of the information it does gather. In unstable times, the media may subordinate themselves to the government.[161]

These findings could lead to the conclusion that the press was lackadaisical about protecting rights only because an ethnic minority was affected. But it has also been found that in seven national issues after the Japanese-American war experience—in the Cuban missile crisis, the *New York Times v. Sullivan* decision, the Pentagon Papers case, Watergate, the *Progressive* magazine's H-bomb article, the invasion of Grenada, and the 200th anniversary observance in 1991 of the adoption of the Bill of Rights—four newspapers across the country rarely used their editorials to profess rights or responsibilities for the press. When the Constitution was mentioned at all, it was to reaffirm press freedom rather than the governmental watchdog function or the marketplace-of-ideas role also inherent in the First Amendment.[162]

The studies examined here indicate that the press too often has served as an uncritical conduit of hostile government or public opinion. Even when it was not overtly hostile to Japanese Americans, the press expressed racism by the silence of its news pages and editorial columns. Its failure of social responsibility and its silence on Constitutional issues demonstrate a continuing crisis for all of us.

NOTES

1. Joe R. Feagin and Clairece Booher Feagin, "Japanese Americans," in *Racial and Ethnic Relations,* 5th ed. (Upper Saddle River, N.J.: Prentice-Hall, 1996), 385–86.

2. Tetsuden Kashima, "Japanese American Internees Return, 1945 to 1955: Readjustment and Social Amnesia," *Phylon* 41 (Summer 1980), 109.

3. Ibid.

4. Peter Irons, *Justice at War* (New York: Oxford University Press, 1983), 9.

5. Ibid., quoting Roger Daniels.

6. Gary Y. Okihiro, *Cane Fires: The Anti-Japanese Movement in Hawaii, 1865–1945* (Philadelphia: Temple University Press, 1991), 25.

7. Ibid.

8. John Gerald Tamashiro, "The Japanese in Hawaii and on the Mainland during World War II As Discussed in the Editorial Pages of the *Honolulu Advertiser* and the *Honolulu Star-Bulletin*" (Master's thesis, University of Hawaii, 1972), 2.

9. Okihiro, *Cane Fires,* 57.

10. Bill Hosokawa, *Nisei: The Quiet Americans* (New York: William Morrow, 1969), 41, as quoted in Timothy Olmstead, "Nikkei Internment: The Perspective of Two Oregon Weekly Newspapers," *Oregon Historical Quarterly* 85 (Spring 1984), 6.

11. Yamato Ichihashi, *Japanese in the United States: A Critical Study of the Problems of the Japanese Immigrants and Their Children* (Palo Alto, Calif.: Stanford University Press, 1932), 94.

12. S. Frank Miyamoto, "The Forced Evacuation of the Japanese Minority during World War II," *Journal of Social Issues* 29, no. 2 (1973), 18.

13. *Personal Justice Denied: Report of the Commission on Wartime Relocation and Internment of Civilians* (Washington, D.C.: U.S. Government Printing Office, 1992), 32.

14. Charles A. Siegel, "West Coast Press Opinion and Propaganda and the Japanese Exclusion Act of 1924" (Master's thesis, Washington State University, 1949), 62.

15. Brad Hamm, "They Work Too Hard: How Newspapers Justified the 1924 Exclusion of Japanese Immigrants" (Paper presented at the Association for Education in Journalism and Mass Communication Southeast Colloquium, Gainesville, Florida, March 1995), 5, quoting Immigrant Act of 20 February 1907, *Administrative Procedure Act: Statutes at Large* 34 (1907), 898.

16. Hamm, "They Work Too Hard," 5.

17. Rita J. Simon, *Public Opinion and the Immigrant: Print Media Coverage, 1880–1980* (Lexington, Mass.: Lexington Books, 1985), 109.

18. This and subsequent population figures are taken from respective years of the

Statistical Abstracts of the United States (Washington, D.C.: U.S. Department of Commerce, Economics, and Statistics, Bureau of the Census).

19. The term "yellow peril" was probably first used by Kaiser Wilhelm II about 1895, according to Roger Daniels, *Concentration Camps: North American Japanese in the United States and Canada during World War II* (Malabar, Fla.: R. E. Krieger Publishing, 1981), as quoted in Claus-M. Naske, "The Relocation of Alaska's Japanese Residents," *Pacific Northwest Quarterly* 74 (July 1983), 126.

20. Carey McWilliams, *Prejudice: Japanese Americans: Symbol of Racial Intolerance* (Boston: Little, Brown, 1944), 52.

21. *Personal Justice Denied*, 37.

22. McWilliams, *Prejudice*, 51.

23. Ibid., 54–55.

24. Okihiro, *Cane Fires*, 130.

25. Cf. "Hundreds of Japs Taking the Place of White Men As Section Hands," *Spokesman-Review*, 6 May 1899, 5, and "Jap Laborers in Washington; There Are 2500 Men Employed by Great Northern," *Spokesman-Review*, 29 October 1900, 8.

26. Jacobus tenBroek, Edward N. Barnhart, and Floyd W. Matson, *Prejudice, War and the Constitution* (Berkeley: University of California Press, 1954), 60.

27. G. Edward White, "The Unacknowledged Lesson: Earl Warren and the Japanese Relocation Controversy," *Virginia Quarterly Review* 55 (Autumn 1979), 618.

28. Okihiro, *Cane Fires*, 78.

29. Tom Brislin, "Weep into Silence/Cries of Rage: Bitter Divisions in Hawaii's Japanese Press," *Journalism & Mass Communication Monographs* 154 (December 1995), 1–2.

30. "Will You Help to Keep This a White Man's Country?," *Seattle Star*, 22 July 1920, 1.

31. U.S. Congress, House Immigration and Naturalization Committee, Immigration Hearings, 66th Cong., 2d sess., pt. 4 (1920), 1057–58.

32. James Bow, "Removing the Japanese, 1913: An Editor's Mediation in California's Asian Exclusion Movement," unpublished 1991 research paper, 7, quoting Chester Harvey Rowell's article, "The Japanese in California," *World's Work* 26 (June 1913), 195–201. Bow is on the journalism faculty of Central Michigan University.

33. Audrie Girdner and Anne Loftis, *The Great Betrayal: The Evacuation of the Japanese-Americans during World War II* (New York: Macmillan, 1969), 67.

34. Douglas Roscoe Pullen, "The Administration of Washington State Governor Louis F. Hart, 1919–1925" (Ph.D. diss., University of Washington, 1974), 232, quoting the *Morning Olympian* of 20 November 1920.

35. Thomas H. Heuterman, *The Burning Horse: The Japanese-American Experience in the Yakima Valley 1920–1942* (Cheney: Eastern Washington University Press, 1995), 25.

36. Ibid.

37. The *Christian Science Monitor* editorial is quoted in "Americanism and the Albany Case," *Wapato Independent* (Washington), 5 February 1920.

38. Heuterman, *The Burning Horse*, 26.

39. Ibid., 32–33.

40. Pullen, "The Administration," 231–32.

41. "Consider the Source," *Seattle Post-Intelligencer*, 17 February 1921.

42. Heuterman, *The Burning Horse*, 60. The Yakama Indian Tribe has recently re-

verted to an earlier spelling of its name. Yakima continues to be the correct spelling of the city, valley, river, and county.

43. Heuterman, *The Burning Horse*, 60.

44. Ibid., 64.

45. Thomas H. Heuterman, " 'We Have the Same Rights As Other Citizens': Coverage of Yakima Valley Japanese Americans in the 'Missing Decades' of the 1920s and 1930s," *Journalism History* 14 (Winter 1987), 97.

46. Heuterman, *The Burning Horse*, 72–73.

47. Hamm, "They Work Too Hard," 1, 5, 18.

48. C. N. Reynolds, "Oriental-White Race Relations in Santa Clara County, California" (Ph.D. diss., Stanford University, 1927); E. S. Bogardus, "Social Distance: A Measuring Stick," *Survey* 56 (1927), 169–71. Both are cited in Edward Strong, Jr., *The Second-Generation Japanese Problem* (Stanford, Calif.: Stanford University Press, 1934), 109, 128.

49. Hillary Conroy and T. Scott Miyakawa, "Foreword," in *East Across the Pacific*, ed. Hillary Conroy and T. Scott Miyakawa (Santa Barbara, Calif.: ABC-CLIO, 1972), xiv–xv.

50. Tamashiro, "The Japanese in Hawaii," 5–6.

51. Ibid., 4.

52. Heuterman, "We Have the Same Rights," 97.

53. Heuterman, *The Burning Horse*, 94.

54. Ibid., 100.

55. Susie Sato, "Before Pearl Harbor: Early Japanese Settlers in Arizona," *Journal of Arizona History* 14 (Winter 1973), 323–24.

56. Tamashiro, "The Japanese in Hawaii," 144.

57. tenBroek, Barnhart, and Matson, *Prejudice, War and the Constitution*, 68.

58. Bob Kumamoto, "The Search for Spies: American Counterintelligence and the Japanese American Community 1931–1942," *Amerasia Journal* 6, no. 2 (1979), 47.

59. Miyamoto, "The Forced Evacuation," 22.

60. Tamashiro, "The Japanese in Hawaii," 14–15.

61. Kumamoto, "The Search for Spies," 57.

62. Ibid., 58.

63. Ibid., 69.

64. Morton Grodzins, *Americans Betrayed: Politics and the Japanese Evacuation* (Chicago: University of Chicago Press, 1969 reprint of 1949 edition), 19.

65. Lloyd E. Chiasson, "The Japanese-American Encampment: An Editorial Analysis of 27 West Coast Newspapers," *Newspaper Research Journal* 12 (Spring 1991), 95.

66. Grodzins, *Americans Betrayed*, 224.

67. Chiasson, "The Japanese-American Encampment," 95.

68. Roger Daniels, *The Decision to Relocate the Japanese Americans* (Philadelphia: J. B. Lippincott, 1975), 12.

69. Okihiro, *Cane Fires*, 231. Also see Jim A. Richstad, "The Press under Martial Law: The Hawaiian Experience," *Journalism Monographs* 17 (November 1970), 18.

70. Dorothy Swaine Thomas and Richard S. Nishimoto, *The Spoilage*, Japanese American Evacuation and Resettlement Series (Berkeley: University of California Press, 1946), 17–19.

71. Miyamoto, "The Forced Evacuation," 25.

72. Irons, *Justice at War*, 6–7.

73. Tamashiro, "The Japanese in Hawaii," 47.

74. Olmstead, "Nikkei Internment," 18, 22–23.

75. Daniels, *The Decision to Relocate*, 47.

76. Sharon Bramlett-Solomon and Patricia Mah, "The Press as Accessory: Editorial Treatment of the Japanese-American Internment Issue" (Paper presented at Southwest Symposium, Southwest Education Council for Journalism and Mass Communication, Texas Tech University, Lubbock, 10–11 October 1993).

77. Grodzins, *Americans Betrayed*, 75–76, 90.

78. Ibid., 90–91.

79. Milton S. Eisenhower, *The President Is Calling* (Garden City, N.Y.: Doubleday, 1974), 110.

80. Ibid., 110.

81. Michi Weglyn, *Years of Infamy: The Untold Story of America's Concentration Camps* (New York: William Morrow, 1976), 29. In the introduction, author James A. Michener reports on page 29 that he found Knox to be a "pompous, simplistic business operator[,] most of whose utterances were as bombastic and foolish as the statements he issued to justify the imprisonment of Japanese American civilians."

82. Leonard J. Arrington, *The Price of Prejudice: The Japanese-American Relocation Center in Utah during World War II* (Logan: Utah State University Press, 1962), 6.

83. Feagin and Feagin, "Japanese Americans," 383.

84. ten Broek, Barnhart, and Matson, *Prejudice, War and the Constitution*, 119.

85. Thomas and Nishimoto, *The Spoilage*, 10.

86. Ibid., 11; also Girdner and Loftis, *The Great Betrayal*, 135.

87. Feagin and Feagin, "Japanese Americans," 386.

88. Tamashiro, "The Japanese in Hawaii," 49–50, 60, 64, 87–88, 159. Also see *Personal Justice Denied*, 6.

89. Roger Daniels, "The Conference Keynote Address: Relocation, Redress, and the Report: A Historical Appraisal," in *Japanese Americans: From Relocation to Redress* ed. Roger Daniels, Sandra C. Taylor, and Harry H. L. Kitano, rev. ed. (Seattle: University of Washington Press, 1991), 8.

90. *Wapato Independent*, 7 May 1942, 4. For a description of the Hollywood war effort, see Clayton R. Koppes and Gregory D. Black, *Hollywood Goes to War: How Politics, Profits, and Propaganda Shaped World War II Movies* (New York: Free Press, 1987).

91. Jean Folkerts and Dwight L. Teeter, Jr., *Voices of a Nation: A History of Media in the United States* (New York: Macmillan, 1989), 344–45, quoting John D. Stevens, *Shaping the First Amendment: Development of Free Expression* (Beverly Hills: Sage, 1982), 46.

92. Feagin and Feagin, "Japanese Americans," 386, citing Thomas and Mishimoto, *The Spoilage*, 8–16; tenBroek, Barnhart, and Matson, *Prejudice, War and the Constitution*, 118–20.

93. John W. Dower, *War without Mercy: Race and Power in the Pacific War* (New York: Pantheon Books, 1986), 82.

94. *Wapato Independent*, 10 June 1942, 4.

95. Lloyd Chiasson, "Japanese-American Relocation during World War II: A Study of California Editorial Reactions," *Journalism Quarterly* 68 (Spring/Summer 1991), 264–66, 268.

96. Grodzins, *Americans Betrayed*, 224, 377–99; Girdner and Loftis, *The Great Betrayal*, 20.

97. Chiasson, "The Japanese-American Encampment," 100.

98. Gary Y. Okihiro and Julie Sly, "The Press, Japanese Americans, and the Concentration Camps," *Phylon* 46 (March 1983), 78.

99. Tamashiro, "The Japanese in Hawaii," 23, 96–98, 106.

100. Takeya Mizuno, "The *New Republic* and Japanese Mass Internment during World War II, 1941–1945: The Liberal Magazine's Uniqueness and Limitations" (Paper presented at Association for Education in Journalism and Mass Communication Convention, Anaheim, California, August 1996), 23–25.

101. William Cary Anderson, "Early Reaction in Arkansas to the Relocation of Japanese in the State," *Arkansas Historical Quarterly* 23 (Autumn 1964), 198–99, 201.

102. Douglas W. Nelson, *Heart Mountain: The History of an American Concentration Camp* (Madison: State Historical Society of Wisconsin for the University of Wisconsin Department of History, 1976), 4.

103. Ibid., 6–8.

104. Valerie Matsumoto, "Japanese American Women during World War II," *Frontiers* 8, no. 1 (1984), 8.

105. Bill Hosokawa, *Thirty-Five Years in the Frying Pan* (New York: McGraw-Hill, 1978), 16.

106. Ibid., 17.

107. Nelson, *Heart Mountain*, 58–61.

108. Ibid., 62.

109. Lynn Thiesmeyer, "The Discourse of Official Violence: Anti-Japanese North American Discourse and the American Internment Camps," *Discourse & Society* 6, no. 3 (July 1995), 346, quoting General John L. DeWitt's *Final Report: Japanese Evacuation from the West Coast 1942*.

110. Nelson, *Heart Mountain*, 68.

111. Patricia A. Curtin, "Go for Broke: Press Coverage of the 442nd Regimental Combat Team" (Paper presented at Association for Education in Journalism and Mass Communication Convention, Atlanta, August 1994), 5.

112. Ibid., 9.

113. Ibid., 11–14.

114. *Hawaii: Paradise Found* (Chicago: Questar Video Productions, 1992), video.

115. Curtin, "Go for Broke," 16–17.

116. Gordon H. Chang, " 'Superman Is About to Visit the Relocation Centers' & the Limits of Wartime Liberalism," *Amerasia Journal* 19, no. 1 (1993), 37, 42–43, 51. The journal issue is devoted to the fiftieth anniversary of Japanese-American internment.

117. Ibid., 51–55.

118. Ibid., 55.

119. Folkerts and Teeter, *Voices of a Nation*, 452–53.

120. Simon, *Public Opinion and the Immigrant*, 34.

121. Louise Merrick Van Patten, "Public Opinion on Japanese Americans," *Far Eastern Survey* 14 (1 August 1945), 208.

122. Kashima, "Japanese American Internees Return," 109.

123. Feagin and Feagin, "Japanese Americans," 387, 388.

124. Ibid., 394.

125. Ibid., 397.

126. Carolyn Martindale, "Only in Glimpses: Portrayal of America's Largest Minority Groups by the *New York Times*, 1934–1994" (Paper presented at Association for Education in Journalism and Mass Communication Convention, Washington, D.C., August 1995), table 7.

127. Ibid., 22.

128. Feagin and Feagin, "Japanese Americans," 388–89.

129. Ibid., 389.

130. Daniels, "Relocation, Redress, and the Report," 5.

131. Ibid., 5; see also Geoffrey S. Smith, "Racial Nativism and Origins of Japanese American Relocation," in *Japanese Americans: From Relocation to Redress*, ed. Roger Daniels, Sandra C. Taylor and Harry H. L. Kitano, rev. ed. (Seattle: University of Washington Press, 1991), 84.

132. Roger Daniels, "Redress Achieved, 1983–1990," in *Japanese Americans: From Relocation to Redress*, ed. Roger Daniels, Sandra C. Taylor, and Harry H. L. Kitano, rev. ed. (Seattle: University of Washington Press, 1991), 219–20.

133. Howard D. Garber, "Apology, Reparations Are Based on Lies," *Los Angeles Herald Examiner*, 5 October 1987, as reprinted and duplicated by Citizens for Truth, Anaheim, Calif.

134. S. I. Hayakawa, personal letter to U.S. Senator Larry Pressler, 17 May 1988.

135. Raymond Y. Okamura, "The American Concentration Camps: A Cover-Up through Euphemistic Terminology," *Journal of Ethnic Studies* 10 (Fall 1982), 98–103.

136. Feagin and Feagin, "Japanese Americans," 384.

137. Ibid., 378, 381, 387.

138. Ibid., 395.

139. U.S. Commission on Civil Rights, *Success of Asian Americans: Fact or Fiction?* (Washington, D.C.: U.S. Government Printing Office, 1980), 14–15.

140. Feagin and Feagin, "Japanese Americans," 390.

141. Ronald Takaki, *Strangers from a Different Shore: A History of Asian Americans* (Boston: Little, Brown, 1989), 474.

142. Feagin and Feagin, "Japanese Americans," 394.

143. Ibid., 397.

144. Darrell Y. Hamamoto, *Monitored Peril: Asian Americans and the Politics of TV Representation* (Minneapolis: University of Minnesota Press, 1994), 70–72.

145. Ibid., 91–96.

146. *Perspectives on Affirmative Action . . . and Its Impact on Asian Pacific Americans* (Los Angeles: Asian Pacific American Public Policy Institute, 1995), 31, quoting Benjamin Seto, national vice president of the Asian American Journalists Association. Seto is a business reporter for the California *Fresno Bee*.

147. Virginia Mansfield-Richardson, "Asian Americans and Mass Communication in the United States: A Wake-up Call" (Paper presented at Association for Education in Journalism and Mass Communication Convention, Washington, D.C., August 1995), 5.

148. *Project Zinger: A Critical Look at News Media Coverage of Asian Pacific Americans* (San Francisco: Center for Integration and Improvement of Journalism and Asian American Journalists Association, 1993), 1, 5–6, 10.

149. *Project Zinger* (Washington, D.C.: Center for Integration and Improvement of Journalism and Asian American Journalists Association, 1992), 5, 12.

150. *Project Zinger*, 1993 ed., 5.

151. James A. Banks, *Teaching Strategies for Ethnic Education*, 2d ed. (Boston: Allyn

and Bacon, 1979), 301–02. Regarding the model minority image, also see "Asian Americans: Media Image Polarized by Good and Bad," *News Watch: A Critical Look at Coverage of People of Color* (San Francisco: Center for Integration and Improvement of Journalism, San Francisco State University, 1994), 40, and Takaki, *Strangers from a Different Shore*, 474–75.

152. Feagin and Feagin, "Japanese Americans," 395–96.

153. Gerald Kato and Beverly Deepe Keever, "Prejudice and the Press: The 1983 Case of Fred Korematsu," in *Media Reader: Perspectives on Mass Media Industries, Effects & Issues*, ed. Shirley Biagi, 3d ed. (Belmont, Calif.: Wadsworth, 1996), 290.

154. Kato and Keever, "Prejudice and the Press," 291.

155. Ibid., 292.

156. Beverly Keever, ed., *Military Secrets: A Case of Government Misconduct in the Wartime Internment of Japanese Americans*, 2d ed. (Honolulu: Hawaii Chapter of the Asian American Journalists Association, 1992), 14–15.

157. Kato and Keever, "Prejudice and the Press," 293, 296.

158. James Phillip Jeter, "The News Magazines and Their Coverage of the Internment of Japanese-Americans during World War II" (Research paper in progress), 25. Jeter is on the faculty of the Division of Journalism at Florida A&M University.

159. James Phillip Jeter, "The News Magazines and Their Coverage of the Quest for Reparations for Japanese-Americans Interned during World War II" (Research paper in progress), 16–17.

160. Chiasson, "The Japanese-American Encampment," 104.

161. Ibid., 105.

162. James B. McPherson, "Crosses Holding Off a Vampire: How Four Newspapers Used Editorials to Define Their First Amendment Functions" (Paper presented at American Journalism Historians Association Convention, Roanoke, Virginia, 6–8 October 1994), 1.

SELECTED BIBLIOGRAPHY

Chang, Gordon H. " 'Superman Is About to Visit the Relocation Centers' & the Limits of Wartime Liberalism." *Amerasia Journal* 19, no. 1 (1993), 37–60.

Chiasson, Lloyd E. "The Japanese-American Encampment: An Editorial Analysis of 27 West Coast Newspapers." *Newspaper Research Journal* 12 (Spring 1991), 92–107.

———. "Japanese-American Relocation during World War II: A Study of California Editorial Reactions." *Journalism Quarterly* 68 (Spring/Summer 1991), 263–68.

Daniels, Roger. *Concentration Camps: North American Japanese in the United States and Canada during World War II*. Malabar, Fla.: R. E. Krieger Publishing, 1981.

———. *The Decision to Relocate the Japanese Americans*. Philadelphia: J. B. Lippincott, 1975.

Daniels, Roger, Sandra C. Taylor, and Harry H. L. Kitano, eds. *Japanese Americans: From Relocation to Redress*, rev. ed. Seattle: University of Washington Press, 1991.

Girdner, Audrie, and Anne Loftis. *The Great Betrayal: The Evacuation of the Japanese-Americans during World War II*. New York: Macmillan, 1969.

Grodzins, Morton. *Americans Betrayed: Politics and the Japanese Evacuation*. Chicago: University of Chicago Press, 1969 reprint of 1949 edition.

Hamm, Brad. "They Work Too Hard: How Newspapers Justified the 1924 Exclusion of Japanese Immigrants." Paper presented at Association for Education in Journalism and Mass Communication Southeast Colloquium, March 1995.

Heuterman, Thomas H. *The Burning Horse: The Japanese-American Experience in the Yakima Valley 1920–1942.* Cheney: Eastern Washington University Press, 1995.

———. " 'We Have the Same Rights As Other Citizens': Coverage of Yakima Valley Japanese Americans in the 'Missing Decades' of the 1920s and 1930s." *Journalism History* 14 (Winter 1987), 94–103.

Hosokawa, Bill. *Nisei: The Quiet Americans.* New York: William Morrow, 1969.

———. *Thirty-Five Years in the Frying Pan.* New York: McGraw-Hill, 1978.

Ichihashi, Yamato. *Japanese in the United States: A Critical Study of the Problems of the Japanese Immigrants and Their Children.* Palo Alto, Calif.: Stanford University Press, 1932.

Irons, Peter. *Justice at War.* New York: Oxford University Press, 1983.

Kato, Gerald, and Beverly Deepe Keever. "Prejudice and the Press: The 1983 Case of Fred Korematsu." In *Media Reader: Perspectives on Mass Media Industries, Effects & Issues,* edited by Shirley Biagi. 3d ed. Belmont, Calif.: Wadsworth, 1996.

Keever, Beverly, ed. *Military Secrets: A Case of Government Misconduct in the Wartime Internment of Japanese Americans.* 2d ed. Honolulu: Hawaii Chapter of the Asian American Journalists Association, 1992.

Kumamoto, Bob. "The Search for Spies: American Counterintelligence and the Japanese American Community 1931–1942." *Amerasia Journal* 6, no. 2 (1979), 45–75.

Mansfield-Richardson, Virginia. "Asian Americans and Mass Communication in the United States: A Wake-up Call." Paper presented at Association for Education in Journalism and Mass Communication Convention, Washington, D.C., August 1995.

Miyamoto, S. Frank. "The Forced Evacuation of the Japanese Minority during World War II." *Journal of Social Issues* 29, no. 2 (1973), 11–31.

Nelson, Douglas W. *Heart Mountain: The History of an American Concentration Camp.* Madison: State Historical Society of Wisconsin for the University of Wisconsin Department of History, 1976.

Okihiro, Gary Y. *Cane Fires: The Anti-Japanese Movement in Hawaii, 1865–1945.* Philadelphia: Temple University Press, 1991.

Okihiro, Gary Y., and Julie Sly. "The Press, Japanese Americans, and the Concentration Camps." *Phylon* 46 (March 1983), 66–83.

Olmstead, Timothy. "Nikkei Internment: The Perspective of Two Oregon Weekly Newspapers." *Oregon Historical Quarterly* 85 (Spring 1984), 5–32.

Personal Justice Denied: Report of the Commission on Wartime Relocation and Internment of Civilians. Washington, D.C.: U.S. Government Printing Office, 1992.

Project Zinger: A Critical Look at News Media Coverage of Asian Pacific Americans. Washington, D.C., 1992, and San Francisco, 1993, Center for Integration and Improvement of Journalism and Asian American Journalists Association.

Simon, Rita J. *Public Opinion and the Immigrant: Print Media Coverage, 1880–1980.* Lexington, Mass.: Lexington Books, 1985.

Takaki, Ronald. *Strangers from a Different Shore: A History of Asian Americans.* Boston: Little, Brown, 1989.

Tamashiro, John Gerald. "The Japanese in Hawaii and on the Mainland during World

War II As Discussed in the Editorial Pages of the *Honolulu Advertiser* and the *Honolulu Star-Bulletin*.'' Master's thesis, University of Hawaii, 1972.

tenBroek, Jacobus, Edward N. Barnhart, and Floyd W. Matson. *Prejudice, War and the Constitution*. Berkeley: University of California Press, 1954.

Thiesmeyer, Lynn. ''The Discourse of Official Violence: Anti-Japanese North American Discourse and the American Internment Camps.'' *Discourse & Society* 6, no. 3 (1995), 319–52.

The Other Asian Americans
VIRGINIA MANSFIELD-RICHARDSON

> The scant media coverage there is [on Asian Americans] is always devoted to either the Chinese Americans or Japanese Americans. Filipino Americans, for example, constitute the second largest ethnic group of Asian-Pacific descent, but it's as if they do not count. Another example would be the issue of race-related violence. While violence against Chinese Americans has, to a certain extent, been publicized in the mainstream media, this much can't be said regarding similar incidents involving Vietnamese Americans.
> —Marites Sison-Paez, editor,
> Special Edition Press, New York City[1]

The proper place to begin, when discussing news coverage of "other Asian Americans," is to determine which ethnic groups of Asian Americans fall into this category. Sadly, the answer is that no one expert or organization seems to know the answer, and it is an area fraught with controversy among Asian-American scholars. The 1990 U.S. Census definition of persons of Asian or Pacific Islander descent included ten ethnic categories for Asians, plus twenty categories under the term "other Asian," and three categories for Pacific Islanders, plus eighteen categories under "other Pacific Islander."[2] However, the nineteen ethnic groups now considered to be Asian Americans, according to the *Asian Americans Information Directory*, differ from the Asian and Pacific Islander ethnic groups of the U.S. Census.[3] Many groups representing Asian Americans, including the Asian American Journalists Association (AAJA) and the Asian American Studies Center at the University of California, Los Angeles, carefully refrain from adopting an official definition of "Asian Americans" and, thus, allow members to determine whether they fall into the classification.[4]

In general, the countries of origin for Asian Americans included in many definitions span more than half the globe—from the Indian continent to the Hawaiian Islands—which makes this ethnic group more broadly defined geo-

graphically than any other ethnic category in the U.S. Census. The real controversy of recent years is whether to include Middle Eastern Americans in the
definition. The AAJA accepts Middle Eastern Americans as an ethnic subcate-
gory of Asian American, yet in the AAJA official map of countries of origin of
Asian Americans provided in their media guide *Asian American Handbook*, the
Middle East is not included, nor are any issues affecting Middle Easterners
included in the AAJA's "sensitivity tips" for journalists covering Asian Americans.[5]

So, discussing "other Asian Americans" seems to involve only two constants:
(1) the definition of who these people are is vague, and (2) most "official"
definitions of Asian Americans are extremely broad.

For purposes here, other Asian Americans include those people who are not
Chinese Americans or Japanese Americans. Middle Eastern Americans are also
not included in this section, partly due to space constraints and partly because
the verdict appears to still be undecided, even among Middle Eastern Americans,
as to whether they are Asian Americans.

Before examining the news coverage of some specific ethnic groups of Asian
Americans, it is helpful to look at a recent content analysis of mainstream newspaper coverage of Asian Americans in twenty of the largest newspapers in the
United States for the year spanning March 1, 1994, to February 28, 1995.[6] An
exhaustive review of literature conducted for the study indicated that the study
appears to be the only content analysis ever conducted to look at newspaper
coverage of all Asian Americans, with coding for fourteen ethnic groups of
Asian Americans, as opposed to studies of coverage of one ethnic segment of
Asian Americans, such as Chinese Americans.[7] This extensive lack of research
on media coverage of Asian Americans, as outlined in the content analysis,
mirrors a lack of coverage in mainstream newspapers of Asian Americans and
issues facing Asian Americans.

Using a slight modification of Paul Deutschmann's ten categories for content
analyses, and Guido Stempel's fourteen such categories, thirteen news article
types were coded for the content analysis, and each story was coded as falling
into one of fourteen ethnic categories or as covering the Asian-American community as a whole. A category for stories on Asian-American personalities was
included since it was often impossible to determine what ethnic background a
personality held just by reading his or her name.[8] The content analysis searched
193 keywords and 123 names of prominent Asian Americans.

Overall, the content analysis turned up only 635 stories on Asian Americans
and issues facing Asian Americans in the twenty newspapers searched for that
year. Since a correlation was established in the study between cities with large
populations of Asian Americans and newspapers in those circulation areas giving
more coverage to Asian Americans, it was not surprising that the newspapers
with the most articles on Asian Americans were the *Seattle Times*, with 215
stories, followed by the *Los Angeles Times* with 73 articles, the *San Francisco
Chronicle* with 70, and the *New York Times* with 54.[9]

It is unfortunate to learn that large newspapers, such as the *Washington Post* (with twenty articles for the year), in cities that have significant populations of Asian Americans (the Washington, D.C., metropolitan area has a large population of Vietnamese Americans) had very few articles. No articles on Asian Americans or any ethnic group of Asian Americans were published that year in the *Detroit Free Press* or the *Washington Times*, and less than ten articles were published in each of the following newspapers: The *Detroit News and Free Press*, the *St. Louis Post-Dispatch*, the *Christian Science Monitor*, the *Detroit News*, and the *Wall Street Journal*.[10]

The study found three strong positive correlations between: (1) the percent of Asian Americans in a city's population and percent of Asian Americans working at a newspaper covering that particular city, (2) the percent of Asian Americans in a city and the coverage of Asian Americans by a newspaper covering that city, and (3) the percent of Asian Americans working in a newsroom and the coverage of Asian Americans by that newspaper. The content analysis did not find an abundance of stereotypical articles, such as stories on gang violence or Asian Americans as the model minority, even though 520 Asian-American journalists surveyed for the research predicted an excess of such article topics.[11]

The study became even more revealing when the amount of coverage given to ethnic groups of Asian Americans other than Chinese Americans and Japanese Americans was examined. Of the total 635 articles, the largest chunk, 256 stories, covered Asian Americans as a whole, and the next largest amount of coverage, 76 stories, covered prominent Asian-American personalities such as cellist Yo-Yo Ma, comedian Margaret Cho, and tennis star Michael Chang.[12]

The content analysis found the most coverage to be on Asian Americans as a whole entity, followed by articles on personalities, and then on each of the five largest ethnic groups of Asian Americans, according to the U.S. Census: Chinese Americans, fifty-eight articles; Japanese Americans and Vietnamese Americans, fifty-three articles each; Korean Americans, forty-seven; Filipino Americans, twenty-four; Asian Indians, twelve; Hawaiians and other Pacific Islanders, eleven articles each; Cambodian Americans, nine; Hmong Americans, seven; Thai Americans and Pakistani Americans, six each; and Laotian Americans and other Asian Americans, three each.[13]

The type of coverage these other Asian Americans received, according to the study, helps in understanding how certain stereotypes are reinforced and how large areas of life among Asian Americans are not receiving much coverage in mainstream newspapers. For the entire content analysis, the type of story published the most dealt with entertainment (156 articles out of the total 635); followed by general human interest articles, which did not include success stories on Asian Americans often associated with the model-minority stereotype (131 stories); followed by crime articles (79); articles on the classic arts (77); articles on politics at all levels, including local and international (66); and articles on public moral problems, which includes race relations (45) and public health and welfare articles (35).[14]

The large amount of coverage given to popular entertainment, which did not include classical arts, was slightly skewed due to that year's premiere of the television program "All American Girl," which was the first prime-time television program with an all-Asian cast. The show was later canceled, but twenty-nine articles on the show were published in the twenty newspapers examined. Only one article in the entire 635 dealt with Asian Americans and the sciences, yet large numbers of Asian Americans have careers in all areas of the hard sciences. Only ten articles out of the total dealt with economic issues. Of the nearly eighty articles published on crime, forty-two dealt with Asian Americans as a whole, followed by ten on Vietnamese Americans. Of the total fifty-three articles published on Vietnamese Americans, one-fifth dealt with crime. It is not surprising, then, to see why the incorrect stereotype of many Vietnamese being associated with gangs and violence continues to be perpetuated in the minds of American newspaper readers.

The study included a survey of 520 Asian-American journalists from print, radio, and television. Of those surveyed, nearly 500 worked in mainstream media, while 20 were the editors of leading Asian-American publications. The survey asked four questions about positive and negative job experiences that the respondents felt were related to their ethnicity, and asked how well the respondents thought the media covered Asian Americans and issues relating to Asian Americans. The responses were alarming at times, telling of incidents in which Asian Americans were called "gooks" and "chinks" in private meetings with superiors, and of more subtle racist comments made among the respondents' colleagues and by news sources.[15]

SOUTHEAST ASIAN AMERICANS

It is particularly important to understand the difference between immigrants and refugees when looking at the media coverage of Southeast Asian Americans, since the majority of those Southeast Asians who arrived in the United States after the 1965 Immigration Act are refugees, and the majority of Southeast Asians arrived in the United States after 1975. One of the "Asian American Issues" cited in the Asian American Journalists Association's media guide, the *Asian American Handbook*, is a complaint that the terms "immigrant," "emigrant," and "refugee" are often improperly used in the media when describing Asians living in the United States. The guide stated that a refugee "is a person admitted to the United States from abroad due to that person's well-founded fear of persecution on account of race, religion, nationality, membership in a particular social group, or political opinion."[16] Most Vietnamese, Laotians, Cambodians, Hmong, and Mien who arrived in the United States after the Vietnam War are refugees; most of the other Asians who have come to this country in the past 150 years have come by their own choice, which made them immigrants. Media coverage of the refugee groups is often quite different from coverage of other Asian groups simply because some, such as the Mien and Hmong, have suffered poverty and severe adjustment problems to American life, partly because they typically were mountain dwellers in Cambodia, Laos, Vietnam, and southern China and had a native language that was mostly oral and not written.

Media coverage on the Vietnamese in the United States has also reflected the large refugee population that flooded into this country after the Vietnam War. In 1964 only 603 Vietnamese were living in the United States; most of them were students, language teachers, and diplomats.[17] But just over a decade later, the U.S.–backed regime in South Vietnam fell in April 1975. Then began one of the most intense, and unique, periods of immigration to the United States in recent history. From April 29 to December 31, 1975, approximately 130,000 refugees from Vietnam, Cambodia, and Laos entered the United States.[18] While this surge of refugees represented mostly the educated classes, the flood of Southeast Asian refugees that followed consisted of poorer refugees forced from their homelands. The media frequently discussed the "Little Saigons," or refugee communities, that subsequently cropped up in large cities nationwide. Unfortunately, as newer generations have emerged, media attention on non-Filipino Southeast Asian Americans continues to focus mainly on model-minority success stories and crime-related news.[19]

FILIPINO AMERICANS

Filipino Americans have a legitimate complaint that they are not given as much attention in the media as Chinese Americans and Japanese Americans, yet Filipino Americans make up the second largest ethnic group of Asian Americans, according to the 1990 U.S. Census.[20] In 1990 the United States had 1.4 million Filipino Americans, compared to 1.6 million Chinese Americans, approximately 866,200 Japanese Americans, and 7.2 million total Asian Americans and Pacific Islanders.[21] Unfortunately, no specific studies that examine the full history of the coverage of Filipinos in the American media have been done.[22] However, some studies, such as Christopher Vaughan's look at the print coverage of Filipinos from 1898 to 1902, are useful in understanding how stereotypes of Filipinos developed and continue today in the media.[23]

Filipino immigration to the United States has occurred in three stages, beginning in the 1920s and 1930s when Filipino immigrants became the backbone of the West Coast agricultural business. On the rare occasion of a newspaper's reporting on Filipino immigrants specifically it was usually in a derogatory reference. In the 1930s and 1940s, Filipinos migrated more inland in the United States and north to Alaska, where they worked in salmon canneries. By the 1940s and 1950s, significant Filipino communities had developed in Chicago, Detroit, Philadelphia, and New York, but no studies have been done on the newspapers in these cities to examine the coverage of Filipino Americans living there. The second wave of Filipino immigrants, between 1946 and 1967, consisted again of mostly unskilled laborers. The third wave of Filipino immigration began after the 1965 Immigration Act and continued through 1980; many of these immigrants were professionals, such as engineers, physicians, and technical workers.

KOREAN AMERICANS

Korean Americans are plagued in U.S. media coverage with stereotypes of mom-and-pop convenience store owners who become involved in crimes with African Americans. Much of this grew out of the riots that swept Los Angeles following the Rodney King verdict, where several Korean-owned businesses were burned or vandalized. Korean Americans, who number approximately 800,000, represent the fourth largest ethnic group of Asian Americans.[24] A backlash has developed recently in the Korean-American community against what is perceived as the media's incessant coverage of crime-related stories and their communities. Lisa Chung, executive director of the AAJA, complained in a 1994 interview that the news media typically do not send an interpreter to cover stories dealing with Korean immigrants, and, consequently, "these very articulate and intelligent people are portrayed as inarticulate as they struggle with the English language rather than being interviewed in their native language."[25] Scholar Edward T. Chang explained the problem in the following way: "The media has [sic] continued to portray the 1992 riots as an extension of the ongoing conflict between Korean merchants and African American residents, despite the fact that more than half the looters arrested were Latinos."[26]

Numerous other issues have arisen concerning the media coverage of Korean Americans, including the fact that a larger percentage of Korean Americans are Christian than percentages of any other ethnic group of Asian Americans, but this is not reflected in the media's coverage of Koreans in the United States.

ASIAN INDIAN AMERICANS

Also underrepresented in the U.S. media, in comparison to their proportion of total Asian Americans, are Asian Indians. In 1990 the United States had approximately 786,700 Asian Indian Americans, making them the fifth largest ethnic group of Asian Americans, following the Japanese Americans—who number about 866,200—as the third largest group.[27] It was not until the 1980 U.S. Census that a separate category was established for Asian Indians. That same census indicated that 52 percent of adult Asian Indians living in America were college graduates, compared to 35 percent of all Asian Americans aged twenty-five and older.[28] Asian Indians differed from other Asian Americans in other ways; for example, only 19 percent of Asian Indians lived in the West Coast states as of 1980, compared to 60 percent of all Asian Americans.[29] Also, nearly 50 percent of all foreign-born Asian Indian adults in the United States work as managers, professionals, or executives, and Asian Indians are a dominant force in hotel management.[30] Also unlike other Asian Americans, Asian Indians have remained out of politics, and they tend to live separately in middle-class neighborhoods, compared to other Asian Americans who often live in ethnic communities.

Some of these facts are reflected in the media coverage of Asian Indians. A rash of articles and news features have been published on the growth of Asian Indians in hotel management in recent years. In the content analysis of twenty U.S. dailies for one year, only one article on Asian Indians and crime was published, but seven human interest stories, and only a total of twelve stories overall, were found.[31]

PACIFIC ISLANDER AMERICANS

Finally, media coverage of Pacific Islanders, particularly when the Hawaiian media are excluded, is seriously scant and does not reflect either the diversity of this ethnic group or the complexities of these people's lives. Currently a move is afoot among Pacific-Islander Americans to reclassify that group as being Native Americans, since many Pacific Islanders in Hawaii were natives of what is now American soil. According to the 1990 U.S. Census, the United States includes 350,000 Pacific-Islander Americans, with the largest subgroups being 205,501 Hawaiians, 57,679 Samoans, and 47,754 Guamanians.[32] Incredibly, Pacific Islanders have been classified as a separate ethnic group in the U.S. Census only since 1980. Serious undercoverage of Pacific Islanders is seen in the earlier mentioned newspaper content analysis, which showed only six articles on non-Hawaiian Pacific Islanders and only eleven on Hawaiians published in twenty of the largest U.S. dailies (not located in Hawaii) for one year.[33]

Migration from the Pacific Islands to the United States reflects the political history of the region, but this is rarely a part of any media coverage on Pacific Islanders. Migration from many islands in the Pacific to Hawaii and the mainland United States often increased when the islands became trust territories of the United States. A disproportionate number of articles concern athletes of Samoan descent, which is not reflective of any Pacific-Islander community issues other than the unimportant "fact" that some Samoans have become good football players.[34] Many scholars also note that Pacific Islanders are the only Asian Americans who became Asian Americans because their homelands, specifically Hawaii, American Samoa, and the U.S. Trust Territories in the Pacific, became part of the United States. Again, this is rarely reflected in the minuscule media attention given to Pacific Islanders. Also, most likely at least partly due to the lack of coverage on Pacific Islanders, most Americans are sorely lacking in their knowledge of the history and culture of the Pacific Islands.

This section on "other Asian Americans" would not be complete without explaining that the ethnic Asian press, with the exception of the Japanese ethnic press, is growing rapidly in the United States, due in part to the lack of coverage given Asian-American ethnic groups in the mainstream media. Magazines such as *Filipinas*, which caters to a young, urban professional Filipino-American readership, and the literally hundreds of ethnic newspapers catering to Korean Americans, Asian Indians, Southeast Asian Americans, Pacific Islanders, and other Asian-American ethnic groups are growing at faster rates in the 1990s than ever before, often due to the ease and lower costs of desktop publishing.[35]

SCHOLARSHIP IS LACKING

Sadly, the media are not the only institutions in society to contribute to perpetuating false stereotypes of Asian Americans, as well as ignoring the importance of Asian Americans in news coverage. The study mentioned earlier indicated a serious lack of scholarship on Asian Americans by media scholars at universities. According to the *Index to Journals in Mass Communication*, which chronicles all research articles in thirty-five leading academic journals for mass communication, only ten articles dealing with Asian Americans and the media were published from 1988 to 1993.[36] Of those ten articles, only four dealt with the entire Asian-American community rather than a segment of the community, such as Korean Americans or Chinese Americans. The thirty-five journals published nearly as many articles (nine) on Native Americans and the media as they did on Asian Americans, yet there are 7.2 million Asian Americans and Pacific Islanders in the United States compared to 1.8 million Native Americans.[37]

Also, none of the leading journals in the communication field, such as *Journalism Quarterly*, *Journalism Educator*, *Mass Comm Review*, *Media, Culture and Society*, or *Journalism Monographs*, published research on the Asian-American community during this six-year period. In fact, in the twenty-nine-year history of *Journalism Monographs*, a highly selective publication of the Association for Education in Journalism and Mass Communication (AEJMC), no one study has ever dealt with the entire Asian-American community. However, one monograph was published that dealt with the Hawaiian press under martial law, and another concerned the Japanese press in Hawaii.[38]

Only four articles that dealt with the entire Asian-American community were found among the thousands of articles published from 1978 to 1994 in the nearly 200 journals indexed in *Communication Abstracts*. Also, only eighteen articles were published on specific ethnic subgroups of Asian Americans in the journals, even though Asian Americans were the fastest-growing ethnic group in the United States during much of that time frame.

Of the eighteen articles, the most coverage went to Pacific Islanders, with six articles published. Japanese Americans and Korean Americans each had five articles, and one article each was devoted to Chinese Americans and to Laotian, Hmong, and Vietnamese refugees in the United States.[39]

For the past twenty-two years, the AEJMC has published in *Journalism Abstracts* abstracts of all the master's theses and doctoral dissertations written each year in the United States that pertain to mass communication. An examination of these abstracts from 1963 to 1994 revealed only four masters' theses and no doctoral dissertations that dealt with the topic of Asian Americans as an entire community.[40]

CONCLUSION

Asian Americans constitute many ethnic groups other than Chinese Americans, Japanese Americans, Korean Americans, Vietnamese Americans, and Pacific Islanders. Little research has been done on Native Hawaiians and other Pacific Islanders, Indian Americans, Hmong Americans, Filipino Americans, and many other peoples who represent ethnic subcategories of Asian Americans. Considering the rich history of these people in the United States, as well as the vital contribution they make to American society today, it is sad that so little attention has been paid to them by mass communication scholars.

NOTES

1. Virginia Mansfield-Richardson, "Asian Americans and the Mass Media: A Content Analysis of Twenty U.S. Newspapers and a Survey of Asian American Journalists" (Ph.D. diss., Ohio University, 1996), 702.

2. *U.S. Census 1990: Social and Economic Characteristics 1993* (Washington, D.C.: U.S. Department of Commerce, Economics and Statistics Administration, Bureau of the Census, 1992), B-30. The ethnic categories for "Asian" are Chinese, Filipino, Japanese, Asian Indian, Korean, Vietnamese, Cambodian, Hmong, Laotian, and Thai. The categories for "other Asian" are Bangladeshi, Bhutanese, Bornean, Burmese, Celebesian, Ceram, Indochinese, Indonesian, Iwo Jiman, Javanese, Malayan, Maldivian, Nepali, Okinawan, Pakistani, Sikkimese, Singaporean, Sri Lankan, Sumatran, and Asian Not Specified. The ethnic categories for Pacific Islander are Hawaiian, Samoan, and Guamian. The categories for "other Pacific Islander" are Carolinian, Fijian, Kosraean, Melanesian, Micronesian, Northern Mariana Islander, Palauan, Papua New Guinean, Ponapean, Polynesian, Solomon Islander, Tahitian, Tarawa Islander, Tokelauan, Tongan, Trukese, Yapese, and Pacific Islander Not Specified.

3. Karen Backus and Julia Furtaw, *Asian Americans Information Directory* (Detroit: Gale Research, 1992), 11–12.

4. For example, Lisa Chung, executive director of the Asian American Journalists Association, explained in a 1995 telephone interview with the author that her organization had no precise definition of who constitutes an Asian American. She said, however, that people from the Middle East are included as members of AAJA and that several Middle Eastern American members had been very active in writing pamphlets and other literature on biases in the American media during the coverage of the Oklahoma City federal building bombing.

5. Asian American Journalists Association (AAJA), *Asian American Handbook* (Chicago: Asian American Journalists Association, Chicago Chapter, and National Conference of Christians and Jews, Chicago and Northern Illinois Region, 1991), 2.3, 2.1–3.13, 4.1–4.4.

6. Mansfield-Richardson, "Asian Americans and the Mass Media." Newspapers re-

searched in the study were the *Atlanta Constitution, Atlanta Journal, Atlanta Journal-Constitution* (all three counted as one newspaper in the study), *Boston Globe, Christian Science Monitor, Chicago Tribune, Denver Post, Detroit Free Press, Detroit News, Detroit News and Free Press, Houston Chronicle, Houston Post, Los Angeles Times, New York Times, San Francisco Chronicle, Seattle Times, St. Louis Post-Dispatch, Times-Picayune, USA Today, Wall Street Journal, Washington Post,* and *Washington Times.*

7. Mansfield-Richardson, "Asian Americans and the Mass Media," chapter 3 on Related Studies,186–226.

8. Paul Deutschmann, *News-Page Content of Twelve Metropolitan Dailies* (Cincinnati: Scripps-Howard Research, 1959) 58–62; and Guido Stempel III, "Gatekeeping: The Mix of Topics and the Selection of Stories," *Journalism Quarterly* 62, no. 4 (1985) 791–96. The thirteen coding categories used in the content analysis were politics and government acts, war and defense, economic activity, crime, public moral problems, accidents and disasters, science and invention, classic arts, popular amusements, public health and welfare, education, general human interests, and other. The coding categories for ethnic groups of Asian Americans were all Asian Americans, Chinese, Japanese, Koreans, Filipinos, Asian Indians, Pakistani Americans, Vietnamese, Hmong, Laotian, Cambodian, Thai, Hawaiian, other Pacific Islander, other Asian American ethnic group, and Asian-American prominent personality.

9. Mansfield-Richardson, "Asian Americans and the Mass Media," 268.

10. Ibid., see ch. 5, 267–370.

11. Mansfield-Richardson, "Asian Americans and the Mass Media," 321, 700–722.

12. Ibid., 270.

13. Ibid.

14. Ibid., 323.

15. Ibid., 727–50.

16. AAJA, *Asian American Handbook*, 3.3.

17. Ronald Takaki, *Strangers from a Different Shore: A History of Asian Americans* (Boston: Little, Brown, 1989), 448.

18. Hyung-chan Kim, *Dictionary of Asian American History* (New York: Greenwood Press, 1986), 40; Takaki, *Strangers from a Different Shore*, 451.

19. Mansfield-Richardson, "Asian Americans and the Mass Media," 323, 325.

20. *U.S. Census 1990*, table 4.

21. Ibid.

22. Mansfield-Richardson, "Asian Americans and the Mass Media," ch. 3, 186–226.

23. Christopher Vaughan, "The 'Discovery' of the Philippines by the U.S. Press, 1898–1902," *Historian* 57, no. 2 (1994), 303–12.

24. *U.S. Census 1990*, table 4.

25. Lisa Chung interview with author, November 1994.

26. Karin Aguilar-San Juan, ed., *The State of Asian America: Activism and Resistance in the 1990s* (Boston: South End Press, 1994), 110.

27. *U.S. Census 1990*, table 4.

28. Harry Kitano and Roger Daniels, *Asian Americans: Emerging Minorities* (Englewood Cliffs, N.J.: Prentice-Hall, 1988), 99.

29. Ibid., 98.

30. Ibid., 110; Edwin McDowell, "Hospitality Is Their Business: Indian-Americans' Rooms-to-Riches Success Story," *New York Times*, 21 March 1996, D1.

31. Mansfield-Richardson, "Asian Americans in the Mass Media," 323.

32. *U.S. Census 1990*, table 4.

33. Mansfield-Richardson, "Asian Americans and the Mass Media," 323.

34. Ibid., ch. 5, 265–370.

35. Aly Colon, "News outside the Mainstream—Ethnic Papers in the Area Find a Loyal and Growing Following," *Seattle Times*, 26 February 1995, final ed.

36. Mansfield-Richardson, "Asian Americans and the Mass Media," 571.

37. *U.S. Census 1990, 1992*, 323–25.

38. Jim Richstad, "The Press under Martial Law: The Hawaiian Experience," *Journalism Monographs* 17 (1970), 1–41; Tom Brislin, "Weep into Silence/Cries of Rage: Bitter Divisions in Hawaii's Japanese Press," *Journalism and Mass Communication Monographs* 154 (1995), 1–29.

39. Mansfield-Richardson, "Asian Americans and the Mass Media," 545–66, 580–82.

40. Ibid., 609–618.

SELECTED BIBLIOGRAPHY

Asian American Journalists Association. *Asian American Handbook*. Chicago: Asian American Journalists Association, Chicago Chapter, and the National Conference of Christians and Jews, Chicago and Northern Illinois Region, 1991.

Backus, Karen, and Julia Furtaw. *Asian Americans Information Directory*. Detroit: Gale Research, 1992.

Deutschmann, Paul. *News-Page Content of Twelve Metropolitan Dailies*. Cincinnati: Scripps-Howard Research, 1959.

Kim, Hyung-chan. *Dictionary of Asian American History*. New York: Greenwood Press, 1986.

Kitano, Harry, and Roger Daniels. *Asian Americans: Emerging Minorities*. Englewood Cliffs, N.J.: Prentice-Hall, 1988.

Mansfield-Richardson, Virginia. "Asian Americans and the Mass Media: A Content Analysis of Twenty U.S. Newspapers and a Survey of Asian American Journalists." Ph.D. diss., Ohio University, 1996.

Stempel, Guido, III. "Gatekeeping: The Mix of Topics and the Selection of Stories." *Journalism Quarterly* 62, no. 4 (1985), 791–815.

Takaki, Ronald. *Strangers from a Different Shore: A History of Asian Americans*. Boston: Little, Brown, 1989.

U.S. Census 1990: Social and Economic Characteristics 1993. Washington, D.C.: U.S. Department of Commerce, Economics and Statistics Administration, Bureau of the Census, 1992.

6

The Pacific Islanders

BEVERLY ANN DEEPE KEEVER

The greatest evil the papers do is not with their reporting, but that they tell
us what we ought to think of this or that, about our high chiefs or the high
chiefs of other lands, about what other people do and what happens to them.
They want to fashion every mind to the same pattern, which is against my
beliefs.

—Samoan Chief Tuiavi'i, circa 1910[1]

We can style writing a "secondary modeling system," dependent on a prior
primary system, spoken language. Oral expression can exist and mostly has
existed without any writing at all, writing never without orality.

—Walter J. Ong[2]

He was only 19 when we learned that he had radiation sickness. They took
him away to the United States, to their big American hospitals and the way
they treated him . . . it was certainly thorough. But to my mind they used
him as if he was an animal. They continuously punctured his body in the
way you might cut up a chicken. He bled from the things they stuck into
him. He was like a laboratory animal.

—Mother of Marshall Islander who died after exposure
to the 1954 U.S. hydrogen bomb test[3]

Like the Native Americans and many Hispanics on the North American continent, the Pacific Islanders did not immigrate to the United States. Instead they
were overcome by U.S. expansion into their home regions. Before Western
contact, all had oral cultures that fostered consensus and communalism; even
today these values of Pacific Islanders are often at odds with U.S.–styled adversarial courts and investigative journalism.[4]

The total population of the Pacific Islands under U.S. strategic protection is
small, about the size of Philadelphia with 1.56 million people. But despite their

small numbers, groups of Pacific Islanders unwillingly became the avant-garde of the Atomic Age. Unlike the world's first three atomic explosions that were shrouded in wartime secrecy,[5] postwar nuclear tests that began at Bikini Atoll in 1946 provide a unique window on U.S. government–press relations that proved detrimental to these Pacific Islanders—and ultimately to people world-wide as well. The Pacific Islanders became what one scholar called a case history of U.S. bureaucratic incompetence and neglect.[6] And they became a case history of U.S. news media deficiencies in covering a racial minority on the outermost rim of the American periphery, where a new power of mass destruction was being tested far from the centers of Western populations, governments, and civilization. Despite the shortcomings in initial U.S. news coverage, the world belatedly recognized the killing power of lingering radioactive fallout and of a doomsday-type weapon of biological extinction.[7] As one historian explained, Pacific Islanders who experienced these first peacetime nuclear tests are impor-tant because "they have already lived in what might be our common future."[8]

U.S. jurisdiction in the Pacific region now covers:[9]

• Hawaii, a territory in 1898, following the overthrow of the Hawaiian monarchy by businessmen and U.S. troops, that became the nation's fiftieth state in 1959; it has housed two nuclear weapons storage areas and an airbase for nuclear-armed intercep-tors.[10]

• Guam, acquired in 1898 from Spain; now an unincorporated territory. Before the Stra-tegic Air Force Wing was deactivated in 1989, a communication scholar reported that Guam contained "the most nuclear weapons in any single location on earth."[11]

• American Samoa, obtained in 1899 through negotiations with Germany without any consideration of the wishes of the Samoans.[12] It is now an unincorporated territory consisting of five main islands and two atolls.

• Federated States of Micronesia, a constitutional government of four states—Yap, Chuuk, Pohnpei, and Kosrae, consisting of hundreds of islands and atolls—tied to the United States in a compact of free association.

• Republic of the Marshall Islands, a sovereign, self-governing entity of thirty-four is-lands and 870 reefs operating in a compact of free association with the United States. Included are the one-time atomic-testing sites of Bikini and Enewetak plus the Kwa-jalein Atoll, originally a base supporting the nuclear test program[13] but since 1983 significant in research in the "Star Wars" Strategic Defense Initiative,[14] which began the militarization of space.[15]

• Republic of Belau (formerly Palau), about 200 islands in a compact of free association with the United States since 1994. Earlier, Belau's voters, in seven plebiscites since 1983, refused to approve by the constitutionally required 75 percent margin a compact with the United States that permits the presence of nuclear vessels and overflight of planes carrying nuclear weapons.[16]

• Commonwealth of the Northern Mariana Islands (CNMI), an archipelago of seventeen islands that, in 1976, became self-governing in union with the United States under a covenant that gave U.S. citizenship to its people and that integrated the islands into the union.[17]

- Military islands, such as Wake, Johnston, and Midway, uninhabited by indigenous people. Midway is designated as a national wildlife refuge; Johnston is a site for the disposal of chemical weapons.

- Numerous unincorporated, unpopulated islands such as Palmyra, which has become newsworthy as a potential nuclear-waste dumping site or a nuclear fuel reprocessing enterprise.[18]

The compacts of free association with the Federated States of Micronesia, the Republic of the Marshall Islands, and the Republic of Belau are described by anthropologist Robert Kiste as legalistic documents defining "an arrangement in which the island nations grant the United States strategic prerogatives in exchange for financial subsidies and certain federal services."[19] Self-governing on internal matters, the islands serve as an outer defense periphery for the U.S. heartland 6,000 miles away. The U.S. nuclear presence in the Pacific is evolving with advances in ballistic missile technology and in space-tracking networks.

These islands, because of their oral-tradition heritage and exceptional pattern of coming under U.S. governance, are given separate treatment in this volume although the Census Bureau in 1990 classified them in the same category as Asian Americans. The term Native Hawaiian is used in this chapter to mean any individual who is a descendent of the aboriginal people inhabiting the present-day state of Hawaii before 1778, when the islands were "discovered" by English Captain James Cook.[20]

The U.S. interest in the region is largely strategic. The Pacific Ocean, covering about one-eighth of the world's surface, gives unity and name to the unique region, which is a sea dotted with about 25,000 islands, more than those in all other oceans combined.[21]

The first descriptions of Pacific Islanders for Westerners came from explorers' accounts, travelers' letters, or missionaries' reports. These early images fixed made-in-the-Atlantic perceptions of Pacific Islanders in three ways. First, Westerners' words and images were of the "noble savage," a popular theme of eighteenth-century romantic naturalism in Europe and the United States, which suggested a closeness to nature, including Biblical notions associated with the Garden of Eden and earthly paradise.[22] This image was used and memorialized by writers like Robert Louis Stevenson and was captured in movies as the backdrop for a romantic native paradise with exotic women for the adventures of mostly male Euro-Americans.[23] It is an image that buoys today's tourist trade.[24]

Second and simultaneously, this noble savage image was distorted to mean an ignoble inhabitant of "the Pagan Islands of the Pacific," in the words of a U.S. evangelical missionary seeking converts.[25]

Third, Westerners perceived the Pacific Islands as a scientific laboratory with its people, plants, and animals as specimens to be scrutinized. This perception began with botanists, artists, and cartographers who accompanied the first white explorers and later inspired Charles Darwin's theories of evolution.[26] Islands proved to be especially instructive because their small, isolated areas "make patterns of evolution stand out starkly," one writer explained. "Islands give clarity to evolution"—and to extinction.[27] The increased role the Pacific Islands came to play in scientific discovery was witnessed by the whole world in 1946 when tests at Bikini Atoll introduced the Atomic Age of unparalleled destructiveness.

Islands also give clarity to the work of humanities and communication scholars.[28] In Hawaii the introduction of the Hawaiian alphabet and the printing press began the transformation of an oral culture to a writing-based one and brought to this communal society the commercialism and imperialism made possible by writing and print. Newspaper historian Helen Chapin noted Harold Innis's theory, discussed in Chapter 1 of this volume, that "print itself is the great colonizer and empire builder."[29]

By 1820 Protestant missionaries from the East Coast had arrived in Hawaii and twenty months later had succeeded in converting spoken Hawaiian words into a seventeen-letter alphabet. The power of the alphabet is its ability to code phonetically in visual symbols the spoken word independent of the language being transcribed.[30] To Westerners, the introduction of writing was essential because of their belief that without writing there is no civilization[31] and thus that oral-tradition peoples were inferior beings. By relying on writing to propagate their religious and cultural messages, the Protestant missionaries embodied in Hawaii two of the biases that later led to negative portrayals of Native Hawaiians in the English-language press founded by their church or by their offspring. These two biases, as detailed in Chapter 1, were the missionaries' sense of religious and mode-of-communication superiorities over Native Hawaiians. Epitomizing these parallel biases was this observation made in 1843 by one of the first U.S. missionary teachers in Hawaii:

As representations to the eye are more vivid and permanent than those communicated to the ear, it may not be useless to insert here the traditional genealogy of the Hawaiian chiefs. The table is, of course, liable to be erroneous, since it is the product of oral tradition and not of written records. There are many traditions relating to these ancient chiefs, but few would be interesting to an English reader.[32]

By 1822 one scholar noted, "Hawaiian had overnight become a written language," and the missionaries had succeeded in printing "a spelling book in the vernacular."[33]

The first impact of transforming the oral language into written form was on education. Traditionally, in Hawaii, knowledge was transmitted apprenticeship style from generation to generation by practice, ritual, and memorization, often with youngsters learning from their elders.[34] But, under the missionaries, learning was transferred to schools and knowledge was transmitted in written or visual form. At first, the missionaries taught adults, especially the Hawaiian chiefs and the upper classes of the hierarchal social order, and then children.

A second impact was the establishment of a Hawaiian-language press. The missionaries shipped their Ramage flatbed to Maui, where it was used to publish the first Hawaiian-language newspaper, *Ka Lama Hawaii*, on February 14, 1834.[35] The paper was used to teach students at the Lahainaluna School, which in turn became the center for training native teachers and other intelligentsia. Other printed materials followed, including commercial Hawaiian-language newspapers. Newspaper articles written by early Native Hawaiians preserved much information about the oral culture.[36] By 1910 nine secular newspapers were published in Hawaiian, by 1920 five were published, by 1930 there were two, and by 1948 there were none.[37] Paralleling the growth of the Hawaiian-language press was the development of English-language newspapers that amplified the missionaries' ethnocentrism. By 1840 *The Polynesian* had been founded by Bostonian James Jarves, who used it to describe Native Hawaiians as racially inferior to whites and to denigrate the Hawaiian culture, saying that it consisted of "only a few misty traditions, oral records of the sensualities and contests of barbarous chiefs."[38] In 1856 Henry M. Whitney, a missionary descendant, founded the *Pacific Commercial Advertiser*. He liked Hawaii and the language, but he disliked Native Hawaiians and detested the hula.[39]

Third, the written Hawaiian language served as a platform that made possible the recording of land transfers and other transactions involving the kingdom, Native Hawaiians, and foreigners that were much too complex to be memorized and retained in the oral-only tradition. By 1840 the missionaries had persuaded the Hawaiian monarchy to adopt a U.S.–styled constitution that ushered in the rule of law used to impose the missionaries' sense of morality, which was applied, for example, to adultery and relations between the sexes. The courts began to define and then enforce the missionaries' version of conduct and lifestyles to which Hawaiian rulers and ruled were expected to adhere, thus sparking a social transformation. The courts promoted this social transformation through a process of changing human behavior that one scholar described as "the criminalization of everyday life."[40] With the advent of Hawaii's newspapers, a circular process began. What happened in Hawaii's courts was used in the newspapers to justify community concern, which led to more assiduous prosecution of what was considered a danger to the community. Thus, the scholar explained, "You had prosecution, concern, prosecution."[41]

Fourth, this sociopolitical transformation coincided with an economic one. In 1843 the missionaries at Lahainaluna also engraved and printed Hawaii's first paper money, creating an alternative that ended the native system of sharing. By 1880 Hawaii was pulled into the U.S. monetary system[42] and then incorporated into a world-system of production.[43] The centerpiece of this economic transformation occurred about 1848 with the *Mahele*, the monarchy's decision to permit undivided Hawaiian communal lands to be cut into individual portions, which paved the way for private property rights that began leaving Native Hawaiians without the economic means to sustain themselves. According to historian Lilikala Kameʻeleihiwa, the *Mahele* proved to be "a tragic historical event, a turning point that had catastrophic negative consequences for Native Hawaiians."[44] By 1886 two-thirds of all government-allotted land was owned by foreigners.[45]

Fifth, noting that the missionaries were among the few foreigners who bothered to learn Hawaiian, language specialist Richard Day explained that paradoxically the missionaries also played an important role in the death of the Hawaiian language. He says in 1854 they switched from their earlier position of advocating teaching in Hawaiian in all public school instruction and instead voted that the government should make "immediate and strenuous efforts to import a knowledge of English language to the natives of these islands."[46]

The missionaries' switch resulted in the near demise of the Hawaiian language so severe that it exemplified "linguistic genocide," which Day defined as "the systematic replacement of an indigenous language with the language of an outside, dominant group, resulting in a permanent language shift and the death of the indigenous language."[47] By 1854 regular government schools taught in English were opened and began to compete with the Hawaiian-language schools for the Department of Education's attention.[48] The number of Hawaiian-language schools and students dropped dramatically until by 1902 there were none.[49] "Hawaiian was strictly forbidden anywhere within school yards or buildings, and physical punishment for using it could be harsh," one researcher wrote. "Teachers were sent to Hawaiian-speaking homes to reprimand parents for speaking Hawaiian to their children."[50]

The decline of the Hawaiian language coincided with the increasing invisibility of Native Hawaiians in their own homeland, largely because of the introduction of new diseases against which the Native Hawaiians had no immunity. By 1853, amidst the *Mahele*, the Native Hawaiian population had been reduced by at least three-quarters.[51] The more than 500,000 pure-blooded Native Hawaiians living in the islands in 1778, when they accounted for 100 percent of the population, decreased by 98.25 percent in the next 215 years until in 1993 they numbered only 8,711, or less than 1 percent of the state population. A documentary informed a national television audience that the number of pure Native Hawaiians in Hawaii would be none by the year 2044.[52] This decline "deepened the feeling of hopeless discouragement in the face of Western culture," one scholar wrote. "The people were dying, the language was dying with the people."[53]

Sixth, a decisive political transformation occurred in 1893 with the overthrow of Queen Liliʻuokalani and the monarchy. The action led to the formation of a new republic, the seizure of all her lands, and the promulgation of a new constitution. The overthrow was led by an oligarchy composed mostly of businessmen, including the sons and grandsons of U.S. missionaries, such as lawyer and soon-to-be newspaper publisher Lorrin Andrews Thurston. Day noted the new "constitution contained a clause which had the effect of requiring voters to be able to read, write, and speak English."[54]

Finally, in 1898, Hawaii was annexed as a territory by a joint resolution of Congress[55] when the Senate was unable to muster the two-thirds vote required by the Constitution for legitimate treaty adopting.[56] The lands seized from the queen five years earlier were handed over to the U.S. government. It is these lands from which the indigenous people more than a century later want to derive more benefit.[57]

In 1900 Hawaii's Organic Act, which served as the governing document for annexation, directed legislators to do their business in English. Thus, this Organic Act "made official what had been happening since the 1820s," Day explained. "The Hawaiian language, in competition with English . . . was relegated to a secondary role in its own homeland."[58]

As another scholar summed it up, the "result of annexation was the total appropriation of the Hawaiian islands by American economic and political interests."[59]

Also in 1898, at the end of the Spanish-American War, Guam passed from Spanish to American control. Soon the missionaries from the same Boston-based interdenominational agency that had converted so many Native Hawaiians arrived on Guam. By 1901 the first Protestant mission and church had been founded on the island where many had already been converted to Catholicism.[60] The story of the Chamorros in Guam losing their language to English is similar to the story of the Native Hawaiians.[61] In 1922, one scholar reported, "Chamorro was prohibited on school grounds and Chamorro dictionaries were collected and burned."[62]

By 1921, when the Native Hawaiians were losing the battle to save their cultural distinctiveness, the U.S. government set aside homestead lands for persons of at least 50 percent Hawaiian blood. These lands, amounting to at least 188,000 acres, gave rise to small enclaves of Native Hawaiians fortunate enough to receive awards. But, in 1990, fewer than 3,800 families reside, farm, or ranch only 17.5 percent of the lands originally set aside. More than 19,000 Native Hawaiians are on the waiting list. And at least 62 percent of the land is used for nonhomestead purposes, mostly by nonbeneficiaries.[63]

The steep decline in the number of the pure-blooded indigenous Hawaiians also resulted from the rise in the number of marriages outside the pure native strain so that by 1920 the number of part-Hawaiians had begun to increase.[64] Most Native Hawaiians now are of mixed ethnicity. The 1980 U.S. Census listed 115,500 Native Hawaiians—or 12 percent of the state's population—and the 1990 federal census listed 138,742—or 12.5 percent of the state's population.[65] Native Hawaiians are a minority in their own homeland.

On May 11, 1922, two radio stations, both owned by Honolulu's two dailies, broadcast commercially for the first time. By Christmas of 1930, for the first time, a Hawaiian program was transmitted internationally when a ten-minute holiday segment was sent by short wave to California.[66] Radio in Hawaii also played a vital role in the historical development of Hawaiian music.[67]

A fourth image of Native Hawaiians developed suddenly in 1931 with the news of what Chapin called "the most famous crime case in Hawaii."[68] It began as an alleged rape of Thalia Massie, the twenty-year-old wife of a U.S. Navy officer and daughter of a U.S. socialite, on September 12, 1931. She told police she was raped by young Hawaiian men; she later identified five. Honolulu newspapers described them as gangsters and degenerates. A jury deadlocked, declining to convict the defendants. While another trial was pending, one of the defendants, a Hawaiian named Joseph Kahahawai, was found murdered. Thalia Massie's husband and mother were charged with the murder. The trial was covered—often sensationally with racist overtones—by New York newspaper reporters, among others. Found guilty and sentenced to up to ten years in prison, the defendants served only one hour of time—amidst a festive atmosphere in the chambers of Governor Lawrence Judd, who years later said he had been pressured by persons in Washington, D.C., to release them. The Japanese-English newspaper *Hawaii Hochi* wrote that Native Hawaiians "are asking whether Hawaii, their own homeland, is now safe for Hawaiians!"[69]

The Massie affair coincided with the 1931 Scottsboro Boys landmark case in which nine young African-American men were accused of raping two white women and barely escaped lynching by a posse in Alabama. The men were tried for rape—one woman later admitted she had lied—and were convicted by all-white male juries.[70] One scholar noted that the cry of rape of a white woman was often used to justify mob violence and even lynching of black men because "white women were the forbidden fruit, the untouchable property, the ultimate symbol of white male power."[71]

As journalism scholar Helen Benedict summarized,

One of the most pervasive traditions of the mainstream press is to assume that crime against whites is newsworthy while crime against blacks and other minorities is not. The result of this racism is twofold: rapes by black men against white women receive a disproportionate amount of coverage, even though they represent only four to twenty percent of rapes in this country; the rapes of black women are largely overlooked, even though they are significantly more likely to be raped than women of any other race.[72]

1934 FEDERAL COMMUNICATIONS ACT TO PEARL HARBOR ATTACK, DECEMBER 7, 1941

No scholarly research was found about U.S. mainstream news coverage of Pacific Islanders on Guam, American Samoa, or Midway during this pre–World War II period. But a 1995 study examined coverage of Native Hawaiians in the *Honolulu Advertiser* from 1934 to 1990, the last sample year the newspaper was owned and published by descendants of the first Protestant missionaries to Hawaii.

The study showed that, in 1934, a century after Hawaii's first newspaper was published, the Native Hawaiians were nearly invisible in the pages of the successor of the oldest existing English-language daily in the Hawaiian Islands, the *Honolulu Advertiser.* For example, in 1934 and 1938, the study found, each of the twenty-eight newspapers sampled devoted to Native Hawaiians an average of four column inches,[73] out of approximately 815 column inches of news content in each newspaper.[74]

1941 PEARL HARBOR ATTACK TO ATOMIC BOMBING OF HIROSHIMA, AUGUST 6, 1945

The bombing of Pearl Harbor on Sunday, December 7, 1941, made Hawaii and other Pacific Islands a dateline for bulletins worldwide, but it resulted in little coverage of the native peoples. "The press during the war covered the Pacific, but they didn't cover the Pacific Islanders," one specialist in the region explained. "These were the forgotten people."[75]

As the Japanese warplanes departed the smoldering Honolulu skyline, word of the attack reached Manila. Nine hours later, waves of Imperial Japanese warplanes knocked out the Far East Air Force that the United States had counted on to defend the Philippines, and on Christmas Eve General Douglas MacArthur prepared to evacuate Manila.[76]

On Guam, no commercial radio or newspaper existed to flash the Pearl Harbor news to local residents. Later that day, Japanese bombers attacked and, on December 10, thousands of Japanese forces arrived. The governor surrendered, Americans were taken prisoner, and Guamanians began thirty months of Japanese rule.

Although the most bitter fighting of World War II often occurred in the Pacific region, the news media and later historians seldom included information about the effects of wartime operations on local people.[77] Yet some Japanese-held areas were subjected to U.S. saturation bombing that is reported to have caused many civilian casualties.[78] The concentration of fire directed at Kwajalein Atoll exceeded any other artillery barrage in both world wars.[79] U.S. servicemen were widely accepted on these islands. They were friendly and thus upset the European prewar colonialists' code of racial separation and superiority.[80]

Although the U.S. news media may have forgotten the Pacific Islanders, military photographers did not. A scholarly fifty-year retrospective of Pacific Islanders, as portrayed in military and official archival photographs, provides insights into what might have been newsworthy enough to cover. The cultural-studies researchers noted that World War II was the best documented of any war and that "never before had so many cameras, in so many places, been pointed at Pacific Islanders doing so many things."[81] Ironically, researchers indicated, given the inhumanity of the Pacific War in particular, "Most pictures during World War II that included nonsoldiers did so to underscore the humanity of the American GIs."[82] The researchers noted that "the photographic record is also largely silent on the experiences of villagers, especially women and children, who often supported, and more often suffered, the war effort.'' The islanders were most often photographed in the supporting role of loyal helpers. ''Brave scouts and hardworking laborers both fit this image and received significant attention from the wartime myth-machines,'' researchers explained. ''Villagers who suffered bombing, dislocation, and starvation did not.''[83]

In Hawaii, within hours after the bombing of Pearl Harbor, news media were placed under historic, unique martial law. Martial law in Hawaii was the first time that U.S. military forces governed an unconquered U.S. area, in effect treating the islands as ''occupied enemy territory,'' communication scholar Jim Richstad wrote, and controlling all government functions except the federal courts. ''Constitutional rights vanished, and the press was caught in the tide.''[84] Aspects of this martial law were held unconstitutional in 1946.[85] The press was under martial law controls for almost the entire war and required licensing from the military for almost half the war.[86] Licensing involved deciding which publications and radio stations were permitted to operate, a practice one authority called a direct violation of the First Amendment and a practice the English ended in 1694.[87]

The military in Hawaii censored all that was published in the territory, including cookbooks. Unlike voluntary censorship, under which the continental U.S. press complained,[88] Hawaii's variety prohibited publication of news items of general interest that were related to the rule of the military government as well as items about the conduct of the war.[89]

The *Advertiser*'s coverage of Native Hawaiians in 1942 during the days of censorship is illuminating for both its quantity and its content.[90] Quantitatively, a content analysis of fourteen randomly selected issues in 1942 found that the *Honolulu Advertiser* published nine news items about Native Hawaiians. These nine items totaled 155 column inches, or an average of 11 column inches devoted to Native Hawaiians in each paper out of about 867 column inches of news in each paper. This 1942 coverage of Native Hawaiians was nearly three times more than in the 1930s and far more than in some of the sampled postwar years.[91] Four photographs—two of them supplied by the U.S. military—accounted for the bulk of the coverage of Native Hawaiians. Each photograph showed U.S. servicemen being entertained, often by several female hula dancers in grass skirts. Strikingly missing from the photos were Hawaiian men.

The martial-law censorship went far beyond news of military consequence, however. Other news deemed unfit to print involved the prostitution that accompanied martial-law rule.[92] This censorship rendered invisible the illegal, exploitive relations between the mostly Caucasian servicemen and nonwhite women.[93] Two scholars who researched prostitution in wartime Hawaii wrote, '' 'Shack-jobs' were common with local women, especially those of Hawaiian or Filipino descent.''[94]

One of the harshest critics of martial law and the licensing of the press was J. Garner Anthony, who was appointed territorial attorney general in the fall of

1942. In a report he prepared for the governor, he charged that the press was not permitted to print certain kinds of news—unrelated directly to the war effort—such as news about prostitution and crime. Richstad also found that the Honolulu newspapers mostly "acted as if prostitution did not exist."[95]

Not until June 17, 1943, after the lifting of licensing constraints on the press, did Honolulu's newspapers begin reporting incidents related to local prostitution.[96] But even when the *Star-Bulletin* began news coverage and editorial-page campaigning about prostitution, the *Advertiser* did not, because publisher Lorrin P. Thurston considered prostitution "a necessary evil with so many military men stationed in Hawaii."[97]

The close cooperation between the press and the military was reflected in Thurston's background. He had been in the military intelligence reserve since World War I, was close to the island intelligence work, and in November 1942 was appointed as public relations adviser to the military governor.[98] Richstad quoted Thurston as describing the cooperation with the military this way: "We all worked closely together," Thurston said. "We were all so accustomed to working together that it didn't take long to learn what they wanted and what they didn't want."[99]

A highly visible strike by Honolulu prostitutes illustrated news suppression. During the first year of the war, prostitutes were confined to living near Honolulu's Chinatown section. But then they demanded the right to live where they pleased in Honolulu and organized a twenty-two-day strike, Richstad reported, adding, "It was possibly the first organized prostitutes' strike anywhere, but the Honolulu newspapers did not carry a word about it for more than two years."[100]

Anthony described the press omissions graphically: "Honolulu was treated to the spectacle of a three weeks' strike by prostitutes who picketed the police station and the office of the military governor with placards announcing their grievances. Nothing appeared in the press in regard to this incident."[101]

1945 ATOMIC BOMBING OF HIROSHIMA TO LITTLE ROCK INTEGRATION, SEPTEMBER 1957

In the postwar era, U.S. jurisdiction expanded to cover other Pacific Islanders. The United States expanded its control in the Marshall Islands beyond Guam to include Bikini and Enewetak; it added the nearby archipelagos of the Carolines and the Marianas. But Pacific Islanders under U.S. jurisdiction, including Native Hawaiians, remained largely invisible in the postwar mainstream media even though the region remained the center of history-making events.

Ten months after the atomic bombing of Hiroshima and Nagasaki ended World War II, the Pacific Islands became what one scholar described as a "nuclear playground."[102] On July 1, 1946, the United States conducted the fourth nuclear explosion in history at Bikini Atoll, some 2,000 miles southwest of Hawaii in the Marshall Islands of the central Pacific. In the thirteen years that followed, the U.S. military conducted sixty-five additional nuclear tests at Bikini

Atoll and at neighboring Enewetak.[103] It also conducted a dozen upper-atmosphere tests at Johnston Island, 800 miles southwest of Honolulu, which Hawaii's tourists and residents could view from Waikiki. After one test, a Thor missile exploded on the launch pad, spewing plutonium into the environment.[104] As one medical doctor explained, "Plutonium lives for 500,000 years and is so toxic that one-millionth of a gram is carcinogenic."[105]

Like all oral-tradition peoples, the Bikinians had deep ties to their land. A scarce resource on volcanic islands and on atolls like Bikini,[106] land largely defined their lifestyle and linked them with their ancestors.[107] The Bikinians' land consisted of twenty-six islands with a total land area of 2.32 square miles that enclosed a lagoon of about 243 square miles. On March 7, 1946, the 261 inhabitants of Bikini Atoll were relocated due to scheduled nuclear testing. For the next half-century, they became nuclear nomads,[108] as they remain today.

Scholars have not systematically studied U.S. news coverage of these Pacific Islanders. But news coverage is sometimes assessed in the voluminous scholarly literature on the early U.S. nuclear tests in the Marshall Islands through the 1960s. Discussed below is the news coverage of three key tests: the first two Operations Crossroads atomic tests held on July 1 and July 25, 1946, and the Bravo hydrogen-bomb test held on March 1, 1954.

Scholarly literature indicates that U.S. news coverage of the Bikinians vacillated between two poles—star status and periods of invisibility. The Bikinians' star status sprang from their forced migration[109] from their homes. But beyond that, an analysis of the scholarly assessments suggests three broad shortcomings of the U.S. news coverage of the three historic experiments that affected Marshall Islanders: (1) failure to ask the most significant question at the right time, (2) failure to follow up on the effects of radiation on human beings, principally Pacific Islanders, and on the environment, and (3) failure of East Coast news organizations to cover the Marshall Islanders' story even when that story was told on the media's home turf in Washington, D.C., before Congress. Only a few antiadministration stories were reported by the media, and those were the result of news leaks.

In Washington, in early 1946, journalists neglected to ask the most significant question of U.S. officials—why should Operation Crossroads be held at all, thus necessitating the forced migration of the Bikinians? The first Crossroads test at Bikini Atoll, dubbed Able, consisted of the military's A-bombing ninety-five battleships—then the size of the world's fifth largest navy—to prove that atomic warfare could not destroy the effectiveness of a naval task force and thus would not render the U.S. Navy obsolete. Few journalists questioned the necessity for the test, although a resolution to cancel the test was introduced in the Senate, and supporting senators noted that leading atomic scientists opposed the proposed detonations.[110] Instead news reporters and columnists covered to the hilt the postwar interservice rivalries that were the driving force behind the testing. Some journalists portrayed the tests as being a conflict between the U.S. Navy and the atomic bomb.[111] Syndicated columnists Joseph and Stewart Alsop warned of "another grim struggle between Navy and Air Forces."[112] Ironically, as lawyer-historian Jonathan M. Weisgall noted, the military factions did agree with the atomic scientists that industrial sites rather than ships would be more likely sites for enemy A-bombs.[113]

Such an unquestioning beginning by the press facilitated what researchers described as "an intensive media buildup,"[114] with government public relations specialists setting the tone for press coverage of the nuclear experiments soon after Bikini Atoll was picked as the A-bomb test site. According to these researchers, "With the mass media uncritically relaying the military's line, the public image of Operations Crossroads became one of self-defense and even humanitarianism." Publicists were responsible for "defining the formative notions of atomic weapons for most citizens," researchers noted. "Motivations for U.S. atomic tests were increasingly depicted as benign, circumscribed, and well-meaning."[115]

The press often echoed this line. *Newsweek* headlined a preview with "Significance: The Good That May Come from the Tests at Bikini."[116] But, researchers noted, "missing from the press billing of Operation Crossroads were any serious suggestions that subjects of the atomic test experiments included human beings,"[117] such as those indigenous people removed from their ancestral homelands.

One exception was the *Los Angeles Daily News*, which headlined its editorial: "The Lunatics at Bikini."[118] The editorial, which sympathized with the Bikinians, indicated that U.S. officials were duping "this unsuspecting, troubled race of men for whom the world already holds so much more than they can understand."[119]

About four months before the July 1 test, the forced migration of the Bikinians from their home islands thrust them onto the world's center stage in what Weisgall called "a major media event."[120]

Popular photographic magazines such as *Life* and *National Geographic* gave the Bikinians and the tests much space. The *New York Times* gave the Bikinians more attention in photographs than in text. For example, one *Times* photograph showed King Juda of Bikini in military uniform next to a U.S. Naval officer who was explaining the relocation process. The photo overline read, "His Kingdom Is at Stake," and the caption described the officer's talking with "King Juda of Bikini Atoll."[121] But Juda was not a king,[122] and military uniform was not his normal attire. Significantly, a *Life* photographer, providing the first documentary evidence that the Bikinians considered their relocation to be temporary, reported that the islanders had told him "that they would come back to Bikini someday."[123]

With the arrival of commercial newsreel teams and a Navy photographic crew, one scholar noted, the "Bikinians had learned the meaning of the motion picture camera and were enjoying the novelty of posing for photographers."[124] The military governor's negotiations with the people were reenacted for the photographers, and at a later date the negotiations were again staged at least eight times for the Navy's newsreel cameramen.[125]

Later in U.S. movie theaters, newsreels, using footage the Navy and others had so carefully filmed, showed scenes of daily life on Rongerik, including the community singing its version of "You Are My Sunshine." A California film studio that was assisting the Navy to garner favorable public perceptions about its treatment of the Bikinians helped script the newsreels, which followed the publicist's recommended narration about how the U.S. military "showed such great care and humane treatment in the evacuation."[126]

Navy officials served as the spokesmen for the Bikinians, and accounts given to the press often masked the sorrow the Bikinians later expressed to researchers and others. The Navy had mounted a campaign in the press to state that the Bikinians were actually going to be much better off in their new home on the island of Rongerik, 140 miles east of their atoll. For example, one Associated Press story quoted a Navy spokesman indicating that the move was actually a blessing in disguise, thus drowning out the islanders' expressions of homesickness. Weisgall noted that the press continued to follow the Navy line, and "reporters were not permitted access to the Bikinians except in the presence of Navy officials, so the islanders' unhappiness on Rongerik was not taken seriously."[127]

For example, a *New York Times* article titled "The Strange People of Bikini" said, in a two-column subhead, "Primitive they are, but they love one another and the American visitors who took their home."[128] That article, published in the Sunday magazine section, was illustrated with a two-column photograph of the U.S. flag being raised over a building. The article carried the byline of a Navy lieutenant, junior grade.[129] A small bold-faced box said the Bikinians "will probably be repatriated if they insist on it, though the United States military authorities say they can't see why they should want to: Bikini and Rongerik look as alike as two Idaho potatoes."[130]

The Navy arranged for 168 newsmen to visit Bikini. It was an all-male corps, chosen from 6,000 press requests.[131] Those reporting from Bikini included the best print and radio reporters of the era.[132] The most influential reporter covering the emerging Atomic Age was William L. Laurence, of the *New York Times*, described by several researchers as "an enthusiastic promoter of the sunny side of the atom."[133] Laurence criticized those scientists who questioned Operation Crossroads, and, among correspondents, Weisgall explained, "dissenters either agreed with Laurence or dropped out of the inner circle of reporters."[134]

The Navy's chief press officer found the overall result of the coverage was beneficial to the government's interests.[135] Journalists met with Crossroads officials only at mob press conferences. "A petition by thirty correspondents asking for permission to speak to scientists in small groups or one-on-one was turned down," Weisgall wrote. "The Navy had opened up the tests to reporters, but strictly on its terms."[136]

Even so, when *Newsweek* quoted a senior admiral who made the rare public admission that some humans "might yet be overexposed to radiation," researchers found that the statement received no substantive news media follow-up.[137]

At fourteen seconds before 9 A.M. on July 1, with live radio broadcasting around the world, the fourth atomic bomb in history was dropped. A voice over the radio implored: "Listen world, this is Crossroads!"[138] The detonation was anticlimactic for newsmen, however, partly because the Navy had given onlookers such darkly tinted glasses that they could barely see the flash, leading some to write that the test had been a dud.[139]

Three weeks later, on July 25, the second Crossroads test, dubbed Baker, was held, and "it was truly a spectacle beyond imagination," Weisgall wrote. It was the world's first underwater test—one that had been opposed by many scientists. It created so much radioactivity over such an immense area that years later it was called "America's Chernobyl."[140] Unaware of the longevity of radiation, the Navy ordered sailors to scrub down the contaminated vessels.[141] By the time dangerous radioactivity levels had forced the Navy to leave the test site, most reporters had already departed.[142]

"The Baker shot had revealed the true dimensions of fallout as a biological weapon of terror, but the media and the military had focused more on the instant effects of the bomb on the target ships," Weisgall noted.[143]

In Honolulu, the mainstream press covered the first atomic tests nonchalantly. In 1947, on the anniversary of the bombing of Pearl Harbor, the commercial newspapers ran U.S. Navy photos of evacuated Bikini children. The accompanying caption described them as "pretty husky and happy and much like happy-go-lucky Hawaiian children when they were asked to smile for the photographer."[144]

But the Bikinians were far from happy. Their wretched living conditions on Rongerik were exposed by the news media—due to a leak. In mid-1947, a critical Navy evaluation was leaked to newspaper columnist Harold Ickes, who had resigned as President Harry Truman's secretary of interior. "The natives are actually and literally dying of starvation," he wrote, describing them as "forgotten." He accused the Navy of "arrogant injustice to a native people," and said their plight was "an international question."[145] The column caused an uproar. Eventually, the Bikinians returned home for five years; then medical tests indicated that they had to be moved again. By then, they "may have ingested the largest amounts of radioactive material of any known population."[146] Fifty years after Operation Crossroads, they live on an island without a lagoon or fishing area, which forced them to change to a farming-based lifestyle.[147]

In summing up media performance, Weisgall wrote, "For reporters and the public, the story of Operation Crossroads was the heat, blast, and tally of sunken ships, but the real story was the powerful, uncontrollable—and invisible—radiation."[148]

Other researchers explained, "The limitation of visible physical impact was in the spotlight; little attention was devoted to invisible radioactive fallout,"[149] including its impact on the heavily exposed Marshall Islanders. In fact, the researchers indicated, "American media eagerly lacquered events even indirectly linked to the atomic test with thick coats of patriotic heroism."[150]

Eight years after Baker, on March 1, 1954, testing returned to Bikini when the even more disastrous Bravo test was conducted—the first U.S. test of a hydrogen bomb delivered by aircraft. It was the largest nuclear test ever conducted by the United States,[151] equal to the force of 750 Hiroshima bombs.[152] So dangerous it could not be exploded in the continental United States,[153] the bomb was designed to catch up with the Soviets who, in August 1953, had exploded their first hydrogen bomb that could be delivered by aircraft. As Weisgall wrote, the Bravo bomb "created a fireball nearly four miles wide that literally vaporized the entire test island and parts of two others," with "serious-to-lethal radioactivity falling over an area almost equal in size to the entire state of Massachusetts."[154]

Included in those receiving the fallout—what the Japanese term *shi no hai* or "ashes of death"[155]—were twenty-eight U.S. servicemen and 236 inhabitants of Rongelap and Utrik atolls. All were moved two and three days later. U.S. officials at first kept the evacuation secret, according to Weisgall. But when a Cincinnati newspaper broke the news—based on the letter of a sailor who wrote to it—officials explained that "during the course of a routine atomic test," some Marshallese "were unexpectedly exposed to some radioactivity" but that "there were no burns" and "all are reported well."[156]

The *New York Times* carried an Associated Press article on the official evacuation on the front page and below the fold. The story added without attribution, "Exposure to mild radiation is not necessarily dangerous." Reaction to that story was recalled later by the head of the U.S. medical team sent immediately after the Bravo test to treat Marshallese. In an interview four decades later with a presidentially appointed committee, he said he told Lewis Strauss, the chairman of the Atomic Energy Commission in 1954, of his concern that the *New York Times* and others had reported a "downright lie" by saying that the fallout hazard was minimal.[157] The doctor recalled Strauss's response: "Young man, you have to remember that nobody reads yesterday's newspapers."[158]

Instead of minimal fallout, Weisgall wrote, within days the islanders developed "the classic symptoms of radiation poisoning—hair loss, skin lesions, and lowered white blood cell counts."[159] Years later, in 1982, U.S. officials admitted that "acute radiation effects" were observed among some people contaminated by the fallout and that Bravo was, in the words of the Defense Nuclear Agency, "the worst single incident of fallout exposures in all the U.S. atmospheric testing program."[160]

Also receiving Bravo's fallout were twenty-three crewmen of a Japanese fishing boat, the *Lucky Dragon*. One scholar reported that the crewmen made Bravo "an international scandal."[161] Seven months later, one crewman died from the effects of the radiation.

Six hours before the test, U.S. officials knew that the winds had shifted, putting the islanders in the fallout pattern, but they proceeded with the detonation anyway. That information—plus the time lag of several days before the U.S. ships evacuated the islanders—later led an Australian documentary to suggest that U.S. officials had deliberately used the Marshallese as human guinea pigs.[162]

Over the years, others told Congress the same thing, but those grievances received virtually no news coverage even when voiced on the home turf of the East Coast press.[163] For example, Weisgall, acting as the legal counsel to the Bikinians, told a U.S. House subcommittee in Washington, D.C., on May 4, 1984, "[T]he crime of Bravo, and I do not use that term lightly, is that the U.S. Government knew in advance of the shot that the winds were headed in the wrong direction. The explanation about the unpredicted wind shift is a lie."[164] In the same hearing, former magistrate of Rongelap Atoll, John Anjain, reminded the committee of the importance of the islanders to the accumulation of U.S. medical knowledge over decades. He told House members of the findings of the Brookhaven medical team that had regularly examined the islanders: "The medical findings provide the *only* knowledge about the effects of radioactive fallout on human beings from detonation of nuclear devices."[165]

Four years earlier, in a 1980 report titled "The Forgotten Guinea Pigs," the House oversight subcommittee included—in a footnote—the Pacific Islanders in its conclusion: "The greatest irony of our atmospheric nuclear testing program is that the only victims of U.S. nuclear arms since World War II have been our own people." The *New York Times* carried a story on the committee report—thought to be the first Congressional study in twenty years on the effects of the testing—and the story carried this quote, but without mentioning the Pacific Islanders.[166] The subcommittee also found that all evidence suggesting radiation was having harmful effects on people or animals "was not only disregarded but actually suppressed" by the U.S. government. Moreover, it noted, the U.S. government had refused to collect data, as proposed by the U.S. Public Health Service, that would have confirmed the adverse health effects of radiation on people and animals.[167]

In October 1995, the Advisory Committee on Human Radiation Experiments, appointed by President William Clinton, "found no evidence that the initial exposure of the Rongelapese or their later relocation constituted a deliberate human experiment." But the committee did note the difficulties the Marshallese have had in obtaining information related to their own health, adding that "their own medical records are only now being made readily available to them."[168]

Bravo set off a huge debate within the United States and internationally. Massive, regional fallout from the test and the furor in Japan caused by the sickness experienced by the *Lucky Dragon*'s crew and the possible contamination of seafood revealed to the world the dangers of radiation the press had failed to cover during the Baker test eight years earlier, Weisgall reported. He added that Bravo finally revealed to "the American public and the world the realization that the killing power of radioactive fallout from a thermonuclear bomb greatly exceeds the fiery blast and heat of the direct explosion that causes it."[169] In mid-1996, the Rongelap people surviving Bravo were living on Majetto Island in Kwajelein Atoll, afraid to return to their radioactive homeland.

In Hawaii, after the fallout and radiation dangers revealed by the 1954 Bravo test, the shortcomings of Honolulu's mainstream newspaper coverage of nuclear issues became glaring. Newspaper historian Chapin made a close reading of the press and then contrasted the performance of Honolulu's two dailies with that of the University of Hawaii's student-run newspaper. Again, the adverse effects of nuclear testing on Marshall Islanders—and others in the Pacific Basin—were ignored by the mainstream press.[170]

In the aftermath of the Bravo test, Chapin found, "the low level of mainstream press discourse" was spotlighted by the more distinguished performance of the university's student-produced newspaper, *Ka Leo O Hawaii*. She described *Ka Leo* as "among the few truly independent papers in the Islands' history."[171]

In contrasting the establishment press with the student newspaper, she found that, in 1958, *Ka Leo* provided "the most independent coverage" about a post-Bravo major nuclear testing protest. With evenhanded news coverage, antinuclear opposition by outsiders going into the Pacific Basin could have helped to spotlight the medical and other problems of the Marshall Islanders. The protest occurred when two small ships visited Hawaii en route to the Pacific nuclear testing grounds to protest experiments. Chapin found *Ka Leo* was "among the few local newspapers to let divergent voices speak in the news section" and to reserve opinion for the editorial page. It did so "in the face of an enormous public relations effort on the part of various government agencies to make nuclear testing palatable."[172]

Chapin's assessment of the contrasting coverage by the commercial newspapers and by *Ka Leo* of the two protest ships is instructive. She found:

1. Trivialization versus manufacturing news. "Establishment papers trivialized what was a bold idea," Chapin noted, when on April 8, 1958, the *Golden Rule*, a thirty-foot ketch, stopped in Honolulu en route to the Enewetak nuclear testing zone. "In the grand tradition of local photojournalism, the commercial press threw an aura of tourism over the subject, posing the *Golden Rule* and crew at Ala Wai Yacht Harbor against a Diamond Head background."[173] In contrast, she noted, the *Ka Leo* staff arranged for the crew members to speak to the student body, thus generating its own news, and gave them extensive front-page coverage.

2. Superficiality versus enterprise reporting. Reporters for the establishment press only superficially addressed the reasons behind the protests. In contrast, *Ka Leo*'s extensive story with the headline "Men, a Boat, an Ocean and a Principle" summarized the crew's mission. She explained, "It gave background information omitted by the daily press."[174] Another student interviewed two university presidents, past and present, and reported their differing views. One, former president Gregg Sinclair, was unconvinced of the danger of radiation in the atmosphere. Chapin explained that "President

Laurence Snyder, who developed the first course in medical genetics to be required in a medical school in the U.S. and had served as president of the American Association for Advancement of Science, had another view: he knew that nuclear testing caused genetic harm and thought that testing would eventually have to be stopped by all countries."[175] *Ka Leo* also printed letters to the editor on both sides of the issue, sponsored a debate between students and faculty, and conducted a campuswide opinion poll, reporting that opinion was "split" on the necessity of continued testing.

3. Placement. The placement of stories in establishment newspapers violated objectivity and reinforced editorial opinion. For example, a *Star-Bulletin* front-pager on April 24, 1958, juxtaposed the headline "Court Blocks Sailing of Golden Rule" and "U.S. Intercontinental Missile Is Hurled 5,000 Miles." In contrast, *Ka Leo* gave the front page of its tabloid to coverage of the *Golden Rule's* mission.[176]

Chapin found the following four deficiencies in mainstream news coverage of the *Golden Rule*:

1. *Labeling*. Mainstream newspapers in their news columns described the crew as "pacifist" and they did little to explain the principle of civil disobedience, "an idea as old as the Boston Tea Party."[177]

2. *Asking loaded questions*. Chapin found that the reporters asked such loaded questions of the crew as "Why weren't crew members opposed to Russian testing? Didn't Americans have to catch up to Russian tests? Why were the crew 'pacifists'?"[178]

3. *Failing to go beyond official sources*. The dailies reported opposition to testing only if doubters held prominent positions, such as Territorial legislator Patsy Mink, who decried "public apathy" upon the arrival of the *Golden Rule* and asked people "to stop and think."[179] Earlier, when the results of Bravo's H-bomb tests moved closer to Hawaii—and as radiation victims were flown to a hospital in Honolulu for checking—"the dailies, with little comment, printed official releases aimed at allaying public fears, such as the Board of Health's assurance that the Hawaiian Islands were 'safe from contamination.' "[180]

4. *Resorting to guilt by association in editorials*. The commercial press in an editorial said that the "Red Chinese already hail the Quakers as heroes for peace, which puts the American voyagers in very bad company indeed."[181]

Thus, in contrast to the mainstream dailies, Chapin concluded, "Recognizing the need for fairness toward a subject of such importance, it was *Ka Leo* that responsibly addressed the 'stop and think' plea, sought objectivity in content and placement, and achieved a leadership role in questioning knee-jerk patriotism."[182]

In Hawaii, the end of World War II also witnessed military servicemen returning to their home islands. But, as one influential Hawaiian scholar observed, in the justified publicity given to the highly decorated units of Americans of Japanese ancestry, "the Hawaiian and part-Hawaiian servicemen went almost unnoticed."[183]

The post–World War II era also saw the beginning of the arrival of jet planeloads of tourists, "primed by advertising."[184] Interestingly, 1950 was the year in which the *Honolulu Advertiser* printed the most news items and the greatest average column inches about Native Hawaiians for each newspaper coded from 1934 through 1990.[185] News coverage of tourist-related activities accounted for some of the increased emphasis. Examples were extensive photographic coverage and an editorial given to the Kamehameha Day pageant and festivities named for Hawaii's first king.[186] Also accounting for more coverage were numerous short items published under a standing column titled "From our Files." This column described such bygone events as the closing of a Hawaiian seminary, sanitary instructions for Native Hawaiians, and "native" women being charged with practicing kahuna-ism—or the Hawaiians' animistic-type religion.

The postwar era also brought television to Hawaii.[187] No scholarly literature assessing early television news coverage of the Pacific Islanders was found. In 1948 the last secular Hawaiian-language newspaper closed, leaving only one religious newspaper published in that language.[188] The military in Hawaii in the 1950s became the leading industry, edging out sugar and pineapple production. By the 1960s the new industry of tourism had surpassed that of sugar production.[189]

1957 LITTLE ROCK INTEGRATION TO NIXON'S RESIGNATION, AUGUST 9, 1974

Hawaii was admitted as the nation's fiftieth state in 1959, overcoming the opposition of members of Congress who objected to including more non-Caucasians within the nation or who remembered the Massie-case specter of imperiled Navy wives and of endangered prospects for self-government.[190] In Hawaii the final vote was nearly seventeen to one in favor of statehood. In contrast, the *Honolulu Advertiser* carried a front-page story saying that persons on the privately owned island of Niihau, which is almost exclusively populated by Native Hawaiians, voted against statehood by a four-to-one margin, the only one of the state's 240 precincts to reject statehood[191] and the state's only predominantly Native Hawaiian precinct. Statehood also meant the transfer from the United States to the state government of those lands that had once belonged to the Hawaiian monarchy.

During this period, the mainstream news media initially left coverage of the plight of the Native Hawaiians to what Chapin called the opposition newspapers. Integral to Hawaiian history, Chapin explained, this category of press has included newspapers published in languages other than English that served Native Hawaiians, Samoans, and other ethnic groups. Since the 1960s this opposition press produced counterculture papers that challenged and changed conventional U.S. values such as supporting environmentally damaging projects.[192]

Noting that "a paradoxical quality of the American press is that it fosters dissent,"[193] Chapin indicated that, by the mid-1850s, Native Hawaiians and sympathizers with the indigenous culture had created a Hawaiian nationalist press that resisted U.S. political and economic domination. This press was 100 years ahead of its time, but its arguments resurfaced in the late 1960s "to force discussion of sovereignty into the mainstream press and successfully modify the latter's opinion."[194]

In the 1960s these opposition newspapers were "an effective organizing tool for grassroots groups coming together with a renewed sense of cultural identity," she explained. "A different political climate meant that the establishment press, although initially resistant, came to view the Hawaiian cause with some sympathy."[195]

As an example, Chapin detailed the Kalama Valley issue that was downplayed by the establishment press but was publicized by opposition publications as "a problem of concentrated land ownership that was contributing to the urbanization of Oahu and the dispossession of Hawaiians from their land."[196] In 1970 *Hawaii Free People's Press* exposed the disappearing rural life of Native Hawaiians and others in the Kalama Valley, where industrialist Henry Kaiser planned to develop 6,000 acres of land into 4,300 homesites, shopping centers, golf courses, hotels, and restaurants.[197]

But the protest lost and the valley was developed. Chapin found the mainstream papers mostly repeated the establishment line that the residents, who had been served eviction notices, were "trespassers."[198]

Chapin credited Native Hawaiian reporter Pierre Bowman with writing especially sensitive articles for the *Honolulu Star-Bulletin*, noting it is a matter "of record that the major dailies over two centuries have employed very few Hawaiian journalists."[199]

"Bowman's approach to Kalama Valley shows the ambiguities of being in the pay of the establishment while one's heart remains with the victims," Chapin explained. To Bowman the resisters were "gentle rebels" attacking the roots of the social and economic structure of "the new plantation," she wrote, adding that "Bowman's coverage contributed to public awareness and won adherents for future confrontations over land and water issues throughout the Islands."[200] Simultaneously, "an obvious shift" in the viewpoint of the mainstream press occurred. Chapin noted that the *Advertiser* recognized "the special problems of Hawaiians" and proposed giving "serious thought to land use in the Islands."[201] Between 1970 and 1971, the two dailies doubled the number of articles published on the evictions and gave more prominent placement of articles.[202] Later, the mainstream press helped to defeat other development proposals.[203]

The Kalama Valley struggle, even though unsuccessful, set the stage for what one Hawaiian Studies scholar described as "a cultural flowering" for Native Hawaiians so that "along with the push for a land base came the growth of cultural pride"[204] and of the Hawaiian language.

Meanwhile, as post–Vietnam War military expenditures decreased, Hawaii's reliance on tourism gradually increased, accompanied by fresh objections about the media. One Hawaiian Studies scholar criticized "TV and radio propaganda" disseminated by commercial broadcasting and daily newspaper advertisements, both of which were viewed as the main channels for the tourist industry.[205] Moreover, in the news and feature sections of the Honolulu dailies, postcard-like photographs were often published of Hawaiian women performing the hula[206] with captions suggesting parallels with postcards created for tourists.[207] Such postcard depictions and captions were severely criticized by an art historian because they tended to render Native Hawaiians timeless. She said this time-lessness denied Native Hawaiians "the historical importance and context of the dance"[208] and extracted them from their native culture in which the dance was used for religious and ritualistic purposes, not to entertain tourists.

A popular editorial-page column on Hawaiian heritage was also cut back from the *Honolulu Star-Bulletin* shortly after that daily was sold to the Gannett Cor-poration in 1961. The column was reduced from daily to Saturdays only when Gannett began cutting costs.[209]

In contrast to the Kalama Valley split, Chapin noted, the perspectives of Hawaii's establishment and opposition press united and intensified their influ-ence on the issue of Kahoolawe, the smallest of the eight major Hawaiian Is-lands. Some Native Hawaiians considered it a sacred place, especially for the ocean god Kanaloa.[210] During World War II, the military began using it for bombing practice to prepare for landings at Tarawa, Okinawa, and Iwo Jima. In 1953 President Dwight Eisenhower placed it under the jurisdiction of the U.S. Navy, and the military continued the bombing practices.[211]

The interest of the establishment press in Kahoolawe began in 1969. Then, Chapin wrote, Maui County Mayor Elmer Cravalho, who also governed Ka-hoolawe, "awoke one night to his home being rocked by a series of bombs."[212] Planes from an aircraft carrier had apparently dropped their hardware too close to Maui, about seven miles away. A 500-pounder had landed in the mayor's pasture—prime undeveloped land suitable for swank development.[213] The *Maui News* interviewed an enraged mayor and others who opposed the bombing[214] and the Honolulu papers followed. In 1976, when the Protect Kahoolawe Ohana was formed by Native Hawaiians to halt the bombing of a sacred site and to initiate lawsuits against federal officials, establishment and opposition newspa-pers gave serious coverage to the 'Ohana, to its activities, and to multitudes of guerrilla-type landings on the target island and other passionate protests.[215] In 1990 President George Bush ordered a halt to the bombing of Kahoolawe. In 1994 title to the island was returned to the state of Hawaii to be held in trust as a natural and cultural reserve until the formation of "a sovereign Hawaiian nation."[216]

Beginning in the 1970s, much political activity advocated remedies for the historical and current grievances of the Native Hawaiians. Even so, by 1994, a report prepared by a University of Hawaii sociology professor noted, "The Hawaiian population continued to have more persons living in families with lower total income, to be concentrated in lower paying jobs, and to enter and complete higher education less often than other ethnic groups."[217]

Yet this long-term socioeconomic condition of the Native Hawaiians was virtually ignored by the *Honolulu Advertiser*, according to a content analysis of 210 newspapers during the fifty-six-year period from 1934 through 1990.[218]

The articles on the socioeconomic conditions of Native Hawaiians were based on breaking news events, such as Hawaiians causing trouble in public places or comments of a prominent person in a public forum, rather than on newsroom-initiated enterprise stories that explained trends or conditions.

That study also found that the *Honolulu Advertiser* included virtually no coverage of Native Hawaiians in crime-related news. Victims or perpetrators were described as "local" or "Polynesian." This invisibility in the news may have resulted in part because many Native Hawaiians plea-bargained their cases, rather than going into an open courtroom accessible to the news media and the public to contest the criminal charges against them. It may also be due to the high number of interracial marriages, which made it difficult for police officers to determine the ethnicity of Hawaiians or part-Hawaiians.

Whatever the reasons, the scant news coverage concealed from the public the disproportionate numbers of Native Hawaiians in prison. It is also surprising because Native Hawaiians are frequently stereotyped as being conspicuously engaged in crime.[219] On January 1, 1977, Native Hawaiians accounted for 46.6 percent of the persons incarcerated in state correctional facilities, although they then constituted only 13.5 percent of the adult population. Of those Native Hawaiians in prison, 69.3 percent were dropouts; many had never attended high school.[220] In the 1990s this overrepresentation continued, causing an official report to describe it as "too great a disparity to be ignored."[221]

A sociology professor's report summarizing the causes for this Native Hawaiian overrepresentation indicated the following:

The external factors most cited include the devastation of the Hawaiian culture and suppression of Native Hawaiians, their low socio-economic status, family breakup, and lack of cultural identity that lead to negative individual attitudes and behaviors such as aggression, substance abuse, and attempts through illegal means to gain what one thinks is one's share of society's benefits.[222]

The subordinate status of the Native Hawaiians in their own homeland is similar to the condition of other native Pacific Islanders under U.S. jurisdiction. As one expert in the region noted, "In the Pacific as well as North America, [white] Americans have assumed a cultural and racial superiority which they believe justifies their disruption of the lives of dark-skinned peoples and the seizure of the latter's real estate for American ends."[223]

Such nonchalance may be rooted in an attitude toward the Pacific Islanders and their homelands that was summed up by the 1969 statement of then-presidential adviser Henry Kissinger: "There are only 90,000 people out there. Who gives a damn?"[224]

1974 RESIGNATION OF NIXON TO LOS ANGELES
UPRISING, APRIL 29, 1992

During this post-Watergate period, several scholars have assessed the main-stream news and public affairs coverage of Pacific Islanders generally, of Native Hawaiians, and of Chamorros in Guam.

An example of the mainstream newspapers' failure to cover Pacific Islanders and their region surfaced as part of a large-scale study made of news flow throughout the region. The study was undertaken when satellite communication was being introduced, thus linking the Pacific region with the rest of the world in a new way and opening up new patterns of information exchange between island societies. The author reported that the *New York Times* and *Los Angeles Times* carried no stories about the Pacific region during a sample week from November 1 to 7, 1976, indicating "the one-way news flow was absolute" from the dominant center to the dependent periphery.[225] Thus, he wrote, these two mainstream newspapers "blanked out the Pacific Islands completely."[226]

Starkly contrasting with blanking out the Pacific Islands is the study of 600 randomly selected *National Geographic* photographs from 1950 to 1986 made by a sociologist-anthropologist team. The Pacific Islands had more than fifty times the number of articles expected on the basis of their population, the study found, or 67 of 592 non-Western area articles. Researchers found four themes in the photographs of Micronesia; the most important was the "toplessness" of its women, followed by "the exoticism of its dancers, the romance of its nav-igators, and the juxtaposition of things native and things modern or Western," including World War II debris. Articles on the Pacific featured far more bare-breasted women than articles on other regions, and 32 percent of all photographs in the sample that included one woman or more also included toplessness—more than three times the rate for any other region. Perhaps this over-representation resulted from an editorial attempt to bring the remote corners of the world into U.S. homes less through spot news than through popular culture as well as through a magazine that is "the product of a society deeply permeated with racism as a social practice and with racial understandings as ways of view-ing the world," the team wrote. "It sells itself to a reading public that, while they do not consider themselves racist, turn easily to race as an explanation for culture and for social outcome."[227]

Sometimes the quantity of news coverage of Pacific Islanders and their region is ample, but the news content is criticized on other grounds. For example, a detailed study examined the news coverage of what one newspaper called "Guam's Trial of the Century" involving Ricardo Jerome (Ricky) Bordallo, the Democratic governor of Chamorro extraction. Soon after taking office in 1983, Bordallo began trying to obtain for Guam commonwealth status that would give the island more leverage with administrators in Washington, D.C., a political stance frowned upon by the U.S. government.[228]

On September 3, 1986, just three days before his reelection primary, he was summoned before a federal grand jury. He refused to answer questions. Later that day he was indicted on eleven counts, including extortion, bribery, obstruction of justice, witness tampering, and various conspiracy and wire fraud charges.[229] At a news conference and in three days of television ads, Bordallo described the investigation as "political lynching" steeped in "colonialism" and "bordering on racism."[230] He indicated that the federal government was trying to remove him from the political scene because he was an advocate for indigenous rights, for which he had campaigned passionately in English and Chamorro. He won the primary election. On October 30, in a radio debate broadcast just five days before the general election, Bordallo admitted taking the money listed in the indictment, but said it was the culturally acceptable practice of *chenchule*, a gift in Chamorro tradition to help another in need. That *chenchule* defense, communication scholar Peter De Benedittis wrote, illuminated "a cross-cultural clash between the U.S. system of justice in an American colony and the values, traditions and rights of those who have been colonized. . . . Bordallo's trial represented a head-on foray against cultural imperialism."[231] Bordallo lost the November 4 general election.

De Benedittis studied the English-language local news output from one radio station, three television stations, and two newspapers, especially the Gannett-owned *Pacific Daily News* (*PDN*).

The first of De Benedittis's four key findings indicated that the role of businessmen in the kickback and bribery schemes was underrepresented in the news, thus ignoring the monied interests' considerable influence on political decision makers. "Guam's media suggested corruption was the fault of politicians, not businessmen," De Benedittis explained. "The media focused on the people who took the bribes, not the people who gave them."[232]

One *PDN* editorial did acknowledge a one-to-one relationship, noting that "it takes two to tangle"[*sic*]. Only seven of the nearly 200 *PDN* articles and editorials published during the five-month period focused on the role business and businessmen played in the scandal.

The *PDN* also labeled Bordallo as being criminally charged or convicted, but it labeled Ken Jones, who admitted giving Bordallo $10,000, as a businessman and founder of a company. De Benedittis noted, "In one case a person who could be labeled as a governor was a criminal, and in the other, a person who could be labeled as a criminal was a businessman."[233]

The second finding indicated that much news content tended to discredit Bordallo and his arguments. Bordallo's *chenchule* defense was examined in only one program by one media outlet, which was KGTM TV-14's program the night before Bordallo's sentencing. A KGTM-TV part-owner was quoted in the study as saying that executives consciously adopted special procedures to "bend over backwards" to be fair to the ex-governor, not necessarily because he deserved it, but because other media were not "doing everything they could to be fair."[234]

A third finding indicated news-content bias that served to buttress the position of the U.S. government, thus preserving its hegemonic grip on Guam. For example, the news media generally failed to question the timing of the indictment, three days before the primary election, and thus failed to question whether the integrity of the electoral process had been violated. The *PDN* also produced over twice as many trial or corruption stories than election stories or editorials between the primary and general election. Journalists defined corruption so loosely, De Benedittis noted, that they sensationalized as corrupt "many normal occurrences in Guamanian culture."[235]

In a fourth finding, the nonintegration of journalists in Guam's culture and Bordallo's claims of being singled out for crimes "created a climate where both the federal government and the press were seen by many as outsiders," De Benedittis noted.[236] Newsroom personnel policies hinged on a revolving door phenomenon characterized by:

• Island reporters who stayed such a short time that they were unable to understand Guam's community

• Residents driven from journalism by low wages into higher-paying jobs

• Local media's rotating newsroom personnel as "a hegemonic insurance mechanism" to keep the social norms of the reporters in line with the interests of mainland corporate owners.[237]

Such practices have a price, De Benedittis stated: "The residents of Guam, according to journalists themselves, do not trust the news media. They do not trust it to be culturally sensitive or skillfully fulfill its function."[238]

Bordallo's allegation that U.S. racism spurred his indictment was later given some credence in interviews with two Chamorros, a scholar and an activist, with De Benedittis's noting their "charges of racial overtones in the treatment of non-whites by both the judicial system and the media."[239] Paraphrasing the Chamorro scholar, who was a University of Guam professor and dean, De Benedittis indicated that "white people who were convicted as part of the trial received no jail time—in fact one guilty white businessman was praised by both the judge and the press—while browns and Asians were nearly all sentenced to serve time and lost their licenses to do business."[240]

Both Chamorros reported that the press reduced its coverage of an indigenous rights group when it became a greater threat to U.S. interests. The University of Guam professor explained that the media give big coverage to fringe groups, because they are unusual, but when these groups begin to challenge the hegemony promoted by the news media, they are ignored. Thus, the Chamorro is quoted as saying, "The problem is that you don't get beyond being recognized as a fringe group."[241]

Bordallo was found guilty and sentenced to four years in prison; he appealed. All appeals failed. On January 31, 1990, the day he was to report to federal prison, Bordallo chained himself to a statue in the capital city, wrapped himself in a Guam flag, pointed a .38 caliber pistol at his head, and killed himself. A nearby placard he had made read: "I regret that I only have one life to give to my island."[242] He was sixty-three years old.

1992 LOS ANGELES UPRISING TO PRESIDENTIAL ELECTION, NOVEMBER 1996

In January 1993, Hawaii's history became news, a researcher noted. A century after the overthrow of Queen Liliuokalani, Native Hawaiians by the thousands gathered at Iolani Palace. Draped in black, the former royal palace was transformed into a place of mourning in memory of where their queen had been dethroned, losing her crown, her people, and her lands, and where she was later imprisoned after having been found guilty on charges of treason. Her overthrow marked the end of the monarchy, removed the political base of the Native Hawaiian people, and led in 1898 to annexation as a territory of the United States followed by statehood in 1959.

A week after the 1993 gathering at Iolani Palace, *Honolulu Advertiser* publisher Thurston Twigg-Smith countered by writing, "The overthrow of the monarchy and subsequent relationship with America are the best things that ever happened to Hawaii and its people."[243] Twigg-Smith is the grandson of Lorrin A. Thurston, a principal leader of the group that overthrew the monarchy and the publisher of the *Honolulu Advertiser* from 1898 to 1931. Both were descendants of two of the first missionaries who arrived in Hawaii in 1820.

The overthrow was justified and beneficial, Twigg-Smith argued; it and the subsequent annexation "were neither illegal nor do they call for apology by anyone."[244]

Four days after the article appeared, John D. Waihee III, Hawaii's first governor of part-Hawaiian descent, in a "brief, but dramatic ad-lib"[245] at the conclusion of his State of the State Address, reached under the lectern for a copy of Twigg-Smith's article. He called attention to the half-page article and read aloud the banner headline: "Overthrow: No Apology Needed"; then Waihee responded, "Well, you can own a newspaper but you cannot own history, and an apology is the least that needs to be done."[246]

Applause drowned out his final words. Twigg-Smith later retorted in print: "Even a governor shouldn't attempt to rewrite history."[247]

Nine months later, President Clinton, siding with Waihee, signed a joint Congressional resolution of "Acknowledgment and Apology" for the "illegal overthrow" of the Kingdom of Hawaii, "which resulted in the suppression of the inherent sovereignty of the Native Hawaiian people."[248] Rejecting Twigg-Smith's version of history, the resolution also noted that the Congregational Church had offered its separate public apology to the Native Hawaiian people and had recognized the "historic complicity" of its missionaries—which included the ancestors of the *Honolulu Advertiser*'s two publishers—"in the illegal overthrow of the Kingdom of Hawaii."[249]

These events spotlighted the media coverage of Native Hawaiians' quest for sovereignty. All nineteen major U.S. newspapers in the NEXIS on-line services file carried news or religious articles in 1993 about these apologies from the U.S. government or the church, an on-line survey indicated.[250]

A decisive turning point for the sovereignty movement occurred in the mid-1990s. As a means of rectifying past injustices that occurred when the Hawaiian monarchy was overthrown in 1893, the state established a mechanism to permit only Native Hawaiians to vote on whether steps should be taken for their own self-government. In mid-1996 about 80,000 ballots were mailed to Native Hawaiians in and out of the state to vote on whether they should begin to elect delegates to propose a Native Hawaiian government. The historic vote was one of the first times in the 103 years since the overthrow of the monarchy that the Hawaiian people as a whole had the opportunity to express their will regarding self-determination. This plebiscite was itself controversial. Some groups urged a voter boycott, arguing against state sponsorship and advocating instead negotiations at the federal level on a government-to-government basis as were used with Native American Indian tribes. Of the nearly 82,000 ballots mailed out, about 33,000 were returned by voters; this low return rate of 40 percent fueled opponents' claims that the state-sponsored balloting had yielded no mandate among Hawaiians to continue the self-determination process. Of the ballots eligible to be counted, over 73 percent voted yes ('ae).[251]

The next step is expected to be a convention of Native Hawaiians to determine how they will manage their own affairs, including ways to derive more benefit from the lands once belonging to the monarchy. Several lawsuits are also pending, including one by a fifth-generation Caucasian rancher, who argues that using state funds and permitting only Native Hawaiians to vote violates the U.S. Constitution.[252] He said he may be receiving funds from a Washington, D.C.–based Campaign for a Color-Blind America.[253]

The flowering of Hawaiian culture begun in the 1970s continues. The Hawaiian language has made a comeback, and in 1992 the state Department of Education approved a policy of allowing public school students to be taught almost entirely in the Hawaiian language through high school.[254] Hawaiians had become more politically active than at any time since annexation,[255] and a striking Center for Hawaiian Studies was inaugurated at the University of Hawaii with promise of becoming the world's premier institution for the study of Hawaiian history, mythology, culture, and language. But the 1990 Census showed that Native Hawaiians had made no progress since 1980 in education, occupation and income attainment; they were still at the bottom of Hawaii's socioeconomic ladder.[256]

Also in the mid-1990s, as discussed below, several scholars assessed Hawaii's news media or media portrayals of Native Hawaiians. In addition, indigenous peoples took steps to begin telling their own stories in their own voices and to set their own agenda for public affairs programming.

Hawaii's news media and journalists have received "relatively little research attention," one scholar found, even though the state is "intrinsically important because of its strategic location." His findings were based on data obtained from surveys distributed to Hawaii's entire full-time news workforce of English-language and ethnic newspapers, radio stations, and network-affiliated television stations. The scholar reported, "Particularly under-represented are the native Hawaiian or part-Hawaiian group."[257] He found that 1.9 percent of the journalists were Hawaiian or part-Hawaiian, although these groups constituted at least 12 percent of the state's population. Caucasians represented 70 percent of the journalists but 23.4 percent of the state population. Moreover, journalists were far more likely than the resident population to be born outside of Hawaii, but were strongly committed to staying in the state.[258] He also quoted a document of the Asian American Journalists Association stating that Pacific Islanders, as well as those of Asian descent, "are often inaccurately or insensitively portrayed in the news."[259] This survey also found that a greater proportion of Hawaii's journalists than the national average considered it "extremely important to investigate government claims, to provide analysis of complex problems . . . and to serve as an adversary of both government and business."[260]

Questioning this view of above-average adversarial reporting was an assessment published just a year later in the *Columbia Journalism Review* (*CJR*). It criticized Hawaii's news media for uncritically accepting government and business views and for being less persistent than the University of Hawaii journalism students who pursued Honolulu Police Department records naming disciplined police officers. The article also criticized the mediocrity of the two Honolulu dailies when they were gaining reportedly huge profits from their public-relations-oriented promotion of Hawaii's tourism—or "selling the state as paradise on earth."[261] The *Honolulu Advertiser*'s president and publisher said that the newspaper will continue to play that role because tourism is seen as the economic driving force in Hawaii through 2015.[262] The *CJR* article also detailed an earlier evaluation of the state's two key newspapers and three major television stations that found "poor coverage of native Hawaiian issues."[263] Hawaii's two largest dailies are "sheltered by the newspaper equivalent of the Endangered Species Act—a joint operating agreement that lets them carve up reportedly huge profits."[264] These reported profits spurred the state legislature and governor in 1995 to enact a statute requiring these profits be disclosed to the public and to the state government; that law is now being litigated. The scholar also wrote that it took an outsider, the *Wall Street Journal*, to "stir up some of the biggest media controversy in recent years" and to expose the "state program that was failing to fulfill promises to give land to native Hawaiians."[265]

Another scholar documented the lack of news attention in Hawaii given to Native Hawaiians across news media types on one single day. Her study provided a snapshot of selected Hawaii television, radio, and print media's local news coverage of racial and ethnic groups on January 18, 1995.[266]

• News coverage of Native Hawaiians was a "significant anomaly" to their proportion of the population. "Of the 131 instances of newspaper and television interviews, only one Hawaiian was directly interviewed, making this group the most under-represented ethnic or racial group in Hawaii." Interviews with nine Native Hawaiians would have been required that day to have made them proportional to the 12.5-plus percent they represent in Hawaii's population.[267]

• Fundamental cultural differences between the indigenous value system and Western values may account for the reluctance of many Native Hawaiians to take advantage of the programming services offered through 'Olelo, a state-mandated public-access studio and channel for community television. Most residents attracted to 'Olelo's training program for public-access productions are Caucasian males.

• In contrast, Native Hawaiians are among the top three racial/ethnic groups that have shown the greatest interest in viewing public access programs that are produced by community groups. The potential for the viewing of a diversity of local ethnic programming may be significant for those with access to cable.[268]

Broadcast Coverage

Among those cablecasting via the public access channel open to community members is a group of Hawaiian activists who have organized a monthly discussion of issues and events largely affecting the indigenous people. Called "First Friday, The Unauthorized News," it is described by one scholar as being "unique in its confrontation of controversial issues." Hawaii's network-affiliated television stations show relatively little that represents the Hawaiian people.[269]

Also empowering Pacific Islanders to tell their own story is a federally funded public broadcasting organization, Pacific Islanders in Communications. It has produced twenty-minute documentaries about Native Hawaiians, Guamanians, and Chamorros.

Drawing an emotional outpouring of sympathy from audiences in the continental United States was the documentary "And Then There Were None," which was shown nationally in 1996 on public broadcasting television stations.[270] The twenty-minute documentary presented the decrease in the numbers of pure-blooded Native Hawaiians in the state from 500,000 in 1778, when they formed 100 percent of the population, to 8,711, or less than 1 percent of the state's population, in 1993. This decline amounts to a 98.25-percent drop in 215 years. A newspaper account indicated the film used "images of at the very least cultural sublimation, at the worst, cultural genocide."[271] Film director Elizabeth Kapuuwailani Lindsey, a descendant of Hawaiian high chiefs and English seafarers, said the work conveys the Hawaiians' "untold story that contradicts the successful marketing image of an island paradise."[272]

The marketing image was also momentarily punctured on Ted Koppel's special ninety-minute live edition of "Nightline" televised in late 1991 from Tokyo on the fiftieth anniversary of the Japanese attack on Pearl Harbor. According to one scholar, "[A] national audience received unexpected exposure to the grievances of Pacific Americans"[273] when native Hawaiian activist Haunani-Kay

Trask asked a panel of "Japanese public relations flak-catchers about the displacement of native Hawaiians by the international tourist industry led by Japan." She asked about the moral responsibility to the native people on the Pacific Islands who were being dispossessed and evicted from their lands so that golf courses and resorts could be built by Japan. Panelists politely answered that local populations should be consulted in making these decisions. But, the scholar noted, Trask's blunt question that was "so at odds with network standards of 'objectivity' " provided one of those rare "television moments" that sometimes "slip through the network *cordon sanitaire* during live broadcasts."[274]

A half-century after the first Bikini Atoll test of 1946, nuclearization reigns in, under, or over the Pacific. At least 312 known atomic tests have been conducted in the Pacific by France, Great Britain, and the United States,[275] and more than one-eighth of the 817 known U.S. nuclear-weapons tests worldwide were conducted there.[276] Radioactivity caused by the initial testing in the Pacific was augmented by that from accidents and waste disposal. In 1962 two known accidents occurred during high-altitude testing of intercontinental ballistic missiles over the Pacific. As researchers noted, one accident left "a radioactive hot spot on the fringe of the Pacific" that may mark it for centuries.[277] Later *Apollo 13*, carrying a payload of 8.2 pounds of plutonium 238—one pound of which could induce lung cancer on every person on earth—splashed down about 1,000 miles southwest of American Samoa and deposited plutonium that now works its way through the aquatic food chain.[278] In 1980, to dispose of radioactive waste resulting from decades of testing, U.S. officials dug a huge pit on an islet near Enewetak, buried a huge pile of sand, debris, and cement that will remain radioactive for 25,000 years and encased it in a twenty-inch-thick concrete dome.[279] Options being considered include emplacement of nuclear wastes in subsediment bedrock[280] or in the world's deepest canyon, the 36,000-foot-plus Marianas Trench.

Today's news media are still failing to cover adequately radiation-related illnesses that were dramatized by Marshall Islanders over the past fifty years, according to Helen Caldicott, a pediatrician, author, and cofounder of the Nobel Peace Prize–winning Physicians for Social Responsibility. When asked about the quality of the news coverage of the Pacific Islanders evolving over the half century, she replied, "I think the news media stink." Recalling Thomas Jefferson's assertion that a truly responsible government depended on an informed public, Caldicott stated, "The media aren't educating the people" about radiation-related dangers. "And so therefore we'll die ignorant."[281]

And the news media might be even more timid in covering these issues thoroughly in the future, she said, because two of the major commercial television networks are now owned by corporations that manufacture nuclear weapons, construct nuclear power plants, or hold related business interests.[282] Thus, on nuclear and defense-related issues, she said, news media "impartiality appears impossible."[283]

One scholar studied thirty-three post–World War II documentary videos and films made for American audiences. He found that the common Western perception of the Pacific as a paradise is being replaced by new images that take "the opposite extreme: that Micronesia is a wasteland." He stated that the United States' abuse of its authority in the islands is portrayed visually in scenes of detonated bombs and disenfranchised islanders that convey a sense of irony and betrayal. But, he noted, "Filmmakers select fragments of social realities while ignoring others; by selecting fragments of life they miss the fullness and complexity of any group's experience."[284]

Decades of these nuclear activities have produced grassroots movements, backed by Christian organizations, trade unions, university students, and some political leaders, calling for a nuclear-free and independent Pacific. As one scholar explained, "From one end of the Pacific Islands region to the other, governments and people alike have a tradition of being anti-nuclear."[285] The sentiments were summed up in a poster reading: "If it's so safe, store it in Washington, dump it in Tokyo, and test it in Paris."[286]

In early 1996, the South Pacific Nuclear Free Treaty, which bans nuclear testing in the zone, had been agreed to by the three powers that had most used the region for experiments—France, the United Kingdom, and the United States. But the treaty is silent on the presence or transit of nuclear-powered vessels, the export of uranium, inadequately protected nuclear-power generation, or the testing of delivery vehicles.[287] Globally, a Comprehensive Test Ban Treaty was adopted by the United Nations' General Assembly and made available in September 1996 for signature by member governments.

CONCLUSION

The English-language scholarly literature reviewed for this chapter is scattered widely across decades, disciplines, geography, and perspectives. And it is relatively sparse. Nonetheless, several observations can be made.

First, Pacific Islanders and their region have generally received even less news coverage than the nation's least covered states. This finding is consistent with and extends earlier research on the geographical patterns of U.S. news coverage. That research found an unequal distribution of U.S. domestic news with California and New York receiving proportionately more stories than their population and as much coverage as the thirty least-covered states.[288] This chapter also lends support to political scientist Michael Parenti's assertion that "the single most common form of media misrepresentation is *omission*."[289]

But Pacific Islanders, although miniscule in numbers, may be considerably more newsworthy than scholarly research shows mainstream U.S. media have acknowledged them to be during the past sixty years. Evidence indicated some Pacific Islanders who experienced nuclear testing serve as the avant-garde announcing the adverse effects of radioactivity on today's human beings and tomorrow's. By slighting coverage of these Pacific Islanders, the mainstream news media may have shirked their surveillance function of serving as sentinels for the public against threats. In shirking this responsibility, the media left unreported decades of U.S. government abuses that are just now coming to light and well-documented mistreatment and neglect of Pacific Islanders.

Recommended ways to improve news coverage of persons in remote geographical areas include increasing background and trend materials in the total media output, decreasing event-oriented articles, reporting everyday occurrences and trends, emphasizing continuity and follow-up, focusing more on nonelite areas and nonelite people within those areas, spotlighting nonpersonal causes of events and more positive events,[290] plus assessing the performance of criminal justice and other agencies.

Second, this chapter provided research evidence that the U.S. mainstream media have slighted or distorted news coverage of some indigenous people from the oral-tradition heritage of the Pacific. Historical data suggest the U.S. print-based sense of cultural superiority may be inferred to be a contributor to this skewing of reality. Evidence indicated that Honolulu's English-language dailies in a variety of ways and over decades tended to slight or ignore coverage of Native Hawaiians, including their decades of overrepresentation in the criminal justice system, their dismal existence at the bottom of the socioeconomic ladder, and their underrepresentation as news sources. Research evidence also suggested that the U.S. mainstream news media undercovered the sacrifices Pacific Islanders made during World War II and the adverse impact that U.S. nuclear testing had on Marshall Islanders—who unknowingly served as an early worldwide warning to others.

The research evidence assembled in this chapter contributes to and advances some theories of influences on news media content, as formulated by communication scholars Pamela Shoemaker and Stephen Reese. They describe five levels of analysis that shape news content. They illustrate these levels with a diagram of a dartboard with the bull's-eye center representing individuals. The next ring represents the media-routines level, then the organizational level, the extra-media level (such as advertisers or government), and the ideological level on the outer rim.

Ideology represents a societal-level phenomenon, and its level of analysis is the most macro or encompassing of the five levels. Shoemaker and Reese wrote that the ideological level represents a total structure, in which "all the processes taking place at lower levels are considered to be working toward an ideologically related pattern of messages and on behalf of the higher power centers in society."[291]

This chapter synthesized research that extends part of Shoemaker and Reese's definition of basic U.S. ideology. That part is the economic ideology component, which is defined as "a belief in the value of the capitalist economic system, private ownership, pursuit of profit by self-interested entrepreneurs, and free markets. The system is intertwined with the Protestant ethic and the value of individual achievement."[292] The influence of these economic beliefs is borne out in this chapter through research presented on Guam's news media. These media, a study found, minimized or masked the role of businessmen in the kickback and bribery transactions that led to the conviction and subsequent suicide of indigenous Chamorro Governor Bordallo and that corrupted Guam's political environment during boom times.

Also at the ideological, societal level of analysis, this chapter spotlighted the need for probing the root causes of why nonwhites, such as the indigenous, oral-tradition Native Hawaiians, are underrepresented on socioeconomic success scales or are overrepresented at almost every stage within the criminal justice process. Decades of ignoring or slighting these socioeconomic conditions—and the factors giving rise to these conditions—suggest a pattern of cultural, if not racial, bias.

Third, this chapter examined the case of KGTM-TV, Guam's sole media outlet whose executives consciously decided to examine Governor Bordallo's *chenchule* claim that accepting businessmen's gifts was a culturally accepted Chamorro practice. The KGTM-TV case illuminates and extends Shoemaker and Reese's organizational level of analysis, which emphasizes the influences on content made by ownership, goals, and policy. Shoemaker and Reese assume that "the ultimate power in a media organization comes from the owner," who sets the direction and ultimate policies.[293] Conversely, this chapter presented another example at the organizational level of analysis by examining Gannett's twinned policies in the 1980s of paying its reporters on Guam so little that personnel turnover was great and of rotating nonlocal editors in and out of the community. Both Gannett policies, research suggested, served to lower the quality of the news product, diminish the credibility of the media, and tighten the corporation's hegemonic control over its workforce.

News organizations largely failed to recognize that *time*, a cornerstone of the news business, was perceived differently with the advent of the Atomic Age, which produces radioactivity and nuclear wastes that linger up to a half-million years. Yet this new order of magnitude spurred no increased surveillance for the benefit of the public by news organizations. Research indicated the adverse impact on Pacific Islanders resulting from early nuclear tests received no urgent media follow-up and only scant critical questioning by the news organizations that toed the U.S. government line on matters that became increasingly vital to the health of the public as well as to national security. Although the U.S. government regularly examined the Marshallese for path-breaking medical evidence about the effects of radioactivity, the news media failed to recognize these Pacific Islanders as pioneers of a new and deadly age.

Fourth, this chapter revealed numerous media practices that biased news coverage favoring the U.S. government or dominant-culture interests to the detriment of Pacific Islanders. Media practices included repeated references to Bordallo as the "indicted governor" but buried or omitted focus on businessmen who gave illegal funds. Newsroom practices used to distort coverage of 1960s nuclear protests in Hawaii included trivialization and superficiality of news, bias in placement and composition of articles or photographs, use of loaded questions, labeling and poor choice of language, failure to go beyond official sources, and use of guilt by association in editorials. Thus, this chapter adds to and expands Shoemaker and Reese's media-routines level of the analysis of influences shaping news content.

Finally, this chapter provided research evidence of the value of diversity in the cultural, racial, or ethnic background of newsroom personnel. One of the few Native Hawaiian reporters employed by Honolulu's dailies in a century covered indigenous-rights issues in a culturally commendable and politically significant way. Negatively, however, research indicated many majority-culture journalists in Guam were often viewed as outsiders with little knowledge about or concern for the local community. Such evidence in this chapter thus contributes to and extends Shoemaker and Reese's individual level of analysis of influences shaping news content.

For the approaching millennium, this chapter suggests, the U.S. globalizing news media might better learn from and report on one-time oral-tradition islanders, including those who reconnoitered the Atomic Age.

NOTES

1. The words of a Samoan chief to his villagers after visiting and critiquing a modern nation—probably Germany before World War I, as described in Beverly Ann Deepe Keever, "On Windwagons and Sky Bursters: Final Regrets of a Mass Communications Pioneer," *Mass Comm Review* 18, no. 1–2 (1991), 11.

2. Walter J. Ong, *Orality and Literacy: The Technologizing of the Word* (London: Methuen, 1982), 8.

3. From English-language subtitles translating the words of an unnamed Marshallese woman speaking in *Half Life: A Parable for the Nuclear Age*, 86-minute videocassette (Los Angeles: Direct Cinema, 1986).

4. Norman Meller, "Pacific Polities and Communications," in *Communication in the Pacific*, ed. Daniel Lerner and Jim Richstad (Honolulu: East-West Center, 1976), 25–29.

5. Jonathan M. Weisgall, *Operation Crossroads: The Atomic Tests at Bikini Atoll* (Annapolis, Md.: Naval Institute Press, 1994), 1–4. An adjunct professor and a contributor to scholarly journals, Weisgall served as legal counsel to the Bikinians for twelve of the fourteen years from 1975 to 1988.

6. Ibid., 4.

7. Ibid.

8. Stewart Firth, *Nuclear Playground* (Honolulu: University of Hawaii Press and Pacific Islands Studies Program, 1987), xi.

9. The United States has also governed the following Pacific areas: the Philippines from 1898 to 1946, when independence was granted, and, after World War II, the Ryukyu (Okinawan) and other Japanese islands until the last of them were returned to Japan in 1972.

10. Thomas Cochran, William M. Arkin, and Milton M. Hoenig, *Nuclear Weapons*

Databook, vol. 1, *U.S. Nuclear Forces and Capabilities* (Cambridge, Mass.: Ballinger Publishing, 1984), 82.

11. Peter De Benedittis, "Guam's Trial of the Century: News, Hegemony, and Rumors in an American Colony" (Ph.D. diss., Pennsylvania State University, 1992), 7.

12. Donald D. Johnson (with Gary Dean Best), *The United States in the Pacific: Private Interests and Public Policies, 1784–1899* (Westport, Conn.: Praeger, 1995), 153.

13. Robert C. Kiste, "New Political Statuses in American Micronesia," in *Contemporary Pacific Societies: Studies in Development and Change*, ed. Victoria S. Lockwood, Thomas G. Harding, and Ben J. Wallace (Englewood Cliffs, N.J.: Prentice-Hall, 1993), 67–80.

14. John C. Dorrance, "Strategic Cooperation and Competition in the Pacific Islands: An American Assessment," working paper no. 203 (Canberra: Australian National University, 1990).

15. Christopher Campbell, *Nuclear Weapons Fact Book* (Feltham, England: Hamlyn Publishing, 1984), 184–85.

16. Kiste, "New Political Statuses," 75.

17. Ibid., 73.

18. Political statuses and populations of these areas are taken from *Pacific Islands Yearbook*, ed. Norman Douglas and Ngaire Douglas, 17th ed. (Suva: Fiji Times, 1994).

19. Robert C. Kiste, "United States," in *Tides of History: The Pacific Islands in the Twentieth Century*, ed. K. R. Howe, Robert C. Kiste, and Brij V. Lal (Honolulu: University of Hawaii, 1994), 234.

20. This definition covering pure Hawaiians and part-Hawaiians follows that used in the U.S. Senate Resolution of Apology to Native Hawaiians, U.S. Public Law 103–150, 103 Cong., 1st sess., November 1993, as reprinted in *The Apology to Native Hawaiians* (Honolulu: Ka'imi Pono Press, 1994).

21. Robert C. Kiste, "Pre-Colonial Times," in *Tides of History: The Pacific Islands in the Twentieth Century*, ed. K. R. Howe, Robert Kiste, and Brij V. Lal (Honolulu: University of Hawaii, 1994), 4.

22. Albert J. Schütz, *The Voices of Eden: A History of Hawaiian Language Studies* (Honolulu: University of Hawaii Press, 1994), 3, 4.

23. Luis I. Reyes, *Made in Paradise: Hollywood's Films of Hawai'i and the South Seas* (Honolulu: Mutual Publishing, 1995).

24. Robert C. Kiste, "The Pacific Islands: Images and Impacts" in *The Pacific Islands in the Year 2000*, ed. Robert C. Kiste and Richard A. Herr (Honolulu: Pacific Islands Studies Program Working Paper Series, 1985), 1–21.

25. Lucy G. Thurston, *Life and Times of Mrs. Lucy G. Thurston*, 3d ed. (Honolulu: The Friend, 1934), 14. Originally published in 1882.

26. Kiste, "The Pacific Islands," 1–21.

27. David Quammen, *The Song of the Dodo: Island Biogeography in an Age of Extinctions* (New York: Scribner, 1996). The author appreciates Robert C. Kiste's calling this recent work to her attention.

28. Helen Geracimos Chapin, *Shaping History: The Role of Newspapers in Hawai'i* (Honolulu: University of Hawaii Press, 1996), 2.

29. Ibid., 6.

30. Robert K. Logan, *The Alphabet Effect: The Impact of the Phonetic Alphabet on the Development of Western Civilization* (New York: William Morrow, 1986), 20.

31. Ibid., 66.

32. Sheldon Dibble, *A History of the Sandwich Islands* (Honolulu: Thos. G. Thrum, 1909), 413. Dibble's preface is dated 1843.

33. John E. Reinecke, *Language and Dialect in Hawaii: A Sociolinguistic History to 1935*, ed. Stanley M. Tsuzaki (Honolulu: Social Science Research Institute and University of Hawaii Press, 1988), 28, 27. Originally published in 1969.

34. Native Hawaiians Study Commission, *Report on the Culture, Needs and Concerns of Native Hawaiians*, vol. 1 (Washington, D.C.: Native Hawaiians Study Commission, 1983), 45.

35. Reinecke, *Language and Dialect in Hawaii*, and Chapin, *Shaping History*.

36. Esther Mookini (aka Kikue Takakura), "A Brief Survey of the Hawaiian Language Newspapers" (Paper submitted to the Committee on Library Prizes for Pacific Island Area Research, 1967), 14–15.

37. Schütz, *The Voices of Eden*, 362–63. For translations into English of some Hawaiian-language newspapers, see Rubellite Kinney Johnson, ed., *Kukini 'Aha'Ilono* [Carry On the News]: *Over a Century of Native Hawaiian Life and Thought from the Hawaiian Language Newspapers of 1834 to 1948* (Honolulu: Topgallant Publishing, 1976).

38. Chapin, *Shaping History*, 27.

39. Ibid., 57, quoting the *Pacific Commercial Advertiser*, 21 April 1859.

40. Sally Merry, "Sexuality and Sovereignty: Transition in 19th Century Hilo" (Address given at the Judiciary History Center, Honolulu, 5 February 1996).

41. Ibid.

42. Chapin, *Shaping History*, 80.

43. Gary Y. Okihiro, *Cane Fires: The Anti-Japanese Movement in Hawaii, 1865–1945* (Philadelphia: Temple University Press, 1991), 280.

44. Lilikala Kame'eleihiwa, *Native Land and Foreign Desires: Pehea La E Pono Ai?* (Honolulu: Bishop Museum Press, 1992), 8.

45. Elizabeth Buck, *Paradise Remade: The Politics of Culture and History in Hawai'i* (Philadelphia: Temple University Press, 1993), 71, footnoting a half dozen sources.

46. Richard R. Day, "The Ultimate Inequality: Linguistic Genocide," in *Language of Inequality*, ed. Nessa Wolfson and Joan Manes (Berlin: Mouton Publishers, 1985), 166, cited by Chapin.

47. Ibid., 164.

48. Larry L. Kimura, "The Hawaiian Language," in *Report on the Culture, Needs and Concerns of Native Hawaiians*, 193.

49. Schütz, *The Voices of Eden*, 352.

50. Kimura, "The Hawaiian Language," 196.

51. Riley M. Moffat and Gary L. Fitzpatrick, *Surveying the Mahele: Mapping the Hawaiian Land Revolution*, vol. 2 (Honolulu: Editions Limited, 1995), 11–12.

52. *Then There Were None*, 26-minute videocassette (Honolulu: Pacific Islanders in Communication and LLB Productions); O. A. Bushnell, *The Gifts of Civilization: Germs and Genocide in Hawaii* (Honolulu: University of Hawaii Press, 1993). Bushnell indicates pure-blooded Hawaiians represented only about 1 percent of the state population in 1970, when U.S. Census officials eliminated that category because they were few in number and of questionable identity, 271–72. See also Kekuni Blaisdell, "Statistics on Kanaka Maoli (Indigenous Hawaiians)" (Paper presented at the Ethnic Studies Community Conference, Honolulu, May 1995).

53. Reinecke, *Language and Dialect in Hawaii*, 30.

54. Day, "The Ultimate Inequality," 169.

55. Howard Zinn, *A People's History of the United States* (New York: Harper Perennial, 1990), 305.

56. Marion Kelly, "The State of Hawaii Responds to the Hawaiian Sovereignty Movement: OHA, HSAC, HSEC, and the Native Hawaiian Vote" (Paper presented at a conference sponsored by the Pacific History Association and the University of Hawaii Pacific Islands Studies Center, Hilo, Hawaii, July 1996), 10.

57. Ibid.

58. Day, "The Ultimate Inequality," 169.

59. Buck, *Paradise Remade*, 76.

60. Robert F. Rogers, *Destiny's Landfall: A History of Guam* (Honolulu: University of Hawaii Press, 1995).

61. Day, "The Ultimate Inequality"; Rogers, *Destiny's Landfall*.

62. Day, "The Ultimate Inequality," 175.

63. Alan Murakami, "The Hawaiian Homes Commission Act," in *Native Hawaiian Rights Handbook*, ed. Melody Kapilialoha MacKenzie (Honolulu: Native Hawaiian Legal Corporation and Office of Hawaiian Affairs, 1991), 43–76.

64. Marylyn M. Vause, "The Hawaiian Homes Commission Act, 1920: History and Analysis" (Master's thesis, University of Hawaii, 1962), 2–4.

65. U.S. Bureau of the Census, *1980 Census of Population, General Population Characteristics, Hawaii* PC80–1–B13 (July 1982), tables 15 and 16; U.S. Bureau of the Census, Release CB91–42 (February 1991) and Summary Tape File 1A, as published in *The State of Hawaii Data Book 1992* (Honolulu: Department of Business, Economic Development and Tourism, March 1993), 44. These censuses counted mixed-race people by self-identification or by the race of the mother.

66. Robert C. Schmitt, "Some Transportation and Communication Firsts in Hawaii," *The Hawaiian Journal of History* 13 (1979), 99–123.

67. George S. Kanahele, ed., *Hawaiian Music and Musicians: An Illustrated History* (Honolulu: University Press of Hawaii, 1979), 320.

68. Chapin, *Shaping History*, 152.

69. Theon Wright, *Rape in Paradise* (New York: Tower Books, 1966), 225.

70. Helen Benedict, *Virgin or Vamp: How the Press Covers Sex Crimes* (New York: Oxford University Press, 1992), 27–29.

71. Ibid., 25, quoting Hall.

72. Ibid., 8–9.

73. Beverly Ann Deepe Keever, "The Alphabet, *The Honolulu Advertiser* and the Hawaiians: A Quintessential Process of Cultural Racism?" (Paper presented at Association for Education in Journalism and Mass Communication Convention, Washington, D.C., August 1995). To be counted, the news item needed to mention the Hawaiian identity or to provide other identifiable information such as birthplace or membership in a Hawaiian group.

74. The figure of 815 is based on this researcher's measuring the newshole—the space devoted to news—in a representative sample of seven of the twenty-eight newspapers studied in 1934 and 1938.

75. Robert C. Kiste, University of Hawaii professor and director of the Center for Pacific Islands Studies, interview with the author, Honolulu, 15 May 1996.

76. William Manchester, *American Caesar: Douglas MacArthur 1880–1964* (Boston: Little, Brown, 1978), 205, 209–212.

77. Lin Poyer, "Micronesian Experiences in the War in the Pacific" in *Remembering the Pacific War*, ed. Geoffrey M. White, occasional paper no. 36 (Honolulu: Center for Pacific Islands Studies, 1991), 86.

78. Geoffrey M. White, "Preface" in *Remembering the Pacific War*, ed. Geoffrey M. White, occasional paper no. 36 (Honolulu: Center for Pacific Islands Studies, 1991), vi.

79. Douglas and Douglas, *Pacific Islands Yearbook*.

80. White, "Preface," vi–ix.

81. Lamont Lindstrom and Geoffrey M. White, *Island Encounters: Black and White Memories of the Pacific War* (Washington, D.C.: Smithsonian Institution Press, 1990), 10.

82. Ibid., 6, quoting Moeller.

83. Ibid., 4.

84. Jim A. Richstad, "The Press under Martial Law: The Hawaiian Experience," *Journalism Monographs* 17 (November 1970), 39.

85. *Duncan v. Kahanamoku*, 327 U.S. 304 (1946).

86. Richstad, "The Press under Martial Law," 1.

87. Ibid., 9.

88. Materials suppressed included the White House's ordering federal agencies in late 1943 to hand over all photographs and negatives showing First Lady Eleanor Roosevelt in a hula skirt, according to George H. Roeder Jr., *The Censored War: American Visual Experience during World War Two* (New Haven, Conn.: Yale University Press, 1993), 123.

89. J. Garner Anthony, *Hawaii under Army Rule* (Stanford, Calif.: Stanford University Press, 1955), 39.

90. Keever, "The Alphabet."

91. Keever, "The Alphabet," app. 2.

92. Anthony, *Hawaii under Army Rule*, 39–41; Jim Richstad, "The Press and the Courts under Martial Rule in Hawaii during World War II—From *Pearl Harbor to Duncan v. Kahanamoku*" (Ph.D. diss., University of Minnesota, 1967).

93. Beth Bailey and David Farber, *The First Strange Place: Race and Sex in World War II in Hawaii* (Baltimore: The Johns Hopkins University Press, 1992).

94. Ibid., 36, citing personal interview with retired U.S. Army Colonel Herman Gist.

95. Richstad, "The Press and the Courts," 200.

96. Ibid., 201.

97. Ibid., 209, paraphrasing Thurston.

98. Ibid., 173, citing Thurston and General Order no. 165.

99. Richstad, "The Press under Martial Law," 26.

100. Richstad, "The Press and the Courts," 200, citing *Honolulu Star-Bulletin*, 21 September 1944.

101. Anthony, *Hawaii under Army Rule*, 40.

102. Firth, *Nuclear Playground*; quote is from book title.

103. The Chugoku Newspaper, *Exposure: Victims of Radiation Speak Out*, trans. Kirsten McIvor (Tokyo: Kodansha International, 1992), 128. Originally published in Japanese as *Sekai no Hibakusha* by Kodansha, 1991.

104. Spark M. Matsunaga Institute for Peace, "50 Years with the Bomb" (Honolulu: 1995), 13.

105. Helen Caldicott, "Nuclear Shadow: The Weapons, the Power, the Waste," *The*

Nation 262, no. 17 (29 April 1996), 14. Bikini gave rise to two diverse words: "fallout" and "bikini." Fallout is discussed later in this chapter; bikini resulted from comparing the effects wrought by a woman in a scantily clad bathing suit to the effects of an atomic bomb, according to Weisgall, *Operation Crossroads*, 4.

106. Kiste, "Pre-Colonial Times," 11, 14–16.

107. Ibid.

108. The term comes from the title used by Jonathan M. Weisgall, "The Nuclear Nomads of Bikini Atoll," in *Foreign Policy* 39 (Summer 1980), 74–98; also see Weisgall, *Operation Crossroads*, 314.

109. From the subtitle in Robert C. Kiste, *The Bikinians: A Study in Forced Migration* (Menlo Park, Calif.: Cummings Publishing, 1974).

110. Weisgall, *Operation Crossroads*, 96.

111. Ibid., 161.

112. Ibid., 154.

113. Ibid, 155.

114. Harvey Wasserman and Norman Solomon with Robert Alvarez and Eleanor Walters, *Killing Our Own: The Disaster of America's Experience with Atomic Radiation* (New York: A Delta Book, 1982), 37.

115. Ibid., 38.

116. Ibid., quoting *Newsweek*, 1 July 1946, 21.

117. Ibid.

118. Weisgall, *Operation Crossroads*, citing *Los Angeles Daily News*, 10 May 1946, 159.

119. *Los Angeles Daily News*, "The Lunatics at Bikini," 10 May 1946, editorial page.

120. Weisgall, *Operation Crossroads*, 112.

121. Photo titled "His Kingdom Is at Stake," *New York Times*, 28 February 1946, 12.

122. Kiste, *The Bikinians*, 31.

123. Ibid., 34, citing *Life*, 25 March 1946, 105–9.

124. Ibid., 32.

125. Weisgall, *Operation Crossroads*, 113.

126. Ibid., 161.

127. Ibid., 309.

128. Ibid., 114.

129. Lt. (jg) E. J. Rooney, "The Strange People from Bikini," *New York Times Magazine*, 31 March 1946, 23.

130. Weisgall, *Operation Crossroads*, 309.

131. Ibid., 141.

132. Ibid.

133. Stephen Hilgartner, Richard C. Bell, and Rory O'Connor, *Nukespeak: Nuclear Language, Visions, and Mindset* (San Francisco: Sierra Club Books, 1982), 38.

134. Weisgall, *Operation Crossroads*, 151.

135. Fitzhugh Lee, "The Press at Crossroads," *Army Information Digest* 2, no. 3 (March 1947), 25–31.

136. Weisgall, *Operation Crossroads*, 142.

137. Wasserman and Solomon, *Killing Our Own*, 42, quoting *Newsweek*, 8 July 1946, 20.

138. Weisgall, *Operation Crossroads*, 185.

139. Ibid., 187–88.

140. Ibid., 224.

141. Numerous books such as Wasserman and Solomon's *Killing Our Own* have been written about the plight of these radiation-contaminated sailors, who for years were denied help from the government for which they had fought.

142. Weisgall, *Operation Crossroads*, 243.

143. Ibid., 306.

144. Chapin, *Shaping History*, 214, citing the *Honolulu Advertiser*, 7 December 1947.

145. Weisgall, *Operation Crossroads*, 311–12.

146. Weisgall, *Operation Crossroads*, 314–15.

147. Robert C. Kiste, "The Relocation of the Bikini Marshallese," in *Exiles and Migrants in Oceania*, ed. Michael Lieber, (Honolulu: University Press of Hawaii, 1977), 87. As a result of several lawsuits and some Congressional action, the Bikinians receive some U.S. funds and medical care.

148. Weisgall, *Operation Crossroads*, 244.

149. Wasserman and Solomon, *Killing Our Own*, 39.

150. Ibid., 305, footnote 60.

151. Thomas B. Cochran, William M. Arkin, Robert S. Norris, and Milton Hoenig, *Nuclear Weapons Databook*, vol. 2, *U.S. Nuclear Warhead Production* (Cambridge, Mass.: Ballinger Publishing, 1987), 42.

152. Weisgall, *Operation Crossroads*, 302.

153. Ibid., 301.

154. Ibid., 302, 303, 306.

155. The Chugoku Newspaper, *Exposure*, 141.

156. Weisgall, *Operation Crossroads*, 303–4; Firth, *Nuclear Playground*, 17–18.

157. The Associated Press, "264 Exposed to Atom Radiation after Nuclear Blast in the Pacific," *New York Times*, 12 March 1954, 1, 3; Advisory Committee on Human Radiation Experiments, *Final Report* (Washington, D.C.: U.S. Government Printing Office, October 1995), 587.

158. Advisory Committee on Human Radiation Experiments, *Final Report*, 587.

159. Weisgall, *Operation Crossroads*, 304.

160. Ibid., citing medical studies and the *New York Times*, 3 July 1968 and 12 November 1972.

161. Firth, *Nuclear Playground*, 20; see also Weisgall, *Operation Crossroads*.

162. *Half Life*, videocassette; Firth, *Nuclear Playground*, 19–20.

163. On 2 May 1984, according to the *New York Times*, Weisgall told the House Appropriations Subcommittee on the Interior that Congress should provide yearly appropriations for the Bikinians. But that article carried no Washington, D.C., dateline, indicating that the congressional session was not covered by the reporter. The article was based on the lawsuit brought by the Bikinians against the Reagan administration.

164. Testimony of Weisgall, 98th Cong., 2d sess., *Hearing before the Subcommittee on Public Lands and National Parks of the Committee on Interior and Insular Affairs House of Representatives on Section 177 of the Proposed Compact of Free Association: Compensation for Victims of U.S. Nuclear Testing in the Marshall Islands*, 8 May 1984, 998–56, II, 23.

165. John Anjain, *Hearing before the Subcommittee*, 235. Emphasis in original.

166. A. O. Sulzberger, Jr., "U.S. Responsible in Atom Testing, House Unit Says," *New York Times*, 7 August 1980, A14.

167. House Committee on Interstate and Foreign Commerce and Its Subcommittee on Oversight and Investigations, *"The Forgotten Guinea Pigs": A Report on Health Effects of Low-Level Radiation Sustained as a Result of the Nuclear Weapons Testing Program Conducted by the United States Government,* 96th Cong., 2nd sess., 1980, Committee Print 96-IFC 53, 37, 26.

168. Advisory Committee on Human Radiation Experiments, *Final Report,* 597.

169. Weisgall, *Operation Crossroads,* 306.

170. Chapin, *Shaping History.*

171. Ibid., 212, illus. on 217.

172. Ibid., 212.

173. Ibid., 214, 215, citing the *Honolulu Star-Bulletin,* 19 and 20 April 1958.

174. Ibid., 216.

175. Ibid., citing *Ka Leo,* 20 and 30 April 1958.

176. Ibid., citing the *Honolulu Star-Bulletin,* 3 July 1958; and *Ka Leo,* 22 April 1958.

177. Ibid., 215, citing the *Honolulu Star-Bulletin* and the *Honolulu Advertiser,* 19 and 21 April 1958.

178. Ibid.

179. Ibid., 215, citing the *Honolulu Star-Bulletin,* 9 April 1958.

180. Ibid., 214, citing the *Honolulu Advertiser,* 20 March 1954.

181. Ibid., 215, citing the *Honolulu Advertiser,* 19 April 1958.

182. Ibid., 216.

183. Mary Kawena Pukui, E. W. Haertig, and Catherine A. Lee, *Nana I Ke Kumu,* vol. 2 (Honolulu: Hui Hanai of the Queen Lili'uokalani Children's Center, 1972), 305, citing G. Allen.

184. Ibid., 306.

185. Keever, "The Alphabet," apps. 1, 2.

186. Ibid., 25.

187. Television came to Hawaii in 1952. Color television arrived on 5 May 1957; see Robert C. Schmitt, "Some Firsts in Island Leisure," *The Hawaiian Journal of History* 12 (1978), 99–119.

188. Schütz, *The Voices of Eden,* 362–63.

189. Okihiro, *Cane Fires,* 275.

190. Paul Alfred Pratte, "Ke alaka'i: The Role of the Honolulu 'Star-Bulletin' in the Hawaiian Statehood Movement" (Ph.D. diss., University of Hawaii, 1976), 189–95.

191. Sanford Zalburg, "Hawaii's Dream Becomes Historic Fact," *Honolulu Advertiser,* 28 June 1959, 1.

192. Chapin, *Shaping History,* 220.

193. Ibid., 3.

194. Ibid., 3–4.

195. Ibid., 340.

196. Ibid.

197. Ibid.

198. Ibid., 341, citing the *Honolulu Advertiser,* 10 July 1970; and the *Honolulu Star-Bulletin,* 29 July 1970.

199. Ibid.

200. Ibid.

201. Ibid., citing the *Honolulu Advertiser,* 12 May 1971.

202. Ibid.

203. Ibid., 342.

204. Haunani-Kay Trask, "Kupaa Aina: Native Hawaiian Nationalism in Hawaii" in *Hawaii: Return to Nationhood*, ed. Ulla Hasager and Jonathan Friedman (Copenhagen, Denmark: International Work Group for Indigenous Affairs, Document no. 75, 1994), 19.

205. Trask, "Kupaa Aina," 16; Haunani-Kay Trask, *From a Native Daughter: Colonialism and Sovereignty in Hawai'i* (Monroe, Maine: Common Courage Press, 1993), 181.

206. An early example of such a typical photograph of a Hawaiian female hula dancer appeared in the statehood edition of the *Honolulu Advertiser*, 23 June 1959, sec. 7, p. 8.

207. Christin J. Mamiya, "Greetings from Paradise: The Representation of Hawaiian Culture in Postcards," *Journal of Communication Inquiry* 16, no. 2 (Summer 1992), 86–101.

208 Ibid., 95.

209. Denby Fawcett, "What Happens When a Chain Owner Arrives," *Columbia Journalism Review* 11, no. 4 (November/December 1972); also cited by Chapin, *Shaping History*, 312.

210. *Kahoolawe Na Leo o Kanaloa: The Voices of Kanaloa*, comp. and intro. Rowland B. Reeve (Honolulu: Ai Pohaku Press, 1995), xix.

211. *Kahoolawe*, 113.

212. Chapin, *Shaping History*, 342.

213. Peter MacDonald, "Fixed in Time: A Brief History of Kahoolawe," *The Hawaiian Journal of History* 6 (1972), 69–90.

214. Chapin, *Shaping History*, 342, citing the *Maui News*, 23 August 1969.

215. Ibid., 343.

216. *Kahoolawe*, 113.

217. Gene Kassebaum, *Criminal Justice and Hawaiians in the 1990s* (Honolulu: Alu Like, 1994).

218. Keever, "The Alphabet," 28.

219. Pukui, Haertig, and Lee, *Nana I Ke Kumu*, 306.

220. Alu Like, *Study on Native Hawaiians in the Criminal Justice System* (Honolulu: Alu Like, 1977).

221. Kassebaum, *Criminal Justice and Hawaiians*, 7.

222. Ibid.

223. Kiste, *The Bikinians*, 198.

224. Ibid., citing a remark made by Kissinger, who later became secretary of state, from Walter J. Hickel, *Who Owns America?* (New York: Coronet Communications, Paperback Library, 1972).

225. Jim Richstad, "News Flow Factors in the Pacific Islands Press" in *Publishing in the Pacific Islands*, ed. Jim Richstad and Miles J. Jackson (Honolulu: Graduate School of Library Studies, 1984), 107.

226. Ibid., 109.

227. Catherine A. Lutz and Jane L. Collins, *Reading National Geographic* (Chicago: University of Chicago Press, 1993), 136–37, 156–57.

228. Kiste, "New Political Statuses," 76.

229. Rogers, *Destiny's Landfall*, 279.

230. De Benedittis, "Guam's Trial of the Century," 9.

231. Ibid., 26.

232. Ibid., 241, 260.

233. Ibid., 222.

234. Ibid., 217.

235. Ibid., 241.

236. Ibid., 197.

237. Ibid., 168; see also Jacqueline Korona Teare, "The 'Pacific Daily News': The Small Town Newspaper Covering a Vast Frontier" (Master's thesis, Michigan State University, 1980).

238. De Benedittis, "Guam's Trial of the Century," 234–35.

239. Ibid., 241.

240. Ibid., 257–58. Rogers in *Destiny's Landfall* (p. 279) pointed out that the prosecutors recommended lenient sentencing for those who cooperated in developing the government's case.

241. De Benedittis, "Guam's Trial of the Century," 261, 263.

242. Ibid., 24; Rogers, *Destiny's Landfall*.

243. Keever, "The Alphabet," citing Thurston Twigg-Smith, "Overthrow: No Apology Needed," the *Honolulu Advertiser*, 24 January 1993, B1.

244. Ibid., quoting Twigg-Smith, "Overthrow."

245. Ibid., citing the *Honolulu Advertiser*, 28 January 1993, A6.

246. Ibid., citing the *Honolulu Advertiser*, 28 January 1993, A6.

247. Ibid., citing the *Honolulu Advertiser*, 28 January 1993, A6.

248. U.S. Public Law 103–150, 103rd Cong. 1st sess., section 1 (1), n.p.

249. Ibid., Whereas Clause no. 36.

250. Crystella Kauka, "Media Coverage of Hawaii in the National and International Press" (Paper prepared for the University of Hawaii School of Library and Information Service, Honolulu, spring 1994).

251. Deborah Ward, "Native Hawaiian Vote—the 'Aes Have It," *Ka Wai Ola O OHA*, October 1996, 1; Pat Omandam, "Native Vote Opponents Rap Results," *Honolulu Star-Bulletin*, 13 September 1996, A7.

252. *Harold F. Rice v. Benjamin J. Cayetano*, Civil no. 96–00390, consolidated with Civil no. 96–00616, U.S. District Court for the District of Hawaii.

253. Rod Thompson, "Rice Convinced We Should All Vote on Sovereignty," *Honolulu Star-Bulletin*, 16 September 1996, A6.

254. Vilsoni Hereniko, "Representations of Cultural Identities," in *Tides of History: The Pacific Islands in the Twentieth Century*, ed. K. R. Howe, Robert C. Kiste, and Brij V. Lal (Honolulu: University of Hawaii, 1994), 423.

255. Kiste, "The United States," 227–57.

256. Herbert Barringer and Nolan Liu, *The Demographic, Social, and Economic Status of Native Hawaiians*, 1990 (Honolulu: Alu Like, Inc., 1994), EX-8, 97.

257. John P. Henningham, "Multicultural Journalism: A Profile of Hawaii's Newspeople," *Journalism Quarterly* 70, no. 3 (Autumn 1993), 553. The survey was distributed in 1988.

258. Ibid., 522, 555–56.

259. Ibid., 551, quoting Asian American Journalists Association Fact Sheet (San Francisco: AAJA, 1988). No specifics were provided.

260. Ibid., 554.

261. Spencer A. Sherman, "Letter from Hawaii: Where the Breeze Is Soft and the

Media Are Mellow,'' *Columbia Journalism Review* 33, no. 3 (September/October 1994), 31.

262. Larry Fuller (Audiotaped address to the Honolulu Community Council, Honolulu, 18 July 1996).

263. Sherman, ''Letter from Hawaii,'' 33.

264. Ibid., 31.

265. Ibid., 32. The exposé of one-and-a-half pages was written by Susan C. Faludi and published in the *Wall Street Journal*, 9 September 1991.

266. Dineh Davis, ''Does the Local Media Provide an Accurate Representation of Hawaii's Diversity?'' (Paper presented at the Ethnic Studies Community Conference, Honolulu, 20 May 1995).

267. Ibid., 13, 14.

268. Ibid., 19.

269. John Henningham, ''Flaws in the Melting Pot: Hawaiian Media'' in *Ethnic Minority Media: An International Perspective*, ed. Stephen Harold Riggins (Newbury Park, Calif.: Sage, 1992), 158–59; Gerald Kato, ''Re-Defining News about Hawaiians in the Age of Information'' (Paper presented at the Ethnic Studies Community Conference, Honolulu, 20 May 1995).

270. Lurline McGregor, ''The Pacific POV (Point of View)'' (Address given at the Pacific History Association Regional Conference, Hilo, Hawaii, 12 July 1996).

271. Tim Ryan, ''The Proud Few,'' *Honolulu Star-Bulletin*, 30 October 1995, B1.

272. Ibid., quoting Lindsey.

273. Darrell Y. Hamamoto, *Monitored Peril: Asian Americans and the Politics of TV Representation* (Minneapolis: University of Minnesota Press, 1994), 20.

274. Ibid., 21.

275. Stu Dawrs, ''Playing with Fire,'' *Honolulu Weekly*, 17 July 1996, 8.

276. Cochran et al., *Nuclear Weapons Databook*, vol. 2, 41, 42. Statistics for the 817 U.S. tests are as follows: 108 in the Pacific, 689 at the Nevada Test Site, 3 over the South Atlantic, and 17 others in various states and Alaska. In addition, 212 U.S. atmospheric tests were conducted from 1945 to 1962; some were conducted in the Pacific, but the number is unspecified. In late 1993, U.S. Department of Energy Secretary Hazel O'Leary announced for the first time that her agency had secretly conducted 204 underground nuclear tests in Nevada from 1963 to 1990. See Tod Ensign and Glenn Alcalay, ''Duck and Cover(up): U.S. Radiation Testing on Humans,'' *Covert Action* 49 (Summer 1994), 29.

277. Robert C. Williams and Philip L. Cantelon, eds., *The American Atom: A Documentary History of Nuclear Politics from the Discovery of Fission to the Present 1939–84* (Philadelphia: University of Pennsylvania Press, 1984), 243.

278. ''Radiation Therapy,'' *Honolulu Weekly*, 19 June 1996, 9. See also the ''Apollo Nuclear Device Falls off New Zealand,'' *New York Times*, 18 April 1970, 13.

279. Douglas and Douglas, *Pacific Islands Yearbook*, ''Marshall Islands,'' 393.

280. Ronnie D. Lipschultz, *Radioactive Waste: Politics, Technology, and Risk* (Cambridge, Mass.: Ballinger Publishing, 1980), 84–88.

281. Helen Caldicott, ''What *Apollo 13* Left Out: Nukes in Space'' (Address given at the University of Hawaii summer session's ''Sakamaki Extraordinary Lecture Series,'' Honolulu, 21 June 1996).

282. Ibid. She identified the two as NBC, owned by General Electric, which owns a missile-making unit, and CBS, which is owned by Westinghouse.

283. Helen Caldicott, *If You Love This Planet: A Plan to Heal the Earth* (New York: W. W. Norton, 1992), 180. See also Robert D. Bullard, ed., *Unequal Protection: Environmental Justice and Communities of Color* (San Francisco: Sierra Club Books, 1994), 9–11, 292–97.

284. James Mellon, "Images of Micronesia on Film and Video," paper presented at Pacific History Association conference, Guam, December 1990, 10, 15. See also *Moving Images of the Pacific Islands: A Guide to Films and Videos*, ed. Diane Aoki; comp. by Diane Aoki and Norman Douglas (Honolulu: Center for Pacific Islands Studies, 1994).

285. Stewart Firth, "Strategic and Nuclear Issues," in *Tides of History: The Pacific Islands in the Twentieth Century*, ed. K. R. Howe, Robert C. Kiste, and Brij V. Lal (Honolulu: University of Hawaii, 1994), 311.

286. Jonathan M. Weisgall, "Micronesia and the Nuclear Pacific since Hiroshima," *SAIS* (School of Advanced International Studies, Johns Hopkins University) *Review* 5, no. 2 (Summer-Fall 1985), 54.

287. Sophie Foster, "An Epic Moment?," *Pacific Islands Monthly*, May 1996, 6–9.

288. Pamela J. Shoemaker and Stephen D. Reese, *Mediating the Message: Theories of Influences on Mass Media Content*, 2d ed. (New York: Longman, 1996), 50.

289. Michael Parenti, *Inventing Reality: The Politics of News Media*, 2d ed. (New York: St. Martin's Press, 1993), 192. Emphasis in the original.

290. Johan Galtung and Mari Holmboe Ruge, "The Structure of Foreign News," *Journal of Peace Research* 2, no. 1 (1965), 64–91.

291. Shoemaker and Reese, *Mediating the Message*, 222–23.

292. Ibid., 222.

293. Ibid., 262.

SELECTED BIBLIOGRAPHY

Anthony, J. Garner. *Hawaii under Army Rule*. Stanford, Calif.: Stanford University Press, 1955.

Buck, Elizabeth. *Paradise Remade: The Politics of Culture and History in Hawai'i*. Philadelphia: Temple University Press, 1993.

Chapin, Helen Geracimos. *Shaping History: The Role of Newspapers in Hawai'i*. Honolulu: University of Hawaii Press, 1996.

Davis, Dineh. "Does the Local Media Provide an Accurate Representation of Hawaii's Diversity?" Paper presented at the Ethnic Studies Community Conference, Honolulu, 20 May 1995.

Day, Richard R. "The Ultimate Inequality: Linguistic Genocide." In *Language of Inequality*, edited by Nessa Wolfson and Joan Manes. Berlin: Mouton Publishers, 1985.

De Benedittis, Peter. "Guam's Trial of the Century: News, Hegemony, and Rumors in an American Colony." Ph.D. diss., Pennsylvania State University, 1992.

Henningham, John P. "Multicultural Journalism: A Profile of Hawaii's Newspeople." *Journalism Quarterly* 70, no. 3 (Autumn 1993), 550–57.

Keever, Beverly Ann Deepe. "The Alphabet, *The Honolulu Advertiser* and the Hawaiians: A Quintessential Process of Cultural Racism?" Paper presented at Association for Education in Journalism and Mass Communication Convention, Washington, D.C., 11 August 1995.

Kiste, Robert C. *The Bikinians: A Study in Forced Migration*. Menlo Park, Calif.: Cummings Publishing, 1974.

Kiste, Robert C., and Richard A. Herr, eds. *The Pacific Islands in the Year 2000*. Honolulu: Pacific Islands Studies Program Working Paper Series, 1985.

Lutz, Catherine A., and Jane L. Collins. *Reading National Geographic*. Chicago: University of Chicago Press, 1993.

MacKenzie, Melody Kapilialoha, ed. *The Native Hawaiian Rights Handbook*. Honolulu: Native Hawaiian Legal Corporation and Office of Hawaiian Affairs, 1991.

Native Hawaiians Study Commission. *Report on the Culture, Needs and Concerns of Native Hawaiians*. Vol. 1. Washington, D.C.: Native Hawaiians Study Commission, 1983.

Richstad, Jim. "News Flow Factors in the Pacific Islands Press." In *Publishing in the Pacific Islands*, edited by Jim Richstad and Miles J. Jackson. Honolulu: Graduate School of Library Studies, 1984.

———. "The Press and the Courts under Martial Rule in Hawaii during World War II—From Pearl Harbor to *Duncan v. Kahanamoku*." Ph.D. diss., University of Minnesota, 1967.

———. "The Press under Martial Law: The Hawaiian Experience." *Journalism Monographs* 17 (November 1970).

Schütz, Albert J. *The Voices of Eden: A History of Hawaiian Language Studies*. Honolulu: University of Hawaii Press, 1994.

Sherman, Spencer A. "Letter from Hawaii: Where the Breeze Is Soft and the Media Are Mellow." *Columbia Journalism Review* 33, no. 3 (September/October 1994), 31–33.

Teare, Jacqueline Korona. "The 'Pacific Daily News': The Small Town Newspaper Covering a Vast Frontier." Master's thesis, Michigan State University, 1980.

Trask, Haunani-Kay. *From a Native Daughter: Colonialism and Sovereignty in Hawai'i*. Monroe, Maine: Common Courage Press, 1993.

Weisgall, Jonathan M. *Operation Crossroads: The Atomic Tests at Bikini Atoll*. Annapolis, Md.: Naval Institute Press, 1994.

7

Investigative Reporting

TIM GALLIMORE AND LILLIAN RAE DUNLAP

> In uncovering evidence, establishing facts, and searching for truth in as impartial a manner as possible, investigative reporting appeals to a higher moral order, an innate sense of right and wrong that ultimately will punish institutional malfeasance.[1]
>
> —Matthew C. Ehrlich

This chapter documents the contributions of investigative journalists in publicizing the complete picture of minority groups in the United States. Several computer databases and journalistic archives were searched to identify investigative reports on minorities. The focus was placed on how the mainstream news media covered four topics of particular interest to minorities. The chapter also provides a brief history of investigative reporting to place in context the coverage of American minority groups.

Some scholars trace the tradition of investigative reporting back to the New Testament writers who tried to counter the official version of the Roman government. Early fiction writers like Charles Dickens wrote exposés of social injustices that appeared first as newspaper serials.[2]

Nellie Bly, a woman who wanted to break into daily journalism that was monopolized by men, tried out for a position at the *New York World* in 1887. The managing editor commissioned Bly to feign insanity and get herself committed to a lunatic asylum on Blackwell's Island outside New York City. Bly spent ten days in the asylum doing "stunt" journalism, part of Joseph Pulitzer's new technique of exploiting crime and scandal to write sensational stories that described a "shocking circumstance with the spirit of a crusade."[3] The *World* ran her two-part series exposing the crowded, harsh, unsanitary conditions and abusive staff at the asylum. The series was credited with convincing the city to provide funds to improve facilities and end the overcrowding and abuse at Blackwell's asylum.

The investigative reporting tradition in America, called "muckraking," can be traced back to 1900 when conscientious newspaper publishers and some popular magazines turned their attention to more aggressive reporting on the increasing problems of the cities and urban life. In 1902, *McClure's* magazine printed articles by Ida Tarbell, Ray Stannard Baker, and Lincoln Steffens, who focused on governmental wrongdoing. Dubbed the "muckrakers" in a 1906 speech given by President Theodore Roosevelt, the reporters embarked upon a crusade to expose corruption in both business and government, expose abuses of basic individual rights, and focus attention on the inequitable distribution of wealth.

The golden era of the muckrakers lasted until 1912; however, the tradition of practicing journalism for moral and social improvement continued through the 1920s and 1930s with the work of such lone crusading journalists as Heywood Broun, Upton Sinclair, and Paul Y. Anderson of the *St. Louis Post-Dispatch*. Others like George Seldes and I. F. Stone, and some from small-circulation magazines like *The Nation*, continued the muckraking tradition through the 1940s and 1950s until its rebirth as investigative reporting in the late 1960s.[4]

Individual journalists like freelancer Seymour Hersh and columnist Jack Anderson were a bridge between the muckrakers of the past and the famous *Washington Post* reporting team of Bob Woodward and Carl Bernstein, whose work on the Watergate case perhaps marks the apex of investigative reporting. These journalists exposed corruption and wrongdoing. Their work was complemented by the activities of citizen-activists like Ralph Nader and government "whistle-blowers" like Senator William Proxmire, who gave annual "golden fleece" awards to what he believed were the most wasteful government programs.[5] The Freedom of Information Act, which became law in 1967, and its amendments gave journalists a powerful tool with which to pry open files and conduct their investigations of the executive agencies of the federal government.[6]

Facing competition from television news in the late 1960s, newspapers saw reform or investigative journalism as a way to maintain their edge in informing the public. In a 1970 article describing the reemergence of investigative journalism, Carey McWilliams, editor of *The Nation*, wrote, "In general both newspapers and magazines have begun to feel that muckraking or investigative journalism is a useful means of countering network news."[7] Starting in 1967, publications like *Newsday* and the Associated Press assembled teams of reporters dedicated to investigative reporting.[8]

Later, network television news divisions produced investigative reports and documentaries every bit as powerful as the traditional muckraking magazines. The 1971 CBS documentary "The Selling of the Pentagon" is one example. Today, most major newspapers have investigative reporting teams, and television newsmagazine programs like "60 Minutes," "20/20," and "Dateline NBC" continue the broadcasting tradition of investigative reporting.

Investigative journalism got a boost in 1975 with the founding of Investigative Reporters and Editors (IRE). The nonprofit educational organization today has 4,500 members and is headquartered at the University of Missouri School of Journalism. The organization helps working journalists, journalism students, and educators practice and teach techniques of investigative reporting through conference workshops, newsroom seminars, and a bimonthly magazine, *The IRE Journal*. The IRE also provides telephone and computer assistance to members who can access its holdings of 10,000 print and broadcast reports and produces *The Reporter's Handbook: An Investigator's Guide to Documents and Techniques*. Most important, however, is its annual competition to recognize the best investigative reporting.

THE JOURNALISM OF OUTRAGE

Definitions of investigative reporting typically focus on how journalists obtain information "rather than its societally relevant results," several scholars have noted.[9] Investigative reporting has been called "the journalism of exposure" because of its emphasis on the watchdog function of a vigilant media eager to expose corruption. The authors of the most widely used textbook on newswriting define investigative journalism as the "pursuit of information that has been concealed, such as evidence of wrongdoing."[10]

Investigative reporting requires a reporter to use enterprise, skills, and techniques beyond those used in normal news gathering to obtain and report information of importance to the public. Often such information is gathered from original documents and data that uncooperative or reluctant sources attempt to conceal. Investigative reporters use scientific methods for gathering information and testing hypotheses. This approach for uncovering facts and establishing truths is sometimes called precision journalism. Philip Meyer, an early practitioner of precision journalism, used social scientific methods to uncover alienation as the key cause behind the 1967 riot in Detroit. "The story's reporting techniques enabled the *Free Press* to explode the myth that the rioters were Southern immigrants who could not adjust to big city life," one source stated.[11]

Reporters have now added the computer to their arsenal of investigative tools. Don Barlett and James Steele, pioneers in using computers for investigative reporting, used computers to analyze Philadelphia criminal court records for a 1972 investigative series. The series exposed unfair sentencing practices and other irregularities in the local criminal justice system.[12]

Another important element of investigative reporting is its focus on exposing social injustice. In 1983 the IRE adopted this definition of investigative reporting:

It is the reporting, through one's own work product and initiative, of matters of importance which some persons or organizations wish to keep secret. The three basic elements are that the investigation be the work of the reporter, not a report of an investigation made by someone else; that the subject of the story involves something of reasonable importance to the reader or viewer; and that others are attempting to hide these matters from the public.[13]

Members of the IRE have disagreed about the requirement that investigative reports concern information that others want to conceal. This part of the definition has been attacked because investigative reporters, with the aid of the computer, have been able to uncover bits of seemingly insignificant information that, when assembled, reveal important societal issues and problems that do not involve coverups. Often the custodians of the information and records themselves do not realize the important truths that are buried in the data analyzed by investigative journalists for their reports.

Steve Weinberg edited out the requirements of evasion or stonewalling from the definition of investigative reporting when he edited the 1996 edition of the IRE *Reporter's Handbook*.[14] In it he quoted veteran investigative reporter Gene Roberts, who said that "investigative reporting is 'not so much catching the politician with his pants down' or focusing on a single outrage. It's digging beneath the surface so we can help readers understand what's going on in an increasingly complex world."[15]

Historians and media scholars have noted that "the purpose of investigative journalism historically has been to tell stories of wrongdoing that will stir moral outrage."[16] In 1988 communication researchers James Ettema and Theodore Glasser termed investigative reporting "the journalism of outrage" and demonstrated how investigative journalists use language to provoke this sense of moral outrage.[17] Investigative journalists count on this sense of outrage to bring about change in the circumstances and issues they report on to the public.

The focus on societal reform, which is supported by the concept of a watchdog press, is a special mission of the investigative journalist.

More than a news-gathering process, the journalism of outrage is a form of storytelling that probes the boundaries of America's civic conscience. Published allegations of wrongdoing—political corruption, government inefficiency, corporate abuses—help define public morality in the United States. Journalistic exposés that trigger outrage from the public or policy makers affirm society's standards of misconduct. . . . Investigative journalists *intend* to provoke outrage in their reports of malfeasance. Their work is validated when citizens respond by demanding change from their leaders. Similarly, corrective policy actions provide official legitimacy to an investigative story.[18]

The results of investigative reporting have so far been inconsistent.[19] At times, laws have been changed and corruption has been rooted out; at other times, the work of the investigative journalist has been ignored by the public. However, experts agree that "muckraking, a perennial force in American life, will no doubt continue to inspire reform where there exists a basis of popular indignation."[20]

INVESTIGATIVE REPORTING AND MINORITIES

In one sense, reporting on the condition of minorities in America began not with investigative reporting by white journalists working for mainstream newspapers, but with the appearance in the eighteenth century of tracts condemning the institution and practice of slavery. Samuel Sewell's 1700 pamphlet, *The Selling of Joseph*, rejected legal recognition of slaves as property. But Sewell, not unlike many of his time, never discussed the equality of blacks and whites or the integration of the races.

Perhaps the most horrific details of slavery became part of early slave narratives. Some of the published narratives include *The Address of Abraham Johnstone: A Narrative of the Uncommon Sufferings and Surprising Deliverance of Briton Hammon, a Negro Man* (1760); *The Life and Dying Speech of Arthur* (1768); and the *Narrative of the Life of Olaudah Equiano by Gustavus Vassa, the African* (1789). Often the narratives were written with the help of abolitionists from the North. They were sometimes published as pamphlets or in newsletters as well as in newspapers.[21]

The next platform for exposing the struggle against slavery was the black press, beginning with the appearance of *Freedom's Journal* in 1827. Dissatisfied with how mainstream papers covered the issue of slavery, John Russwurm and the Reverend Samuel Cornish started publishing *Freedom's Journal* so that blacks could plead their own cause and illuminate the conditions under which they were forced to live. The tradition continued with the publication of other abolitionist pamphlets and newspapers, including William Lloyd Garrison's *Liberator* (1831) and Frederick Douglass's *The North Star* (1847).

Ida Wells Barnett defied Southern white supremacy with her antilynching crusade of the 1890s. This African-American teacher-turned-journalist began her investigation after a close friend was lynched with two other black men. The men's "crime" was that they had a more successful grocery store than their white competitors. Wells Barnett discovered that between 1882 and 1892, 726 black men and women were hanged. She concluded that the lynchings were part of a larger effort to reestablish white supremacy following Reconstruction. She traveled around the South collecting sworn statements from witnesses to lynching, then wrote about the lynchings in her weekly paper, *Free Speech*, and later for other black papers around the country. She wrote a series of pamphlets and gave antilynching speeches across the North and in Europe. Antilynching leagues were organized in the United States and England. Because of the increased public scrutiny resulting from her work, the number of lynchings declined from a peak of 241 in 1892 to 107 in 1899.[22]

The publishers of other black newspapers, such as the *Baltimore Afro-American* and the *Chicago Defender*, continued to muckrake on behalf of their race. They were joined in 1905 by W.E.B. DuBois, who founded and edited *The Crisis*, the magazine of the National Association for the Advancement of Colored People (NAACP).

Muckraking in the mainstream press entered a new phase when it started to focus on racial issues in 1908. "Not content merely to arouse public opinion, individual muckrakers attempted to translate indignation into positive programs for change," stated scholars John Harrison and Harry Stein.[23]

During the muckraking era, Charles Edward Russell investigated racial and industrial conditions in the South for the *New York Herald*. Revolted by segregation and the poor treatment of blacks, Russell joined with Lincoln Steffens and others to support the founding of the NAACP.[24]

Since then, investigative journalism has matured to include more detailed and substantive reporting on the nation's minority groups. In fact, the mass protest against the deplorable socioeconomic conditions of African Americans known as the Civil Rights Movement is credited with the revival of investigative journalism in the 1960s.[25] This contribution includes the *New York Times v. Sullivan* Supreme Court decision that made it more difficult for public officials to sue the media successfully for libel when they report on public figures and controversial social issues.

Through its reporting, television played a key role in forwarding the Civil Rights Movement. Viewers across the country were horrified at live pictures of black civil rights demonstrators, including children, being beaten, set upon by police dogs and blasted with high-pressure fire hoses in the South. On January 21, 1959, CBS television presented a documentary on the closing of six Norfolk, Virginia, high schools to avoid federally ordered desegregation. The series was hosted by Edward R. Murrow. By using such a high-profile correspondent to report on the program, CBS gained for the civil rights issue tremendous credibility with whites.

During the early 1960s, NBC aired several "NBC White Papers." One program in late 1960 turned the cameras on desegregation efforts in Nashville. In 1962 the series focused on the effects of the tightening of the welfare code in Newburgh, New York. In 1968 ABC aired a six-part special on "Bias and the Media," which exposed racism in the ranks of journalists. Ed Bradley hosted a 1975 CBS special, "Blacks in America: With All Deliberate Speed?," which examined conditions since the 1954 U.S. Supreme Court school desegregation case *Brown v. Board of Education of Topeka, Kansas*.

Exemplary investigative reporting was done in the 1972 exposé of the forty-year Tuskegee experiment conducted by the U.S. Public Health Service (PHS) to observe the effects of untreated syphilis on 400 black men in Macon County, Alabama. The experiment was started in 1932 when the results of untreated syphilis were already known to medical science. Promising free health treatment and a proper burial, the Public Health Service and Tuskegee Institute recruited poor black men infected with the disease to participate in the study. The men, mostly sharecroppers, were not told they were part of an experiment. Neither were they given any treatment, even after penicillin was discovered as a cure for syphilis in the 1940s. Doctors conducting the experiment simply observed and documented the progression of the disease until the subjects died. After the subjects died, the doctors conducted autopsies on the men and compared their medical condition to that of 200 healthy black men in a control group.

The experiment continued until Jean Heller, an investigative reporter with the Associated Press, broke the story on July 25, 1972, in the *Washington Star*.[26] "The exposé generated national press attention and a swift public reaction of outrage," one source stated.[27] Once the news of the forty-year experiment was made public, the Centers for Disease Control and Prevention, which had inherited the project, the Tuskegee Institute, and most of those involved over the years started to deny involvement and distanced themselves from the affair. Others justified their participation on the basis of the racist views of black inferiority that were prevalent when the experiment began.

"When the Associated Press broke the story in 1972, a shocked public drew comparisons with the Nazis' Nuremberg experiments. Neither contrite nor apologetic, most of the study's senior physicians offered inadequate scientific defenses and improbable moral ones," noted one journalist.[28] Major newspapers carried the exposé and editorial comments condemning the experiment, especially the federal government's involvement in it. The government appointed a blue-ribbon panel to investigate the experiment.

The study was terminated in October 1972. A class-action suit for $1.8 billion was filed against the government on behalf of the men involved in the experiment. The case was settled out of court for $12 million. Syphilitic survivors of the experiment got $37,500 each; those in the control group got $15,000 each; and the estates of the deceased got lesser amounts.[29]

Because of the experiment, the sexual partners of the syphilitic men had not been told that they too were exposed to the disease; as a result, many black children were born with congenital syphilis. This led to charges that the government experiment amounted to genocide against blacks. Similar charges have been made that the government is responsible for the introduction and spread of AIDS among African Americans.[30] These latter accusations, although unconfirmed, may also lead to future investigative reporting on African Americans and other minority groups.

STUDIES ON MINORITIES, INVESTIGATIVE REPORTING

In order to identify the studies that scholars have already published on minorities and investigative reporting, a bibliographic search was conducted using several computer databases. Among them were PAIS International, ERIC, Journalism/Communication Abstracts, and Dissertation Abstracts. The searches revealed that very few academic studies have been done on this specific topic. Dissertation Abstracts listed only two pertinent theses: "Geographic Discrimination in Mortgage Lending: An Empirical Investigation" by Paul R. Goebel (University of Georgia, 1980); and "At the Bar of Judge Lynch: Lynching and Lynch Mobs in America" by John R. Ross (Texas Tech University, 1983). The

Ross thesis includes investigative reports of the NAACP and other civil rights groups as well as newspaper reports in the archives of the Tuskegee Institute.

The most comprehensive analysis of investigative reporting and minorities is found in *Muckraking: Past, Present and Future*, edited by John Harrison and Harry Stein. Chapter 3, "Race Relations and the Muckrakers," is devoted to the topic. The chapter points out that muckraking on urban corruption had a greater impact on the public than did stories on the plight of the disenfranchised Negro. *Pearson's* and *Hampton's* were two magazines that distinguished themselves during the muckraking era with their specific focus on racial discrimination and injustice.

Although historians disagree about the contributions of muckraking to the cause of equality for American minorities, some argue that "the muckrakers made a considerable contribution to the cause of Negro rights."[31] Among the early works cited in the Harrison and Stein chapter is Ray Stannard Baker's 1908 series, "Following the Color Line." The muckraking magazines—*McClure's, The Nation, The New Republic, Cosmopolitan*, and the *Atlantic Monthly*—published stories about lynchings, riots, the selling of convict labor, and what was generally referred to as "the race question."

But apparently the great muckrakers largely ignored racism and segregation as they exposed the other evils of their times. Some muckrakers, like Will Irwin and Ray Stannard Baker, were accused of racism and complicity with the social order of inequality. Harrison and Stein wrote, "Steffens and Russell, whatever their personal views, barely mentioned Negroes in their published work."[32] Both muckrakers subscribed to the popular conception of a hierarchy of the races and viewed the Negro as inferior. In his private letters, Lincoln Steffens referred to Negroes as "niggers."[33]

Herbert Shapiro's article on "The Muckrakers and Negroes" in the Spring 1970 issue of *Phylon* chronicles the early muckrakers' attempts to report the conditions of African Americans.[34] Shapiro concludes that what the muckrakers wrote was more of a coverup than an exposé of America's treatment of African Americans. Shapiro's analysis of their writings showed that the muckrakers from Baker to Upton Sinclair disseminated racist stereotypes about blacks and condoned the racial hierarchy of their times. "Whatever evaluation is made of what the muckrakers had to say about Negroes, it should be observed that only rarely does it appear as a central theme in the crusade."[35] But despite the shortcomings in the muckrakers' attention to racial injustice, Shapiro concluded that they "punched a hole in the wall of ignorance and silence meant to keep Negroes from the attention of the entire country."[36] The muckrakers also did not investigate the situation of Native Americans, Hispanics, or Asian Americans.

Because the literature about investigative journalism and minorities is so sparse, research was done on the topic to document the contributions of the mainstream media in this arena. Several searches were conducted to identify investigative reports on minorities. Race relations, criminal justice, environmental racism, and redlining were chosen as special topics for this analysis.

Investigative stories that appeared in the print media were identified through computer searches of the Expanded Academic Index (1980–1995), the Nexis database, and the National Newspaper Index (1993–1996). The IRE database was used to find investigative reports that appeared in both broadcast and print media between 1975 and 1995. The analysis also included stories from the Radio and Television News Directors Association Edward R. Murrow Awards competitions. Tapes from the regional and national winners since 1984 are indexed and archived in the broadcast news department at the University of Missouri's School of Journalism.[37]

In identifying investigative stories, the authors focused on reporting that went beyond the normal beat story or coverage of the breaking news event. Included in the analysis are stories that exposed problems, issues, and trends that were reported on by using interviewing and documentation techniques common to extended and extensive investigation. These stories uncovered new information of significance to understanding the larger issues, the context, and the conditions of minority populations in the United States. The reporter had to dig up the facts rather than rely on reports from government or private nonjournalistic institutions. Only a few of the stories found dealt with the problems of U.S. minorities other than African Americans. The impact that the reporting had, especially changes in law or social practice that resulted, also was assessed.

FINDINGS

Eighty-seven investigative stories were found. The bulk of them, seventy-one, were published in newspapers of all circulation sizes and from all regions of the country. Eleven of the stories were produced by broadcasters; five were published in magazines. Of those five, only one general circulation magazine, *U.S. News & World Report*, published an investigative report on the four issues focused on for the study. This was a surprising finding given the central role that magazines have played historically in investigative journalism. The specifics of the findings are reported by topic below and in four accompanying tables.

Race Relations

According to Sig Gissler, former editor of the *Milwaukee Journal*,

Race—it is America's rawest nerve and most enduring dilemma. From birth to death, race is with us, defining, dividing, distorting. . . . Yet despite the importance of race and the deep public interest in it, the media's coverage tends to be fragmented, episodic, confused, misdirected and sometimes cowardly. . . . In short, the media in America too regularly mangle their crucial mission as regards race.[38]

However, the media in many large cities have done investigative reports on the relations between the minority and majority populations. Also common are as-

Table 1
Investigative Reporting on Race Relations

IRE #	DATE	MEDIA/LOCATION	TOPIC/ISSUE
10373	Feb. 28-Dec. 29, 1994	*Akron Beacon-Journal*	race relations
9704	May 19, 1993	WTTW-TV (Chicago)	cost of racism
10095	May 8, 1993	*Times-Picayune*	race relations in New Orleans
9545	Feb. 21-28, 1993	*Indianapolis Star*	race relations
8827	Oct. 3, 1991	KUCR-Radio (Riverside, Calif.)	Korean-black conflict
8409	Sept. 26, 1991	ABC News, "Primetime Live"	blacks treated with suspicion
6959	Feb. 28-Jan. 13, 1989	*Birmingham News*	race relations
6650	Sept. 24-29, 1989	*York (Pa.) Daily Record*	Spanish language discrimination
8543	Oct. 22-28, 1989	*Times Union* (Albany)	racial attitudes
6046	Oct. 30, 1988	*Kalamazoo Gazette*	discrimination against black renters
5526	Jan. 25-Feb. 5, 1988	KMOX-Radio (St. Louis)	racial hatred
6868	May 22-27, 1988	*Rocky Mountain News* (Denver)	condition and history of blacks
5133	June 13-19, 1987	*Cincinnati Post*	progress of blacks
	1986	WSMV-TV (Nashville)	race relations 20 yrs. after Civil Rights Act
728	Feb., 1985	*Dallas Morning News*	low-quality subsidized housing for blacks
2725	Dec. 30, 1984	*Asbury Park* (N.J.) *Press*	discrimination against black renters
------	Apr. 24-Dec. 25, 1983	*Boston Globe*	status of blacks in workplace
2287	July, 1981	*The Record* (Hackensack)	discrimination in funeral arrangements
308	Jan., 1979	*The Record* (Hackensack)	real estate discrimination

TOTAL = 19

sessments of the conditions of African-American citizens over a period of time, usually from the death of Martin Luther King, Jr., or some major riot that the city experienced during the civil rights era. About twenty such articles that appeared between 1975 and 1995 were found (see Table 1).

The year-long public journalism project on race relations published by the *Akron Beacon-Journal* in 1993 won a Pulitzer Prize for public service. The project encompassed five series of articles that appeared throughout the year. The series surveyed conditions of blacks and whites thirty years after Martin Luther King, Jr., described his vision of a color-blind American society. The examination revealed that relations between the races had changed little. The socioeconomic conditions of African Americans had not improved significantly. More important, the series documented that "regardless of income level, blacks are less likely to get mortgage or business loans."[39]

The *Boston Globe* won a Pulitzer Prize in 1984 for its six-part series on race relations published throughout 1983. The *Globe* won in the "special investigative" category for its local reporting on conditions in Boston. The series was the result of a decision taken by the editors after the violence of the 1970s over school busing periodically to examine race relations in the city's institutions. The focus of the *Globe*'s series was on the hiring and promotion of blacks in high technology, banks, newspapers, crafts unions, universities, and government.

The investigative team of seven journalists used statistics and interviews with African-American and Hispanic residents and leaders of the city's most powerful institutions to gather information. The *Globe*'s investigation found that Boston was the hardest metropolitan area in America for an African American to hold a job or to earn a promotion.

Broadcasters have also contributed to exposing the state of America's race relations. KMOX Radio in St. Louis won a George Foster Peabody Award for its series, "Hate Crimes: America's Cancer," which examined race relations in Missouri. The reports aired in January and February of 1988. The reporting resulted in the state legislature's strengthening Missouri statutes dealing with ethnic intimidation.

Similar stories on race relations were broadcast or published in Nashville (WSMV-TV, 1986); Chicago (WTTW-TV, 1993); Indianapolis (*Star*, 1993); Cincinnati (*Post*, 1987); New Orleans (*Times-Picayune*, 1993); and elsewhere. A radio station in Riverside, California, investigated black and Korean conflict, and a Pennsylvania newspaper examined Spanish language discrimination. Among the more outrageous findings from these investigative projects was one in the *Record* (Hackensack, N.J.) documenting discrimination by cemetery operators who refused to bury blacks and whites in the same cemeteries in Hackensack and neighboring cities.[40]

Crime, Law, and Justice

The journalists of the muckraking era filled the popular magazines with stories about lawlessness in America. However, they demonstrated "little knowledge of the subcultures and functioning of the justice-delivery system," according to Harrison and Stein.[41] Their accounts included stories about judicial, political, and business corruption; lynchings; police brutality; rioting; and slave-labor contracting. Although they chronicled the disparity in the legal treatment of whites and blacks, the muckrakers were more concerned about unchecked economic power and the corruption of capitalism than about injustices inflicted on the Negroes in their society.

In assessing thirteen years of IRE investigative reporting award winners, former IRE executive director Steve Weinberg found in 1992 that today's investigative journalists write about the same topics and themes as did the muckrakers. The top three categories among fifty-two winning entries concerned waste, fraud, abuse, and corruption in all levels of government and in local law enforcement.[42] During the thirteen years of competition, only four awards were given to investigative stories about racial discrimination. However, the trend did show that journalists reported on racism in the judicial system when it involved arrests, bail, and sentencing, as well as other types of discrimination stories involving housing rental and mortgage lending. Inspired by the 1991 Rodney King beating in Los Angeles, many journalists wrote stories about police bru-

Table 2
Investigative Reporting on Criminal Justice

IRE #	DATE	MEDIA/LOCATION	TOPIC/ISSUE
9816	Dec. 19, 1993	*Sarasota Herald-Tribune*	pretrial release skewed to favor whites
------	Aug.-Oct., 1993	WSFA-TV (Montgomery)	FBI cover up murder of black man
9923	Aug.15, 1993	*New York Newsday*	criminal justice
9663	July-Aug., 1993	*Houston Chronicle*	minority traffic arrests
9706	May, 1993	*Chicago Reporter*	disparities in community policing
9290	Aug. 25, 1992	*Delaware County Daily Times* (Primos, Pa.)	racial profiles, blacks arrested
9340	Nov.15-20, 1992	*Daily Progress* (Charlottesville, Va.)	drug law, black males
9233	July 22, 1992	*Seattle Post-Intelligencer*	police brutality
8049	Dec. 8-10, 1991	*Florida Times-Union*	longer sentence for killing whites
8571	Dec. 8, 1991	*San Jose Mercury News*	minorities get worse plea bargain deals
8274	Nov./Dec., 1991	*Dallas Morning News*	military justice
8133	June 9-14, 1991	*Evansville* (Ind.) *Courier*	jail term for minority drug offenders
8025	June 16-22, 1991	*Hartford Courant*	inequities in bonds
8175	Apr. 17, 1991	*Charleston News & Courier*	police brutality
9435	May 12-15, 1991	*West County Times* (Richmond, Calif.)	higher percentage of black men convicted
8348	May 19-20; Dec. 22-23, 1991	*Times Union* (Albany)	minorities more likely to be sent to jail
7673	Apr. 29-May 2, 1990	*Indianapolis Star*	minorities get more time for same offences
7344	Nov. 7, Dec. 16, 1990	*Los Angeles Daily News*	police use guns, dogs on minorities
6350	Oct. 1, 1989	*Dallas Times Herald*	minorities punished more severely
6789	July 30, 1989	WWOR-TV (Secaucus, N.J.)	police stop minorities in expensive cars
5673	Feb.-June, 1988	*Asbury Park* (N.J.) *Press*	few minority prosecutors
5098	Dec.13-16, 1987	*Atlanta Constitution*	double standard of justice for blacks
4445	July 22, 1986	*Princeton Packet*	arbitrary police searches
4299	Mar. 9-11, Dec. 21, 1986	*Dallas Morning News*	exclusion of black jurors
1217	July 7-12, 1985	*Herald & Review* (Decatur, Ill.)	exclusion of black jurors
3421	Nov.11-13, 1985	WTSP-TV (St. Petersburg, Fla.)	FBI, Justice Dept. cover up murder
2730	July 15, 1984	*Miami Herald*	racially balanced jury system exists
2023	June, 1984	*Philadelphia Inquirer*	police use dogs on minorities
4001	March, 1983	*Fayetteville* (N.C.) *Times*	judges changing verdicts after trial
2627	Dec., 1978	*Clarion-Ledger* (Jackson, Miss.)	Mississippi hostile justice
239	Mar., 1976-Apr., 1978	*Charleston* (W.Va.) *Gazette*	court inequities, disparate sentencing

TOTAL= 31

tality. "Almost all of the brutality stories contain elements of racial discrimi-nation," Weinburg observed.[43]

For the period examined for this study, the IRE database and the RTNDA archives contained thirty-one investigative reports about minorities and all as-pects of the criminal justice system (see Table 2). With one exception, these reports demonstrate over and over that racial bias and inequalities permeate the nation's judicial system. The reporting produced evidence that minorities are questioned, harassed, arrested, abused, and brutalized by police in greater per-centages than whites. Minorities have less access to bail and adequate legal counsel than whites and often are given longer prison sentences than whites who are convicted of the same type of crime. An early example of these reports is the *Charleston* (W.Va.) *Gazette* series, which appeared between March 1976 and April 1978. The series uncovered questionable practices among judges and court inequities, including disparate sentencing, especially for black defendants.

The investigative reports on criminal justice document that there are few minorities among prosecutors and judges. The investigations also chronicle the trend by courts to exclude black jurors. The one exception to the finding of bias and inequality in the judicial system came in a 1984 *Miami Herald* report based on a computerized study of the Dade County Circuit Court's jury system. The report found that, contrary to charges of being unfair and discriminatory against blacks, the Dade County system is actually racially balanced.[44]

However, evidence of rampant injustice and abuse was more typical of the stories found in this project. For example, in 1989, WWOR-TV documented the persistent practice by the New Jersey State Police of stopping, harassing, and falsely arresting African and Hispanic Americans. New Jersey police stopped and searched minorities in disproportionate numbers and often detained them for hours. More than 70 percent of those whom police stopped were minorities, while a check performed by WWOR-TV showed that only 7 percent of the motorists regularly using the targeted strip of highway were minorities. WWOR's investigation encouraged some local newspapers to report on allegations of racism among the New Jersey State Police.

Environmental Racism

The term environmental racism embodies a new concern for American minorities. Industrialization and the nuclear age have produced an increasing volume of toxic waste products that must be disposed of somewhere. The location of plants that produce these hazardous waste products and how and where society disposes of the materials are important questions being investigated by journalists. Their findings to date indicate that minority communities are disproportionately chosen as locations for the production and disposal of hazardous waste. Journalists have documented that the federal government is among the perpetrators of environmental racism.

From 1993 to 1996, six stories about environmental racism run in major newspapers were indexed in the National Newspaper Index. Between 1980 and 1996, twenty such stories were indexed in the Infotrack and Expanded Academic Index databases. Most of these stories appeared in legal, scientific, or environmental journals. The only mass circulation magazine that even reported on the topic was *U.S. News & World Report*, which ran a two-page article in 1992.[45] Only one of these stories was considered an investigative report based on the definition used for this study. That story, which is discussed below, also won an IRE award. The IRE database was used to identify eight other investigative stories on environmental racism (see Table 3).

A team of *National Law Journal* reporters won a 1993 IRE award for their reporting on environmental racism. The story, titled "Unequal Protection: The

Table 3

Investigative Reporting on Environmental Racism

IRE #	DATE	MEDIA/LOCATION	TOPIC/ISSUE
10408	July/Aug., 1994	The Humanist (Amherst, N.Y.)	environmental racism
10077	Jan./Feb., 1994	E Magazine (Norwalk, Conn.)	Cherokees shut down unsafe nuclear plant
9702	May-Dec., 1993	Dallas Morning News	govt. forces blacks into toxic dump ghetto
8847	Sept. 21, 1992	National Law Journal (N.Y.)	environmental racism and the EPA
8695	May/June, 1992	E Magazine (Norwalk, Conn.)	minority areas targeted for toxic dumps
8699	Spring 1992	Covert Action (Washington, D.C.)	toxic waste disposal on Native American lands
8637	Nov. 17-21, 1991	St. Louis Post-Dispatch	federal govt. polluted American Indian lands
8010	April, 1991	The Crisis (NAACP)	hazardous waste in minority neighborhoods
7411	June, 1990	The Chicago Reporter	illegal garbage dumping in city's black wards

TOTAL = 9

Racial Divide in Environmental Law,'' was published in September 1992. The team was able to prove a disparity in how the federal government cleans up toxic waste sites and punishes polluters. The article demonstrated that the most dangerous pollution was in minority communities and that the Environmental Protection Agency (EPA) was much more vigorous in prosecuting and heavily fining polluters for polluting in white communities than in minority communities.

As a result of the article, Congress pledged to hold hearings on the findings, and a manufacturer canceled plans to build the world's largest pulp plant in a small black community featured in the article. In addition, the EPA's enforcement chief sent a memo to field offices warning them to guard against bias in all stages of the enforcement process.[46]

In 1993 the *Dallas Morning News* exposed a government housing plan that would have forced thousands of African-American families to live in a crime-ridden, government-owned ghetto that was about to be declared a Superfund toxic contamination site. As a result of the exposé, the project was abandoned.

A 1991 series published in the *St. Louis Post-Dispatch* reported how the federal government polluted Indian lands, including Mohawk land in New York and uranium mining sites in the Southwest. The reports indicated that federal authorities also gave polluted land to unsuspecting Native Americans in Alaska. A 1994 series in *E Magazine* in Connecticut explained how Cherokees shut down an unsafe nuclear plant.

In 1986 WGN-TV in Chicago aired ''My Toxic Neighbor,'' which identified a perfect example of environmental racism. The journalists investigated the effects of a nearby chemical plant on residents and plant workers. Most of the neighbors were African Americans. The series and follow-up reports caused the EPA to focus attention on the problem and speed up steps to protect plant employees and the public. Results also included accelerated EPA testing and Senator Alan Dixon's call for immediate off-site testing.

Redlining

Many laws came out of the civil rights era that were aimed at eliminating racial segregation and discrimination in all aspects of American society. Among them were the Fair Housing Act and the Equal Credit Opportunity Act guaranteeing minorities equal access to housing and to the financing to afford it. Noncompliance with these laws was widespread, and the nation continued its historical pattern of segregated housing as financial institutions denied mortgage loans to African Americans. This practice, known as redlining, is defined as the refusal by financial institutions to make mortgage loans to residents of certain neighborhoods because of the area's racial composition, the income level of the residents, or the age of the housing.

The Home Mortgage Disclosure Act of 1975 was added to the arsenal of legal weapons available to combat the discriminatory practice of redlining. The act mandated the collection of demographic data on mortgage lending to identify better the patterns of discrimination. In 1977 Congress passed the Community Reinvestment Act to help outlaw redlining. The act requires financial institutions to invest in all geographic areas served by their branches and also requires lenders to meet the credit needs of all segments of the community.

Through monitoring compliance with these laws and through their own investigations, journalists are able to report on the level of access minorities have to mortgage loans and other kinds of credit. The media have had their greatest impact on improving the conditions of American minorities through their coverage exposing the continuing practice of redlining. From 1993 to 1996, thirteen stories on mortgage discrimination were published in the major newspapers indexed in the National Newspaper Index. The Expanded Academic Index listed sixty-five news stories on the topic between 1980 and 1996. The Nexis database included 428 items on redlining and minorities between 1989 and 1995. The contribution of investigative reporting on this topic is seen in the twenty-eight stories listed in Table 4. Although most of the stories focused on redlining in African American communities, one 1993 story published in the *Anchorage Daily News* was concerned with redlining against Native Americans.

With the coming of the information age, "information redlining," also called "electronic redlining," became a new method used by financial institutions and information service providers to discriminate against minority and poor communities. Just as with mortgage loans, a pattern is developing wherein minorities are systematically being denied access to information technology and the infrastructure that will deliver information services in the future. Some regional telephone companies have been charged with redlining on the high-tech information highway. The phone companies are systematically bypassing low-income and minority neighborhoods as they install the digital dial tone network to deliver "video-on-demand" services.

As early as 1981, journalists were investigating charges of electronic redlining by the cable television industry. It appeared that cable providers were selectively

Table 4
Investigative Reporting on Redlining

IRE #	DATE	MEDIA/LOCATION	TOPIC/ISSUE
------	April 17, 1995	*U.S. News & World Report*	new redlining, minorities still shortchanged
10424	May 29, 1994	*Santa Rosa Press Democrat* (Santa Rosa, Calif.)	redlining of high-income minorities
10519	Feb. 27, 1994	*Hartford Courant*	minority mortgages twice as likely to be rejected
9742	Dec. 5, 1993	Cable News Network	insurance company won't cover blacks
9909	Nov. 14, 1993	*Anchorage Daily News*	redlining Native Americans
10133	Sept. 12, 1993	*Tribune-Review* (Greensburg, Pa.)	bias in banking system
9510	Aug. 8, 1993	*News & Record* (Greensboro, N.C.)	redlining
9936	June 6-8, 1993	*Washington Post*	no improvement in lending to minorities
9965	Apr. 25, 1993	*St. Paul Pioneer Press*	Twin City blacks can't get mortgages
9705	Jan., May, 1993	*Chicago Reporter*	redlining
9555	Nov. 30, 1992	*Wall Street Journal*	redlining
8573	Nov. 30, 1992	*Wall Street Journal*	blacks and loans in largest cities
------	Nov. 15, 1992	CBS, "60 Minutes"	minority homeowners pay higher interest
9389	July 5-6, 1992	*Evansville* (Ind.) *Courier*	redlining
8334	May 14-17, 1991	WHDH-TV (Boston)	redlining on second mortgages
7329	Sept. 9-11, 1990	*The Oregonian* (Portland)	redlining is common
6557	Sept. 11-12, 1989	*Boston Herald*	discrimination in rental
6599	Aug. 20-23, 1989	*Birmingham News*	Alabama mortgage problems
7162	Oct. 29, 1989	*Kansas City Star*	redlining studied in 59 cities
7939	Aug., 1988	*Detroit Free Press*	redlining
5788	July 24-27, 1988	*Detroit Free Press*	redlining
4705	May 1-4, 1988	*Atlanta Journal-Constitution*	redlining Atlanta's middle-income blacks
4662	July 20, 1987	*Atlanta Journal*	blacks barred from buying property
267	May, 1984	*Knickerbocker News* (Albany)	insurance redlining
702	June 22-26, 1980	*Chicago Tribune*	black community pays more but gets less
408	Feb., 1979	*Evening Independent* (St. Petersburg, Fla.)	real estate steering segregates city
114	Nov., 1976	*Los Angeles Magazine*	redlining, speculation in poor areas
151	July, 1975	*Kansas City Star*	redlining in inner-city neighborhoods

TOTAL = 28

wiring to bypass large sections of minority communities, threatening to deprive them of important services that cable promised to deliver. These services included security and fire alarm systems, electronic banking, shopping, and news delivery.

Black Enterprise magazine reported on the selective marketing of cable television to upscale groups to the exclusion of others. The reporter warned that the selective cable wiring and marketing practices would create a new kind of black ghetto isolated by a lack of information. The reporter concluded, "Electronic redlining is not a fantasy. It is as real as the economic redlining practiced by many banks."[47]

Insurance redlining is another continuing practice of financial discrimination against minorities and the poor in America. This type of redlining is carried out by insurance companies that refuse coverage or charge more for covering properties in minority communities. Getting insurance coverage has been a historic problem for African Americans. Shut out of the mainstream financial system,

African Americans formed economic cooperatives to care for the sick and the poor and to bury the dead. Fraternal organizations carried on this work until the establishment of black-owned banks and insurance companies such as North Carolina Mutual in 1898 and Atlanta Life Insurance Company in 1905.[48] These insurance companies developed because white-owned companies refused to do business with blacks.

Today, investigative journalists reporting on redlining often examine minority access to, and the cost of, insurance as part of their investigations. On July 20, 1994, the House of Representatives passed legislation focusing on insurance redlining.[49] However, insurance representatives argue that, just as is the case with mortgage lending, insurance coverage involves assessment of financial risk and appropriate denial of applicants deemed too risky. They say that redlining does not exist and that institutions are just practicing good financial management and are not engaged in racial discrimination.

More recent media exposés on the topic show that the new redlining is different from the old but that minorities are still getting shortchanged in banking, insurance, and other economic activities. A 1995 investigative story published by *U.S. News & World Report* came to this conclusion after a six-month investigation of banking, lending, and home insurance coverage in poor and minority neighborhoods. The report was based on an analysis of 24 million mortgage records, nine sets of banking and insurance industry data, and 200 interviews in twelve cities. The investigation demonstrates that not much has changed. Minorities of all income levels are denied mortgages and home insurance coverage at more than twice the rate of whites with comparable incomes.[50]

Successful Series

For the last ninety-six years, muckrakers of all types have been stirring up moral outrage and calling for social progress for minorities. Their success has been limited. Past investigative reporting on race relations might have pricked the nation's conscience momentarily, but the continuing poor situation and treatment of American minorities indicate that few lasting changes have resulted. Exposés of corruption and inequities in the criminal justice system at times have produced more just and humane treatment for single individuals caught up in the web of the law. However, systemic bias, neglect, and abuse still characterize minorities' relationship to the system. Reporting on the new scourge of environmental racism seems to be having more of an impact, but it is too early to tell if it will be lasting.

It is in covering economic discrimination, or redlining, that investigative journalism seems to have made its greatest contribution to exposing and improving conditions for American minorities. The impact of journalists' work in this area can be seen in the actions that legislators and the business community have taken as a direct result of the reporting. Often the media outlets that conducted the investigations run follow-up stories about these actions.

A June 1980 *Chicago Tribune* series showed how members of the black community pay higher insurance rates and lose out on federal block grant funds and bank money as government officials and investors choose to funnel that money into "safer" investments in the white neighborhoods of Chicago (see Table 4, IRE no. 702).

The series, called "The Black Tax," was based on a three-month investigation of how, despite antidiscrimination laws, the black community still pays more and gets fewer services. Within days of publication, the Illinois Legislature, the Chicago City Council, and Cook County officials took action to solve these problems. Hearings were held on mortgage lending, insurance rating, tax assessments, government housing rehabilitation, and tenant displacement in the black community. This was an example of how the new investigative journalism produced reform and positive social change.[51]

In 1991 WHDH-TV in Boston produced a three-part series on redlining, "Signed, Sealed and Suckered," that led to Congressional hearings on the regulation of home improvement companies in Massachusetts. Reports revealed that banks were refusing to provide home improvement loans in targeted black communities. Banks were then buying up the loans extended to some of the homeowners by high-priced home improvement companies. The investigation began after people complained about shoddy workmanship, unexplained fees, and loan interest rates of 24 percent. In many instances, people lost their homes, but the state legislature refused to pass any bills to control the banks or the home improvement companies. After the series aired, two bills passed out of committee, and congressional hearings were scheduled.

The best-known investigative reporting on redlining is the "The Color of Money" project. The *Atlanta Journal-Constitution* won the 1988 Pulitzer Prize for this series on redlining in Atlanta's African-American neighborhoods. Written by Bill Dedman, the series ran between May 1 and 4 with follow-up stories between May 5 and 16 (see Table 4, IRE no. 4705). Dedman used database reporting and help from university researchers to document how Atlanta banks routinely discriminated against middle-class African-American applicants for housing loans.

Besides informing its readers, the series led to changes in the system just as in the muckraking days of the past. "The banks set up a $72 million fund to enable Atlantans with modest incomes to gain access to mortgages. . . . Beyond that, the banks increased in various ways their receptivity to black loan applicants to the extent that over the next five years the turn-down ratio was cut nearly in half," reported one source.[52] As a result of the series, national attention was focused once again on redlining, and some reform was made in the banking industry. The most important regulatory reform that resulted was a change in how lending institutions must report data on loans. These institutions must now disclose the race of successful and denied loan applicants so that federal bank examiners can more easily assess compliance with the lending laws.

Many government agency reports and studies of lending in other areas of the country resulted from "The Color of Money" series. The longer-term results are seen in the number of articles in professional publications warning the lending community that it needed to comply with the law and to better report on lending in minority communities. "Potential for CRA Trouble Just Doubled" appeared in the November 1989 *ABA Banking Journal* (81:11, p. 26), crediting "The Color of Money" series with having a sudden and "massive impact" on the banking industry's compliance and reporting on mortgage and home improvement lending. In "Watching Out for Number One," a compliance report that appeared in the May 1990 *ABA Banking Journal* (82:5, p. 71), the writer warned that "Too few bank CEOs are familiar with 'The Color of Money.' "

In addition to receiving the usual accolades that accompany winning the Pulitzer Prize, Bill Dedman and his series were praised by the profession for making a difference and breathing life back into investigative journalism. "The Color of Money" was cited as an example of how to use computer-assisted reporting methods for performing investigative journalism.[53]

Other journalists and media outlets followed the lead of the *Journal-Constitution* and started investigating lending in their locales. Two "Frontline" documentaries, "Race and Credit" and "Your Loan Is Denied," ran in June 1992 on public television stations. The documentaries, produced by the Center for Investigative Reporting, indicated renewed interest in exposing discriminatory practices in mortgage lending.

"The Color of Money" series was cited in a July 1993 *Black Enterprise* article.[54] Several academic journals in various disciplines also published articles on redlining following the publication of "The Color of Money" series. Many of these articles mention or quote from the series. They include "What Do We Know about Racial Discrimination in Mortgage Markets?" in *Review of Black Political Economy* 22: 1 (Summer 1993), 101; and "Perspectives on Mortgage Lending and Redlining," in *Journal of the American Planning Association* 60: 3 (Summer 1994), 344–54.

In a 1993 three-part series, the *Washington Post* exposed the racially biased system of home lending that exists in the Washington, D.C., area. The series showed that local banks and savings and loans provided mortgages to white neighborhoods at twice the rate they did to comparable African-American neighborhoods.

Other Series

Several other notable investigative reports on minority groups other than African Americans were found that were not part of the databases or time periods searched. They are mentioned here as examples of investigative reporting on other minorities.

The *Arizona Republic*'s extensive 1987 series called "Fraud in Indian Country" was nominated for a Pulitzer Prize. It revealed that, in many cases involving oil and gas companies, the federal government has sided with business interests

and had bilked Native Americans of profits rightfully theirs. Also, despite spending $30 billion on Indian programs in the previous decade, the series said, the
federal government had failed to improve the economies of the reservations and
had provided seriously substandard education and housing and "the worst health
care tax money can buy."[55]

In 1983 and 1984 the Detroit news media produced a variety of investigative
stories on the circumstances of the death of Vincent Chin, a Chinese-American
man who was bludgeoned to death by an auto worker wielding a baseball bat.
The stories were triggered by protest rallies held by Detroit Chinese Americans
after the admitted killer and his stepson received only a $3,000 fine and pro-
bation. Although the stories were not the work of a single news organization,
the Chinese-American woman who headed the protest group said she thought
the stories, which investigated various aspects of the case, represented "investigative journalism at its best moment."[56] The stories and rallies led to a federal
trial for violating Chin's civil rights; the killer was found guilty and sentenced
to prison. A new federal trial was ordered, however, and in 1987 in Cincinnati
he was found not guilty.

In 1984 a team of Latino reporters, editors, and photographers at the *Los
Angeles Times* won a Pulitzer Prize Gold Medal for public service for its twenty-
nine-part series on Latinos in southern California. The series covered the conditions of Latinos in employment, housing, education, health care, discrimination,
and other aspects of life.[57]

CONCLUSION

Investigative reporting has adopted the lofty goal of creating moral outrage
that can inspire positive change and reform based on information uncovered and
the social conditions that reporters expose to an engaged public. However, it is
difficult to link improvement in race relations to the work of investigative reporters. In fact, the weight of evidence suggests that not much significant improvement has taken place despite the rhetoric and legislation of the past thirty
years. For example, the criminal justice system still appears to be as corrupt and
racist as ever in its treatment of minorities. This lack of effect perhaps occurs
because it is far more difficult to change societal attitudes and rogue individual
behavior than it is to measure compliance with the law and to embarrass institutions with a financial incentive into treating minorities justly and fairly.

This study has found that a variety of media outlets has been active in investigating and reporting on minorities and minority issues over the years. The
participants include large- and small-circulation newspapers; radio and television
stations; and the legal, professional, and advocacy journals. Unlike the previous
muckraking magazines that began exposé and outrage reporting, today's general
circulation magazines are doing much less investigative reporting. Although this
analysis focused on databases and the IRE organization, which may tend to
include more newspaper stories, a search of the *Readers' Guide to Periodical*

Literature, which indexes magazines, did not uncover any investigative reports on the four topics examined for this study.[58]

This research on the topic of investigative journalism and its contributions to publicizing the complete picture of minority groups in the United States indicates that much work has been done by the media, but more analysis of this kind of journalistic work by scholars is needed.

NOTES

1. Matthew C. Ehrlich, "The Journalism of Outrageousness: Tabloid Television News vs. Investigative News," *Journalism and Mass Communication Monographs* 155 (February 1996), 19.

2. William Gaines, *Investigative Reporting for Print and Broadcast* (Chicago: Nelson-Hall Publishers, 1994), 3.

3. Brooke Kroeger, *Nellie Bly: Daredevil, Reporter, Feminist* (New York: Random House, 1994), 87–88.

4. See James L. Aucoin, "The Re-emergence of American Investigative Journalism 1960–1975," *Journalism History* 21, no. 1 (Spring 1995), 3–15.

5. Walter M. Brasch, *Forerunners of Revolution: Muckrakers and the American Social Conscience* (Lanham, Md.: University Press of America, 1990), 142–45.

6. The Freedom of Information Act can be found at 5 U.S.C.A. Sect. 552.

7. Carey McWilliams, "Is Muckraking Coming Back?" *Columbia Journalism Review* 9 (Fall 1970), 12.

8. John M. Harrison and Harry H. Stein, eds., *Muckraking: Past, Present and Future* (University Park: Pennsylvania State University Press, 1973), 129.

9. David L. Protess, Fay Lomax Cook, Jack Doppelt, James Ettema, Margaret Gordon, Donna Leff, and Peter Miller, *The Journalism of Outrage: Investigative Reporting and Agenda Building in America* (New York: Guilford, 1991), 4.

10. The Missouri Group, *News Reporting and Writing*, 5th ed. (New York: St. Martin's Press, 1996), 537.

11. Aucoin, "The Re-emergence of American Investigative Journalism," 11.

12. Ibid.

13. Investigative Reporters and Editors, *The Reporters' Handbook* (New York: St. Martin's Press, 1983), vii–viii.

14. 14. Rosemary Armao, "It's No Secret . . . Or Is It?" *The IRE Journal* 19, no. 1 (January/February 1996), 3.

15. Ibid.

16. Ehrlich, "The Journalism of Outrageousness," 9.

17. See J. S. Ettema and T. L. Glasser, "On the Epistemology of Investigative Journalism," in *Mass Communication Review Yearbook* 6, ed. M. Gurevitch and M. R. Levy (Newbury Park, Calif.: Sage, 1987), 183–206; J. S. Ettema and T. L. Glasser, "Narrative Form and Moral Force: The Realization of Innocence and Guilt through Investigative Journalism," *Journal of Communication* 38, no. 3 (1988), 8–26.

18. Protess et al., "The Journalism of Outrage," 5.

19. See Bruce Porter, "Pulitzer Prize-winning Exposés and Their Sometimes Dubious Consequences," *Columbia Journalism Review* 33, no. 6 (March/April 1995), 41–47.

20. Harrison and Stein, *Muckraking*, 60.

21. For excellent information about slave narratives in a historical context, see Charles H. Nichols, *Many Thousand Gone* (Bloomington: Indiana University Press, 1963).

22. Miriam DeCosta-Willis, ed., *The Memphis Diary of Ida B. Wells* (Boston: Beacon Press, 1995).

23. Harrison and Stein, *Muckraking*, 49.

24. Robert Miraldi, "Charles Edward Russell: 'Chief of the Muckrakers'," *Journalism and Mass Communication Monographs* 150 (April 1995), 4.

25. Aucoin, "The Re-emergence of American Investigative Journalism," 9.

26. James H. Jones, *Bad Blood: The Tuskegee Syphilis Experiment* (New York: Free Press, 1981), 204.

27. Tom W. Shick, "Race, Class, and Medicine: 'Bad Blood' in Twentieth-Century America," *Journal of Ethnic Studies* 10, no. 2 (1982), 97.

28. "An Experiment with Lives," *New York Times*, 21 June 1981, sect. 7, p. 9.

29. "Foster Disputes Alleged Link to Tuskegee Syphilis Experiment," *Washington Post*, 25 February 1995, A10.

30. David L. Kirp, "Blood, Sweat, and Tears: The Tuskegee Experiment and the Era of AIDS," *Tikkun*, May-June 1995, 50.

31. Harrison and Stein, *Muckraking*, 45.

32. Ibid., 50.

33. Ibid., 53.

34. Herbert Shapiro, "The Muckrakers and Negroes," *Phylon* 31 (Spring 1970), 76–88.

35. Ibid., 78.

36. Ibid., 81.

37. For more information about the tapes, call the broadcast news department at 573-882-4205. Transcripts of many of the RTNDA tapes are also in the IRE archives. Copies of stories and other materials in the IRE archives may be obtained by calling 573-882-2042, sending a fax to 573-882-5431, or writing to the IRE at 138 Neff Annex, Missouri School of Journalism, Columbia, Missouri 65211.

38. Sig Gissler, "Newspapers' Quest for Racial Candor," *Media Studies Journal* 8, no. 3 (Summer 1994), 123–24.

39. "Hard Truths: We Now Have Facts about How Skin Tone Colors Many Facets of Life in the Akron Area," *Akron Beacon-Journal*, 30 December 1993, A12.

40. Barbara Roberson Gardner, "Discrimination in Death: The Final Blow," *The Record*, 13 July 1981, B17.

41. Harrison and Stein, *Muckraking*, 77.

42. Steve Weinberg, "Tracing the Trends: 1991 Award Winners," *The IRE Journal* 15, no. 3 (May/June 1992), 8.

43. Ibid., 8.

44. "Circuit Court Jury System Is Racially Balanced," *Miami Herald*, 15 July 1984, A10.

45. "A Whiff of Discrimination?," *U.S. News & World Report*, 4 May 1992, 34.

46. Weinberg, "Tracing the Trends," 7.

47. Udayan Gupta, "Electronic Redlining," *Black Enterprise*, October 1981, 94.

48. James B. Browning, "The Beginnings of Insurance Enterprise among Negroes," *Journal of Negro History* 22, no. 4 (October 1937), 417–52.

49. See "Anti Redlining in Insurance Disclosure Act," H.R. 1188, 103d. Cong., 2d. sess., 21 July 1994.

50. "The New Redlining," *U.S. News & World Report*, 17 April 1995, 51.

51. See "House Will Investigate 'Black Tax' Findings," *Chicago Tribune*, 27 June 1980, sec. 2, p. 1; "Plan Council Move to Stop Tenants' Displacement by Rehab," *Chicago Tribune*, 1 July 1980, sec. 1, p. 7; "Probing the 'Black Tax'," *Chicago Tribune*, 2 July 1980, sec. 4, p. 2; "Bill Would Assist Displaced Tenants," *Chicago Tribune*, 9 July 1980, sec. 6, p. 3; "State House Panel to Probe Redlining," *Chicago Tribune*, 25 July 1980, sec. 1, p. 5.

52. Porter, "Pulitzer Prize-Winning Exposés," 46.

53. Cecilia Friend, "Daily Newspaper Use of Computers to Analyze Data," *Newspaper Research Journal* 15, no. 1 (Winter 1994), 63–72.

54. Carolyn Brown and Matthew S. Scott, "How to Fight Mortgage Discrimination . . . And Win!!!" *Black Enterprise*, July 1993, 48–59.

55. "Fraud in Indian Country: A Billion-Dollar Betrayal," *Arizona Republic* (Phoenix), 4–11 October 1987.

56. *Who Killed Vincent Chin?*, film by Christine Choy and Renee Tajima, nominated for the Academy Award and named Best Film and Best Documentary at international film festivals in 1988. (New York: Filmmakers Library, 1988).

57. "Latinos in Southern California," *Los Angeles Times*, 24 July–14 August, 1983.

58. The same keywords were used to search the *Readers' Guide to Periodical Literature* from 1932 to 1989, which were used to conduct computer database searches on each ethnic minority group and the four topics covered in the study. In addition, the keywords "Black," "Negro," "Afro American," and "colored" were used to search the earlier volumes of the *Readers' Guide* during the years when those terms were used to refer to African Americans.

SELECTED BIBLIOGRAPHY

Aucoin, James L. "The Re-emergence of American Investigative Journalism 1960–1975." *Journalism History* 21, no. 1 (Spring 1995), 3–15.

Brasch, Walter M. *Forerunners of Revolution: Muckrakers and the American Social Conscience*. Lanham, Md.: University Press of America, 1990.

Chalmers, David M. *The Muckrake Years*. New York: D. Van Nostrand, 1974.

Downie, Leonard. *The New Muckrakers*. Washington, D.C.: New Republic Book, 1976.

Ehrlich, Matthew C. "The Journalism of Outrageousness: Tabloid Television News vs. Investigative News." *Journalism and Mass Communication Monographs* 155 (February 1996).

Ettema, J. S., and T. L. Glasser. "Narrative Form and Moral Force: The Realization of Innocence and Guilt through Investigative Journalism." *Journal of Communication* 38, no. 3 (1988), 8–26.

———. "On the Epistemology of Investigative Journalism." In *Mass Communication Review Yearbook* 6, edited by M. Gurevitch and M. R. Levy. Newbury Park, Calif.: Sage, 1987, 83–206.

Harrison, John M., and Harry H. Stein, eds. *Muckraking: Past, Present and Future*. University Park: Pennsylvania State University Press, 1973.

Investigative Reporters and Editors. *The Reporters' Handbook*, 3d ed. New York: St. Martin's Press, 1996.

Jones, James H. *Bad Blood: The Tuskegee Syphilis Experiment*. New York: Free Press, 1981.

Meyer, Philip. *Precision Journalism*, 2d ed. Bloomington: Indiana University Press, 1979.

Miraldi, Robert. "Charles Edward Russell: 'Chief of the Muckrakers'." *Journalism and Mass Communication Monographs* 150 (April 1995).

Protess, David L., Fay Lomax Cook, Jack Doppelt, James Ettema, Margaret Gordon, Donna Leff, and Peter Miller. *The Journalism of Outrage: Investigative Reporting and Agenda Building in America*. New York: Guilford, 1991.

Regier, D. D. *The Era of the Muckrakers*. Chapel Hill: University of North Carolina Press, 1932.

Rosen, Jay. "Making Things More Public: On the Political Responsibility of the Media Intellectual." *Critical Studies in Mass Communication* 11, no. 4 (December 1994), 363–88.

Shapiro, Herbert. "The Muckrakers and Negroes." *Phylon* 31 (1970), 76–88.

Swados, Harvey, ed. *Years of Conscience: The Muckrakers*. Cleveland: World Publishing, 1962.

Weinberg, Arthur, and Lila Weinberg, eds. *The Muckrakers*. New York: Simon & Schuster, 1961.

Wells Barnett, Ida B. *Crusade for Justice*. Chicago: University of Chicago Press, 1970.

8

Racial Minorities and the FCC's "Public Interest" Mandate: Defining and Redefining Their Role, 1934–1996

WILLIAM J. LEONHIRTH

We have generally thought that if many individual voices are heard, our society will be better informed than if only a few voices are heard. The greater the diversity in our broadcast media, the more likely it is that truth will emerge.
                        —1979 Federal Communications Commission Report[1]

The Communications Act of 1934 provided the foundations of U.S. communications policy for more than sixty years. The enactment of the Telecommunications Act of 1996 has offered the first comprehensive revision of the 1934 act that, in succession to the Federal Radio Act of 1927, established the "broadcasting" model for regulation of mass communication.[2] The hallmark of the 1927 and 1934 acts, which the 1996 act retained, is the provision that holders of broadcasting licenses have to operate in "the public interest, convenience, and necessity."[3] Since 1934, the "public interest" provision has raised the questions of who is the "public" in whose interests broadcast license holders are to act and what are the stakes of minority groups in the population in that constituency. Racial minorities may be among a number of competing voices heard as the Federal Communications Commission (FCC) conducts at least eighty rule-making sessions on the implementation of the Telecommunications Act of 1996.[4]

Analyses of news coverage of minority groups in the United States have centered on the relationships between the minority groups and mass media institutions, such as newspapers, radio stations, and television stations. Issues of contention have included portrayals of minorities in news coverage, access of minorities to the mass media to present their viewpoints, employment of minorities in the mass media and minority ownership of media outlets. Inherent in these issues are questions both of the role of news media in the formation of public opinion and of the access of the public, including members of minority groups, to news media institutions. In the 1990s, the traditional news media are facing challenges from new communications technologies that allow interaction between audience members on the same scale as the transmission of news media messages. The changing media environment may alter significantly the relationships between racial minorities, as individuals and groups, and the news media.

Also present is a news media environment of concentration, with new alliances between corporate giants such as Disney and ABC-Capital Cities, Time-Warner and Turner Broadcasting, and Westinghouse and CBS, and between former components of the old Bell system. The Telecommunications Act of 1996 allows greater entry of existing media companies into new media endeavors and expands the opportunities for greater dominance of their holdings. For example, the new act permits regional Bell companies to engage in electronic publishing of news, entertainment, legal notices, advertising, educational and instructional materials, and other kinds of information.[5] Such concentrations may preclude greater minority ownership of communication properties, particularly as the FCC, Congress, and the courts reverse previous policies that aided entry of minorities and women into the mass media and telecommunications field.

LOOKING BACK

Inauguration of broadcasting in the 1920s created a new communications environment in the United States. Audience members were for the first time simultaneous recipients, on a broad scale, of transmissions of information and entertainment through broadcasting, rather than reading printed materials at their own pace or convenience. The "broadcasting" model for regulation of mass communication, which the Communications Act of 1934 helped to establish, stands in contrast to the "print" model and the "common-carrier" model.[6] The print model provides generally that the First Amendment protects most of the content of mass circulation publications. Exceptions to this protection have included libel, sedition, and obscenity. The common-carrier model, which derives from transportation regulation, provides for the regulation of routes and rates but makes no provision for the regulation of content. This model generally has applied to point-to-point communication systems such as the telephone and telegraph and not to mass communication systems. Regulation of cable television, which provides broadcasting content through a common-carrier system, continues to raise questions about which is the appropriate model for its regulation: print, common carrier, or broadcasting.[7]

At issue since the 1920s has been whether the public-trustee system of broadcasting makes the best use of a public resource, the electromagnetic spectrum, and best represents all segments of the public, including racial minorities. At odds, essentially, have been a social and an economic model of communication. The notion of public interest or common good varies as to the model. For those who support an economic model, the common good is an aggregate of what individuals see as in their best interests. Consumers vote with their fingers on the dial and with their purchases of advertisers' products, and the broadcasting system maintains programming that has strong consumer support. Counter to this notion are arguments, from those who support the social model, that private station owners, in their attempts to gain the most support from audience members and customers of advertisers' products, will avoid controversy and views that are outside of the social and economic mainstream, including the views and interests of racial minorities. More important, the market system, particularly if only a few providers of content exist, gives consumers only a limited choice of entertainment and information options, and options that may not be in their best interest, supporters of the social model argue. The common good in the social model is collective improvement that broadcasting can further, whether in education, culture, or political consensus.

The Communications Act of 1934 included social goals[8] but did not spell out these goals or how they might affect social life or groups in the nation. The act required the FCC to "generally encourage the larger and more efficient use of radio in the public interest."[9] The act prohibited censorship[10] but at the same time barred profane or indecent speech.[11] Through its licensing power, the commission received its regulatory authority. The Supreme Court in the *NBC v. US* case[12] in 1943 upheld the FCC's authority to regulate mass communication, and in the *Red Lion Broadcasting Co. v. FCC* case[13] in 1969 the court upheld the FCC's authority to regulate speech through the Fairness Doctrine, which required broadcasters to provide competing viewpoints on public issues. Opponents of a Mississippi television station with discriminatory programming practices, including failure to air black viewpoints even on network programming, successfully used the Fairness Doctrine to challenge the station's license.[14] But the FCC abandoned the Fairness Doctrine in 1987.

Also at issue for the past sixty years has been what right the public, or components of the public, has to participate in the mass communication process, whether through dissemination of viewpoints or ownership of media outlets. The Communications Act of 1934 left unresolved questions about content and First Amendment protection, the definition of public interest, media concentration and diversity of media ownership, employment, and content.[15] On issues of access and diversity, the FCC has dealt with racial-minority ownership, racial-minority employment, and programming of interest to racial minorities. One challenge to increase diversity resulted in the opportunity for greater public participation in license renewals. The decision in *United Church of Christ v. FCC*,[16] which challenged discriminatory programming practices at a Mississippi television station in 1966, resulted in a federal appeals court decision that allowed the public to intervene in license renewals. The United Church of Christ's Office of Communication, in the Mississippi case, challenged the practices of WLBT in Jackson, Mississippi, of using derogatory on-air references to blacks and failing to carry network programs on race relations.[17] The UCC Office of Communication also assisted the Rosebud Sioux in challenging the license of

KELO in South Dakota because of its failure to serve the interests of the Sioux. The challenge resulted in the negotiation of agreements with KELO and another South Dakota station, KPLO.[18] The *United Church of Christ* decision in the WLBT case helped to put the public in the "public" interest[19] and forced the FCC to change its policy that the only interveners with standing were those who had a direct financial stake in the license renewal. After 1968 and the release of the Kerner Commission Report on urban violence, the FCC instituted policies to increase opportunities for minorities in broadcasting. Tools included affirmative action requirements and advantages in comparative hearings for license renewals, distress sales of broadcasting properties, and tax certificate policies, which allowed those who sold broadcasting licenses to minorities to defer capital gains and receive a financial advantage.

The portrayal of minorities on television and the employment of racial minorities in the broadcasting industry were subjects of a 1977 study by the U.S. Commission on Civil Rights, *Window Dressing on the Set: Women and Minorities in Television*. In its 1979 follow-up to that report, the commission reported that blacks had made some gains with positive portrayals after the Civil Rights Movement of the 1950s and 1960s, but "Hispanic Americans, Asian and Pacific Islanders, and Alaskan natives continued to be virtually absent from television drama."[20] The commission recommended in 1979 that all holders of broadcast licenses, as well as networks and groups of broadcasting stations, should provide affirmative action programs to guarantee representative employment of minorities and women at all levels of the broadcasting industry, including top decision making.[21]

In 1978 the FCC released its *Statement of Policy on Minority Ownership of Broadcasting Facilities* and launched initiatives, including tax certificates and distress sales, to promote racial minorities' ownership of broadcast properties. A 1979 FCC report contended that minority ownership was vital to the promotion of diversity: "The greater the diversity in our broadcast media, the more likely it is that truth will emerge. To the extent that minorities have been excluded from participation in the broadcast industry—and they have been excluded—diversity has suffered."[22]

The FCC reported in 1979 that racial minorities—Native Americans, Alaska natives, Asians, Pacific Islanders, African Americans, and Hispanics—owned less than 1 percent of 9,600 broadcast properties, AM and FM radio stations and television stations, in the United States.[23] The National Telecommunication and Information Administration (NTIA), in its 1996 report on minority ownership of broadcasting properties, found that, in 1995, African Americans, Hispanics, and Native Americans constituted 27 percent of the population and owned 2.9 percent of 11,000 broadcast properties in the United States. NTIA officials noted that access to capital was the principal barrier of racial minorities to ownership of broadcast stations.[24] Racial minorities' ownership of broadcast stations has remained relatively unchanged since 1993.

Efforts to increase opportunities for racial minorities in broadcasting have received reverses in recent years. Congress eliminated the tax certificate policy in 1995.[25] The Telecommunications Act of 1996 eliminated the comparative hearing requirement for broadcast renewals[26] so that license holders will not have to defend their performance against competing financial or social policy interests. Affirmative action provisions, including preferences for distress sales, are under assault in Congress and the courts. The Supreme Court, in its *Adarand Constructors v. Pena* decision in 1995,[27] required the use of strict scrutiny for affirmative action programs. Under strict scrutiny, use of racial classifications is "constitutional only if they are narrowly tailored measures that further compelling government interests."[28] The high court overturned the *Metro Broadcasting v. FCC* decision,[29] which, in 1990, permitted the use of intermediate scrutiny for affirmative action and allowed the FCC to provide racial advantages for comparative hearings and to allow distress sales to racial minorities. Under intermediate scrutiny, the court allowed the use of racial classifications if they were "substantially related to the achievement of the government's interests."[30] The court in *Metro Broadcasting* had held that support of racial minority ownership of broadcasting stations supported a long-standing Congressional mandate to promote diversity of views and interests in broadcasting.[31] As a result of the *Adarand* decision, the FCC suspended minority preferences for participation in spectrum auctions, which could have given women and racial minorities more opportunities to participate in new communication systems such as microwave-based personal communication services.[32]

The Telecommunications Act of 1996 provides a Telecommunications Development Fund, which may provide racial and other minorities with a financing resource for telecommunications businesses.[33] But the overall impact of the law on minorities in broadcasting may be detrimental because of support for the concentration of media holdings.[34] The law does require periodic assessments of barriers to entry of small telecommunication businesses, including female-owned and minority-owned businesses, into the competitive marketplace.[35] Still unresolved in the law is the role of minority interests in the public interest. Also unresolved is any clarification of the public interest itself.

NEW ON-LINE MEDIA

Participation of African Americans and other minorities in cyberspace is increasing,[36] but an editorial exchange in *Boardwatch*, a leading chronicler of Internet events, indicated that questions exist about racial identity in computer-mediated communication. Walter Findlator, the system operator of the Afra-Span Network, an African-Cuban bulletin board system (BBS) offered in a letter to the editor to provide assistance to consumer on-line systems such as America Online and Prodigy in creating cultural-interest services. "As you know, as the world of computers emerges into each household, more modems will be bought and used and people of color will wonder where are the black BBS's, or the

Hispanic, Jewish, or Asian, etc.''[37] *Boardwatch* editor Jack Rickard criticized Findlator for bringing racial issues onto the Internet:

If you are against racism, why are you calling for areas on-line specifically for people of color and Latin heritage, and damning larger services for not supplying them? In most of the on-line communities I haunt, I would be hard-pressed to tell what ethnicity most of the participants are unless they specifically make a point of telling me. One of the distinct advantages I find in electronic communication, and specifically in some of its limitations, is that we have to deal with each other based on the expression of minds and the content of our character, and our race or what we drive has little bearing.[38]

Despite scholarly interest in the social effects of computer-mediated communication, few examples exist, so far, of analyses of specific contents of on-line communication. In 1993 Christine Ogan conducted an analysis of the Turkish Electronic Mail List, a list server with more than 300 subscribers, during the Persian Gulf War in 1991.[39] List servers automatically transmit posted messages to subscribers' electronic-mail accounts. Ogan used a goal typology that Sandra Ball-Rokeach and Kathleen Reardon explicated in 1988[40] to classify the messages that participants posted on the list server during January 1991.[41] Ogan found that the list server provided ''a specialized medium, resembling a publication, to serve the debate, association, and exchange functions of that community.''[42] Ogan argued that the list server provided an arena for group decision making and mobilization for a larger number of people than would be possible with traditional mass media:

Mass media cannot be effectively used for mass decision-making or deliberation, and face-to-face decision-making has an upper limit on the size of the group that can participate. But electronic deliberation may be able to produce a written document or come to some decision on an action to take on which a great many of the members can agree. This allows members to work as a very large team of reporters or editors to produce a document, almost in the same manner as they might if they were having a face-to-face meeting.[43]

CONCLUSION

New communications technologies provide the opportunity for individuals and groups to distribute messages on a mass-circulation basis, but access to these opportunities will depend on current and future efforts to put the technologies into the hands of those who, in the past, have not been full participants in the U.S. media environment.

What still remains in question is whether these communication opportunities will bring minorities more into the social, economic, and political mainstream, if that is their goal, or will eliminate that mainstream, so that minorities and other groups become direct competitors with other societal groups for needed resources. Concentration of media resources into fewer and fewer hands may result in less, not greater, opportunity for a diversity of viewpoints and interests. Legal, regulatory, and economic barriers may prevent the realization of "collaborative" participation of audience members in the creation of media information and entertainment and priorities. What is available in the future may be akin to the similar network offerings of CBS, NBC, and ABC in the 1950s, 1960s, and 1970s. Even if individual options are available, will they be available to only a limited number in the population? The Telecommunications Act of 1996 offers evidence, with further concentration of media ownership and indecency regulations for Internet content, of support for top-down provision of information and entertainment rather than the lateral participation espoused by many Internet supporters.

Convergence of media has created a new communication environment in the United States, and the role or roles of racial minorities, as individuals and groups, in this environment still is in development. Future directions will depend on the social, political, and economic context of the U.S. media environment and the place of minorities in this context.

NOTES

1. Office of Public Affairs, Federal Communications Commission, *Minority Ownership of Broadcast Facilities: A Report* (Washington, D.C.: U.S. Government Printing Office, 1979), 5.

2. Don R. Pember, *Mass Media Law*, 4th ed. (Dubuque, Iowa: William C. Brown, 1987), 545.

3. 47 U.S.C. Sec. 302(a) (1996).

4. Richard Schaefer and J. R. Rush, "A Policy Analysis of the Telecommunications Act of 1996" (Paper presented at Association for Education in Journalism and Mass Communication Convention, Anaheim, California, August 1996), 27.

5. Ibid., 16.

6. Ithiel de Sola Pool, *Technologies of Freedom* (Cambridge, Mass.: Harvard University Press, 1983), 2.

7. See *Turner Broadcasting System v. FCC*, 114 Sup. Ct. 2445 (1994).

8. Erwin Krasnow, Lawrence Longley, and Herbert Terry, *The Politics of Broadcast Regulation*, 3d ed. (New York: St. Martin's Press, 1982), 15.

9. 47 U.S.C. Sec. 303(g) (1996).

10. 47 U.S.C. Sec. 315 (1996).

11. 47 U.S.C. Sec. 303 (1996).

12. 319 U.S. 190 (1943).

13. 395 U.S. 367 (1969).

14. *Office of Communication of the United Church of Christ v. FCC*, 425 F.2d. 543 (DC Cir. 1966).

15. Harvey Zuckman and Martin Gaynor, *Mass Communication Law in a Nutshell*, 2d ed. (St. Paul, Minn.: West, 1983), 323.

16. 359 F.2d. 994 (DC Cir. 1966).

17. Clint Wilson II and Félix Gutiérrez, *Race, Multiculturalism, and the Media: From Mass to Class Communication*, 2d ed. (Thousand Oaks, Calif.: Sage, 1995), 219–20.

18. Ibid., 221.

19. Although the public participation had little direct effect on the renewal of licenses, citizen groups used their participation to affect commission procedures and policies and to negotiate changes in station programming. Kent Middleton and Bill Chamberlin, *The Law of Public Communication*, 2d ed. (New York: Longman, 1991), 556.

20. U.S. Commission on Civil Rights, *Window Dressing on the Set: An Update* (Washington, D.C.: U.S. Government Printing Office, 1979), 1.

21. Ibid., 63–65.

22. Office of Public Affairs, *Minority Ownership of Broadcast Facilities*, 5.

23. Ibid.

24. National Telecommunications and Information Administration, *Minority Commercial Broadcast Ownership in the United States* (Washington, D.C.: Department of Commerce, 1996), 1.

25. Self-Employed Health Insurance Act of 1995, Pub. Law No. 104–107, Sec. 2, 109 Stat. 93 (1995).

26. Telecommunications Act of 1996, Pub. Law No. 104–104, Sec. 204(4), 110 Stat. 56 (1996).

27. 1995 U.S. Lexis 4037.

28. Ibid., 51.

29. 49 U.S. 547 (1990).

30. 49 U.S. 547, 569 (1995).

31. 49 U.S. 547, 600 (1995).

32. Action in Docket Case. FCC Proposes Rules for Auctioning the Remaining Broadband PCS Licenses, 60 Fed. Reg. 37,786 (1995).

33. Telecommunications Act of 1996, Pub. Law No. 104–104, Sec. 714, 110 Stat. 56 (1996).

34. Ibid., Sec. 202.

35. Ibid., Sec. 2257.

36. Stafford V. Battle and Rey L. Harris, *The African-American Resource Guide to the Internet* (Edison, N.J.: USCCCN Publishers, 1994); "A New Gain in Power: Two Entrepreneurs Guide Blacks onto the Computer and into the Future," *Washington Post*, 1 February 1995, final edition, D1; Jube Shiver, Jr., "Busting Barriers to Cyberspace: On-Line Activists Fight to Keep the Poor, the Elderly, and Minorities from Being Left Out of the Information Age," *Los Angeles Times*, 29 March 1995, A1.

37. Letter to the editor, *Boardwatch*, November 1994, 10.

38. Ibid.

39. Christine Ogan, "Listserver Communication during the Gulf War: What Kind of Medium Is the Electronic Bulletin Board?," *Journal of Broadcasting and Electronic Media* 37 (1993), 177.

40. Sandra Ball-Rokeach and Kathleen Reardon, "Monologue, Dialogue, and Telelogic: Comparing an Emergent Form of Communication with Traditional Forms," in *Advancing Communication Science: Merging Mass and Interpersonal Communication*, ed. Robert Hawkins, John Wiemann, and Suzanne Pingree (Newbury Park, Calif.: Sage, 1988).

41. Ogan, "Listserver Communication," 188–91.

42. Ibid., 192.

43. Ibid.

SELECTED BIBLIOGRAPHY

Krasnow, Erwin, Lawrence Longley, and Herbert Terry. *The Politics of Broadcast Regulation*. 3d ed. New York: St. Martin's Press, 1982.

Middleton, Kent, and Bill Chamberlin. *The Law of Public Communication*. 2d ed. New York: Longman, 1991.

Office of Public Affairs, Federal Communications Commission. *Minority Ownership of Broadcast Facilities: A Report*. Washington, D.C.: U.S. Government Printing Office, 1979.

Ogan, Christine. "Listserver Communication during the Gulf War: What Kind of Medium Is the Electronic Bulletin Board?" *Journal of Broadcasting and Electronic Media* 37 (1993), 177.

Pool, Ithiel de Sola. *Technologies of Freedom*. Cambridge, Mass.: Harvard University Press, 1983.

Schaefer, Richard, and J. R. Rush. "A Policy Analysis of the Telecommunications Act of 1996." Paper presented at the Association for Education in Journalism and Mass Communication Convention, Anaheim, California, August 1996.

U.S. Commission on Civil Rights. *Window Dressing on the Set: An Update*. Washington, D.C.: U.S. Government Printing Office, 1979.

Wilson, Clint II, and Félix Gutiérrez. *Race, Multiculturalism, and the Media: From Mass to Class Communication*. 2d ed. Thousand Oaks, Calif.: Sage, 1995.

9

Conclusion

MARY ANN WESTON, CAROLYN MARTINDALE, AND
BEVERLY ANN DEEPE KEEVER

Taken as a whole, the studies of news coverage of the five racial and ethnic groups compiled in this volume paint a fairly devastating picture of the American news media. News coverage of these groups by media of the white mainstream has ignored, stereotyped, and distorted them. In a few cases newspaper editors even have campaigned actively against these groups—for example, for the exclusion of Chinese workers, or the internment of Japanese Americans, or the extermination of native peoples.

While this is not a particularly new revelation, the accumulation of evidence in these studies points to some disturbing conclusions and some hopeful directions for further research. The studies brought together in this book show clear patterns in the press's flawed dealings with minority groups. The studies show remarkably similar shortcomings in coverage across groups and over time. These problems have received more attention but have not evaporated as the twentieth century nears its end. The patterns of news media shortcomings are all the more disturbing when weighed against the press's self-professed ideals of independence, accuracy, fairness, and fearlessness. Again and again, studies of Native Americans', African Americans', Asian Americans', Hispanics', and Pacific Islanders' treatment at the hands of the mainstream news media have revealed violations of those ideals.

To some extent such behavior may be explained—though not condoned—by putting the news media in the cultural contexts of their times. Clearly, past newspaper publishers and broadcasters reflected the contemporary ideology of white dominance, reinforcing the truism that the news media generally follow, rather than lead, public opinion. But, as the studies described here show, the news media frequently amplified and enflamed public prejudices, too.

At the same time, the news media seldom examined the economic forces that brought groups such as the Chinese and Mexicans to the United States, as well as the economic value to the dominant society of the exploitation of the cheap labor of Chinese, African, and Mexican Americans. Nor, often, were these groups' considerable contributions to the nation's economic growth and American culture emphasized in the news.

But blanket indictments such as this do injustice to the relatively rare instances where journalists or news organizations went beyond their communities' prejudices to pursue the truth. Examples include those Southern newspaper editors who defied community pressure to tell the stories of the treatment of African Americans at the hands of white segregationists in the 1950s and 1960s South, or the local newspapers in South Dakota in the 1930s or Wisconsin in the 1950s that treated Native Americans as responsible members of their communities. Investigative journalism of the 1970s and later has exposed other glaring examples of mistreatment of some of these groups. Sometimes this exposure spurred action; too often, it did not.

While contemporary mind-sets and prejudices undoubtedly played a part in the poor performance of the news media presented in this book, the studies show an even more disturbing finding: journalistic conventions, habits, traditions, and values contributed to the distorted news coverage of racial and ethnic groups. The patterns of these distortions are strikingly similar among the groups studied.

The ways in which news has been—and to a large extent still is—defined have worked in powerful ways to misshape the coverage of these groups. When applied to the coverage of minorities, the values that make news—that which is out of the ordinary, timely, involving celebrities or famous people, important (which is often defined in the context of government actions), and oriented to events as opposed to trends or issues—actually have distorted these groups' lives and stories.

For example, study after study took the news media to task for ignoring groups until they were involved in conflict or crisis: Mexican Americans involved in the "zoot suit" incidents of the 1940s, African Americans' civil rights demonstrations in the 1960s, Native Americans protesting at Wounded Knee in the 1970s, and so on. Even when these groups made their brief appearances on the news agenda, the issues—often economic and legal—that underlay the clashes were buried or omitted. The news value of conflict became a primary focus, and historical information that would have put the crisis in context seldom appeared.

The news value that highlights the unusual or bizarre or exotic often led journalists to focus on superficial appearances or differences, rather than substantive issues. Aggrieved groups soon learned that a colorful or threatening protest demonstration would bring them notice in the news media when peaceful petitioning would not. Thus, Indians occupying Alcatraz Island to demonstrate for their treaty rights, or African Americans taking to the streets to protest police brutality, attracted prominent coverage, although the underlying issues that led to the demonstrations did not command the same attention.

The news ideal of "objectivity," which in operation often meant reliance on provable, observable facts and which sought to balance one view against a counter position, also at times worked against accurate coverage of the groups studied in this book. This journalistic technique of providing balance by airing views on two opposing sides of issues has tended to obscure complex issues of Native American sovereignty, for example, and to lump an internally diverse group, such as Hispanics, into a monolithic entity.

The unspoken values that underlie the objectivity ideal of the mainstream press were listed by Jack Newfield as "belief in welfare capitalism, God, the West, Puritanism, the Law, the family, property, the two party system and . . . the notion that violence is only defensible when employed by the state."[1] Journalists working under the constraints of these assumptions can be hard pressed when covering people from cultures who may not share those values. Cultures that are traditional, that value cooperation over competition, that place the welfare of the family or group above that of the individual, that have religious beliefs different from those of Protestant Christianity too seldom see sensitive and accurate depictions of themselves in the news media, the studies indicate.

The powerful mythologies and stereotypes that surround each of the minority groups, which have been vividly dramatized in the entertainment media, also found their way into the framing of news stories about them. Thus, journalists covering twentieth-century Native Americans sometimes unconsciously fit them into the mold of the Hollywood Indians of Western movies. Similarly, stories involving African-American men too often cast them in the stereotype of sexual or athletic prowess or criminality. Another aspect of the power of stereotypes is that, according to minority journalists working in the white media, stories that conform to the stereotypes often are more likely to be used than those that do not.

All these ways of identifying, reporting, and organizing the news collectively yielded distorted portrayals of minority group members as people with problems who were culturally exotic and separate from the larger community. Without adequate reporting of the social and economic roots of these groups' problems, media coverage could convey the misleading impression that the victims caused their own distress. A related pattern found in the studies was consigning minority groups to news "invisibility." For example, the oppression that prevented blacks in the South from voting for nearly a century went virtually unreported until civil rights demonstrations began in the 1960s.

The news media's habit of giving weight and credibility to government policies also worked against balanced coverage of these groups, the studies show. In fact, some of the most prominent coverage came in response to government policies that were of questionable wisdom and legality. Examples include the internment of Japanese Americans in World War II and the atomic testing in the Pacific that displaced and endangered islanders there.

Examination of media coverage has shown that the government's position was emphasized more and questioned less than that of the affected minority. Few in the media, for example, questioned the government plans of relocating

Pacific Islanders for atomic testing, or the government's assertion that the tests were safe. Few news organizations questioned the obvious violation of civil and human rights when Japanese Americans were uprooted from their homes and businesses and sent to internment camps during World War II or, initially, when the government tried to terminate the tribal status of some Native American groups. Such studies show news organizations less as independent watchdogs of government than as megaphones for government propaganda.

The studies also have revealed a pattern of news media passivity that belies the ideal of aggressive scrutiny of agencies of power. For example, in the 1960s, when blacks were denied the vote in many parts of the South, this fact, which could be verified from public records, was turned into an allegation that simply required a countering quote.

If the patterns revealed in these studies show sins of commission on the part of the news media, there are sins of omission, too.

These racial and ethnic groups' contributions to the common good, stories that did not fit easily into crisis or event-oriented frameworks, often were ignored. The newsworthy aspects of everyday lives of whites—births, marriages, deaths, opening of businesses, school honors—that filled pages of local newspapers for much of the period of this study, often excluded the achievements of the community's Japanese or Chinese or African Americans or Hispanics or others of color. Sometimes, a minority group was virtually erased from a community's history because it was not covered in the local press.

And white racism, identified by the Kerner Commission as the underlying cause of the racial violence of the 1960s, was seldom mentioned, much less examined, in news coverage.[2] Such an omission is not surprising if one views the mainstream white-owned media as institutions acting in the service of perceived white interests. Historically this can be seen in newspaper support for the extermination of Native Americans, for the exclusion of Chinese immigrants, or for the internment of law-abiding Japanese Americans.

The consequences of such coverage can be inferred easily. If readers and viewers are given misleading or distorted pictures of a group—or no pictures at all—they will have little opportunity to develop insights into the group or to help form sensible public policies concerning the group. The sad fact of daily American life is that many citizens are isolated from those of different racial or ethnic backgrounds, whether in segregated suburbs, urban ghettos, rural towns, or remote reservations. Thus the news media have a heavy responsibility to bring to America a true picture of its diversity.

To a distressingly large extent, research has shown, groups such as African Americans, Native Americans, Hispanics, and others are portrayed in the news as a threat or a problem, as being outside American society rather than a part of it. Given the kinds of coverage detailed in this volume, it is little wonder that perception gaps exist between and among these groups and the dominant society. Vivid examples of spontaneous actions growing from this perception gap include the violent eruptions of outrage at the acquittal of the Los Angeles police officers accused of beating Rodney King in 1992 and the racially divided reactions to O.J. Simpson's acquittal on murder charges in 1995.

Public officials, too, are affected by perceptions fostered by the news media. The peril of using or exploiting flawed views of minorities in making public policy can be seen in such disastrous actions as the Japanese internment, the tribal termination policies of the 1950s, and the assaults on affirmative action and immigration in the 1990s.

Perception gaps also contribute to the erosion of the credibility of the news media. How can people who do not see themselves portrayed realistically in the news believe other things they read and watch in the same media?

To the extent that members of these racial and ethnic groups are separated from one another and from the dominant society, the news media have an increased obligation to help them know and understand one another.

The studies compiled here suggest many avenues for further research. Much of the previous research has provided snapshots—small pebbles in the mosaic that give only a glimpse of the larger picture. Valuable as these studies are and will continue to be, scholars could and should explore other avenues.

Some groups, such as Asian Americans in general as well as their various subgroups, are too little studied. Scholars in the field perceive that, in the mid- to late twentieth century, their treatment in the news has been different from that of African Americans and Native Americans, for example. But not enough research has been done to know if the perception is valid. Systematic studies of the news coverage of Pacific Islanders also are needed. The coverage of some other groups, including Native Americans, has been studied more in the previous century than in the present one. Such studies provide important historical reference points for much-needed continued analysis; additional studies of more recent coverage could provide a valuable longitudinal picture. Some perceive that the mainstream coverage of the 1990s debates over welfare, affirmative action, and immigration policies repeat past mistakes of the news media: passive acceptance of official pronouncements, using benign code words such as "reverse discrimination" to advance racist policies, and more. Clearly, research is needed to document or disprove these perceptions.

Little research has been done to compare the news coverage of more than one group in a particular location. Also, while content analyses can give us valuable quantitative information about coverage of these groups, more research is needed on the quality of that coverage. Far more research has been done on news from the print media than from television, the medium from which most Americans get their news. One obvious reason for this is the difficulty in finding and analyzing archival television news footage, a difficulty that is fading as technology develops.

And more research is needed into the managerial and decision-making dynamics that have led to the flawed coverage shown in this book. If racism in the news media is institutional, that institutionalization should be revealed and dissected.

Scholars who study news coverage of minorities also have the responsibility to assess media performance realistically. This means taking into account the real-life constraints with which news workers must deal. Clearly, news coverage of racial and ethnic groups has been flawed. But it is equally clear that numerous journalists in newsrooms today are working hard to remedy those flaws. Scholars should take into account those efforts and, through their research, help news workers find ways to improve their coverage. Such research could begin to answer the question: How can the news media truly apply their ideals of fairness, accuracy, and independence to make coverage of minorities better reflect reality?

The news media are in the unique position of being a Constitutionally protected, profit-making commercial enterprise. Their responsibility to present what the Hutchins Commission called a "representative picture of the constituent groups in the society" is clear.[3] Citizens in a democracy—of all colors and backgrounds—need accurate information about their society in order to act and vote intelligently. Most media managers, at least in their public pronouncements, take that responsibility seriously.

But like any commercial enterprise, the news media act in their economic self-interest to maximize profits. The trend in the 1980s and 1990s to combine media into huge conglomerates of which news organizations are a small component has increased the emphasis on the bottom line.

The irony in the late twentieth century is that, with regard to news coverage of minorities, the right thing and the profitable thing may be converging. It has been estimated that minorities will constitute 32 percent of the U.S. population by 2010 and that by 2060 or earlier whites will no longer be in the numerical majority. Moreover, it has been predicted that 87 percent of the population growth between 1992 and 2000 would occur among nonwhites.[4] As the population becomes more diverse, media seeking to attract readers and viewers would do well to cover minority racial and ethnic groups in meaningful ways that go beyond patronizing window dressing.

One reason the coverage of minorities has not improved faster is that old news habits die hard. Newsroom cultures, molded for the last century and more by entrepreneurial white men, are slow to change—despite the good intentions of many. Even when people of color and Hispanics make it into mainstream news organizations, the influence they can exert may be minimal. Those with truly original and radical approaches to the coverage of underrepresented people and causes have great difficulty in getting their ideas translated into journalistic action. In most newsrooms today, Hispanics and people of color are still in the minority; many newsrooms are still all white. This does not mean, however, that recruiting racially and culturally diverse news workers is an exercise in futility. When journalists from these and other underrepresented groups reach critical mass and make inroads into the managerial suites, change will accelerate. The responsibility, however, should not be on them to redress the white news media's problems. All those who take seriously the mission of the news media in a democratic society have the obligation to make their coverage reflect accurately the nation's diversity. Those who educate journalists, both in the academy and in the newsrooms, must see knowledge of and sensitivity to the multicultural world as an essential part of that training.

NOTES

1. Quoted in Michael Schudson, *Discovering the News* (New York: Basic Books, 1978), 184.

2. National Advisory Commission on Civil Disorders (Kerner Commission), *Report of the National Advisory Commission on Civil Disorders* (New York: Bantam Books, 1968).

3. Commission on Freedom of the Press (Hutchins Commission), *A Free and Responsible Press* (Chicago: University of Chicago Press, 1947).

4. Ted Pease, "Philosophical and Economic Arguments for Media Diversity," in *Pluralizing Journalism Education: A Multicultural Handbook*, ed. Carolyn Martindale (Westport, Conn.: Greenwood Press, 1993), 8.

Index

About the Editors
and Contributors

THE EDITORS

BEVERLY ANN DEEPE KEEVER is an associate professor of journalism at the University of Hawaii, where she teaches courses in public affairs reporting, specialized reporting, and the history of mass communications. She coauthored with Gerald Kato a chapter in *Media Reader* (1996) and has contributed to *Biographical Dictionary of American Journalism* (Greenwood, 1989) and to the periodicals *Mass Comm Review*, *Journalism Educator*, and *International Communication Bulletin*. A former newspaper and magazine correspondent, she covered the Vietnam War for seven years for *Newsweek*, the *New York Herald Tribune*, and the *Christian Science Monitor*. Her reporting on Khe Sanh and other coverage for the *Monitor* was nominated in 1969 for a Pulitzer Prize on international affairs. She was later a reporter for Capitol Hill News Service in Washington, D.C., where she was also a freelance writer. She holds degrees from the University of Nebraska, Columbia University Graduate School of Journalism, and the University of Hawaii. She has received the University of Hawaii Regents' Medal for Excellence in Teaching and freedom-of-information awards from the Hawaii chapters of the Society of Professional Journalists, Common Cause, and Women in Communications, Inc.

CAROLYN MARTINDALE is a professor emerita of Youngstown State University, in Ohio, where she served as director of the journalism program and advisor to the student newspaper for more than twenty years. She is the author of *The White Press and Black America* (Greenwood, 1986) and the editor of *Pluralizing Journalism Education: A Multicultural Handbook* (Greenwood, 1993). Her articles on press portrayals of African Americans and on bringing information about various racial and ethnic groups into the journalism curriculum have appeared in Paul Lester's *Images That Injure* (Greenwood, 1995),

Facing Difference: Gender, Race and Media (1997), and in *Journalism Quarterly*, *Newspaper Research Journal*, *Journalism Educator*, *College Media Review*, *Student Press Review*, and *Educational Record*. She has twice received Youngstown State's Distinguished Professor Award, and was honored for her contributions to multiculturalism at the university. She holds a B.A. and an M.A. in journalism from Kent State University.

MARY ANN WESTON is an associate professor at the Medill School of Journalism, Northwestern University, where she teaches courses on reporting, writing, and the history of mass communications. She has also done research on Chicago journalism of the twentieth century and on portrayals of women in newspaper editorials. She is author of *Native Americans in the News* (Greenwood, 1996) and has contributed to the *Dictionary of American Biography*, *Dictionary of Literary Biography*, *Journalism History*, and *Newspaper Research Journal*. A former newspaper reporter and freelance writer, she has reported for newspapers in England and for the *Detroit Free Press*, among others. She was a member of the *Detroit Free Press* staff that won a Pulitzer Prize for coverage of the 1967 Detroit riots. She is also a former assistant curator of the Mitchell Indian Museum. She received her undergraduate and graduate degrees from the Medill School of Journalism.

THE CONTRIBUTORS

ANN ELIZABETH AUMAN is an associate professor of journalism at the University of Hawaii at Manoa where she teaches news editing, writing, and publication design. Her publications focus on change in newspapers, including technological, structural, and cultural change. She has studied and conducted research in China and Taiwan and has nine years of professional journalism experience. She has worked for *The Toronto Star* and the *Globe and Mail*, as well as in television and public relations. She is currently pursuing her doctorate in political science at the University of Hawaii. She holds a master's degree in Asian Studies from the University of Hawaii and an M.B.A. from the University of Toronto.

JOHN M. COWARD is an assistant professor of communication at the University of Tulsa, where he teaches both journalism skills and media theory courses. A former newspaper reporter and editor in east Tennessee, he completed his M.S. at the University of Tennessee and his Ph.D. degree in communication at the University of Texas at Austin. He has taught journalism and mass communication at Emory & Henry College in Virginia and at the University of Oklahoma in Norman. Most of his research examines media representations of Native Americans in the mainstream and native press. He has contributed chapters on Indian images to *Media/Reader* (1996), *Outsiders in Nineteenth Century*

Press History (1995), and *Pluralizing Journalism Education* (Greenwood, 1993), and he has published articles in *Journalism Quarterly* and *Journalism History*. He is currently completing a book called *The Newspaper Indian* on Native American identity in the nineteenth-century press.

LILLIAN RAE DUNLAP is an assistant professor of broadcast news at the School of Journalism at the University of Missouri-Columbia. She holds a B.A. degree in music from Defiance College, in Ohio, and an M.M.E. (music) and Ph.D. in speech and mass communications from Indiana University-Bloomington. Her research interests include the portrayal of African Americans in television news. She is a former director of the Afro-American Arts Institute at Indiana University, a former television news reporter/producer/anchor for WTTV Channel 4 in Indianapolis, and the former director of the Audio Video Communication Center and lecturer at Institut Teknologi MARA/Indiana University in Shah Alam, Selangor, Malaysia. She served as music research consultant for the award-winning PBS documentary "Eyes on the Prize II." She has been a visiting faculty member at the Poynter Institute for Media Studies, in Florida, a resident faculty in the RTNDA-Missouri School of Journalism Management Seminars for News Executives, a visiting scholar at Pennsylvania State University, and a consultant to a major international telecommunications corporation. She is currently working on a ten-year study of African-American images in local television news.

TIM GALLIMORE is an assistant professor at the School of Journalism at the University of Missouri-Columbia. Before joining the Missouri faculty in 1990, he was an assistant professor at Ohio University. He holds a Ph.D. in mass communications from Indiana University. His teaching and research interests include First Amendment theory, international broadcasting, communication policy and law, and access to public information. His published work appears in *In the Camera's Eye: News Coverage of Terrorist Events* (1990), *The Oxford Companion to the Supreme Court of the United States* (1992), *Global Journalism: Survey of International Communication* (1995), and the periodicals *Gazette*, *Journalism Quarterly*, and *Media Development*. He has traveled to Hungary and Poland as a Fulbright scholar and has conducted workshops for journalists and journalism educators in the Czech Republic, the Slovak Republic, Romania, and Mauritania, West Africa. He has worked as a newspaper reporter at the *Indianapolis News* and the *Bloomington Herald-Telephone* (Indiana).

OSCAR H. GANDY, JR., is professor of communication at the Annenberg School for Communication at the University of Pennsylvania. He is the author of *The Panoptic Sort* (1993), which examines bureaucratic uses of personal information, and *Beyond Agenda Setting* (1982), which examines the use of information subsidies in the formation of public policy. He is preparing a textbook on communication and race, and he recently completed a fellowship at the

Freedom Forum Media Studies Center at Columbia University, where he began a project that explores the way in which the press covers racial difference in exposure to social risks. He previously served as director of Howard University's Center for Communications Research and coordinator of the broadcast production sequence. He received his Ph.D. in public affairs communication from Stanford University. Before entering the academic world, he was a writer and producer for WCAU-TV in Philadelphia.

THOMAS H. HEUTERMAN retired in 1996 as a professor in the School of Communication at Washington State University, where he served as chair from 1977 to 1986. His books are *Movable Type* (1979), a biography of frontier editor Legh Freeman, and *The Burning Horse* (1995), a history of the Japanese Americans in the Yakima Valley. He also has written various articles about Japanese Americans. He is president of the American Journalism Historians Association and is a former chair of the History Division of the Association for Education in Journalism and Mass Communication. He received a B.S. in journalism from Washington State University, a master's degree in communication from the University of Washington, and a Ph.D. in American Studies from Washington State University. He was a reporter for the *Yakima Herald-Republic* from 1957 to 1965.

WILLIAM J. LEONHIRTH is an assistant professor of communication at the Florida Institute of Technology in Melbourne. He worked for twenty years as a newspaper reporter and editor in Tennessee and Alabama, and for five years he edited and published a science and technology newsletter with a national circulation. He began his doctoral studies at the University of Florida in 1992. While there, he worked as an administrative assistant for the university's Interactive Media Lab and electronic newspaper project. Leonhirth's research interests include new communication technologies and their effect on mass communication, social organization, and the understanding of communication itself.

VIRGINIA MANSFIELD-RICHARDSON is an associate professor of communication at Pennsylvania State University's College of Communications, where she teaches news writing, advanced news writing, and media ethics. She specializes in communication theory and international media, and speaks and writes Chinese. Her work has appeared in *History of the Mass Media in the United States: An Encyclopedia* (1997), *Statistics: An Inferential Approach* (1984), and *The Best of Style Plus* (1984). A reporter and editorial aide at the *Washington Post* for eleven years, she has written for two other newspapers and two magazines in the United States and Europe. She was the assistant director of American University's Brussels program, the largest study-abroad program in Europe, for a year. She has worked at the World Bank and as a caseworker for a U.S. congressman. She holds a B.S. and Ph.D. from Ohio University and an M.P.A. from George Mason University, in Fairfax, Virginia.

GREGORY YEE MARK is an associate professor of Ethnic Studies at the University of Hawaii at Manoa. His primary area of interest is the Chinese in the United States, with an emphasis on Hawaii. His other research topics and publications focus upon opium and the anti-Chinese movement, pioneer Chinese families in Hawaii, Chinatown gangs, and the Chinese involvement in sugar and coffee cultivation. A longtime scholar and community activist, he has been involved in issues concerning the Asian-American community since the 1960s. He is currently president of the Chinese Community Action Coalition, an organization that upholds and promotes the civil rights of the Chinese in Hawaii. He has a doctorate and a master's degree in criminology from the University of California, Berkeley.

MICHAEL B. SALWEN is a professor of communication at the University of Miami, Coral Gables, Florida. His research interests include international communication and the social effects of the mass media. He is an associate editor of the *Journalism and Mass Communication Quarterly* and book review editor of *World Communication*. He is the author of *Radio and TV in Cuba: The Pre-Castro Era* (1994) and coauthor of *Latin American Journalism* (1991) with Bruce Garrison. He is also coeditor of *An Integrated Approach to Communication Theory and Research* (1996) with Don Stacks. His work has appeared in the *Journalism and Mass Communication Quarterly*, the *Journal of Broadcasting & Electronic Media*, *Studies in Latin American Popular Culture*, *Critical Studies in Mass Communication*, and elsewhere. He holds a Ph.D. from Michigan State University. He worked for four years as a journalist in New Jersey and Pennsylvania before going into academia.

GONZALO R. SORUCO is an associate professor of communication at the University of Miami, Coral Gables, Florida. His research interests include international communication, public opinion, and social effects of the mass media. He is the author of *Cubans and the Mass Media in South Florida* (1996). His work has appeared in *Marketing Research*, *Encounter*, *Opinion*, and elsewhere. He has worked as consultant to several marketing and media research companies in the United States and Latin America. He holds a Ph.D. from Indiana University.

ISBN 0-313-29671-5

HARDCOVER BAR CODE